PERSONALITY DEVELOPMENT

SECOND EDITION

PERSONALITY DEVELOPMENT

HENRY CLAY SMITH
Professor of Psychology
Michigan State University

McGRAW-HILL BOOK COMPANY

New York St. Louis San Francisco Düsseldorf
Johannesburg Kuala Lumpur London Mexico Montreal New Delhi
Panama Paris São Paulo Singapore Sydney Tokyo Toronto

PERSONALITY DEVELOPMENT

1 2 3 4 5 6 7 8 9 0 K P K P 7 9 8 7 6 5 4

This book was set in Melior by Black Dot, Inc.
The editors were Robert P. Rainier and Renée E. Beach;
the designer was Nicholas Krenitsky;
the production supervisor was Bill Greenwood.
Kingsport Press, Inc., was printer and binder.

Library of Congress Cataloging in Publication Data

Smith, Henry Clay, date
    Personality development.

    First published in 1961 under title: Personality
adjustment.
    Bibliography: p.
    1. Personality. 2. Adjustment (Psychology)
3. Interpersonal relations. I. Title.
[DNLM: 1. Personality development. 2. Social
adjustments. 3. Students. BF698 S649p 1974]
BF698.S576 1974   155.2   73–16409
ISBN 0–07–058902–X

HUM
R

10.95

ACKNOWLEDGMENTS

Quotations on page 9–10, 17 from *Experiencing Youth: First-Person Accounts* by George W. Goethals and Dennis S. Klos, pp. 107–108. Copyright © 1970 by Little, Brown and Company.

Quotation on pages 10–11 from *L.S.D. Psychotherapy* by W. V. Caldwell. Copyright © 1968 by W. V. Caldwell. Reprinted by permission of Grove Press, Inc.

Quotation on page 15 from *Civilization and Its Discontents* by Sigmund Freud. Translated from the German and edited by James Strachey. Copyright © 1961 by James Strachey. Used with permission of W. W. Norton & Company, Inc.

Quotations on page 19 from *Leftover Life to Kill* by Caitlin Thomas. Copyright © 1957 by Little, Brown and Company. Reprinted by permission of Little, Brown and Company.

Quotation on page 32 from "Swann's Way" from *Remembrances of Things Past* by Marcel Proust, translated by C. K. Scott Moncrieff. Copyright © 1962 by Random House, Inc. Reprinted by permission of Random House.

Quotations on pages 39–40, 95 from *Memories, Dreams, Reflections* by C. G. Jung and translated by Richard and Clara Winston. Copyright © by Random House, Inc. Reprinted by permission.

Quotation on pages 85–86 from *The Summing Up* by W. Somerset Maugham. Copyright © 1938 by W. Somerset Maugham. Reprinted by permission of Doubleday & Company, Inc.

Quotation on page 91 from *Autobiography* by Mark Twain, edited by C. Neider. Copyright © 1959 by Harper & Row Publishers, Incorporated.

Quotations on pages 142, 467, 476–477, 481 from *Future Shock* by Alvin Toffler. Copyright © 1970 by Alvin Toffler. Reprinted by permission of Random House, Inc.

Quotation on page 186–187 from *Varieties of Religious Experience* by William James. Copyright © 1902 by William James, renewed 1929. Reprinted by permission of David McKay Company, Inc.

Quotation on pages 187–188 from *Thomas Jefferson: The Apostle of Americanism* by Gilbert Chinard. Copyright © 1930 by Little, Brown and Company.

Quotation on page 227 from *Infants and Institutions* by S. Provence and R. Lipton. Copyright © 1962 by International Universities Press Inc., reprinted by permission of International Universities Press, Inc.

Quotation on page 316 from *Abnormal Psychology and Modern Life* by James C. Coleman. Copyright © 1964 by Scott, Foresman and Company, reprinted by permission of Scott, Foresman and Company.

Quotation on pages 359–360 from "Playboy Interview," *Playboy Magazine*, September 1971. Copyright © 1971 Playboy.

Quotation on pages 368–369 from *Psychotherapy and Culture Conflict* by Georgene Seward. Copyright © 1956 by The Ronald Press Company.

TO NANCY, OUR CHILDREN,
AND OUR CHILDREN'S CHILDREN

CONTENTS

PREFACE

Personality Development is a text for courses in the psychology of personality and adjustment and for introductory psychology courses that stress personality and interpersonal relationships. Most students take these courses to gain a better understanding of themselves and others; many instructors teach these courses as a survey of the science of personality. The question guiding this edition even more than earlier ones is: how can the science be best presented to meet the needs of the student?

The book approaches the question from four related but distinctive points of view. Part One, "The Science of Personality," compares and contrasts the common-sense view of personality with the goals, theories, and methods of the scientific view. Part Two, "Traits as Personality," considers five basic traits: boldness, emotionality, future-mindedness, practicality, and empiricism. Each chapter in this part defines a trait, shows how it is measured, explains why people differ on it, and examines the significance for the student of his position on it. Part Three, "The Self as Personality," deals in turn with the autistic, impulse-ridden, opportunistic, conforming, conscientious, and self-actualized stages of self-development. It answers these questions about each stage: What are its key symptoms? How do people develop to the next higher stage? Why do some people never develop beyond the stage? Why does everyone sometimes regress to the stage? Part Four, "Roles as Personality," builds upon the sex, marital, parental, leadership, and citizen roles that everyone plays. The questions here are: Why do people play roles? How do they differ in the ways they play them? What determines their success in playing them?

Each view of personality is organized around the concepts and relationships assumed by one readily understood theory. Each concept is approached with the same basic questions in mind. Each question is answered with the help of recent research. The student is presented with ways of assessing where he stands in relation to the theory. And the book examines the relationships of the theoretical concepts to such great ideas of mankind as happiness, freedom, and love as well as their implications for the solution of personal and social problems.

The book has a symbolistic bias. It assumes that man is the only symbol-using animal, that this fact makes him as different from the ape as the ape is different from a tree, and that no symbols are more important to the individual than the words he uses to describe himself, his differences from others, and his relationships with others.

Henry Clay Smith

ONE

THE SCIENCE
OF PERSONALITY

When Fan Che asked Confucious, "What is humanity?"
the master answered, "To love men."
When he asked, "What is knowledge?"
the answer was, "To know men."

INSCRIPTION IN A CHINESE TEMPLE

1

PERSONALITY AND THE PURSUIT OF HAPPINESS

We hold these Truths to be self-evident:
That all Men are created equal,
that they are endowed by their Creator
with certain unalienable Rights,
that among these are Life, Liberty, and the Pursuit of Happiness.

DECLARATION OF INDEPENDENCE

Everyone is concerned with understanding personality: the parent wants to understand the personality of his child; the teacher, of his student; the executive, of his employee; and all of us want to understand our own personalities. The science of personality, and this book, seek to contribute to this understanding. But what is personality? Why do we seek to understand it? How is it determined? The general answers given in this chapter to these questions form the book's skeleton. To begin with, though, who are the psychologists whose work provide its heart and muscles?

Since 1920, the number of professional psychologists in the United States has increased from less than 1,000 to more than 25,000. About half of them work in colleges and universities; a quarter, in governmental agencies; and the rest, in private organizations. Wherever they work, they are concerned with increasing our knowledge of behavior and experience or with using the knowledge they have to help solve human problems. Some study animals; some are concerned with educational and school problems; some are concerned with personnel and industrial problems; some are concerned with problems of human engineering and the development of psychological tests. Most, however, are concerned with counseling and clinical work.

The typical clinical psychologist works in an agency: a mental hospital, an institution for the feeble-minded, a prison, a juvenile-court, a mental-health clinic, a college or university health service. In these agencies, he often works with psychiatrists and psychiatric social workers. A *psychologist* has typically earned a Ph.D. degree in a university psychology department. A *psychiatrist* is a physician who has typically spent several years studying and treating disorders of behavior after receiving his M.D. A *psychiatric social worker* is a graduate of a school of social work, and usually has the degree of Master of Social Work for which two years of graduate study are required and has specialized in mental-health problems.

In spite of their different professional affiliations, clinical psychologists, psychiatrists, and social workers come from similar backgrounds and have very similar attitudes on most social questions (Henry, Simms, and Spray, 1971). (Complete references are listed alphabetically at the end of the book.)

All develop and use the theories, facts, and methods of the science of personality. All wish to help individuals live happier lives. All seek to change the society so that it will be a happier place in which to live. None think that a person can be, or should try to be, happy all the time. None doubt, however, that some people lead happier lives than others. And none doubt that all can learn to deal with life's troubling experiences in ways that will lead to happier and more constructive lives.

WHAT IS PERSONALITY?

"Personality" has dozens of meanings: popular, legal, grammatical, ethical, religious, economic, and psychological (Allport, 1937). At the core of all these different meanings, however, is a common feeling: A person is both unique and important. Thus, the word gives direction and energy to the vague human desire for individuality. Today, this desire seems almost as tangible as the desire for food. Yet only rarely in human history, apparently, has man been even aware of this desire. The historian Burckhardt (1960, p. 121) concludes that the Renaissance in Italy was one of these rare times:

In the Middle Ages both sides of human consciousness—that which was turned within and that which was turned without —lay as though dreaming or half awake beneath a common veil. The veil was woven of faith, illusion, and childish prepossession, through which the world and history were seen as clad in strange hues. Man was conscious of himself only as a member of a race, people, party, family or corporation—only through some general category. It is in Italy that this veil dissolved first; there arose an *objective* treatment and consideration of the State and of all the things of this world, and at the same time the *subjective* side asserted itself with corresponding emphasis. Man became a spiritual *individual*, and recognized himself as such. In the same way the Greek had once distinguished himself from the barbarian, and the Arab had felt himself an individual at a time when other Asiatics knew themselves only as members of a race.

To the ancient Greeks, a *person* was something very concrete: a theatrical mask which actors took on and off as they played different roles. The present most popular definition has shifted the meaning of personality from something an individual puts on to the way he appears to his audience: "The social characteristic of commanding notice, admiration, respect, or influence through personal characteristics." As actors, then, our personality changes with our audience. We have a different personality when we are talking to our mother than when we are talking to our wife, our children, our friends, or our enemies. We may be admired by our mothers but not by our wives; we may be admired by our friends but not by our enemies. We may be respected by our children but by no one else. We are always influenced by what others think we are; we are not always what others think we are.

The psychologist, however, is not primarily interested in what we seem to others to be; he is interested in what we have been, are, and will become. To begin with, therefore, he tries to define personality as the total of all a person's responses: the way he walks, talks, brushes his teeth, etc. For example, observers of Raymond, a boy who lived in a Midwestern town with his parents, attempted to record everything that he did in one day. The following sequence was recorded as Raymond was getting dressed (Barker and Wright, 1951, pp. 16–17):

7:01   Raymond picked up a sock and began tugging and pulling it on his left foot. As his mother watched him she said kiddingly, "Can't you get your peepers open?" Raymond stopped pulling on his sock long enough to rub his eyes again. He appeared to be very sleepy. He said plaintively, "Mommie," and continued mumbling in an unintelligible way something about his undershirt.

7:02   His mother asked, "Do you want to put this undershirt on or do you want to wear the one you have on?" Raymond sleepily muttered something in reply. (His mother left the room and went into the kitchen.) Raymond struggled out of the T-shirt which he had on. He put on the clean striped T-shirt more efficiently.

7:03   He pulled on his right sock. He picked up his left shoe with slow deliberation, looking intently at the shoe as he worked steadily until he had it all laced.

7:04   He put on his right shoe . . .

This is a few minutes of Ray's interactions with his environment. The report of the whole day is a book. Obviously, defining personality as the "total" of responses is too broad.

A better definition of personality would suggest what should be observed, why it is important to observe it, and how the observations can be made and interpreted. "Intervening variable" definitions are of this type. Such definitions consider personality as something that intervenes between the person as a stimulus to others and the person as a responder. The following definition, adapted from the classic one of Allport (1937), is of this type:

Personality is the dynamic organization of traits within the self that determine the individual's unique way of playing his social roles.

The definition stresses what a person is, not what others see him to be. It stresses the units of personality ("traits"), the way these units are fitted together ("dynamic organization . . . within the self"), and what purpose the traits and their organization serve

("... determine the individual's unique way of playing his social roles"). Thus, a study of Raymond's personality *would* pay attention to his traits (his boldness, his emotionality, etc.), to the way these traits are organized, and the influence of the organization on his interactions with the world around him (fights with his mother, dominates his playmates, etc.).

A Trait Definition

Personality does have units, these units are organized, and the organization does determine interactions with the environment. However, it is practically impossible to focus simultaneously upon units, organization, and interaction. Is it best, then, to concentrate upon units, organization, *or* interaction? Those psychologists who answer "units" approach personality from a trait point of view and adopt a trait definition of personality like the following:

A personality is a distinguishable individual who is defined by the traits that differentiate him from other individuals.

As Figure 1-1 suggests, the trait definition leads to a hunt for those dimensions that are of most help in distinguishing individuals from each other. If, for example, we look at Tom, Dick, and Harry from the trait point of view, we are interested in the common traits that distinguish them from one another. Thus, we might find that Tom was bolder than Dick or Harry, Dick was more emotional than Tom or Harry, and Harry was more future-minded than Dick or Tom. We approach personality from this point of view in Part 2 of this book.

An Organizational Definition

Those who believe that the greatest progress will come from paying attention to the whole rather than the parts, stress that personality is a dynamic organization. They emphasize that individuals are living organisms, that organisms are not a sprawling mass of loosely related parts, but primarily a system of structures and activities under coordinated control.

A structure, in general, is the arrangement of parts into a whole: floors and walls are parts of a building; nouns and verbs are parts of a sentence; and boldness and emotionality are parts of the whole personality. Similar structures may be made of dissimilar parts: the same house may be built with wood or with brick; the same kind of declarative sentence may be written with different words; and individuals with equally immature or mature personality structures may have quite different traits. Psychologists concerned with the weakneses

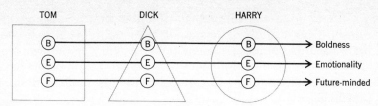

Figure 1-1   Trait definitions emphasize differences between people, deem-phasize the organization of the self and its interactions with the environment.

and strengths of the personality organization, prefer a definition like the following:

> *A personality is a dynamic whole that is defined by the distinctive structural attributes of the self.*

A structural view of personality does not stress the ways in which Tom, Dick, and Harry differ. As Figure 1-2 suggests, it shows rather the ways in which Tom's boldness, emotionality, and other traits are related to each other and how effectively they are organized. We approach personality from this point of view in Part 3.

An Interactional Definition

Interactionists assert that man is a social animal and can only be fully understood by considering the social context in which he lives and develops. They also assert that nothing is as important as other people in determining the nature of the individual, and they further assert that the most important and valuable thing in understanding a person is his general way of interacting with others. Such psychologists prefer a definition like the following:

> *Personality is an organism-environment field that is defined by its distinctive way of playing social roles.*

The definition assumes that Tom, Dick, and Harry have traits that differentiate between them and that organization of these traits within each of them is different. The definition stresses, however, as Figure 1-3 indicates, the interactions of each of them with other people. It is personality from the interpersonal view that will be our concern in the last part of the book.

Trait, organizational, and interactional views of personality each have their proponents and opponents, their particular weaknesses and strengths. Each one opens a new horizon and shows us a new aspect of personality. Overall, they do not conflict but complete and

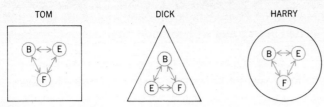

Figure 1-2   Structural definitions emphasize the dynamic organization within the self; deemphasize traits and roles.

complement one another. Part 2, therefore, looks at personality from the trait point of view; Part 3, from the organizational point of view; and Part 4, from the interactional point of view.

WHY DO WE TRY TO UNDERSTAND PERSONALITY?

The shortest, the most popular, and, on the whole, probably the best answer is: To make ourselves and others happier. But what is happiness? Webster's Third International Dictionary says it is "a state of well-being characterized by relative permanence, by dominantly agreeable emotion ranging in value from mere contentment to deep and intense joy in living, and by a natural desire for its continuation." The state is easiest to identify by its opposite, by *un*happiness so painful that the individual desires the *dis*continuation of his life.

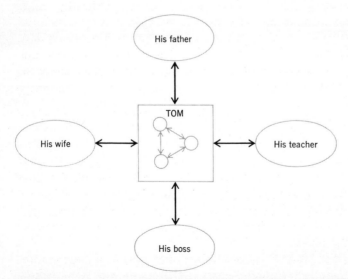

Figure 1-3   Adjustment definitions emphasize the interactions between an individual and those around him, deemphasize his distinguishing traits and his personality structure.

Jim, a college junior, describes his attempted suicide after his rejection by a girl he had been going with for more than a year (Goethals and Klos, 1970, p. 107):

> She said she never wanted to see me again. . . . I tried to reason with her again on the way to the train station. She left me at the train depot and the ache within me was worse than physical pain. It was too much to take! What could I do? . . . I had a gun in my room, a little .22 caliber rifle. . . . I went into the living room and played a couple of records that had been meaningful to me and the girl. I started to cry once more. I went back into my room and picked up the rifle. I aimed it at my stomach and started putting pressure on the trigger. No, no, I couldn't do it! . . . Finally, I pointed the gun and jerked. . . . "Oh, oh God, what have I done?" The gun was on the floor and I hurt. I made it to the phone and called for help. It seemed like it took years for the doctor, then the ambulance to come. Oh, I hurt so much, but they couldn't give me anything for the pain until they knew exactly what was wrong with me. This was the beginning of two weeks with a shot every hour on the hour. Weeks that were full of intravenous tubes, a consuming thirst, and no sleep. In the course of six weeks I had three operations. Due to advances in medicine and my youth I recovered. A few years ago, a few discoveries ago, and I would have died. . . .

Happiness is not an impermanent state of bliss like those reported by drug users (Caldwell, 1968, p. 36–38):

> . . . their minds relaxed into a wide-angle view which considered the largest contexts and patterns: they might sense the weight and balance of a whole room, as an artist, by squinting, can evaluate a whole picture rather than its details.

> Suddenly colors were stunning in their intensity, as though for each shade of indigo and vermillion and emerald there were some archetype, some platonic essence, beyond all previous experience. Music assumed elaborate spatial forms of joyous multiplicity; the sounds of the instruments glowed with vibrant colors, rasped and slithered with textures strange to the touch, burned steadily in the darkness of silence or exploded in skyrocket showers of delight. There was nothing like it in all of life, of dreams, or art.

> There were other avenues of experience almost as beguiling. Men looked at flowers, at trees, at the ocean; and suddenly it seemed they had never seen them before—never grasped the

radiant beauty, the dazzling ordered complexity of the rhyth-
mical forms. These adventurers had somehow escaped the
barren aseptic depot of modern life and wandered in the
Chinese landscape of the sages. They sighed at the flowers,
gaped at the waterfalls, and rolled in drunken hilarity by the
mist-shrouded lake of dreams.

Such states are often followed by relatively permanent states of
*un*happiness as is seen in the deaths of popular rock-music performers.
Janis Joplin, blues-singing idol of thousands, died in October 1970 at
the age of twenty-seven of an overdose of drugs. The month before, the
equally well-known Jimi Hendrix was found dead in a London apartment as a result of suffocation from vomiting while unconscious,
presumably from the effects of drugs. Al Wilson, guitarist with the rock
group Canned Heat, died from an overdose of sleeping pills. Brian
Jones of the Rolling Stones drowned in the swimming pool of his home
in England while under the influence of drugs and alcohol.

In his novel *Brave New World*, Huxley (1932) described a
society in which most people existed in a permanent state of mild
contentment:

The world's stable now. People are happy; they get what they
want, and they never want what they can't get. They're safe,
they're never ill; they're not afraid of death; they're blissfully
ignorant of passion and old age; they're plagued with no
mothers or fathers; they've got no wives, or children, or lovers
to feel strongly about; they're so conditioned that they practically can't help behaving as they ought to behave. And if
anything should go wrong, there's *soma*.

Soma is a highly developed tranquilizing drug that the citizens of the
Brave New World learn to use as they repeat slogans. To prevent anger:
"A gramme is better than a damn." To avoid thinking about the past or
the future: "Was and will make me ill, I take a gramme and only am."
To avoid strong feelings: "When the individual feels, the community
reels." They are encouraged in a continuous round of sexual and
sensuous pleasures: "Never put off until tomorrow, the fun you can
have today."

The happiest person feels a joyous and enduring sense of
physical and mental well-being; of being "all together" as an individual
and as a part of something larger than himself; of being acutely aware of
all that is going on within and around him; of being free; and of being
sure of why things happen and how to control the things that happen
(Figure 1-4). Business, art, religion, science, and, indeed, all man's
institutions, grew out of his desire to experience these feelings.

Figure 1-4 Happiness is more than amusement on a superslide. It comes from being everything you can be and doing everything you can do. The happiest person is the most fully human: he has the competence and freedom to be himself. (Michigan Tourist Council)

Measurement is an ideal in psychology as it is in every science, applicable to happiness as it is to every other psychological state. The Happiness scale (Table 1-1) is one effort to approach this ideal. It uses self-ratings of variations in the positiveness, the intensity, the permanence of the emotional states that characterize happiness. The happiness score is the total of the numbers checked. Thus, the most unhappy person would score 0; the happiest, 16. The person who sees himself as neither happy nor unhappy would score 8. More than three-fourths of college students typically report themselves as at least mildly happy.

Measurements of this sort are always imperfect, often premature, and sometimes even harmful. What good are they, then? In his study of happiness, the psychologist searches for its causes. He looks for the things that are *related* to happiness. He has faith that such relationships can eventually be discovered and communicated to others. He knows that numbers are much better suited to his purpose than words. A word is detached, has a meaning of its own, and has no systematic relationship to other words. A number, on the other hand, is

TABLE 1-1 The Happiness Scale

A. Check the statement which best describes your feelings:

_____0 I am very dissatisfied and unhappy.

_____1 I am a little dissatisfied and unhappy.

_____2 I am neither happy nor unhappy.

_____3 I am fairly satisfied and happy.

_____4 I am very satisfied and happy.

B. Check the statement which shows how much of the time you feel this way:

_____0 I am seldom happy.

_____1 Occasionally.

_____2 About half of the time.

_____3 A good deal of the time.

_____4 Most of the time.

C. Check the statement which best tells how you think your feelings compare with others:

_____0 I am much less happy than the average person.

_____1 I am somewhat less happy than the average person.

_____2 I am about as happy as the average person.

_____3 I am somewhat happier than the average person.

_____4 I am very much happier than the average person.

D. Check the statement which best describes your life experiences up to the present time:

_____0 My life has been very unpleasant.

_____1 My life has not been pleasant.

_____2 My life has been neither pleasant nor unpleasant.

_____3 My life has been pleasant and enjoyable.

_____4 My life has been very enjoyable.

[*Source*: Hoppock, 1935]

not detached, has no meaning by itself, but does have a systematic *relationship* to other numbers. Numbers, in other words, have a purely *relational* meaning.

What is related to happiness? Watson (1930) tried to find an answer. He first isolated the 50 students with the lowest happiness scores and the 50 students with the highest scores in a large college population. He gave these students a long questionnaire concerning many aspects of their attitudes and behavior and then analyzed the replies to each question to determine in what ways the happy students differed from the unhappy ones. The happy students, for example, reported much more often than the unhappy students that they were able to give a talk to high school pupils about sex; were able to supervise a large group of workers; were able to lead an effective group discussion; would prefer to live with others rather than alone at the age of sixty; preferred a job with responsibility to one which would leave them free; were not particularly sensitive to the opinions of others, unduly shy, or bothered by strong fears. Tennis was the only sport in which the happy were different from the unhappy—more of the happy group were able to play it. Only 8 percent of the unhappy group could replace an electric fuse, whereas 35 percent of the happy group reported that they could. In interpreting these numerous details, Watson [1930] concluded:

> The essentials of happiness for most people are among the stable elements of life (friends, work, nature), not among the stimulants (alcohol, clubs, churches, dancing, cards, automobiles, or arts). Happiness is associated with serious, deliberate, responsible, earnest, hardworking living rather than with impulsive, light, amusing dilettantism.

The approach of the psychologist to the relationship between happiness and personality depends on his definition of personality. From the trait point of view, for example, he may ask: Is happiness, itself, a trait? From the structural point of view, he may ask: Does the happy person have distinctive structural attributes? From the interpersonal view, he may ask: Does the happy person interact with others in a distinctive way? Here we briefly describe these points of view and suggest some general answers to these questions.

The Trait View of Happiness

Traits distinguish people from each other. A trait is any stable aspect of a person's behavior or experience. The word has many synonyms: complex, interest, mode of adaptation, style of life, general attitude, generalized habit, personality trend, etc. The dictionary is a vast storehouse of trait names: abrupt, absent-minded, academic, accommodating, accurate, acquiescent, acquisitive active, adventurous, etc. Some of these traits bear the name of a particular person because they originally were used to describe an aspect of that person's behavior that was unique with him: Beau Brummell, Cassandra, Don Juan, Lesbian, Narcissistic, Napoleonic, Rabelaisian, Sadistic, and Shylock. Most of the names, however, refer to *common traits*, stable aspects of behavior that have much the same form for everyone but that differentiate between people because some have more and some have less of the quality.

Is happiness a trait? William James, the father of American

psychology, suggested that it might be: "There are men who seem to have started life with a bottle or two of champagne inscribed to their credit; whilst others seem to have been born close to the pain-threshold, which the slightest irritants fatally send them over" (1929, p. 133). Psychologists, like men in general, vary in the pain they feel and see in the world. Sigmund Freud (1961, p. 58–59) was impressed by the evil in the world:

... men are not gentle creatures who want to be loved, and who at the most can defend themselves if they are attacked; they are, on the contrary, creatures among whose instinctual endowments is to be reckoned a powerful share of aggressiveness. As a result, their neighbour is for them not only a potential helper or sexual object, but also someone who tempts them to satisfy their aggressiveness on him, to exploit his capacity for work without compensation, to use him sexually without his consent, to seize his possessions, to humilate him, to cause him pain, to torture and to kill him. . . . Who, in the face of all his experience of life and of history, will have the courage to dispute this assertion? . . . Anyone who calls to mind the atrocities committed during the racial migrations or the invasions of the Huns, or by the people known as Mongols under Jenghiz Khan and Tamerlane, or at the capture of Jerusalem by the pious Crusaders, or even, indeed, the horrors of the recent World War—anyone who calls these things to mind will have to bow humbly before the truth of this view.

Allport (1954, p. 14) takes a quite different view:

Normal men everywhere reject, in principal and by preference, the path of war and destruction. They like to live in peace and friendship with their neighbors; they prefer to love and be loved rather than to hate and be hated. . . . While wars rage, yet our desire is for peace, and while animosity prevails, the weight of mankind's approval is on the side of affiliation.

We do differ in the amount of goodness we see in the world, the confidence we have in ourselves, and the optimism with which we approach life's inevitable problems. We not only differ but these differences are large, develop early, and remain relatively stable. Happiness, however, is not so much a matter of how we see the world as a matter of how well we can deal with it. It is good to see good, but it is also good to see bad when it is there to harm us. Happiness, in other words, depends upon the ability to meet *the realistic demands of situations*. In a general way, we all recognize this fact as did the chief mate in *Moby Dick* (Melville, 1961, p. 122):

> "I will have no man in my boat who is not afraid of a whale." By this he seemed to mean, not only that the most reliable and useful courage was that which arises from the fair estimation of the encountered peril, but that an utterly fearless man is a far more dangerous comrade than a coward.

Happiness is not a trait though the trait view may aid us in achieving it. It can help us to know and accept the fact that we are different from other people and that other people are, and will remain, different from us. We often feel that others are more like us than they actually are. We also often feel, though we may not admit it to ourselves, that other people *ought* to be like us. Rogers (1961), one of America's best known psychotherapists, has told how hard it is for him to accept the uniqueness of others:

> Can I be strong enough as a person to be separate from the other? Can I be a sturdy respecter of my own feelings, my own needs, as well as his? Can I own and, if need be, express my own feelings as something belonging to me and separate from his feelings? Am I strong enough in my own separateness that I will not be downcast by his depression, frightened by his fear, nor engulfed by his dependency? Is my inner self hardy enough to realize that I am not destroyed by his anger, taken over by his need for dependence, nor enslaved by his love, but that I exist separate from him with feelings and rights of my own? When I can freely feel this strength of being a separate person, then I find that I can let myself go much more deeply in understanding and accepting him because I am not fearful of losing myself.
>
> ... Am I secure enough within myself to permit him his separateness? Can I permit him to be what he is—honest or deceitful, infantile or adult, despairing or over-confident? Can I give him the freedom to be? Or do I feel that he should follow my advice, or remain somewhat dependent on me or mold himself after me?

The Self View of Happiness

Viewed as an organized whole, personality is constantly growing and changing with the years. Here, for example, a black student describes her growth from her freshman to her senior year (Goethals and Klos, 1970, p. 150–153):

I am a black woman. It's not something that you discover, it's something that you know. What you don't know sometimes is how it means . . . this place was a mass of "never-before-possibilities." You know, to be here presupposes some ability. In the case of black women, it presupposes an added ability. The ability to survive. Why not? They had made it through high school, largely on the fringes of things. . . . So you, the bright black promise child, come here. And you get out of the cab and you take a deep breath and you look around. . . . You fool yourself at first. You think you can divorce your blackness from your selfness. How many times did we tell ourselves in those first few weeks "I am me, myself first. And then a black woman, second." Somewhere, the two things can no longer be dichotomized. This place helps you to find that somewhere. Some people might call it personality integration, whatever that implies. . . . It is almost the end of the second year, and the nine of you are assembled to recount the year past. Your eyes are wider now than before. And you are tired. But you are free. You are free to realize your worth. But in freedom is nakedness and coldness and pain. You are stripped of illusions. You are nothing if not realistic.

Your talk turns to things which concern every woman, but which have a special cast for black women. You talk about your freshman hangups, and you laugh bitterly. "The end of man is to know." Okay, so you know, now. What?

This year has been pain. Last night or the night before, a black man heard a black woman cry. And that black woman broke because things here got to be too much. It is too much to be a teacher-educator, confessor to all the white guilt complexes, initiator, perpetrator, painful reminder to all the black men with their white women in their arms or on their minds. . . . It is too much sometimes, because you are expected to cope with it all and to integrate it all into some cohesion. And you do, somehow. Somehow, you prevail. . . .

This place, with all its negation of you, affirms you. You can laugh at it in the end. You will transcend it. You will grow, in spite of it. And this is what this is all about. Your beauty is your being. You are marred a little by conflict and you are more than a little sorry that it has been so hard. But you are, and you are black and you are moving. And that's the wonder of it.

Philosophers and psychologists have generally taken the dynamic view of happiness. Socrates said: "The best man is he who most tries to perfect himself, and the happiest man is he who most feels that he is perfecting himself." In his essay "What Makes a Life Significant?" William James stressed that happiness was dynamic, not static, that the road was always better than the inn:

> The solid meaning of life is always the same eternal thing—the marriage, namely, of some unhabitual ideal, however special, with some fidelity, courage, and endurance; with some man's or woman's pains—and, whatever or wherever life may be, there will always be the chance for that marriage to take place.

From the organizational point of view, we often fight being happy. We resist, sometimes successfully, the pushes and pulls that lead us toward increased competence. The pulls may be too slight and the pushes become too hard. Pain and anxiety push us toward the development of our personalities. But development is a long, uncertain, and disturbing process. The pain and the anxiety are here and now. We want immediate relief and we can get it: alcohol reduces anxiety; drugs reduce anxiety; and psychological mechanisms reduce anxiety.

The Role View of Happiness

Skill in getting along with and helping others is one aspect of general competence. Of all of an individual's competencies, however, interpersonal competence is most central in influencing the course of his life and the satisfactions he derives from it. The infant is utterly dependent upon other human beings for his physical survival. The adult's success in attracting a desired mate, establishing a happy marriage, raising children, making friends, and achieving occupational advancement depends upon his skill in dealing with other people. People fail in their work, ruin their marriages, and raise maladjusted children because they do not possess this skill.

We relate to others to obtain food, to gain shelter, to protect ourselves from physical harm, and to express and satisfy our feelings and emotions. Fromm (1963, p. 6) has stressed that above and beyond all of these needs man has the need to escape from loneliness by relating to others:

> This awareness of himself as a separate entity, the awareness of his own short life span, of the fact that without his will he is born and against his will he dies, that he will die before those whom he loves, or they before him, the awareness of his

aloneness and separateness, of his helplessness before the forces of nature and of society, all this makes his separate, disunited existence an unbearable prison. He would become insane could he not liberate himself from this prison and reach out, unite himself in some form or other with men, with the world outside.

The unhappiest experience in the lives of many is the ending of a relationship. The poet, Dylan Thomas, died at the age of thirty-nine, his health ruined by chronic alcoholic intoxication. Caitlin, his wife, describes her grief and reaction to it (Thomas, 1957, pp. 6, 15–16):

Dylan and dying, Dylan and dying, they don't go together; or is it that they were bound to go together; he said so often enough, but I did not heed him. I was as foolish as women are supposed to be, paid no attention, took him for granted, was only concerned with how to express my own aggressive, demanding, frustrated, vile, jealous self. And look what he had done to me! How brutally cruelly am I punished; surely out of proportion to my disdoing (p. 6.)

. . . I did all the things a Lady should not do, and showed them, aggressively, just how unladylike a Lady can be. I gave myself up with selfless abandonment to being awful. . . .

I stole their sons and husbands, doing violence to both our diversely raw feelings; violating purposefully my most precious holy vows to Dylan; saying his golden endearing words for me to them, making the same familiar sweet affectionate gestures . . . inciting a deliberate sacrilege, a shameful sacrifice of our love that was too stubborn to be put out. And all this fervour of destruction, to no, not one, flickering twinge of improvement, curative effect in my buried, unremitting black burning world; the ridiculous reverse; an increase in my inescapable dedication to Dylan and a mutilated, guilt-soaked, pride-stripped body.

Most students anticipate that their marital and family relationships will be the greatest source of their personal happiness. Students at American colleges and at foreign colleges were asked: "What three things or activities in your life do you expect to give you the most satisfaction?" (Jacob, 1957). They had six choices: family relations, career, recreational activities, religious activities, community affairs, and participation in national and international affairs. More American students (89 percent) than students from any other country picked family relations. Gillespie (1954) asked students from the United States and nine other countries to write an autobiography entitled *My Life from Now until the Year* A.D. *2,000.* The replies of American youth indicated that they were far more preoccupied with their future family life than the youth of any of the other nations.

The classic study of Terman (*Psychological Factors in Marital Happiness,* 1938) provided the measurement model that has been used for generations. In obtaining a "happiness score," he used answers to a series of items such as: engaging in outside interests together; agreeing on how to handle finances; agreeing on religion, on show of affection, on recreation; regrets about getting married; and subjective ratings of happiness. The nearly 800 couples also checked a list of complaints and these (if checked) became a part of the score. The answers of the individual from one part of the measure to another were in considerable agreement, i.e., an individual who checked many complaints was highly likely to indicate that he disagreed with his wife about religion and to say that he regretted getting married. Extreme efforts were made to protect the anonymity of the respondents and to convince them how impossible it would be for their questionnaires to be identified. The happiness scores of husbands and wives based on their completely separate replies were still highly correlated ($r = .67$).

Figure 1-5 shows the distribution of scores for all couples. The vast majority said they were at least mildly happy. About 15 percent, however, said they were at least mildly unhappy. A more recent study (Lear, 1972) reports almost identical figures. McKinney (1939) asked college students to estimate anonymously the happiness of their parents. Fifteen percent admitted that their parents were unhappy, and more than twice as many said that their parents frequently quarreled and that their mothers were dissatisfied with their lot. Bossard and Boll (1955) had marital happiness of 440 married persons rated by their brothers and sisters. Overall, 14 percent were rated unhappily married.

The divorce rate suggests a rapid decline in marital happiness. The United States Public Health Service (*New York Times Almanac,* 1972, p. 494) reports that the number of divorces per year per 1,000 married women increased almost 50 percent between 1960 and 1970. During the same decade, however, the average duration of a marriage remained at a steady 7 years, the percentage of unmarried getting married increased somewhat, and the percentage of divorced who remarried increased a great deal. On the whole, it seems that the state of marriage is at least as attractive as it ever was but that the small minority of the unhappily married are less and less inclined to endure their misery.

In general, whether husbands and wives are happy or unhappy in their marriages or in any other relationship depends, to a large degree, on the way they play their social roles. Part 4 develops the theory that the more considerately and responsibly people play their roles, the happier and more helpful they are likely to be.

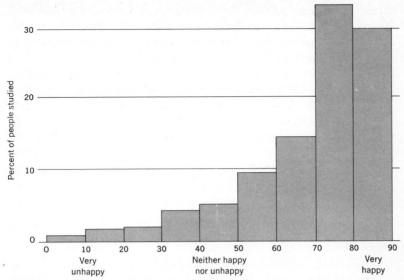

Figure 1-5 Percent of married persons reporting varying degrees of material happiness. (Adapted from Terman, 1938)

WHAT DETERMINES PERSONALITY?

"Being" and "becoming" are equally vital but entirely separate problems. We may know what a person is without knowing how he became what he is; we may know what processes determined what a person became without being able to describe what it is he became. This book draws a sharp line between ways of describing and ways of explaining personality. Thus far, we have said, we can describe a person by his traits, his self, or by the way he plays his roles. But what determines the traits we have, the self we develop, the way we play our roles?

Psychologists with an interactional view stress the influence of cultural environment. It is the power of social institutions, they imply, that tends to mold us all into "Citizen Sams" (Allport, 1945):

Citizen Sam . . . moves and has his being in the great activity wheel of New York City. Let us say that he spends his hours of unconsciousness somewhere in the badlands of the Bronx. He wakens to grab the morning's milk left at the door by an agent of a vast dairy and distributing system whose corporate maneuvers, so vital to his health, never consciously concern him. After paying hasty respects to his landlady, he dashes into the transportation system whose mechanical and civic mysteries he does not comprehend. At the factory he becomes a cog in a set of systems far beyond his ken. To him (as to everybody else) the company he works for is an abstraction; he plays an unwitting part in the "creation of surpluses" (whatever they are), and though he doesn't know it, his furious activity at his machine is regulated by the "law of supply and demand" and by "the availability of raw materials" and by "prevailing interest rates." Unknown to himself he is headed next week for the "surplus labor market." A union official collects his dues; just why he doesn't know. At noontime that corporate monstrosity, Horn and Hardart swallows him up, much as he swallows one of its automatic pies. After more activity in the afternoon, he seeks out a standardized day-dream produced in Hollywood, to rest his tense but not efficient mind. At the end of his day, he sinks into a tavern, and, unknowingly victimized by the advertising cycle, orders in rapid succession Four Roses, Three Feathers, Golden Wedding, and Seagram's which "men who plan beyond tomorrow" like to drink.

Those who focus upon the influence of the external world see man as controlled by the stimuli that come to him through his senses. Social institutions determine the most frequent and vital of these stimuli and, therefore, the development of personality. Personality is not what is left when these stimuli are removed; it is a product of these stimuli. The human infant has almost infinite potentialities. Whether he becomes saint or sinner, hero or rapist, scientist or minister, the actualization of evil or good depends upon the social institutions of which he is a member.

Clinical psychologists, on the other hand, are impressed by the way a man is driven by his heart and guts, his emotions and his instincts, to create a "life space," a private world, that often ignores and sometimes contradicts the pressures of the society. They note the way in which a client's past experiences and present motives determine what he sees and does. They observe how much he selects the social environment and the people who best fit his needs. They see how much he distorts realities to fit his needs. As a consequence, they tend to conclude that the actual physical and social worlds of most people are almost irrelevant in determining their own life, their own psychological worlds. Their personalities are formed by the particular genes they have inherited, the unique life experiences they have endured, and, above all, by the highly individualistic perceptions they have of the world.

However, it is the *interaction* between the internal and external worlds that largely determines what happens to the individual and what happens to the society.

The most realistic question to ask, then, is not whether heredity *or* environment determines personality, nor how much of personality is determined by differences in heredity and how much by differences in environment. It is: How do the hereditary and environmental influences interact? The answer is that they interact through the operation of: (1) direct genetic mechanisms; (2) indirect genetic mechanisms; (3) general environmental mechanisms; and (4) specific environmental mechanisms.

Direct Genetic Mechanisms

Heredity may influence behavior directly or indirectly. The mechanism by which genes interact with environment to create differences in a trait may be quite direct. In one kind of feeble-mindedness, for example, genes that are essential for normal intellectual development are defective. The causal chain from defective gene through metabolic disorder and consequent cerebral malfunctioning to feeble-mindedness has been examined step by step. In our present state of knowledge, there is no environmental factor which can completely counteract the genetic deficiency. The individual will be mentally retarded, regardless of the type of environmental conditions under which he is reared. Even in this rare case, however, there is some interaction with the environment. Intellectual development shows some variations with the type of care and training available to the individual.

Indirect Genetic Mechanisms

The influence of genetic mechanisms is generally less direct than in the kind of feeble-mindedness just described. Hereditary deafness, for example, often leads to severe intellectual retardation. The causal chain, however, is much more complex and indirect: (1) deafness may interfere with normal social interaction; (2) poor social interaction leads to poor language development; (3) poor language development leads to poor performance in school; and (4) poor language ability and poor school achievement lead to poor performance on intelligence tests. Training can offset these handicaps. The degree of intellectual retardation due to deafness is, in fact, an index of the state of development of special instruction facilities: the better the facilities, the less the retardation.

Genes may influence behavior even more indirectly but just as powerfully through the operation of social stereotypes. Blood types, for example, are directly determined by genes. Suppose there was a country in which carriers of blood group AB were considered aristocrats and those of group O, laborers. In such a country, genes determining blood types would have a strong influence on behavior. Of course, the genes would only influence behavior in that particular country. Such specificity of influence, however, is the essential property that differentiates indirect from direct mechanisms. In our country we do not have stereotypes about people in different blood groups. We do have stereotypes about people with different colored skins.

General Environmental Mechanisms

The most direct of hereditary mechanisms do not immediately influence behavior. All environmental influences do. However, environmental influences may be narrow or broad, limited or pervasive, temporary or enduring. The narrower, the more limited, the more temporary the influences, the more *specific*. The broader, more pervasive, and more permanent the influence, the more *general*.

Social-class membership is a general environmental mechanism, for its influence is both pervasive and relatively permanent. A person's social-class membership determines the range and nature of intellectual stimulation provided by home and community through books, music, art, and play activities. It determines the person's interest in performing abstract intellectual tasks, surpassing others in school, and gaining social approval.

Specific Environmental Mechanisms

Food, alcohol, and drugs may influence behavior dramatically, but their influence quickly wanes. Formal training programs also are specific environmental influences. While their influence may have a permanent impact, it is almost always very limited in scope. The border between general and specific mechanisms is hard to define. Still, the distinction is useful, for it emphasizes that the influence of specific mechanisms that are available to the teacher, counselor, or the individual must be seen against the background of the broader and more permanent pressures exerted upon the individual by his general environment.

In sum, both direct and indirect genetic and environmental mechanisms determine personality. These mechanisms have a different influence on traits than they have on personality structures or interpersonal relationships. They also have different influences on particular traits, structures, and relationships. For example, differences in boldness are caused by quite different mechanisms than those that determine the practicality of a person. In the following chapters, therefore, we shall consider the varying influence of each of the four mechanisms on each aspect of personality.

Before considering these specifics, however, it is essential that we examine the critical differences between common-sense and scientific theories of personality.

SUMMARY

This book assumes that the better an individual understands his personality, the happier he is likely to be. It defines personality as "the dynamic organization of traits within the self that determine the individual's unique way of playing his social roles." This chapter introduces the three major ways in which psychologists approach the problem of understanding personality: traits as personality, the self as personality, and roles as personality. These perspectives divide the book. The chapter also introduces the major causes of differences in personality: direct and indirect genetic mechanisms; general and specific environmental mechanisms; and interactions between these mechanisms. Throughout the book, differences in personality are first described in terms of traits, stage of self development, or ways of playing roles, and then the differences are explained in terms of the mechanisms.

SUGGESTIONS FOR FURTHER READING

The readings here and in the following chapters are arranged in order of their general interest and readability. Those marked with an * are from a list of "psychological thrillers" compiled by McCollom (1971) from the ratings of hundreds of students. In these cases, typical comments of students are included.

Goethals, G. W., and Klos, D. S. (1970). *Experiencing youth: first-person accounts.* Boston: Little, Brown. Twenty-six brief but gripping accounts by college students of their problems in becoming autonomous, developing an identity, and achieving sexual intimacy.

Russell, B. (1968). *The conquest of happiness.* New York: Bantam. Simple, wise, and earthy advice by a great mathematician and philosopher.

*Adcock, C. J. (1964). *Fundamentals of psychology.* Baltimore: Penguin, 1964 (paperback, Pelican edition). Shows the relation of the science of personality to psychology in general. This book provides a brief and interesting account of the field as a whole: "extremely valuable as a general review . . . far more interesting than anticipated . . . a really good book."

Smith, H. C. (1973). *Sensitivity training.* New York: McGraw-Hill. A summary of research concerned with the ability to understand people and with methods for improving the ability.

2

THEORIES OF PERSONALITY

Science aims to give man an understanding, a power of prediction,
and a power of control, beyond that which he can achieve
through his own unaided common sense.

GORDON ALLPORT

A theory is a set of concepts with *assumed* relationships between them. Einstein's theory, for example, is such a set of concepts and assumed relationships between them ($E = mc^2$). The science of psychology is a vast enterprise devoted to the development of theories about human behavior and experience, of ways of testing these theories, and of ways of applying them to the solution of human problems. This book is primarily devoted to describing and applying a trait theory, a self theory, and a role theory. These theories are not particularly difficult to understand. They are, however, extremely difficult to use because they conflict with the common-sense theories that we have learned to use. The main purpose of this chapter, therefore, is to make the reader aware of the nature of the personality theory he is already using, why he uses it, and how his theory differs from scientific ones.

COMMON-SENSE THEORIES

Common-sense theories use concepts and assumed relationships as do scientific theories. Like science, common sense seeks to test its theories. Science, however, uses different kinds of concepts, assumes different kinds of relationships, and uses a different kind of method for testing its theories. Above all, science *knows* that it is using theories but common sense does not. Common sense does not believe that it is using theories; it believes that it is describing reality.

Concepts

What concepts do we use in our common-sense theory? The dictionary lists about 18,000 words that are possible personality concepts. Anderson (1968) gave college students 555 of these and asked them to think of a person being described by each word. He then asked them to rate the person from "least favorable or desirable" to "most favorable or desirable." He determined the average rating of each word. The words were then ranked from "1," the word with the highest average rating to "555," the word with the lowest average rating. Table 2-1 is a sample from the complete list. It shows that "sincere" was the most desirable trait and "liar" was the least desirable trait.

Everyone of the 555 words has an emotional, a descriptive, and a predictive meaning. Calling a person "friendly," for example, implies that we like him, describes how he behaves toward us, and predicts that we would expect him to behave in the same way in the future. However, words vary a great deal in the amount of emotional, descriptive, or predictive meaning they convey. "Sincere" and "liar" are saturated with emotional meaning but only tinted with descriptive and predictive meaning. "Talkative," on the other hand, is high in descrip-

TABLE 2-1   The Emotionality of Traits

College students rated 555 personality-trait words on likeableness as personality characteristics. The mean ratings of
50 of these are given below. The number in front indicates
the rank among the 50 from the most desirable to the least
desirable. The number in parentheses indicates the rank of
that trait among the original 555.

1.	Sincere (1)	26.	Bold (237)
2.	Honest (2)	27.	Cautious (239)
3.	Understanding (3)	28.	Impulsive (252)
4.	Intelligent (7)	29.	Emotional (264)
5.	Open-minded (9)	30.	Opportunistic (274)
6.	Considerate (12)	31.	Conformist (306)
7.	Warm (16)	32.	Radical (307)
8.	Friendly (19)	33.	Unemotional (347)
9.	Responsible (28)	34.	Nervous (367)
10.	Ambitious (59)	35.	Pessimistic (410)
11.	Conscientious (65)	36.	Dominating (432)
12.	Cooperative (79)	37.	Neurotic (438)
13.	Capable (83)	38.	Cold (486)
14.	Punctual (93)	39.	Incompetent (492)
15.	Tolerant (100)	40.	Irresponsible (499)
16.	Calm (179)	41.	Unreliable (504)
17.	Artistic (183)	42.	Boring (514)
18.	Scientific (185)	43.	Hostile (523)
19.	Orderly (186)	44.	Selfish (532)
20.	Religious (195)	45.	Greedy (540)
21.	Nonconforming (212)	46.	Dishonest (551)
22.	Middle-class (221)	47.	Cruel (552)
23.	Talkative (226)	48.	Mean (553)
24.	Excited (227)	49.	Phony (554)
25.	Moderate (228)	50.	Liar (555)

(*Source*: Anderson, 1968)

tive and predictive meaning but low in emotional meaning. "Bold" has
little emotional meaning, more descriptive meaning, and a great deal of
predictive meaning.

Theories use concepts that are meaningful. But do we prefer
words that are saturated with emotional, descriptive, or predictive
meaning? Anderson asked his students to rate the meaningfulness of
words from 0 ("I have almost no idea of the meaning of this word") to 4
("I have a very clear and definite understanding of the meaning of this
word"). Result: The more emotional the word, the more likely it was to

be judged as meaningful to us. If we see a person at all, we tend to see him with some emotion. We see him through an emotional atmosphere of some boredom or excitement, fear or anger, hate or love. Consequently, we do use personality concepts that primarily describe how we feel about him.

Assumed Relationships

Common-sense theory favors concepts with high emotional loadings. What relationships between these concepts does it assume? The answer is: It assumes a *close* relationship. If we say that someone is "honest" and "understanding," it is highly *un*likely that we will say he is either "mean" or "phony." If we say that he is a "liar," it is highly likely that we will also say that he is "greedy" and "cruel." It is highly *un*likely that we will say he is "intelligent" and "open-minded."

Why do we assume such an intimate relationship between the concepts of our common-sense theory? Our conceptions reflect our perceptions. We see a person as an instant emotional whole and then differentiate parts within the whole. The parts are not independent of the whole. They are integrated with it. Our first verbal picture of a person, then, is a brief and simple whole. As we talk or write about him our picture becomes more elaborate and more differentiated. However, the words we use are intimately related to each other because they reflect the integrated whole we perceive.

Every part of our perception of a person is related to every other part. Consequently, every part of our conception tends to be related to every other part. For example, the concepts we use to describe appearance are related to the concepts we use to describe traits. McKeachie (1952) had six men rate six women on 22 different personality traits. They were told that the purpose of the study was to determine the reliability of personality ratings made on the basis of a 10-minute interview. Actually, the purpose was to determine the influence of lipstick on personal impressions. Each man interviewed three girls with and three without lipstick; each girl appeared in three interviews with and in three without lipstick. Result: Without lipstick, a girl was more often judged as being conscientious, serious, talkative, and not interested in men. After the interviews the men were asked what things they thought had influenced their ratings. None mentioned lipstick.

The reverse is also true: Knowing the traits of a person generates a description of his physical appearance.

Students were given these two descriptions (Secord, 1958):

A.   This man is warmhearted and honest. He has a good sense of humor and is intelligent and unbiased in his opinion. He is responsible and self-confident with an air of refinement.

B.   This man is a ruthless and brutal person. He is extremely hostile, quick-tempered, and overbearing. He is well known for his boorish and vulgar manner and is a very domineering and unsympathetic person.

The students were then asked to rate 32 facial *features* of the two fictitious men on a 7-point scale. They not only did this quickly and without difficulty but also generally agreed on the differences between them. The warmhearted man had a more direct gaze, a smoother brow, more relaxed nostrils, and hair more neatly groomed. The ruthless man had a darker complexion, more tense face, a squarer jaw, and a rougher texture to his skin.

Relationships are structured: a few central concepts organize the peripheral ones within a unified framework. The warmth of a person is one of these central concepts. Asch (1946) read list A to one group and list B to another:

List A: Intelligent, skillful, industrious, *cold*, determined, practical, cautious

List B: Intelligent, skillful, industrious, *warm*, determined, practical, cautious

The two groups were asked to write an imaginative sketch of the kind of person who would have such a combination of traits. The substitution of warm for cold made a big difference in how the other traits were viewed. The following sketches are typical:

COLD GROUP: A very ambitious and talented person who would not let anyone or anything stand in the way of achieving his goal. Wants his own way, he is determined not to give in, no matter what happens.

WARM GROUP: A person who believes certain things to be right, wants others to see his point, would be sincere in an argument, and would like to see his point won.

The groups were also given a list of additional traits and asked to check those which fitted their impression of the person. The warm person was more often checked as generous, wise, happy, sociable, popular, and humorous. The cold person was more often checked as shrewd, irritable, ruthless, and self-centered. Asch concludes:

The moment we see that two or more characteristics belong to the same person they enter into dynamic interaction. We cannot see one quality and another in the same person without their affecting each other. . . . From its inception the impression has structure, even if rudimentary. The various characteristics do not possess the same weight. Some become central, providing the main direction; others become peripheral and dependent. Until we have found the center—that part of the person which wants to live and act in a certain way, which wants not to break or disappear—we feel we have not succeeded in reaching an understanding.

Our theories, then, mirror our momentary perception of a person. They also do something less obvious but more important. Perceptions may be intense and vivid, but they are brief. We may dimly recall how we perceived a person yesterday. In a week we may not remember at all. Our theory gives *expression* to a perception. This fact implies a radical change. What was dim becomes bright, what was passive becomes active, and what was readily forgotten is now easily remembered. The novelist Proust (1922) has described the way in which our conceptions influence our perceptions:

> Even the simple act which we describe as "seeing someone we know" is, to some extent, an intellectual process. We pack the physical outline of the creature we see with all the ideas we have already formed about him, and in the complete picture of him which we compose in our minds those ideas have certainly the principal place. In the end they come to fill out so completely the curve of his cheeks, to follow so exactly the line of his nose, they blend so harmoniously in the sound of his voice that these seem to be no more than a transparent envelope, so that each time we see the face or hear the voice it is our own ideas of him which we recognize and to which we listen.

The Common-Sense Test of Theories

The holder of a common-sense theory is as eager to test it as the holder of a scientific one (Figure 2-1). The crucial difference is that the ultimate test of common sense is subjective: "of, related to, or determined by the mind, ego, or consciousness." The scientist knows that his theory does not *determine* reality but only fits or does not fit it. His ultimate test, therefore, is objective: "independent of mind, ego, or consciousness."

The pitfalls of subjective tests are illustrated by a personnel manager being "taken" by an unethical salesman (Stagner, 1958).

Figure 2-1 A nineteenth century labyrinth garden near Versailles. Dense hedges separated the paths in this garden, and multiple deadends and blinds made solving the maze even more difficult. A person trying to find the exit would form and test many "theories" about the correct route. Scientific theories must also be testable. Only if explicit predictions are made can the theory be compared with actual results of experiments. (Ron Junttonen)

"Let me give you a real demonstration. You take this personality test yourself, and I'll give you the report based on your scores. If you don't agree that it is amazingly accurate I won't even try to sell it to you." The gullible manager takes the test, reads the report, is amazed by its accuracy, and spends a lot of his company's money for a device not worth the paper and printing.

The salesman can achieve his results by including in his "report" statements like the following:

You prefer a certain amount of change and variety and become dissatisfied when hemmed in by restrictions and limitations (91%).

While you have some personality weaknesses, you are generally able to compensate for them (89%).

You have a great need for other people to like and admire you (85%).

You have a tendency to be critical of yourself (82%).

The percentages after the statement indicate the proportion of 68 personnel managers who agreed that the statement was either a "rather good" or an "amazingly accurate" picture of themselves. About the same percentage of college students will agree. In fact, few people will choose their own personality diagnosis based on objective test data when given a choice between it and vague generalities like those above.

The subjective tests of experts do not escape the pit. Oskamp (1965) gave increasing amounts of information about a person to a group of psychologists. The psychologists first studied just a few general facts about a man and then predicted how he would behave in 25 different situations. Afterward, they were asked: How many of your predictions do you think were correct? Subjectively, the psychologists expected 33 percent of their predictions to be correct. Objectively, 26 percent were actually correct. The psychologists were given increasing amounts of information. Each time, they reported how many of their predictions they thought would be correct. At the final stage, they read more than a thousand words about a person. The more they read, the more confident they became about the accuracy of their predictions. Objectively, however, their accuracy remained about the same. Thus, at the final stage, the typical psychologist expected to get 53 percent of his predictions correct. He actually got 28 percent correct. The author concluded: "The judges' confidence ratings showed that they became convinced of their own increasing understanding of the case. . . . Their certainty about their own decisions became entirely out of proportion to the actual correctness of those decisions."

SCIENTIFIC THEORIES

All scientific theories of personality must start from common-sense ones. Without our feelings and thoughts about people and without the expression of those feelings and thoughts in concepts and assumed relationships, we would not even be aware of the field of personality. With them, we communicate our feelings about people, describe them, and indicate how we expect them to feel and behave toward us. A scientific theory of personality, though, has a specialized purpose. It concentrates upon the advancement of our understanding of how we can expect people to feel and behave. In pursuit of this end, scientific theories focus upon fewer, less emotional, and more explicit concepts and relationships that can be objectively verified. In exemplifying these requirements here we will use the trait theory that is elaborated in the next section of this chapter. However, the same requirements apply to the self and role theories that we consider in later chapters.

The Fewer the Concepts, the Better

The development of a scientific trait theory begins with the thousands of trait names in the dictionary. The first task is to reduce them to a reasonable number. About a fourth can be eliminated because they describe temporary rather than stable qualities: *ablaze, alarmed, awed*, etc. Another fourth can be eliminated because they reflect purely emotional reactions to a person: *asinine, addle-brained, atrocious*, etc. Still another fourth can be eliminated because it is uncertain whether they refer to people: *abysmal, autumnal, arctic*, etc. Even after these reductions, about 5,000 names remain, beginning with *absent-minded, abstemious*, and *academic.*

The list can be further reduced by eliminating synonyms and by grouping opposites. For example, active and inactive can be thought of as opposite ends of one trait—*active* and *inactive*; similarly, *sensitive* can be grouped with *insensitive*; pessimistic with *optimistic*, *inhibited* with *expressive*, etc. By such ingenious armchair processes, the 5,000 can be reduced to several hundred. Psychologists for decades have struggled with the problem of reducing the several hundred to a more manageable number. In the process, they have discarded some traits that cannot be measured, some that proved to be so changeable as to be uncertain guides to permanent personality trends, and still others that were found to be too similar to others.

As a result of these processes, Gough (1954) isolated 10 traits: *impulsivity, flexibility, self-acceptance, social presence, intellectual efficiency, social participation, tolerance, dominance, social responsibility*, and *delinquency*. Edwards (1954), following slightly different procedures, isolated 14 traits: *endurance, heterosexuality, exhibitionism, intraception, achievement, order, change, affiliation, autonomy, nurturance, dominance, deference, abasement*, and *aggression*. Cattell (1956) identified 16 traits: *nervous tension, emotional sensitivity, surgency, calm trustfulness, sophistication, self-sufficiency, radicalism, positive character, general intelligence, emotional stability, will control, adventurous cyclothymia, accessibility, dominance*, and *Bohemianism.*

"Dominance" is the only name that appears in all three trait lists. However, many of the same traits merely have different labels. Thus, Gough's *social participation*, Edwards' *affiliation*, and Cattell's *adventurous cyclothymia* all involve gregariousness. Again, Gough's *tolerance*, Edwards' *nurturance*, and Cattell's *adventurous cyclothymia* are related to warmth in human relationships. Still, some of the traits in each of the theories have no counterpart in the other theories. For example, there is no obvious match in the other theories of Gough's *flexibility*, of Edwards' *heterosexuality*, or of Cattell's *radicalism*.

Matching all the traits that could be matched, Grossman (1967) still found 22 different traits described in the three different theories.

Of course, it is not the primary aim to have the smallest number of traits. The aim is to have the smallest number that is still able to describe the stable and significant ways in which people actually differ from each other. By processes that we shall examine in the next chapter, Grossman concluded that five traits were adequate for this task: *cautious* versus *bold*, *unemotional* versus *emotional*, *present-minded* versus *future-minded*, *artistic* versus *practical*, and *religious* versus *scientific*.

The Less Emotional the Concepts, the Better

Common-sense theories reflect the fact that our feelings about other people are among the most meaningful and important things in our lives. However, our present feelings tell us little about our past or future ones. The person we were indifferent to yesterday, we may love now and hate tomorrow. Our present feelings about him tell us little or nothing about his feelings toward us. The science of personality aims to make our predictions about others more accurate so that what we expect them to do they will do. Common-sense theory satisfies our powerful and urgent need to express how we feel about a person. Scientific theory satisfies a less urgent, but, in the long run, a more powerful need to have realistic expectations about what we and others will feel, think, and do. In the pursuit of this end, it seeks concepts that are as impersonal and unemotional as possible.

The traits identified by Grossman (1967) approach the ideal of neutrality, for not only are the traits of moderate desirability but the opposite ends of the traits seem nearly equal in desirability to the typical student. Thus, "cautious" and "bold" stand next to each other in the middle of Table 2-1; while "unemotional" is judged somewhat less desirable than "emotional," its close synonym, "calm," is judged as more desirable. Again, the artistic and practical, the impulsive and the controlled, and the religious and the scientific are typically judged to be of almost equal desirability.

Impersonality and unemotionality are scientific ideals. Scientists, themselves, find it hard to adhere to these ideals. To be useful, a theory must be used. It must be exciting and vital enough to get psychologists to talk about it, to accept or fight it, to use it or abuse it, and most important, to try to prove or disprove it. Like other people, psychologists are inclined to be most interested in those personality theories that use emotional rather than unemotional concepts.

The More Explicit the Concepts, the Better

Like scientific theories, common-sense theories use concepts in describing people, assume relationships between these concepts, and make predictions about what people will feel and how they will behave from these concepts and relationships. Generally, however, we are only dimly aware of our common-sense theories, we use concepts without realizing it, assume relationships without stating them, and unconsciously make predictions about people based on these relationships. Thus, the students using the lipstick theory were unaware that they were doing so. Their theories were *implicit*. A valuable theory fits reality. To know that it does fit reality, we must be able to show that it does. We cannot even think about testing our implicit theories because we do not even know that we have them. Thus, the first and most obvious step toward the development of a scientific theory is that it be made explicit, i.e., stated in words, numbers, or formulas.

The Explicitness of Psychoanalytic Theory

Freud's psychoanalytic theory is explicit. It defines three basic concepts (the id, the ego, and the superego), states relationships between these concepts, and explains how people should feel and behave if the assumed relationships are correct. The central concepts are pictured in Figure 2-2 and briefly defined below.

The *id* consists of everything psychological that is present at birth; it is in close touch with the body processes, and it is a reservoir of psychic energy that furnishes all the power for the operation of the ego and the superego. The id cannot tolerate discomfort. Consequently, when the tension level of the organism is raised, the id attempts to discharge the tension immediately. Its method of tension reduction is called the *pleasure principle*, which operates either through *reflex action* or through what is called the *primary process*. Sneezing and blinking illustrate the reduction of tension through reflex action. The primary process is an attempt to discharge tension by forming an image of an object that will remove the tension. The hallucinatory experience in which the desired object is present in the form of a mental image is called *wish fulfillment*. The best example of the primary process is the dream, which Freud believed always represented the fulfillment or the attempted fulfillment of a wish. The primary process, however, is not capable of reducing tension—the hungry person cannot eat mental images of food.

The id knows only the subjective reality of the mind; the *ego* distinguishes between things in the mind and things in the external

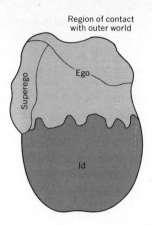

Figure 2-2 Structural elements in the psychoanalytic theory of Freud. The id is entirely unconscious; the superego and the ego are mainly conscious. The ego carries out the demands of the id and the super-ego represents most of the region of contact with the outer world. (After Healy, Bronner, and Bowers, 1931)

world. The ego, the executive of the personality, obeys the *reality principle* and operates by means of a *secondary process.* The pleasure principle is only concerned with whether an experience is painful or pleasant; the reality principle is also concerned with whether it is true or false, that is, whether it has external existence or not. The secondary process is the realistic thinking by means of which the ego formulates and tests a plan for satisfying a need. Thus, the hungry man thinks of a place where food may be found and then looks in that place. This is *reality testing* in its simplest form.

The ego exists to forward the aims of the id. It is part of the id, derives its power from the id, and never becomes completely independent of the id. As executive, the ego tries to integrate the conflicting demands of the id, the superego, and the external world. Since this is a difficult task, the ego is often under a great strain. Thus, its weakness or strength becomes crucial in maintaining the integrity of the organism. The more mature a person becomes, the greater becomes his *ego strength.*

The id is the biological side of personality; the ego, the psychological; the *superego,* the social. The superego is the internal representative of the ideals of society; it is the moral judge of conduct; it represents the ideal rather than the real; and it strives for perfection rather than pleasure. Although the superego has its own functions, they are so closely related to the functions of the id and the ego that it is difficult to disentangle their effects. The main concern of the superego is to decide whether an act is "right" or "wrong." Its most difficult task is to control the sexual and aggressive impulses of the id, the impulses whose expression is most likely to be condemned by society.

Some theories are more explicit than others. The more fully a theory is expressed in words and symbols, the more exactly these words and symbols are defined, and, above all, the more measurable the concepts and relationships assumed by the theory, the more explicit the theory becomes. Einstein's theory, for example, is more explicit than Freud's. The former is expressed in exact mathematical symbols; the latter, only in verbal symbols. There is little argument about what Einstein meant by his concepts or the relationships his theory assumed; there is still, more than half a century after Freud's theory was formulated, considerable doubt about what he meant by some of his concepts and what relationships he assumed. The concepts and assumed relationships of Einstein's theory have been measured; many of Freud's concepts and relationships still have not been.

Psychoanalytic theory looks at personality not from the trait view but from the organizational view. As we shall see in Part 3, theories of the development of the self are more comprehensive than trait theories. They are also, however, less explicit about the concepts they employ and the relationships between these concepts that they assume. A research psychologist is forced to chose between working with the less comprehensive but more exact trait view of personality and the more comprehensive but less exact dynamic view of personality. The reader, however, is not forced to make such a choice; each of these views offers him a different but valid perspective on human personality.

The More Testable a Theory, the Better

No theory is simpler and more explicit than the theory that there is a life after death. Early in his career Carl Jung was an admirer and friend of Freud (Figure 2-3). In 1914, however, he broke completely with Freud and formed his own theory of psychoanalysis and method of psychotherapy that has become known as *analytic psychology*. In his autobiography (1965, pp. 301–302), he has this to say about the theory of a life after death:

For most people it means a great deal to assume that their lives will have an indefinite continuity beyond their present existence. They live more sensibly, feel better, and are more at peace. One has centuries, one has an inconceivable period of time at one's disposal. What then is the point of this senseless mad rush? Naturally, such reasoning does not apply to everyone. There are people who feel no craving for immortality, and who shudder at the thought of sitting on a cloud and playing the harp for ten thousand years! There are also quite a few who have been so buffeted by life, or who feel such disgust for their own existence, that they far prefer absolute cessation to continuance. But in the majority of cases the question of immortality is so urgent, so immediate, and also so ineradicable that we

Figure 2-3 Carl Jung, the Swiss psychiatrist, at the age of seventy-nine. In his youth a follower of Freud, he later developed his own analytical theory, which stressed the individual's need for a sense of meaning and personal worth. (The Bettman Archive)

must make an effort to form some view about it. But how?

My hypothesis is that we can do so with the aid of hints sent to us from the unconscious—in dreams, for example. . . . What the myths or stories about a life after death really mean, or what kind of reality lies behind them, we certainly do not know. We cannot tell whether they possess any validity beyond their indubitable value as anthropomorphic projections. Rather, we must hold clearly in mind that there is no possible way for us to attain certainty concerning things which pass our understanding . . . I do not know for what reason the universe has come into being, and shall never know. Therefore, I must drop this question as a scientific or intellectual problem. But if an idea about it is offered to me—in dreams or in mythic traditions—I ought to take note of it. I even ought to build up a conception on the basis of such hints, even though it will forever remain a hypothesis which I know cannot be proved.

The theory that there is a life after death is not a scientific theory because it cannot be verified (Marx, 1951):

Testability is the absolutely essential characteristic of any scientifically useful hypotheses. . . . Without some degree of willingness to subject all concepts to a critical, operational analysis the essential self-correcting processes in science can hardly function effectively. It is in just such a tight and exclusively speculative atmosphere that cultlike and anti-empirical tendencies thrive. . . . A major obstacle to more effective scientific progress seems to be a general disinclination to submit constructs and theories to a critical and rigorous operational analysis (whether or not that particular term is used) and a corresponding failure explicitly to recognize the invidious infiltration of emotional beliefs and extra-scientific values throughout all phases of theory construction.

The number and importance of the relationships that can be assumed from a theory and then tested determine its potential value. Can predictions from psychoanalytic theory be checked? Yes, and here are two examples.

Freud deduced from his theory that a man would be afraid of losing his penis and that a woman would envy the penis of a man and wish to castrate him. Hall and Van de Castle (1965) had 60 male and 60 female students report two dreams per week. If a dream indicated that the dreamer had suffered the loss, removal, or injury of any specific part of his body (hair, teeth, arm, etc.), it was classified as indicating *castration anxiety*. If loss or injury occurred to someone who was not the dreamer, it was classified as *castration wish*. If the dreamer acquired some object like a penis (a pencil, rake, etc.), then the dream was classified as *penis envy*. The frequency of the three types of dreams for men and women were then counted. Freud's deduction was supported: 80 percent of the men had more castration anxiety than other types of dreams; only 36 percent of the women had more castration anxiety. Three times as many women as men had more castration wish or penis envy dreams than castration anxiety dreams.

Patients under psychoanalytic treatment lie on a couch during their therapy hours. The theory behind the procedure is that the lying-down position encourages the recall of early experiences. To check this, Berdach (1965) had 42 undergraduate men recall any memories that came to mind in a 20-minute period. Half of the men were tested in a sitting-up position; the other half, in a lying-down position. The results supported the hypothesis: "The mean number of memories in the age 0–3 years category was significantly greater in the lying-down than in the sitting-up position."

Some inferences from psychoanalytic theory can be verified. However, some cannot. For example, Freud postulated a death wish in human beings. To test the postulate, we need to make predictions from it about what is going to happen before it happens. It seems impossible to derive any testable propositions from the assumption of a death wish in people. After a person commits suicide we can say that he had a death wish. However, this is like betting on a horse after the race is over.

The more precisely a theory specifies the kinds of predictions to be made from it and the more exactly these predictions can be measured, the better. Freud wrote of fascinating and sensational ideas (sex, aggression, death) in an exciting literary style which is rare among scientists. But how many cases of a particular type did he study and from what backgrounds did they come? What measures or criteria did he use for assigning a case to a particular category? How intense does an experience have to be before it is traumatic? How weak does the ego have to be before it is overridden by an instinctual impulse? Freud gave only imprecise answers.

The strength of psychoanalytic theory from the common-sense point of view is that its complexity matches the complexity of real people much more closely than a simple trait theory. However, it is harder for a person to see how the theory applies to a concrete person. By contrast, it is easy to apply the five-trait theory. Here, for example, is its application to Freud himself. The ratings shown under the headings are based in part on the quotations from Freud and from the biography of Freud by Jones (1957):

Average Boldness

Work of some sort was daily bread to Freud. . . . He was never in bed before one in the morning and often much later. . . . Freud never had a serious illness before his late sixties. . . . He was a remarkable walker, light, swift and tireless.

It is possible to criticize Freud's education of his children on one point only—it was unusually lenient.

Freud had a modest enough estimate of himself . . . Marie Bonaparte told him she thought he was a mixture of Pasteur and Kant. He replied: "That is very complimentary, but I can't share your opinion. Not because I am modest, not at all. I have a high opinion of what I have discovered, but not of myself. Great discoverers are not necessarily great men. Who changed the world more than Columbus? What was he? An adventurer."

He was certainly a cheerful person, so the worst that might be supposed was that perhaps he was one of those "cheerful pessimists."

Very Unemotional

Two things . . . we find exemplified in a high degree with

Freud: Tolerance of anxiety, i.e., such mastery of it that it affects one but little, and a firm apprehension of reality.

One sensed an invisible reserve behind which it would be impertinent to intrude, and no one ever did. . . . He never spoke to his children about his youth and early years; most of the knowledge they have of it has come from the present work . . . quite complete reticence on the matter of his love life.

Though not demonstrative by nature, he had, it was not hard to perceive, a deep fund of tenderness as well as kindness. It is not surprising that he inspired devotion.

Very Future-Minded

Freud's apparel was invariably neat and correct, though not smart or fashionable. . . . Freud led a quiet and regular life. . . . Freud once told Jung that were he ever to suffer from a neurosis it would be of the obsessional type. His excessive cigar smoking was evidence of such an obsessional quality. In spite of repeated operations for throat cancer that were directly related to his smoking, he was never able to give up the habit though he tried often.

Very Artistic

I knew already from his writings of his astonishing knowledge of literature; of his memory, especially for Shakespeare; and of his other tastes, his love of all antiquities, of Greece and Rome, and the art of earlier cultures.

Now Freud had inherently a plastic and mobile mind, one given to the freest speculations and open to new and even highly improbable ideas. But it worked this way only on condition that the ideas came from himself; to those from outside he could be very resistant, and they had little power in getting him to change his mind.

Very Scientific

Freud would have been in favor of any obvious social reforms, but in a longer view he was not sure that they would produce a really satisfactory civilization. Something more radical was needed, and he was a revolutionary rather than a reformer.

He disliked pathological types or extremes of any kind. From this attitude of mind his intolerance of religion in my mind largely derived; for religion tends to see life in black or white and cannot accept the compromises and complexities in it which are the subject matter of scientific psychology.

About one thing Freud was serious above all else and it became the driving force of his life. That was the search for knowledge. His mind was not of the philosophic or contemplative kind; it was a restless, inquiring mind.

Freud's indifference to the views of other people was one of his most highly developed characteristics, one so striking as to be observed in ordinary life by those who met him even casually.

These ratings of Freud reflect the judgments of the author. That is, they are the result of using the subjective method of common sense. Science requires not only objective methods of determining where a person stands on a trait but also objective methods of determining whether the traits really reflect stable differences between people and whether they are actually as independent of each other as the theory assumes. The next chapter reviews some of these objective methods.

SUMMARY

A personality theory is a set of concepts with assumptions regarding the relationships between them. Everyone makes daily use of common-sense theories to intensify, illuminate, and stabilize his perceptions of himself and others. Everyone also tests his theories by subjective ("of, related to, or determined by the mind, ego, or consciousness") means. A psychologist develops a scientific theory of personality from a common-sense one by using unemotional concepts, by defining them as concretely and explicitly as possible, by measuring them, by reducing their numbers, and by testing the relationships he assumes between the concepts by objective means, i.e., by means that are *independent* of his opinion about what the actual relationships are.

SUGGESTIONS FOR FURTHER READING

Fromm, E. (1957). *The art of loving.* New York: Harper. A very popular account of personality from a role point of view.

*Hall, C. H. (1955). *A primer of Freudian psychology.* Paperback, New American Library. A very frequently read book about the world's best-known self theorist: "More informative than entertaining."

Allport, G. W. (1937). *Personality: a psychological interpretation.* A classic in the field of personality that stresses the trait point of view but defends the complexity of personality from rigid and simplistic scientific methodologies.

Peirce, C. S. (1957). *Essays in the philosophy of science.* New York: Liberal Arts Press. A small book that contains almost all that was written by probably the greatest and certainly the most neglected American philosopher of science. Contains the brilliant essay: "How to make our ideas clear." He was never able to get a job at a university.

3

THE TESTING
OF THEORIES

The fundamental hypothesis of science is this:
There are real things, whose characters are entirely
independent of our opinions about them.

CHARLES S. PEIRCE

To survive and grow, some animals rely on the number of their offspring; others, on speed; and still others, on poisons, and camouflage. Man is unique in his heavy reliance upon *self-direction*, upon knowing who he is, where he wants to go, and how to get there. Understanding himself, therefore, is central for his survival and well-being. Problems of self-direction trouble these students as they do all of us:

Conrad   My ambitions are high and wide: I want to make a lot of money, I want to be a successful engineer who contributes something of worth to mankind, I want to become an outstanding bowler and golfer, etc. But I am lazy. At times, an iron deficiency and a bad sinus condition sap my energies. But even if I could correct these ailments, I think that I would still be indolent. For example, I want very much to take flying lessons after my college classes. Instead, I just go to sleep. I don't see how I can achieve the goals I have set for myself.

Howard   My early religious training made a deep impression upon me but the value of money I have learned bitterly as a result of my participation in society. It seems to me many men resolve the conflict by first making themselves economically secure in any way they can and then reconstructing their ideas around a core of religious beliefs which wipe their smeared consciences clean. Is it better to follow this popular plan or to guide yourself via the golden rule and, when other men pass you on the way up the economic ladder, to say to yourself that it doesn't matter because you are doing your job the Christian way?

Joseph   I pride myself on having original ideas, and I would like to express them to people I meet. But I haven't got the courage of my convictions or enough self-confidence to do it. I can't buck the group. Besides, I know I'll have to conform if I am ever going to be a business success. I have always dreaded being an organization man, but it doesn't look as if I will have much choice.

Mabel   I like most people, and I get a great deal of satisfaction from helping people when they are in trouble and letting them know that I understand them and want to do what I can for them. But I am shy about expressing my feelings, and friends have told me that I seem rather cool and secretive. It makes me very uncomfortable when I think that others seldom realize how sympathetic I am toward them or how much I would enjoy doing things for them.

Margaret   Because I am orderly, I like things to be well-planned, neat, and carefully done. But I like to be different, to have novel ideas, and to do unexpected things. As a consequence, I often scorn my own orderliness and try to do things in an unmethodical and haphazard way.

Sarah I am often with people and generally enjoy social gatherings of all sorts. When I have a chance to go to parties, I usually say "yes" without even thinking about it. But I also enjoy having a chance to think my own thoughts and meditate about things. Sometimes at a party, I will suddenly think how silly it is for me to be sitting around drinking, smoking, and talking about ridiculously unimportant things when I could be enjoying myself just being alone and thinking. Then I feel like jumping up and leaving.

Thomas I have a tremendous desire to get good grades, but I am frustrated because I would like to get married and can't afford it. Sometimes with some subjects I can concentrate pretty well, but most of the time I can't. I just sit and daydream about my girl instead of doing my work. I think I'll just try harder to concentrate and just not think about my girl.

To direct himself toward the happy solution of such problems, the individual needs the ability to make realistic predictions about himself: How am I different from other people and how likely are these differences to endure? How do I need to change to become the person I would like to be? How do I relate to other people now and how would I like to change? Inevitably, he must use a theory in answering these questions, for, unlike any other creature, man is a theory-using animal.

The kind of theory the individual uses has enormous influence on the goodness of the solutions he finds for his problems. Common-sense theories, as we saw in the last chapter, are of little value for this purpose, for we do not use them as guides for our actions in the future. We use them primarily to describe our feelings right now. Even more important, we test them by our opinions, not by methods that are independent of our opinions. Scientific theories of personality are oriented in an entirely different direction, for they aim to help the individual predict future behavior by the use of theories tested by objective means.

The first job in testing a theory is to measure the set of concepts proposed by the theory. It is only when this task has been performed that we can determine whether the relationships assumed by the theory match the actual relationships. In this chapter, we consider the general methods that psychologists use in testing all theories and illustrate them by showing how they were applied in the development of the five-trait theory.

THE MEASUREMENT OF CONCEPTS

The five-trait theory asserts that there are relatively large and permanent differences between people in their degree of boldness, emotionality, time orientation, practicality, and scientific interests. But do people actually differ in these ways?

The measurement of psychological concepts is never entirely successful. Psychologists, like all scientists, are engaged in the endless task of making their imperfect measures more perfect. The process is like a hurdle race in which the hurdles get higher and higher. If a measure does not make the first easy hurdle, it is eliminated. If it does, it goes on to the next. In measurement, internal consistency is the easiest hurdle; reliability, the next; and validity, the hardest.

In the last chapter, we defined and illustrated boldness, emotionality, future-mindedness, practicality, and scientific interest. In the next five chapters, inventory measures of each of these traits are separately presented. Here we shall consider how well these inventory measures get over the measurement hurdles.

Internal Consistency

Internal consistency is the degree to which different parts of a measure agree with each other. For example, a ruler on which the distance from one to two inches is not the same as the distance from two to three inches would lack internal consistency. The greater the discrepancy, the greater the inconsistency. Personality measures have much lower internal consistencies than rulers. The most commonly used index of internal consistency is the correlation between one part of a measure and another. Correlation is the statistical process by which scores on one measure are related to scores on another. A correlation of .00 means that the scores on one measure have *no* relationship to scores on another; a correlation of 1.00, a perfect relationship. Correlations between the parts of a physical measure such as a ruler are very close to 1.00. Correlations between the parts of an intelligence test are generally above .90. The internal consistencies of standard achievement tests are generally above .80. The internal consistencies of personality tests are generally less than .80 and often much less.

The most frequent way of determining the internal consistency of a personality test is to obtain two subscores; the first, by adding the odd-numbered items; the second, by adding the even-numbered items. The greater the agreement between the scores on these two parts of the test, the higher its internal consistency. The index of agreement between the two halves can be computed in a few hours by hand and in a few seconds by a computer. If the correlation is low, the validity is almost certain to be very low. If scores on half of a test are not related to the scores on the other half, it is nearly impossible for scores on the whole test to be related to anything else. If the correlation is high, the first hurdle is over. The race, however, is far from won.

Table 3-1 shows the internal consistency correlations for each of the five 40-item inventories. The first step in obtaining each of these correlations was to obtain a subscore for the odd items (1, 3, 5 . . . 39) and a subscore for the even items (2, 4, 6 . . . 40). These two subscores were then correlated. The higher the correlations, the higher the agreement between parts of the measure. Note, first, that the correlations for two different groups are approximately the same. With the exception of the .78 for the larger group in the "control" scale, all the correlations are .80 or higher. The correlations are about as high as are obtained with the best personality inventory measures and some are as high as those obtained by intelligence tests. Generally, the battery appears to get over the lowest hurdle with some room to spare.

The scales must be consistent to be valid. However, they may be consistent and still be invalid. One way in which this can happen is by restricting the range of content covered by a scale. We might, at the extreme, have a scale with zero range. Thus, replying "yes" to the statement, "I enjoy speaking in public," is an indicator of boldness. Suppose that this statement was repeated in exactly the same form 40 different times. Obviously, a person's score on the odd items (unless he makes a clerical error) would be identical with his score on the even items. No inventories, of course, repeat identical items. Some, however, have only slight variations in content or wording from a single theme. The procedure does increase the consistency of the scale but does not increase its validity, the ultimate goal. Grossman (1967) avoided this trap by selecting a wide range of statements that were still internally consistent. The scale includes statements not only about public speaking but about self-confidence, optimism, activity level, and leadership.

High internal consistency without validity may also result if

TABLE 3-1   The Internal Consistencies of Inventory Measures of Five Traits

	Odd-even correlations	
Traits	First group (N = 100)	Second group (N = 300)
Cautious vs. bold	.88	.86
Unemotional vs. emotional	.88	.86
Present-minded vs. future-minded	.80	.78
Artistic vs. practical	.90	.88
Religious vs. scientific	.90	.85

(*Source*: Grossman, 1967)

the scale is loaded with questions that have one answer that obviously has greater *desirability*. In statements like "I hate my mother," "I dislike most people," and "I have frequent and violent nightmares," the desirable answer is obviously "false." Now there are wide differences between individuals in their tendency to choose the desirable answer. Some people almost always give the desirable answer, while others are strongly inclined to choose undesirable answers in describing themselves. As a result, scales thought to measure neuroticism, psychopathic tendencies, or boldness may be highly consistent without actually measuring any of these qualities. To avoid the problem, the authors of the scales first administered possible statements for the scales to students and asked them—regardless of what they would answer for themselves—which would be more desirable. Statements for which approximately the same number chose the "true" as the "false" answer were assumed to be neutral. Statements on which the vast majority of students chose the same answer as the most desirable one were either discarded or revised.

Variations in acquiescence may also produce high internal consistency at the expense of validity. Some people are "yea-sayers" and some are "nay-sayers." That is, some have a strong tendency to answer "true" to questions, while others have an equally strong tendency to answer "false." As a result, if the "bold" answer to the statements in an inventory were always "true," then the acquiescent people would score as very bold. If the "bold" answer were always "false," the acquiescent people would score as very cautious. To reduce the influence of acquiescence, Grossman selected statements for each of the scales so that the lowest and highest scores could only be obtained by answering 20 of the statements "true" and 20 of the statements "false." The procedure gives the extremely acquiescent or nonacquiescent person an average score rather than an extreme one. In summary, Grossman widened the range, reduced the influence of social desirability, and controlled the influence of acquiescence in the development of his scales. Each of these efforts increases the probability that the scales will be valid.

Repeat Reliability

Repeat reliability is the agreement between two scores on the same measure at different times. The different parts of a ruler must not only be consistent with each other, but also measurements made with the same ruler of the same object at two different times must agree with each other. The repeat reliability of a ruler is rarely a problem. The repeat reliability of personality measures often is a problem. The measurement of repeat reliability takes more time than the measurement of internal consistency; internal consistency can be determined

TABLE 3-2   Repeat Reliability of Inventory Measures of the
Five Personality Traits

Traits	Correlations on the same test taken two months apart
Cautious vs. bold	.83
Unemotional vs. emotional	.81
Present-minded vs. future-minded	.80
Artistic vs. practical	.92
Religious vs. scientific	.94

(*Source*: Linden, 1965)

by administering a test to a group of people once, whereas the determination of repeat reliability requires administering the same test to the same group of people on two different occasions.

The most comprehensive determination of repeat reliability requires that the same test be given to the same people many times over a long period. Is self-confidence a stable trait? A group first took an inventory test of self-confidence when they were in college, then took it again a year later, and a third time 20 years later. The reliabilities were as high as have ever been achieved in the area of personality measurement: after a year, .80; after 20 years, .60 (Kelly, 1955).

Low repeat reliabilities may be due to defects in the measuring instrument. On the other hand, the instrument may be in order but what is being measured may actually change a great deal from one time to another. Whatever the reason, low reliabilities are a handicap. Thus, scores on an intelligence test would be useless if the IQ a person obtained one day had no relationship to the IQ he obtained the next day (Figure 3-1).

Table 3-2 shows that the scales measuring the five traits have reliabilities as high as their internal consistencies. That is, students completing the same scales a second time two months later tend to achieve the same scores. The tendency is stronger with the practical and the religious scales than with the other three. All the scales, however, have sufficient reliability so that we can predict that most students will get about the same scores on the scales after several months. Reliabilities decline with the length of time between administrations. Nonetheless, we can assume with some confidence that the qualities measured by these scales are quite dependable.

Validity
Validity is the degree to which a measure is actually measuring what it is supposed to measure. The most convincing index of the validity of a

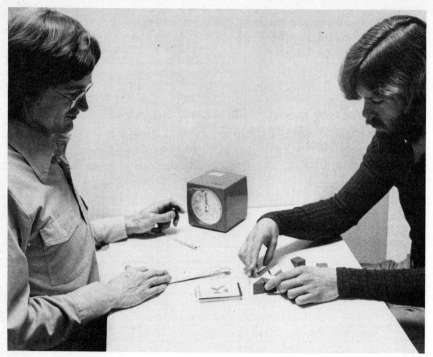

Figure 3-1 Administering the Block Design Test. A part of the Wechsler Adult Intelligence Scale, this test is used to measure both intelligence and special ability. If this test has high repeat reliability, the subject will obtain a similar score each time he takes the test. (Ron Junttonen)

measure is the size of its correlation with an independent measure of what it is supposed to be measuring. Intelligence tests are supposed to predict performance in school. Are they valid for this purpose? Thousands of correlations between scores on hundreds of tests of intelligence and grades in elementary, high school, college, and graduate school have been calculated to find answers to the question. In general, while the correlations are never perfect and sometimes low, they are always positive. That is, intelligence test scores have some validity for predicting academic performance.

The validity of a measure is not just the most important thing about it; it is the *only* thing of importance. Why, then, do psychologists concern themselves with the internal consistency, repeat reliability, and independence of a measure? The first part of the answer is that it is always a hard job to determine the validity of an intelligence test given to five-year-olds to predict their success in college. We have to wait nearly 20 years to obtain a direct measure of the test's validity.

The second part of the answer is that a test never has one validity; it has many. Thus, intelligence test scores are used in predicting the performance of first graders and graduate students, in predicting the job success of executives and ditch diggers, and in predicting the success of military officers and privates. The validity of intelligence tests for these different purposes is also different: high for first graders, low for graduate students; high for executives, low for ditch diggers; and high for officers, low for privates.

The greatest difficulty of all in determining the validity of a measure directly is to find a good measure of what the test is supposed to be predicting. School grades of students are easy to come by, but how do we measure the success of executives? Of ditch diggers? Of officers? Of privates? Such questions are still harder to answer in the field of personality. How can we find out whether a person is bold in his everyday life? Incompetent or competent? Unsuccessful or successful in his relationships with other people? None of these questions are unanswerable, but it may take many years of hard work to find the answers. The work will have been largely wasted if it turns out that the measure has no validity.

It is to save unnecessary work, therefore, that psychologists first determine the internal consistency and repeat reliability of their measures. It may take decades to determine validity; it takes only hours to determine consistency and reliability. The small effort eliminates many measures that cannot be valid. A measure of no internal consistency can have no validity; one of low consistency can, at best, have only very low validity. A measure with no repeat reliability can have no validity, one of low reliability can, at best, have only a very low validity.

The five trait scales may not have been valid because they lacked internal consistency or repeat reliability. However, the results already reported indicate that these sources of low validity have been drastically reduced. Consequently, it is now in order to consider the most important question: How valid are the scales; i.e., how well do they measure what they are supposed to measure? In its most general form the question is: What can we predict about a person from knowing his scores on the scales?

One way of validating the scales is to determine whether a person's actual behavior fits his score. For example, the author asked for volunteers to be interviewed by him on a stage before 400 students. He then examined the boldness scores of the 10 who volunteered. All of them had boldness scores above the average of the class and two of them were in the 99th percentile in boldness. As we examine each of the traits in the next chapters, evidence on the complex question of the validity of the trait scales will be presented.

THE MEASUREMENT OF RELATIONSHIPS

The five-trait theory *assumes* that the traits are independent, i.e., that there is no relationship between where a person stands on one trait and where he stands on another. Do the facts fit the assumption? Does a person's boldness really have no relationship to his practicality? Does a person's present-mindedness really have no relationship to whether he has a scientific point of view? To find the answer, it is only necessary to measure where a group of people stand on each of the traits and then correlate the measures. The closer the correlations are to zero, the more independent the traits are.

What are the correlations between scores on the bold, emotional, future-minded, practical, and scientific scales? The scores of 300 students on the five scales were intercorrelated. Table 3-3 gives the results. Scores on the different scales are almost totally independent. From knowing the boldness score of a person, for example, it would be impossible to predict whether he would be unemotional or emotional, present-minded or future-minded, artistic or practical, religious or scientific. The only relationship is that between practical and scientific scores; i.e., there is a slight tendency for a person to be less scientific as he becomes more practical.

The reader should bear in mind, however, that we are now concerned, not with dictionary definitions of these traits, but with *operational* definitions. That is, boldness *is* what is measured by the boldness scale; emotionality *is* what is measured by the emotional scale, etc. In the following chapters we will examine the details of each of these scales. All the operational definitions of the traits, however, are based on self-definitions. That is, the scale scores are based on what people say about themselves.

The reader should also bear in mind that it is no surprise that the traits measured by the scales are independent, for they were laboriously constructed to *be* independent. Why? The more independent traits are, the more information we get. We get more information about a room from knowing its width *and* length than from having two measures just of its width. We get more information about

TABLE 3-3   Correlations between Measures of Five Traits

	Emotional	Future-minded	Practical	Scientific
Bold	−.04	.05	−.02	−.06
Emotional		−.19	−.16	.00
Present-minded			−.03	−.12
Practical				−.37

(*Source*: Grossman, 1967)

the physique of a person from having measures of his height *and* weight than having two measures of his height. In the same way, we get more information about an individual's personality from knowing his boldness *and* emotionality than from having two measures of his boldness.

THE ULTIMATE TEST OF A THEORY

We improve our understanding of others by improving the theories we use. Consequently, this book describes and applies theories: a theory about the traits that distinguish people from each other (Part 2); a theory about the way the self develops (Part 3); and a theory about the development of love (Part 4). It takes some effort to learn these theories; it takes more effort to practice applying them; but it takes the most effort to learn to control the common-sense theories we habitually use. The only scientific way of knowing that a theory has actually improved our understanding is by the improvement of our accuracy in making predictions about others. But how can the accuracy of the predictions we make about people be measured?

Prediction, in referring to a person, implies judgments about what we do not know about him from what we do know. Predictions of this sort can be made about a person's past, present, or future feelings and behavior. In the measurement of predictive accuracy, the best method might seem to be to have judges meet people and then make predictions about them. The face-to-face method is closest to everyday reality. However, it presents almost insurmountable practical problems: the same person cannot be presented to different judges in the same way; the measures can rarely be checked because the person is usually not available for a second appearance. Showing judges sound films or having them listen to taped interviews of people and then make predictions is a much more convenient approach to the measurement of understanding through predictive accuracy. The use of written cases is still more convenient, although they are yet another step away from everyday realities.

The Test of the Ability to Understand People, shown in Exhibit 3-1, illustrates the written case method for making judgments. The typical accuracy score among more than 300 college students was 51 although some had scores as low as 34 and some as high as 67. The test has the virtue of being internally consistent, i.e., students who get one answer correct tend to get the other answers correct. It also has repeat reliability; i.e., students tend to get about the same scores on different occasions. The correct answers for the test are given at the end of the chapter.

Is the test a valid measure of the ability to apply a theory in understanding people? The internal consistency and reliability as well as the way the test is constructed suggests that it is. However, the ability to understand others depends not only upon how well we can use a theory. It also depends upon how well we look at and listen to a person, how well we understand the groups to which he belongs, and how interested we are in understanding him (Smith, 1973). Furthermore, high internal consistency and reliability only suggest that the test is valid; they do not prove it. The validity of a test can only be confidently established by showing its relationship to an independent measure of what the test is supposed to be measuring. Where are we to obtain such an independent measure of understanding? Certainly not from common-sense criteria, i.e., our subjective estimate of how well we understand people. The problem is complex, and, so far, largely unsolved. However, psychologists act upon the basic faith that even in such complicated cases, measures of understanding can be developed and evidence of their validity found that will be generally convincing.

EXHIBIT 3-1

TEST OF THE ABILITY TO UNDERSTAND PEOPLE

Directions: How well can you predict the feelings and behavior of people? In each of the following actual cases some information is given about a person. Study the facts, then pick the answer to each statement that you think is correct. The correct answers are known from more complete information about the individuals.

Amos   Amos is the traffic manager for a Milwaukee brewery. He was promoted from the driver ranks and possesses a fourth-grade educational background. He is very loyal to the company and has high moral standards. When working in the ranks, he gained the reputation of being the hardest-working driver. He is a big man and says that "Hard work never hurt anyone."

T F   1.   He works 10 to 12 hours a day and 6 to 7 days a week.
T F   2.   He believes his employees should be paid on a commission basis.
T F   3.   He feels that the union's seniority rule is as good a basis as any for promoting helpers to drivers.
T F   4.   He tries to promote his product at all times, even to the point of losing friends.

Betty   Betty is the tall and slender receptionist of a university dean. Thirty-nine years old, she has top seniority among the seven girls in the office. The job requires that she meet the large number of students who have been asked to see the dean or who come to him for advice. She refers to students as "dumbbells," openly blames them for their errors, and swears when she is angry, which she often is.

T F 5. She consults the other girls about the regulation of the heat and ventilation in the office.

T F 6. She compliments the other girls when they do a good job.

T F 7. She was an only child.

T F 8. She is dependable about passing along phone messages she received for the other girls.

Christopher Christopher's parents live in a small Western town where his father teaches school and his mother is librarian. Both parents are shy and quiet, fond of reading and natural history. His brother, five years older, is now a lawyer. Christopher has always been thin and frail but seldom ill. He began to talk early, but did not walk early. He seldom cried and required little discipline as a child. His intelligence test scores are considerably above those of the average college student.

T F 9. Christopher seldom daydreamed.

T F 10. He enjoyed his school gang.

T F 11. He feels that he is not a true participant in life.

T F 12. While in college he went to many movies.

T F 13. He creates imaginary friends.

T F 14. He enjoyed high school activities.

T F 15. Occasionally, when excited, he loses his voice.

T F 16. His college grades are lower than the grades of other students of his intelligence.

Dorian When he first came to Harvard, Dorian was a tall, narrow-shouldered twenty-four-year-old graduate student in engineering. He was born on a farm in Wisconsin, the youngest of a large family. He received most of his education at country schools until he entered engineering college. Recalling his family and childhood, Dorian said:

My earliest impressions of life that I can remember now were to a large extent miserable. As a baby I was constantly ailing, apparently having one childhood disease after another, starting off with measles at the age of six weeks. Mother was an intelligent, gentle, loving woman, and was much thought of by friends and neighbors. My father was at times a brutal man and inclined, when drinking, to be unpleasant to me. At such times he would make fun of me, call me all sorts of unpleasant names and say that I probably wouldn't live the year out, and that it would be better if I didn't. . . . My father had become an invalid, I forgot to mention before, shortly after Mother died. He was in acute need of a job, for he had no money, and was living on what he could borrow from a brother. He was earning his meals by working in a restaurant.

Dorian was one of 540 college students hired for an intensive study of personality at Harvard in the 1930s.

T F 17. In an experiment involving a mild electric shock, Dorian was unusually disturbed.

T F 18. He had some difficulty in recalling the names and ages of his brother and sisters.

T F 19. Dorian was a good conversationalist.

T F 20. He had recently become a Christian Scientist.

Edgar Edgar is sixteen years old. A bit slight for his age, he is a medium-brown Negro boy, the oldest of four children in a middle-class New Orleans family. His mother is a physically powerful woman, religious, dominant, and thrifty. She has been the head of the family since the father deserted seven years ago. She insists on well-mannered and obedient children. Edgar's father was a semi-skilled worker. Before he deserted the family, the mother had decided that Edgar would be a doctor. Now she works to keep up appearances and to keep the children in school. Edgar was not to bring "lower-class" children home or play with them. He had to stay in the yard after 4 P.M. His mother frequently used beatings in disciplining her children. In spite of money problems, she arranged for Edgar to attend a private Negro prep school. He was above average intelligence and maintained good academic and athletic records throughout school.

T F 21. He is severely punished by his mother when he exhibited curiosity about sex.

T F 22. He shows few signs of anxiety or worry.

T F 23. He saves money to buy good clothes.

T F 24. He feels strongly that lower-class Negroes are unfairly persecuted.

T F 25. He says: "I'm as good as anybody in the world."

T F 26. He is boastful.

T F 27. He is verbally but not physically aggressive.

T F 28. He is proud of his mother.

Frank Frank entered Dartmouth College from a private school and graduated as an economics major. He was of slight build, average height, good health, a very superior intelligence. An observer who had known him and his family for a long time commented:

The only child of very admiring and doting parents. During his pre-college life, he was brought up to be a perfect gentleman; so much so, in fact, that he failed to reveal the usual boyish traits as completely as he should have. As he grew older, he veered from the exemplary behavior and developed a reputation of being a great ladies' man, a somewhat reckless driver, and indifferent to the serious aspects of living. At times, his appearance is very smooth, and then again he is quite neglectful and looks extremely seedy. The mother has been a semi-invalid during all the boy's life and has dominated him, and I believe imposed upon him beyond reason.

THE TESTING OF THEORIES

T F 29. When asked what superpoliteness expressed, he replied: "Contempt!"
T F 30. Fellow students think of him as a "snob."
T F 31. Frank received high grades in college.
T F 32. Frank has few artistic interests.

George   George was the second son of Irish immigrant parents who had grade school educations. His father's earnings were meager at first, but improved when encouraged by his wife. He invested a small inheritance in a flower shop. George's mother felt that education was less important than religion, but necessary for getting ahead socially. She was very affectionate, but dominating. George's parents decided he should be a doctor. His father was rather passive, but capable of outbursts. Punishment of the children was severe. It included shaming, denying of affection, spanking, and denying of pleasure. As a child George was his parents' favorite, and was often the center of attraction. He was good-looking, and was considerably above average intelligence. Later, however, he lost favor when his brothers made more social progress.

T F 33. He found it easy to make decisions.
T F 34. He had very strong guilt feelings about masturbation.
T F 35. He acted childish in high school.
T F 36. He was a "show off" in kindergarten.
T F 37. He bragged about his sexual conquests.
T F 38. He bragged about being so young in high school.
T F 39. He was very studious.
T F 40. He found it much easier to get along with boys than girls.

The Harrisons   Margaret Harrison is the owner and manager of an independent woman's ready-to-wear shop in a suburb of Cleveland. She also does all the buying, which means leaving the shop in charge of a saleswoman twice a year while she is in New York. She is married to a man who is lame. Because of this he has refused to work for quite some time. He does odd jobs around the store and gives orders to the employees. He drinks heavily. Mrs. Harrison is about fifty-five years old. She is large, sturdy and extremely intelligent. She has had a great deal of experience in the retail field. She is in the upper middle class. She is industrious and ambitious, but has a quick temper and never admits a mistake.

There are five saleswomen, two maids, and ten alteration women working for her. They receive excellent pay and work from 9 A.M. to 5:30 P.M. with an hour off for lunch. The merchandise in the shop is extremely highly priced and consequently for customers who are wealthy, high-society people.

T F 41. Mrs. Harrison is liked by her employees.
T F 42. She is constantly enlarging her shop.
T F 43. She lets her employees take a 10-minute break in the afternoon.

T F 44. She doesn't hesitate to state her opinion if she disagrees with a customer's taste in clothes.

John John, at fifteen, was 5'4" tall and weighed 105 pounds. He had a childhood record of ill health. John was usually reserved but sometimes expressed himself forcefully. He was not at home in social gatherings, though he often attended. He enjoyed talking about books, art, politics, and movie stars. He got good marks in Literature and Language, but poor ones in Math. John grew up in a middle-class suburban area. His father provides a modest income as a plumber. He is patient and friendly with John. John's mother, the dominant figure in the household, is often apprehensive about his safety and demands much of his time.

T F 45. John is unusually fearful of his emotional impulses.
T F 46. John stated: "I wish my mother could be happier."
T F 47. John saw himself as seldom worrying about "things which he had done, but never told to anyone."
T F 48. John felt that radical agitators should not be allowed to make public speeches.

Karl Karl, a Dartmouth student, was a cheery, sociable, and conventional young man of average intelligence, who was earnest and dilligent in his college work. He graduated, however, in the lowest tenth of his class. He had considerable feelings of inferiority and a fear of making independent judgments. His completions of incomplete sentences ("artificial as *the ice cream in a soda fountain window*," "exciting as *a battle between a mongoose and a cobra*," "Idealistic as *the life of a nun*," etc.) indicated that Karl had a creative capacity that had not been used in his academic work. Both of his parents were talented musicians but he could not carry a tune or play an instrument.

T F 49. In his autobiography he wrote that he was "the most even-tempered cuss that has ever walked on two feet."
T F 50. About the same number of friends described him as "even-tempered" as described him as "quick-tempered."
T F 51. Karl was unable to organize and present ideas clearly.
T F 52. He clearly distinguished between what he thought and what others expected him to think.

The Lawrences William Lawrence, twenty-four, and Laura, twenty-three, have been married for a year and a half. Both his and her parents had approved of their marriage. Their parents were foreign-born, similar in social and economic backgrounds, and lived in the same community. At the time of their marriage, William had had only irregular employment since his graduation from high school. William is proud of his dead mother. She had run her husband's affairs, planned her seven children's vocational and social activities, and faced death with an unsagging spirit. The youngest of his three sisters, all of whom were much like their mother, took care of him when their mother died. Laura, although she wanted to teach kindergarten, had worked as a store clerk for two years before her marriage and continued to work at the same job afterward. Her father had been a successful merchant. However, he had developed an interest in gambling and had given up several good positions impulsively. He often gave Laura and her mother tongue-lashings. Her mother was patient and long-suffering. The Lawrences had few friends and belonged to no social organizations.

T F 53. William expected his wife to do many things for him.

T F 54. His mother was also named Laura.

T F 55. He feels that his childhood was happy.

T F 56. He knows that he wants to depend on his wife as he used to depend upon his mother and sisters.

T F 57. William, commenting on getting married, said: "With superhuman effort I forced myself to go to the courthouse and say, 'I want my license.'"

T F 58. Laura continued to respect her father even after he had ceased to support the family.

T F 59. William considers his marriage a mistake.

T F 60. William still greatly admires his wife's appearance and personality.

The Medford Twins Earl and Frank, identical twins, were born in a Midwestern city, of uneducated and unmarried parents. When the boys were six months old, they were turned over to their mother's sister. She kept Frank but placed Earl with a family who had advertised their wish to board a baby. This family soon assumed full responsibility for Earl and took him to a city in the Northwest without consulting the aunt of the two boys. Earl's foster father was a college graduate and a successful salesman; Frank's, a streetcar conductor. Earl graduated from college; Frank attended high school only six months, though later he attended night school. Earl was raised in comfort; Frank was brought up by his fond aunt with little economic security in the neighborhood where he was born. Both twins had happy homes with only moderate discipline.

They were both interviewed and tested by psychologists in 1941 when they were thirty-seven years old. The twins were remarkably similar in many respects: same height, same color hair, same fingerprints, same good health, same poor spelling, same ratings on many personality traits, very similar vocational interest scores, etc. In some respects, however, they were different. For each of the statements, indicate the name of the twin to whom you think the statement applies. Mark "1" for Earl and "2" for Frank.

1 2 61. Was less pompous and affected.

1 2 62. Said that what he wished for most was the happiness of his family.

1 2 63. Was more eager to impress people.
1 2 64. Said that what he wanted most in life was a good business with men working for him.
1 2 65. Was more emotional.
1 2 66. Was more timid and self-conscious.
1 2 67. Was more disturbed by his failure to achieve his ambitions.
1 2 68. Was more friendly in his personal relations.

The Nelson Twins Fred and John, identical twins, had very similar backgrounds and personalities. Their father, an unsuccessful and alcoholic son of a well-to-do father, had gone to Cuba to make his fortune. He failed there as a farmer and also failed in Florida where the family had moved when the boys were four. He eventually returned to New England to live with the twins' grandmother. The mother of the twins was industrious and long-suffering. Though she was, for the most part, responsible for rearing the children, their father was sporadically a demanding and cruel disciplinarian. The twins left school after the eighth grade and went to work in the same factory on semiskilled jobs. They are working at identical jobs today. They have the same eye and hair color, and look very much alike. Both have type O and Rh-positive blood. Both are shy, dependent, passive, and anxious.

The twins came to the attention of physicians at the age of forty-six because John had developed a severe duodenal ulcer while Fred remained in good health. For each of the statements below indicate the name of the twin to whom you think the statement applies. Mark "1" for Fred and "2" for John.

1 2 69. Had better understanding of himself and of other people.
1 2 70. Was more optimistic.
1 2 71. Showed greater hatred of his father.
1 2 72. Described his wife as a good cook and mother.
1 2 73. While the level of gastric secretion was much higher than normal in both twins, his level was higher than his brother's.
1 2 74. Was more resentful that their mother had not given them more from the $100,000 she inherited about ten years ago.
1 2 75. Was a warmer and more tender person.
1 2 76. Was readier to accept blame.

Norms for the Test of Understanding

Percentile	0	10	20	30	40	50	60	70	80	90	100
Number right	33	42	45	47	50	51	53	55	57	59	68

SUMMARY

Scientific personality theories seek to give better answers to the same questions that common-sense theories try to answer. The ultimate test of any theory is its accuracy in predicting how a person will feel, think, or behave. The first step toward this test is to measure the concepts assumed by the theory. The better these measures, the better the test can be. In developing a good measure, psychologists first try to eliminate or improve measures where one part does not agree with another part, i.e., where they lack *internal consistency*. They also try to eliminate or improve measures that give different results from one time to another, i.e., where they lack *repeat reliability*. Finally, they eliminate or improve measures that do not agree with independent measures of what they are supposed to be measuring, i.e., where they lack *validity*. It is only when valid measures of the concepts proposed by a theory are available that it is possible to determine whether the relationships assumed by the theory agree with the actual relationships. The development of the five-trait theory was used to illustrate these phases in the theory-testing process.

SUGGESTIONS FOR FURTHER READING

*Dethier, V. F. (1962). *To know a fly*. San Francisco: Holden-Day. A fascinating account of methods of testing theories: " . . . a good example of how to conduct experiments, formulate hypotheses, fix up dependent-independent variable situations, and finally how to interpret the findings and come to conclusions." Every student who read this found it interesting, amusing, and enjoyable. Many students found it impossible to swat a fly after reading it.

*Lorenz, K. (1952). *King Solomon's ring*. New York: Thomas Y. Crowell. Another excellent introduction to theory testing via animals. The book appeals as art and autobiography as well as science: "This has got to be the best way to learn about methods of studying animal behavior . . . the charm of the book lies as much with the author as with the subject . . ."

Lyman, H. B. (1963). *Test scores and what they mean*. Englewood Cliffs, N.J.: Van Nostrand (paperback). A readable presentation of some of the fundamentals involved in using and interpreting tests.

Huff, D. (1954). *How to lie with statistics*. New York: Norton. An entertaining account of the misuses of statistics that will aid in learning their proper use.

KEY TO THE TEST OF THE ABILITY TO UNDERSTAND PEOPLE

1. T	2. T	3. F	4. T	5. F	6. F	7. T	8. F
9. F	10. F	11. T	12. T	13. T	14. F	15. T	16. F
17. T	18. T	19. F	20. T	21. T	22. F	23. T	24. F
25. T	26. T	27. T	28. F	29. T	30. T	31. F	32. F
33. F	34. T	35. T	36. T	37. T	38. T	39. F	40. F
41. F	42. T	43. F	44. T	45. T	46. T	47. F	48. F
49. T	50. T	51. T	52. F	53. T	54. T	55. T	56. F
57. T	58. F	59. T	60. F	61. (2)	62. (2)	63. (1)	
64. (1)	65. (2)	66. (1)	67. (1)	68. (2)	69. (1)	70. (1)	
71. (2)	72. (1)	73. (2)	74. (2)	75. (1)	76. (1)		

TWO

TRAITS AS PERSONALITY

Will people ever learn that there is no other
equality possible than the equal right of every
individual to become and to be himself, which
actually means to accept his own difference
and have it accepted by others?

OTTO RANK

4

THE CAUTIOUS AND THE BOLD

A stitch in time saves nine.
Nothing ventured, nothing gained.

OLD PROVERBS

From the trait point of view, our personality is the pattern of traits that differentiate us from others. Boldness is the best known and most often measured of all traits. The very cautious, like Ibsen (Table 4-1 and Figure 4-1), lack self-confidence, are pessimistic, physically inactive, and socially aloof people who avoid leadership positions. The very bold, like Shackleton (Table 4-2 and Figure 4-2), are self-confident, optimistic, energetic, and gregarious people who seek and enjoy leadership. How bold are you? Why do we differ in boldness? How well can you judge the boldness of others? Is it better to be cautious or bold? This chapter tries to answer these questions.

HOW BOLD ARE YOU?

The boldness scale (Table 4-3) provides one way of answering this question. Boldness is one of the traits defined by the five-trait theory that was discussed in both Chapters 2 and 3. Of the 40 statements in the scale, 12 concern leadership tendencies; 9, self-confidence; 8, optimism; 6, activity level; and 5, gregariousness. These are clusters of subordinate traits that define the cautious versus bold trait. The number of statements indicate the relative influence of a subordinate trait on the basic trait.

These subordinate traits are related empirically, not logically. Logically, a person could be strongly motivated to be a leader without being self-confident, optimistic, energetic, or gregarious. In fact, some leaders do have this pattern. It is also logical, and occasionally occurs, that a person is extremely high on one of the subordinate traits and low on the others. In general, however, people who are high on one of the traits in the cluster tend to be high on the others.

It is hard to estimate our own boldness since it is dependent upon how bold others are. The norms at the end of the table permit you to compare your own image of yourself with the image that others have of themselves. But note that our boldness depends upon with whom we are comparing ourselves. Men are bolder than women. Thus, we are bolder if we compare ourselves with women than with men. The more education a person has, the bolder he tends to be. Thus, we are bolder in comparison with the uneducated than with the educated.

Honesty, of course, is essential in answering the statements. In general, the big problem with inventories is that people tend to ascribe desirable and not to ascribe undesirable qualities to themselves. However, this is a small problem with cautiousness and boldness, for the average student sees these traits as almost identical in desirability.

Chapter 2 outlined how the boldness trait was isolated; Chapter 3, how the validity of the scale was determined. In these discussions,

TABLE 4-1   The Caution of Ibsen

Henrik Ibsen, the Norwegian dramatist, was very timid and cautious in his daily life. He scorned the rich in his plays; he acted as his own astute businessman when fame and money finally came to him. He was attracted to women; he had a terror of scandal, was careful to observe the conventions, and once fled from a girl he had arranged to meet when her father approached. His plays viewed the lot of women in marriage as degraded; his work was based on the devotion of a wife who spent her life to ensure him the best conditions for his writing.

As a boy, he was lonely and shy. As a man, he cut himself off from his parents and lived for almost 30 years in Italy and Germany in virtually complete social isolation. What he liked best was to go alone to his place in a cafe and watch people. He trusted no one, perhaps not even his wife. He was pessimistic and often depressed, once being saved by his wife from committing suicide. He generally viewed men as miserable creatures. Yet he was an indignant pessimist, for he believed that society could become better if men would only struggle, accept pain, and fight against adversity. He wrote a series of great plays between 1850 and 1900 that aimed to resolve the conflicts between human nature and society. They were simultaneously psychological, social, and cosmic. Many dramatists believe they approach in power the dramas of ancient Greece and of Shakespeare.

Figure 4-1 Henrik Ibsen, 1828–1906. (Norwegian Embassy Information Service)

TABLE 4-2   The Boldness of Shackleton

Sir Ernest Henry Shackleton was the son of an English physician, who became a noted Antarctic explorer (Lansing, 1959). His restless energy, his supreme self-confidence, his optimism, and his insatiable desire for excitement made him inept in many everyday situations. He was constantly involved in new schemes, each of which he was sure would win his fortune. None ever did. At various times he planned to manufacture cigarettes, run a fleet of taxicabs, mine in Bulgaria, organize a whaling factory, and dig for buried treasure. He joined the British Merchant Navy at the age of 16 and rose steadily through the officer ranks. He was of medium height but broad-shouldered, had small hands but a powerful grip, and talked in a quiet slow voice that could terrify men when he raised it in anger. Becoming bored with the routine of the Navy, he joined Scott's 1901 National Antarctic Expedition. In 1907 he led three companions to within a hundred miles of the South Pole but had to turn back in a desperate race with death because of a shortage of food. In 1915, at forty, he became the leader of the 28-man Imperial Trans-Antarctic Expedition. Their ship was crushed in the pack ice and sank. Shackleton camped his men on the ice for five months, then led them across to the open ocean, and from there sailed to deserted Elephant Island. With one companion in a leaking 22-foot boat he then journeyed for three weeks across a thousand miles of ocean filled with ice floes, winds up to fifty miles an hour, and waves that reached as high as a hundred feet to South Georgia Island where he organized a rescue party. Every man was saved and the only casualty was a frozen foot. He was described by one of his men as "the greatest leader that ever came on God's earth, bar none." An experienced explorer remarked: "For scientific leadership give me Scott; for swift and efficient travel, Amundsen; but when you are in a hopeless situation, when there seems no way out, get down on your knees and pray for Shackleton."

Figure 4-2 Sir Ernest Henry Shackleton, 1844–1922. (United Press International)

TABLE 4-3 The Cautious vs. Bold Scale
A definition of the traits is given below with 40 statements that measure it. The statements are grouped under subordinate traits in the cluster and the answer for the "bold" end of the scale indicated. Your total score is the number of bold answers that you make. Norms for 100 college men and 100 college women in 1970 are given after the statements. The two most discriminating items in the scale are indicated with an asterisk.

Definition
The cautious person is a physically inactive, quiet, and aloof individual who avoids leadership positions, lacks confidence in himself, and takes a pessimistic view of the world. The bold person is an energetic, talkative, and gregarious individual who is self-confident and optimistic and who seeks and enjoys positions of leadership and responsibility.

Directions
If you think a statement is "true" or more true than false as far as you are concerned, underline "T." If you think a statement is "false" or more false than true as far as you are concerned, underline "F."

Nonleader vs. leader
<u>T</u> F   1.* I am generally regarded by others as a leader.
<u>T</u> F   2. I enjoy speaking in public.
<u>T</u> F   3. There are few things I enjoy more than being a leader of people.
<u>T</u> F   4. I have frequently assumed the leadership of groups.
<u>T</u> F   5. I enjoy taking full responsibility for introducing people at a party.
<u>T</u> F   6. I am always taking on added social responsibility.
<u>T</u> F   7. I am generally the leader of the people I know.
<u>T</u> F   8. I am often called upon to settle arguments between people.
T <u>F</u>   9. I am seldom the center of attention in a group.
T <u>F</u> 10. I would rather listen to a story than tell one.
T <u>F</u> 11. I sometimes find it hard to lead people and maintain them in order.
T <u>F</u> 12.* I generally keep in the background at social functions.

Low vs. High Self-Confidence
<u>T</u> F 13. I am very self-confident.
<u>T</u> F 14. I am almost never embarrassed.
T <u>F</u> 15. I am often lacking in self-confidence.
T <u>F</u> 16. I am cautious about undertaking anything which may lead to humiliating experience.
T <u>F</u> 17. I feel somewhat inferior as a person to a few of my friends.
T <u>F</u> 18. I am frequently discouraged by my own inadequacies.
T <u>F</u> 19. When I meet a stranger, I sometimes think he is a better person than I am.
T <u>F</u> 20. I am somewhat more shy than the average person.
T <u>F</u> 21. I generally feel self-conscious in the presence of important superiors.

Pessimistic vs. Optimistic
T F 22. Most of the time, I am extremely carefree and relaxed.
T F 23. I am a rather carefree person.
T F 24. I am very optimistic.
T F 25. Some people I know can look forward to a happier life than I can.
T F 26. I have quite a few fears about my future.
T F 27. I am at least as much of a pessimist as an optimist.
T F 28. I sometimes become melancholy without very good reasons.
T F 29. I have some feelings of inferiority.

Inactive vs. Active
T F 30. I am generally active in my everyday life.
T F 31. I spend myself freely as I have plenty of energy.
T F 32. I frequently become involved in too many activities.
T F 33. I am a very adventurous person.
T F 34. I prefer quiet games to extremely active ones.
T F 35. I generally talk very quietly.

Socially Aloof vs. Gregarious
T F 36. I like to have people around me practically all the time.
T F 37. I always like to be with people rather than be alone.
T F 38. I always prefer to work with others.
T F 39. I am inclined to limit my friends to a few people.
T F 40. I dislike it when I am with people constantly.

	Percentiles										
	Cautious										Bold
	0	10	20	30	40	50	60	70	80	90	99
Men	3	9	15	16	18	20	23	25	27	30	34
Women	4	8	10	12	15	18	20	22	25	28	38

however, a critical step in Grossman's work to which we now return was by-passed. "The five clusters he located and the names given to each of them are shown . . ." But how are these names arrived at? In general, by intuition based on information. It is assumed that each of the subordinate traits is "saturated" with a core trait to which they are all pointing. What is this core trait that is a mixture of leadership, confidence, optimism, activity, and gregariousness? It has most frequently been labelled "dominance." Dominance, however, is interpersonal; i.e., we must have some one to dominate before we can be dominant. We have preferred the label "boldness" because it is not necessarily interpersonal; it is a perception of an approach to the world

in general. However, a single word is always an incomplete description. The best definition is what the scale as a whole measures.

How valid is the scale? That is, does a person's estimate of his
boldness correspond to his actual boldness? Scores on scales like these
certainly have some validity: people who are in leadership positions
obtain higher scores than people who are not; people who volunteer to
speak before groups obtain higher scores than those who do not; and
successful door-to-door salesmen obtain higher scores than the unsuccessful.

Inventory measures of boldness like this one also agree with
scores on quite different measures of boldness. College students, for
example, completed the Thematic Apperception Test (Uleman, 1966).
The TAT consists of a series of ambiguous pictures covering a variety of
human relationships and situations. When presented with a picture
(see Figure 4-3) the subject is asked to make up a story about the
picture: What is happening? What led up to the scene? How does it
come out? Most people identify themselves with one of the characters
in the picture. Their stories, therefore, become thinly disguised autobiographies. Thus, some see in the picture a conflict between the older
and the younger woman. They see it as a scene that has been preceded
by many quarrels between the two because the older woman has always
sought to dominate the younger one. Others perceive a friendly
relationship, with the older woman giving sympathetic support to the
younger one.

For the particular group of students being considered, their
stories were rated for signs of boldness: attempts in the story of a bold
person to influence a less bold one; the presence in the stories of people
of position, wealth, fame, or glamour; optimistic outcomes of stories;
and indications that the people in the story were perceived as self-
confident and competent. The more signs of boldness in a student's
stories, the higher his rating in boldness. These ratings from the TAT
were then correlated with scores on a personality inventory measuring
boldness and with ratings of boldness made by friends of the students.
The higher a student's boldness score on the inventory, the higher he
was rated in boldness by his friends, and the greater the number of
boldness "themes" in his TAT stories. Furthermore, those with the
highest scores were actually bolder in a laboratory gambling situation
where they were expected to dominate others. They reported themselves as more comfortable in the role of manipulator. They also won
more money.

Of course, boldness scores do not always agree with actual
boldness. Some individuals may have a very erroneous self-image: they
may see themselves as bold when they are actually quite cautious; or
they may see themselves as submissive to the wishes of others when

Figure 4-3 What is happening? What led up to the scene? How does it come out? These are questions that the person taking the Thematic Apperception Test answers in responding to the ambiguous pictures that make up the test. (By permission Harvard University Press, copyright 1943, from H. A. Murray Thematic Apperception Test)

they are actually overbearing. Some individuals may realize they are cautious or bold but choose for some reason to report that they are not. The majority of people, however, do seem to understand where they stand on this trait and do report accurately their standing.

WHY DO WE DIFFER IN BOLDNESS?

Direct and indirect genetic mechanisms interact with general and specific environmental mechanisms to create differences in boldness as they interact to create differences in all traits. Heredity is only one of the determiners of differences in boldness. However, the present evidence indicates that heredity has *more* influence in creating differences in boldness than in any of the other traits we shall consider.

Direct Genetic Mechanisms

Activity level, one of the elements in boldness, is heavily influenced by direct hereditary mechanisms. The most certain evidence comes from studies of the boldness of animals. Rundquist (1933) first put a large group of rats, one at a time, in an activity cage and measured the number of times each rat turned a wheel in a given period of time. He then interbred the rats who made the largest number of turns and, separately, the rats who made the smallest number of turns. He repeated the process for 15 generations. At this point, the energetic rats were about four times as active as the lethargic ones. Dogs too differ in their activity levels: Royce (1955) gave pedigreed dogs a battery of physiological, psychological, and social tests; the general level of activity was one of the characteristics in which the dogs most clearly differed from one another. The steps by which boldness may develop from activity level is suggested by a study of dogs (Figure 4-4). James (1951) split litters of wire-haired terriers and beagles: three beagle and two terrier puppies were raised by a terrier mother; three beagle and three terrier puppies were raised by a beagle mother. At the end of a year, dominance tests were conducted. Result: All the terriers dominated all the beagles. Why?

The terriers are highly active and excitable animals. They would invariably come forward as the experimenter entered the runs and begin to jump up as if trying to get attention. The beagles, on the other hand, would remain in the background. . . . When cornered they would take the passive defense attitude. They are definitely of a more inhibited type than the terriers.

A similar mechanism appears to operate in human beings. Sheldon and Stevens (1945) found that those people with powerful and muscular physiques (mesomorphs) were active, energetic, and dominating (somatotonic); those with thin and fragile physiques (ectomorphs) were shy, hypersensitive to pain, and restrained and inhibited (cerebrotonic). The methods and interpretations of Sheldon and Stevens have been severely criticized. However, more recent evidence acquired by more careful methods (Cortes and Gatti, 1965) lends some support to their conclusions. Mesomorphs, for example, reported themselves as confident, energetic, enterprising, and adventurous where ectomorphs reported themselves as detached, tense, shy, and reserved. Similar relationships between physique and temperament have been found among boys and girls (Davidson, McInnes, and Parnell, 1957), " . . . ectomorphic boys and girls of seven were more anxious, more submissive, and more meticulous than children of the other body types."

The influence of hereditary mechanisms on boldness is harder to isolate in human beings. Still, boldness often appears at an early age and becomes painfully easy to identify. Consider, for example, the following case of a nursery school child (Woolley, 1925):

The most outstanding characteristic of Agnes on entrance—and

Figure 4-4 "The terriers are highly active and excitable animals. . . . The beagles . . . are definitely of a more inhibited type." (Wide World Photos, Evelyn M. Shafer)

indeed as long as we knew her—was her egoism and her desire to dominate and boss others, and secure her own advantage by any method available. She had no notion of occupying any position but that of center of the stage. The first personality study made of her makes this comment. "At first she wanted literally to run the school." Whenever anything was to be done, Agnes was the first to volunteer. Her constant expressions were "I want to—I am going to." Her voice was loud and rasping, and was constantly sounding out above the others. Indeed so insistent and ubiquitous was she that it was difficult to conduct the school with her in it. She had no conception of her own limitations. . . .

Activity level seems to be the key in human beings as well as in lower animals. Differences in activity level are readily observed in the first few days of life and remain remarkably stable (Shirley, 1931).

Indirect Genetic Mechanisms
American men are bolder than American women, i.e., more dominating, more active, more self-confident, and more optimistic. Direct

mechanisms are in part responsible, for males of mammalian species have more red blood corpuscles and are regularly more active than females. However, the influence of genetic differences also operates indirectly through social stereotypes. Men in our society are expected to be bolder; the women, more cautious. Here, as elsewhere, individuals tend to behave in the way that society expects them to behave. Among college students, the men were only slightly bolder than the women, i.e., only slightly more dominating, self-confident, and energetic. Yet studies of more representative groups of men and women consistently show the greater boldness of men to be among the largest of sex differences (Cattell, 1965). Furthermore, genetic mechanisms are largely responsible for the differences in activity level that are intimately related to boldness among animals.

Education provides a key. Trier (1959) gave a boldness inventory to 242 housewives in Michigan, selected to be representative of the socioeconomic levels of families in the community. From the total group, he picked the 57 with the lowest and the 57 with the highest scores in boldness and divided them according to their education. Table 4-4 shows the major result: the more educated the housewife, the bolder she was. More than three times as many of the housewives with some college education were in the bold group. Other results were consistent: the larger the income of the family, the bolder the wife; the higher the occupational status of the husband, the bolder the wife; and the younger the housewife, the bolder she was. Furthermore, housewives who worked were bolder than those who did not. It seems that differences in the boldness of men and women are largely due to the differences in their social status. The status differences persist. A cross-section of more than 3,000 women were asked about sex differences in energy, an important aspect of the trait: "Do you feel that men have more physical stamina than women?" "Yes" was answered by 68 percent of those with an eighth grade education or less, 55 percent of those with high school education, and 38 percent of those with college education (Reistrup, 1972).

TABLE 4-4   The Boldness of Women in Relation to Their Education

Education	57 Cautious housewives, %	57 Bold housewives, %
Less than high school	20	16
High school	68	47
More than high school	12	37
Total	100	100

(*Source*: Trier, 1959)

General Environmental Mechanisms

The effects which general environmental influences may have on boldness are suggested by the case of the identical twins Mary and Mabel (Newman, Freeman, and Holzinger, 1937). Since they were identical twins and therefore had the same genes, hereditary mechanisms could not account for any of the differences between them. The twins, however, were separated soon after birth. Mary lived all her life in town and finished school in a large city; she devoted herself to music and music teaching. Mabel lived on a large and prosperous farm, finished the eighth grade in a small country school, and participated actively in all the work commonly done by an able-bodied farm woman. They were both interviewed and tested when they were twenty-nine years old. Mabel weighed 138 pounds and was hard-muscled; Mary weighed only 110 pounds, and her muscles were soft and poorly developed. Mabel was bolder. She walked with a firm masculine stride; Mary had a ladylike step and manner. Mabel was also more aggressive, more of a leader, less fearful, and less readily shocked by unpleasant words and ideas.

Parents, a vital part of the general environment of a child, may have a profound influence on his boldness. Severe parental discipline, for example, tends to develop bold children. Schutz (1958) divided 60 Harvard students into 12 groups with 5 students in each group. Each group met for 14 one-hour meetings over a period of six weeks and discussed the same topics, performed the same tasks, and solved the same problems. Observers sat in at each meeting and completed extensive ratings. The instruction for one of the ratings was stated like this:

> In many groups there is someone who, regardless of how good his ideas are, seems to have tremendous influence on the final group decision. . . . In your opinion was there any member (or possibly two members) of the present group who tried to behave in this way?

The 60 students were asked to rate the severity of the discipline they had received as children. At the end of the sessions, parental discipline was related to attempts to influence group decisions. Result: The severely disciplined students more often tried to dominate group decisions. A different study of the same relationship yielded a similar result. Mothers who reported that they disciplined their children severely also reported that their children were bold and aggressive (Sears, Maccoby, and Leven, 1957).

The general social environment influences the boldness of dogs as well as men and women. Twenty-one Scottish terriers were reared separately in cages covered by heavy cardboard. They saw human beings only during their daily feeding period. Litter-mates were raised as pets in homes or in the laboratory. The relative boldness of the isolated dog and his normally reared litter-mate was tested by putting them together in opposite corners of the testing room when neither had had food for 24 hours. Either a large bone or a dish of food was placed in the center of the floor. An experimenter led each of the dogs up to the food and allowed him to smell it. They were then returned to their corners and released at the same time. A dog scored a *win* when he drove the second dog away from the food by growling or barking, and remained in control of the food for all or most of the time. Result: The dogs with a normal social environment won 89 percent of the 64 matches (Thompson and Melzack, 1956).

Specific Environmental Mechanisms

From an impersonal point of view, specific environmental mechanisms are of minor concern compared to the pervasive influences of genes and of general environment. From.·a personal and practical point of view, however, they are of major concern. The individual can do nothing about the genetic and general environmental influences that have molded him. It is only specific environmental mechanisms that are within his control. At best, these mechanisms can only produce small changes. Such small changes, however, may be very important to the individual, as the results of McFall and Marstan (1970) suggest.

These authors read the following announcement to their undergraduate classes:

We are now beginning an experimental program for persons who feel that they would like to be more assertive in various social situations. For example, such a person might find it difficult to deal with one of these salesmen who call you on the phone. We want volunteers who seriously want to change this aspect of their behavior, and who would be willing to work in a guided training program for a period of several weeks, with once-a-week meetings with the experimenter. Of course, we can't promise miraculous changes, but these procedures have been effective in other studies.

Several precautions were taken to make it easy for extremely cautious people to sign up. They were told that they could sign up in a booklet or by telephone. They were also told that they would not have to commit themselves finally even if they expressed an initial interest. Eighteen men and twenty-four women agreed to participate, but six dropped out before the end of the experiment.

Ten of the thirty-six subjects were placed in a control group.

They were told that more students than anticipated had signed up for the study, that they were being placed on a temporary waiting list, and they would begin treatment as soon as it could be arranged. However, like the students who did take the treatment, the assertiveness of the control was assessed at the beginning and the end of the study. The assessment tests included a battery of tests designed to measure their assertive behavior, an inventory measure of their anxiety, and a measure of their pulse rate during the test situation.

Nine of the subjects were given four hours of individual therapy. The first hour was devoted to an exploration of the student's problems of not being able to assert himself and ended with these remarks by the therapist: "You are too concerned with what other people think of you. You must stop worrying about making everyone like you and stand up for your rights!" In the next three sessions, attempts by the student to assert himself between sessions were discussed, he was given a common-sense rationale for his nonassertiveness, taught to recognize when he was engaging in nonassertive behavior, and strongly encouraged to behave more assertively.

The remaining 17 students participated in a behavioral-rehearsal technique for developing assertiveness. Determining the effectiveness of this technique, in fact, was the purpose of the study. The first behavior-rehearsal treatment session began with a brief, tape-recorded statement of the treatment rationale. This statement stressed that the best way for a person to become more assertive was for him to *learn* what constituted an assertive response and to *practice* making such responses in a nonthreatening situation like that provided by the experiment. At the end of the first session and during all the following three sessions, the student listened to six different assertiveness situations. He was asked to imagine himself in each situation and to make an assertiveness response to it. The following indicates the type of situations:

NARRATOR: And as the two people squeeze in line between you and their friend, one of them looks at you and says:

NEWCOMER: "Excuse me. You don't mind if we cut in, do you?"
(Bell sounds as cue for student to respond)

As the sessions progressed, the assertive encounters were intensified. Throughout the behavioral-rehearsal treatment, students worked on their own, relying entirely on rehearsal and self-evaluation of their assertive behavior.

Did the training increase assertiveness? The control group showed no differences in their assertiveness on the behavior test, in their reported anxiety during the test situation, or in their pulse rate from the pretest to the end-test. The therapy group showed no improvement on the behavior test, in their reported anxiety, and their pulse rates actually increased although their reported satisfaction with the way they behaved increased. The authors concluded that students in therapy: ". . . changed in their verbal self-appraisals of their assertive behavior, that is, were more satisfied with it, but showed no appreciable change in their actual behavior." The behavioral rehearsal, however, did significantly increase their assertiveness. Conclusion: "The results of the present study indicate that an automated and standardized response rehearsal treatment was effective in improving assertive performance."

Would the increased assertiveness in the laboratory transfer to life? To find out, all subjects in all the groups were telephoned two weeks after the posttreatment tests by an experimental assistant posing as a magazine salesman. They were given the "opportunity" to obtain their "choice of three nationally acclaimed magazines free for the rest of the school year" when they subscribed to two other magazines offered at "special college prices." The calls were tape recorded and four judges who did not know which group any of the subjects had participated in, rated the speed with which each subject showed resistance. Results: The behavioral-rehearsal group expressed "resistance to the 'salesman' at a relatively earlier point in the telephone interaction."

Did the behavioral-rehearsal training increase general boldness? Probably not. All subjects took the Taylor Manifest Anxiety Scale before and after the treatment period. None of the groups showed any appreciable change. It seems unlikely that such training would make generally cautious people more likely to enjoy leadership positions, to take a more optimistic view of life, to be physically more active, or to take a generally more favorable view of themselves.

HOW WELL CAN YOU JUDGE THE BOLDNESS OF OTHERS?

Our own boldness blocks our understanding of the boldness of others: the cautious judge others cautiously while the bold judge them boldly. In general, our own personalities are *the* major obstacle to understanding the personalities of others. Since this obstacle occurs with every trait and with every approach to personality, we shall try to make clear at the beginning the nature of this largely unrecognized but potent barrier to understanding others.

The Centrality of Good and Bad

Hit on the back of the head, we *sense* blinding flashes of light and color. Hit in a slightly different place, we *perceive* stars and butterflies. Sensation is the registration of stimuli in the brain; perception is an awareness of objects, qualities, or relationships by way of these sensations: we sense heat but perceive fire; we sense loudness but perceive a drum; and we sense sourness but perceive vinegar. Perception, then, is the interpretation of sensations, the prediction of a substance from sensory clues. We are so used to predicting the substance from its sensory shadow that we normally feel that the shadow *is* the substance: we do not see green, but a pea; we do not hear high-pitched voice sounds, but a child; we do not smell smoke, but a cigar. Generally, we do not observe a person; we perceive him.

Common sense views perception as a quite passive affair: the eye is a motion-picture camera; the ear, a tape recorder. What we see a person do and hear him say is transcribed on the slate of our awareness. The records are then sorted, edited, and evaluated. Contrary to this common-sense view, our feelings about a person are central, not the facts. We do not primarily and typically perceive that a person is tall or short, but that he is friendly or unfriendly. We do not perceive that he is thin or heavy, but that he is fascinating or boring. We do not perceive that he is quiet or loud, but that he is helpful or harmful. Above all, we do not perceive that he is cautious or bold, but that he is likeable or unlikeable, good or bad.

This instant whole impression that a person makes upon us we shall call his *expressive* quality. This quality that we perceive is not an inference we make from our observations; it is not something added to our original perception; it is not, in other words, a minor and dispensable aspect of our impression but a major and essential one. When we have met a person for the first time, we rarely have a clear idea about how old the person is, how tall, how heavy, or how blonde. We generally have a clear idea of his expressive quality, i.e., how much we liked him and whether we thought he was a desirable person.

Boldness and Goodness

All of us perceive some people as good and others as bad. Some of us, however, perceive *most* people as good and some of us perceive *most* people as bad. Some of us generally perceive the world as having a benign expressive quality, seeing it as largely filled with friendly, helpful, fascinating, familiar, kind, warm, and good people. On the other hand, some of us see it as malignant, as filled with unfriendly, harmful, boring, strange, cruel, and bad people.

The cautious tend to perceive others as threatening and evil. A college girl, for example, says (Maslow and Mittlemann, 1951, pp. 132–133):

I don't trust anybody in the world, not even my mother. After all, people are all selfish deep down and are out only to get, not to give. If you relax for a minute they will take advantage of you. Even the people I have called my friends have always turned out this way and I have decided that the best thing to do is never to be too close to anybody and keep my secrets to myself. . . . Women are catty and jealous and all the men I have ever known have been out to get from me whatever they could. . . . That was the way it was with my father and mother. My mother was weak so my father took advantage of her all his life. . . . My parents never really wanted me or loved me, and nobody else ever has either. If I died tomorrow there would not be anybody in the world who would be sorry for more than a few minutes, and there would be a lot of people who would be glad.

On the other hand, the bold, tend to perceive the world as good, as John exemplified (Maslow and Mittlemann, 1951, p. 134):

I have the feeling of being at home in the world and at home with people. I realize now that I have always assumed that a person was nice until he had proven himself to be otherwise. I like them, therefore they like me. I have always had a lot of friends, and as a matter of fact, I can think of very few people whom I have ever called enemy. One friend of mine once told me that I have such a nice view of the world because I bring out the best side of everybody I know. He tells me that the same people I like and who behave so decently and nice with me, behave in a very different fashion with other people. I think it is because they realize that I have no desire to threaten or to hurt them, that I really like them, and that I am really pleased when something nice happens to them. In other words, they have nothing to worry about as far as I am concerned.

The judgments of the cautious and the bold reflect what they see the world to be. Thus, the cautious, in judging the ambiguous case of Jim Nelson (Table 4-5), tend to rate him lower on desirable qualities than do the bold. The bold see others as *actually* being better people than do the cautious.

TABLE 4-5 How Good Is Jim Nelson?

For the last 10 years Jim Nelson has been the foreman in the shipping department of an automobile parts manufacturing company. When Jim was appointed foreman, several others with more seniority were also considered for the job. Jim got the job because he had had more education than the others. Some of the men resented this and made Jim's task as supervisor a pretty tough one at first. However, this has been forgotten now and Jim gets along with the men very well. Jim's greatest handicap as a supervisor is the fact that he is somewhat shy. Also, he occasionally has difficulty expressing himself. His strongest quality is his sincere interest in his job.

On the basis of the information given, do you think Jim has the following qualities? Mark each one as follows: (1) Quite unlike him; (2) A little unlike him; (3) A little like him; (4) Rather like him; (5) Quite like him.

1 2 3 4 5   (1) Realistic
1 2 3 4 5   (2) Ambitious
1 2 3 4 5   (3) Flexible
1 2 3 4 5   (4) Practical

Assume that you are Jim's supervisor and must give him a merit rating on the following qualities. Mark each quality as follows: (1) Poor; (2) Fair; (3) Average; (4) Good; (5) Superior.

1 2 3 4 5   (5) Initiative
1 2 3 4 5   (6) Potentiality
1 2 3 4 5   (7) Industriousness

Jim filled out an anonymous personality inventory when he was hired. He responded to each of the statements below by marking them: (1) Strongly disagree; (2) Disagree; (3) Neither agree of disagree; (4) Agree; (5) Strongly agree. Answer the following three statements as you think Jim answered them.

1 2 3 4 5   (8)   I like reading about business trends.
1 2 3 4 5   (9)   I am systematic in caring for my personal property.
1 2 3 4 5   (10) I never neglect serious things in order to have a good time.

In judging the boldness of others the situation reverses. The cautious, who feel inferior, tend to think that others feel more optimistic and self-confident than they actually do. The judgments of the cautious, however, tend to have critical overtones. That is, they see others as being too conceited, too self-confident, too arrogant, too egotistical. The bold, on the other hand, are likely to think others do not have as good opinion of themselves as they should have and are, therefore, likely to underestimate their self-confidence and optimism.

Good or Bad versus Good and Bad

Some instructors give most of their students the same grade; other instructors give many F's and A's. Some supervisors give most of their employees the same merit rating; others rate many as "outstanding" and many as "improvement essential." In general, some people always see others as either "very good" or "very bad," while others generally see them as a mixture of both, neither very good nor very bad.

Complex thinkers more often see people as a mixture of goodness and badness than do those who are simple thinkers. College students saw a brief film in five scenes of a young woman (Gollin, 1954). Two scenes suggested that she was promiscuous and immoral: (1) being picked up in front of a run-down hotel and (2) entering a glass-fronted store that might have been a bar and coming out with a man who was not the same man who had picked her up in front of the hotel. The middle scene was neutral: (3) walking along and talking to a female companion. The other two scenes suggested that she was kind and considerate: (4) giving money to a beggar, and (5) helping a woman who had fallen on a public stairway. After they had seen the film the students were asked to:

Write down on the paper given to you the impression you have formed of the person who appears in all the scenes. Please be as detailed as you can; that is, write your impression as if you were telling someone about this individual's personality.

Result: 49 percent of the students had *simplified* impressions of the girl. They described her as immoral *or* kind, but not both; 30 percent had *aggregated* impressions—they described the girl as immoral *and* kind, but did not try to explain how the two qualities could appear in the same girl; and 21 percent had *related* impressions—they described the girl as having both qualities and gave some account of how the two might be related to each other.

We tend to see people as unified and simple wholes. It is only slowly and gradually that we learn to differentiate the parts within the complex whole. The impulse toward unity is so strong that it blinds us to facts that are inconsistent with the unified impression. The novelist Somerset Maugham (1938) reached a similar conclusion:

I suppose it is a natural prepossession of mankind to take people as though they were homogeneous. . . . It is evidently less trouble to make up one's mind about a man one way or the other and dismiss suspense with the hrase, "He's one of the best of he's a dirty dog." It is disconcerting to find that the savior of his country may be stingy or that the poet who has opened new horizons to our consciousness may be a snob. Our natural egoism leads us to judge people by their relations to ourselves. We want them to be certain things to us, and for us that is what they are; because the rest of them is no good to us, we ignore it.

However natural the "prepossession," it leads to many errors in understanding.

The Need for Feedback

The common-sense approach to people centers upon a subjective, personal, and emotional question: How do I feel about him? The scientific approach centers upon an objective, impersonal, and unemotional question: How does he see himself? We are generally confident that we understand what a person thinks of himself. But is our confidence justified? How can we tell whether a person is as bold as we think he is? The answer is that we need feedback from him. To get this feedback we need to listen to what he says about his boldness. A more precise form of feedback is to compare our estimates of his score on the boldness scale to the score that he actually obtains. The cases of Joan and Mary (Table 4-6) give one example of this kind of feedback.

TABLE 4-6   The Cases of Joan and Mary

Joan Dellard, a twenty-year-old sophomore majoring in psychology, and Mary Bernard, a forty-three-year-old senior majoring in home economics, both completed the boldness scale and wrote a brief autobiography of themselves. After reading the thumbnail sketches of them based on their autobiographies, try to decide which is the bolder of the two and then try to decide how you think their boldness scores would compare with those of other college women.

Joan Dellard   Joan has three older brothers, and all of the children were raised by her grandmother because her mother was working. Her mother always compared her to her brothers, and she never measured up to their achievements. Her father, the vice president of a small company, was respected and obeyed by all the children, and gave no physical disciplining. Her brothers considered her as the "kid" or a tag-along. Joan had negative feelings toward her grandmother because she sided with her mother, and often berated Joan's father. She had few friends as a child, and got along better with boys than with girls.

Joan says her ideas on religion are in the process of changing, but she is anti organized religion. She is a curious person, doesn't get bored easily, is interested in practically everything, and likes to read and learn. But she is inconsistent, often needs reassurance from her close friends and relatives, and is sometimes frightened by external conditions like the possibility of World War III.

Mary Bernard Mary's childhood was difficult because her parents were very strict and expected much of her, and permitted no deviation from their high standards. As a result, she tends to avoid trouble, became independent early in life, and has some difficulty establishing relationships with people. As she says, "nothing offered; nothing accepted." She spent her summers with her aunts and uncles who were very religious, and thus has developed very high ethical and religious standards for herself. She is tolerant of other people, can deal easily with abstract theories, and has an almost unlimited amount of physical energy to do what she wants to do.

She lists her favorable characteristics as "impeccable honor and integrity, very empathic, extremely tenderhearted, organized, persistent, very fastidious, respect for the dignity of man." On the other hand, she is somewhat conceited, is unable to compromise, often attempts to do too much, and tries too hard to be perfect. She finds it difficult to balance recreation and work, wants to be a complete person, and feels she is obligated to no one person and holds no person obligated to her.

Who is the bolder?* (Circle)   JOAN   MARY

How does their boldness compare with that of other college women?*
(Circle the percentile that you think each girl matches)

	Percentile									
Cautious			Average				Bold			
Joan 0	10	20	30	40	50	60	70	80	90	99
Mary 0	10	20	30	40	50	60	70	80	90	99

*Correct answers are given at end of chapter.

IS IT BETTER TO BE CAUTIOUS OR BOLD?

In his everyday life, the psychologist, like everyone else, lives in an emotional, personal, and subjective world where the goodness and badness of people, actions, and ideas are primary. In this world, the neutrality of "cautious" and "boldness" is a dubious abstraction, for it is based on what a nonexistent "average" person thinks. Individuals do not react to the trait in a neutral way. Some people see cautiousness as a quite undesirable trait, whereas others see it as a quite desirable one. The same is true for boldness.

What influences whether we see caution or boldness as more

desirable? Probably the most general answer is that we like ourselves and, consequently, we like the traits that we have. Thus, the cautious like caution; the bold like boldness. We like the traits we have even though we see they have undesirable as well as desirable aspects. A cautious student, for example, says:

> I feel like the man who, when asked what he was planning to do next year, replied: "I don't know, but I'm sure I'm not going to like it." My pessimism is an asset in that there is little chance of being surprised by the jolts of life—it prepares me for the worst and prevents me from being tumbled from a pink cloud. On the other hand, my pessimism makes it difficult for me to enjoy any immediate pleasure. I am too expectant of a later catastrophe. Also, my pessimistic outlook has occasionally alienated friends who do not care to share my gloom. However, I do feel that pessimism points out the truth: the imperfections in life, society and the world more than balance the good things.

On the other hand, a bold student says:

> I have a great deal of self-confidence. But because my feelings are not easily hurt, I have a tendency to neglect the feelings of other individuals. I do not picture myself as a cold, heartless person, although I have heard this is the opinion some people hold of me. The source of this opinion is people with whom I have worked in various group activities. When working on project committees, I often find myself in the position of chairman. I have been informed that I tend to be too businesslike in carrying out my duties, frequently expressing opinions which injure the feelings of others. I know I must correct this habit by employing tact and realizing that all people are not like myself, if I'm to succeed.

We tend to like the traits we have; we also tend to like people who have traits similar to our own. Byrne and his colleagues conducted a wide-ranging series of studies to find out whether people like people who were similar to dissimilar to themselves. For example, in one of these studies (Byrne, Clore, and Worchel, 1966) 84 students of low or high socioeconomic status met each other in small groups for a short time. Each student later indicated how much he liked the other individuals in his group. Result: Those of low status liked best those of low status; those of high status liked best those of high status. In generalizing from their numerous studies the authors concluded: "It seems quite possible that in any type of social comparison with other human beings (e.g., traits, tastes, income, overt behavior, etc.) similarity is preferred to dissimilarity." If so, then the cautious like the cautious; the bold, the bold.

Why do we like people like ourselves so much? Perhaps it is because they confirm our view of reality. When we are uncertain about what is real and what is not real, what is important and what is not important, what we should do and what we should not do, we become confused, disoriented, and fearful. Our certainty increases when we find people who agree with our answers. We like people who are like us because they confirm our views of reality. The friends of a student agree with him that art courses are better than economics courses or vice versa, that religion is more important than science or vice versa, that blondes are better than brunettes or vice versa, etc. Even more important than these external matters, friends support a person's view of *himself.* Specifically, the cautious see the present as threatening and the future filled with uncertainties. The bold challenge their view of reality. On the other hand, the bold who see this as a good world in which evil can be subdued are chilled by the gloomy view of the cautious.

The universality and durability of differences in boldness indicate that both the cautious and the bold see an aspect of reality that the other does not, and both have their strengths as well as their weaknesses. The strength of the bold is that they like to make decisions and are ready, and often eager, to accept responsibility. Decisions, however, involve risks. The energy, optimism, and self-confidence of the bold encourage them to take unnecessary risks that may endanger both themselves and others. Sometimes any fast decision is better than none or a slow one. In general, however, the weakness of the bold lies in their tendency to plunge ahead without thought and without awareness of dangers. Their tendency to be tough-skinned is also likely to anger others. The strength of the cautious lies in their tendency to make careful decisions; their weakness, their tendency not to make any decisions at all.

In general, then, the question of whether it is better for a person to be cautious or bold can only be answered: It depends. It depends on whether his cautiousness or boldness is effective. The most effective person is one who is cautious *or* bold *according to the demands of the situation.* We like bold explorers but we prefer cautious bankers. It is not so important to us that a man is cautious or bold as it is how and when he is either. Some situations require caution, others, boldness. The effectiveness of a person seems to depend more upon finding a situation that fits his level of boldness than upon the level itself. The Shackletons are ineffective in routine situations but effective in hazardous and novel ones; the Ibsens make poor explorers but may make great writers. The effectiveness of our cautiousness or boldness also depends upon who is in a particular life situation with us. The bold husband and the cautious wife may make a more effective team than if both were bold or both cautious. The effectiveness of any level of boldness depends upon the demands of the particular situation we are in and upon who is in the situation with us. Above all, however, it depends upon the total personality structure of which boldness is only one element.

Both the cautious and the bold have problems, but they have different kinds of problems. A problem is a personal thing. A person has a problem if what he is doing is not moving him toward the goal he seeks; he has a serious problem if what he is doing is moving him *away* from the goal he seeks. A problem, then, is not an impersonal characteristic of a situation, for what is a serious problem to a cautious person may be no problem at all to a bold person in the same situation. And vice versa.

What can the cautious and bold do about their different kinds of problems? One thing they *cannot* do is to change their degree of boldness in any radical way. The cautious cannot make themselves reckless or the bold make themselves prudent. Some people are believers in heredity, others are believers in environment. The former consider efforts to alter boldness as a waste of time, while the latter see them as overwhelmingly important. The facts about boldness, however, require us to recognize that genes have an important influence on boldness but that this influence may be significantly modified by the environment. Modifications of boldness cannot be achieved easily, nor can they be drastic. Furthermore, the older a child becomes, the less influence changes in his environment are likely to have. By the time he is a college student, big changes may have little general effect.

What the cautious and the bold *can* do is to better understand how bold they are, accept both the weaknesses and strengths of their particular trait, plan their lives to avoid their weaknesses and to use their strengths, and, finally, to work at correcting small but critical weaknesses. Socrates said that self-knowledge was the highest aim of philosophical inquiry. No one has ever really disagreed with him, but everyone has found it a difficult kind of knowledge to obtain.

Introspection is a necessary but insufficient method for gaining self-knowledge. It reveals that which is accessible to our individual experience. The inventory measure of boldness reveals how our experience compares and contrasts with the experiences of others. Even more, it isolates an area of human experience in which we do differ in profound and significant ways. Thus, this approach permits us to find out about ourselves by noting the similarities and differences between ourselves and others. The better we understand who others are and what they want, the better we understand what we are and what we want. It also works the other way: the better we understand what we are and want, the better we understand what others are and want. It would be pleasant to be cautious *and* bold, as careful as Ibsen and as daring as Shackleton. None of us are, or can be.

However, many charlatans make a successful living by appealing to our wish to possess desirable but incompatible traits. Mark Twain (1961, p. 71) reported a typical experience with a phrenologist, a reader of bumps on the head:

Fowler received me with indifference, fingered my head in an uninterested way and named and estimated my qualities in a bored and monotonous voice. He said I possessed amazing courage, an abnormal spirit of daring, a pluck, a stern will, a fearlessness that were without limit. I was astonished at this, and gratified, too; I had not suspected it before; but then he foraged over on the other side of my skull and found a hump there which he called "caution." This hump was so tall, so mountainous, that it reduced my courage-bump to a mere hillock by comparison, although the courage-bump had been so prominent up to that time—according to his description of it—that it ought to have been a capable thing to hang my hat on; but it amounted to nothing, now in the presence of that Matterhorn which he called my Caution. He explained that if that Matterhorn had been left out of my scheme of character I would have been one of the bravest men that ever lived— possibly the bravest—but that my cautiousness was so prodigiously superior to it that it abolished my courage and made me almost spectacularly timid. He continued his discoveries, with the result that I came out safe and sound, at the end, with a hundred great and shining qualities; but which lost their value and amounted to nothing because each of the hundred was coupled up with an opposing defect which took the effectiveness all out of it.

The more able an individual is to accept his limitations, the more competent he becomes. Sixth-grade children, for example, were asked to check anonymously which of twenty statements of undesirable behavior were true of them (Taylor and Combs, 1952). All statements described behavior likely to be true of all children: "I sometimes waste time when I should be working," "I sometimes talk back to my mother," etc. The children also took the California Test of Personality, a measure of personal adjustment. The average child in the lower half of the test checked less than six of the undesirable statements, the average child in the upper checked about nine—50 percent more than the less adjusted children. In general, any level of any trait has possible weaknesses and strengths. The more realistic we are about ourselves, the more able we are to use our strengths and protect ourselves from our weaknesses.

SUMMARY

The cautious person is a physically inactive, quiet, and aloof individual who avoids leadership positions, lacks confidence in himself, and takes a pessimistic view of the world. The bold person is an energetic, talkative, and gregarious individual who is self-confident and optimistic and who seeks and enjoys positions of leadership and responsibility. Genes create differences in boldness through their influence upon activity levels; they also influence such differences indirectly by their interaction with racial, sexual, and other social stereotypes. Such general environmental influences as parental attitudes and social class also create profound differences in boldness. Specific environmental mechanisms can make only small differences in the boldness of adults. However, these differences may make large differences in the happiness and well-being of the individual. The boldness of a judge of boldness interferes with his judgments—the cautious tend to see others as bolder than they are; the bold, less bold than they are. Both the cautious and the bold have weaknesses and strengths. However, the weaknesses of the cautious are the strengths of the bold, and the strengths of the cautious are the weaknesses of the bold. Each, therefore, must find a different way of compensating for his weaknesses, utilizing his strengths effectively.

SUGGESTIONS FOR FURTHER READING

Lansing, A. (1959). *Endurance*. New York: McGraw-Hill. A gripping account of Shackleton's leadership of the 1915 Imperial Trans-Antarctic Expedition. Boldness at its best.

Boswell, J. (1965). *The Life of Samuel Johnson*. New York: Modern Library. The greatest biography ever written. This eighteenth century literary figure was not only very bold but also wise and fascinating. Boswell lets Johnson, a great talker, talk about himself.

Fuller, J. L. (1960). *Behavior genetics*. New York: Wiley. The genetic bases of behavioral characteristics such as intelligence, personality, temperament, and behavior disorders are lucidly discussed.

Anastasi, A. (1958). Heredity, environment, and the question "How?" *Psychological Review*, **65**, 197–208. A readable account of the interaction view that is taken throughout the present book.

*Correct answers for Table 4-6: Joan scored at the 10th and Mary at the 80th percentile. Consequently, Mary is much bolder than Joan.

5

THE UNEMOTIONAL
AND THE EMOTIONAL

Temperament refers to the characteristic phenomena
of an individual's emotional nature, including his susceptibility
to emotional stimulation, his customary speed of response,
the quality of his prevailing mood, and all peculiarities of
fluctuation and intensity of mood.

GORDON ALLPORT

Our perceptions of ourselves and others are impregnated with emotion. Some of us, though, are more pregnant than others. Some perceive the world with more intense, frequent, and varied emotions than others. The emotional atmosphere in which some of us live is either bright sunshine or heavy rain, joy or grief, excitement or anguish, exultation or depression. Others of us spend most of our lives in a partly cloudy climate. Psychologists like William James (Table 5-2 and Figure 5-2) are very emotional. Others like Sigmund Freud (Table 5-1 and Figure 5-1) are relatively unemotional. How emotional are you? Why do we differ? How well can you judge the emotionality of others?

HOW EMOTIONAL ARE YOU?

You *cannot* tell how emotional you are from knowing how bold you are. The bold person is as likely to be very unemotional as he is to be emotional. The bold may be placid about the general good he sees around him or he may be filled with excitement about it. The cautious person may be agitated by the evil he sees in the world around him or he may calmly say: So what?

Table 5-3 presents an inventory scale which enables the reader to compare the level of his emotionality with those of college men and women. Common sense suggests that people who have the most frequent emotional states are also more likely to have intense ones, to have a wider variety of emotions, and to express their feelings more fully. Facts verify common sense, for those who answer one question in the emotional direction are likely to answer the others in the same direction.

Physiological Measures of Emotionality

Inventories measure emotionality by means of systematic self-reports. Instruments that measure heart rate, blood pressure, rate of breathing, and the electrical responsiveness of the skin provide an indirect means of measuring emotionality. Of these, the GSR (the galvanic skin response) has been most widely used.

The GSR is very sensitive to changes in emotionality. For example, college men drew pictures of an automobile, a man, and a woman. While making the drawings, the men were seated in a chair with double armrests and electrodes were attached to the fingers of the nonpreferred hand. A polygraph provided a continuous record of changes in skin resistance throughout the testing session (Figure 5-3). Decreases in the electrical resistance of the skin are an index of increasing emotionality. The mean of readings taken at the beginning, middle, and end of each type of drawing was calculated. Result:

Drawing the auto created the least emotionality; the man, next; and the woman, most (Handler and Reyher, 1966).

GSR measures are best known as "lie detectors." In fact, however, judgments about lying made on the basis of such measures are only about 75 percent correct. They are much more accurate in detecting the presence of "guilty knowledge" (Lykken, 1959). College men were asked to enact two mock crimes, one a "murder." For the murder enactment, a student was taken to the second floor of a building and required to knock on the door of one of the offices. The door was opened by an assistant who, after some preliminary conversation, invited the student to play a hand of poker. The assistant got the better hand, remarked that the student now owed him a hundred dollars, and walked over to stand looking out the window. Taking a weapon from his pocket, the student went through the motions of killing the assistant, hid the weapon in a drawer of the desk, and left the office. Later, the student was seated in the interrogation room, GSR electrodes attached to his dominant hand, a blindfold put over his eyes, and a pair of headphones adjusted to his ears. He was instructed to listen to the questions that were asked but not reply to any of them. All students (including the "innocent" group who had not been in the murder room) were asked six questions such as:

The murderer hid the weapon in one of the drawers of a desk. Which drawer was it? Was it the (a) upper left (b) lower right (c) upper right (d) middle (e) lower left?

A sufficient time after each alternative was allowed to permit the GSR activity to dissipate. The scoring was simple and objective. If a student's largest GSR was to the relevant alternative, he was given a score of 2; if his second largest response was to the relevant alternative, he was given 1; any other response was scored as 0. Thus, a perfect "innocent" score was 0 and a perfect "guilty" score was 12. Scores of 6 or less were scored as innocent; those over six as guilty. None of the 48 innocent in the various phases of the study scored more than 6; 44 of the 50 guilty (88 percent) obtained guilty scores. Counting the guilty and innocent together, there were 94 percent correct classifications. Conclusion: "Detection of guilty knowledge, while less widely applicable, is a more reasonable, objective, and generally defensible technique and is demonstrably capable of very high validity in those situations where it can be used."

Both inventories and instruments measuring physiological processes provide measures of emotionality. How well do these two ways of measuring emotionality agree? Cattell (1965) first measured emotionality by various objective tests: urine analysis, handwriting pressure, increase in pulse rate on plunging an arm into ice water, and response to newspaper headlines. He than compared these measures with an inventory measure of emotionality. The objective test scores were related to the inventory measures in the following order:

Over-all susceptibility to annoyance
Tendency to agree
Admission of common frailties
Confidence about skill in untried performance
Severity of criticism
Handwriting pressure

Conclusion: "One can therefore use questionnaire or objective tests according to circumstance." The study also corrected some common misunderstandings about the nature of emotionality. Thus, the most emotional people had the *least* handwriting pressure. Emotional people have greater muscular tension at the back of the neck and shoulder but less tension in the feet and hands.

TABLE 5-1   The Unemotionality of Freud
Freud, the father of psychoanalysis, was calm. He had none of the violent mood oscillations, none of the unpredictability, and none of the unstable equilibrium that seemed so central to the personality of James. Freud was extremely reserved and emotionally undemonstrative.

Figure 5-1 Sigmund Freud, the world's best known personality theorist, is shown here at the age of seventy-two. His psychoanalytic theory stresses the sexual and aggressive aspects of behavior, early childhood experience, and unconscious processes. (Wide World Photos)

His general calmness, however, did not extend to his ideas. Jung (1965, p. 150), at one time a student of Freud's, comments:

There was no mistaking the fact that Freud was emotionally involved in his sexual theory to an extraordinary degree. When he spoke of it, his tone became urgent, almost anxious, and all signs of his normally critical and skeptical manner vanished. A strange deeply moved expression came over his face. . . .

I can still recall vividly how Freud said to me, "My dear Jung, promise me never to abandon the sexual theory. That is the most essential thing of all. You see, we must make a dogma of it, an unshakable bulwark." He said that to me with great emotion, in the tone of a father saying, "And promise me this one thing, my dear son: that you will go to church every Sunday."

TABLE 5-2   The Emotionality of James

William James at the turn of the century was "the foremost scholar in America" and is today known as the father of American psychology. He was one of the founders of the American Psychological Association, and his *Principles of Psychology* is one of the world's greatest books. James's early education was fitted into his father's migrations between New York, Europe, and Newport. As an adolescent he studied painting under John La Farge but he soon gave up art in favor of philosophy and science. He received his medical degree from Harvard in 1870. As an adult, he became a citizen of the world. In spite of chronic ill-health, he spent much time in traveling, spoke French and German fluently, and had many friends in many lands.

Figure 5-2   William James, 1842–1910. (The Bettman Archive)

James was a late starter: he did not begin teaching until after he was thirty, he did not marry until he was thirty-six, he did not settle upon psychology as his major interest until after forty, and most of his writing was done after fifty.

James was very emotional. He was nervous, unpredictable, and spontaneous. He varied from moods of deep depression to moods when he was radiant, vivid, gay, loving, and companionable. He was very sensitive to both his physical and social environment. It is the unanimous testimony of all who knew him that he lived much through the eyes. He was an unceasing observer of all that lay about him—of nature and art, as well as of life. He wanted to see people he knew and exchanged photographs with many of his friends. Although he described himself as a "musical barbarian" he was quick to discriminate nuances of sound, especially in the quality of a human voice. His sensitivity to his social surroundings is suggested by his humorous remarks about taking children to Europe (Perry, 1954, p. 146):

It seems to me that the most solemn duty I can have in what remains to me of life will be to save my inexperienced fellow-beings from ignorantly taking their little ones abroad when they go for their own refreshment. To combine novel anxieties of the most agonizing kind about your children's education, nocturnal and diurnal contact of the most intimate sort with their shrieks, their quarrels, their questions, their rollings-about and tears, in short with all their emotional, intellectual and bodily functions, in what practically in these close quarters amounts to one room—to combine these things (I say) with a *holiday* for *oneself* is an idea worthy to emanate from a lunatic asylum.

TABLE 5-3   The Unemotional vs. Emotional Scale

A definition of the emotionality trait is given below with 40 statements that measure it. The statements are grouped under subordinate traits in the cluster, with the answer underscored for the emotional end of the scale. Your total score is the number of emotional answers that you make. Norms for 100 college men and 100 college women in 1970 are given after the statements. The two most discriminating items in the scale are indicated with an asterisk.

Definition
Calm people have infrequent, moderate, and limited emotional states that they suppress rather than express. Emotional people have frequent, intense, and wide-ranging emotional states that they freely express.

Directions
If you think a statement is "true" or more true than false as far as you are concerned, underline "T." If you think a statement is "false" or more false than true as far as you are concerned, underline "F."

Frequency of Emotional States
<u>T</u> F   1. I rather frequently find myself getting emotional about some-
          thing.

<u>T</u> F   2.* I become emotional fairly easily.

<u>T</u> F   3. My feelings and emotions are very easily aroused.

<u>T</u> F   4. I experience rather frequent pleasant and unpleasant moods.

<u>T</u> F   5. I rather easily get stirred up.

<u>T</u> F   6. I am easily moved to laughter or tears.

<u>T</u> F   7. I am considered rather emotional by my friends.

T <u>F</u>   8. I am a rather objective and matter-of-fact person.

T <u>F</u>   9. My emotional life is marked by great moderation.

T <u>F</u>   10. I am moderate in my tastes and sentiments.

T <u>F</u>   11. I am almost never extremely excited or thrilled.

T <u>F</u>   12. It takes a great deal to make me emotional.

T <u>F</u>   13. I believe I am less emotional than most people.

T <u>F</u>   14. I find that my life moves along at an even tenor without many ups and downs.

Expression of Emotional States

<u>T</u> F   15. I like having someone with whom I can talk about my emotional problems.

<u>T</u> F   16. I am rather spontaneous in speech and action.

<u>T</u> F   17. I am a fairly impulsive person.

<u>T</u> F   18. I like to discuss my emotions with others.

<u>T</u> F   19. I sometimes speak on the spur of the moment without stopping to think.

<u>T</u> F   20. I have sometimes corrected others, not because they were wrong, but only because they irritated me.

T <u>F</u>   21.* I usually prefer to keep my feelings to myself.

Figure 5-3 The polygraph measures physiological changes. Emotional arousal is detected by monitoring changes in heart rate, electrical resistance of the skin, eye movements, brain waves (EEG), and other body processes. (Ron Junttonen)

Table 5-3 (Continued)

T **F** 22. I suppress my emotions more often than I express them.
T **F** 23. I think much and speak little.
T **F** 24. I usually express myself objectively, with considerate caution and restraint.
T **F** 25. I never complain about my sufferings and hardships.
T **F** 26. I am practically always tolerant even in dealing with people I don't like.
T **F** 27. I consider most matters from every standpoint before I form an opinion.

Range of Emotional States
I **F** 28. Quite a few things make me emotional.
I **F** 29. I have occasional difficulty getting the temperature of my bath the way I like it.
I **F** 30. Sometimes I become so emotional that I find it a little hard to get to sleep.
T **F** 31. I am seldom disturbed by sexual matters.
T **F** 32. I almost always do about as well as I expected in competitions.
T **F** 33. I almost never notice minor physical injuries.
T **F** 34. I can stand pain better than the average person.
T **F** 35. I have never been seasick, plane sick, or car sick.

Intensity of Emotional States
I **F** 36. I have sometimes gotten so angry that I felt like throwing and breaking things.
I **F** 37. I have occasionally had to make an effort not to cry.
I **F** 38. I have very strong likes and dislikes.
I **F** 39. I have sometimes screamed for joy.
T **F** 40. I usually do things in a leisurely sort of way, seldom getting excited.

	Percentiles										
	Unemotional									Emotional	
	0	10	20	30	40	50	60	70	80	90	99
Men	2	8	11	16	20	22	24	28	30	32	35
Women	5	13	20	21	23	25	28	30	32	34	40

WHY DO WE DIFFER IN EMOTIONALITY?

Like differences in boldness, differences in emotionality are influenced by direct and indirect genetic and by general and specific environmental mechanisms. However, the weight of each of these influences, and the ways that they interact are decidedly different.

Direct Genetic Mechanisms

The emotional person behaves in a different way from the unemotional person. Such behavioral differences are not inherited. All that is inherited are different genes that control the synthesis of proteins in different ways. The path from genes to behavior is thus very complex. What can be inherited is a differential susceptibility to the same experience. For example, all human beings are susceptible to common diseases; some, however, are more susceptible than others. Furthermore, susceptibility to some diseases is more influenced by genetic differences than susceptibility to others. Thus, susceptibility to measles seems only slightly influenced by genetic differences: 87 percent of fraternal twins (who have different genetic endowment) contracted measles when their twin contracted them; 95 percent of identical twins (who have the same genetic endowment) contracted them when their twin did. But susceptiblity to tuberculosis is strongly influenced by genes: only 28 percent of fraternal but 74 percent of identical twins contracted tuberculosis when their twins contracted it (Strickberger, 1968). The question here, then, is: How much are differences in susceptibility to emotional stimulation due to differences in genes?

The emotionality of rats is heavily influenced by direct hereditary mechanisms. Hall (1938), for example, developed an emotional and a calm strain of rats in one generation. To begin with, he placed 145 unselected rats in a brilliantly lighted circular enclosure 7 feet in diameter (a fear-provoking situation for rats). Each rat was placed in the middle of the circle for two minutes on each of 12 different days. Emotionality was measured by counting the number of days on which the rat urinated or defecated while in the circle. The average rat urinated or defecated on 4 of the 12 days. Hall then mated 7 of the most emotional male rats with 7 of the most emotional female rats, who had 40 offspring. He also mated 7 of the calmest males with 7 of the calmest females, who had 35 offspring. When the 75 offspring were three months old, they were tested for emotionality in the same way as their parents. For the total group, there were 139 occurrences of emotional defecation or urination. Of these, 12 percent occurred among the offspring of the calm parents; 88 percent, among the offspring of the emotional parents. More recent studies show that emotional rats have larger adrenal glands and smaller kidneys (Fever and Broadhurst, 1962). (See Figure 5-4 for the names and positions of the endocrine glands in the human body.)

Differences in the emotionality of dogs seem also based upon

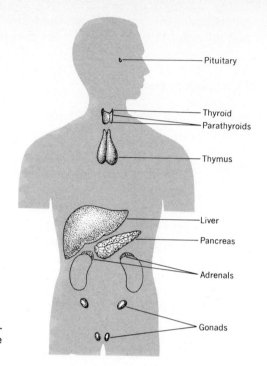

Figure 5-4 The names and positions in the body of the endocrine glands.

direct heredity mechanisms. Mahut (1958) observed the reactions of more than 200 dogs to fear-provoking stimuli: a mechanical snake that was dragged across the floor, an umbrella that was suddenly opened, and a balloon inflated in front of the dog. She noted the number of times that each dog attempted to avoid or to escape from the fear-provoking stimuli. Working and hunting dogs were much more emotional than fighters and ratters. Collies and shepherds showed ten times as many fear responses as boxers and Scotch terriers. In the same breed, emotional dogs have larger and heavier endocrine glands than calm ones (Stockard et al., 1941).

Chimpanzees are more emotional than gorillas (Figure 5-5). Schaller (1963) observed mountain gorillas in their native African habitat. He noted that, unlike chimpanzees, the gorillas never had diarrhea in response to his tracking them. He reports: "Most gorillas possess an outwardly placid nature which is not easily aroused to excitement. Their usual facial and bodily expressions, even in disturbing situations, are ones of repose." His field impressions are consistent with the description of one captive female gorilla given by Yerkes (1927):

Figure 5-5 Animal studies show the influence of direct genetic mechanisms on emotionality: gorillas like the one above are less emotional than chimpanzees; some breeds of dogs are less emotional than others; both calm and emotional rats can be bred. (Foldes/Monkmeyer; Charles Belinsky/Photo Researchers, Inc., Black Star)

Whether lacking in affectivity or merely inexpressive of her emotions, she appeared to be strangely calm, placid, even-tempered, and self-dependent. It seemed at times as though she were repressing or inhibiting acts. Especially when confronted with trying situations such as insoluble problems, disappointment, or disagreeable stimuli, she often exhibited a degree of self-control which was suggestive of stolidity. Her aloofness and air of independence suggested also superiority. She seldom acted impulsively, and a fit of temper such as young chimpanzees and orangutans frequently exhibit was never observed.

The inference from these rat, dog, and gorilla studies is that the emotionality of men should also be heavily influenced by genetic differences in the ease with which the autonomic nervous system can be aroused. The inference, however, is hard to verify. The measurement of emotionality in men is difficult; relating such differences to heredity is even more difficult. Above all, the influence of general and specific environmental influences on emotionality is both enormously greater and more difficult to control in human beings than in animals.

An excellent study by Scarr (1966) shows that what is true for animals is true for humans. He had mothers as well as observing psychologists rate 28 fraternal and 24 identical pairs of twin girls between the ages of six and ten on the emotionality they showed in the presence of other people. There was no relationship between the emotionality of one fraternal twin and the other. There was a high relationship between the emotionality ratings of the identical twins. These differences had nothing to do with varying attitudes of parents toward fraternal and identical twins. Fraternal twins who were mistakenly thought to be identical were no closer in their emotionality scores than those who were correctly identified as fraternal. Identical twins who were mistakenly thought to be fraternal were just as close in their emotionality ratings as those who were correctly identified as identical (Scarr, 1968).

Indirect Genetic Mechanisms

Genes directly determine differences in emotionality by making some of us more sensitive than others to the *same* experiences. They also may indirectly determine differences by exposing us to *different* experiences. Thus, differences in genes determine differences in physique. In turn, these differences in physique determine differences in the way that other people react to us and thus selectively expose us to different social experiences. People do not respond to a big and strong boy the way they respond to a small and weak one. People do not respond to a girl that matures early in the same way they respond to a girl who matures late. An individual who is physically mature is frequently treated as an adult regardless of his age. Consequently, those who mature early tend to be more dominating and less emotional than those who mature later.

The most profound of these indirect influences are those genetic differences that make half of the world male and half female. Women are more emotional than men. Ratings of two-year-old nursery school children showed that, even at this age, the girls were more emotional than the boys (Hattwick, 1937). College women are also more emotional than college men (Table 5-3). Other inventory studies have shown the same result (Guilford and Martin, 1944), and interview ratings of emotionality have shown women to be even more emotional than their inventory scores indicate (Darley, 1937). Women also show much greater galvanic skin response to emotional stimuli (Berry and Martin, 1957). But female rats are *less* emotional than males ones (Hall, 1938).

The greater emotionality of women is certainly due in part to an indirect hereditary mechanism. That is, genes create the biological differences between males and females, social stereotypes about men and women create the emotional differences between them. The training of girls and boys for their different roles in life starts at birth. Girls are given different clothing and toys, and are expected to behave in "feminine" ways. Girls are rewarded more often for helping their mothers in household tasks, for looking pretty, for being interested in dolls, and for caring for household pets and plants. The differences in sex role training are great. The difference in emotionality between men and women is small. The former may well account for all of the latter.

General Environmental Mechanisms

People of different countries show large differences in emotionality (Figure 5-6). Hundreds of citizens in each of six countries completed the same anxiety inventory or an exact translation of it (Cattell, 1965, p. 122). Citizens of the United States had the lowest emotionality score (7.1). The averages for France (14.1) and India (15.1) were twice as large. Scores for the United Kingdom, Japan, and Italy were between these extremes (9.8, 12.5, 13.5). Countries on the border between a free enterprise and a communist zone had the highest scores. Reports of these countries were not published, in order to avoid political pressures on their scientists who had gathered the data. The general economic conditions, cultural values, and political tensions of a country appear to have a profound influence on levels of emotionality. The increased emotionality scores of the typical college man and woman may reflect increasing tensions in the United States. The norms shown in Table 5-3 are based on the replies of students in 1970. Their emotionality scores are higher than those of students taking the same scale in the same class in 1966.

Status in our own society influences emotionality. Children of laborers report more fears and greater emotional disturbances than children of professional fathers (Maddy, 1943). High school students of low socioeconomic status are more fearful than students of high status.

The emotionality of individuals also varies with their place in the life cycle. Studies of age differences show the peak emotional period to be in the early twenties, when the individual is commonly struggling with establishing his occupational, marital, and social roles. There is also a later rise in the emotionality of housewives as they approach middle age, the time when their active role as a mother is reduced or eliminated. After sixty, the anxiety levels for both men and women begin to climb (Cattell, 1965).

Specific Environmental Mechanisms

Positive emotions create no problems: we would all like to feel happier, gayer, and more affectionate than we are. It is the negative emotions of anger, disgust, sadness, and—above all—fear and anxiety that are the problems.

Alcohol is the best known and most widely used mechanism for changing disturbing emotional states. However, many new kinds of tranquilizing drugs are now available. Three of the most used are *reserpine*, *chlorpromazine*, and *meprobamate*. All tend to make the

Figure 5-6 General environmental mechanisms influence emotionality: Are Americans less anxious than Frenchmen or Indians? (H. Armstrong Roberts; Weston Kemp; Marilyn Silverstone/Magnum)

fearful or anxious person quieter, and to make him feel less tense and miserable. Reserpine so relaxed a group of monkeys that for several hours they did not respond to the test situation provided by the psychologists (Hall, Warren, and Harlow, 1955). The effect of chlorpromazine on more than 300 patients in a mental hospital was summarized as follows (Feldman, 1957): "Its capacity to convert highly disturbed behavior into docile tractability has remained an impressive phenomenon." The drugs do not appear to interfere with vision, steadiness, driving, or performance on college examinations (Marquis, Kelly, Miller, and Rapoport, 1957). The use of tranquilizers with schizophrenics resulted in improvements that "far surpassed that accomplished by previous forms of treatment in these patients" (Hollister, Traub, and Beckman, 1956, pp. 72–74).

Tranquilizers reduce emotional tension, pain, and distress of anxiety. They do not resolve the conflicts that cause the anxiety. They do permit a hospital staff to do away with various forms of physical restraint otherwise needed with agitated patients. They can also prepare patients for forms of treatment that deal with the causes of anxiety.

"Docile tractability" is a dubious goal for more or less normal people. However, millions of Americans are spending hundreds of millions of dollars each year on tranquilizers to reduce anxiety and to achieve instant "happiness."

The Reduction of Fear through Training   Fear of illness, of failure, of the disapproval of others, and of the loss of friends and relatives are among the most serious and pervasive of emotional problems. Most of us also have specific fears: of snakes, of high places, of closed places, of dogs, of darkness. Brief training periods are often successful in reducing or eliminating such specific fears.

Training may be directed at giving the fearful person more control of the fear-arousing situation. A dentist reduced the fears of his patients by providing them with a buzzer which they could sound whenever they wanted him to stop drilling. Military experts train soldiers so thoroughly in how to behave in combat that in actual battle the combatants perform the learned acts. Performing as they have been taught dissipates their emotional energy, provides them with the maximum control over their situation, and, consequently, does the most to reduce their fears (Glavis, 1946). For the same reason, experienced steelworkers, coal miners, and automobile racers are generally less fearful in action than the inexperienced. Although before their performances skilled actors and public speakers may be as emotional as inexperienced ones, they are less so during the performance.

Training may also reduce or eliminate the fear itself by "desensitization." Two dozen college students, who had an intense fear of nonpoisonous snakes, were selected by their replies to a widely distributed questionnaire. The experimenters, Lang and Lazovik (1963), verified the intensity of these fears by personal interviews with each student. All of them reported feeling very uncomfortable when they were asked to look at a photograph of a snake.

During the desensitization training, each student met with a trainer five times for less than an hour each time. In the initial session an "anxiety hierarchy" of 20 steps was established. The first step in the hierarchy was the reference to snakes that was least provocative of anxiety; the last, the reference that aroused the most intense emotion. The hierarchy varied somewhat from student to student. Typically, "writing the word *snake*" and "looking at a picture of a snake" were at the bottom of the hierarchy, while "stepping on a dead snake accidentally" and "picking up a live snake" were at the top. In the desensitization program, the students were first asked to imagine the least fearful reference to a snake, i.e., "imagine the word *snake* written out." With some variation, the student repeated this process until he reported that it did not make him feel uncomfortable. At this point, the program would advance to the next step. And so on.

The program was successful. At the end of the fifth meeting, 54 percent were able to hold a snake without feeling disturbed. Six months later, 45 percent of the group were still able to repeat the performance. By contrast, in a control group who were equally fearful but did not go through the desensitization program, less than one in five was willing to touch a live snake. The authors concluded:

1.   It is not necessary to explore with a subject the factors contributing to the learning of a phobia or its "unconscious meaning" in order to eliminate the fear behavior.

2.   The form of treatment employed here does not lead to symptom substitution or create new disturbances of behavior.

3.   In reducing phobic behavior it is not necessary to change basic attitudes, values, or attempt to modify the "personality as a whole."

HOW WELL CAN YOU JUDGE THE EMOTIONALITY OF OTHERS?
Our ability to predict the emotionality score of another is a convincing test of our understanding of his emotionality. The exercise in Table 5-4 asks you to judge the emotionality of Susan Edgar as well as the two college women introduced in the last chapter, Joan Dellard and Mary Bernard. In completing this test bear in mind that "unemotional" does not mean no emotion but *less* emotion than most college women and that "emotional" does not mean always emotional but *more* emotional than most college women.

Why do we make errors in judging the emotionality of others? The last chapter discussed a major source of errors in judging any aspect of personality. We are so preoccupied with whether we like or dislike a person or with trying to decide whether we like or dislike him

TABLE 5-4 How Well Can You Judge the Emotionality of Others?
Susan Edgar, a nineteen-year-old social work major, completed the trait
scales. Her boldness was slightly higher than that of the typical college
woman. After reading the sketch below based on her autobiography, judge
her emotionality, first in comparison with Joan Dellard and Mary Bernard and
then in comparison with college women in general. Remember that emotionality is independent of boldness. That is, you cannot predict with any
accuracy where people stand in emotionality from knowing their boldness
scores.

Susan Edgar Her family was not very close because the members were
individualistic, and shared few common interests. At an early age she
developed a liking for animals and she had as many and as varied an
assortment of pets as her parents would allow. Her parents didn't understand
where this interest came from (they were both teachers) and disliked her
spending so much time with her animals. Susan says, "I told my animals my
secrets and how I felt, and can't see why I should tell people who might take it
the wrong way or not understand."

Susan didn't date much till she came to college, and gets along
better with older people than with people of her own age group, who seem
immature to her. She believes in two religions—God and Mother Nature—and
understands the latter better; "I just don't know what side God is on." She
likes cooking, skating, swimming, and horseback riding. Her interests are
broad, and she feels she often expects too much of herself. She respects
other people's beliefs, but is persistent. She says she can be a tomboy, or a
lady, when called for.

Joan Dellard Joan Dellard is the cautious psychology major described
earlier (p. 86). As a child, her parents were always comparing her unfavorably
with her three older brothers. She often needs reassurance, and is sometimes
frightened by such things as the possibility of World War III.

Mary Bernard Mary, the bold middle-aged major in home economics, was
also described earlier (p. 86). Among other things, she says that she became independent early in life and feels obligated to no person and
holds no person obligated to her.

How do these three women compare in their emotionality?* Below, rank
"1" the woman that you think is *least* emotional; "2" the one in the middle;
and "3" the one that is most emotional.

Susan Edgar   _____
Joan Dellard   _____
Mary Bernard   _____

Table 5-4 (Continued)
*How does their emotionality compare with that of other college women?**
(Underline the percentile that you think each girl matches)

	Percentile										
	Unemotional				Average				Emotional		
Susan Edgar	0	10	20	30	40	50	60	70	80	90	99
Joan Dellard	0	10	20	30	40	50	60	70	80	90	99
Mary Bernard	0	10	20	30	40	50	60	70	80	90	99

*Correct answers are given at end of chapter.

that we are uninterested and unaware of how he sees himself. Further-more, the cautious are more likely to see a person as threatening and unlikeable and the bold to see him as helpful and good regardless of his emotionality or any other trait.

The last chapter also stressed that the good judge is able to think in a complex way about others; i.e., he is able to see *both* the good and the bad in others. This is a particularly hard thing for those who react to others in a highly emotional way to do. Ehrlich and Lipsey (1968) used statements like those in Table 5-5 to determine differences in the affective style of people in relating to others. They found wide and consistent differences. They also found that the stronger a person's emotional reactions to new people tended to be, the more concerned he was about making a good first impression himself, the more likely he was to make judgments based on little information, and less likely he was to change his first impressions on the basis of later information.

CAN WE EDUCATE OUR EMOTIONS?

It is certainly better to have some emotion than none, for our feelings determine the worth and meaning of our lives. If we had no feelings, if ideas were the only things our minds could entertain, nothing would be seen as having any more value than anything else. Everyone, of course, has some feeling about something. The real questions, then concern the intensity of the emotions we experience, the kind of emotions we have, our awareness of our emotional states, and, above all, the extent of our emotional education.

Expressed versus Repressed Emotion

As Freud and James testify, extremely mature and constructive persons can be unemotional *or* emotional. We generally like what we are and like those who are like ourselves—the unemotional prefer the unemotional; the emotional, the emotional. Less often, we envy and admire our opposites. Both ends have their weaknesses: the emotional may be paralyzed by the intensity of their emotions; the calm may be so bland and placid that they respond to nothing and improve nothing, either in themselves or in the world around them. A common and grave weakness of the apparently unemotional is that they are really extremely emotional but are repressing or suppressing their feelings. Freud

---

TABLE 5-5   What Is Your Emotional Style in Relating to Others?*
When we met a person for the first time, some of us respond quickly and intensely while others respond more slowly and calmly. How do you react?

Read each of the statements below. Indicate whether you "strongly disagree" (SD), "disagree" (D), are "uncertain" (?), "agree" (A), or "strongly agree" (SA) that the statement describes your typical reaction when meeting new people. Circle the number in the column below, SD, D, ?, A, or SA that corresponds to your level of disagreement or agreement with the statement.

SD	D	?	A	SA		
1	2	3	4	5	1.	When I meet people for the first time, I know immediately if I like or dislike them.
1	2	3	4	5	2.	I immediately have a strong reaction to them.
1	2	3	4	5	3.	Even when I talk to a person for just a few minutes, I am likely to have a strong reaction to them.
1	2	3	4	5	4.	I find that certain new people turn me on—almost immediately.
1	2	3	4	5	5.	I know immediately if I like or dislike them.
5	4	3	2	1	6.	My reactions to new people are very neutral.
5	4	3	2	1	7.	It takes me quite a while to make up my mind about how I feel about a person.
5	4	3	2	1	8.	I do not make judgments about people until I am sure of the facts.
5	4	3	2	1	9.	I feel that one needs to know a person for a long time before he has a good idea of what a person is really like.
5	4	3	2	1	10.	It takes more than one meeting for me to decide if I like or dislike a person.

Scoring. Count the numbers you have circled. Ten is the least emotional response to others and fifty is the most emotional. An average score is about 30.

Source: Ehrlich and Lipsey 1968.

called repression "the pillar upon which the edifice of psychoanalysis rests."

Repression and Suppression

Repression is motivated forgetting. We remember triumphant moments, "forget" embarrassing ones; remember the times we have been intelligent, forget the times we have been a fool; remember our altruistic decisions, forget our selfish ones. We "forget" what makes us feel inferior, ashamed, guilty, and anxious.

What is learned in school may be lost through physiological processes or through interference by new material with the retention of old material. Memories which have been repressed, however, can be fully recalled under certain conditions. They can also have marked effects upon behavior. During hypnosis, for example, a confirmed smoker was instructed to feel that smoking was a bad habit, that he both loved and hated it, that he wanted to get over the habit but that he felt it was too strong a habit to break, that he would be very reluctant to smoke and would give anything not to smoke, but that he would find himself compelled to smoke (Erickson, 1939). He was also instructed that when he awakened he would experience all these feelings but not remember that he had been told to have them. After he was awakened, he was offered a cigarette but he refused, saying he preferred his own brand. He spent considerable time searching through his pockets for his own, finally finding them in their usual place. The procedure was repeated with matches. Finally, he started to light his cigarette but became engrossed in a conversation so that the match burnt his finger. Lighting another match, he offered to demonstrate how to save matches by splitting them down the middle and using only half. The trick didn't work. When a member of the audience offered him a light, he sneezed and blew the light out. The next time, he had put the wrong end of the cigarette in his mouth, so that the wet end would not light. When it was finally lighted, he took a few deep puffs and then let the cigarette burn undisturbed. While smoking another cigarette, he knocked off the burning tip in making an expansive gesture.

In *suppression*, we consciously decide to exclude an idea from our thoughts, our conversation, and our actions; in *repression*, an idea is unconsciously and automatically excluded. In the following case, Albert was suppressing:

> I was stationed in Japan, flying combat missions with a B-29 squadron over North Korea. I had been there about three months and had flown 14 missions. Each one seemed to get worse than the one before, and each time I was more afraid that something might happen. I dared not express my feelings for

fear of being left on the ground and taken off the crew. I managed to pull myself together and make that fifteenth mission. We were over the target when one of our highly explosive bombs failed to release properly and "hung" in the bomb bay armed. My first thought was to get out of the plane, but this would have resulted in a panic. Since I was the one person who could reach the bomb, I climbed into the open bomb bay and disarmed it. . . . Oddly, I never again was afraid to fly a combat mission.

But in the following case, Elmer was repressing:

When I was about six years old my mother and I went for a walk in the small Pennsylvania town where we lived. My curiosity was aroused by a small blacksmith shop; and I cautiously proceeded to investigate it. The blacksmith offered to set me up on one of the horses. As he picked me up, he left great black handprints on my clean shirt. I was terrified by the size and movement of the horse, and my mother scolded me for getting dirty after I was lifted down. From that time until my mother accidentally recalled the incident to me when I was in high school, I was much afraid of horses and felt strongly that they were particularly dirty animals.

Fear versus Anxiety

Fear is a painful state. But, generally, it is momentary, we understand what causes it, and we know what we need to do to reduce or eliminate it. Anxiety is a worse state: it is generally enduring, we do not understand what is causing it, we often do not know what to do about it, and we are often not even aware that we *are* anxious. "Anxiety" has many different meanings. Popularly, the word is used as if it were identical with fear. As psychologists define the term, however, it is quite different: *Anxiety is a vague fear aroused by internal conflicts.* A study that exposed students to fear-arousing and anxiety-arousing situations makes clear the important differences between these two painful states.

Twenty men at Yale University were placed in a *high fear* situation (Sarnoff and Zimbardo, 1961). When they came into the laboratory room, the experimenters told them:

Our present experiment deals with the skin as an organ of sensation. In order to measure your physiological reactions, we are now going to attach some instruments to your arm and finger. These instruments are electrodes which are connected

to a machine which records exactly the strength of your response to each stimulus.

They were then led to believe that they would be given electrical shocks that would last for two minutes. The experimenters assured them that the shocks would not cause damage or injury. However, there was a small sign posted on the wall: "Danger/High Voltage." They were shown a series of slides of "typical" subjects "listening to the instructions," "about to receive his first shock," etc. In order to provide a reasonable basis for asking the subjects to wait in other rooms, the experimenters told them that it would be necessary to assess their basal rates of responding before applying the actual shocks:

> Now that your basal rates have been recorded, it will take us about ten minutes while we tally the data and reset our measuring instruments. While we are doing these things, we are going to ask you to wait in other rooms which are available to us . . . we have found that some of our subjects prefer to do their waiting alone, while others prefer to wait together with other subjects. Therefore, we are going to give you your choice of waiting alone or with others.

The subjects were never actually shocked. The aim of the study was to find out whether fearful people prefer to be with others or alone. An experimenter later fully explained this aim individually to each subject. Result: 95 percent chose to wait with others before being shocked.

Twenty-two other men were placed in a *high anxiety* situation. The setting was the same as in the high fear situation. However, the experimenters told them this time that the study concerned the sensitivity of the lips. They were led to believe that they would have to suck on a number of objects. In front of the subjects were the following items: baby bottles, oversized nipples, pacifiers, breast shields, and lollipops. They saw slides of a "typical" subject with his tongue hanging out and his lips puckered, about to suck his thumb (another object of stimulation). They then were given the choice of waiting alone or with someone else before the actual experiment. The experimenters assumed that the desire to obtain pleasurable gratification by sucking on the female breast or on objects closely related to this infantile experience, such as nipples and pacifiers, had been repressed by most of the subjects. They further assumed that the chance to satisfy the desire would arouse an internal conflict, i.e., anxiety. Result: Only 45 percent of the high anxiety group chose to be with others during the waiting period, less than half the percentage of the high fear group who

made this choice. How can these radically different responses to fear and anxiety be explained?

Like fear, anxiety is a "stirred-up" state of the organism. Both fearful and anxious people, if the stimulus is intense enough, show the same bodily symptoms: pounding heart and rapid pulse, tense muscles, dryness of the throat, "butterflies" in the stomach, "nervous perspiration" or "cold sweat," trembling, and feeling sick to the stomach.

Unlike fear, however, the anxious person has only a vague idea of what he is anxious *about*. The "high fear" group knew exactly what there was to be afraid of—the painful electric shock. The "high anxiety" group, on the other hand, were much less aware of what was causing their disturbance. Anxious people in everyday life, like the anxious people in the laboratory, do not understand the source of their anxiety. For example (Cameron and Magaret, 1951, pp. 311–312):

An ambitious but overdependent patient developed a typical anxiety attack in which gastrointestinal symptoms were prominent. One day at work, just after his convalescence from a severe attack of "grippe," he learned that he had not been granted an expected salary increase. To this information, which he angrily considered evidence of unfair discrimination, he reacted characteristically with nausea and diarrhea, which he attributed to food poisoning; and because of his heightened anxiety level, the gastrointestinal symptoms persisted. The patient then became greatly concerned over the possibility that he had a gastric ulcer, or perhaps cancer of the stomach. He consulted one physician after another, tried innumerable sorts of medication, and insisted upon repeated gastrointestinal investigations, in spite of the discomfort they entailed. The consistent medical reassurances he received that there was no evidence of organ pathology gave him no lasting relief. Finally, he left work and stayed home in bed for a period of nine weeks, convinced that he was suffering from an obscure but fatal illness. . . . Therapy, aimed not at the symptoms of anxiety, but at the conflict between passive and aggressive reactions which had induced them, brought him eventually to full social recovery.

Like fear, anxiety arises when we are blocked from getting what we want. The "high fear" group felt blocked in their efforts to avoid the electric shock. The "high anxiety" group felt blocked in their desire to gain oral satisfaction.

Unlike fear, the anxious are blocked, not by obstacles in the external world, but by an internal conflict. Wild animals, bolts of

lightning in a thunderstorm, or a burning forest block men from safety and make them fearful. The man lost in the desert or the farmer in a flooded field is blocked by his physical environment and becomes fearful. The unemployed, the segregated black, and the slum dweller are blocked by their social environment and become fearful. The anxious, however, are blocked from within by their inability to go in two different directions at the same time. Such conflicts may arise from incompatible needs: a person cannot eat and sleep, fight and flee, submit and dominate at the same time. Conflicts may arise from incompatible goals: a person cannot go to the movies and to a dance or be a selfless hero and look after his own best interests all at the same time. And conflicts may arise from incompatible methods: a person cannot earn a living by being a crook and an honest worker at the same time.

It is easier to define fear and anxiety theoretically than it is to distinguish between them in daily life. In everyday life, specific fears fade into vague fears and vague fears into anxieties. A boy, for example, may have a specific fear of the dog next door because he knows that the dog bites almost everyone. The specific fear may become a general and vaguer fear, for he does not know when he will meet the dog, whether the dog will bite him when he does, or what to do if the dog does try to bite him. Furthermore, the fear of one dog may generalize into a vague fear of all dogs or even of all animals. The vague fear may become an anxiety, a fear of his own impulses. The laughter of friends and neighbors may make him so ashamed of his fear that he "acts brave," denies to others that he is afraid of dogs, and, eventually, denies his fear to himself. Afraid to admit his anxiety to himself, he may still become very disturbed under circumstances that seem entirely safe—a discussion about someone else who is afraid of dogs, or the presence of a man who looks like the owner of the dog.

The ability to distinguish between fear and anxiety is helped by noting what a person does about his stirred-up state. Almost all of the "high fear" group, for example, chose to wait with others. Being with others when we are afraid gives us a chance to evaluate the soundness of our fears, to gain release through talking about them, and to remove the causes of fears through joint action. Less than half of the "high anxiety" group, on the other hand, chose to wait with others. Why? Partly, because while we do not know exactly what is causing our anxiety, we do know that the intensity of our feelings is disproportionate to the external threat. We realize that others may judge our feelings to be undesirable or strange, so that we are hesitant to talk about them. Most important of all, when we are anxious, we are disturbed about our inner selves, not about the external world. We are at least dimly aware, therefore, that joint action with others cannot help us.

Anxiety is the result of internal emotional conflicts. Such

conflicts arise because our feelings about ourselves and the world are too simple, too incomplete, too inconsistent. Such conflicts are reduced as our understanding of our feelings becomes more complex, complete, and consistent. Anxiety, in other words, is an inevitable part of personality development: immaturity causes anxiety; maturity reduces anxiety. Carl Rogers (1951) suggests that the central task of psychotherapy is to reduce anxiety by encouraging personality development:

... The organism moves through struggle and pain toward enhancement and growth. The whole process may be symbolized and illustrated by the child's learning to walk. The first steps involve struggle, and usually pain. Often it is true that the immediate reward involved in taking a few steps is no way commensurate with the pain of falls and bumps. The child may, because of the pain, revert to crawling for a time. Yet, in the overwhelming majority of individuals, the forward direction of growth is more powerful than the satisfactions of remaining infantile. The child will actualize himself, in spite of the painful experiences in so doing. In the same way, he will become independent, responsible, self-governing, socialized, in spite of the pain which is involved in these steps. Even where he does not, because of a variety of circumstances, exhibit growth of these more complex sorts, one may still rely on the fact that the tendency is present.

Psychology versus Art

Our happiness depends more upon our awareness of our emotions than upon their intensity. As we become emotionally educated, we learn to recognize and face our feelings of anger, shame, disgust, fright, and longing. As we face and study our emotions, they become less vague and diffused, more differentiated and individualistic. As we study them, we become more skillful in dealing with them. The ability to represent our emotional states in symbolic form is essential to all of these processes. Words and numbers can represent the relationships between emotions and their causes and consequences; they cannot represent the emotions themselves. Art can. Music, painting, fiction, poetry, architecture, movies, and dancing intensify, illuminate, and objectify feelings so that we can see, study, and deal with them.

Anxiety results from an emotional conflict of which we have little awareness and less understanding. One of the tasks of psychology is to increase our awareness and understanding by showing us what is related to anxiety. Art sails an entirely different course. Increasing our understanding of our feelings is the primary task of art. It does not approach this task by showing us what is related to our feelings; it seeks to show us our feelings. This chapter has been concerned with clarifying the scientific view of emotions—the relationships between genetic and environmental mechanisms and enduring emotional states. Chapter 7 returns to the problem of how art clarifies and educates our emotions.

SUMMARY

The unemotional are seldom stirred to express their feelings. The emotional have frequent, intense, and wide-ranging emotional states that they like to talk about. Genes create differences between individuals in their susceptibility to the same emotional stimulation and in the emotional stimuli to which they are likely to be exposed. Drugs can temporarily and training can permanently alter some of these differences. While fear is among the most painful of emotional states, anxiety (a vague fear aroused by internal conflicts) creates more enduring and more disruptive emotional states. Psychology seeks to clarify the causes and consequences of such emotional states so that they can be dealt with more effectively. Art seeks to objectify these states so that they be seen and felt, illuminated and harmonized.

SUGGESTIONS FOR FURTHER READING

Perry, R. B. (1954). *The thought and character of William James*. Boston: Atlantic–Little, Brown. The authoritative biography of the emotional father of American psychology and of his unusual and unusually creative family.

Jones, E. (1957). *Life and work of Sigmund Freud*. 3 vols. New York: Basic Books. A detailed and comprehensive picture of the man and the myth.

Cannon, W. B. (1929). *Bodily changes in pain, hunger, fear, and rage*. Appleton-Century-Crofts. A short and readable psychological classic.

Answers for Table 5-4: Edgar (1), Dellard (3), and Bernard (2). Edgar, 10th percentile; Dellard, 90th percentile; and Bernard, 60th percentile.

6

THE PRESENT-MINDED
AND THE
FUTURE-MINDED

Religion admonishes man not to be fearful of the day to come,
and human wisdom advises him to enjoy the present day, not
caring for the future. But man could never follow this
advice. To think of the future and to live in the future
is a necessary part of his nature.

ERNST CASSIRER

We cannot imagine any real thing that did not exist or occur at some time. Man shares with all life the influence of *organic* time, for all life preserves some traces of its past which influence its future. Man shares with the higher animals a sense of *perceptual* time, a sense of the passage and transience of time. Man, alone, is aware of *abstract* time, of time as a pure sequence of time, of time as measured by sun dials, water clocks, or watches. As a result of this unique ability, man is aware of events that happened before he was born and that may happen after he dies. An awareness of the future seems to exert an important influence on even the young child. As he develops, his fears and hopes for the future play a more and more important part.

The future dominates our lives. However, it rules the lives of some much more than others. Dylan Thomas (Table 6-1 and Figure 6-1) was present-minded: he seemed to live in the moment, thinking and planning very little for the future. George Washington (Table 6-2 and Figure 6-2) was future-minded: he set goals for the future, organized his time for their achievement, and spent his time and efforts to achieve them. How future-minded are you? Why do we differ in our future-mindedness? How well can you judge the future-mindedness of others? Is it better to be present-minded or future-minded?

HOW FUTURE-MINDED ARE YOU?

We can study visual perception by studying the functioning of the eye. We can study auditory perception by studying the functioning of the ear. We cannot study time perception in the same way, for there is no special system in the body to sense time. If an interval of time is filled with experience, it is perceived to pass quickly. Time perception, however, is not primarily a function of exposure to experience; it is a function of the ability to integrate experience. For example, a piece of music, when first heard, is unfamiliar and not easily coded, therefore time seems to pass slowly. After a number of repetitions, the music becomes more familiar and is more easily coded, and time passes more quickly. Finally, when the listener has heard the piece many times and is thoroughly familiar with it, his attention to the music suffers, and consequently the stimulus is no longer completely coded. Time passes slowly again. Music which is rhythmic and repetitive is very easily coded, becomes familiar very quickly, and also becomes boring quickly. Thus, when we first hear a popular song, time seems to pass slowly; the next few times, time passes much more quickly; soon, however, time slows down again.

Our concern, though, is not with the similar ways in which we perceive time, but with the different orientations we take toward

Figure 6-1 Dylan Thomas, 1914–1953. (Bunny Adler/Pix, Inc.)

TABLE 6-1 The Present-Mindedness of Dylan Thomas

Dylan Thomas, a Welsh poet, died in 1953 at the age of thirty-nine in St. Vincent's Hospital, New York. His poems (*A Child's Christmas in Wales, Quite Early One Morning*, etc.) and his poetic dramas (*Adventures in the Skin Trade* and *Under Milk Wood*) place him among the most talented of modern poets. His notoriety in the United States, however, rests upon his poetry-reading trips to hundreds of American colleges and universities. These were accompanied by legendary drinking bouts and sexual adventures that were dramatized in the play, *Dylan*, in which Alex Guinness originally played the leading part.

Dylan's father was a man of literary and intellectual ability, but he spent most of his life teaching at the Swansea Grammar School. Dylan quit this school at sixteen, an almost total academic failure. He was later described by one of his teachers as "clever, but intellectually almost incredibly lazy." His home life was a solitary one and his loneliness was intensified by chronic illness. His mother pampered and cuddled him.

On his arrival in London before twenty, he set the daily pattern that persisted through his life: loafing in the morning, writing in the afternoon, drinking and talking in the evening. He was an incessant smoker, his clothes had the appearance of an unmade bed, and he was ineffective in dealing with the details of day-to-day life. A favorite breakfast was ice cream in a glass of beer. He appeared not to believe in private property: The money he made he spent immediately and sometimes lost, he borrowed the personal belongings of friends without asking them and even took such things as sewing machines and rugs from their homes. He did believe in following his impulses.

His friend and biographer (Fitzgibbon, 1965) remarked: "Not to have indulged his desire to the full would have been, in his eyes, to be untrue to himself as he saw himself, and a denial of that personal freedom on which he set so high a value." He liked people: He liked to be with people, he liked to talk with people, and, above all, he liked to drink with people. His dramatic ability was so great and his desire to be what people expected him to be so intense that he developed to a high degree the capacity his friends described as "Instant Dylan." He could instantly detect what people wanted him to be and act the part so convincingly that they were confident he *was* that way.

abstract time. The first five statements in Table 6-3 deal directly with these differences in time orientation. It turns out that those who are present-minded also see themselves as relatively impulsive, focused upon immediate satisfactions, and little concerned with planning and organizing their activities. The future-minded, on the other hand, are also controlled, work-centered, and methodical.

Cattell (1965) isolated a similar inventory trait but labeled it, following Freud's terminology, as "low and high superego strength." In describing the qualities of those high in superego strength he says (pp. 94–95):

> It is obviously not just a rational politeness or conformity but a somewhat fierce "categorical imperative" (to use Kant's description) of the kind exemplified at its strongest by the biblical saints. It is not wholly responsible for determining persistence and perseveration, since these may arise also in the service of personal ambition, but it has much to do with persistence in super-personal goals and ideals, and with attempts to exercise powerful self-control.

Impulsivity has also been measured by noninventory methods. Preference for color over form is one such method. Students performed tasks that involved sorting a circular red object into a circular blue box or a square red box. Those who consistently sorted by color rather than by shape showed many evidences of impulsivity: They were faster in their responses, they were more disrupted when they were assigned an unexpected task, and they more often described themselves as impulsive (Murray and Jackson, 1964). The impulsivity of children has also been measured by rating their speed of response and errors in a visual-sorting task (Kagan, 1966). (See also Figure 6-3.) Those classified as impulsive by this method made more errors in reading. One reason

Figure 6-2 George Washington, 1732–1799. (New York Public Library)

TABLE 6-2 The Future-Mindedness of George Washington

Washington's control was evident to all who knew him. President Thomas Jefferson, in writing to a friend, described the first President in these terms (Lipscomb and Bergh, 1903):

His mind was great and powerful without being of the very first order; his penetration strong, though not so acute as that of a Newton, Bacon, or Locke; and as far as he saw, no judgment was ever sounder. It was *slow in operation*, being little aided by invention or imagination, but sure in conclusion. Hence the common remark of his officers, of the advantage he derived from councils of war, where hearing all suggestions, he selected whatever was best; and certainly *no general ever planned his battles more judiciously*. But if deranged during the course of action, if any member of his plan was dislocated by sudden circumstances, he was slow in readjustment. The consequence was, that he often failed in the field, and rarely against an enemy in station, as at Boston and York. He was incapable of fear, meeting personal dangers with the calmest unconcern. Perhaps the strongest feature in his character was prudence, never acting until every circumstance, every consideration, was maturely weighed, refraining if he saw doubt, but when once decided, going through with his purpose, whatever obstacles opposed. His integrity was most pure, his justice the most *inflexible* I have ever known, no motives of interest or consanguinity, of friendship or hatred, being able to bias his decision. He was, indeed, in every sense of the word, a good, and a great man.

His temper was naturally irritable and high toned; but reflection and resolution had obtained *a firm and habitual ascendency over it.* If ever, however, it broke its bonds, he was most tremendous in his wrath.

In his expenses he was honorable, but exact; liberal in contributions to whatever promised utility; but frowning and unyielding on all visionary projects, and all unworthy calls on his charity. . . . Although in the circle of his friends, where he might be unreserved with safety, he took a free share in conversation, his colloquial talents were not above mediocrity, possessing neither copiousness of idea, nor fluency of words. In public, when called on for a sudden opinion, he was unready, short and embarrassed. Yet he wrote readily, rather diffusely, in an easy and correct style. This he had acquired by conversation with the world, for his education was merely reading, writing and common arithmetic, to which he added surveying at a later day. His time was employed in action chiefly, reading little, and that only in agriculture and English history. His correspondence became necessarily extensive, and, with journalizing his agricultural proceedings, occupied most of his leisure hours within doors.

---

that impulsive people, like Dylan Thomas, do so poorly in their school work may lie in their reading difficulties.

Estimates of time in a laboratory situation distinguish between the impulsive and the controlled. The controlled see time as a valuable commodity that should not be wasted. The impulsive put less value upon time and are less concerned about wasting it. The 40 most impulsive and the 40 most controlled freshmen in a class of nearly 300 completed 12 trials on a maze while they were blindfolded (Meade, 1966). The fictitious scores reported to half of each group after each trial indicated that they were making very little progress. The fictitious scores reported to the other half of each group indicated that they were making very rapid progress. After exactly 15 minutes all of the men answered the question: How long did it seem to you that you were working on the test? Table 6-4 summarizes their answers. Time passed quickly (12 minutes) when the controlled felt that they were making rapid progress. When they thought they were making little progress, time passed slowly (18 minutes). The estimates of the impulsive were almost unaffected by their supposed rate of progress (16 and 14 minutes).

Cottle (1967) gave more than 500 young men and women these instructions:

Think of the past, present, and future as being in the *shape* of circles. Now arrange these circles in any way you want that best shows how you feel about the *relationship* of the past, the present, and the future. You may use different size circles. When you have finished, label each circle.

The typical man and woman were oriented toward the future; i.e., their future circles were much larger than those for the past or the present. The past circles were the smallest. As with the Present-minded versus Future-minded Scale, women were more present-minded than men, their circles of the present being larger and their circles of the past, smaller, than those of the men.

Braley and Freed (1971) used a different but equally simple device. They asked respondents to report 10 personal events that they expected to happen in the future. They then calculated the time interval between the time of reporting and the time of the expected future event. The measure of future-mindedness was the total elapsed time: the greater the time, the greater the future-orientation of the respondent was assumed to be.

TABLE 6-3   The Present-Minded vs. The Future-Minded Scale
A definition of the trait is given below with 40 statements that measure it. The statements are grouped under subordinate traits in the cluster and the answer for the future-minded end of the scale is indicated. Your total score is the number of future-minded answers that you make. Norms for 100 college men and 100 college women in 1970 are given after the statements. The two most discriminating items in the scale are indicated with an asterisk.

Definition
"Now" people live in the moment, obeying their present feelings and ignoring the future. "When" people live for the future, setting hard goals for themselves and planning, working, and controlling their feelings to achieve them.

Directions
If you think a statement is "true" or more true than false as far as you are concerned, circle "T." If you think a statement is "false" or more false than true as far as you are concerned, circle "F."

Present vs. Future Time
<u>T</u> F   1. I live more for the future than the present.
<u>T</u> F   2. I spend a great deal of time thinking about my plans for the future.
T <u>F</u>   3. I generally seek whatever makes me happy here and now.

T <u>F</u>   4. I like to be with people who are not preoccupied with the future.

T <u>F</u>   5. I am much more interested in activities that I can enjoy for their own sake than in activities that are of long-range benefit.

Impulsivity vs. Control

<u>I</u> **F**   6. I never lose my head.

<u>I</u> **F**   7. I always keep control of myself in an emergency situation.

<u>I</u> **F**   8. I can always do a good job even when I am very excited.

<u>I</u> **F**   9. I am considered extremely "steady" by my friends.

<u>I</u> **F**   10. I believe that what a person does about a thing is more important than what he feels about it.

T <u>F</u>   11. I frequently obey whatever impulse is strongest.

T <u>F</u>   12. I am greatly influenced in my minor decisions by how I happen to feel at the moment.

T <u>F</u>   13. I find that my minor likes and dislikes change rather frequently.

T <u>F</u>   14. I find it difficult to keep my mind on one detail for very long.

T <u>F</u>   15. I accept my feelings as the best guide for my actions.

T <u>F</u>   16. I have some difficulty in concentrating my thoughts on one thing for a long time.

Pleasure vs. Work

<u>I</u> **F**   17. I enjoy work more than play.

<u>I</u> **F**   18. I set very difficult goals for myself.

<u>I</u> **F**   19.* I am extremely ambitious.

<u>I</u> **F**   20. I am guided in all my conduct by firm principles.

<u>I</u> **F**   21. I really don't like to drink alcoholic beverages.

T <u>F</u>   22. Most of my spare money is used for pleasure.

T <u>F</u>   23. I believe that I have the disposition of a pleasure-seeker.

T <u>F</u>   24. I like to be with people who don't take life too seriously.

T <u>F</u>   25. I feel that friendship is more important in life than anything else.

T <u>F</u>   26. I occasionally neglect serious things in order to have a good time.

T <u>F</u>   27. I believe in getting as much fun as I can out of life.

T <u>F</u>   28. I would rather see a musical comedy than a documentary film.

Less vs. More Planning

<u>I</u> **F**   29. I like to make a very careful plan before starting in to do anything.

<u>I</u> **F**   30. Whenever I have to undertake a job I make out a careful plan of procedure.

<u>I</u> **F**   31. I like to keep all my letters and other papers neatly arranged and filed.

<u>I</u> **F**   32. I am extremely systematic in caring for my personal property.

<u>I</u> **F**   33. I like to have my life so arranged that it runs smoothly and without much change in plans.

Figure 6-3 A child's drawing of a house and a nineteenth century engraving of an English cathedral. The impulsivity and lack of planning in the child's drawing give it freedom and spontaneity, while the control and planning in the engraving give it greater detail and realism. The present-minded are more original; the future-minded are more ambitious. (Ron Junttonen)

I F   34. I like to have my meals organized and a definite time set aside for eating.

I F   35. I keep my workplace very neat and orderly.

I F   36. I always finish one task before taking on others.

T F   37.* I generally go from one thing to another in my daily life without a great deal of planning.

T F   38. I find it rather hard to keep to a rigid routine.

T F   39. I am not particularly methodical in my daily life.

T F   40. I am occasionally disorganized if I am called on suddenly to make a few remarks.

	Percentiles										
	Present-Minded								Future-Minded		
	0	10	20	30	40	50	60	70	80	90	99
Men	2	9	11	13	16	19	20	23	24	27	32
Women	5	8	11	13	15	16	19	21	23	25	32

TABLE 6-4   Estimates of a 15-Minute Interval by Impulsive and Controlled Students

	Slow progress in learning	Fast progress in learning	Difference
The impulsive group	16	14	2 minutes
The controlled group	18	12	6 minutes

Source: Meade, 1966.

WHY DO WE DIFFER IN FUTURE-MINDEDNESS?

Dependable differences in future-mindedness occur early in life. Mac-Arthur (1955) gave more than 100 thirteen-year-old English secondary school boys a battery of tests that had in common the necessity of continuing boring, fatiguing, and discomfort-producing tasks. Among the tasks were standing with heels slightly raised from the floor, sitting with one leg extended horizontally, and holding a pair of dumbbells at arm's length. Even at this age, the scores on the test were highly interrelated, suggesting a general trait of control. The best single measure was the rating given a boy by his classmates. A boy who was rated as a good "sticker" tended to get high scores on the other tests. Other studies indicate that differences in the trait can be measured as early as the age of five (McClelland, 1961, p. 340). Why do differences in future-mindedness occur so early?

Direct Genetic Mechanisms

Do genes influence sensitivity to the here and now? Unexpectedly, studies of fat and thin people strongly suggest that they might (Schacter, 1971). In general, these studies show that the eating habits of fat people are controlled by external stimuli, i.e., food, while the eating habits of thin people are not. Both fat and thin people swallowed a balloon that contracted when stomach muscles contracted. Both groups were regularly asked: "Are you hungry?" The thin people reported they were hungry when their stomach contracted. The answers of the fat people had no relationship to their contractions. Unfed fat and thin people were sometimes given tasty milk shakes and sometimes milk shakes with quinine added. The fat people drank more of the tasty and less of the quinine milk shakes than did the thin people. In another study, 20 fat people were given a chance to eat shelled almonds and 20 were given the chance to eat unshelled ones. The same number of thin people were exposed to the same conditions. Only one of the fat group tried the nuts with shells; 19 out of 20 tried the shelled ones. Among the thin people, as many ate the shelled as the unshelled nuts. Fat and thin people were also observed in an oriental restaurant where they could chose to eat with chopsticks or a fork. More of the fat people chose to eat with a fork. Schacter concludes that fat people are more stimulus-bound than thin people and suggests that differences in the ventromedial hypothalmus cause the difference. If so, then being bound to food stimuli may be just one example of being generally bound to the present.

Indirect Genetic Mechanisms

Sex and physique are related to time orientation. Women (Table 6-3) are somewhat more present-minded than men. The strong are more persistent than the weak (Sheldon, Stevens, and Tucker, 1940). However, society reacts to strong males in quite a different way than to weak females. It seems more likely, therefore, that these small differences in future-mindedness are due to these large differences in treatment rather than to the greater susceptibility of weak females to immediate stimuli.

General Environmental Mechanisms

Independence training seems largely responsible for the development of future-mindedness. Between 500 and 400 B.C., the Athenians shifted from an extremely future-minded to an extremely present-minded society. From both cross-cultural and family studies, McClelland (1961) concludes that such shifts are the result of a shift from child-rearing practices that stress the development of early independence to practices that do not. He measured future-mindedness ("need for achievement") by the analysis of imaginative stories (Mc-Clelland, Atkinson, Clark, and Lowell, 1953). In one study in the United States, he first isolated a group of present-minded and a group of future-minded boys. He contrasted the attitudes of the mothers of the boys in the two groups. The mother with a future-minded son more often had expected him to do the following things when he was eight years old:

> To know his way around the city
> To try new things for himself
> To do well in competition
> To make his own friends

That is, she earlier and more strenuously encouraged her son to solve his own problems. Protestant families expected their sons to be responsible and independent much earlier than did Irish and Italian families. Parents who were college graduates emphasized independence training more.

The stress a mother places upon independence training is heavily influenced by the society into which she is born. Among the Kwoma, for example, a mother typically fosters the child's dependence upon her by being with him and cuddling him constantly. Among the Ainu, on the other hand, the child is placed in a cradle at an early age and neglected by the mother for long periods of time.

The greater the stress upon independence training in a society, the higher its achievement motivation is likely to be. Friedman (McClelland et al., 1953) reached this conclusion by correlating child-rearing practices among eight American Indian cultures with the amount of achievement imagery revealed by their folk tales of Coyote, a popular Indian trickster hero. Although all the tales concerned Coyote, the achievement imagery reflected in them varied from tribe to tribe. In the order of achievement imagery, from highest to lowest, the tribes ranked as follows:

1. Navaho
2. Chiricahua-Apache
3. Western Apache
4. Comanche
5. Flatheads
6. Hopi
7. Paiute
8. Sanpoil

The following Comanche tale illustrates a moderate amount of achievement imagery (McClelland et al., 1953):

Coyote was always knocking about hunting for something. He
came to a creek, where there was nothing but green willows.
Two little yellow-birds were playing there. He came up to
them. Laughing, they pulled out their eyes and threw them on
the trees,while they stood below. "Eyes, fall!" they said. Then
their eyes fell back onto their sockets. Coyote went to them. *He
greatly admired their trick.* "O brothers, *I wish to play that
way, too.*" "Oh, *we won't show you,* you are too mean. You
would throw your eyes into any kind of a tree and lose them."
"Oh, no! I would do just like you." At last the *birds agreed to
show him.* They pulled out his eyes, threw them up, and said,
"Eyes, fall!" They returned to their places. "Let us all go along
this creek!" said the birds. *"Other people will see us and take a
fancy to us."* They went along playing. Coyote said, "I am going
over there, I know the trick well now." He left them. He got to
another creek. A common willow tree was standing there.
"*There is no need to be afraid of this tree.* I'll try it first." He
pulled out his eyes, and threw them at the tree. "Eyes, fall" he
shouted. His eyes did not fall. He thus became blind. He tied
something around his eyes, and left.

In contrast to the six images here, a Paiute tale of Coyote had only two
images. The ranking of the tribes on achievement imagery paralleled
their ranking on independence training: the higher the ranking on
independence training, the greater the achievement imagery.

From an examination of a vast array of such psychological and
anthropological data, McClelland (1961, p. 345) finally concludes that
future-mindedness ("I set very difficult goals for myself," "I am
extremely ambitious," and "I live more for the future than the present")
results from an early, but not too early, emphasis upon mastery: ". . . a
stress on meeting certain achievement standards somewhere between
the ages of six and eight . . . neither too early for the boy's abilities nor
too late for him to internalize those standards as his own."

The findings of Abegglen (1958) support the conclusion. He
interviewed and tested 20 top executives of large corporations with
low-status fathers: 5 of the fathers were unskilled laborers; 10, skilled
laborers; 5, clerks or salesmen. He matched each of these executives
with an executive of equally high position who had a high-status father.
The two groups were similar in intelligence. The low-status group,
however, were not only more controlled but also more dominating,
more exhibitionistic, and more eager to avoid blame. They were also
less interested in women.

The fathers of the low-status group had had little influence on
their sons. Two of the 20 fathers had died when their sons were infants;
5 had been chronically ill; and 6 had had serious business and financial

difficulties. On the whole, the sons felt hostile toward their fathers and saw them as inadequate:

> It bothered me quite a bit, now that I think about it, that the other kids were told they couldn't play with me because I was a gambler's son.

> I never knew him when he wasn't an invalid . . . a meek, mild, extremely honest man.

> My father was one of the most underpaid men. He was that way all his life; it must have been a complex; he never wanted to make a dollar—and he never made a dollar.

Their mothers, on the other hand, were viewed as supportive but as setting high standards:

> My mother was a very determined person, strictly disciplined. She was a person of the old school who believed in bringing up her children along a straight line. She had all the responsibility of bringing up the kids. My mother was very religious. She was a marvelous person . . .

> My mother was very ambitious for us. I'll give her credit for that. No, she didn't tell us what to do, but secretly I think she wanted one of us to be a preacher. . . . Mother always wanted more cultural things. She had great ideas. I avoided Father most of the time. I always went to her for advice. She wanted me to get ahead.

The sequence appeared to be this: the low-status fathers, who were low in ambition possibly because of their own harsh and restrictive backgrounds, were either absent or unimportant in the home. The mothers demanded early independence in their children, but not in order to remove the children as a burden or trouble to them. Rather, they had a deep involvement in their children and a high interest in their development of self-reliance and their achievement of difficult goals.

In general, ambition, the ability to make and stick to long-range plans, seems to depend most directly upon the standards set by the parents and indirectly upon the standards set for the parents by their culture. The absence of such standards leads to present-mindedness. Present-mindedness, however, may be exaggerated by genetic and physical elements.

Specific Environmental Mechanisms

Kipnis and Resnick (1971) measured the future-mindedness of a large number of college students by several inventories of the type shown in Table 6-3. They then isolated 60 present-minded underachievers and matched them with 60 future-minded achievers. Half the members of each group were paid 10 dollars each to attend in groups of six for an hour weekly either remedial math or counseling sessions. The other 30 of each group were used as controls. They attended neither session. The leaders of the sessions later reported that the present-minded did not seem interested in the sessions and attended primarily for the money. Still, both sessions were effective, and about equally so. At the end of the semester, only 16 percent of the present-minded in the control group received grades above the median. Four times as many of those who attended the tutorial math or the counseling sessions received grades above the median. The future-minded did a little better with the sessions than without them. The authors concluded that the sessions forced the present-minded to focus upon their course work and grades at much more frequent intervals than they would otherwise have done. The lesson seems clear: the student who knows he is present-minded and wants to improve his grades should set up a system that requires him to pay frequent attention to his incompleted work.

HOW WELL CAN YOU JUDGE THE FUTURE-MINDEDNESS OF OTHERS?

Understanding what other people think of themselves is extremely important in developing constructive relationships with them. However, such understanding is hard to check for we almost never find out whether our judgments are right or wrong. Table 6-5 offers the reader a chance to apply what he has now learned about future-mindedness to Carol Form as well as to the women introduced in earlier chapters.

Earlier chapters have given some of the reasons for our difficulties in understanding others: we assume that they have the same dim or bright view of themselves as we have of them when most of them do not; we assume that people are "pretty much alike" when they are not; or we may assume that our instant whole impression of others is accurate when it seldom is. Another basic reason for our failures in understanding is our approach to the question: What is he like?

In approaching this question, we may ask: What does he think of himself? Most of us most of the time, however, ask: What do *I* think of him? Our only preoccupation with what he thinks tends to focus on the question: What does he think of *me*? We often say that we have an "opinion" about a person. The word too weakly states the case. We generally have a confident perception, a firm conviction, of what he is "really" like. Reality, however, is elusive. A person's view of himself is sometimes false, often distorted, and always incomplete. Still, just as we generally understand ourselves better than other people do, other people understand *themselves* better than we do. Time and again, psychologists have shown that *the closer we stick to what a person says about himself, the more accurate our understanding of him is likely to be* (Giedt, 1955). The principle is especially valid in estimating a person's position on traits like future-mindedness.

TABLE 6-5 How Well Can You Judge Future-Mindedness?

Carol Form, a twenty-year-old sophomore, completed the trait scales and wrote an autobiography. She was considerably bolder and calmer than the typical student. After reading the sketch below, judge her future-mindedness in comparison with Susan Edgar, Joan Dellard, and Mary Bernard and then in comparison with other college women.

Carol Form She comes from an upper middle-class family, and feels that her parents (who are "snobby") were strict, but that the discipline was good for her. Her relationship with her parents was "terrible" during adolescence, but improved when she started dating. She doesn't like to be pushed around by her friends, and feels that she has often been persuaded (fairly easily) to do things she would not normally do.

　　　　Her ethical and moral standards are very high; she does not smoke or drink. Religion means a lot to her, but she doesn't go to church often during the school year. She wants to teach Home Economics, and has to study hard to get good grades. She tries to be friendly and get along with everybody, and doesn't deliberately hurt people's feelings. She says she is considerate, responsible, and sincere, but also is very sensitive, and gets hurt easily. She also gets moody and depressed easily for no reason.

Susan Edgar Susan is the extremely calm and moderately bold sophomore described earlier (p. 109). She said that she likes animals, has broad interests, and is persistent.

Joan Dellard Joan is the cautious and emotional psychology major described earlier (p. 86) who said that she was interested in practically everything but was not very consistent.

Mary Bernard Mary is the middle-aged senior described earlier (p. 86) who lists as her favorable characteristics an impeccable honor and integrity. She is quite bold and somewhat more emotional than the typical college woman.

How do these four women compare in their future-mindedness? Rank "1" the woman that you think is most present-minded; "2" next; "3" next; and "4" the one who is most future-minded.

Carol Form   _____
Susan Edgar   _____
Joan Dellard   _____
Mary Bernard   _____

*How does their future-mindedness compare with that of other college women?**
(Circle the percentile that you think each girl matches most closely)

Percentile										
Present-Minded					Average		Future-Minded			
Carol Form 0	10	20	30	40	50	60	70	80	90	99
Susan Edgar 0	10	20	30	40	50	60	70	80	90	99
Joan Dellard 0	10	20	30	40	50	60	70	80	90	99
Mary Bernard 0	10	20	30	40	50	60	70	80	90	99

*Correct answers are given at end of chapter.

IS IT BETTER TO BE PRESENT-MINDED OR FUTURE-MINDED?

The answer: It depends. Any position on any of the five traits has both weaknesses and strengths. Which is more prominent in the life of the individual depends upon the way his traits are organized in his developing self. How good this organization is depends upon how well the individual understands the promises and dangers of his position on the traits and what he does about them. What are the weaknesses and strengths of different time orientations?

The Past-minded

Few American college students are preoccupied with the past. Even small children seem naturally to become conscious of the future before the past. As they grow older, their doubts and fears, their anxieties and hopes, their thoughts and actions are focused upon the future. Since the past cannot be changed, their energies are directed toward dealing with present and future problems. But the seriously maladjusted are generally more preoccupied with what they did or what was done to them in the past than they are in their present and future problems (Braley and Freed, 1971).

Lack of awareness of the past does not mean that the past lacks influence. We are what our past has made us as the stability of our positions on the basic traits exemplify. In a more general way, the past dominates the lives of those in primitive cultures (Cassirer, 1944, p. 224):

What has existed from immemorial times, is firm and unquestionable. To call it into question would be a sacrilege. For the primitive mind there is no more sacred thing than the sacredness of age. It is age that gives to all things, to physical objects and to human institutions, their value, their dignity, their moral and religious worth. In order to maintain this dignity it becomes imperative to continue and to preserve the human order in the same unalterable shape.

In times of personal and social stress, modern man readily returns to this primitive view.

Our feelings about the past are quite distinct from our consciousness of the past. History is an effort to make us conscious of our past. Nietzsche condemned history for its possible paralyzing effect on dealing with present and future problems: the man who escapes into history is like a "snake that has swallowed a rabbit whole and lies still in the sun, avoiding all movement not absolutely necessary." However, a new understanding of the past gives us at the same time a new prospect for the future. Historical knowledge is the answer to definite questions, an answer that must be given by the past; but the questions themselves are put and dictated by the present—by our present personal and social problems. Thus, psychotherapy is largely directed toward making the disturbed person conscious of his past and of its influence upon him. History is concerned with making people conscious of their common past and of its influence upon them. Personal or social history cannot tell the individual or the society what to do next. However, historical knowledge often reveals what *not* to do.

Present-mindedness

Even to their friends, the present-minded often seem to be too lazy, disorganized, and unambitious. Keith, for example, had this to say about his 250-pound and six-foot-five-inch friend, Paul:

> Nine years ago Paul and I both qualified for academic scholarships to a private high school. Still, Paul elected to attend the public high school. He had the highest IQ in his class, but he graduated with a D average. Many universities offered him football scholarships; he stayed home and drove a truck for a year and then went into the service. After this, although he had the GI Bill to help him through school, he took a job on an assembly line with no chance of promotions. With his stature, power, and intelligence he could be very successful in many fields. However, these are of little worth while he lacks ambition and is content with mediocrity.

The present-minded not only seem to be too fat but also too frequently users of drugs. A comparison of 50 heavy-cigarette-smoking college men with 50 nonsmokers showed the heavy smokers to be more present-minded (Plath, 1959). The present-mindedness of college drinkers compared to nondrinkers was even more pronounced (Kukuk, 1960). The present-minded are also more frequent users of marijuana (Hogan and Manking, 1970).

On the other hand, the present-minded often succeed in their desire "to get as much fun as they can out of life." Their impulsivity gives them daily sources of release and satisfaction, as Carol's picture of herself suggests:

I have no trouble explaining how I feel. When something bothers me a great deal, I enjoy talking it over with my family or friends. When I become upset, I cry easily. I find this a great help in relieving my tensions. When I am happy, I laugh easily and often. I enjoy giving speeches when the topic is one on which I have strong feelings. I talk easily with strangers and enjoy telling people about myself. When I am angry, I say how I feel, but I also find it easy to say I am sorry and admit my mistakes. As far as I know, I have always been this way. I think my family background accounts for this trait, because I am daughter number four in a family of six girls. My parents and my sisters have always been very close, and we have all freely expressed our emotions to each other.

The present-minded are also relatively immune to many of the irritations, worries, and discontents that afflict the extremely future-minded. Since the future-minded are commonly very punctual, they are often annoyed by being kept waiting, by delays in restaurants, at airports, or in traffic. Since they feel they have much to do and little time in which to do it, they are impatient with people who don't come quickly to the point. As a result, they frequently engage in two lines of thought at once, and are poor listeners, particularly in conversations that they do not see as being relevant to their immediate goal.

The future-minded are chronically worried about meeting deadlines. They seldom feel that they can spare the time for recreation or hobbies. When they do spend the time, it is likely to be on highly competitive games or in gambling. They hate to waste time in performing essential but repetitive tasks and often try to do several of these simultaneously (reading while eating or shaving, for example).

No matter how much a future-minded person has achieved, he is generally dissatisfied with his socioeconomic status. More ominous for his happiness, he is inclined to become obsessed with numbers (points made, grades achieved, percentages obtained, merchandise sold, awards granted, money made, etc.). He is thus inclined to value his life by these number values. As a result, he often pays little more than lip service to the human values of love, affection, and friendship—values that are central to the lives of the present-minded.

The present-minded are more original. Barron (1957) gave a variety of objective tests of originality to 100 veteran Air Force officers between the ages of twenty-seven and fifty. He combined scores on the tests to obtain a composite originality score. He then selected an "original" group (the 25 officers with the highest scores) and an "unoriginal" group (the 25 officers with the lowest scores). All the officers completed series of aptitude, interest, and personality tests and were rated by staff psychologists on a variety of traits. The original officers were more intelligent, bolder, and more artistic. Above all, however, they were more present-minded.

In sum, Dylan Thomas reflects the weaknesses and strengths of the present-minded. He was "incredibly lazy" and disorganized. But he was original. He enjoyed his many friends and a zestful absorption in his daily activities. He did not die of a heart attack, he died of alcoholism.

Future-mindedness

The future-minded are often dissatisfied with their future-mindedness. Jacqueline complains:

> My control makes it easier for me to restrain myself when necessary. Other than this, I can see no advantage. Since I have difficulty expressing my feelings, my acquaintances often think I am unfriendly—many times I cannot express how happy I am or how delighted I am over some happening. Similarly, when something is sad and I express little emotion, people often think I am cold and unfeeling. Although I have been this way for a long time, I find little value in it.

Sandra makes a similar complaint:

> A great deal of my behavior is governed by my ambition. I have achieved an outstanding academic record, I have been very successful in outside jobs, and my score on the recent personality test of ambition was among the highest. The primary source of the trait is the training I received from my parents, who held

the middle-class belief that ambition is a virtue. The attitude was so emphasized in my formative years that I now find that I am incapable of purposely doing a poor job, even though I may despise the work and inwardly revolt against it.

In grade and high school my home training was reinforced by the competitiveness and above-average ability of my peer group, whom I felt I must surpass. In college I have felt that the one way to gain recognition in the anonymity of an overlarge institution is through scholastic achievement.

The strength of my ambition has forced me to do things at a high level of excellence, even though the things in themselves are confining and unsatisfying to me. On the other hand, my ambition has brought me a high degree of personal success in college and acclaim at home. My ambition creates a conflict between what I feel I must do and what I would much rather do.

The grimness of the lot of the future-minded becomes especially apparent when their aspirations are unrealistically high. A person's *level of aspiration* is his immediate goal: something almost within reach, a possible success near at hand. Where a high jumper sets the bar after he has cleared 6 feet measures his level of aspiration. The level set is a compromise between the desire for success and the desire to avoid failure, the first pushing the level up and the second pulling it down. However, there is no feeling of failure if the level is set too high; the high jumper who fails to clear the bar at 10 feet does not experience failure. And there is no feeling of success if the level is set too low—if the jumper clears the bar at 3 feet, he does not experience success. Thus, the levels of aspiration we set fall within the range where we feel we might succeed or fail.

Aspirations tend to conform to expectations, past successes raising them and past failures lowering them. There are wide individual differences, however, for some have ambitions far below and some far above what they might reasonably expect to achieve. Some quickly change their aspirations to fit their experiences of success and failure; others stick tenaciously to their high goals in the face of repeated failure. For example, Ausubel and Schiff (1955) had 50 high school boys and girls take a speed-of-reading test, an arithmetic test, a test involving digit symbols, and one using a stylus maze. Each subject was asked before each test: "How many sentences (examples, units) like this do you think you could do in 90 (60) seconds? Make the very best estimate you can." The subject then took the test. Regardless of how well he had done, the subject was told that his score was 75 percent of what he had aspired to. The same procedure was repeated four times.

A *goal-discrepancy* score and *goal-tenacity* score were calculated for each subject for each test. Goal discrepancy was measured by
subtracting the score he was told he had made from the score that he set
himself to obtain on the next trial. Goal tenacity was measured by the
amount of change in the level of aspiration from the beginning to the
end of the experiment. Discrepancy and tenacity scores were consistent
from one test to another; those who had high discrepancy and tenacity
scores in speed of reading, for example, had similar scores in the other
tests. Also, those who had high discrepancy scores had high tenacity
scores.

Those who hold to unrealistic goals tend to be emotionally
unstable. Klugman (1948) obtained goal-discrepancy scores for 30 adult
subjects. The subjects also completed an inventory designed to measure emotional stability. Result: The higher the goal discrepancy, the
greater the emotional instability (correlation, .46).

Raifman (1957) discovered that peptic-ulcer patients at a VA
hospital had more unrealistic ambitions than either neurotic or normal
subjects. He concludes:

> The ulcer patients were significantly higher in their attainment
> than either of the two control groups, and more inclined than
> the normal subjects to over-estimate their ability at the begin-
> ning of the problem. All of these differences appear to indicate
> that ulcer patients are an ambitious lot who cannot achieve
> their aspirations because they set goals which to others seem
> insurmountable.

Raifman's results are in accord with the widespread clinical
impressions that the typical ulcer patient, as in the following case,
tends to be extremely ambitious (Kapp, Rosenbaum, and Romano,
1947):

> A hard-working young executive of twenty-six came to the
> hospital with a bleeding duodenal ulcer. His father had died in
> the patient's early childhood, and he had grown up in an
> atmosphere of personal, family, and economic insecurity, but
> with marked overdependence on his mother. He married and
> was overdependent on his wife also. They had to live with his
> wife's parents, which added to his feeling of insufficiency. His
> apparent aggressiveness and independence in the business
> world were probably compensatory: underneath he seethed
> with hostility against his wife, mother, and mother-in-law. He

felt really insecure and dependent, but was unable to accept his own dependency needs. He hated those to whom he felt tied emotionally, but could not express his antagonism against them openly.

Normally, the future-minded, while they do not reach the occasional zestful peaks of the present-minded, do gain a regular flow of satisfaction, as Keith suggests:

As long ago as I can remember I have always set difficult goals for myself. In grade school I worked for a scholarship to a private prep school. Once there I set my goal to graduate with honors. I did. In college I am doing the same thing. In sports, though I am not a natural athlete, I won a golden glove in boxing and honors in hockey, track, and football. In the service my goal was to be the best soldier on the post, and this I was. During the summer months I strive for distinction as the best man on a well-drilling crew; this goal I've always shared with my brother.

A nagging problem for the future-minded in creative fields is that their ambition, planning, and organization can make them good, but it cannot make them great. The future-minded Trollope (1923), for example, became a good but not a great novelist. In a period of 32 years he wrote 54 novels, most of them while he was also an active full-time employee of the British Post Office. Of his writing, Trollope says:

When I have commenced a new book, I have always prepared a diary, divided into weeks, and carried it on for the period which I have allowed myself for the completion of the work. In this I have entered, day by day, the number of pages I have written, so that if at any time I have slipped into idleness for a day or two, the record of that idleness has been there, staring me in the face, and demanding of me increased labor so that the deficiency might be supplied. . . . I have allotted myself so many pages a week. The average number has been about 40. It has been placed as low as 20, and has risen to 112. . . .

As I journeyed across France to Marseilles, and made thence a terribly rough voyage to Alexandria, I completed the allotted number of pages every day. On this occasion more than once I left my paper on the cabin table rushing away to be sick in the privacy of my stateroom.

The future-minded are like beavers who chew steadily through large tree trunks. Their weakness is that they tend to be unimaginative. They are too tightly bound to the immediate situation and the old solution. In the words of Oscar Wilde, the future-minded easily "falls into careless habits of accuracy, or takes to frequenting the society of the aged and well-informed." The present-minded, like chameleons, can change their color to fit the outer world. Though more flightly, they also tend to be more flexible and imaginative.

The future-minded person of college age can be aware of and can modify his future-minded tendencies. However, he is not free to decide to become present-minded, for his position on the trait has been largely determined by his past experiences. Even if he were free, it would be hard to decide: the future-minded seems as likely to have as happy a life as the present-minded.

Should a society be present-minded or future-minded? In a stable society where the future will be like the past, the better answer would appear to be: present-minded, for tomorrow will bring it no problems that yesterday's solutions will not fit. In modern society, however, the answer seems emphatically the opposite. Today, we have serious new problems which cannot be solved by old methods. In the future, the number, size, and seriousness of these new problems will continue to accelerate.

Toffler (1970) suggests that the senses of Americans have been already so bombarded, their capacity to absorb new information so overloaded, and their decisions made so numerous by the increasing transience, novelty, and diversity in their lives that they are already suffering from "future-shock." The future-shocked do not become future-minded, or even present-minded, but past-minded:

> The Barry Goldwaters and George Wallaces of the world appeal to his quivering gut through the politics of nostalgia. Police maintained order in the past; hence, to maintain order, we need only supply more police. Authoritarian treatment of children worked in the past; hence, the troubles of the present spring from permissiveness. The middle-aged, right-wing reversionist yearns for the simple, ordered society of the small town—the slow-paced social environment in which his old routines were appropriate. Instead of adapting to the new, he continues automatically to apply the old solutions, growing more and more divorced from reality as he does so.

Toffler proposes detailed personal, educational, and governmental approaches to the problem. The core of these proposals lies in the development of "anticipatory" democracy, i.e., a future-minded citizenry devoted to deliberately choosing and developing the extremely diversified and decentralized kind of future society they want.

SUMMARY

Humans seem naturally oriented toward the future. However, the present-minded live much more in the moment than the future-minded who suppress their impulses in working toward distant goals. Parental standards account for most of these differences although genes may play an important part in creating differences in susceptibility to immediate stimuli. Every time orientation has its danger and its promise. The past-minded may brood over their failures and those responsible for them or they may use history as an aid in solving their problems. The present-minded may enjoy the moment but fall victims of cigarettes, alcohol, and other drugs. The future-minded may achieve more but be more dissatisfied with their achievements and drive themselves to collapse by their unrealistically high aspirations. Whatever the orientations of its citizens, however, modern society must cope with the problems generated by the accelerating speed with which technology is pressing the future upon men.

SUGGESTIONS FOR FURTHER READING

Hardy, T. (1950). *The mayor of Casterbridge*. New York: Modern Library. Henshaw, the mayor in this short fictional classic, reveals the warmth and impulsiveness of the present-minded but also the possible tragic consequences of the trait. The story begins with the sale of his wife to a stranger while drunk.

Fixgibbon, C. (1965). *The life of Dylan Thomas*, Boston: Little, Brown. The life and drunken death of a creative but present-minded poet.

McClelland, D. C. Atkinson, J. W., Clark, R. A., and Lowell, E. (1953). *The achievement motive*. New York: Appleton-Century-Crofts. Original studies that trace the origins and causes of future-mindedness.

Answers to Table 6-5; Form (1), Edgar (3), Dellard (2), and Bernard (4). Form, 20th percentile; Edgar, 75th percentile; Dellard, 30th percentile; and Bernard, 90th percentile.

7

THE ARTISTIC
AND THE PRACTICAL

Everyone whose attitude is introverted thinks, feels, and acts
in a way that clearly demonstrates that the subject is the chief
factor of motivation while the object at most receives only a
secondary value. . . . The state of extroversion means a strong,
if not exclusive, determination by the object.

CARL JUNG

Everyone is a subject and an object, has a mind and a body, and lives in a private inner world and a public outer world. Some people, like Thoreau (Table 7-1 and Figure 7-1), pay most attention to their inner worlds and to art. Some people, like Morgan (Table 7-2 and Figure 7-2), pay most attention to their outer worlds and to business. This chapter is concerned with the measurement, the causes, and the consequences of these differences between the artistic and the practical.

ARE YOU MORE PRACTICAL THAN ARTISTIC?

The Artistic versus the Practical scale (Table 7-3) with the accompanying norms permits the reader to compare his artistic and practical leanings with those of college men and women. The statements in the scale were derived in the following manner. First, scores on a scale designed to measure *thinking* introversion-extroversion (" . . . an inclination to meditative or reflective thinking, philosophizing, analysis of one's self and others, versus an extroverted orientation of thinking" Guilford, 1940) were related to scores of more than 20 other traits. In an analysis of the interrelationships, thinking extroversion appeared in a cluster with low artistic values, high economic values, and interest in the opposite sex. The 40 statements in the scale consist of those from the four subordinate traits that were most closely related to each other.

The artistic person, as the scale defines him, is a person of high artistic values and low-economic values who has a strong inclination toward meditative and reflective thinking; the practical person is low in aesthetic values, high in economic values, and has a strong *dis*inclination toward reflective thinking. Thus defined, differences in the trait are *not* related to differences in emotionality, emotional control, or gregariousness. It is vital to keep the definition in mind, for authorities view the trait in rather different ways. Cattell (1965), for example, says:

> We see the extrovert as sociable, optimistic, talkative, group-dependent, a bit thick-skinned, trusting, and adaptable. The introvert is shy, not very fond of people *en masse*, individualistic, and a bit rigid and suspicious.

Guilford (1959), on the other hand, feels that the trait is best described by inattentiveness versus alertness:

> . . . Alertness versus inattentiveness is a matter of keeping in rapport with the environment versus being inattentive or absentminded. A person high on this dimension says that he keeps in close touch with things going on around him, that he is

Figure 7-1 Henry David Thoreau, 1817–1862. (The Bettman Archive)

TABLE 7-1 The Artistry of Thoreau

Henry David Thoreau died at forty-five of tuberculosis in Concord, Massachusetts, in 1862. At that time, he was looked upon as a minor disciple of Ralph Waldo Emerson. Fifty years ago he was thought of as an "also-ran" who was rapidly being forgotten. Today, however, modern leaders rate him as one of the giants of American thought (Harding, 1965):

Mahatma Gandhi: There is no doubt that Thoreau's ideas greatly influenced my movement in India.

Robert Frost: In Thoreau's declaration of independence from the modern pace is where I find most justification for my own propensities.

Justice Douglas: Thoreau lived when men were appraising trees in terms of board feet, not in terms of watershed protection and birds and music. His protests against that narrow outlook were among the first heard on this continent.

Sinclair Lewis: *Walden* is one of three or four unquestionable classics in American Literature.

Thoreau believed that everything arises from inwardness—life, education,

TABLE 7-1 (Continued)

thought, religion, culture, and government. He had an almost total indifference to material things (Thoreau, 1950, p. 13):

Most of the luxuries, and many of the so-called comforts of life, are not only not indispensable, but positive hindrances to the elevation of mankind. . . . None can be an impartial or wise observer of human life but from the vantage ground of what we should call voluntary poverty. . . .

His poetry, his essays, his books, and the millions of words in his private journals reveal a deep inward and aesthetic view of life. While living for several years alone in a dirt-floored cabin that he built on the shores of Walden Pond, he wrote (p. 101):

Sometimes, in a summer morning, having taken my accustomed bath, I sat in my sunny doorway from sunrise till noon, rapt in a revery, amidst the pines and hickories and sumachs, in undisturbed solitude and stillness, while the birds sang around or flitted noiselessly through the house, until by the sun falling in at my window, or the noise of some traveller's wagon on the distant highway, I was reminded of the lapse of time.

Thoreau earned a frugal living as a maker of pencils. He liked his family and friends, but he never married. He preferred to be alone: "I have never found the companion that was so companionable as solitude."

---

not less attentive than the average person, and that he is alert to things in his immediate surroundings.

Inkblot Responses as a Measure of practicality

The Rorschach Ink Blot Test provides a much more indirect measure of the trait. The test consists of ten cards with inkblots: five in black and gray, two in black and red, and three entirely in colors. Like an inkblot, they are unstructured. The cards are presented one at a time with questions like: "What might this be?" "What does this remind you of?" After the subject has responded to all the cards, he goes back and describes each response in detail, telling what part of the inkblot and what characteristics of it suggested his answer. The interpretation of the subject's personality is based upon the *location* of the things he perceives, upon the *determinants* of what he sees, and, to a lesser degree, upon the *content* of what he sees. A critical aspect of location, for example, is whether the subject characteristically locates what he sees in the whole ("The whole thing reminds me of a bat") or in a part ("The small white space there looks like a goose"). Color ("Here's a green grasshopper"), form ("A pair of pliers"), and movement ("A pair

Figure 7-2 John Pierpont Morgan, 1867–1943. (United Press International)

TABLE 7-2   The Practicality of Morgan

Even as a boy, John Pierpont Morgan found the mechanics of business fascinating. When he was 12, he organized a *Grand Diorama of the Landing of Columbus*, sold tickets to family and friends, and afterward prepared an accurate balance sheet of the whole operation. During his business career, he was responsible for the reorganization of American railroads and the building of the Cathedral of St. John the Divine in New York City. Morgan spent millions on art objects and ruled the Metropolitan Museum of Art. However, his approach was not an aesthetic one. A curator of the museum later said that "a crude historical imagination was the only flaw in his otherwise perfect insensibility." A magazine assessed his contribution to art as follows (Allen, 1949):

. . . In the world of art quite as much as in the world of finance, Mr. Morgan was above everything a man of action. His successful raids upon the private collections of Europe were organized and carried out with the rapid decisive energy of a great general. He believed in military methods; he regarded rapidity and irrevocability of decision as more important than accuracy of judgment; he considered discipline more effective than a nice discrimination.

On his return from Europe in 1912 he was called before a congressional house committee before Christmas to answer the charge that the money and credit resources of his company controlled the American economy. Morgan insisted that what ruled the financial world was not money.

Counselor: Is not commercial credit based primarily upon money or property?

Morgan: No sir, the first thing is character.

Counselor: Before money or property?

Morgan: Before money or anything else. Money cannot buy it. . . . Because a man I do not trust could not get money from me on all the bonds in Christendom.

---

of raccoons racing") are different determinants that are interpreted in different ways. For content, one of the useful classification schemes is to divide it into animal ("bat," "goose," "raccoon") or human.

The test gives a comprehensive and structured interpretation of a personality. How valid the interpretations are is still a subject of considerable disagreement among psychologists. The measure of *introversive* tendencies is among the most consistent and stable scores derived from the test. The score consists of the ratio of movement (M) responses to color (C) responses: The more movement responses and the fewer the color responses, the higher the introversive score. M responses ("Two women trying to pull something apart," "dancing and frolicking fawns") are interpreted as responses to inner impulses; C responses ("blood," "emerald," "green bug") as responses to external stimulation. The M/C ratios tend to be the same from one set of inkblots to another (Thornton and Guilford, 1936) and people even after intervals of years have similar ratios (Hertz, 1942).

Compared to inventory measures, the Rorschach has the practical difficulty of taking much more time to give and much more skill to interpret. One possible alternative projective measure is the ratio of verbs to adjectives in a person's speech or writing. Like M responses, verbs suggest an orientation toward inner realities. Like C responses, adjectives suggest an orientation toward outer realities. Records of spontaneous speech would probably be more revealing than carefully written material. While the ratio would be simpler to calculate than Rorschach scores and seem to have validity, little actual use has thus far been made of it (Sanford, 1942).

WHY DO PEOPLE DIFFER IN THEIR PRACTICALITY?

Genetic mechanisms may be part of the answer. However, a child's early environment seems to be the primary determinant.

TABLE 7-3 The Artistic vs. the Practical Scale

A definition of the trait is given below with 40 statements that measure it. The statements are grouped under subordinate traits in the cluster and the answer for the practical end of the scale indicated. Your total score is the number of practical answers you make. Norms for 100 college man and 100 college women in 1970 are given after the statements. The two most discriminating items in the scale are indicated with an asterisk.

Definition

The artistic are introverted in their orientation, aesthetic in their attitudes, and artistic in their interests. The practical are extroverted in their orientation, practical in their attitudes, and economic in their interests.

Directions

If you think a statement is "true" or more true than false as far as you are concerned, underline "T." If you think a statement is "false" or more false than true as far as you are concerned, underline "F."

Introverted vs. Extroverted Set

I **F** 1. I can deal much better with actual situations than with ideas.

I **F** 2. Sports generally interest me somewhat more than very intellectual affairs.

I **F** 3. I am mainly interested in ideas that are very practical.

I **F** 4. I only work for concrete and clearly-defined results.

I **F** 5. I tend to judge people in terms of their concrete accomplishments.

T _F_ 6. I like to discuss abstract questions with my friends.

T _F_ 7. I sometimes think more about my ideas than about the routine demands of daily life.

T _F_ 8. I spend a lot of time philosophizing with myself.

T _F_ 9. My head is always full of imaginative ideas.

T _F_ 10. I often think for a long time about an idea that has occurred to me.

T _F_ 11. Daydreams are an important part of my life.

Aesthetic vs. Practical Attitude

I **F** 12. I am an extremely practical person.

I **F** 13.* I would rather be a salesman than an artist.

I **F** 14. I think there are few more important things in life than money.

I **F** 15. I would particularly enjoy meeting people who had made a success in business.

I **F** 16. I tend to accept the world as it is and not worry about how it might be.

I **F** 17. I am really only interested in what is useful.

I **F** 18. I believe that competitiveness is a necessary and desirable part of our economic life.

TABLE 7-3 (Continued)

I F 19. I prefer the friends of my own sex to be very efficient and of a practical turn of mind.

I F 20. I always keep my feet solidly on the ground.

T F 21.* Artistic experiences are of great importance in my life.

T F 22. I prefer friends who have well developed artistic tastes.

Few vs. Many Artistic Interests

I F 23. I have never tried to collect pictures of paintings I like.

I F 24. Magazines such as *Arts and Decorations* bore me.

I F 25. I would rather read "Business Week" than "Atlantic Monthly."

I F 26. In a discussion, I tend to lose interest if we talk about serious literature.

I F 27. I would rather see a movie than read a book.

I F 28. I have seldom enjoyed an art course.

T F 29. I enjoy going to art galleries very much.

T F 30. I would like to hear a popular lecture on contemporary painters.

T F 31. If I had unlimited leisure and money, I would enjoy making a collection of fine sculptures or paintings.

T F 32. I like to visit exhibits of famous paintings.

T F 33. I like abstract paintings.

T F 34. If I had the ability I would enjoy teaching poetry at a University.

T F 35. I like to read poetry.

T F 36. I would like to take a course in the modern novel.

T F 37. I like ballet performances.

T F 38. I think I would like to decorate a room with flowers.

T F 39. I get an intense pleasure from just looking at a beautiful building.

T F 40. I would rather read an article about a famous musician than a financier.

					Percentiles					
Artistic										Practical	
0	10	20	30	40	50	60	70	80	90	99
Men	2	8	10	12	14	16	20	22	26	29	33
Women	1	6	9	10	12	14	16	18	20	23	35

Direct Genetic Mechanisms

Some infants appear to be born with a "thin skin"; i.e., they are physically inactive but physiologically over-responsive. Some, on the other hand, are born with a "thick skin"; they are physically active, placid, and cheerful. The former, Cattell (1965) believes, tend to become artistic and the latter, practical. Whether the genetic mechanism is a tendency toward general inhibition or just social inhibition is not clear. All agree, however, that direct genetic mechanisms play only a small part in creating differences in practicality.

Indirect Genetic Mechanisms

Women are more inner-oriented in their thinking and more artistic. Men are more object-oriented and more utilitarian. Other studies reveal the greater introversion of women and the greater extroversion of men to be one of the largest of the trait differences between the sexes (Allport, Vernon, and Lindzey, 1951). Differences in the early rearing of boys and girls is the most obvious determinant. The more protected, playful, and limited environments of typical girls lead them in an introverted direction. The more stressful, serious, and gregarious environments of boys lead them to a greater concern with happenings in the external world.

The influence of genetic differences, though less obvious, may also be more profound. Men may respond to an introversive rearing like dogs in an art museum. William James (1890) stressed that the same environmental influences do not have the same effect:

If such an account were true, a race of dogs bred for generations, say in the Vatican, with characters of visual shape, sculptured in marble, presented to their eyes, in every variety of form and combination, ought to discriminate before long the finest shades of these peculiar characters. In a word, they ought to become, if time were given, accomplished *connoisseurs* of sculpture. Anyone may judge of the probability of this consummation. Surely an eternity of experience of the statues would leave the dog as inartistic as he was at first, for the lack of an original interest to knit his discrimination on to. Meanwhile the odors at the bases of the pedestals would have organized themselves in the consciousness of this breed of dogs into a system of "correspondences" to which the most hereditary case of *custodi* would never approximate, merely because to them, as human beings, the dog's interest in these smells would for ever be an inscrutable mystery . . . subjective interest may, by laying its weighty index-finger on particular items of experience, so accent them as to give to the least frequent association far more power to shape our thought than the most frequent ones possess.

The *interaction* between genetic and environmental influences may be even more influential. Females may be more easily molded by the pressures of the environment for both genetic and environmental reasons. There is, for example, evidence that the intelligence of girls is more influenced by the education of their parents than the intelligence of boys (Honzik, 1963).

General Environmental Mechanisms

The artistic are daydreamers. They fall into reveries, do a great deal of "wool-gathering," and construct many "castles-in-Spain." The day-dreamer shifts his attention away from external to internal stimuli. It is dangerous to make this shift when activities in the external world are pressing in upon us. Daydreaming, therefore, is least frequent during meals, during sexual activity, or in times of emergency. It is most frequently reported occurring as the person is falling asleep. The novelist Katherine Mansfield (1928, pp. 135–136) illustrates the pattern:

> It often happens to me now that when I lie down to sleep at night, instead of getting drowsy, I feel more wakeful and, lying here in bed, I begin to *live* over either scenes from real life or imaginary scenes. It's not too much to say they are almost hallucinations as they are marvellously vivid. I lie on my right side and put my left hand up to my forehead as though I were praying. This seems to induce the state. Then, for instance, it is 10:30 P.M. on a big liner in mid-ocean. People are beginning to leave the Ladies Cabin. Father puts his head in and asks if "one of you would care for a walk before you turn in. It's glorious up on deck." That begins it. I am there. Details: Father rubbing his gloves, the cold air—the *night* air, the pattern of everything, the feel of the brass stair-rail and the rubber stairs. Then the deck—the pause while the cigar is lighted, the look of all in the moonlight, the *steadying* hum of the ship, the first officer on deck, so far aloft the bells, the steward going into the smoking-room with a tray, stepping over the high, brass-bound step. . . . All these things are far realer, more in detail, *richer* than life. And I believe I could go until . . . there's no *end* of it.

Children daydream much more than adults (Singer, 1966). One very likely reason is that the pressures from the external environment increase with age. Those intensely preoccupied with becoming educated, raising a family, or doing a job have less time to shift their attention from the external to the internal world.

    Are children from stressful homes more practical? Do benign and effective parents have children who are more likely to be artistic daydreamers while hostile and ineffective parents have children who are much more attentive to the external world? The answer seems to be "yes." Children reared under the stresses of institutional care from early childhood are more active, less capable of delay, less able to rely on inner experiences, and have lower Rorschach M responses (Goldfarb, 1949). High activity and low imagination generally go together. Imaginative persons are better able to inhibit their physical actions, deliberate longer in solving problems, remain quieter during waiting periods, and use fewer gestures in defining verbs (Singer, 1960).

Play The infant first explores his own body and then the physical objects closest to him. When he has mastered these simpler perceptual and motor tasks, he turns to more complex forms of play with toys and other material things. If his needs are regularly well satisfied by a natural schedule of feeding, sleeping, cleaning, and social stimulation, he will gradually turn from the exploration of the physical world to the internalization of play through make-believe, daydreaming, fantasy, and storytelling. The full development of internalized play, however, requires not only a freedom from external pressures but also positive encouragement to play.

Women are more artistic than men. Mothers are not only with their children more than fathers, but also create a more playful atmosphere. They say funny things to their infants, play peek-a-boo games, and bounce them on their knees in ways that provide a novel but startling stimulus to the child. Later, their singing, their storytelling, and their use of games to persuade their children to do things may further encourage a game-playing attitude. We would expect, therefore, that children who had the most contact with their mothers would be most artistic. The expectation is supported by the results of a study of frequency of daydreaming among six cultural groups in the New York area. The six cultures were first ranked from those where children had the greatest contact with the mother to those where they had the least. The rank order was: (1) Negro; (2) Italian; (3) Jewish; (4) Irish; (5) German; and (6) Anglo-Saxon. A daydreaming questionnaire was then administered to 400 college students representing these cultural groups. The average frequency of reported daydreaming was almost identical with the order of frequency of contact with the mother, i.e., the Negroes and Italians were first and the Germans and Anglo-Saxons were last (Singer and McCraven, 1962).

Identification of a child with his parent is less objective than the amount of contact, but probably a more important determinant of his behavior. Identification is the process by which a person practices acting like another person without being deliberately encouraged or taught. Thus, a son may put on his father's clothes and pretend that he has his father's occupation and responsibilities. A daughter asks that her dolls eat their cereal and hang up their clothes as she has heard her mother ask. Identification is important in the development of extroversion as well. The students in the six cultural groups also filled out a Parental Identification scale, reporting the degree to which they felt they were like their fathers. The Negroes and Italians reported themselves to be much less like their fathers than did the Germans and the Anglo-Saxons. In a complementary study, women who reported themselves as more like their mothers than their fathers were more frequent daydreamers than those who reported that they were more like their fathers than mothers (Singer and Schonbar, 1961). Greater contact between the American father and his children and the consequent greater frequency with which his children identify with him may account for the practicality of American culture. At any rate, our culture is extremely practical. The Japanese, for example, are much more artistic than Americans and this difference persists even for second and third generation Japanese-Americans in Hawaii. Even British university students and school-children are more artistic than their American counterparts (Cattell, 1965).

Solitude   The child's exploration of his inner world requires not only freedom from external stresses but also inner world explorers to imitate. It would seem too to require being left alone to explore. Do those who are left alone the most tend to become most introverted? The best evidence in support of a positive answer comes from a comparison of oldest or only children with children who had older siblings. Children between the ages of six and nine were questioned about their play patterns, imaginary companions, and "pictures in their heads." On the basis of their replies they were put into a low- and high-fantasy group. The oldest and only children were much more often in the high-fantasy group (Singer, 1961). Suburban children are less often alone than children raised in the country or in big cities. They are caught up in a round of Brownies or Cub Scouts, music and dance lessons, Little League games and father-son dinners. The suburban children daydream less than either of the other groups (Singer, 1961).

If solitude is a requirement for the development of introversion, then prisoners with long terms of solitary confinement should become more introverted. Some observers think they do, although we have no objective evidence on this point. Biographical studies suggest that many of our greatest thinkers had lonely childhoods. John Stuart Mill, for example, was educated away from other children because of his father's intellectual program for him. Bertrand Russell has also described a long period of social isolation in his childhood when he found most of his stimulation in self-created games and in his library (Egner and Dennon, 1962). A study of eminent scientists reveals that they spent much time alone as children and that their social development was slow rather than rapid (Roe, 1953). The author concludes:

Practically all current psychological theory of development stresses strongly the central importance in any life of the richness of personal relations as a basis for "adjustment." But the data of this study demonstrate, and it seems to me quite conclusively, that a more than adequate personal and social adjustment in the larger sense of an adjustment which permits a socially extremely useful life and one which is personally deeply satisfying is not only possible, but probably quite common, with little of the sort of personal relations which psychologists consider essential.

These general determinants of introversion can be readily applied to Thoreau. He himself felt that he had the constitution of an introvert. Recalling his first visit as a child to Walden Pond, he remarked: "That sweet solitude my spirit seemed so dearly to require at once gave the preference to this recess among the pines, where almost sunshine and shadow were the only inhabitants." His father was a quiet and lovable man who read and listened to music a great deal. A friend described him as "far too honest and scarcely sufficiently energetic for this exacting yet not over scrupulous world of ours." His mother, an excellent woman with a compassion for the downtrodden, necessarily dominated the family life. She shared a deep common interest with her husband in nature. In his childhood, Thoreau seems to have been loved but left alone. Classmates in grammar school later recalled that he was a spectator at social games of so solemn a nature that they called him the "Judge." As an adult, his quest for solitude at Walden Pond provided the basis for his best-known book.

Specific Environmental Mechanisms

A child in a sober and threatening early environment crowded with people is forced to be practical, i.e., forced to pay particular attention to the people and things around him and not to become preoccupied with his thoughts. On the other hand, a lonely but secure and playful environment encourages him to be artistic, i.e., encourages him to pay attention to his inner feelings and thoughts and to exercise his imagination. Children from such an environment are likely to be interested in art, to have their interests encouraged, and to develop artistic skills.

The more art education a person has, the greater his artistic sensitivity is likely to become. Child (1965) developed a measure of aesthetic judgment and tested this common-sense hypothesis. The final test consisted of 128 pairs of pictures projected by means of slides before the group being tested. The pictures in a pair were of similar theme and content. However, one of each pair had been unanimously chosen by a panel of 14 art experts as being of higher aesthetic value. The choice of the experts was the "correct" answer.

Several hundred Yale men took the test. Their scores ranged from 44 to 104. The internal consistency of the test was very high. (r = .87). The same students also spent three hours taking a wide variety of personality tests. A study of the relationships between personality and aesthetic judgment scores led to the conclusion that those of high aesthetic judgment had an exceptional "willingness to be aware of anxiety and report it." The following is a thumbnail sketch of a typical high-scorer on the judgment test:

> . . . A person of actively inquiring mind, seeking out experience that may be challenging because of complexity or novelty, ever alert to the potential experience offered by stimuli not already in the focus of attention, interested in understanding each experience thoroughly and for its own sake rather than contemplating it superficially and promptly filing it away in a category, and able to do all this with respect to the world inside himself as well as the world outside.

The amount of art education, however, was much more closely related to scores on the test than any of the personality measures. Furthermore, Child found that poor judges became good judges after only a few hours of intensive training with feedback.

Do art experiences, themselves, help people? The growth of art therapy, the use of a patient's reactions to works of art or his own art productions to reveal unconscious pathological symptoms, implies a positive answer to this question. Art therapy, however, stresses the use of art as a diagnostic tool rather than a therapeutic device. Art counseling, on the other hand, stresses the use of art experiences as a way of increasing a normal individual's awareness, understanding, and acceptance of his inner thoughts and feelings.

Does art counseling help? Fifteen sixth-grade boys participated in an art counseling class at the North Carolina Advancement School as one part of their summer program (White and Allen, 1971). They attended the class an hour and a half each day for five days a week during the eight-week summer term. The class was presented to the boys as a visual-arts course designed to help them understand themselves and the world around them better. No grades were given, but no grades were given in any of the classes.

The art teacher-counselor designed activities to aid the boys in developing a more positive self concept through artistic expression (Figure 7-3). The tasks were short and each boy was encouraged to work with material with which he could be successful. The boys were encouraged to question their motives in their production and to

Figure 7-3 Artistic expression aids individuals in developing a more positive self concept. (Michigan Department of Mental Health)

evaluate the product in relation to what they were trying to communicate. Most of the teacher's time was spent with individuals.

To measure the success of the program, the boys completed the Tennessee Self Concept Scale at the beginning and at the end of the summer program and again 14 months later. The scale measures the general degree of acceptance of the self. Its 10 subscales include Physical Self, Personal Self, Family Self, Social Self, and Moral-Ethical Self. The scores at the end of the course were much higher on all 10 scales. The follow-up tests were administered in the local schools of the boys by their local counselor. The results showed that the boys had maintained their improved self-acceptance for more than a year after the art course.

Is art counseling better than traditional counseling? The 15 boys in the art-counseling program also participated in the regular counseling program, as did all boys at the school. Some type of counseling, either individual or small group, was received every day by everybody. Fifteen boys who had had the regular counseling but not the art counseling also took the self-concept scale before and after the summer session and again later. These boys showed no change as a result of their summer school experiences and no change 14 months later. Art counseling succeeded in making stable improvements in the self-concepts of the boys while traditional counseling failed in making even temporary improvements.

HOW WELL CAN YOU JUDGE THE PRACTICALITY OF OTHERS?

The reader can find an answer to this question by completing the exercise in Table 7-4 that presents the same four women introduced in earlier chapters. Bear in mind that one can tell nothing about where a person stands on this trait from how bold, how emotional, or how future-minded he is. It is very hard to remember this in making judgments, for it conflicts with our experience in using common-sense theories where traits are intimately related to each other. For example, we know that when someone describes another person as "sincere" he is extremely likely to also describe him as "honest," "cooperative," and "dependable" and extremely *un*likely to describe him as "cruel," "mean," and a "liar."

"Empathy" is the process of assuming that another person is like us (Table 7-5). It is the foundation of our understanding of others: we assume that another person will think about himself as we think about ourselves. However, empathy is also the foundation of our *mis*understanding of others for we often think a person is like us when he is not. These misunderstandings arise because we have great difficulty separating how much we like a person from how much he is actually like us, how close we feel to a person from how close he actually is.

We may make two quite different kinds of empathic errors: we may err by assuming that people whom we feel close to have traits close to our own when they do not; we may err by assuming that people from whom we feel distant have traits unlike ours when, in fact, their traits are very much like our own. Some of us are much more prone to make one kind of error than the other. That is, we differ a great deal in our empathic tendencies. How do the empathic and the nonempathic differ? From a group of several hundred college students, 25 who consistently assumed a great deal of similarity were matched with 25 of the same sex and intelligence who consistently assumed little similarity. Both groups asnwered the 200 statements in the five-trait scale. The answers of the empathic and the nonempathic groups were compared and the 48 statements that they answered most differently were isolated. These 48 statements were answered by a second group of empathic and nonempathic students. The 24 statements shown in Table 7-5 are those that most sharply separated the high-empathy from the low-empathy groups (Smith, 1973). The reader may obtain some suggestion of his own tendencies by answering these statements and

TABLE 7-4 How Well Can You Judge Practicality?

In this exercise you are asked to judge the practicality of the four women introduced in earlier chapters. Here is a brief sketch of each of these women.

Joan Dellard Twenty-year-old psychology major, the youngest of four children. She is highly cautious and emotional, and quite present-minded. She says that she is a very cautious person, doesn't get bored easily, is interested in practically everything, and likes to read and learn.

Mary Bernard She is forty-three years old and majoring in home economics. She is quite bold, somewhat emotional, and very future-minded. She says that she has been independent from early in life, has an unlimited amount of physical energy, and finds it difficult to balance recreation and work.

Susan Edgar She is a social work major who is the youngest of the women. She is moderately bold, extremely calm, and quite future-minded. She likes skating, swimming, and horseback riding and can be a tomboy, or a lady, when called for.

Carol Form She is a young sophomore who describes her family as "snobby" and her relationships with them during adolescence as "terrible." She is bold, emotional, and present-minded. She says she is considerate, sincere, and tries to get along with everybody.

How do these women compare in their practicality? * Rank "1" the woman that you think is most artistic in her orientation; "2" the next; "3" the next; and "4" the woman who is most practical.

Joan Dellard   _____

Mary Bernard   _____

Susan Edgar   _____

Carol Form   _____

How does their practicality compare with that of other women? *

			Percentile							
	Artistic				Average					Practical
Joan Dellard	0	10	20	30	40	50	60	70	80	90	99
Mary Bernard	0	10	20	30	40	50	60	70	80	90	99
Susan Edgar	0	10	20	30	40	50	60	70	80	90	99
Carol Form	0	10	20	30	40	50	60	70	80	90	99

*Correct answers are given at end of chapter.

checking his answers against those given by the empathic person.

The empathic personality revealed by the answers to the 24 statements is consistent with the results of a similar study (Chance and Meaders, 1960). This concluded that a high empathizer had a "highly

TABLE 7-5 Are You too Empathic?

We are "empathic" when we assume that another person is feeling and thinking what we would feel and think if we were in his shoes. If he is, we understand him; if he is not, we *mis*understand him. Some people are extremely unempathic, assuming that almost no one is feeling and thinking what they would feel and think. Others are extremely empathic, assuming that almost everyone is feeling and thinking what they would feel and think. Both make mistakes in judging others, for one assumes too little and the other too much similarity between themselves and others. Which kind of mistakes are you more likely to make? Extremely unempathic people answer the statements below in the opposite direction from extremely empathic people. The answers of the empathic people are given at the end of the chapter. Extremely unempathic people score below 7; the typical student, 12; and the extremely empathic, over 16.

Cautious vs. Bold
1. I like having people around me practically all of the time.
2. I always prefer to work with others.
3. I would rather listen to a story than tell one.
4. I am cautious about undertaking anything which may lead to humiliating experiences.
5. I am almost never embarrassed.

Unemotional vs. Emotional
6. I am fairly easily moved to laughter or tears.
7. I am moderate in my tastes and sentiments.
8. I think much and speak little.
9. I have strong likes and dislikes.
10. I become emotional fairly easily.
11. It takes a great deal to make me emotional.
12. I have sometimes corrected others, not because they were wrong, but only because they irritated me.

Present-minded vs. Future-minded
13. I generally seek whatever makes me happy here and now.
14. I always keep control of myself in an emergency situation.
15. I find it rather hard to keep a rigid routine.

Artistic vs. Practical
16. I am mainly interested in ideas that are very practical.
17. I get an intense pleasure from just looking at a beautiful building.

Religious vs. Scientific
18. It is necessary to retain the belief that God exists as a personal being.
19. In matters of conduct I conform very closely to custom.
20. The thought of God gives me a complete sense of security.

21. I control my sexual impulses by instituting prohibitions and restrictions.
22. Some of my friends think my ideas are a bit wild and impractical.
23. I am temperamentally more a skeptic than a believer.
24. The European attitude toward mistresses is more sensible than ours.

developed need for social interactions although strongly tinged with dependence upon and conformity to the constraints that others impose," while the low empathizers tended to be "nonconforming, impatient with custom and authority, disinclined to plan and to accept schedules, wanting to be in the limelight, not strongly motivated toward seeking contacts with others, seeking new experiences, and preferring aggressive modes of behavior."

IS IT BETTER TO BE ARTISTIC OR PRACTICAL?

Is it better to be cautious or bold? Unemotional or emotional? Present-minded or future-minded? The pluses of any particular answer are balanced by potent minuses. Is it better to be artistic or practical? Either answer is a plus: we must be practical to survive; we must be artistic to flourish. The need to understand and to deal with the external world of people and things is apparent to all: the better we can drive a car and operate a typewriter, the better we understand how to make and keep money, and, above all, the greater our practical understanding of people, the happier we are likely to be. We need to be practical about others not only for our sake but also for theirs: the mother needs practical understanding to get her sick child to take medicine, the husband needs it to get his fat wife to eat less, and the teacher needs it to get his students to learn.

Does art help us? The purely practical answer: No. Among those who answer "yes," there is little agreement about why. Art counseling, we have seen, helped young boys gain a happier acceptance of themselves. There is a common belief held by some psychologists as well as laymen that introverted and artistic children are more likely to develop into withdrawn and schizophrenic adults. But the opposite of this belief seems to be true. More than half of the patients in mental hospitals are diagnosed as schizophrenics. The outstanding characteristic of such people is their indifference and unresponsiveness to other people. The common assumption is that such people lead lives of very active fantasy, that they live in a private world rather than a social world. Consequently, it is also assumed that introverted children are prone to become schizophrenics. The assumption does *not* seem to be true. Recently, various childhood traits were related to pathological outcomes (Singer, 1966). Children showing the most introverted tendencies (shyness, quiet behavior, and daydreaming) *least* often became schizophrenics.

One reason for this contradiction between the facts and general opinion is that schizophrenics are not the daydreamers they have been assumed to be. The childhood traits that were found to be related to adult schizophrenia were more extroverted than introverted— hyperactivity, antisocial behavior, and an extreme external orientation. In any case, it is not the amount but type of daydreaming that is important. The daydreams of schizophrenics, compared to those of normal people, were more concrete and less imaginative; more fearful and less happy; more fragmented and less integrated. The daydreams of the schizophrenics are filled with vague memories, and ideas associated with feelings of guilt and self-recrimination that flit uncontrollably across their consciousness.

However, the introverted may use fantasy as an end in itself. Fantasies may replace normal social contacts. As a result, the dreamer may never develop social skills necessary for normal interpersonal relations. Fantasies may also create an unreal view of social situations. Thus an introverted man may develop a fantasy about sexual intercourse based upon no dating and much reading. His fantasies may picture it as an experience of overwhelming excitement and deep romantic communication. When intercourse does occur, his hesitant performance may seem so unsatisfying that he may withdraw even more completely from social contacts into his fantasy world.

Fantasies may also disturb otherwise normal human relationships. The introverted wife may dream of the romantic entrance of her husband on his return from work, his passionate embrace, and his words of devotion and reassurance. The introverted husband, on his way home from a harassing day, may dream of the relaxed quiet of his home, of a fine dinner, and of the enveloping feminine warmth that awaits him. When he slumps into his chair on arrival, the wife may launch into a recital of her day's misfortunes in an effort to gain his sympathy. When his own dream is broken, the husband may himself start a quarrel that leads to a bitter review of old grievances.

The practical person may also use his interest as an end and not as a means. As the introverted may escape into the inner world of fantasy, the practical may escape into the outer world of action (Dewey, 1939, p. 44):

> Zeal for doing, lust for action, leaves many a person, especially in this hurried and impatient human environment in which we live, with experience of an almost incredible paucity, all on the

surface. No one experience has a chance to complete itself because something else is entered upon so speedily. What is called experience becomes so dispersed and miscellaneous as hardly to deserve the name. Resistance is treated as an obstruction to be beaten down, not as an invitation to reflection. An individual comes to seek, unconsciously even more than by deliberate choice, situations in which he can do the most things in the shortest time.

The novelist Henry Miller (*Tropic of Capricorn*) suggests the narrow view of the purely practical man:

To walk in money through the night crowd, protected by money, lulled by money, dulled by money, the crowd itself a money, the breath money, no least single object anywhere that is not money, money, money, everywhere and still not enough, and then no money, or a little money or less money or more money, but money, always money, and if you have money or you don't have money it is the money that counts and money makes money, but *what makes money make money*?

The introvert may be stalled in a life of fantasy. Normally, however, introversion leads to an interest in the arts. But what function does art serve? Beauty, said Santayana (1955), is pleasure objectified and "art is the response to the demand for entertainment." Art is a pleasure and is often entertaining. But primitive man did not paint animals on the walls of caves or Michelangelo build St. Peter's Cathedral to entertain themselves or others.

Art, says Langer (1962), satisfies man's universal desire to intensify, illuminate, and harmonize his inner thoughts and feelings. Its primary function, therefore, is not to imitate nature, to give pleasure, or to entertain. It is to "objectify feeling" so that we can contemplate and understand it. Love, hate, joy and sadness, anger and tenderness are subjective: they are inner formless states of organic excitement or depression. How can such states be objectified so that we can capture, hold, and handle them? By creating art objects in which the feelings are so embedded that people cannot help but experience the feeling when they are confronted with the object. A feeling that is formless within us becomes formed in works of art so that we can study and learn about the feeling: "On a foggy night you see dimly moving forms in the mist; one of them emerges clearly, and is the form of a man. . . . It is in this sense of an apparition given to our perception that work of art is form. . . . Like a natural being, it has a character of organic unity, self-sufficiency, individual reality." Practical training educates our actions and scientific training educates our thoughts. Artistic training educates our emotions: "Few people realize that the real education of emotion is not the 'conditioning' effected by social approval and disapproval but the tactic, personal, illuminating contact with symbols of feeling."

The 1972 top TV show, "All in the Family," objectifies the feelings of a racist, sexist, and bigot. Archie Bunker expresses, illuminates, and intensifies feelings of the viewer that were vague and ephemeral. Through Archie, he sees, can talk about, and think about feelings that, before, he could scarcely see, could rarely speak about, and never think about seriously. In the process, he becomes aware of his own anxieties about members of the opposite sex, different races, and different religions. As a consequence, he becomes better able to harmonize his conflicting emotions. In general,

> Thanks to man's capacity to be infected with the feelings of others by means of art, all that is being lived through by his contemporaries is accessible to him, as well as the feelings experienced by men thousands of years ago, and he also has the possibility of transmitting his own feelings to others (Tolstoi, 1960).

Other novelists have expressed a similar view of their primary function. Farrell (1954) said:

> Reading a novel intelligently, we can live through our experiences which are a kind of test of our own moral standards, our judgments, our way of seeing characters and events. . . . We are able to live imaginatively as though we were inside the skin of another. Deep and unconscious desires, wishes, fantasies, are all stimulated and we achieve a sense of living anew, of living differently, and of living in a world other than our own private world or our own immediate world.

Conrad (1912) spoke of the function of the artist in the same vein:

> He speaks to our capacity for delight and wonder, to the sense of mystery surrounding our lives; to our sense of pity, and beauty, and pain; to the latent feeling of fellowship with all creation—and to the subtle but invincible conviction of solidarity that knits together the loneliness of inummerable hearts, to the solidarity in dreams, in joy, in sorrow, in aspirations, in illusions, in hope, in fear, which binds men to each other, which binds together all humanity—the dead to the living and the living to the unborn.

As there are artistic and practical individuals, so there are artistic and practical societies. Morris (1956) compared the values reported by several thousand college students in the United States with over a thousand students in India, over seven hundred students in Nationalist China in 1948, and with somewhat smaller but comparable groups of students in Japan and Norway. The instrument used to measure values was a questionnaire entitled "Ways to Live." The English version was used in India, and translations were used in China, Japan, and Norway.

In making their choice between the ways the students were instructed as follows:

Remember that it is not a question of what kind of life you now lead, or the kind of life you think it prudent to live in our society, or the kind of life you think good for other persons, but *simply the kind of life you personally would like to live.*

More than students of any other country, the Chinese stressed the practical way:

The stress is upon delight in vigorous action for the overcoming of obstacles. The emphasis is upon the initiation of change rather than upon the preservation of what has already been obtained. The orientation is outward toward society and to nature.

The Japanese placed the greatest emphasis upon the artistic way:

The stress is upon a rich inner life of heightened self-awareness. The self, rather than society, is the focus of attention. The emphasis is upon the simplification and purification of the self in order to attain a high level of insight and awareness.

The artistic and the practical stress equally valid but entirely different needs and, consequently, use different ways of satisfying them. Much more than students of any other country, American students preferred a balanced way of life. Almost half of American women and more than a third of American men chose this way (Morris, 1956):

We should at various times and in various ways accept something from all other paths of life, but give no one our exclusive allegiance. At one moment one of them is the more appropriate; at another moment, another is the most appropriate. Life should contain enjoyment and action and contemplation in about equal amounts. When either is carried to extremes we lose something important in our life. So we must cultivate flexibility, admit diversity in ourselves, accept the tension which this diversity produces, find a place for detachment in the midst of enjoyment and activity. The goal of life is found in the dynamic interaction of enjoyment, action, and contemplation, and so in the dynamic interaction of the various paths of life.

SUMMARY

Everyone must deal with his inner private world as well as the external world. The artistic, however, pay most attention to their inner worlds and are aesthetic in their attitudes and interests; the practical, to the outer world and are utilitarian in their attitudes and interests. Which world a person concentrates upon seems largely determined by early experiences. The artistic come from secure and solitary childhoods in which playfulness is encouraged; the practical, from insecure and gregarious childhoods in which serious work is stressed. Art seems to be a powerful but neglected method for helping both the artistic and the practical to understand their feelings and to educate their emotions.

SUGGESTIONS FOR FURTHER READING

*Cantril, H., and Bumstead, C. H. (1960). *Reflections on the human venture*. New York: New York Univ. Press. It is a long book, but students who read it liked it: "Uses literature to illustrate concepts of psychology. . . . It shows man as a human, breathing, feeling animal, a picture of him that is somehow lost in the laboratory."

Hall, C. S. (1953). *The meaning of dreams*. New York: Harper. Informative and easy to read.

Singer, J. L. (1966). *Daydreaming: an introduction to the experimental study of inner experience*. New York: Random House (paperback). A review and interpretation of studies of the nature, antecedents, and consequences of daydreaming. Concludes with a discussion of daydreaming in psychopathology and daily life.

Humphrey, G. (1948). *Directed thinking*. New York: Dodd, Mead. A report of experiments in the field of creative thinking that contains many suggestions for improving one's own thinking.

Answers for Table 7-4; Dellard (1), Bernard (3), Edgar (2), and Form (4); Dellard, 10th percentile; Bernard, 50th percentile; Edgar, 40th percentile, and Form, 60th percentile.

Answers for Table 7-5: 1 (T), 2 (T), 3 (T), 4 (T), 5 (F), 6 (T), 7 (T), 8 (T), 9 (F), 10 (F), 11 (F), 12 (F), 13 (T), 14 (F), 15 (F), 16 (T), 17 (F), 18 (T), 19 (T), 20 (T), 21 (T), 22 (F), 23 (F), 24 (F).

8

THE RELIGIOUS
AND THE SCIENTIFIC

Science says things are; morality says some things are better
than other things; religion says the best things are the eternal
things. The scientist has nothing to fear for his own interests
from the liveliest possible state of fermentation in the
religious world of his time so long as he is willing to allow
that some religious hypothesis *may* be true.

WILLIAM JAMES

Religion is the expression of man's belief in and reverence for a superhuman power. Science is the expression of man's belief in the value of observation, experimental investigation and natural phenomena. The "religious," as we shall use the term, are those who put more faith in the principles embodied in traditional religious and social customs than they do in the facts derived from science. The "scientific" are those who put more faith in facts.

ARE YOU MORE SCIENTIFIC THAN RELIGIOUS?
Martin Luther King (Table 8-1 and Figure 8-1) had deep religious convictions growing out of his faith in the teachings of Christ. David Hume (Table 8-2 and Figure 8-2) placed his faith in science and his hope in the changes that scientific facts would produce in religion and society.

The statements in Table 8-3 are derived from a factor analysis (Linden, 1965). The analysis showed high religious values appearing in the same cluster with resistance to social change, conformity to social norms, and low interest in science. Those students who were skeptical about religion also tended to be the most ready for social change, nonconformists, and scientific in their orientation. The 40 statements in the scale are those from the various subordinate scales that were most closely related to each other and, therefore, to the core meaning of the cluster. They are arranged under three headings: principles versus facts, old versus new religions, and old versus new customs.

Psychologists have long been aware of this cluster of traits. It is, for example, close to the traits that William James associated with rationalism and empiricism more than fifty years ago (1955):

Rationalistic (going by "principles")	**Empirical** (going by "facts")
Intellectualistic	Sensationalistic
Idealistic	Materialistic
Optimistic	Pessimistic
Religious	Irreligious
Free-willist	Fatalistic
Monistic	Pluralistic
Dogmatical	Skeptical

Consistently, those who obtain high rationalistic scores on the inventory are firm believers in principles ("I think I have a more rigorous standard of right and wrong than most people"), more intellectualistic ("I am more interested in general ideas than specific facts"), and more optimistic ("The thought of God gives me a complete sense of secur-

Figure 8-1 Martin Luther King, 1929–1968. (United Press International)

TABLE 8-1   The Religious Martin Luther King

King was born in 1929 in Atlanta, Georgia. His grandfather, his father, and he, in turn, were pastors of the Ebenezer Baptist Church. All were also pioneers in the modern Negro resistance movement. From childhood, King was deferential to his elders and considerate of his peers. He was also a model student in the public schools, in the private laboratory school at Atlanta University, and in Booker T. Washington High School. He graduated from the Crozer Theological Seminary in Chester, Pennsylvania, with a straight A average.

His personality and work were molded by ideas: the idea of Christian love and brotherhood, the idea of nonviolence, and the idea of confrontation, the bringing out into the open of submerged evils by forcing face-to-face meetings between man and man, Negro community and white community (Bennett, 1964, p. 2):

What King did now—and it was a huge achievement—was to turn the Negro's faith in the church to social and political account by melding the image of Gandhi and the image of the Negro preacher and by overlaying all with Negro songs and symbols that bypassed cerebral centers and exploded in the well of the Negro psyche.

Negro empiricists had been contemptuous of the redemptive power of love and of the effectiveness of nonviolence. E. Franklin Frazier, the Negro sociologist, expressed the view of the majority in 1924: "If the masses of Negroes can save their self-respect and remain free of hate, so much the better for their moral development. [But] I believe it would be better for the Negro's soul to be seared with hate than dwarfed by self-abasement."

In January, 1956, King was arrested in Montgomery on a charge of traveling 30 miles an hour in a 25-mile zone. In June, 1964, he was arrested in St. Augustine, Florida, on a charge of violating the state's anti-trespass law. If arrests are evidence of self-abasement, King had ample facts to support his self-abasement. Between 1956 and 1964 he was arrested, fined, or jailed more than two dozen times. Yet in the latter year, following his visit with the Pope, Sweden awarded him the Nobel Peace Prize, given annually to the person "who has done most for the furtherance of brotherhood among men."

ity"). The empiricists, on the other hand, are ardent believers in facts ("Science should have as much to say about moral values as religion does"), more materialistic ("I am more interested in what I see and hear . . ."), and more skeptical ("I am temperamentally more a skeptic than a believer").

Conservative versus liberal, conformist versus nonconformist, dogmatic versus undogmatic are other labels given to essentially the same trait.

More subtle measures agree with inventory measures. When those low or high on religious versus scientific scales rate the virtues of others, they place their own values high on the list of virtues. When they scan the newspaper, they observe and remember more news items pertaining to their respective beliefs. When they make associations to words, they make more and faster associations to words related to their beliefs. When they are shown photographs of men labeled "minister" and "scientist" for a tenth of a second, they identify the man related to their beliefs more quickly (McGinnies and Bowles, 1949). The ratings that people give themselves tend to be close to the scores they achieve on the inventories (Stanley, 1951).

Once formed, a religious or scientific orientation seems highly resistant to change. Watson and Hartmann (1939), for example, exposed 10 atheists and 10 theists who were graduate students to 10 carefully selected reasons for believing in God and 10 for not believing in God. Some were appeals to authority, some to scientific evidence, and some to logical arguments both for and against. The theists and atheists were given an attitude scale measuring their religious beliefs before and after exposure to 20 arguments. There was practically no change in their scores. At the end of the study, the students were suddenly asked to recall as many of the 20 arguments as they could. The atheists remembered more of the arguments supporting their view; the theists remembered more of the arguments supporting theirs.

Education seems to leave the basic orientation practically unchanged. Todd (1941) noted practically no change in the religious and scientific values of students between high school and the sophomore year of college. Studies at Franklin and Marshall College, Sweet Briar College, and Springfield College report only slight changes in the scientific and religious values between the freshman and senior years

Figure 8-2 David Hume, 1711–1776. (New York Public Library)

TABLE 8-2   The Scientific David Hume

When he died in 1776, Hume was the author of best-sellers in history, economics, and political science. His greatest achievement, however, was his philosophical writings, which laid the foundations of modern empiricism. His basic assertion that sensory experience was the *only* avenue to the kingdom of knowledge was a "turning point in the history of thought." Two centuries later, Einstein acknowledged his debt to Hume for his own discoveries: "The type of critical reasoning which was required for discovery of this central point was decisively furthered . . . by the reading of David Hume's . . . philosophical writings."

Hume was born in Scotland, ". . . of a good family, both by father and mother. . . . My father, who passed for a man of parts, died when I was an infant, leaving me, with an elder brother and a sister, under the care of our mother, a woman of singular merit, who, though young and handsome, devoted herself entirely to the rearing and educating of her children." He became a tolerant and helpful man who enjoyed the material comforts of life and who was very loyal to his many friends. He liked women, but he never married.

His life reflected his empiricism. He was independent, scientific, nonconforming, and an advocate of vast social changes. The "Science of Human Nature" that he expounded through his life was generally ignored and misunderstood at the time. However, it laid the foundations for searching analyses of the bases for church doctrine and led to his books being placed on the prohibited list by the Roman Catholic Church. Nonetheless, they were read then and are read now by theologians with great interest. His religious skepticism remained with him to the end. During his final year of debilitating illness, he continued to write, to read, and to cheerfully converse and play whist with his friends. His doctor, believing that so happy a man could not be dying, told him that he would write to a mutual friend to report his recovery. Hume replied: "As I believe you would not choose to tell anything but the truth, you had better tell him that I am dying as fast as my enemies, if I have any, could wish, and as easily and cheerfully as my best friends could desire" (Mossher, 1954).

(Jacob, 1957). Kelley (1955) compared the religious and scientific scores of college students with the scores they obtained twenty years later. Result: .60 and .50. Considering the possible errors in measurement, these relationships are extremely high.

WHY DO WE DIFFER ON THE TRAIT?

Both the religious and scientific have faith: "The substance of things hoped for; the evidence of things not seen." (Hebrews, XI:1). Faith is a belief in the value and trustworthiness of a thing, person, principle, or point of view. In facing the routine problems of daily life we are not aware of a need for it. In facing grave situations, however, we become acutely aware of the need. The pilot flying through sleet and fog needs faith in his plane and his copilot. When we are haunted by our past, feel unable to cope with the present, or are frightened about the future, we need some faith that will give us the ability to go on living.

The religious and the scientific have fundamental faiths. The religious have faith in a source of knowledge superior to and independent of facts. They have faith in custom, in the wisdom of tradition, in God. The scientific have faith that even the most disturbing and complicated situations can be understood. They have faith that this understanding can be communicated to others in a useful way. They have faith that this understanding can lead to the ability to predict and control situations for the benefit of mankind (Figure 8-3).

The trait does not measure absolute differences in the amount of faith people have in religion and science. Rather it measures the *relative* differences in their faiths, whether they have *more* faith in one than in the other. What determines the balance of faiths?

Direct Genetic Mechanisms

The five traits have been discussed in the order of the probable influence that genetic mechanisms have upon them. Boldness seems

TABLE 8-3   The Religious vs. the Scientific Scale

A definition of this trait is given below with 40 statements that measure it. The statements are grouped under subordinate traits in the cluster and the answers for the scientific end of the scale indicated. Your total score is the number of scientific answers that you make. Norms for 100 college men and 100 college women in 1970 are given after the statements. The two most discriminating items in the scale are indicated with an asterisk.

Definition:

   The religious, putting their faith in principles developed through tradition, tend to be resistant to change, conforming, and religious. The scientific, putting their faith in facts, tend to be ready for change, individualistic, and skeptical.

Directions:

   If you think a statement is "true" or more true than false as far as you are concerned, underline "T." If you think a statement is "false" or more false than true as far as you are concerned, underline "F."

Principles vs. Facts

<u>I</u>   F   1.   I am more interested in what I see and hear than in abstract principles.

<u>I</u>   F   2.   I am temperamentally more a skeptic than a believer.

<u>I</u>   F   3.   I believe that we should have less censorship of speech and press than we do now.

<u>I</u>   F   4.   Radical agitators should be allowed to make public speeches.

<u>I</u>   F   5.   In the long run, science provides the best hope for solving the world's problems.

<u>I</u>   F   6.   Science should have as much to say about moral values as religion does.

<u>I</u>   F   7.   I like to read scientific articles in popular magazines.

<u>I</u>   F   8.   I would enjoy the kind of work that a scientific research worker does.

T   <u>F</u>   9.   I am more interested in general ideas than in specific facts.

T   <u>F</u>   10.   I carry a very strict conscience about with me wherever I go.

T   <u>F</u>   11.   I think that I have a more rigorous standard of right and wrong than most people.

T   <u>F</u>   12.   I would rather be a salesman than a scientific research worker.

T   <u>F</u>   13.   Divine inspiration is an infallible source of truth.

Old vs. New Religions

<u>I</u>   F   14.   The world might benefit from a new kind of religion.

<u>I</u>   F   15.   It is possible that there is no such thing as divine inspiration.

<u>I</u>   F   16.   I have occasionally doubted the reality of God.

<u>I</u>   F   17.   I haven't yet reached any final opinion about the nature of God.

T   <u>F</u>   18.   It is necessary to retain the belief that God exists as a personal being.

TABLE 8-3 (Continued)

T F 19. A person should develop his greatest loyalty toward his religious faith.

T F 20.* The idea of God must remain absolutely central to the whole plan of human purpose.

T F 21. My faith in God is complete for "though he slay me, yet will I trust him."

T F 22. It is absolutely vital to assume that there is a God behind the universe.

T F 23. I have always been unalterably convinced of the reality of God.

T F 24. The thought of God gives me a complete sense of security.

T F 25. I trust in God to support the right and condemn the wrong.

T F 26. The idea of God means more to me than any other idea.

T F 27. It is as important for a person to be reverent as it is for him to be sympathetic.

Old vs. New Customs

I F 28. Compared to your own self-respect, the respect of others means little.

I F 29. I often act contrary to custom.

I F 30. Some of my friends think my ideas are a bit wild and impractical.

I F 31.* I believe that everybody would be happier if both men and women had more sexual freedom.

I F 32. The European attitude toward mistresses is more sensible than ours.

I F 33. I think that cremation is the best method of burial.

I F 34. Women should have as much right to propose dates to men as men to women.

T F 35. In matters of conduct I conform very closely to custom.

T F 36. I consider the close observance of social customs and manners as an essential aspect of life.

T F 37. I think that it is much more important to learn to control sexual impulses than to express them.

T F 38. I control my sexual impulses by instituting prohibitions and restrictions.

T F 39. No individual, no matter what the circumstances, is justified in committing suicide.

T F 40. I take pains not to incur the disapproval of others.

	Percentiles										
	Religious									Scientific	
	0	10	20	30	40	50	60	70	80	90	99
Men	6	20	23	25	27	28	30	31	33	35	38
Women	7	13	17	20	22	24	27	29	30	33	37

Figure 8-3 What is man's relation to the universe? Man is, or can be, its master, according to American society. The same social values which drove pioneers across the plains to the West still operate in this society: Neil Armstrong's "One small step for man . . ." onto the surface of the moon was just an extension of this philosophy. (New York Public Library)

most heavily influenced by genetic mechanisms, emotionality next, and then future-mindedness, practicality, and, finally, the balance of faith in religion and science. Intelligence influences the degree to which an individual can verbalize, organize, and communicate his faith in religion or science. Neither intelligence nor any other inherited trait seems to influence the balance of his faiths.

Indirect Genetic Mechanisms

Sex makes a big difference. Men are more scientific than women: more interested in facts, less interested in principles; more interested in science, less interested in religion; and more interested in social change, less interested in social conformity. The results of other studies are quite consistent. Men have higher scientific and lower religious values (Allport et al., 1951). Men are more radical and more self-sufficient, i.e., more likely to agree that "Our greatest need today is that all people should learn birth control," and that "It is desirable to have divorce obtainable simply by mutual consent," and more likely to disagree that "The Bible is true in all parts" (Cattell, 1965).

Sons identify more with their fathers' values than their

mothers'; daughters identify more with the values of their mothers. But why are fathers more scientific and mothers more religious? *Sex typing* seems the most likely answer. All cultures establish different attributes as desirable for men and women. In our culture, men are expected to be and encouraged to be interested in mechanics, science, and mathematics; women, in religion.

General Environmental Mechanisms

The dominant values of members of a society reflect the dominant values of the society. Religious values have overwhelmingly dominated the vast majority of societies. Science probably is more prominent in the value system of the United States than in any society in the history of the world. We value a dime and a dollar, but not equally. Both are a part of a system that determines their relative worth and also the relative worth of many other objects that we desire. In turn, our economic values are part of a still larger system that determines the worth not only of material but of religious and scientific goals as well.

The value system of a society, DuBois (1955) suggests, results from its answers to basic questions regarding man's relation to the universe, to time, and to other men. The questions and the answers for American society are:

> **Q.** What is the nature of the universe?
> **A.** The universe is a machine.
> **Q.** What is man's relation to the universe?
> **A.** Man is, or can be, its master.
> **Q.** What is man's relation to other men?
> **A.** All men are equal.
> **Q.** What is the future of man?
> **A.** Man is perfectible.

Because we view the universe as a machine, we are fascinated by machinery. Because we feel that we can master the universe, we build more and better machines. Because we believe that all men should be equal, our most natural heroes are baseball players, movie stars, and quiz winners, for their success does not give them power over others. And because we believe that man is perfectible, we have more psychologists than any other country in the world to aid us in becoming more perfect. Our answers are not verifiable, not complete, and sometimes conflict with each other. On the whole, however, they are harmonious and fit into a value system which is summed up in the phrase "the democratic way of life."

Not all Americans accept the American value system with

equal fervor. Those who accept democratic institutions generally have a scientific view of man in the universe, feel that critical thinking about problems should be encouraged, and think that it is generally a good thing to try out new ideas. Those who reject the "democratic way" feel that the *status quo* should not be disturbed, that personal security should be limited to the upper classes, and that powers outside of, and higher than, man are the dominant force in human life (Harding, 1944).

The values of children are heavily influenced by the values of their parents. Fisher (1948) measured the values of college students and of their parents. Table 8-4 shows the relations. The religious values of children are not only close to those of their parents, but closer than their scientific, artistic, or practical values. The explanation is apparent, for wives and husbands were closer in their religious values than in any other area. Thus, both presented the *same* values to their children. When specific religious attitudes and practices were compared, parents and their children were even closer.

A college senior suggests the family origins of his religious view:

Having taken a good look at myself, I find one thing to be true: I am very conservative. With me, things have a set course along which they must move. In religion, it is: "Faith of my fathers ... I will be true ... till death." In my social activities, liberalism has no place—the rules were set before my time; they could not be wrong! I must confess that I wish it were possible to return to the days of yesteryear and relive those in which even the dust seems to have been in an orderly pattern on the earth. Amid today's changing, undecided, informal, haphazard age, I find it almost impossible to accept the liberal opinions of people who have forgotten their past and long only for a hazy future ... being as I am has caused me to know many embarrassing moments. Why I am this way I am not sure, but I do remember being brought up by my grandparents—good old conservatives, rigid with discipline and proud of formalities.

TABLE 8-4 Relationship between the Religious and Scientific Values of Parents and Children

| Values | Mother | | Father | | Median |
	Daughter	Son	Daughter	Son	
Religious	.49	.40	.60	.45	.47
Scientific	.30	.15	.26	.18	.29

(*Source*: Fisher, 1948).

Children learn their values *early*. Catholic, Jewish, and Protestant children have a marked preference for children of the same faith (Radke, Trager, and Davis, 1949). Studies of eminent scientists reveal one consistent quality: very early development of an intense and persistent energy directed toward scientific discovery (Roe, 1953).

The more considerate a parent, the more likely a child is to learn his values. Payne and Mussen (1956) selected from a large number of high school boys 20 who were closely identified with their fathers and 20 who were little identified with their fathers. The degree of identification was measured by counting the number of items from a 50-item personality inventory that the son and his father answered in the same way. The number of items that the son and his mother had answered in the same way were subtracted from this total. The chief difference between the "high" and "low" identifiers was in their perception of their fathers: those most closely identified saw him as a friendly person; the least identified saw him as someone cold and rejecting.

Catholics are less scientific than Protestants. Knapp and Goodrich (1952) compared the effectiveness of Catholic colleges and universities in producing scientists. They defined a scientist as a man who had received his doctor's degree in science and was listed in the 1944 edition of *American Men of Science*. They measured effectiveness by determining the number of male graduates of each institution between 1924 and 1934 who became scientists. Of every 1,000 graduates of non-Catholic institutions, 12 became scientists. Reed, Earlham, and Oberlin colleges led the list. Of every 1,000 graduates of Catholic institutions, 3 became scientists.

Specific Environmental Mechanisms

Since 1946, the T-group has spread across the country and around the world. More than 100,000 Californians have participated in such experiences (Allen, 1968). Between 1963 and 1968 the number of participants in T-groups conducted by the National Training Laboratory Institute doubled. The method is used in classrooms, in marital counseling, group psychotherapy, and church services. It has been applied to problems of race relations, police training, and executive development. In short, the training is growing and is commercially successful. Why is it so popular? Some evidence points to the conclusion that it is trying to satisfy the need for a scientific motive but actually satisfying a religious one. Before examining some of this evidence, it is necessary to review the history of the T-group idea and its avowed aims.

In 1946 psychologists at the Massachusetts Institute of Technology discovered the T-group idea while running a two-week workshop aimed at reducing tensions in Connecticut communities. Some of the members attending overheard the staff listening to and discussing tapes of the sessions in which they had participated. They thought it was the most valuable part of the workshop. Thus was born the basic T (training)-group idea: to have participants discuss themselves and the ways they see themselves relating to each other in a small unstructured, face-to-face group. The idea is flexible and is called by a variety of other names, including sensitivity, laboratory, and encounter-group training. The activities of these groups are never planned in advance. The role of the leader varies but never includes forceful direction of the group's activities. The T-group stresses "emotional learning" rather than intellectual learning. It stresses the "here and now" rather than the "there and then."

What do such groups try to do? The development of self-insight, of awareness of group processes, and of skill in intervening constructively in group activities is often mentioned. Behind these goals are less explicit but more comprehensive ones: the development of a spirit of inquiry about one's role in the world, of an expanded "interpersonal consciousness," and of "authenticity" in interpersonal relationships. Above all, T-groups try to develop sensitivity to others, i.e., an understanding of others, particularly of their feelings and emotional states.

What do such groups actually succeed in doing? Danish and Kagan (1971) developed a sophisticated measure of "affective sensitivity." The measure uses a videotape situational test containing 41 scenes involving 11 different counselors taken from actual counseling sessions. After seeing a videotape sequence, a subject chooses from several multiple-choice alternatives the one that he thinks describes the affective state that the client was actually experiencing.

Does T-Group Experience Improve Affective Sensitivity?   The test was given to 51 members in six T-groups before and after their training. Result: The average member in two groups improved significantly; in two groups, insignificantly; and in two groups, declined slightly. In the light of these negative results, the authors concluded: "If affective sensitivity is a trait like that of intelligence, then both hereditary potential and environmental conditions may be influential and large gains by groups should probably not be expected to occur. This raises a question about whether or not people can be "taught" to improve their affective sensitivity. . . ." Review of many studies of the same question led to similar negative conclusions (Dunnette, 1969).

T-groups do succeed in making participants feel good about themselves and each other. Trainees almost invariably are enthusiastic about the training. They report that their self perceptions, sensitivity, and interpersonal effectiveness were changed in highly beneficial ways. In general, participants develop a *feeling* of being close to, sympathetic with, and understanding of others in the group. These subjective feelings, however, have no apparent relation to objective understanding of others.

Why do participants feel good as a result of participating? Mintz (1971) suggests that participation is an effective mechanism for dealing with a cultural neurosis:

> ... the pressures of our society produce a syndrome which, though not deviant, is intrinsically pathologic. This syndrome is marked by fear of intimacy and longing for intimacy; fear of self-exposure; difficulty in relating to others without pretense or defensiveness; conflicts around dependency and self-assertiveness; in short, a syndrome most succinctly described as alienation from others and from the self.

Such techniques as lifting and rocking, fall-catch responses, blind contact, arm wrestling, and disrobing are ways of curing the neurosis.

Dunnette (1969) concludes from his study of T-groups that this movement as well as many related activities in our society are propelled by a religious motive:

> I intend something close to the early Christian concept of *agape*, a sense of spontaneous giving of the self, the free expression of self in interaction with others, without calculating of cost or gain to either the giver or the receiver, and a deep commitment to the worth and humanity of man. I refer to the many current social revolts—the New Morality, the Hippies, and in particular to the explosive growth of group training programs ... Intimacy Training ... Sensitivity Training, T-grouping, or Awareness Training.

Participants may attend no church. They may reject all formal religious doctrines and dogmas. Still, they seek and seem to satisfy a religious need through T-group experiences. We shall return to some speculations about the value of this motive at the end of the chapter.

HOW WELL CAN YOU JUDGE THE TRAIT IN OTHERS?

The reader can find an answer to this question by completing the exercise in Table 8-5 that again presents Joan, Mary, Susan, and Carol.

TABLE 8-5   How Well Can You Judge Religious vs. Scientific Orientations?

You are now finally asked to judge the religious vs. scientific interests of the four women introduced in earlier chapters. Here are some of the things that they said about themselves that are relevant to judging this trait.

Joan Dellard   This cautious, emotional, present-minded and artistic psychology major said that her ideas on religion are in the process of changing but that she is anti organized religion.

Mary Bernard   This future-minded, bold, and emotional middle-aged home economics major said that she spent her summers with her aunts and uncles who were very religious, and thus has developed very high ethical and religious standards. She is tolerant of other people and can deal easily with abstract theories.

Susan Edgar   This ambitious, bold, and calm young social-work major says that she believes in two religions—God and mother nature—and understands the latter better because "I just don't know what side God is on."

Carol Form   This calm, bold, impulsive, and practical upper middle-class sophomore says that she had often been fairly easily persuaded to do things she would not normally do. She doesn't smoke or drink, feels that she has high ethical and moral standards, but doesn't go to church often during the school year.

*How do these four women compare in their scientific orientation?**
Rank "1" the woman who you think is most religious; "2" next; "3" next; and "4" the most scientific.

Joan Dellard   _____
Mary Bernard   _____
Susan Edgar   _____
Carol Form   _____

*How do they compare on this trait with other college women?**
Circle the percentile that you think each girl matches most closely

	Percentile									
	Religious				Average					Scientific
Joan Dellard	10	20	30	40	50	60	70	80	90	99
Mary Bernard	10	20	30	40	50	60	70	80	90	99
Susan Edgar	10	20	30	40	50	60	70	80	90	99
Carol Form	10	20	30	40	50	60	70	80	90	99

*Correct answers are given at the end of the chapter.

In approaching this question in earlier chapters we have examined some of the difficulties in making such judgments and suggested ways of overcoming them. Here, we give a tentative answer to the general question: What kind of person is the best judge of others?

Chance and Meaders (1960) tape-recorded 45-minute interviews with two men who had previously completed the Edwards Personal Preference Schedule. Ninety-six undergraduate men, who had also completed the inventory, filled it out as they predicted the interviewed men had filled it out. An accuracy score for each student was obtained by counting the number of times predicted responses agreed with actual responses. The traits of the 18 most accurate students were compared with the traits of the 18 who were least accurate. From an examination of the trait differences the authors drew the following sketch of the sensitive person:

> . . . a person who is active and outgoing in social relationships, who likes other people but is not markedly dependent upon them, who is ascendant but not hostile and competitive, and who is not given to intellectual reflections about his interpersonal relationships. The picture is one of an individual who finds significant satisfaction in social activities and carries on his daily life with a minimum of interpersonal or intrapersonal conflict.

The sensitive pattern (Table 8-6) resulted from a different approach but produced similar conclusions (Smith, 1973). Each statement in this table is a clue to the qualities of the good judge. These clues suggest, first of all, that the sensitive are bold, but with powerful reservation. They are energetic, self-confident, and optimistic; they are *not* dominating or gregarious. They are emotional but not hostile; stable but not rigid; and independent but not unsympathetic. Above all, they seem seriously interested in ideas different from their own and attracted by people different from themselves. These statements give a good idea about the qualities of the sensitive person. However, they are a poor measure of the differences in sensitivity between individuals because of the narrow range of total scores.

IS IT BETTER TO BE MORE RELIGIOUS OR MORE SCIENTIFIC?

History seems to tell us that the better the religion *and* the better the science man has, the more liberated and happier he is likely to be. The age, power, and universality of religious institutions testify that they reflect, and to some degree satisfy, some basic human need. Scientific institutions are a late and refined product of civilization that could only develop under special conditions. Yet the triumph of science in the

TABLE 8-6 The Sensitive Pattern

Three large groups of students answered the items from the same personality inventory but completed different tests of Sensitivity to People. Those who scored high on these sensitivity tests consistently answered the items below differently from those who scored low. The statements are arranged under the trait scales in which they appear. The answers given more often by the sensitive group are at the end of the chapter.

Cautious vs. Bold
1. Some people can look forward to a happier life than I can.
2. I am extremely active in my everyday life.
3. I am somewhat more shy than the average person.
4. I have quite a few fears about my future.
5. I am always taking on added social responsibility.
6. I am quite self-confident.

Unemotional vs. Emotional
7. I have sometimes corrected others, not because they were wrong, but only because they irritated me.
8. I am seldom excited or thrilled.

Artistic vs. Practical
9. In a discussion, I tend to lose interest if we talk about any serious literature.
10. Artistic experiences are of great importance in my life.
11. I am more interested in general ideas than specific facts.

Present-Minded vs. Future-Minded
12. I am not particularly methodical in my everyday life.
13. I always keep control of myself in an emergency situation.
14. I really don't like to drink alcoholic beverages.
15. I almost never lose my head.
16. I consider most matters very carefully before I form an opinion.
17. I am a fairly impulsive person.

Religious vs. Scientific
18. It is just as important for a person to be reverent as it is for him to be sympathetic.
19. Compared to your own self-respect, the respect of others means little.
20. Radical agitators should be encouraged to make public speeches.

modern world is so complete and uncontested that it, too, seems to reflect and satisfy a basic human need.

The principles, methods, and results of science are endlessly disputed. Its general function, however, is not disputed. Science gives us an assurance of a constant world. It seeks to answer the question: What will happen if I do this or that to myself, to others, or to things?

Through its answers, it satisfies man's need for an understandable, predictable, and controllable external world.

The principles, methods, and results of religion are also end-lessly disputed. Unlike science, however, the motive that it seeks to satisfy is also disputed. Freud assumed that the religious motive was the sex motive in disguise. More commonly, the motive has been assumed to be man's effort to allay his fear of death. His study of primitive religious leads Cassirer (1944) to deny that religion originates in either sexual desires or the fear of death. Primitive societies always regard death as accidental, not inevitable: "The whole of mythical thought may be interpreted as a constant and obstinate negation of the phenomenon of death." Rather, all religion is based upon man's "deep conviction of a fundamental and indelible *solidarity of life* that bridges over the multiplicity and variety of its single forms." The development from mythical, to magical, to moral forms of religion could never suppress or eradicate these deep convictions. It had to channel this "sympathy of the Whole" to give scope to a new feeling of individual-ity, a feeling that seems to negate the universality of feeling that is postulated by primitive religion: "It was this difficulty and this riddle that had to be solved by the progress of religious thought." From this point of view, the basic religious motive is man's desire to feel close to, sympathetic with, and in harmony with other men and with the world.

The motive seems fully satisfied in mystical experiences. Here, for example, is a psychiatrists' report of his introduction to "cosmic consciousness" (James, 1929, p. 390):

I had spent the evening in a great city, with two friends, reading and discussing poetry and philosophy. We parted at midnight. I had a long drive in a hansom to my lodging. My mind, deeply under the influence of the ideas, images, and emotions called up by the reading and talk, was calm and peaceful. I was in a state of quiet, almost passive enjoyment, not actually thinking, but letting ideas, images, and emotions flow of themselves, as it were, through my mind. All at once, without warning of any kind, I found myself wrapped in a flame-colored cloud. For an instant I thought of fire, an immense conflagration somewhere close by in that great city; the next, I knew that the fire was within myself. Directly afterward there came upon me a sense of exultation, of immense joyousness accompanied or im-mediately followed by an intellectual illumination impossible to describe. Among other things, I did not merely come to believe, but I saw that the universe is not composed of dead matter, but is, on the contrary, a living Presence; I became conscious in myself of eternal life. It was not a conviction that I would have eternal life, but a consciousness that I possessed eternal life then; I saw that all men are immortal; that the cosmic order is such that without any peradventure all things work together for the good of each and all; that the foundation principle of the world, of all the worlds, is what we call love, and that the happiness of each and all is in the long run absolutely certain. The vision lasted a few seconds and was gone, but the memory of it and the sense of reality of what it taught has remained during the quarter of a century which has since elapsed. I knew that what the vision showed was true. I had attained to a point of view from which I saw that it must be true. That view, that conviction, I may say that consciousness, has never, even during period of the deepest depression, been lost.

Mystical experiences, however, are dramaticized by their brevity. Less intense but more permanent feelings of holiness are frequently reported. James, himself, said (1955, p. 192):

I have written a book on men's religious experiences, which on the whole has been regarded as making for the reality of God . . . I firmly disbelieve, myself, that our human experience is the highest form of experience extant in the universe. I believe rather that we stand in much the same relation to the whole of the universe as our canine and feline pets do to the whole of human life. They inhabit our drawing-rooms and libraries. They take part in scenes of whose significance they have no inkling. They are merely tangent to curves of history the beginnings and ends and forms of which pass wholly beyond their ken. So we are tangent to the wide life of things. But, just as many of the dog's and cat's ideals coincide with our ideals, and the dogs and cats have daily living proof of the fact, so we may well believe, on the proofs that religious experience affords, that higher powers exist and are at work to save the world on ideal lines similar to our own. . . .

Similarly, Thomas Jefferson reports (Chinard, 1957, p. 523):

When we take a view of the universe, in its parts, general or particular, it is impossible for the human mind not to perceive and feel a conviction of design, consummate skill, and indefinite power in every atom of its composition. . . . The truth of the matter is, that nature has implanted in our breasts a love of others, a sense of duty to them, a moral instinct, in short, which prompts us irresistibly to feel and succour their distresses. . . . Some men are born without the organs of sight, or of hearing, or without hands. Yet it would be wrong to say that man is born without these faculties.

The needs that religion and science seek to satisfy are entirely different. Consequently, their principles, methods, and results are entirely different. The religious motive is like a thirst that demands water; the scientific motive, a hunger that requires food. Water does not satisfy hunger, nor does food satisfy thirst. Man needs both water and food; he needs religion and science.

James was well aware that neither the religious nor the scientific have been willing to accept this view, for they have a low opinion of each other (1955, p. 22–23):

> Their mutual reaction is very much like that that takes place when Bostonian tourists mingle with the population like that of Cripple Creek. Each type believes the other to be inferior to itself; but disdain in the one case is mingled with amusement, in the other, it has a dash of fear.

The scientific tend to view religion as a disease rather than a cure. They point out that religion claims to be in possession of an absolute truth, but its history is a history of errors; that it promises a transcendent world but is all too human; that it has offered a communion with nature and brotherhood but has given mankind the most fanatic struggles that the human race has endured. In turn, the religious point out that the applications of science may destroy the world tomorrow. The radical differences in their perspectives are reflected in the readiness of the religious and the resistance of the scientific to accepting ESP as real.

ESP: Real or Unreal?

Can we become aware of the thoughts of others or of events without the aid of our senses? James (1956) argued that the religious and the scientific differ in their answers because of their radically different theories about the relationship between the mind and body, consciousness and the brain. They both agree that consciousness is absolutely dependent upon the brain. Thus, neither doubts that a blow on the head results in the loss of consciousness because of an injury to the brain. However, the scientific implicitly assume that the brain produces consciousness as the fire under a tea kettle produces steam. The religious assume that the brain *receives* consciousness as a TV set receives signals from a transmitter. For the scientific, the man who is hit on the head loses consciousness because the fire is put out; for the religious, because the tube is broken. James felt there was no way of proving or disproving either theory. However, his colleague, Peirce (1955) emphasized that just because a theory was not testable did not mean that it would never be testable:

Who would have said, a few years ago, that we could ever know of what substances the stars are made whose light may have been longer in reaching us than the human race has existed? Who can be sure of what we shall not know in a few hundred years? Who can guess what would be the result of continuing the pursuit of science for ten thousand years, with the activity of the last hundred? And if we were to go on for a million, or a billion, or any number of years you please, how is it possible to say that there is any question which might not ultimately be solved?

Recent experiments suggest that the possibility that ESP exists is much more likely than most scientists are willing to admit.

In a 1933–34 test of ESP, Pratt, an assistant of Rhine who was then at Duke University, and Pearce, a student who was paid for his participation in the experiment, met in Pratt's office. They synchronized their watches and fixed a time for the test to start. Then Pearce walked across the Duke quadrangle to the library, where he sat in a cubicle in the stacks. Pratt went through 50 ESP cards, taking them one at a time and placing each card face down in front of him for one full minute (Figure 8-4). Then he turned over all the cards, made two records of their order, sealed the records in an envelope, and delivered them to Rhine. There were 37 such sittings. Result: The accuracy of Pearce's predictions supported the theory, for they far exceeded chance.

Hansel (1966) was a severe critic of some ESP experiments. Rhine invited him to visit his laboratory. During this visit Hansel asked one of the research assistants to run through a pack of ESP cards while he (Hansel) locked himself in an office down the hall. Result: He scored 22 hits out of 25 cards. Hansel had tiptoed out of the office down the hall, stood on a chair, and peeked through a crack over the door and observed the cards as the assistant looked at them. Hansel does not say that Pearce cheated in this way. He does say:

One would expect that anyone in Pratt's position would have examined the room carefully and have taken elaborate precautions so that no one could see into it. At least he might have covered the windows leading to the corridor. Also, the cards should have been shuffled after they were recorded, and the door of the room might well have been locked during and after the tests.

Figure 8-4 Some of the cards used by Rhine in his studies of extrasensory perception. (Courtesy Dr. J. B. Rhine)

The better the measures and the experimental design used, the more convincing the test of a theory. The ESP cards provide an excellent way of measuring the assumed influence of ESP; the design was not so excellent.

Moss, Chang, and Marc (1970) tested long-distance ESP by measuring the impact of transmissions from 22 subjects in Los Angeles to 28 subjects in another part of Los Angeles, to 15 subjects in New York City, and to 14 subjects in England. They took great care in meeting the objections of both believers and nonbelievers in ESP.

Believers in ESP have generally criticized experiments whose results showed no evidence of extrasensory perception on two grounds. The anecdotal history of mental telepathy suggests that it happens most frequently when deeply dramatic events are involved: the death of a close relative, the devastation of a city by fire, etc. Supporters complain that experimental tests reduce or eliminate what may be the essential emotional element. They also complain that people vary in their sensitivity to ESP and that experiments fail to take this element into account.

To meet the first objection, the transmitters were exposed to a series of six emotional episodes. The exposure consisted of seeing colored slides on a screen with synchronized sounds to heighten the emotional impact. For example, in one episode the 22 subjects looked at a series of nine slides of voracious beasts: boa constrictor, eagle, lion, tiger with bloody mouth devouring his prey. At the same time, they heard excerpts from Antill's *Corroboree* punctuated by the screams and roars of wild animals. In another episode they saw slides of the 1966 Israeli-Arab war accompanied by machine-gun fire, bombing sounds, and an Israeli song of triumph. In still another episode they saw slides of Cape Kennedy with rockets, satellites, and astronauts walking in outer space while listening to electronically distorted music from Holst's *Neptune*. To meet the objection of variations in sensitivity, both transmitters and receivers filled out a fact sheet covering their personal experiences with psychic phenomena as well as information related to their imagination and creativity. It was planned to analyze the results for the possibility that negative results would be obtained because of the individual insensitivity of a particular transmitter or receiver, *groups* of transmitters and receivers were used.

Nonbelievers have generally criticized ESP experiments on methodological grounds. Inadequate number of subjects, poor statistical analysis, clues given to subjects by experimenters who know the correct answers, and the neglect of negative evidence, etc. To meet some of these objections, the experimenter arranged the six emotional episodes into three pairs of contrasting emotions. One of each pair was selected just before transmission by the toss of a coin. For example, the "wild animals" episode was paired with the "space" episode and the "war" episode was paired with a "love" episode. In addition, three control slides were devised to be as nonemotional as possible: letters of the alphabet, a black line drawn at various angles, and a random series of single numbers.

At noon in Los Angeles, the first randomly selected episode was shown to transmitters. Each group of receivers was alerted at the time that the transmission was beginning and asked to write down every impression they received. At the end, the receivers were shown *both* emotional episodes in a pair and asked to chose which slide they thought was the "correct" one. The procedure was repeated for the other two pairs of emotional episodes as well as for the control groups. When the transmitters actually were seeing a control episode, the receivers were still shown an emotional pair and asked to make a choice though neither answer could be correct.

In the control situation, the correctness of the guesses for Los Angeles, New York, and London groups did not exceed chance. In the experimental situation, however, the 57 receivers in the three groups did exceed chance. Furthermore, all three groups did better than chance although only the Los Angeles group (which had most of the subjects) did significantly better. There was no evidence that previous experience with ESP or artistic tendencies had any influence on accuracy.

The experimenters were particularly impressed by the closeness of some of the subjective impressions to the actual episode transmitted. Here, for example, are some of the associations with the "Space" episode when it was being transmitted:

> War of the Worlds, by H. G. Wells? Or the next war, involving death by the use of satellites and flying platforms.

> Giddy . . . hysterical. Movement. Universe, galaxy, stars.

> I can see the world as if I were in a space ship—I'm in a cabin which is very clear and quiet . . . everything is floating. (In parentheses this receiver wrote: "A very definite premonition. Exact image. Incredible!")

The results strengthen the idea that ESP is a reality. They do not finally prove it is real, for there is always the possibility of some unrecognized error.

The scientific put their faith in knowledge derived from the senses; the religious, in knowledge derived from extrasensory sources. *Pragmatism*, the final book of William James (1955), was an effort to describe a way by which hypotheses derived from religion might be tested by scientific means. The pragmatic method, he said, is:

> *The attitude of looking away from first things, principles, 'categories,' supposed necessities; and of looking towards last things, fruits, consequences, facts.* . . . There is absolutely nothing new in the pragmatic method. Socrates was an adept at it. Aristotle used it methodically. . . . The pragmatic method is primarily a method of settling metaphysical disputes that otherwise might be interminable. Is the world one or many? Fated or free? Material or spiritual? What difference would it practically make to any one if this notion rather than that notion were true? If no practical difference whatever can be traced, then the alternatives mean practically the same thing, and all dispute is idle. There can *be* no difference anywhere that doesn't *make* a difference elsewhere—no difference in abstract truth that doesn't express itself in a difference in concrete fact and in conduct consequent upon the fact, imposed on somebody, somehow, somewhere, and somewhen.

Studies of ESP provide a pragmatic test of a religious hypothesis. Is it better for a society to be dominated by religion or science? The answer seems to lie neither in the amount of faith it has in either but in the quality of both. Mankind has advanced as religion and science have advanced. Science has developed from astrology to astronomy, from alchemy to chemistry. Religion has developed from systems of taboos to systems of morality. Taboos dominate the political, social, sexual, and family life of primitive societies. Advanced religions have relieved men of the unbearable burden of the innumerable restrictions and compulsions dictated by taboos and replaced them with a profound sense of religious obligation that is the expression of a new positive ideal of human freedom.

Is it better for the individual to be dominated by his religious or scientific faith? In times of personal crisis, the thirst for religious satisfaction is so powerful that he seems to have little choice in the matter. An experience of Francis Galton (1909), a famous English scientist of the last century, indicates the ease with which the religious motive can overpower the scientific one:

I had visited a large collection of idols gathered by missionaries from many lands, and wondered how each of those absurd and ill-made monstrosities could have obtained the hold it had over the imaginations of its worshippers. I wished, if possible, to enter into those feelings. It was difficult to find a suitable object for trial because it ought to be in itself quite unfitted to arouse devout feelings. I fixed on a comic picture. It was that of Punch, and made believe in its possession of divine attributes. I addressed it with quasi-reverence as possessing a mighty power to reward or punish the behavior of men towards it, and found little difficulty in ignoring the impossibilities of what I professed. The experiment gradually succeeded; I began to feel and long retained for the picture a large share of the feelings that a barbarian entertains towards his idols, and learnt to appreciate the enormous potency they might have over him (p. 276).

In general, however, the development of the self seems to recapitulate the development of religion and science. The autistic child seeks to satisfy his thirst for religion and his hunger for science in the mythical and magical ways of primitive societies. The self-actualized adult satisfies these motives in ways consistent with the most advanced religions and the most modern science. The development of the self is the major theme of the next part.

SUMMARY

Religion and science follow different principles, use different methods, and seek to satisfy enduring, but different, human needs. Because they put their faith in traditional principles, the "religious" tend to be conforming and resistant to change. Because they put their faith in facts, the "scientific" tend to be skeptical, individualistic, and ready for change. The balance of an individual's faith seems largely determined by the values of his parents and the degree of his identification with them. The rise of encounter groups illustrates the concealed strength of the religious motive. The controversy over the reality of ESP demonstrates that the heat of the conflict is generated by the different metaphysical views of the religious and scientific. The development of an individual's religious or scientific views interacts with the development of his self.

SUGGESTIONS FOR FURTHER READING

*Hesse, H. (1951). *Siddhartha*. New York: New Directions. The author's books have attained a high level of popularity among college students and this is their favorite: "Brought me closer to Eastern thinking and beliefs than I have ever been before. . . . Hesse, eighteen years ago, wrote about what college students are searching for today. . . . packed with psychological insights and understanding."

*Allport, G. W. (1960). *The individual and his religion*. New York: Macmillan (paperback, Macmillan edition). Students report: "It provides a rational basis for an individual to evaluate and improve his own religious philosophy. . . . written twenty years ago it is still relevant to today's society."

James, W. (1936). *Varieties of religions experience*. New York: Modern Library. A readable classic on the psychology of religion. Deals, among other things, with the nature of mystical experiences and with the values and dangers of saintliness. Written with the belief that "a large acquaintance with particulars often makes us wiser than the possession of abstract formulas, however deep."

James, W. (1955). *Pragmatism*. New York: Meridian Books. In this famous book, James offers a philosophy for reconciling the conflicts between the religious and the scientific.

Answers for Table 8-5: Dellard (4), Bernard (3), Edgar (2), Form (1). Dellard, 90th percentile; Bernard, 40th percentile; Edgar, 30th percentile; and Form, 10th percentile.

Answers for Table 8-6: 1 (F), 2 (T), 3 (F), 4 (F), 5 (T), 6 (T), 7 (F), 8 (F), 9 (F), 10 (T), 11 (T), 12 (T), 13 (T), 14 (F), 15 (T), 16 (F), 17 (T), 18 (F), 19 (T), 20 (T).

THREE

THE SELF
AS PERSONALITY

The attainment of unity depends more upon
knowing what one wants than upon getting it.
It is striving toward the known goal that
confers unity, not the successful arrival . . .
unity lies only in the struggle for unity.

GORDON ALLPORT

9

THE DEVELOPMENT
OF THE SELF

There is first of all a stream of experiences, which is indifferent in respect to the I-thou and which contains factual contents of the ego and of the other ego in undifferentiated mixture; and in this stream there gradually form the clearly defined eddies which slowly draw new elements of the stream into their circles and in this process are correlated with successive and very gradually differentiated individuals.

MAX F. SCHOLER

Personality traits make valuable distinctions between individuals. They reveal that Ibsen was cautious and Shackleton bold; Freud was calm, James emotional; Thoreau was artistic and Morgan practical; Thomas was present-minded and Washington future-minded; and King was religious and Hume scientific. At best, however, traits only describe how individuals differ from each other. They do not describe how the traits are related to each other within the individual. In fact, where a person stands in relation to other people on any of the traits discussed in the last part of the book has *no* relation to how he will stand on the other traits.

This part views personality from the radically different structural perspective. It stresses the dynamic organization of the self. The trait view stresses the qualities that distinguish *between* individuals; the structural, the organization of qualities *within* the individual.

Some psychologists are enthusiastic advocates of the former approach; some, of the latter. Discussions between the two groups sometimes become heated. Advocates of the trait view are likely to describe it as *objective, reliable, rigorous, scientific down-to-earth, hardheaded,* and *sound,* and to describe the structural view as *mystical, vague, hazy, crude, sloppy,* and *muddleheaded.* In turn the structural advocates use such adjectives as *dynamic, global, sympathetic, genuine, live,* and *true to life* in describing their view and such words as *cut-and-dried, dead, rigid, oversimplified,* and *pseudoscientific* to describe the trait approach. The friction is scientifically valuable, for it generates the heat required to test more fully the usefulness of the two approaches.

This chapter introduces the structural view by examining the questions: What is the self? How does it develop? Why does it develop?

WHAT IS THE SELF?

The "self," says the dictionary, is the total, essential, or particular being of one person. Though often used as a synonym for personality, the word stresses an individual's *consciousness* of what he is. The word is popular. Subjectively, a person experiences the elation and joy of success and the disappointment of failure. He congratulates himself or others for a job well done. He condemns himself or others for mistakes. He feels he makes decisions and he feels the sorrows of bad ones and the joys of good ones. He needs "self" to communicate these feelings that are central in his life. Nearly a hundred hyphenated forms of the word appear in the dictionary, ranging from self-abnegation and self-abuse to self-willed and self-winding.

For the past half century, the word has been unpopular among psychologists. With the development of the empirical orientation and the experimental methods of behavioristic psychology, what a person *does* was increasingly stressed, not what he thought he was. The behaviorists view the self as an "empty black box" whose contents are unimportant, unhelpful, and misleading. They warn against the errors into which a self psychology can lead us. They were convinced that a strictly objective attitude was the only possible way to advance our scientific understanding of people. But decades of radical behaviorism have failed to produce the expected advances. It has clarified the pitfalls in a self psychology; it has not solved the problems raised by it. Without a self, without introspection, and without an immediate awareness of feelings and thoughts, we could not even define the field of human psychology. Consequently, psychologists are returning to the problems of the self raised long ago by William James (1890).

Psychologists have slowly learned a truth taught by the behaviorists—the only scientifically useful concepts are those that are, or can be, measured. The measurement of the real or actual self is a baffling task. A person cannot discriminate between what he thinks he is and what he actually is: How can he know what he does not know about himself? Still, he confidently assumes that what he sees himself to be is what he actually is. However, he does not make this assumption about others, for he sees that the way others perceive themselves is oversimplified, distorted, and often erroneous. Rather, he assumes that the way *he* perceives the other person is the way the other person really is. But this, too, is a dubious assumption, for our impressions of others are also likely to be oversimplified, distorted, and mistaken.

Consequently, the self as here defined is *a person as he feels, perceives, and thinks of himself.* Just as a person sees objects and other people, so he can perceive himself. Just as his perceptions of objects and other people are never entirely complete and accurate, so his perceptions of himself are never entirely complete and accurate. The self defined in this way *does* permit us to measure aspects of the self. Individuals perceive themselves as cautious or bold, unemotional or emotional, present-minded or future-minded, artistic or practical, religious or scientific. With such measures, we can examine the relationships between the perceived self and the actual self. Thus, we can study the relationship between the individual's perception of his boldness and the boldness of his social behavior, the relationship between his perceptions of his emotionality and his physiological behavior, etc. With such measures, we can begin to study the way the self is organized and how the organization develops.

SELF-OTHER DIFFERENTIATION

How does the self develop? Many artists have answered the question. *The Confessions of St. Augustine* portrayed the agonies of development with an intensity that has never been exceeded; James T. Farrell illuminated the developmental struggles of a Roman Catholic boy in *Studs Lonigan* far beyond the powers of a psychologist; Richard Wright described the problems of development for a ghetto Negro with almost physical impact in *Native Son*; Marquand's work pictured with acidity what it was like to develop in the upper strata of New England and New York society; at a simpler level, Robert Anderson's *Tea and Sympathy* dramatizes the way in which one adolescent learned what masculinity is and is not. The list is so impressive that one might conclude that the task is best left to the artists.

The artist and the psychologist, however, are not in conflict, for they seek to describe the developing person from different perspectives, by different methods, and with different goals in mind. The artist strives to illuminate and communicate what a person feels and experiences as he is developing. The scientist tries to answer the questions: What is to happen to him next? The theory of self-other differentiation is one answer to this question. What is going to happen to the self next? A one word answer is: differentiate. Differentiation is the process of developing from the one to the many, from the simple to the complex, from the homogeneous to the heterogeneous. The fertilized cell differentiates; i.e., the single cell divides, redivides, and continues to redivide as the organism develops. Organisms differentiate as they climb the phylogenetic scale. The amoeba produces a mouth, a hand, a foot, or an arm by changing its entire shape. In higher animals biological functions become specialized and assigned to more permanently segregated systems. These differentiated structures adapt more effectively than the more primitive structures. The behavior of the developing infant, too, gradually becomes more differentiated. His random twisting and squirming differentiates into more and more precise patterns of reaching, gesturing, and talking.

Awareness also grows and, in the process, differentiates. The infant, as Figure 9-1 suggests, is conscious of his immediate life space but is not aware of the difference between his self and the external world. As he develops, his awareness expands. As it does, as the dotted circle suggests, the child begins to differentiate his self from the external world. This process begins by his differentiating within the external world; i.e., he sees the difference between his mother, his father, and others in the environment. Later and more gradually, he differentiates within himself, i.e., he becomes aware of the difference between feeling hungry and feeling tired, pained, or angry. Still, the shadowed ellipses suggest he has little ability to differentiate between what he wants and what others want, what he feels and what others feel, between his dreams and reality. As his self develops (the dark and white circles in the "adult" diagram), he develops the ability to differentiate what is inside from what is outside. However, as three dotted lines are meant to show, this process is never complete. The

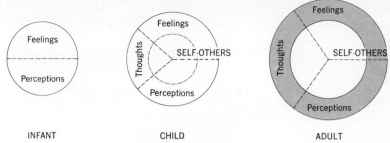

Figure 9-1 A diagram of the theory of self-other differentiation. The infant has awareness, but not of self; the child, an awareness of his self, but not of the difference between himself and others; and the adult, an awareness of the difference between what he sees, feels, and thinks and what others see, feel, and think.

most highly developed individual sometimes fails to differentiate, i.e., confuses what he feels and thinks with what others feel and think.

This theory of self-other differentiation has the virtue of simplicity. It has the greater virtue, as the following chapters indicate, of fitting together many vital facts about the developing self and suggesting new facts to look for. Its least obvious but greatest scientific virtue is that self-other differentiation can be measured.

Differentiation from the Physical World

The body, said James, "is the innermost part of the *material* Self in each of us; and certain parts of the body seem more intimately ours than the rest." The infant, however, seems to have little ability to differentiate between his physical self and his physical environment (Figure 9-2). He treats his own body as if were foreign to him. He plays with his toes like toys and claws his own face until it bleeds. The work of Witkin and his associates (1954) showed that adults still differ widely in their ability to differentiate their physical selves from the physical world. These authors measured "field independence" by a variety of tests, including block designs, embedded figures, and the tilting room described below.

The Tilting-Room–Tilting-Chair Test This device for measuring field independence is shown in the photograph (Figure 9-3). In testing a subject, the room and chair are first tilted to set positions while the subject keeps his eyes closed. The experimenter then asks him to open his eyes. On some trials he is now asked to bring himself and the chair to the true upright while the room remains tilted. On other trials, he is asked to bring the *room* to the true upright while he remains tilted in

Figure 9-2 Self-other differentiation implies that the child learns to impose a certain structure upon the world as she perceives it. At first, she and the sand are the same; as she matures, she will learn that her physical surroundings are not the same as her physical self. Similarly, she will differentiate between her social surroundings—other people—and her self. (Michigan Tourist Council)

the chair. The score in both cases is the difference between the degrees the chair or the room is actually tilted and the degrees the subject tilts them. A high score is a measure of field dependence; a low score, a measure of field independence.

The performance of Oliver, an extreme field-dependent type, was described as follows:

> . . . Again reflects striking field dependence. In both room-adjustment series he accepted the room as upright at extreme positions of tilt. In series 1a (room and chair initially tilted to the same side) the room was tilted an average of 40° when reported to be straight, and in series 1b (room and chair initially tilted to opposite sides) an average of 52°. Thus, here again he passively accepted the prevailing field at or close to the position of tilt in which it was presented (56°) without any

Figure 9-3 Equipment used in the measurement of field independence. The subject sits in the chair which is then tilted from the vertical position. The independent person is not influenced by the tilt of the "room" when he is asked to move his chair back to the vertical position. (Courtesy Dr. H. A. Witkin)

real attempt at actively relating field position to body position . . . he was at the extreme of his group with regard to extent of adherence to the field.

The performance of Hedda, an extreme field-independent type, was described as follows:

She made very effective use of her body in determining the position of the surrounding room. She brought the room, initially tilted a 56°, to within an average of 7° of the true upright in Series 1a . . . and 8° in Series 1b. . . . The greatest amount by which the room was tilted on any trial at the time she reported it to be upright was 12°. In determining the position of her body, she effectively maintained the "separate-ness" of body and field. On retest a year later her performance again showed extreme independence of the field.

The results of the tilting-room–tilting-chair test were quite consistent with other information about Oliver and Hedda. Oliver, for example, was described as follows:

> He has pathetic inferiority feelings, which often make him fearful of his own inadequacy. Consistent with this is his constant anxiety; his tendency to denial and constriction of inner life; his characteristic handling of hostility by repression and reaction formation; his extreme disturbance over, and fear of, sexual impulses; and his conformity to authority's expecta-tions and related concern with the opinion of others of him.

His need to be accepted and liked and his sensitivity to the opinion of others are illustrated by his responses to the sentence-completion test:

> (My greatest worry is) making a hit with people.
>
> (I feel ashamed when) I have to go to a friend's house for the first time.

By contrast, Hedda was described in this way:

> Her autobiography is a very frank document which almost flaunts her "faults" and problems. It contains no apologies—the document itself is a first draft which contains "my thoughts just as they came to me." It states that she was thoroughly "spoiled" as a child and that she very early "exhibited domineering qualities." From the time of childhood playmates she has been the "iron hand in the velvet glove." She still is. She must be in control of a situation, and she obtains considerable pleasure in exerting her power—her chief weapon at the moment being her good looks.

Measures of independence of the physical environment are related to mental and physical health. Studies of obese women, asthmatic children, ulcer patients, and alcoholics show them to be much more field dependent than the average person. In one study, 24 women alcoholics were matched with 24 women of the same age, education, and religion who were not alcoholics. Both groups com-pleted four different tests designed to measure field dependence (Karp,

Poster, and Goodman, 1963). Result: The scores of the alcoholic women showed more field dependence on all four of the tests.

Differentiation from the Social World

The most direct method of measuring self-other differentiation is to ask: How different are you from other people? Wegner (1971) developed a variety of measures of this type. The shortest was to ask: Is your mother similar or dissimilar to you? Is your father similar or dissimilar to you? Those who reported that one parent was similar were highly likely to report that the other parent was similar too.

Wegner also gave the Test of Self-Other Differentiation, the first part of which is shown in Table 9-1. Students were highly consistent in their degree of self-other differentiation. That is, if they said the typical man would like or dislike the same things that they did, they were very likely to say that the typical woman and the particular man and woman would also be similar to them. Furthermore, those who differentiate themselves from their father and mother were also likely to differentiate themselves from the typical man and woman and the particular man and woman.

Those who differentiated themselves from others also differentiated themselves from the physical environment. The students who took the tests of self-other differentiation also completed three tests of field independence (the Embedded Figures Test, the Block Design Test, and the Concealed Figures Test). Those who obtained higher scores on the former also obtained higher scores on the latter three.

TABLE 9-1   Test of Self-Other Differentiation

Your "empathy" is your tendency to assume similarity between yourself and others. That is, when you empathize, you assume that another person's feelings are similar to your own. Without empathy we could not understand others. With empathy, however, we still sometimes misunderstand others because we incorrectly assume similarity.

This is a test of your empathic accuracy, the correctness of your assumptions of similarity and dissimilarity to others. The test has four parts: (1) empathy with the typical man; (2) empathy with the typical woman; (3) empathy with Naomi Warren, a particular woman; and (4) empathy with Harold Warren, a particular man.

Part I. YOU AND THE TYPICAL MAN
The replies of thousands of American men to each of the interests below have been analyzed. In making their replies they were asked to disregard as much as they could considerations of salary, social status, and possibilities of

future advancement. They were asked to consider only whether they would like or dislike the interest, regardless of any necessary skills, abilities, or training.

Ask yourself these two questions about each of the interests below:

    A. Do I like the interest more than I dislike it or do I dislike it more than I like it?

    B. Would the majority of American men say that they liked the interest more than they disliked it or would they say they disliked it more than they liked it?

Mark "1" (like-like)	If you *like* the interest and also think that the typical man would *like* it.
Mark "2" (dislike-dislike)	If you *dislike* the interest and also think the typical man would *dislike* it.
Mark "3" (like-dislike)	If you *like* the interest but think the typical man would *dislike* it.
Mark "4" (dislike-like)	If you *dislike* the interest but think the typical man would *like* it.

1. Auto salesman
2. Talkative people
3. Civil service employee
4. Algebra
5. Dentist
6. Factory worker
7. Jeweler
8. Life insurance salesman
9. Pharmacist
10. Real estate salesman
11. Printer
12. Politician

Note: Algebra is the only one that most men said they liked.

(*Source*: Smith, 1973)

Thus, people vary widely and consistently in whether they see most people as pretty much like themselves or quite different from themselves. Furthermore, the former tend to be field dependent; the latter, field independent. The critical question, however, is: How *accurate* are people in their self-other differentiations? For example, those who would like being an "auto salesman" might assume that the typical man also would like it when he actually does not. On the other hand, those who would dislike being an auto salesman might assume that the typical man likes it when he does not. Wegner obtained the accuracy scores of each of his students on the test in Table 9-1. On the basis of their field independence test scores, he then divided them into a group who were *low* in field independence, *moderate* in field independence, and *high* in field independence. He then determined the accuracy of the self-other differentiations of the three groups. The *moderate* group was most accurate; the *low* and *high* groups, least accurate.

Every person is like every other person in many ways; he is also unlike every other person in many ways. Thus, the development of self-other differentiation is not a simple process of gradually seeing more and more differences between ourselves and others. It is the complex process of differentiating the ways in which we are actually like others and how much we are like them from the ways in which we are unlike them and how much we are unlike them.

Stability of the Self

Those who are undifferentiated change their views as their environment changes. On the other hand, those who clearly and firmly differentiate themselves from the world around them maintain a relatively constant view of themselves. Thus, the less a person changes his view of himself from one time to another, the more likely he is to differentiate himself from others. The Self-Image Questionnaire (Heath, 1965) offers a relatively simple way of measuring self-other differentiation in this indirect way.

The measure consists of a series of rating scales such as the following:

CAUTIOUS

Avoids the strange and new. Looks at all aspects of a situation over-cautiously. Plays it safe.

ADVENTUROUS

Seeks and readily enters into new experiences and situations. May show a good deal of initiative; enjoys risks.

Among the 29 other pairs of adjectives in the scale are: anxious versus placid; imaginative versus unimaginative; undercontrols impulses versus overcontrols impulses; and dependent versus self-sufficient.

In using the questionnaire Heath first asked students to rate themselves on each of the 30 traits on an eight-point scale (i.e., from 1, very cautious, to 8, very adventurous). At a later time, they repeated their ratings on the same traits. The measure of stability of the self-image is the sum of differences between the two occasions. The smaller the sum of these differences, the greater the stability of the self-image.

Haverford College students generally had a tendency to rate themselves in the same way on the Heath scales from one time to another (repeat reliabilities ranged from .64 to .88). They differed, however, in the strength of the tendency. These differences were related to many other aspects of their behavior. The questionnaire measures of stability agreed with ratings of the stability made by professors who knew the students well. Stability scores were also related to academic competence—the higher the scores, the higher their grades. This measure of stability appeared to be the most promising among dozens that were tried. Thus far, however, it has been tried on only a small number of men attending one small private college.

The five-trait scales discussed in the last section could be used in a similar way. As we have seen, most people have a stable view of their degree of boldness, emotionality, future-mindedness, practicality, and scientific orientation. Yet some students do vary markedly from one time to another. The degree of this variation would be a measure of the degree of the stability of the self-image.

STAGES OF SELF-OTHER DIFFERENTIATION

Like the body, the self develops through stages (Figure 9-4). A stage of physical development has three essential characteristics. First, a stage *builds on earlier stages and prepares for future ones.* Thus, the five-year stage of physical development arises from the physique that the child had as an infant and prepares for the physique he will have as an adult. Second, *a later stage is more complex than earlier ones.* The physique of the five-year-old is more complex than the physique of the infant and less complex than the physique of the adult. Third, *each stage is part of an invariable order*—no stage can be skipped by anyone. The physical development of the individual requires that he go through an unchanging and universal series of stages.

The principles that govern the stages of physical development also govern the stages of behavioral development. The standing stage builds upon the creeping stage and prepares for the walking stage. Standing is more complicated than creeping and less complicated than walking. The stages have an invariable order for all people: No infant has ever gone from the creeping stage to the walking stage without going through the standing stage.

The development of self, too, goes through stages that obey the same principles. The assumption, however, is far less certain than for physical or behavioral development. We can observe the stages of physical and behavioral development, whereas we can only infer the stages of personality development. The stage approach provides a simple, comprehensive, and useful way of viewing the complicated total process of personality development.

Loevinger (1966) has advanced the theory that there are six stages of self-other differentiation: the autistic, the impulse-ridden, the opportunistic, the conforming, the conscientious and the self-

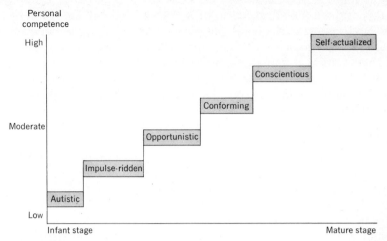

Figure 9-4 Stages in the development of the self.

actualized. These stages occur in an invariable order. One cannot, that is, skip a stage; one cannot be a conformist until one has been an opportunist. Each stage provides the foundation for the next stage. Thus, the techniques developed by the opportunist are needed to build a conformist. Finally, a later stage is more complex and adaptive than an earlier one. The next chapters describe each of these stages in detail. They are introduced here to stress the common thread of developing self-other differentiation that runs through them.

The Autistic Stage

At this stage, there is no self-other differentiation. What the world looks like to an infant at this stage is difficult to imagine. It seems likely that it is not a "blooming, buzzing, confusion." Since the infant cannot shift his attention as rapidly as adults, it is likely that it is a limited and quiet world. When the baby is watching his mother, he probably does not hear sounds around him; when he is attending to a hunger pain, he may not feel his mother's touch. His world may be made up of single perceptions.

Our dreaming world is like the waking world of the autistic. As in our dreams, the autistic cannot distinguish what is on his mind from what is in the world.

The Impulse-ridden Stage

The developing dependence of infants force them to learn to differentiate persons from things and caretaking persons from strangers. While the impulse-ridden have learned to differentiate some aspects of their external environment, they have not learned to differentiate between their desires. The intensity of the desire of the moment is their only guide. They cannot differentiate between what they want now and what they will want in an hour. They cannot differentiate between one kind of wish and another kind. Above all, they cannot differentiate between what they want and what others want. They are solely preoccupied with immediate rewards; they are only deterred by the threat of immediate punishment.

The hallmark of the impulse-ridden stage is the temper tantrum. A tantrum is a violent response to deprivation. The child may kick, beat his head on the floor, scratch himself, or hold his breath. He may do all of these things simultaneously. His rage is sometimes so violent and his contact with reality so slight that he seems to be almost unconscious. To the objective observer, the deprivation generally seems to be slight and out of all proportion to the violence that accompanies it. The child seems totally overpowered by the impulse that has been blocked. Tantrums reach their peak incidence somewhere between the ages of three and six. It is commonly assumed that the child is using the tantrum to manipulate people so that he can get what he wants. Quite often, however, the child attempts to inflict pain upon himself rather than the adult who is frustrating him. That is, the tantrum is a way of punishing *himself*, for he feels that he is the source of his own unhappiness. If he did not want something so badly he would not be so miserable. Thus, it often seems as if the child were beating out of himself the impulses that had brought about the unpleasantness.

The Opportunistic Stage

As with the impulse-ridden, the intensity of their desire is the only guide of opportunists. Unlike the impulse-ridden, however, opportunists can differentiate between their immediate and long-run desires. Most unlike the impulse-ridden, they sharply differentiate between what they want from what others want. Loevinger (1966) describes the stage in this way:

> It is understood that there are rules, but they are obeyed in terms of immediate advantage. Thus the morality is purely an expedient one. What is bad is to be caught. Interpersonal relations are manipulative and exploitive, but there is a marked shift away from dependence. The small child says, "Do it by self," and the adolescent at this stage says, "Who needs them?" Conscious preoccupation is with control and advantage, dom-

ination, deception, getting the better of, and so on. Life is a zero-sum game; what you win, I lose.

The Conformist Stage

Self-development, like physical and behavioral development, is slow and continuous. Consequently, those at the conforming stage differentiate within the external world, within themselves, and between the external world and themselves more fully and realistically than does the opportunist. However, the continuity of differentiation is punctuated by abrupt qualitative shifts. The conformists not only live in a larger world; but also in a different *kind* of world. The center of the worlds of the opportunist and conformist lies in their immediate and primarily biological needs. The new world of the conformist, however, focuses upon a different kind of need, the need to follow the rules (Loevinger, 1966):

At this stage the rules are partially internalized. They are obeyed just because they are rules. Chief sanction for transgression is shame, contrasting with the opportunistic stage preceding, which is often described by others (but not by those in it) as shameless. Genuine interpersonal reciprocity is possible now, reciprocity is, after all, the Golden Rule. In many cases, however, the mutual trust is extended only to a narrowly conceived ingroup. There may be strong prejudice against various outgroups conceived in stereotyped terms. Interpersonal relations are seen primarily in terms of actions rather than of feelings and motives. Conscious preoccupation is with material things, with reputation and status, with appearance, and with adjustment. References to inner feelings are typically stereotyped, banal, and often moralistic.

The Conscientious Stage

From the conforming to the conscientious stage, there is a slow internalizing of rules in the slowly differentiating self. Finally, the psychological world tips as a see-saw shifts when one walks up and past its center. When it does, the rules start coming from a different place. For the conformist, rules are rules: his rules are the group's rules; the group's rules are his rules; the group wants him to follow its rules, and he wants to follow the group's rules. The conscientious person differentiates his rules from social rules. He obeys his own rules, even when his obedience to them is condemned by society (Loevinger, 1966):

Morality has been internalized. Inner moral imperatives take precedence over group-sanctioned rules. The sanction for transgression is guilt. Interpersonal relations are seen in terms of feelings and traits rather than actions; they become more vivid, intensive, and meaningful than in earlier periods. Conscious preoccupation is with obligations, ideals, traits, and achievement as measured by inner standards rather than by recognition alone. Conduct is seen not simply as a series of actions, but as a set of enduring propensities; spontaneous interest in the origins of their conduct is often expressed by unsophisticated subjects at this stage. Capacity for self-criticism characterizes this stage; its absence, the conformist stage.

The Self-actualized Stage

The fully self-actualized self is a theoretical necessity, not a reality, for the process of differentiation is a never-ending one. At the beginning of this stage the characteristic moral issue is how to cope with inner conflicts, conflicting duties, and conflict between needs and duties (Loevinger, 1966):

> Such conflicts, although quite evidently present at earlier periods, including the conscientious one, are not squarely and consciously coped with earlier. Along with coping with one's own conflicts comes greater toleration for those choosing other solutions than one's own, in contrast with the moral condemnation frequent in conscientious and conformist stages. Interpersonal relations remain intense, they involve a recognition of inevitable mutual interdependence, and, a crucial addition, they involve the recognition of other people's need for autonomy.

DIFFERENTIATION THROUGH SYMBOLIZATION

Every human being develops a self. Just as he learns to feel, perceive and think of things, he learns to feel, perceive, and think of himself in an increasingly differentiated way. How does he learn to do so?

No animal develops a self. Why not? Animals, like men, have a receptor system that receives stimuli from the environment and an effector system that responds to them. Man, unlike any animal, has a *symbolic system* between the receptor and effector systems. This system transforms the whole of human life. Compared with other animals, man does not live just in a broader reality; he lives in a new dimension of reality. Through the use of symbols, man may become as different from an ape as an ape is different from a tree. It is through advances in the use of symbols that man advances from the autistic, to the impulse-ridden, to still higher stages of self differentiation. But what is a symbol?

A symbol is anything that *designates* something else. Words are symbols; numbers are symbols; paintings are symbols; maps are symbols; musical compositions are symbols; flags are symbols; funeral services are symbols. A symbol is part of a symbolic *system*: "10" is part of a numerical system; "personality" is part of a language system; and a marriage ceremony is part of a religious symbolic system. Any particular symbolic system is potentially *universal*: anything may be designated by a number, anything may be designated by a word, and anything may be designated by a ritual. Symbolic systems are *versatile*. Not only can the same thing be designated by numbers, words, or rituals but also by different words, different numbers, or different rituals.

A sign is *not* a symbol. A sign does not designate, but operates. It is not social, but physical. It is not functional, but substantive. And it is not part of a system that is versatile and universal. The difference between a sign and a symbol is illustrated by the experience of a major who had a dog which accompanied him on his walks. Whenever the master got ready to go out the animal showed signs of joy and excitement. But one day the major decided to try an experiment. He put on his hat, took his cane, and made the customary preparations— without, however, having any intention of going for a walk. To his surprise, the dog remained quietly in his corner. Why? In the major's room there was a desk with a drawer which contained some valuable and important documents. The major had formed the habit of rattling this drawer before leaving the house in order to make sure that it was safely locked. He did not do so on the day he did not intend to go out. But for the dog this had become a necessary *sign* of the walk-situation. Without this signal, the dog did not react. The rattling was not a product of social invention but a physical activity; not a functional, but a substantive thing. Rattling could not designate anything else; nothing else could designate walking for the dog.

It is a giant step from using signs to using symbols. This is dramatically illustrated by a critical incident in the life of blind and deaf Helen Keller, as told by her teacher. She wrote of Helen at the age of seven (Keller, 1908, p. 815):

I must write you a line this morning because something very important has happened. Helen has taken the second great step in her education. She had learned that everything has a name, and that the manual alphabet is the key to everything she wants to know. . . . This morning, while she was washing, she wanted to know the name for "water". . . . I spelled "w-a-t-e-r"

in Helen's free hand. The word came so close upon the
sensation of cold water rushing over her hand it seemed to
startle her. She dropped the mug and stood as one transfixed. A
new light came into her face. She spelled "water" several times.
Then she dropped on the ground and asked for its name and
pointed to the pump and the trellis and suddenly turning round
she asked for my name. I spelled "teacher." All the way back to
the house she was highly excited, and learned the name of
every object she touched, so that in a few hours she had added
thirty new words to her vocabulary. The next morning she got
up like a radiant fairy. She has flitted from object to object,
asking the name of everything and kissing me for very
gladness . . .

Previously, she had learned to associate a specific thing with a specific
sign of the alphabet. Now, she had learned that manual signs were not
restricted to specific things but were symbols of universal applicability,
that *everything* has a name. The whole human world began to unfold to
her and her self development had begun.

Chimpanzees are on the border between the sign world of
animals and the symbolic world of humans. They can learn relationships; i.e., they can pick the smallest, brightest, or greenest object. With
more difficulty, they can learn to abstract a particular perceptual
quality; i.e., they can pick from a variety of objects all of those with the
same color. They have an emotional language so that they can express
and communicate their feelings by posture, gesture, or cry. They have a
high level of practical intelligence: they can adapt to or modify their
environment by the use of tools and even invent tools. No chimpanzee
has ever learned to speak more than a few words even after the most
assiduous training. Many, however, have been taught more than a
hundred gestures in sign language. Yet they stick to their immediate
needs and their present situation. They can use the language in dealing
with the concrete, but not with the abstract; with the actual, but not
with the possible; and with the real, but not with the ideal. They have
the buds of a symbolic system which has never flowered.

The development of an individual's symbolic ability determines the development of his self. By the use of symbols, he can recall
the past, deal with things not in his immediate environment, and
project his experience into the future. He can learn from the experience
of others, forecast the consequences of his own behavior, and have
ideals. He can learn to control himself rather than be controlled by the
accidents of his environment or the force of external authority. With
symbolic ability, above all, he can develop insight into the world of

physical and social reality as well as into the private world within himself. Studies of age differences in vocabulary support the view that symbolic skill continues to grow throughout the life of the individual. A group of 127 men who as college freshmen took the Army Alpha Test (which stresses the understanding of concepts) took the same test again when nearly fifty (Owens, 1953). Their scores were higher when they were fifty. More than a thousand superior adults took a concept mastery test again after about twelve years (Bayley and Oden, 1955). Scores at later ages were higher than at earlier ones. The oldest subject was a man retested at the age of seventy. He improved.

Language is the oldest symbolic system of man and the one earliest acquired by the child. The infant's transition from the autistic to the impulse-ridden stage is inevitably accompanied by the ability to use language. As his ability to use language increases, his ability to differentiate between himself and the world increases. Language develops to serve human interests and purposes. Since nothing is more interesting and important to the child than other people, he soon learns that some people are "nice" and some are "mean," that some are "friendly" and some are "greedy." As he develops, his common-sense theory of personality becomes more elaborate and precise. As it does, he becomes increasingly able to differentiate between himself and others.

The central importance of linguistic and numerical ability has long been recognized by psychologists. Tests of the ability to understand and use verbal symbols are the oldest, the most numerous, and the most frequently used of all psychological tests. Vocabulary tests of verbal comprehension are the heart of most intelligence tests and an inevitable ingredient of all scholastic aptitude tests. Differences in verbal comprehension are comparatively easy to measure in a quick and dependable manner.

Tests of the ability to understand and use quantitative symbols are almost as prevalent as verbal tests. Differences in this ability are also easily and dependably measured. The range in this ability is at least as great as the range in verbal ability. Consequently, tests may vary from measuring the ability to do simple arithmetic problems to the ability to solve complicated mathematical problems.

While most tests of symbolic ability stress the use of words, some do not. In his analysis of the items occurring in intelligence tests, Thurstone (1938) isolated these relatively independent primary mental abilities:

Verbal comprehension (V): ability to define and understand words

Word fluency (W): ability to think rapidly of words as in extemporaneous speech or solving crossword puzzles

Space (S): ability to draw a design from memory or to visualize relationships

Number (N): ability to do arithmetic problems

Memory (M): ability to memorize and recall

Perceptual (P): ability to grasp visual details and to see differences and similarities among objects

Reasoning (R): ability to find rules, principles, or concepts for understanding or solving problems

Each of these abilities represents skill in the manipulation of different kinds of symbols in different ways. The more completely these different kinds of symbols are represented in a test, the more completely it will measure the individual's general symbolic ability.

The measurement of the ability to use artistic symbols has been neglected. The measurement of the ability to use behavior symbolically has been almost totally neglected.

DEVELOPMENT, RETARDATION, AND REGRESSION

The individual develops by learning to represent and manipulate his feelings, thoughts, and actions by the aid of symbols. How does he learn, or fail to learn, or forget what he has learned about the symbolic systems? What he has learned determines his stage of development. What he *can* learn, however, depends upon his stage of development.

There is an invariable sequence in the development of ways of learning. The autistic can only become impulse-ridden by learning to depend upon others. The impulse-ridden become opportunistic by learning to imitate the behavior of others; the opportunistic can only become conformists by identifying with others; and the conformist can only become conscientious by identifying with ideas. Just as there are lower and higher stages of self-development, so there are lower and higher ways of learning. While the autistic can only learn to be dependent, the impulse-ridden can learn by imitating as well as by depending. The opportunistic can learn by identifying with people as well as by imitating and depending. And the conformist can learn by identifying with ideas as well.

The development of the self may be retarded at any stage. Thus, the autistic can learn to become dependent, but he may not; the impulse-ridden can learn to imitate, but he may not; the opportunistic can learn to identify with others, but he may not; and the conformist can learn to identify with ideas, but he may not. The nature of these retarding conditions are also explored in the following chapters.

The self may develop or it may be retarded. Even when it has developed, it may regress; i.e., it may return to an earlier stage. Under the pressure of physical fatigue and sleeplessness, of continued frustration, or of emotional stress, the self reverts to an earlier stage of feeling, thinking, and behaving—the conformist becomes again an opportunist; the opportunist, impulse-ridden; the impulse-ridden, autistic. Resistance to these regressive pressures vary a great deal, but no one is immune. Under the strain of violent and prolonged emotion, we all move back toward the autistic view of the world. We no longer see people in an objective way. We see them as benevolent or malignant, as friendly or hostile, as familiar or strange, as alluring or threatening. Our selves become submerged in the high seas of undifferentiated awareness.

One of the great services of Freud was his clarification of the mechanisms that the self uses to defend its integrity in times of stress. Indeed, "regression" itself is one of them. The mechanism that Freud considered the key to all the others, "repression," has already been discussed (see Chapter 5). Freud's own definition of the mechanism of repression, suppression, and regression are included in Table 9-2,

---

TABLE 9-2   Freud and the Mechanisms
The quotations below are from Freud's work. The blanks indicate the omissions of words referring to the mechanisms of *repression, suppression, aggression, projection, fantasy,* or *regression.* Fill in the correct words. Correct answers are given at the end of the chapter.

1. _____ is the process by which a mental act capable of becoming conscious (that is, one which belongs to the preconscious system) is made unconscious and forced back into the unconscious system.

2. _____ demands a constant expenditure of energy.

3. We have been concerned exclusively with the fate of the idea to be repressed. . . . But we have so far ignored the question of what happened to the affect attached to this idea . . . it is the immediate fate of the affect to be converted into anxiety. . . . This transformation of affect is, moreover, by far the most important effect of the process of _____.

4. We may say that _____ is to the other methods of defense what the omission of words or passages is to the corruption of a text.

5. The limitation of _____ is the first and perhaps the hardest sacrifice which society demands from each individual.

6.   Now, if I turn back to the dream, I often find it colourless and devoid of any very intense affective tone. . . . I might say that a _____ of the affects has been accomplished by the dream-work.

7.   That is why he takes such pains to _____, i.e., to transfer outwards, all that becomes troublesome to him from within.

8.   A wife who is ignorant of her own impulses to ruin her husband and subjectively convinced that she is most devoted may, because of _____, consider her husband to be a brute wanting to harm her.

9.   It is a matter of everyday experience that fidelity, especially that degree of it required in marriage, is only maintained in the face of continual temptation. Anyone who denies this in himself will nevertheless be impelled so strongly in the direction of infidelity that he will be glad enough to make use of _____ as an alleviation.

10.   This unknown hostility, of which we are ignorant and of which we do not wish to know, is _____ from our inner perception into the outer world and is thereby detached from our own person and attributed to the other.

11.   Dreaming is on the whole an act of _____ to the earliest relationships of the dreamer.

12.   The associations of the patients went back from the scene to be explained, to earlier experiences, and forced the analysis which was to correct the present, to occupy itself with the past. This _____ led even further backward.

13.   When the human being grows up and ceases to play he only gives up the connection with real objects; instead of playing he then begins to create _____.

14.   Object selection is first accomplished in the imagination, for the sexual life of the maturing youth hardly finds any escape except through an indulgence in _____; that is, in ideas which are not destined to be brought to execution.

15.   Analysis enables the mature ego, which by this time has attained a greater strength, to review these old _____ with the result that some are lifted, while others are accepted but reconstructed from more solid material.

---

along with three other mechanisms not yet referred to: aggression, projection, and fantasy. So familiar are these terms, that the reader may already be able to match the mechanisms to Freud's statement about it. Reaction formation and compensation are other Freudian mechanisms that will be referred to in the following chapters.

Figure 9-5 Because the defense mechanisms are unconscious and overlapping, they are hard to separate and identify. The batter thought the pitcher had thrown a "bean ball" (repression and projection?) and started toward the mound (aggression!) but was stopped by the umpire. He is now arguing with him (rationalization?). Later, he struck out (regression?). (Wide World Photos)

The particular mechanisms used by a person under stress give a clue to the stage of development he has reached and is regressing from. Thus, fantasy and projection are associated with the autistic stage and will be discussed in the next chapter; negativism and aggression, with the impulse-ridden stage; rationalization, with the opportunistic stage; reaction formation, with the conformist stage; and compensation and over-compensation, with the conscientious stage (Figure 9-5).

SUMMARY

The self, a person as he sees and thinks of himself, develops in an invariable sequence from the autistic through the impulse-ridden, opportunistic, conforming, and conscientious stages to the self-actualized stage. Each stage provides necessary preparation for the next one. As a person develops through these stages he becomes increasingly able to discriminate himself from others. His capacity to make these discriminations depends upon his mastery of linguistic, quantitative, artistic, and religious symbols and symbolic systems. He may be retarded at any stage of development by his failure to achieve this mastery. He may regress to an earlier stage as a result of physical or psychological stress.

SUGGESTIONS FOR FURTHER READING

*Axline, V. (1964). *Dibs: in search of self*. Boston: Houghton Mifflin (paperback, Ballantine edition). At the top of the McCollom list of books that thrilled student readers: "Even though this book is written about a five year old, it does have a significance to a college student who is trying to find himself and his place in the world." Many students reported that they literally could not put it down until they finished reading it.

*Wilson, J. R. (ed.) (1964). *The mind*. New York: Time. Some students were initially suspicious of a picture-book approach but they liked the bird's eye view of the field. They particularly liked the picture essay on "Strange Landscapes from the Realm of Mental Illness" that includes a section on schizophrenic art.

Evans, Jean (1954). *Three men*. New York: Knopf. Cases which illustrate the effects of frustration and conflict in human development, presented in detail and with literary skill.

White, R. W. (1966). *Lives in progress: a study of the natural growth of personality*. New York: Holt. Fascinating case reports by an outstanding authority.

Answers to Table 9-2: 1. Repression   2. Repression   3. Repression   4. Repression   5. Aggression   6. Suppression   7. Project   8. Projection   9. Projection   10. Projected   11. Regression   12. Regression   13. Fantasy   14. Fantasy   15. Repression

10

AUTISTIC TO IMPULSE-RIDDEN

Every stage has its weaknesses, its problems
and its paradoxes, which provide both a potential
for maladjustment and potential for growth.

JANE LOEVINGER

Every infant begins at the autistic stage. Most develop beyond it, but some are retarded at it, and everyone sometimes regresses to it. What is the world of the autistic like? How do they develop to and beyond the impulse-ridden stage? Why do some fail to develop? When do adults return to this stage?

THE AUTISTIC STAGE

All of us live in two worlds: the subjective and private world of our feelings, perceptions, and thoughts; the objective and public world of things, people, and events. All of us find it hard to discriminate between these two worlds, between what is inside and what is outside our heads. The autistic find it extremely hard. They cannot discriminate mind from body, psychological from physical. Consequently, they believe that physical objects are endowed with consciousness and mental events have physical properties. Thus, a pre-school child may believe that dreams are made of wind. Unable to take the point of view of others, a young boy will admit that he has a brother but deny that his brother has a brother. The autistic think absolutely, not relatively. If they see that a brick is on top of a box, they cannot see that the box is on top of the ground. The less ability the individual has to differentiate between himself and others, then, the more autistic he is.

Autistic Symptoms

Those at the autistic stage cannot be impulse-ridden, opportunistic, conforming, or conscientious. However, those at these higher stages can, and often do, show signs of autism. The most central of these is an indifference to, or fear of, people. Dreaming, hallucinating, fantasizing, and projecting reveal more specific aspects of the autistic syndrome.

Dreams Dreaming is autistic. In a dream we can feel, see, hear, and think intensely; we cannot discriminate between the dream and reality. Everyone dreams, but the autistic live in a dream world. As the child develops beyond this stage he first recognizes that *dreams are not real events*. Soon afterward, he understands that *dreams are experiences that others cannot see*. Much later, he becomes aware that *dreams take place inside himself*. Finally, he sees that dreams are not caused by agencies, but *that he is the cause of his dreams*.

These dream stages seem to occur in all children in all cultures (Kohlberg, 1969). Among the Atayal, a Malaysian aboriginal group on Formosa, adults believe in the objective reality of dreams. Their children follow the same sequence as American children but at a slower pace. They do not reach as high a stage. As adults they regress.

Dream development seems to be an interaction between environmental mechanisms (Kohlberg, 1969, pp. 358–359):

The apparent invariant universal sequence in the development of the dream concept in the absence of adult cultural support cannot be interpreted as being the direct result of maturational unfolding, since the culture can "reverse" it by specific training. . . . A maturational interpretation is also contradicted by the fact that the Atayal children go through the same sequence more slowly than do their Taiwanese and American age-mates, presumably because the Atayal exists in a somewhat cognitively impoverished general culture.

Hallucinations   Hallucinating is another common form of autistic experience. We are hallucinating when we have a compelling sense that we are hearing, seeing, smelling, or touching something when there is nothing there to hear, see, or smell. We are hallucinating when we hear the phone ring when it hasn't, when we "see" someone in a crowd who is not there, when we smell gas when there is no gas. Almost any mother of a young infant will report hearing it cry only to find the baby asleep when she goes to check. Hallucinations are easy to produce experimentally. Ellson (1941), for example, sounded a very low tone 60 times (the subjects were told it was a hearing test) and at the same time a light was turned on. He then presented the light alone. Eighty percent of his subjects reported hearing the tone when there was no tone.

Fantasies   Those daydreams in which a wish is fulfilled are also autistic experiences. Figure 10-1 shows the prevalence and types of daydreams among undergraduate men (Shaffer and Shoben, 1956). In comparison with the men, the women were much less concerned with feats of daring and bravery and much more concerned with dreams of physical attractiveness. The women were also less likely to dream of vocational success or of making a heroic rescue but more likely to dream of being a martyr. Men and women reported sexual, possessive, and destructive fantasies about equally often. The fantasies of a group of graduate students averaging twenty-eight years of age were not markedly different from those of the undergraduates. About half the students reported having systematic fantasies with an elaborate plot which was imagined again and again. Less than 3 percent of the students studied reported no recent daydreams.

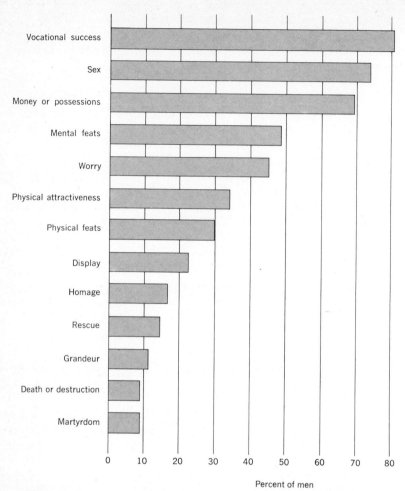

Figure 10-1 Percentage of college men who had recently experienced different types of daydreams. (Data from Shaffer and Shoben, 1956)

Projections   To Freud, projection meant seeing one's own baser qualities or experiences in another person. It is now commonly used to mean the general process of attributing our qualities and experiences, good or bad, to others. In this sense, the purely autistic are purely projective, for they cannot discriminate between their own feelings and thoughts and those of others.

Those at higher stages find it easy to discriminate their own desirable feelings and thoughts from those of others. They find it much harder to discriminate their undesirable ones. For example, a child is given two toys, one he likes and one he does not like. He is asked to give one of them to a playmate. He gives the one he does not like.

Afterward, he judges his playmate as less generous than he did before. The process is about like this: (1) the thought "I am stingy" makes the child feel anxious; (2) he represses the anxiety: "I am not stingy; I am generous" and (3) he projects the undesirable trait: "He is stingy."

The projection of undesirable traits is an everyday phenomenon: a baseball player misses a grounder and scowls at his glove; the housewife burns the dinner and blames the stove. Thelma, a kitchen supervisor, says:

It was my duty to make sure specific duties were performed by my 10 subordinates. During one of the peak rush periods I was transferring hot chowder from the soup kettle. I slipped on some trash on the floor, spilled the soup, and burned my foot. I laid the blame on the maintenance man who was to have cleaned up the kitchen area and threatened to fire him. Later, I realized that he could not be held responsible for every piece of trash and that I had spilled the soup because I had not watched my footing and was trying to work at too great a speed. It hurt my pride to admit I was really at fault.

It is often hard in such everyday situations to assess accurately either motives or guilt. For this reason, projection provides a particularly effective way of concealing emotions from ourselves. Everyone sometimes projects. Some people, however, use projection habitually and excessively. A large number of difficult and eccentric people, faddists, pseudo reformers, inventors, and cantankerous and litigious men and women are masterful projectionists. About one out of fifty cases admitted to mental hospitals is diagnosed as "paranoia." Typically, the person with paranoia shows a good grasp of correct conduct and leads a fairly well-adjusted life. The central quality of such people is the presence of fixed and well-organized delusions resulting from projection.

DEVELOPMENT

The infant cannot discriminate what is him from what is not him, what is internal from what is external. As he develops toward the impulse-ridden stage, he begins to make these discriminations. What does he first learn to discriminate? He does not learn to discriminate symbols; he does learn to discriminate between symbol users. He learns to discriminate his mother from his father and both of them from strangers. Objectively, the infant is totally dependent for his survival upon those around him; subjectively, however, he does not feel dependent. He *learns* to feel dependent.

How does he learn this feeling? The newborn baby can suck

and manipulate and is soon able to hold, babble, and smile. The mother stimulates these responses: she permits the baby to manipulate her hair and fingers; she moves her head and thereby stimulates the baby to follow it with his eyes; she talks and thereby stimulates the baby to babble. The mother monkey allows her young to cling to her hairy undersurface for several months after birth. In a similar way, the human mother satisfies and fosters the attachment needs of her child. Finally, she reduces the discomfort of her child's hunger, thirst, and pain. Through these processes, the infant becomes attached to the mother and learns to recognize her face, form, and voice.

The attachment to the mother *generalizes* to other human beings. Rheingold (1956) selected 16 six-month-old infants living in institutions who were cared for by many volunteers. She played the role of mother for eight of these infants for eight hours a day, five days a week, for eight consecutive weeks. She bathed and diapered them, played with them, smiled at them and generally tried to be as good a substitute mother as possible.

The eight control babies were cared for in the typical institutional way. Several women performing the motherly duties for each child in a routine fashion. Four weeks after the end of the experimental period, the 16 infants were tested for their social responsiveness to the experimenter, to an examiner who administered the tests, and to a stranger. The reactions of the experimental babies to their surrogate mother did generalize. More often than the control babies, they gave some facial reaction or smiled back when the three kinds of adults smiled or talked to them. Monkey studies provide even more convincing evidence of the generalization of responsiveness from the mother to other monkeys (Sackett, Porter, and Holmes, 1965).

The infant who becomes attached to his mother becomes dependent upon her (Figure 10-2). In fact, the most obvious index of his attachment is the intensity of his separation anxiety, i.e., how much he cries when he is separated from his mother. Monkeys raised in isolation from other monkeys become attached to physical objects, such as diapers and metal tubes (Sackett, 1968). They do not become attached to other monkeys. They will not mate, interact appropriately with other monkeys, or care for their own children (Harlow, Harlow, Dodsworth, and Arling, 1966). They avoid all social contact, crouch and clutch at themselves, and seem very fearful.

No child is raised in total isolation so that no child totally lacks dependence upon others. Children, however, vary widely in their degree of dependence. Here is a description of minimally attached Teddy at the age of one year, a typical product of typical institutional care (Provence and Lipton, 1962, p. 26):

Figure 10-2 A child must have social contact in order to grow up to interact successfully with others. The earliest social contact is with mother, and his dependence on her may become a model for his dependence on others throughout his life. (Ron Junttonen)

Outstanding were his soberness, his forlorn appearance and lack of animation. The interest that he showed in the toys was mainly for holding, inspecting, but rarely mouthing. When he was unhappy he now had a cry that sounded neither demanding or angry—just miserable—and it was usually accompanied by his beginning to rock. The capacity for protest which he had earlier was much diminished. He did not turn to adults to relieve his distress or to involve them in a playful or pleasurable interchange. He made no demands. The active approach to the world, which had been one of the happier aspects of his earlier development, vanished.

RETARDATION

Retardation at the autistic stage is the most serious of mental health problems and the hardest to solve. James, an autistic child, had no vocabulary at the age of two. At eight, he was "mute, isolated, with only occasional attempts to relate." At eleven, his mother, who showed little concern for any of her children, reported that he knew four words. His nonidentical twin brother, John, was not as limited in his speech development. He also played well with other children, cooperated with the examiner, and showed none of the stereotyped gestures of James (Vaillant, 1963).

The speech of autistic children is always poor. However, they are often very sensitive to sounds, vibrations, and music. Typically, James was so unresponsive to his parents that they at first thought he was deaf. They noted, however, that he often stood motionless for long periods of time listening to the radio and to records. At the age of seventeen months he repeated in full a well-known aria from *Don Giovanni*. Music is, in itself, satisfying; speech is a means of gaining satisfaction from others. Vaillant (1963) suggests that the musical aptitude of the autistic is due to a neglect of communication and a concentration upon the immediately satisfying end.

The autistic may learn to distinguish himself from the world without learning to distinguish the physical from the social world. He then acts as if he could see no difference that was important to him between people and things. He may show little more interest in communicating with people than he shows in communicating with objects. He may cry or laugh, but not in response to others. He may gesture and talk as much when he is alone as when he is with people. Neither his gestures nor his speech may be comprehensible to others, for he does not intend them as communication. What he does convey to others is his profound desire to avoid them and to avoid communicating with them.

The autistic child becomes the schizophrenic adult. Schizophrenia is (American Psychiatric Association, 1952, p. 26):

> a group of psychotic reactions characterized by fundamental disturbances in reality relationships and concept formations, with affective, behavioral, and intellectual disturbances in varying degrees and mixtures. The disorders are marked by strong tendency to retreat from reality, by emotional disharmony, unpredictable disturbances in stream of thought, regressive behavior, and in some, by a tendency to "deterioration."

One out of four people admitted to mental hospitals in the United States for the first time is diagnosed as schizophrenic; one out of two in mental hospitals at any time falls into this category. The highest rate of admission for this disease is among people in their late teens and early twenties. The average length of their stay is about thirteen years (Wolman, 1965), and the longer they stay the more they "deteriorate."

Consequently, schizophrenia is our major mental health problem. Some aspects of the illness as seen from the inside are indicated by Table 10-1.

TABLE 10-1   Autobiography of a Schizophrenic Experience

In November, 1948, a thirty-six-year-old college graduate and trained social worker was admitted to a private mental hospital. The diagnosis was catatonic schizophrenia. She was the wife of a professional man and the mother of three children. After three weeks she was discharged but was readmitted for three months the following November with the same diagnosis. She was admitted for the third time in July, 1951, and discharged in September, 1952, after electric shock treatments (Anonymous, 1955).

After her discharge she wrote an anonymous autobiography of her experiences. About half the statements below are quotations from the autobiography and half are contradicted by the autobiography. Underline the "T" for the statements that are from the autobiography and the "F" for those that are false. Answers are given at the end of the chapter.

T F   1. I had never had any serious psychological problems until a few months before I was first admitted.

T F   2. My marriage had always been a source of security for me and remained so throughout my illness.

T F   3. I was suddenly confronted with an overwhelming conviction that I had discovered the secrets of the universe.

T F   4. I always had some lingering doubts about the convictions that came so suddenly to me.

T F   5. I talked extensively with an imaginary companion.

T F   6. At no time during my illness did I see any visions.

T F   7. I was taken to the hospital in a rigid condition.

T F   8. Part of the time I was exploring a new planet but it was too lonely, and I had to get back to the earth somehow.

T F   9. I was somehow an indispensable link in preventing total collapse.

T F 10. I thought that my enemies were actively trying to interfere with my activities, and at times even to kill me.

T F 11. The picture of myself which I had during my illness was much different from that which I had always carried around with me during most of my adult life.

T F 12. I felt that I had the power to control the relation of the sun in relation to other astronomical bodies.

T F 13. As I improved I changed from a religious to a nonreligious type of orientation.

T F 14. My relations with people generally became easier and more relaxed.

T F 15. There were changes from a state of chronic sexual desire to semifrigidity.

The hallmarks of the autistic stage, poor communication and indifference to people, are the hallmarks of the schizophrenic. In a *schizoid* person these tendencies are a marked and stable part of his personality, but he is still capable of carrying on a routine life in a fairly acceptable way.

Poor communication and indifference to people are the central qualities of *simple schizophrenia.* A person in whom these qualities are pronounced may be institutionalized as Thomas Bryan was. His mother complained:

> He doesn't shave and lets his beard grow. He won't circulate with anyone. He lies in bed. I've been bringing him his meals. I am afraid he will go away and get caught in a snowstorm.

In less serious forms, such people may drift along in a routine and solitary way of life showing no ambition, little emotion, and no discontent. Some of the more capable persons of this type drift into simple clerical or manual jobs where they resist efforts to change or complicate their routines. Others become idlers, vagrants, or prostitutes.

In *hebephrenic schizophrenia* silliness, inappropriate smiling and laughter, incoherent streams of talk with words made up by the patient, and fleeting bizarre ideas are added to the basic pattern of poor communication and indifference to people. This is the most poorly defined of all schizophrenic categories. It is often used for those who fall somewhere between simple schizophrenia and the catatonic or paranoid categories.

In *catatonic schizophrenia* motility disorders are prominent. In the stuporous phase, the catatonic may not speak, eat, or react to painful stimuli. He may lie with his eyes open without blinking for hours or days. He may show a waxy flexibility, so that his limbs retain the position in which they are placed. In spite of his lack of reactivity, he may be quite observant and able to recall later many of the things that happened. Imagined experiences during this period may be on a cosmic scale, as were those of a patient who later reported that he was the battleground for a struggle between good and evil in the universe in which the forces were so equally balanced that the slightest move on his part would decide the struggle. Afraid to make the wrong move, he lay absolutely still. The stupor may give away in a few moments to violent, frenzied excitement. He may then talk incoherently, impulsively attack and attempt to kill another person, mutilate himself, or commit suicide.

In *paranoid schizophrenia* delusions dominate the picture. The delusions are typically changeable, numerous, and fantastic. The patient may believe that people are persecuting him; that he is Christ,

Napoleon, or George Washington; and that he is being influenced by strange machines. He hears people murmuring against him, sees them lurking at the windows, feels the electric ticklings they are directing against his skin, and tastes the poison that they have slipped into his food.

Is schizophrenia determined by genetic or environmental mechanisms? Psychiatrists opt for the genetic; psychologists, for the environmental. Psychiatrists are more likely to agree with statements like these (Fitzgibbons and Shearn, 1972):

Schizophrenia cannot develop without a genetic predisposition.

Schizophrenia is basically a central nervous system dysfunction.

Physiological factors will one day be established as central to the schizophrenic process.

Psychologists, on the other hand, are more likely to agree with statements like these:

Mothers of schizophrenics prevent their children from gaining a sense of trust in themselves.

The thought disorder in schizophrenia derives from the disordered patterns of interaction within the family.

Schizophrenia probably develops from the learning of faulty patterns of communication.

The disagreements arise from the psychiatrist's sensitivity to data showing genetic causes, of which there is a great deal, and from the psychologist's sensitivity to data showing environmental causes, of which there is also a great deal. Again, it seems, the interaction between genetic and environmental mechanisms is most critical.

Direct Genetic Mechanisms

The evidence for a direct genetic mechanism is extensive. Among fraternal twins of schizophrenics, only 15 percent were schizophrenic; among identical twins, 86 percent (Kallman, 1953). Furthermore, the rates for identical twins reared apart were very similar to those for identical twins reared together (Slater, 1953). The blood chemistry, autonomic functioning, and anatomical details of the body organs of schizophrenics were demonstrably different from those of non-schizophrenics (Hoffer and Osmond, 1959). The possibility that schizophrenia may be the product of a biochemical substance produced by the body is supported by the fact that mescaline drugs and LSD-25 produce behavior that is very similar to schizophrenia (Kety, 1959).

At best, however, this evidence leaves the nature of the direct genetic mechanism in the dark. At the worst, it may merely be a reflection of environmental influences. Thus, the fact that schizophrenic parents have schizophrenic children and that schizophrenic children have schizophrenic siblings may be due entirely to the environments provided by such parents. The fact that schizophrenics are physiologically different from nonschizophrenics may only reflect changes resulting from chronic and intense anxiety states created by early environmental experiences. In any case, even the most ardent biologists do not claim that genes cause schizophrenia, only that predisposing genes *interacting* with environmental stresses create schizophrenia. The critical question is, then, whether there is any innate predisposition and, if so, how powerful it is.

Indirect Genetic Mechanisms

Some infants seem born to be quiet, unsmiling, and socially unresponsive; others, to be babbling, laughing, ticklish, and socially responsive. This apparently genetic difference may operate indirectly to retard the development of dependence by influencing the reactions of caretakers of the child. Mothers and other adults are likely to spend more time and to play more with the responsive than with the unresponsive child.

General Environmental Mechanisms

Sarvis and Garcia (1961) reached the conclusion from their clinical investigation of 80 autistic children that "the difficulties invariably involved the particular developmental stage when the mother was the primary object to the child so that the disturbance caused the child to adopt a basic paranoid attitude toward the mother." The children had an intense fear of people, an intense hostility toward them, and an intense fear of showing their hostility. As a result, they avoided people. The chronic avoidance, in turn, intensified their fear, hostility, and timidity.

Mothers of autistic children seem to have used their children to satisfy their own needs without regard for the welfare of the child. Meyer and Karon (1967) matched six mothers with autistic sons with six mothers of the same age, education, and intelligence who had normal sons. All the mothers completed the Thematic Apperception Test. Stories that concerned a conflict between a dominant and a dependent person were separated, coded, and rated as "benign" or "pathogenic." If the dominant person in the story took the needs of the dependent person into account, it was classified as benign. If the dominant person did not take the needs of the dependent person into account, the story was classified as pathogenic. Result: All six of the mothers with autistic sons had higher pathogenic scores than the normal mothers with whom they were matched. Conclusion:

The schizophrenogenic mother feels inadequate and compensates for her inadequacy by making demands on the child in terms of her own pathological needs without regard for the welfare of the child whenever her needs conflict with his. In many respects, the underlying problems of the schizophrenogenic mother are similar to those of the schizophrenic, but she defends against her anxieties by destroying the child.

How much and how soon an infant learns to depend upon others is determined by this relation with his early caretaker. Cultural differences, however, create differences in the behavior of caretakers. Among the Uganda of east central Africa, for example, the typical infant exhibits separation anxiety at 6 months; among middle-class Americans, not until ten months. Why the difference? The Ugandan baby spends most of his first 6 months being held by someone; the American baby spends them alone in a crib (Ainsworth, 1967).

Studies of general environmental influences are consistent with the view that in those environments most likely to provide warm human relationships for the child there is less autism. In those most likely to provide him with cold human relationships, there is more autism.

The Hutterites of South Dakota have a long-standing reputation as a close and cohesive culture that has achieved "peace of mind." The rate of schizophrenia in their communities is far below that of the general population (Eaton and Weil, 1955). The rate of schizophrenia in Chicago is highest in the central business district, next highest is the adjacent hobo and rooming-house area, and lowest in the residential areas on the edge of the city (Faris and Dunham, 1939). The results were similar for different areas of Providence, Rhode Island, and Worcester, Massachusetts (Gerard and Houston, 1953). In New Haven, Connecticut, the lower class constitutes only 19 percent of the population but 38 percent of the patients in mental hospitals, while the upper classes constitute 3 percent of the population but only 1 percent of the patients in hospitals (Hollingshead and Redlich, 1958).

In summary, it now seems that an infant becomes autistic when he has suffered intense frustration in his infancy. His genetic endowment may make him peculiarly susceptible to such frustrations. However, a painful relationship with his mother appears to be the decisive element. Some social environments are more likely than others to produce mothers of this kind. Such environments are more likely also to create relationships with other people of a similar kind for the infant and so reinforce his early learning. Finally, the pattern of defense against such anxieties spirals. The longer he uses his defenses, the more firmly they become established and the more resistant they become to change. Furthermore, as his pattern of withdrawal and lack of communication becomes fixed, he becomes less and less available to those forces that work for constructive change—such as other people. The autistic child becomes the schizophrenic adult.

Specific Environmental Mechanisms

Genetic and general environmental influences both seem to exercise a potent influence in retarding people at the autistic stage. From the point of view of both society and the autistic, however, the urgent question is: What can be done about it? The basic objectives in the treatment of schizophrenics are simple: to reduce their fear of people, to improve their ability to communicate with others, and to increase their competence in dealing with reality. The obstacles to their achievement, however, are so great that only very modest success has thus far rewarded the most intense efforts. Success is greatest with those whose first illness occurs in adulthood as a result of intense environmental stress. Failure is more likely where symptoms have occurred in early life and slowly intensified.

Psychosurgery   If schizophrenics inherit a tendency to be tense and fearful, then one may attempt to alter the organ that is the transmitter of the inheritance—the brain. *Prefrontal lobotomy* consists of cutting nerve fibers that connect the prefrontal lobe of the brain with the thalamus. The operation is a desperate one that is reserved for "hopeless" cases. Even in such cases, the method is being less and less often used.

Shock Therapy   There are three principal shock methods: insulin, metrazol, and electric. Electroshock, the most recent and most widely used, consists of attaching electrodes to the head and passing controllable electric currents through the brain to produce convulsive seizures. The method does produce temporary improvement among some psychotics but presents the disquieting probability that it also produces brain damage. The frequency and extent of such damage is still unknown.

Drug Therapy   Finding benefits of drugs is complicated by the fact that drugs and personality interact: the same tranquilizer may have different effects on different people. It is even further complicated by the subtle social influences operating in experiments. A new "tranquilizer" and a new "energizer," for example, were administered to 120 hospitalized patients with a variety of disorders. Psychiatrists evaluated their effects on patients by rating the patient before and after taking the drugs. Up to 80 percent of patients in some categories were judged to have benefited from the drugs. When compared with improvement in a matched control group of patients who had not had the "drugs," both "drugs" showed beneficial effects. The patients, the psychiatrists, and the nurses participating in the program thought they were using tranquilizers and energizers. In fact, *all* the drugs used in both experimental and control groups were sugar pills (Loranger, Prout, and White, 1961).

Psychotherapy   It is impossible to counsel a patient who will not talk, who talks in an incomprehensible way, who tries to commit suicide, who fights, or who believes the therapist is in a conspiracy against him. Tranquilizers may relax a patient so that he can communicate more easily and energizers may excite him so that he expresses his emotions more frequently. Psychotherapy for one patient, however, may take many hours a week for many months. Most hospitals have hundreds and many have thousands of patients for each therapist. Consequently, effective drugs may merely expand the already long lists of those waiting for therapy.

Group Therapy   The most common method of group therapy consists of hourly meetings of a small group of patients under the guidance of the therapist (Figure 10-3). The therapist encourages the members to air their problems, feelings, and attitudes, but avoids taking over the meeting. He must, however, prevent patients from making verbal attacks upon one another. Persons in such groups often also have private sessions with the therapist. Besides saving the time of the therapist, the technique has some advantages over individual therapy. It is closer to social reality. It does not require the dependence upon the therapist that some patients find intolerable and others accept too completely. The patient also has a better opportunity to learn that his problems are not unique, to relieve his feelings of isolation and rejection, and to profit from the experiences of others who have similar problems. Most state mental hospitals are now making some use of the method.

Figure 10-3 A group therapy session for the aged. Because the method is both economical and realistic, its use is expanding the treatment of minor as well as major disorders. (Postgraduate Center for Mental Health, New York)

Milieu Therapy Psychosurgery and drug therapy assume that it is best to look at schizophrenia as one looks at physical illness. A physical illness is a disturbance of the organic functions of the body. A cold, a fever, or a heart attack is an abnormal, unpleasant condition which happens to the *individual* person, not to his relationships with other people. Psychotherapy does not stress the physical but it does stress the psychological individual. The central quality of schizophrenia, however, lies in the disturbance of *relationships* between individuals. In general, the idea that mental illness may be most helpfully viewed as a disturbance of interpersonal relationships is spreading (Adams, 1964; Berne, 1964).

Psychosurgery and drugs treat schizophrenia by use of theories and techniques borrowed from the physical and biological sciences. By contrast, "moral" therapy, which reached its peak a hundred years ago, stressed the social environment of the patient. Milieu therapy regarded the insane as normal people who had lost their reason as a result of having been exposed to severe psychological and social stresses. Treatment aimed at relieving the stresses by friendly association, discussion of their difficulties, and the daily pursuit of meaningful work and social activities.

This century-old therapy seems to have accomplished at least as much as more recent methods (Rees, 1957, pp. 306–307):

Moral treatment reached its zenith in the years between 1820 and 1860. The results of treatment during that period were outstandingly good and bear comparison with some of the figures obtainable today. For example, in all patients admitted to the York Retreat (in England) within three months of the onset of illness—between the years 1796 and 1861 the discharge rate was 71%. . . . These are truly remarkable figures, especially when one takes into consideration that a substantial portion of the patients must have been general paralytics, for which there was at that time no effective treatment.

The Joint Commission on Mental Illness and Health (1961) observed that "twentieth-century psychiatry can add little" to Pinel's principles of moral therapy for psychotics,

except to convert them into modern terminological dress, contribute more systematic thought to the significance of various symptoms, intensify the doctor-patient relationship through scientific knowledge of psychological mechanisms, treat the patient as a member of a social group which expects him to behave in accepted ways, and specify that moral therapy has been subject to an incredible amount of distortion and misinterpretation . . .

In mental hospitals using milieu (environmental) therapy today, stress is placed upon the patient as a person having a disturbed social role in a social situation, not as a "case." Milieu therapy is illustrated by the manner in which 42 schizophrenic soldiers were treated at the Walter Reed General Hospital in Washington, D.C. (Artiss, Bullard, and Rioch, 1962). Treatment was based on these assumptions:

1.   The patient will be able to return to successful Army duty within six months.

2.   Since 95 percent of all soldiers complete their Army duty successfully, the cause of the patient's failure will be found in his performance.

3.   The patient will be found to be communicating at all times,

with respect either to the immediate situation, or his chronic problems or both, however bizarre the system he is using.

4.   The schizophrenic patient's symbolic behavior can be understood.

5.   Understanding him helps him.

6.   Working with others is a therapeutic experience for him.

Results: 64 percent of the patients returned to duty. Conclusion: "It seems reasonable to expect that recovery figures in the vicinity of 80 percent may be feasible with further knowledge relative to (1) selection of patients; (2) selection and training of staff members; (3) staff intercommunication systems; and (4) mores and values of patient group."

Community Life for the Mentally Ill (Fairweather, Sanders, Maynard, Cressler, and Bleck, 1969) describes and evaluates a more radical, less expensive, and more effective form of milieu therapy outside a hospital setting. The initial experimental group consisted of 15 volunteers who had been in the hospital for years. The control group consisted of patients who volunteered but remained in the hospital. The experimental group moved to and remained for several years at a former motel near a freeway and in a low-income area. The aim of the experiment was to make the group as financially self-sufficient and self-governing as possible as soon as possible. Analysis of a wide array of economic, social, and psychological data showed the lodge program to be extraordinarily successful. The authors conclude: "The paramount implication of this study for the mental patients, other marginal individuals, and those who manage the society is the urgent need to create new and more participative social statuses and roles for those members who only marginally belong to it."

REGRESSION

The vast majority of us develop beyond the autistic stage, but a tragic few remain at it. Under fatigue, strain, and stress we all return. Some can resist more pressure than others. Under enough pressure, however, all begin to dream, fantasize, hallucinate, or project. When the pressure is relieved, we generally return toward our normal stage, as the following case illustrates (Ewalt, Strecker, and Ebaugh, 1957):

> A fifty-three-year-old woman was admitted to a mental hospital in a highly agitated and deeply depressed condition. She was in a state of almost ceaseless activity, squirming in her chair, walking rapidly about, pulling at her hair, pinching her cheeks, biting her fingers. Her deeply lined face bore an expression of

unutterable woe. At times she was frankly terrified; at other times she shrank from a nurses' hand because she felt herself unworthy to be touched. She made one unsuccessful attempt at suicide.

She was of healthy ancestry and had a good educational background. As a young woman she had been quiet, conscientious, and self-sacrificing. She was distinctly sociable, well-liked by her friends, and a capable manager of the house. But her life had been highly stressful. At twenty-five she had married a man who proved to be a hopeless alcoholic and drug addict. She had been constantly worried about her husband, her children, and the family finances. When the husband's deterioration had made further home life impossible, she had separated from him. She had run a rooming house in order to support herself and the children. For five years before her illness she had been unable to secure help and had been constantly exhausted by the work of the house. As a result she had had severe attacks of grippe every winter and was in a badly run down condition. In spite of her miserable state and violent self-accusations, she was not disoriented, had no hallucinations, and had no apparent gaps in her memory. At the end of a year in the hospital she was well on the way to recovery. She was beginning to understand the distorted nature of her previous ideas. Among other things, hospitalization helped her to recover from her physical exhaustion.

Chronic insomnia produces autistic behavior. The autistic symptoms of students undergoing the stresses of college examinations may be caused by getting very little sleep night after night for many weeks. The autistic symptoms of those who have recently undergone traumatic disaster experiences often clear up rapidly once they are able to return to normal sleep habits. Many old persons suffer from chronic insomnia due to their physical aches and pains or to emotional stress created by rejection, separation from their families, or fear of approaching death. Their regressive symptoms are often assumed to be evidence of senile deterioration. The symptoms are often due to loss of sleep. In general, insomnia is a serious problem. Treatment of insomniacs by drugs or training in methods of sleeping well would prevent many gross errors of judgment that lead to accidents or impulsive suicidal behavior.

Do We Need Autistic Experiences?

Dreaming, at least, seems essential to our well-being. Aserinksy and Kleitman (1953) discovered that distinctive brain-wave patterns occur at periodic intervals during normal sleep and that these patterns correlated with rapid eye movements (REMs) and dreaming. Fisher and Dement (1963) monitored the eye-movement records of sleeping subjects and woke them for a few minutes when they were beginning to dream. During a recovery night when their dreaming was not interrupted, the subjects showed a marked increase in the amount of dreaming. All subjects who were put through the dream-deprivation procedure for five consecutive nights showed a gradual deterioration in their ability to concentrate and became increasingly irritable and anxious. Without dreaming, it seems, hallucinations become frequent, thinking becomes confused, and behavior becomes disorganized.

Can We Use Autistic Experiences?

In their dreams, the mature return to the autistic world. A recent addition to psychoanalytic theory, "regression in the service of the ego," suggests that creative persons exercise constructive control over this return. They have the ability to shift back and forth between the autistic and the later stages. Like a child, the creative person may have ready access to his dreams, fantasies, and vague impulses. Unlike the child, he distinguishes between autistic and later-stage processes. He discriminates between what he sees and hears in his mind and what exists in the external world. He separates what he dreams of being and doing from what he is and has done. He distinguishes between what he feels about a person and what the person has done, is doing, and is likely to do in the future.

The world of the autistic is a world of actions, of forces, of conflicting powers. Whatever is seen or felt is surrounded by a special atmosphere—an atmosphere of joy or grief, of anguish, or excitement, of exultation or depression. The expressive quality of this primitive stage of development is revealed with greater diversity, force, and purity when we are dreaming than when we are awake. Through controlled regression the creative person has access to his primitive world.

Users of psychiatric drugs often assert that they produce a higher form of human experience. The states they produce are often vivid and sometimes extremely satisfying. These states of "oneness," however, seem more like those experienced by a healthy and well-fed infant than by an adult.

THE IMPULSE-RIDDEN STAGE

Loevinger (1966) describes those of the impulse-ridden in the following way:

The child confirms his separate existence from the mother by exercise of his own will. Control of impulse is lacking or at best undependable. Rules are not recognized as such; an action is bad because it is punished. Interpersonal relations are exploitive and dependent, but the dependence is not recognized as such. People are seen as sources of supply. . . . Some manifestations of this stage remain remarkably the same throughout the life span, hence are not age specific, e.g., temper tantrums.

The impulse-ridden can differentiate people from things, helpful people from harmful people, rewarders from punishers. Like the autistic, they are dependent upon others for their survival; unlike the autistic, they *feel* dependent.

Impulse-ridden Symptoms

Psychological differentiation proceeds from the outside to the inside, from the objective to the subjective, from differentiating between people to differentiating within the self. The impulse-ridden, therefore, are preoccupied with concrete and obvious externals. Thus, child or adult, the impulse-ridden is preoccupied with bodily functions. The *form* of the preoccupation is different. The three-year-old makes joking remarks about "going pooh-pooh"; the adult, about sex. Sex for him, however, is largely a fascination with his own physiology, not with the social relationship involved.

The child weeps at the departure of its mother; the impulse-ridden adult is miserable when alone. Typically, they are unaware of their feeling of dependence. In fact, they may aggressively assert that they are very independent. The asserters, however, constantly seek the company of others, may telephone incessantly, and keep the TV on when alone. They feel dependent because they perceive others as suppliers of their every need. Consequently, they are not only fearful of being alone, but also enraged when others do not supply them with what they want.

Impulsive Aggression   When we are aggressive, we attack. We all attack sometimes. However, how much we attack, why we attack, and what we attack varies greatly with our stage of development. The conscientious father may spank his erring son though he dislikes doing it. The conforming soldier may dutifully kill the enemy. The opportunistic business man may destroy the company of his competitor. The impulse-ridden attack impulsively; i.e., without premeditation and without considering the consequences, they seek to hurt or destroy the source of their immediate frustration. They may directly attack what is frustrating them, attack something else, or attack themselves to relieve their feelings.

An extrapunitive response is one in which the individual aggressively attributes the frustration to external persons or things. An intropunitive response is one ". . . in which the individual aggressively attributes frustration to himself." An extrapunitive response may be a physical attack upon an obstacle.

> A man came into a service station to have a muffler installed on his car. Rust and corrosion had frozen the old muffler to the new tail pipe. After 10 minutes of pulling and tugging, the mechanic became so angry that he took a 10-pound hammer and beat the muffler full of holes and ruined the tail pipe. The owner flew into a rage and swore at the mechanic.

Physical attacks, even upon objects, generally bring retaliation, and as a consequence our direct attacks upon others usually take a verbal form, as in the case of Lawrence.

> I hurried home from class at noon so that I could eat lunch before I went to work. Because I only had a few minutes, I didn't remove my food from the tray before eating, which is one of the rules of the dining room. When the resident adviser suggested that I do so, I became angry and left. When he came to my room later to explain why he had made the request, I told him I didn't want to listen to his silly pitter-patter and closed the door in his face. That evening I was telling everyone how he had overstepped his authority and how authoritarian and inhuman he had been.

Verbal aggression also brings retaliation: the child who criticizes his parents may be punished, and the employee who attacks his boss may be fired. But suppression of anger increases tension, which, in turn, increases the feelings of hostility and of anxiety.

The *displacement* of aggression, shifting the attack from a feared object to an unfeared one, is one way out of the circle: the child beats her doll; the employee beats his wife; the student attacks his smaller roommate. Intropunitive aggression is that response in which the individual aggressively attributes frustration to himself. A not infrequent object of aggression is the frustrated person himself. He may feel that he is the primary source of his frustration—and he may be right. Consequently, he criticizes himself, and in extreme cases he may actually inflict physical punishment upon himself. Some situations are so anxiety-provoking that aggressiveness is almost inevitable. However, some individuals are habitually aggressive regardless of the situation: they are *hostile* people. Such people express their aggression in a wide variety of often subtle forms: hypercriticalness, a readiness to belittle and disparage; nagging; the holding of grudges; prejudices; cynicism; suspiciousness of people's motives; "patriotism" that seems to have no content except hatred of some enemy; readiness to exploit and intimidate; contempt for the "soft" enterprises of reconciliation; quickness to see personal opponents as public enemies; and the definition of success in terms of power over others. When the hostility is intropunitive it may find expression in migraine headaches, peptic ulcers, feelings of depression, and self-recrimination. The intropunitive person often feels unworthy of being loved, has a rigid conscience and a high level of aspiration.

Negativism   The pain of frustration is so intense for the impulse-ridden that they not only attack others but also themselves in an effort to find relief. Consequently, they strive to control themselves—but they have no self to control. An early step in developing their self is to *assert* their self, i.e., to assert their independence from those around them. They become negativistic; i.e., they develop a strong and irrational resistance to accepting the suggestions of others. Negativism is more common among boys than girls and normally reaches a peak between the ages of two and three. When her son is three, a mother may have more success in controlling him by reversing her orders: "*Don't* eat your egg," "*Don't* go to bed," etc. The use of negativism gradually tapers off, but there is generally a brief resurgence during early adolescence. Buhler (1933) reports that more than half of a group of thirteen-year-old girls reported having "poor social relations" with their parents, whereas less than 10 percent of nine- and seventeen-year-olds made such a report.

Some adults continue to lean heavily upon negativism. The origin of their negativism generally lies in their early relations with their parents. On the one hand, their parents may have pulled, hauled, hurried, and interrupted them so frequently and unnecessarily that negativism became the only effective method of dealing with their anxieties. On the other hand, their parents may have so regularly given in to their rebellions that they learned to use negativism as a way of getting whatever they wanted, of freeing themselves from unpleasant tasks, and of remaining pleasantly at the center of attention in their families.

Most adults use negativism in milder forms and special situations: they do not openly oppose, but they do resist suggestions; they argue small points in routine; they fail to "understand" what they were told to do; they do what they were told to do in a sloppy manner. Responses of this sort commonly arise in relations with people of authority, for few leave childhood with entirely positive feelings toward people with power. Consequently, most students have some negative feelings toward their teachers; employees have them toward their bosses; the bosses have them toward union leaders; union leaders have them toward managers; and the poor have them toward the wealthy.

Development

The impulse-ridden develop toward the opportunistic stage by imitation. Imitation is the process by which we mold our speech, mannerisms, style, appearance, and, in general, our external behavior to match the behavior of another person. Children share with monkeys and apes the ability to imitate. Before his first birthday, the normal infant begins to copy the speech sounds of those around him and to play such games as peekaboo and pat-a-cake. The influence of imitation seems to reach its peak in childhood and then to wane. The developing individual increasingly confines imitation to the increasingly rare situations in which he is faced with (1) a baffling problem and (2) a trusted person who seems to have a new and successful way of dealing with the problem.

The more rapidly a child learns to feel dependent upon those around him, the more quickly he learns to imitate them. Bandura and Huston (1961) had children play a guessing game with an experimenter. Some of the children had had a nurturant session with the experimenter; some had not. The children from the nurturant session were much more imitative of the experimenter than those who had not had this session.

A second requirement for the development of learning by imitation is that the child experience the rewards of imitation. This normally means the child gradually learns to imitate models who are older and more competent. Andrews (1965) introduced pairs of preschoolers to a "game" in which one child in the pair had to make a series of choices (of various colored forms, Tinkertoy pieces to be assembled, etc.) in order to obtain a prize, while the other child watched. When the game was new to one child (the subject) and the other child (the model) was identified as having played it before, significantly more imitations occurred than when neither child had had previous experience or when both children had had previous experience.

As the dependency motive for imitation weakens, the reward motive strengthens. That is, the dependent child imitates all the behavior of the person imitated; the independent child, only behavior that brings reward. Ross (1966), for example, taught 52 nursery school children one at a time how to run a post office. All the children were eventually tested on how much they imitated the behavior of the experimenter that was *relevant* to running the post office and how much they imitated behavior that was *irrelevant* to running the post office. The amount of relevant and irrelevant imitation was then related to their degree of dependence.

Each child saw the experimenter engaging in seven different sets of behavior relevant to running the post office: collecting and giving change, operating the cash register, dialing the telephone, etc. Each child's imitation was measured when he was made the postman.

Each child also saw the experimenter doing things that were irrelevant to running the post office. For example, when answering the phone, which rang periodically, she (1) picked up a pencil from the counter and stuck it behind her right ear, (2) put her left foot on the telephone chair, (3) tapped a balloon that was hanging near the table, etc. Imitation of these irrelevant behaviors were measured at the same time that the imitation of relevant behaviors was measured.

Five teachers at the nursery school rated differences in the degree of dependence of the children before the experiment began. As a check on the ratings, all the children were observed for the first day of each of eight weeks to see (1) if they sought help while undressing and dressing when arriving and leaving school, and (2) if those who lived within walking distance came and went with adults or older children rather than by themselves. The children who were rated as more dependent by the teachers were also those who sought more help and came with others to school.

Finally, degree of dependency was related to the degree of irrelevant imitation. Result: The more dependent the child, the higher his score in irrelevant imitation. Conclusion: The dependent infant imitates the *person* he feels dependent upon. As he imitates, he learns to imitate less of the behavior that is not relevant. Finally, the amount of imitative learning declines. It declines because the child gradually develops a larger and larger repertoire of behaviors for dealing with his impulses as a result of past imitations. It also declines because the child develops more effective ways of learning than aping in detail the behavior of others.

These results offer an explanation of development from the impulse-ridden to the opportunistic stage. The autistic person cannot learn to be opportunistic directly, for he feels no dependence and therefore pays no attention to others. The impulse-ridden person does pay attention to others. Consequently, he can learn ways of getting what he wants by imitating them.

Retardation

The impulse-ridden have a poor control over their aggressive impulses. The opportunistic have learned to discriminate between when it is safe and when it is *not* safe to be aggressive. The temper tantrum is the most obvious sign of retardation at the impulse-ridden stage. However, those whose aggressive impulses have been completely inhibited are more dangerous. The overcontrolled build up tension that may explode in impulsive acts of murder, manslaughter, or mayhem.

Megargee (1966) studied nine boys who had been institutionalized for extremely assaultive acts: killed mother with a rifle, shot father with pistol, slashed victim with knife, etc. He compared them with 21 boys institutionalized for moderately assaultive acts (hit victim with wrench, struck woman with blunt object), with 20 institutionalized for auto theft, burglary, and other offenses against property, and with 26 institutionalized for unruliness, defiance, and unmanageability in the home. The extremely assaultive group obtained higher scores on a self-control scale than any of the other groups. They also had better school attendance and conduct records, fewer previous incarcerations, and higher ratings on such traits as cooperativeness and friendliness by their counselors during their first 10 days in custody. They were more often described by such adjectives as meek, self-controlled, conscientious, and withdrawn. A review of newspaper accounts and case histories of extremely assaultive individuals suggests that such individuals are extremely overcontrolled: "In case after case the extremely assaultive offender proves to be a rather passive person with no previous history of aggression."

Manics have too little control over their impulses; depressives, too much. Manic-depressives alternate between too little and too much. About 15 percent of the patients admitted to mental hospitals are classified as manic-depressives. Manic patients are impulse-ridden: hyperactive, sleepless, distractable. They aggressively resist any interference with the immediate gratification of their rapidly fluctuating impulses. They often become suddenly depressed, although when and if this will occur is unpredictable. There is, in fact, little certainty about the diagnosis itself. More than half of one group of patients who were diagnosed as manic-depressive were later diagnosed as schizophrenic (Lewis and Pietrowski, 1954). There is little doubt, however, about the basic difference between schizophrenics and manic-depressives. Schizophrenics withdraw from people and from communication with them; manic-depressives are responsive to people and to social expectations, often acutely so.

Clifford Beers (1948) wrote a well-known autobiography of his manic-depressive attack: *A Mind That Found Itself.* He reports that after three years of depression, he suddenly became very excited. His mind was flooded with ideas for a vast program of humanitarian reform. He began writing letters about everything that happened to him and soon exhausted his supply of stationery. He arranged to secure large quantities of wrapping paper, which he cut in strips a foot wide and pasted together into long rolls: "More than once, letters twenty to thirty feet long were written, and on one occasion the accumulation of two or three days of excessive productivity, when spread upon the floor, reached from one end of the corridor to the other—a distance of about one hundred feet. My hourly output was something like twelve feet. . . ."

Writing could absorb only a fraction of his energies. He tried to assume charge of his part of the hospital, to conduct an investigation of hospital conditions, and to invent a machine for overcoming the force of gravity. With the wealth obtained from his invention, he planned to change his home city into a garden spot and center of learning with new parks, cathedrals, libraries, art galleries, theaters, mansions, and the most magnificent university in the world. As with about two out of three manic-depressives, Beers recovered. After his recovery, he dropped his experiments and his plans for changing the city, but he did help to establish the National Committee for Mental Hygiene that was later expanded to international dimensions.

The basic process in many manic-depressives seems to be something like this: They feel like doing something very wrong so they try to do something very good. Their personal sacrifice in doing good is generally not appreciated. They feel more aggressive. They try harder to do good but it is still not appreciated. The cycle is thus set for an acute depression. The passivity of the depressive may represent the final stalemate. He feels so intensely hostile that he can no longer do good. Why do some people fail to learn effective control over their impulses?

Direct Genetic Mechanisms   Manic-depressive psychosis exists in less than 1 percent of the general population. By contrast, 26 percent of fraternal twins and 96 percent of identical twins of manic-depressives also develop manic-depressive symptoms .(Kallman, 1953). At the most, however, genes provide only a predisposing disposition. The disposition must interact with a particular social environment to result in the manic-depression, as these identical twins illustrate (Burks and Roe, 1949):

Clara and Doris were identical twins of below-average intelligence. Their family included many unstable and maladjusted people. They were separated at the age of two and raised by different foster parents.

Clara went to live in the city. She was the only child of her very fond foster parents. The discipline at home was very mild. She went to school regularly until the fifth grade. At seventeen, she married a stable older man.

Doris went to live in a large city with foster parents who were in similar economic circumstances to those of Clara. However, they were extremely harsh and strict in disciplining her and their other two children. Her school attendance was very irregular. Like Clara, she held various odd jobs before her marriage. She was married at twenty-three to a shell-shocked veteran.

The psychologists met the twins when they were thirty-nine years old. At this time, they were living in the same community and were close friends. Clara was leading a normal, happy, moderately active life. Doris, however, was rated as more easily upset, pessimistic, and impulsive. She was discontented and irritable with her children. She was diagnosed as psychotic. A year later she was placed in a mental institution, classified as a manic-depressive.

Convincing evidence of the operation of a genetic mechanism in causing impulsive aggression comes from the study of the chromosomes of inmates in a Scottish state hospital for the dangerously violent. All but a handful of the more than 300 detained in the hospital had criminal records. The use of photomicrographs of blood cells now permits the direct analysis of human chromosomes. The normal number of chromosomes is 46. However, about one in a thousand men in the general population has an extra Y chromosome. This chromosome constitution is known as: 47, XYY. Nine of the men in the hospital, almost three percent of the total group were diagnosed as 47, XYY. (Jacobs, Brunton, Melville, Brittain, McClemont, and Whatmore, 1965; 1968).

The 9 men were compared with 18 men from the same hospital who had a normal (46 XY) constitution (Price and Whatmore, 1967). Those with the 47, XYY had been committed much earlier. In fact, three of the nine had been committed before the age of 10. Among the 31 siblings of the 9, only one had a criminal conviction and that was for a single offense; among the 63 siblings of the control group, about 1 in 5 had a criminal record and the total number of convictions for the group was 139. From these results Court-Brown (1968) concludes:

. . . the picture emerged of psychopathic individuals lacking in any ordinary capacity for feeling, apparently without much depth of emotion, who seemed incapable of making any rational plans for the future, and who on the whole pose behavioral problems from childhood. . . . These individuals, drawn from all the social classes, stood out as the black sheep of their families, and as the apparently inexplicably erring sons in otherwise reasonably well-adjusted families.

Indirect Genetic Mechanisms The 47 XYY group are not only impulsively aggressive; they also have abnormal hormone activity, exhibit neurological abnormalities, are mentally dull, and are excessively tall. People may be afraid of big and dull men and treat them differently from small and bright ones. It may be that this different treatment accounts for the aggressiveness of the group rather than the genetic predisposition of the group to aggressive acts.

Similar difficulties in disentangling direct from indirect genetic mechanisms exist in trying to account for the greater aggressiveness of men.

Females in many species of animals will not fight despite severe provocation unless protecting their young; males fight readily even in the absence of external provocation. Testosterone has a pronounced influence on this difference: males given injections in infancy engage in more adult fighting; female mice who were administered male hormone in the first 24 hours following birth resembled normal male mice in the tendency to fight (Edwards, 1968).

Studies of American school children consistently find aggressive behavior much more frequent in boys than girls. If children are asked which parent is more dangerous or punitive, both boys and girls agree that the father is. If they are shown a picture of a rabbit and tiger, they will say that the rabbit is more like a woman and the tiger like a man.

Individual differences in the aggressiveness of human males are large and stable. Identical twins much more closely resemble each other in aggressiveness than do fraternal twins (Gottesman, 1963). Three-year-old males who are aggressive toward their mothers and prone to loss of control when frustrated tend to be aggressive in adolescence (Moss and Kagan, 1964). Individual differences in the aggressiveness of females, however, tend to be small and unstable.

Aggressiveness in males tends to be approved and encouraged; in females, to be disapproved and discouraged. Genes make a difference in aggressiveness; sex-role training also makes a difference. Are small genetic influences exaggerated by the culture or are large genetic influences diminished by the culture? The best guess seems to be the former.

General Environmental Mechanisms
The impulse-ridden become opportunistic by learning to imitate. However, they only imitate those who are dependable suppliers of their

needs. Consequently, it would seem likely that a warm and cohesive social environment that encouraged the development of dependency would have fewer people retarded at the autistic stage, and more advancing to the impulse-ridden and higher stages. The generalization fits the facts resulting from a study of the mental health of Hutterites (Eaton and Weil, 1955).

The Hutterites migrated from Russia to the United States in 1874. Before 1917 they lived in small communities in the southeastern part of South Dakota. Since they believe in early marriages, encourage large families, consider birth control sinful, and are strongly opposed to divorce, they have one of the highest reproduction rates in the world, their numbers doubling about every sixteen years. In 1950, there were more than eight thousand with communities in Iowa, Montana, Alberta, and Manitoba. They live in communities of about a hundred members which are run on a democratic basis with much emphasis on religion. The black trousers of the men and the polka-dot handkerchiefs of the women are a symbol of their closeness and homogeneity. They believe in communal ownership and control of all property. Their workers are paid no wages, and their attitude is to "do the best you can" rather than to compete.

Eaton and Weil made a careful count of minor and major mental disorders in this culture. The rate of major mental disorders (psychoses) was about the same as in ten other cultures. In fact, only an arctic village and a northern area in Sweden had a higher rate. The rate in a slum area in Baltimore was about the same as among the Hutterites. The authors reached the gloomy conclusion that serious mental disorders may be about the same across wide variations in social environment.

The stage view of personality development offers a more hopeful interpretation. The rate of all psychoses (schizophrenia + manic-depression + others) is no better among the Hutterites. The Hutterites, however, have a lower rate of schizophrenia, and a higher one for manic-depression than is found in less favorable environments (Figure 10-4). If we assume that manic-depression is a disorder at a higher stage of development than schizophrenia, then we can conclude the Hutterite environment is healthier. The Hutterites did have many fewer forms of minor mental disorders: fewer alcoholics, fewer criminals, fewer eccentric personalities, and fewer psychopathic deviates. Retardation at the impulse-ridden stage appears to be higher in societies that encourage cross-identification. "Identification" is the process by which a child learns to mold himself after another person; cross-identification occurs when a boy identifies with a woman or a girl with a man.

The relationship between cross-identification and impulse-

Figure 10-4 Alcoholics, criminals, and schizophrenics are rare among the Hutterites. Manic-depressives, however, are much more common than in the general population. (Religious News Service Photo)

ridden behavior was investigated in 48 nonliterate societies. The frequency of crime was used as the measure of impulsiveness. The societies were first ranked in accordance with the opportunity for boys in the society to form an identification with their fathers. In monogamous societies where the opportunity for father-son identification is highest, both theft and crimes against persons were lowest. In polygynous societies where one husband lives with several wives and their children, the crime rates were higher. In those societies where the mother and her son typically live apart from the father, the crime rates were highest of all. In such societies, it appears that male children identify goodness with femininity and "badness" with masculinity. They rob and assault partly as an effort to establish their image of themselves as masculine (Bacon, Child, and Barry, 1963). The cross-identification is likely to produce strong feelings of anxiety and guilt from two different directions: a boy feels guilty because he hates his father, and he feels guilty because he does not behave like a man.

Specific Environmental Mechanisms
Psychosurgery, shock treatment, drugs, psychotherapy, and milieu therapy, all of which are used in the treatment of schizophrenia, are also used in the treatment of manic-depressives. In fact, psychother-

apists often find it hard to agree with each other or even with themselves from one time to another on whether a particular person is dominantly at the autistic or the impulse-ridden stage.

REGRESSION

Under stress, a person with a highly differentiated self may temporarily return to the undifferentiated world of dreams, hallucinations, fantasies, and projections of the autistic. Under less stress, the person may return to the world of dependency, impulsive aggression, and negativism that characterizes the impulse-ridden stage. Generally, the shorter he falls, the quicker he comes back. Thus, those committed to hospitals as manic-depressives are much more likely to recover completely in a few months than those diagnosed as schizophrenics.

We are not pushed back to lower stages only because of the grimness of our present lives. The earlier stages that we have lived through continue to retain a fascination for us. The person with a highly differentiated self retains a yearning to be freed from the fetters of his individuality, to immerse himself in the stream of universal life, to lose his identity, to be absorbed in the whole of life—as he was in the autistic stage of his development. In the same way, the conscientious may yearn to be as dependent, as free to express his aggressive impulses, and to say "no" to everyone as he did when he was at the impulse-ridden stage. The autistic infant or the impulse-ridden child is more likely to be envied than pitied.

Advocates of psychedelic drugs not only yearn for the autistic stage but espouse it as the ideal stage. Even philosophers have advanced impulsiveness as an ideal. The English philosopher Joad (1928) suggests the primary reason why it does not work:

> Believing that the only way to get rid of temptation is to yield to it, he surrenders his mind to every credo that may tickle the reason, his body to every pleasure that may enthral the sense; holding that not the fruits of experience but experience itself is the end of life, he withholds himself from nothing that will cause him to thrill to the pulsing of a more exquisite excitement. . . . He will seek in art and sensationalism the means to keep his experience always at white-hot intensity, and treating his body as an Aeolian harp, will play upon it for the evocation of novel and exquisite harmonies of sense or feeling. Unimpeachable in theory, the doctrine fails somewhat unexpectedly in practice. The recipe for the production of pleasure does not produce pleasure. Servitude to the senses is found to be a more burdensome and exacting form of slavery than servitude to conscience. . . .

SUMMARY

Everyone needs to dream, but those at the autistic stage live in a dream world, unable to discriminate between what is inside from what is outside their heads. Every infant begins at this stage; schizophrenics are adults who have never developed far beyond it. The critical element in their retardation lies in the failure to develop the feeling of being dependent upon others. Both genetic and environmental mechanisms play a significant part in this failure. However, what part each plays and how it plays it are still unknown. Surgery, drugs, psychotherapy, and group therapy are used to overcome this failure but with only limited success. The development of therapeutic communities is a promising new possibility.

The impulse-ridden have developed dependence, but the strength of their momentary impulses is their only guide. The child has a temper tantrum when his impulses are blocked; some impulse-ridden adults engage in sudden acts of violent rage. The XYY chromosome seems directly related to impulsive behavior, but it accounts for only a few of those retarded at this stage. The impulse-ridden get beyond it by imitating the behavior of others so that anything that prevents learning by imitation tends to retard. The same therapies that are used with the autistic are used with the impulse-ridden, but with greater success. Under fatigue and stress, individuals beyond these stages may temporarily regress to them.

SUGGESTIONS FOR FURTHER READING

*Green, H. (1964). *I never promised you a rose garden*. New York: Holt (paperback, New American Library, Signet). Students report the book to be so vivid as to be almost frightening: "The story of sixteen-year-old Deborah's fight to become a member of the participating world of people, to come out from the sidelines and the private world of her own creation . . . a fantastic book from which to gain an understanding of the nature of mental illness and mental institutions."

Beers, C. W. (1948). *A mind that found itself*. New York: Doubleday.

Brown, H. C. (1937). *A mind mislaid*. New York: Dutton.

Hillyer, J. (1927). *Reluctantly told*. New York: Macmillan. Three well-known autobiographies of persons who recovered from major mental illnesses. The latter half of Beers's book describes his successful efforts to found a mental-hygiene.

Answer to Table 10-1: 1. F   2. F   3. T   4. F   5. T   6. F   7. T   8. T   9. T   10. T   11. F   12. T   13. F   14. T   15. F

11

OPPORTUNIST
TO CONFORMIST

The ideal pecuniary man is like the ideal delinquent in his
unscrupulous conversion of goods and persons to his own ends,
and in a callous disregard of the feelings and wishes of others
and of the remoter effects of his actions.

THORSTEIN VEBLEN

Unlike the autistic, the opportunist can discriminate his wishes and thoughts from the wishes and thoughts of others. Unlike the impulse-ridden, he can imitate those who have learned to control their behavior in order to satisfy their immediate needs. However, he has not learned to identify with the feelings of others, as the conformist does. This chapter traces personality development from the opportunistic to the conforming stage. Again, the questions are: How does the individual develop beyond these stages? What conditions cause him to remain at these stages or to return to them?

THE OPPORTUNISTIC STAGE

Owen Simons, a twenty-five-year-old graduate student, is an opportunist. He is good-looking and always neatly dressed. He is intelligent, fluent in speaking, forceful in writing, and ambitious to achieve a high status in his chosen field. He is keenly aware of the rules governing his advancement toward this status—a high grade point average, politeness in dealing with his teachers, etc. However, his use of the rules is consistently expedient. He copies the work of others into his papers without acknowledging the source. He distorts the opinions of others when he thinks it is to his advantage. He manipulates others to do his work. When caught breaking the rules, he does not lose his poise. He gives fervent lip service to the ideals of honesty and integrity. He asserts that "he didn't understand" that what he had done was wrong, and asks: "Why didn't someone tell me?" He assumes an air of contriteness and humility. He appeals to the sympathies of others when he thinks appeals will work; he makes forceful demands that his rights be protected when he thinks force will work. He feels independent, resourceful, and a master of "How to win friends and influence people." However, he is disliked and avoided by his fellow students. His best friend states that Owen often makes him "want to punch him in the nose."

The Symptoms of Opportunism

Owen is not stupid, not unattractive, and not unaware of what it takes to succeed. He is an imitator, a manipulator, and a rationalizer. Owen understands that there are rules that people follow to get what they want. He can also behave in accordance with the rules. What he does not understand is that there are internal rules that match the external ones. He can behave in accordance with the rules, but he cannot feel in accordance with the rules. He can imitate but he cannot identify; the conformist imitates *and* identifies.

Imitation is the process by which we mold our external behavior to match the external behavior of others. *Identification* is the process by which we mold our feelings, attitudes, and personality to match the feelings, attitudes, and personality of others. Imitation is external, objective, and behavioristic; identification is internal, subjective, and emotional. The transition from imitation to identification, from copying behavior to copying feelings, seems to be the key process determining passage from opportunism to conformity.

The development of honesty illustrates the path to the opportunistic stage and beyond. The autistic have no idea what honesty is. The impulse-ridden slowly develop a series of habits that are unrelated to each other. Thus, one child who has the habit of telling the truth when he is caught may cheat at games or steal pennies. A child who lies may not cheat or steal. The opportunist understands the general rules of honesty. He does not lie, steal, or cheat—if he thinks he will be caught (Figure 11-1). If he does not get caught, he will feel elated rather than ashamed. The conformist who is dishonest feels ashamed. The opportunist is motivated by his immediate self-interest, not by his desire to gain the satisfaction of being honest or to avoid the shame of being dishonest.

Owen has learned how to act like a conformist but not how to feel like a conformist. He can act honest without wanting to be honest; he can act contrite without feeling contrite; and he can act friendly without feeling friendly. In general, he has learned how to imitate but not how to identify with people.

Manipulation   The opportunist only obeys rules when he sees that to do so will be to his immediate advantage. He is preoccupied with and talks about getting the better of, deceiving, and dominating others. His interpersonal relationships, that is, are manipulative and exploitive.

Most college students have generally passed beyond opportunism, and many far beyond. Still, instructors are sometimes dismayed at the appeal of opportunism (Coyle, 1955):

Mr. Coyle, I don't want to criticize you as a psychology teacher but you haven't taught this class one thing about how to fool an employer about our qualifications for the job—or how to pad our job resumes—or, for that matter, how to cut angles in general.

Unfortunately, this college student spoke for possibly the majority of the class, which I daresay was a relatively representative sample drawn from the New York City population. In one of several efforts to develop value consciousness, if not values themselves, *What Makes Sammy Run* was assigned as supplemental required reading. Subsequent class discussion

Figure 11-1 The opportunist knows the general rules of honesty, and adheres to them when he thinks he might get caught. Police use marked cars to visibly announce their presence, keeping the public continuously aware of the possibility of detection. (Ron Junttonen)

of this book and polling revealed that a substantial majority considered Sammy "a pretty good guy," "smart," "nobody's fool," "definitely not a sucker." Several volunteered that they had learned a lot from Sammy that "would come in handy." The three or four students who spoke out against Sammy's values or "unifying philosophy of life" were analyzed by their classmates as being "jealous" or as lacking "the courage Sammy had."

Rationalization In rationalizing, we give a *good* motive for our behavior rather than the real one. Hardly an hour passes in which we do not rationalize some of our behavior: the stumbling child blames the chair; the defeated tennis player restrings his racket; the rejected suitor suddenly finds faults in the girl; the cheating student explains that "everyone does it"; the angry father beats his son because "it will do him good"; the man who betrays his friend for gain explains that "you must be practical"; the avaricious person points out that "the Lord helps those who help themselves." Rationalization is a mild form of repression in which the facts are distorted rather than forgotten. Sometimes it is our motives that are distorted, sometimes their causes, and sometimes our goals. Most of the time it is all three.

The autistic and the impulse-ridden do not rationalize, for they see no need to justify themselves or their behavior. The opportunist does. A child soon learns that his antisocial behavior will not be punished if he can convince his parents that his motives were "good." If he makes his baby brother cry by shoving a rattle into his face but explains that he had found it and was returning it to its rightful owner, he is likely to avoid a spanking. The child gradually expands his understanding of "good" and "bad" motives from his parents, from his friends, and from his teachers.

Like the opportunist, the conformist and the conscientious also rationalize but for different reasons. The opportunist rationalizes for the consumption of others; the conformist, for his own consumption as well as for the consumption of others; and the conscientious, primarily for his own consumption. We rationalize to avoid pain or the threat of pain. The only source of pain for the opportunist is other people, for he feels no shame but only fears that others may punish him. The conformist has partially internalized rules, so he rationalizes to avoid self-punishment as well as the punishment of others. The conscientious person has fully internalized the rules. Consequently, when his behavior violates them, he rationalizes primarily to escape self-punishment. While these discriminations can be made in the abstract, they are difficult to make in the concrete, as the following examples show.

Physical aggression as a result of anger is such an unacceptable act that only an appeal to self-preservation normally makes it acceptable. Frank, a college student, recalling his high school days, says:

Before a football game with our principal rival, I was told that a guard on the opposing team was out to smear me. On the first play of the game, he tried to tackle me. I could have gotten loose, but instead I went down with my knees flying. That was the last game of the season for that guard, for I had broken his jaw and nose. Deep within myself, I knew that my action was not excusable. But I kept telling everyone who would listen that it was done in self-defense.

The love of a mother for her children has such a high social value that she must explain even minor lapses.

When the children get too noisy for my nerves, I tell them to play outside because the fresh air is good for them.

In turn, she may use her maternal feelings to explain behavior that might otherwise be criticized:

> I was planning to attend a PTA meeting one evening. When my husband said he would be away that night, I decided that I would have to stay home, because the boys were apt to stay up too late if I left them alone. This was true enough, but I was really using it as an excuse not to go to a boring meeting. Not to go because I thought I would be bored made me feel like a poor parent who was uninterested in her child and his school, but if I stayed home so that my children would get their proper sleep, then I was still being a good mother.

A person may be somewhat aware of what he is doing as he begins to rationalize. He may also be able to recognize that he was rationalizing after it has served its purpose. However, once a rationalization has been developed and while it is still useful, its origins are largely lost, for the person represses his real feelings. He fools himself even when he may not be fooling others.

Rationalization may also be a way of distorting our view of the causes of our emotions. It may, for example, allow us to shift blame from an actual cause to one that is more acceptable. John says:

> I wanted to make the wrestling team the first year I was in high school. After two weeks of practice, I realized that there were two better men returning in my weight classification and that I would have no chance of being number one in my weight. I quit the team, explaining to my family and friends that I needed the time for study and for other extracurricular activities.

More often the rationalization works indirectly by changing our perception of the obstacle. Kenneth explains how this form of rationalization works:

> In my junior year in high school, I played on the B team during the entire season. In my senior year I knew I wasn't going to make the first string, so I walked off the field the day the coach was cutting the squad. I told my friends that the new coach, who didn't know me but knew some of the other boys, was playing favorites and not giving me a chance.

Some of our purposes that grow from our emotions make us feel tense and uncomfortable. Rationalization is an aid in making their pursuit more acceptable to ourselves and to others. Peter describes it this way:

Ten months ago I wanted a newer car, so I traded in my 1968 Ford and bought a 1973 one. At the time, I had a job which required the use of the car, so I told people that the old Ford could not take the beatings I gave it in my travels on the dirt roads of rural areas. I told about the necessary repairs that were coming due and the foolishness of putting any more money in a car as old as that. I realized later that I had greatly exaggerated the poor condition of my old car.

Rationalizing goals is generally easy, for we normally have many motives for doing what we do. Thus, we need pick only the most pleasant and socially acceptable one as *the* explanation. Murphy (1947, p. 547) gives the following example:

Suppose . . . that in the plans of King Leopold of Belgium relative to the exploitation of the Congo area, the sheer economic motivation constituted actually 90 percent, the love of glory and the status as an empire builder another 5 percent, the fun of power politics 4 percent, and all the more idealistic motives, such as education of the natives, 1 percent. Leopold then needed only to make this last 1 percent the anchorage point or figure, relegating to the ground the other 99 percent.

Development

How does the opportunist who acts without feeling become the conformist who acts with feeling? The child first learns to act like his parents and, in the process, gradually learns to feel and think like them. For example, a two-year study of drug use among nearly 10,000 high school students in Toronto indicates that parents who use drugs have children who use drugs. Students who reported their parents to be regular users of tranquilizers were twice as likely to smoke marijuana, three times as likely to use hallucinatory drugs, and eight times as likely to follow the example of drug use set in their households (Smart and Fejer, 1972). What explains the relationship? The answer suggested here is that the child first learns to use drugs and then gradually learns to feel and think like a drug user.

Imitation produces identification. The more we imitate another person, the more we tend to feel and think like that person. Fourteen women who were heavy smokers played the role of a patient with an experimenter. The experimenter, playing the role of a physician, told the patient she had lung cancer. For an hour they acted out several scenes that focused on the pain of the illness, hospitalization, and early death. Twelve other women played the passive role of listening to a tape-recording of a role-playing session. Eighteen months later members of both groups were telephoned to find out how many cigarettes they were smoking each day. Both groups were smoking less; the active role players were smoking still less than the passive listeners. The smoking habits of a control group who had not role played or listened to the role playing had not changed at all. The reports of participants during the final interview indicate that the active role players identified more completely with the cancer victim. Here is a typical comment by a role player who said that he had not been influenced by the Surgeon General's report linking smoking and lung cancer (Mann and Janis, 1968, p. 342):

> . . . But I was in this other study. A professor was doing this psychological thing and I was one of the volunteers. And that was what really affected me. . . . He was the one that scared me, not the report. . . . I got to thinking, what if it were really true and I had to go home and tell everyone that I had cancer. And right then I decided I would not go through this again, and if there were any way of preventing it I would. And I stopped smoking. It was really the professor's study that made me quit.

Clore and McMillan (1970) obtained similar results in a similar experiment. They had students play the role of a disabled student by wheeling themselves across the campus to the student union, having a cup of coffee, and returning. Here is a typical reaction to the experience:

> My arms had started to bother me and it was hard to go in a straight line. When I got to the ramp at the union, I started to go up and realized I was never going to make it. The looks that I received were very interesting and were consistently the same. People looked out of the corner of their eyes and then a downward glance past my legs. They seemed a bit embarrassed. I am surprised what effect this had on me. I was alone the entire time. I saw no one that I knew, so perhaps this made me take it all very seriously. All I know is that my eyes filled up with tears coming back up alone in that elevator.

Afterward, the role players expressed a greater liking for the handicapped and a more favorable attitude toward spending additional money for facilities for them than did a group who had walked behind a role player as he went across campus. Both groups expressed greater liking and more favorable attitudes toward expenditures than did a control group. Conclusion: The more we imitate another person, the more we tend to identify with him.

The more we assume a person is like us, the more we attend to, imitate, and therefore identify with him. Children assume their parents are more like them than other adults and, therefore, identify more with them. Sons generally assume their fathers are more like them than their mothers and, therefore, identify more with their fathers; daughters, for the same reason, identify more with their mothers.

Similarly, a boy identifies more with boys; a girl, with girls. Boys and girls in the first grade saw a series of slide sequences of seven-year-olds in different emotional situations. Some of them involved happy events (a birthday party, winning a television contest); other slides displayed sadness (a lost dog or social rejection), fear (a lost child or a frightened dog), and the emotion of anger (a false accusation). Some children saw boys and some saw girls in the slide sequence. Afterward, each child told how he felt. Result: Boys identified more with boys; girls identified more with girls. (Feshbach and Roe, 1968). That is, boys were more emotional in responses to situations involving boys; girls were more emotional in their responses to situations involving girls.

The more we identify with a person, the less we differentiate ourselves from him, the more we assume that he is like us and we are like him. Burnstein, Stotland, and Zander (1962) brought more than 100 junior high school boys together in the school gymnasium and asked them to complete a "describe yourself questionnaire." One part of the questionnaire required the boys to rate their excellence in swimming, ability to hold breath under water, etc. Two weeks later, the boys were addressed in groups of a dozen by a "deep-sea diver" (one of the authors) who described his career and stressed his excellence in swimming, ability to hold his breath under water, etc. In some groups, he stressed that he was similar to the boys; he was born and raised in their rural neighborhood, went to the same school, had a father who worked in the same factory that employed most of the fathers of the boys, etc. In other groups, the diver stressed that he was dissimilar: he was born and raised in a big city, went to a large city school, had a father who was a fisherman, etc. At the end of each group meeting, the diver asked the boys to rate themselves again on their excellence in swimming, etc. Result: The boys who had heard the "low similarity" diver rated themselves about as they had two weeks before; the boys who heard the "high similarity" diver changed their ratings of themselves so that they were more like those that the diver described himself as possessing.

The opportunist, then, becomes a conformist by learning to identify with other people. He does this by first learning to model his behavior and then to model his feelings after them. The more completely he imitates another person, therefore, the more likely he is to identify with him. The more he sees that another person is like himself and has the same problems that he has, the more likely he is to pay attention to him, to imitate him, and to identify with him. The more he learns to feel like another person, the less he differentiates between himself and that person. That is, the more he identifies with another person, the more likely he is to feel, think, and behave as if he were the other person and the other person were himself.

Retardation

The psychopath illustrates retardation at the opportunistic stage in an extreme form. The central quality of the psychopath is the absence of identification with other people. He has not made the most elementary values of society a part of himself. In the psychopathic group we find unprincipled businessmen, confidence men, impostors, crooked politicians, prostitutes, and assorted delinquents and criminals. They are generally of normal intelligence and are often quite bright. They know the rules of society and the ways of influencing others. They are, however, deficient in moral and ethical values. They typically have little or no internal conflict about their antisocial behavior. They are frequently in conflict with the law and wind up repeatedly in the courts and jails. The individual described below illustrates many of the common features of the psychopathic personality (Galvin and MacDonald, 1959, pp. 1057, 1059–1061):

> He was admitted to a hospital for psychiatric examination in November, 1955. In talking about his life, the patient said that his mother had placed him in an institution for fatherless boys when he was six years old. When he was nine, his mother married a wealthy rancher but refused his repeated requests to come home. At eleven, he was expelled from school for stealing. At sixteen, he lied about his age and enlisted in the Coast Guard. A few months afterward he went AWOL and was later discharged. In early 1951, he forged over 40 checks for a total value of almost $5,000. Later in the year, he crashed through a road block and was sentenced to 60 days in prison for bootlegging and carrying a concealed weapon.
>
> In 1954, his stepfather died and his mother inherited over $90,000. In 1955, she purchased a drive-in for him and went to live with him. The drive-in was not a financial success. In September, it was closed for the winter months. He then took a job as a night mechanic, his 45th since leaving school. During this period, he became very irritated and short tempered with his mother but remained very dependent upon her.
>
> In November, 1955, eleven minutes after leaving Denver, a 4-engine airliner exploded and crashed with the loss of 44 lives. Two weeks later the patient confessed that he had

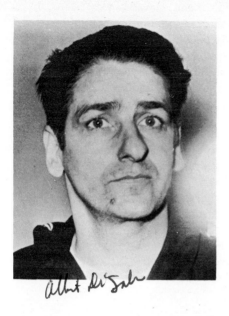

Figure 11-2 A psychopath: this man strangled 13 women in the Boston area (Wide World Photos)

placed a time bomb in his mother's luggage, consisting of a timer, a hot shot battery, blasting caps, and 25 sticks of dynamite. On his admission to the hospital on a plea of insanity, he described his reaction as follows: "I tried to tell her how I felt about it. She just said she wouldn't stay, she wouldn't give me any reason at all, no reason why she didn't want to stay. I thought it was the last time she was going to run off and leave me. I wanted to have her for myself for once. Since I was just a little kid she'd leave me with these people, those people. I wanted to get close to her, everytime I'd get close to her she'd just brush me off like I was a piece of furniture, as if I didn't mean more to her than nothing . . . I just felt if it killed somebody that was tough. It seemed the odds were big enough, there was more fun that way. I just didn't think about the other people on the plane."

The facts suggest the following interpretation. The patient's early close association with his mother led him beyond the autistic stage to a strongly felt dependence upon her. However, there was no opportunity to identify with a father. The prolonged and incomprehensible separation from his mother was painful and probably viewed by the boy as punishment. Because he did not know why he should be punished, he saw no way of avoiding further punishment. Consequently, he acted as if there was no point in restricting his behavior and inhibiting himself. He also developed an intense hostility toward his mother, who had punished him without cause. The situation was probably intensified as he committed more and more serious transgressions. His transgressions brought increasingly severe rejection by his mother and made it increasingly unlikely that he would identify with her or anyone else. Result: A person who stole chronically, was sexually promiscuous, did not respond with guilt to his misdeeds, failed to develop any stable interpersonal relationships, and saw little reason to restrain himself in order to gain the affection of other people.

Eventually he was reunited with his mother. He still had a strong need for an affectional relationship with her. However, once the period of major identification in childhood is passed and internalization of values has not taken place, an individual seems incapable of learning them later. Without such values, he cannot learn in adolescence and maturity that his mode of behavior is punishable by law and society. Under such circumstances, anxiety is rarely present although fear of being caught often is. Such a person is capable of learning what the rules are and the consequences of breaking them. He seems, nevertheless, incapable of using them as guides for his own behavior.

Retarding Mechanisms Mechanisms that retard a person at the autistic or impulse-ridden stage obviously prevent him from developing even to the opportunistic stage. But once at the opportunistic stage, what prevents him from developing beyond it?

To identify with people, the child needs appropriate people with whom to identify. More specifically, he needs people who like and help him and who are like him. The child raised in an institution by indifferent strangers has no one with whom he can identify. The boy raised by an adoring and overprotective mother has no one appropriate with whom to identify. Even the absence of siblings may reduce identification. Thus, Stotland and Dunn (1963) had college students observe a fellow student being berated for his failing performance in a difficult situation. Their emotional reaction was measured with a psychogalvanometer as well as by later subjective reports. First born and only children identified less: "The first and only born . . . react as if they only used the other person's performance level as a guide to self-evaluation and do not really 'feel with' him."

Differences in family organization may create profound differences in the degree of identification. Whiting (1959) divided 28 societies into the following categories:

Monogamous nuclear (7) Societies in which the mother, father, and children eat, sleep, and entertain under one roof. Grandparents and siblings of the parents live elsewhere.

Monogamous extended (6) Societies in which two or more

nuclear families commonly live together under one roof. A typical extended family consists of an aged couple with their married sons or daughters together with their spouses and children.

Polygymous (8) Societies in which the typical family consists of a man living with wives and their children.

Mother-child (7) Polygynous societies in which each wife has a separate house and establishments and lives in it with her children. In these societies, the father either has a hut of his own, sleeps in the men's club house, or rotates among the houses of his various wives.

Type of society was related to degree of guilt. Guilt was measured by the degree to which individuals in the society felt personally responsible for what happened to them, i.e., in this case, for getting sick. That is, the more often members of a society blame themselves for having gotten sick, the greater the guilt in the society. The 28 societies were then divided into the 14 with the highest ratings on guilt and the 14 with the lowest rating. Result: 86 percent of monogamous nuclear societies were in the "high guilt" group; 67 percent of the monogamous extended families; 38 percent of the polygynous societies; and 14 percent of the mother-child polygynous societies. Only 1 of the 7 societies of the monogamous nuclear type was in the "low guilt" group; only 1 of the societies of the mother-child type was in the "high guilt" group.

Members of low guilt cultures are more likely to remain opportunists; members of high guilt cultures are more likely to become conformists. For example, 15 American-born children in a rural public school in Hawaii were given an opportunity to win a prize in shooting a ray-gun. They were given 20 trials and told that they needed 35 points to win. They were also told to keep a record of their performance. However, the experiment was secretly arranged so that all the children received the same score: 32. Only 7 of the 15 children cheated even though they thought there was no way for them to be caught. Samoan society is classified by anthropologists as a "shame" culture. The same study was performed with Samoan children in the same class in the same school in Hawaii. *None* of the 19 Samoans resisted the temptation to cheat (Grinder and McMichael, 1963).

Psychotherapy has had very little success with psychopaths. Psychotherapy requires that patient and therapist enter into a mutual relationship of shared regard and trust. Psychopaths are incapable of either requesting or accepting help. They avoid therapy. They generally react with aggression to therapists, for they perceive therapists as similar to the parents who rejected them. Offers of help are met with demands for even more help. If the demands are not met, an explosion of hate occurs. To the psychopath, manifestations of good will are either signs of an enemy's weakness or tricks designed to deceive him.

Some people think that it is unfortunate that a psychopath should be imprisoned. Society, however, has other people to think of besides him. A man beaten over the head with a piece of lead pipe has only a mild interest in whether his assailant was a simple criminal or a complex psychopath. Many psychopaths do not respond to therapy. The logical conclusion is that they should be locked up with the therapist until they do—maybe for the rest of their lives. Every effort, of course, should be made to expand research that may lead to more effective treatment.

Regression

Conformists understand the Golden Rule and want to follow it. Sometimes, however, they do not. A conformist who must deal with a threatening and authoritarian leader may feel forced to deal with him in a manipulative way. In general, a person's stage of development sets an upper limit to the quality of relationships that are possible for him. This possibility, however, may not become a reality.

We are pushed back to the opportunistic stage by unfavorable circumstances. We are also pulled back to it by its primitive appeal. The behavior of a psychopath often arouses intense anger in others. But this is not the whole story. Sometimes he is idolized and made a hero as in the case of Bluebeard, Morgan the Pirate, and Jesse James. The psychopath's readiness to violate social norms to gratify his wishes and his lack of anxiety about having done so arouse envy. He does things that we would like to do but do not do because of the anxieties that we have and he does not. Our envy is intensified by the social grace and charm he often shows because of his lack of anxiety in the presence of others.

THE CONFORMIST STAGE

When we conform, we obey a law, follow a custom, or yield to social pressures. Motorists who approach an intersection where there is no cross traffic show widely varying behavior: some stop, some slow down, and some continue at the same speed. Increased social pressure changes the pattern. When there is no cross traffic but when a red light and a traffic officer are present, over 90 percent of motorists stop completely. Also, pressures to conform exist in many less obvious places: the failure of college students to participate in class discussions is often a conforming response (Smith and Dunbar, 1951).

Conformity is inevitable. The laws, customs, and values of all societies pervasively and firmly mold the behavior of their members. Conformity is also often desirable from any point of view. The average motorist in the United States conforms more closely to traffic laws than his European brother. Consequently, fatal accidents on the roads of the United States are many fewer per car than in Europe. About 30 people are killed, 50 women raped, 750 robberies committed, and 3,000 burglaries attempted every day in the United States. Few would question that greater conformity to the laws governing these matters would be desirable.

Susan is a conformist:

I would much rather agree and conform than risk the chance of creating a disturbance by not conforming or not going along with the crowd. Many times this has annoyed me, but the desire to conform always seems to win out. I suppose the main reason for my constant conforming is to win or keep friends. I feel that by agreeing with people I am more likely to be accepted by them.

Don is a nonconformist. He feels that "the world is too much with us":

Many people disagree with me, and I do not hesitate to disagree with them. I believe in being uninhibited, and I do not feel it necessary to justify my actions to anyone. I care little whether people approve of what I do or think. Too many people, in my estimation, conform and never think first whether it is right or wrong to conform. I do not agree with a group just because I am a member of it. I admire people like Ernest Hemingway for enjoying life and traveling thru it rather than with it . . . I like flying, driving, music, and just about all recreations. In religion and philosophy I am a liberal and am still searching. . . . I would rather receive a set of drums or something equally impractical for a present than clothes or similar "sensible" items . . . I am an only child and have probably had my way more than is usual in families.

Symptoms of Conformity

The most obvious and measurable symptom of the conformist is that he yields to group norms. The opportunist obeys the norms when he sees that it is to his immediate advantage to do so. The conformist obeys the norms whether it is to his advantage or not. Indeed, he tends to conform even if it is to no one's advantage to do so. Still, he has only *partially* internalized the rules, for the question which often preoccupies him is: What will people say?

Group before Individual Judgment The conformist typically is not aware that he is a conformist, for he conforms because he never seriously thought of doing anything else. He is at one with his surroundings and feels himself to be a part of them. He sometimes thinks of himself as being a nonconformist. Self-ratings, as a consequence, are an undependable measure of conformity. Crutchfield (1955) used an elaborate electrical communication network to measure differences in conformity in a much more objective way.

His method applies a "standard group pressure" to each person taking a test and measures the extent to which the person responds to the pressure. In the test, five persons at a time look at slides projected on the wall in front of them. The slides show lines, arithmetic problems, pretty and ugly objects, and social questions. Each subject is given the same tasks: to judge which is the longest line, to choose which is the correct answer to the problem, to indicate which is the prettiest object, and to give his opinion on a social issue. He reports his answer by closing the proper switch on the table in front of him.

The five persons are not allowed to talk to each other. They are told that their answers are reported to the others by signal lights on their switchboards. They are also told that the order of reporting answers will be varied: sometimes one person will give his judgment first, sometimes second, and so on. Thus, every person will sometimes be the last person to report his answer and will therefore be able to see how the other four answered the problem before he answers. Actually, there is no electrical connection between the switchboards. What the subjects think are the judgments of their fellow members are really being "fed" to them by the experimenter. Consequently, the experimenter can make it appear that the other four members agree on an answer, and this is what he does for each person as many as 50 times in a single session. A subject's conformity score is the number of times he gives the answer that he believes the group has given.

All of the subjects in the principal study were then engaged in professions requiring leadership and most had at least some college training. Few of these subjects conformed on easy problems or questions of personal taste. In general, however, the tendency to conform was striking. For example, subjects outside the group-pressure situation and subjects inside the situation were asked whether they agreed or disagreed with the following statement: "Free speech being a privilege rather than a right, it is proper for society to suspend free speech." Outside, only 19 percent agreed with the statement; inside, 57 percent agreed. There were wide differences among the 50 middle-aged professional men. Some conformed in almost all of the situations; and some conformed in almost none.

Public before Private Laws Unlike the opportunist, the conformist follows the Golden Rule: Do unto others as you would have them do unto you. However, he acts as if what he should do for himself and what he should do for others is what the group norms say he should do. The conformist does not differentiate the group's rules for him from his rules for himself. The Greek word *autonomos* is a combination of "autos" meaning self and "nomos" meaning law. The autonomous person is one who governs himself by his own laws. Thus, the conformist is not autonomous.

The person who is not autonomous lacks freedom. However, the person who *is* autonomous also lacks freedom: "The power to make one's own choices or decisions without restraint from within or without." Freedom has a different meaning at each stage of development. The impulse-ridden have no internal restraints and want no external ones. However, they have external restraints imposed. The conformist has weak internal restraints but powerful external ones. The conscientious have weak external constraints but powerful internal ones, for they seek to devise and conform to their private laws. The German philosopher, Immanuel Kant, tried to formulate the test that all private laws should ideally meet: Act only on private laws that you wish everybody would follow. Autonomy, then, is not a gift, but a task; not a fact, but a possibility; and not easy, but hard to achieve. It has not been achieved by the conformist.

Externals before Internals Obedience to his group reflects and intensifies the conformist's primary preoccupation with externals (Figure 11-3). He is little concerned with internal matters: his feelings, his ideas, or his inner conflicts. Thoughts about inner states, his own or those of other people, tend to be both infrequent and superficial. He is very aware of what he does and others do, little aware of what he feels or what others feel while they are doing it. The absence of serious self-criticism is thus the hallmark of the conformist.

Most people are at the conformist stage. Consequently, their values tend to dominate judgments of normality and adjustment. Conformists are severe in their moral judgments. Their judgments are also heavily influenced by whether behavior leads to the loss or gain of tangible things: money, possessions, college degrees, and status jobs. They are also likely to view violations of customs with greater seriousness than do the conscientious and the self-actualized. On the other hand, they are less concerned with inner motives, feelings, or ethical principles. Conformists judge what people do, not what they intend to do. Consequently, they are likely to judge the unhappy but

MERGING
TRAFFIC

Figure 11-3 The conformist is preoccupied with externals: material possessions, physical appearance, and social status. The "little boxes on the
hillside" are reflections of the conforming individuals inside. (Hugh Rogers/
Monkmeyer)

wealthy man as better adjusted than the poor but happy one. In sum,
"psychological adjustment" has become, in the minds of many, synon-
ymous with conformity.

Development

Some conform in public and disobey in private. Some conform in a
particular situation because they have decided that the customary way
is the best way. The extreme conformist obeys the rules in public or in
private and in all situations because he believes it is *right* to conform.

The conformist is far along the road toward personality development. He is out of sight of the autistic, who not only does not know
that there are rules but also does not even know that he is a person
separate from other persons. The conformist is beyond the impulse-
ridden, who knows that he is a person but does not know that there are
rules that govern interpersonal relationships. He is well ahead of the

opportunist, who knows there are rules but does not know that they apply to him. The conformist is capable of genuine cooperative and reciprocal relationships with others.

By contrast, those at the conscientious stage are confused and troubled. The conscientious person opposes his will against the will of his parents and against the compulsions of the outside world. He seeks his own attitudes towards himself and toward the world. He has lost his comfortable identification with the people and the world around him; he has not found his own identity. His fear of life is intensified by his increased sense of separateness. He is plagued by self-criticism, by feelings of guilt, and by a sense of inferiority.

People may be conscientious who do not violate public laws. They *are* conscientious if they deliberately disobey a public law to obey a private one and take the consequences of their public disobedience. Thus, those who obey the draft law may be conscientious. Those who disobey the draft law may also be conscientious—or opportunistic. However, those who disobey the draft law and willingly go to prison for it *are* conscientious. The novelist Conrad (1912) said: "Those who read me know my conviction that the world, the temporal world, rests on a few very simple ideas; so simple that they must be as old as the hills. It rests notably, among others, on the idea of Fidelity." The conscientious do not merely understand ideas like Fidelity; they identify with them; i.e., their feelings, thoughts, and actions are ruled by them.

What leads some conformists to take the giant step of substituting their own private ideas for publicly accepted ones? Self development, we have asserted, is the slow process of making internal what was originally external. As the autistic infant learns to depend upon his mother he becomes impulse-ridden; as the child learns to imitate the behavior of those around him he becomes opportunistic; as the adolescent learns to identify with the feelings of those around him he becomes a conformist. Finally, he becomes conscientious as he becomes more and more identified with the *ideas* of people rather than with the people themselves. A boy may first feel dependent upon his father, then talk the way he does, then perceive the world as he does, and, finally, love, fight, and work for truth, beauty, and goodness as his father did.

When a person identifies with another person, he responds emotionally as if he were that person: he feels joy when the person triumphs, sadness when he fails, and anger when he is injured. When he identifies with an idea he responds in a similar way: he feels joy when the idea triumphs, sadness when it fails, and anger when it is injured. How does a person move from identifying with people to identifying with their ideas? Just as we move from imitating a person to identifying with him, we may move from identifying with the person to identifying with his ideas. The American philosopher Peirce (1955), for example, described how one might develop an identification with the idea of God in this way:

> Just as long acquaintance with a man of great character may deeply influence one's whole manner of conduct, so that a glance at his portrait may make a difference, just as almost living with Dr. Johnson enabled poor Boswell to write an immortal book and a really sublime book, just as long study of the works of Aristotle may make him an acquaintance, so if contemplation and study of the physical-psychical universe can imbue a man with principles of conduct analogous to the influence of the great man's works or conversation, then that analogue of the mind—for it is impossible to say that *any* human attribute is *literally* applicable—is what he means by "God."

Retardation

Why do most people never develop beyond the conforming stage? Crutchfield (1955) related conformity scores to a wide range of biographical facts, attitude scales, personality inventories, and intelligence tests. Here are some of his conclusions:

> . . . there appears to be a marked difference in the early home background of the conformists and independents. The high conformers in this study come almost without exception from stable homes; the independents much more frequently report broken homes and unstable home environments . . .
>
> Most of the men in the sample are fathers, and it is instructive to see that in their view of child-rearing practices, the conformers are distinctly more "restrictive" in their attitudes, and the independents are distinctly more "permissive" . . .
>
> Previous theoretical and empirical studies seem to converge, though imperfectly, on a picture of the overconformist as having less ego strength, less ability to tolerate his own impulses and to tolerate ambiguity, less ability to accept responsibility, less self-insight, less spontaneity and productive originality, and as having more prejudiced and authoritarian attitudes, more idealization of parents, and greater emphasis on external and socially approved values.
>
> All of these elements gain at least some substantiation in the present study of conformity behavior, as objectively measured in our test situation. The decisive influence of

intelligence in resisting conformity pressures is perhaps given even fuller weight in the present findings.

It appears that those who remain conformists have a strong parental will to oppose because of the constant presence of parents and because of the parents' authoritarian attitudes. They have weak personality structures incapable of withstanding and resolving internal conflicts generated by opposing individuals and groups. To become conscientious, an individual must be intelligent enough to be able to formulate and to apply ideas. Idiots, imbeciles, and morons do not have this ability. However, intelligence alone is not sufficient, for the opportunist has enough intelligence to formulate rules for himself and to apply them. He is just not motivated to do so. The conscientious are motivated to formulate and apply their own rules. Why do most conformists never develop this motivation?

Retardation and Survival   Some situations demand that we obey social norms to survive. The driver who ignores the traffic lights is not long for this world. Some situations, however, demand that we follow our judgment if we want to survive. In general, some societies demand conformity while others demand nonconformity for survival. Members of the former, as a consequence, are more conforming while members of the latter are more conscientious.

The Temne of Sierra Leone are primitive rice farmers whose single annual crop must be rationed out in daily units until the next harvest. Berry (1967) presented 122 Temne with a line-judging task in which each was presented with nine lines and asked to judge which one was the same length as a standard line at the top. Six test sheets, each containing nine horizontal lines, were presented at a distance of four feet. After two sample problems, the subject was told:

Here is another sheet with nine lines on it, one here at the top, and eight beneath it. This time I am going to give you a hint. Most Temne people say this line (experimenter pointing to number 6) is equal in length to the one at the top. Which one do you say?

On that particular test trial the line pointed to was correct. On the next three trials the line pointed to was incorrect. A high proportion of the Temne chose the incorrect but conforming line. In explanation of his choice a typical Temne said: "When Temne people choose a thing, we must all agree with the decision—this is what we call cooperation." The Temne as a people punish individually any deviations from socially accepted behavior.

The same task was given to 122 Eskimos of Baffin Island. Since the area in which they live is without edible vegetation, an individual's survival depends solely upon his skill in hunting and fishing. The Eskimo ignored the "information" about the group choice. Typically, he said nothing during the testing but often gave a quiet, knowing smile as he indicated the line that actually matched the standard line. As a people, the Eskimos are known to be self-reliant, individualistic, and fearful of both dependency and incompetence.

Eskimos survive by learning to trust their own judgment. The more intelligent they are, the better their judgment is likely to be. In general, the more intelligent a person is, the more likely he is to be able to formulate rules that have greater survival value than those of his group. Those who remain at the conformist stage are less intelligent, not only because the less intelligent find it hard to formulate their own rules but also because they find that the rules of the group are better than the rules they can formulate.

Retardation and Shame   Internalized moral values rule the conscientious. If what they think, decide, or do is in conflict with these values, they feel guilty and are ready to accept blame for what they have done. The intensity of guilt feelings, however, varies a great deal from person to person in our society. It also varies from society to society. It is, therefore, to an examination of these cultural differences that we first turn in an effort to understand why some people do and some do not develop from the conforming to the conscientious stage.

All societies satisfy the needs of their members. However, in order to survive they must also punish those who violate the rules that maintain their complex social systems (Whiting, 1959). All societies also learn that policing is not enough, for this method of social control would require that each member have a policeman shadowing him—and who shadows the policeman? Again, all societies have neighbors acting as informal policemen, but none have found this type of control sufficient. All societies, therefore, have developed ways of getting their members to control *themselves*. Shame and guilt are two of these ways.

Shame cultures stress external sanctions; guilt cultures, internal ones (Benedict, 1946, p. 223):

> Shame is a reaction to other people's criticism. A man is shamed either by being openly ridiculed and rejected or by fantasying to himself that he has been made ridiculous. In either case it is a potent sanction. But it requires an audience or at least a man's fantasy of an audience. Guilt does not. In a

nation where honor means living up to one's own picture of oneself, a man may suffer from guilt though no man knows of his misdeed and a man's feeling of guilt may actually be relieved by confessing his sin.

The housewife who feels comfortable when she has swept the dirt under the rug before the guests arrive is motivated by shame. If she feels uncomfortable even though she knows the guests will not see the dirt, she is motivated by guilt.

The early Puritans in the United States based their morality on guilt. Japanese society, on the other hand, stresses that a sense of shame is the root of all virtue. Americans believe men to be neither good nor bad but that they are perfectible; the Japanese believe men to be innately good but that they have the obligation to keep their goodness untarnished. Americans believe that men must develop a conscience to control their evil impulses; the Japanese strive to eliminate the conscience, so that their good impulses may more freely express themselves. Americans feel little obligation to their parents and their society for their care, education, and present well-being; the Japanese feel a great obligation to their forebears and their contemporaries. Americans value the man who rebels against conventions and seizes happiness in spite of obstacles; the Japanese value the man who disregards his personal happiness and fulfills his obligations—the virtuous man is one who divorces his loved wife in order to obey his mother or who sacrifices his life to fulfill his obligation to his family. Americans believe in equality; Japanese believe in a hierarchy of worth based on age, sex, social class, and family. They follow elaborate rituals to show the relationships between persons in different parts of the hierarchy (Benedict, 1946).

Like fish in the sea, neither we nor the Japanese are much aware of the cultural controls under which we live. Yanked from our seas, however, we soon may be gasping for breath. *My Narrow Isle* (Mishima, 1941) is the autobiography of a Japanese girl who went to college at Wellesley. Her reactions were like those of an expert tennis player entered in a croquet tournament (p. 226):

My pride in perfect manneredness, a universal characteristic of the Japanese, was bitterly wounded. I was angry at myself for not knowing how to behave properly and also at the surroundings which seemed to mock at my past training. Except for this vague but deep-rooted feeling of anger there was no emotion left in me. . . . My Japanese training, requiring every physical movement to be elegant and every word uttered to be according to etiquette, made me extremely sensitive and self-conscious in this environment, where I was completely blind, socially speaking.

Her highly developed watchfulness for all the cues in other people's acts and her strong sense that other people were sitting in judgment upon her were largely irrelevant to living in a guilt culture.

Some Japanese have always been motivated by guilt and probably more are today than before World War II. Some Americans have always been motivated by shame and probably more are today than in the Puritan period. In general, however, the more a society stresses guilt as a mechanism of social control, the more guilty the typical member of that society is likely to feel.

Guilt societies use love-oriented techniques to control their children; shame societies, object-oriented techniques. The more object-oriented techniques are stressed in a society, the more likely it is that the typical member will remain at the conformist stage.

Retardation and Identification   Identification with people is essential for the development of the conscientious. Intense identification is not. In fact, intense identification seems to retard development from the conforming to the conscientious stage. Comparisons of children raised in Kibbutz and non-Kibbutz settlements support this conclusion. The Kibbutz child is *not* raised in a traditional family. Shortly after birth he is placed in a nursery with a group of age peers in charge of a nurse caretaker. The mother and the caretaker have quite separate functions. The mother nurses the baby during the first year, cares for him during several periods of the day, and subsequently takes him for short visits to her apartment, to the father, and to brothers and sisters. After the first year, the mother sees the child during daily visits after work and for longer periods on holidays. The caretaker administers to the child's physical needs, to his training, and to his socialization. She teaches the child how to feed himself, toilet trains him, and controls his aggression. As the child grows older, the peers in his group take an active role in his socialization. In general, the role of the parents is much like the role of grandparents in the United States.

Kibbutz children have less severe guilt feelings than the non-Kibbutz children who are raised by their mothers and fathers. Rabin and Goldman (1966) measured the severity of guilt feelings among 100 non-Kibbutz and 110 Kibbutz boys and girls in the seventh grade. The responses the children gave to four incomplete stories were classified as showing low, medium, or high guilt. The stories involved theft, disobedience to mother, death-wishes, and sabotage of group enterprises. On all four of these stories the responses of both the boys and the girls in the Kibbutz showed less guilt than the children in the non-Kibbutz. Conclusion: " . . . Kibbutz children, because of more diffuse and less intense identification, show less severity of guilt upon violation of social norms than non-Kibbutz children."

The immediate consequences of Kibbutz rearing were less favorable than traditional rearing (Rabin, 1958). When studied during childhood, the children from traditional homes were superior in all tests and especially superior in their social development. The long-range consequences, however, favored the Kibbutz rearing. As adolescents, Kibbutz children were slightly more intelligent, had a wider range of interests, and gave considerable evidence of being more mature in their personality organization.

In the long run, it seems, moderate identification is more likely to lead toward the identification with ideas that is characteristic of the conscientious.

Regression

The step down from the conscientious to the conforming stage is attractive and sometimes nearly irresistible. The conscientious person does what his own convictions and his own judgment tell him to do. It is always less effort to let the group decide than to make up one's own mind. However, it is easy to decide for oneself between the better of two goods. It is harder to decide between the lesser of two evils. It is hardest of all in times of accelerating social change and upheaval. In such times the conscientious feel an increasing distrust of their own judgments. They are more than likely to see freedom as a burden rather than a privilege. If the situation becomes acute enough, they may try to throw off the burden—and succeed. In *The March of Fascism*, Raushenbush (1939) relates how he asked a German grocer whether something valuable had been given up when freedom was surrendered. The grocer replied: "But you don't understand at all. Before this we had to worry about elections, and parties, and voting. We had responsibilities. But now we don't have any of that. Now we're free."

SUMMARY

The opportunist can understand and imitate the behavior of others; he cannot understand and identify with the feelings of others. Consequently, he can only follow rules about what he should say and do. Furthermore, he only follows these rules when it is to his immediate advantage or he thinks he will get caught and punished if he does not. Others tend to see the opportunist as a chronic manipulator and rationalizer, for he can only act the way he should and cannot feel the way he should. Retardation at this stage may result from the absence of appropriate models with whom to identify or from a rearing in which only behaving in the right way is stressed. Progress beyond the opportunistic stage is gradual. However, the psychopath reveals the essential qualities of this stage in pure form: he has no capacity to identify with others, no awareness of right and wrong, and no feelings of shame or guilt about the harm he does.

The conformist can identify with others as well as imitate them. Consequently, he follows rules even though it is to his disadvantage to do so and even though he thinks he will not get caught if he breaks them, for he wants to avoid the self-punishment of his own feelings of guilt at the violation of the rules. However, the conformist has limited ability to differentiate between the rules of the group and his own rules and places primary stress on following rules of behavior rather than rules of feeling and thinking. People may remain at the conforming stage because following the rules of the group is essential for survival. As people develop beyond this stage, they identify more and more with the rules and less and less with the makers of rules.

SUGGESTIONS FOR FURTHER READING

Dicker, L. (1957). *My inward journey.* Philadelphia: Westminster Press. An autobiographical report of the six years of psychotherapy undertaken by a young housewife and mother to cure herself of asthma.

Leonard, W. E. (1927). *The locomotive-god.* New York: Appleton-Century-Crofts. A University of Wisconsin professor and poet describes his efforts to discover the childhood origins of his phobia and to cure himself.

Reik, T. (1948). *Listening with the third ear.* New York: Farrar, Strauss. An intimate and informal account of psychoanalytic treatment as seen through the eyes of the analyst.

Devereux, G. (1951). *Reality and dream.* New York: International Universities Press. A report of the psychotherapy of an American Indian that reveals some of the cultural factors that determine the development of the self.

12

CONSCIENTIOUS TO SELF-ACTUALIZED

The most radical division that it is possible to make of humanity is that which splits it into two classes of creatures: those who make great demands on themselves, piling up difficulties and studies; and those who demand nothing special of themselves, but for whom to live is to be every moment what they already are, without imposing on themselves any effort towards perfection; mere buoys that float on the waves.

JOSÉ ORTEGA y GASSET

It is hard to find the common qualities shared by those at the conscientious and self-actualized stages. The Ibsens and Thoreaus, the Freuds and Jameses, the Kings and the Humes are more noteworthy for their differences than their similarities. The desirability of being at these stages compounds the problems. Even the impulse-ridden and opportunists among us are inclined to say and to believe that they are "conscientious." We begin, therefore, by examining two of the few studies of these stages in an effort to find the central qualities of the conscientious and the self-actualized and to discover the processes by which the former become the latter.

THE STUDIES OF MASLOW AND MacKINNON

Maslow (1954) made a strenuous effort to identify the common qualities of self-actualized people. He defined the need for self-actualization as the "desire to become more and more what one is, to become everything that one is capable of becoming." It is a growth need rather than a deficit need like the need for food, water, safety, belonging, or status. He assumes that human needs are in a hierarchy from low to high. It is only when the lower needs are satisfied that the need for self-actualization can emerge to dominate the personality. For example, Thomas Jefferson, born into a well-to-do and respected Virginian family, had his lower needs for physical satisfaction, safety, and belonging fully satisfied. As a consequence, his youth was preoccupied by the need for status. As the young author of the Declaration of Independence, he gained the esteem of his country and the world. These lower and external needs satisfied, his maturity was dominated by the need for self-actualization and his personality reflected the attributes of the self-actualized person: spontaneity, freshness of perception, acceptance of the world, and identification with mankind.

In studying the self-actualized personality Maslow started with people who seemed to be operating at full capacity: fulfilling themselves, making maximum use of their talents, and generally doing the best that they were capable of doing. They were selected from his students, personal acquaintances, and historical figures. His final group consisted of 48 persons: 12 "probable," 10 "partial," and 26 "potential or possible" self-actualizers. Among his 48 were the following 18 public and historical figures:

Jane Addams	Johann Wolfgang von Goethe
Ludwig van Beethoven	William James
Albert Einstein	Thomas Jefferson
George Washington Carver	Abraham Lincoln
Eugene V. Debs	Fritz Kreisler
Thomas Eakins	Eleanor Roosevelt

Sigmund Freud	Franklin D. Roosevelt
Albert Schweitzer	Henry Thoreau
Baruch Spinoza	Walt Whitman

In addition, the group included 10 unnamed contemporaries of Maslow whom he had observed informally over long periods of time and 20 students picked from the 1 percent of the college population showing the most certain signs of becoming self-actualizers. Maslow (1954, p. 203) has described the general method he used in studying the group:

Data here consist not so much in the usual gathering of specific and discrete facts as in the slow development of a global or holistic impression of the sort we form of our friends and acquaintances. It was rarely possible to set up a situation, to ask pointed questions, or to do any testing with my older subjects (although this *was* possible and was done with younger subjects). Contacts were fortuitous and of the ordinary social sort. Friends and relatives were questioned where this was possible.

One of the qualities Maslow distinguishes most sharply between the self-actualized and those at lower stages was their independence, i.e., their tendency to obey their own laws rather than public ones: "independence of culture and environment," "quality of detachment," "need for privacy," and "resistance to enculturation." They were open, realistic, and critical: "spontaneity," "continued freshness of perception," "discrimination between means and ends," "efficient perception of reality," and "problem-centered." They were equalitarian by nature: "democratic character structure," "acceptance of self and others," "identification with mankind." They were also loving people: "fusion of sex and love," "deep and profound interpersonal relations," "oceanic feelings."

The Study of Architects

Maslow's pioneer study was intuitive, unsystematic, synthetic, unquantitative, and limited to the highest stage of development. MacKinnon's study was experimental, systematic, analytic, quantitative, and sheds light upon the conforming and conscientious stages as well as the self-actualized stage.

The Selection of the Groups   The aim of MacKinnon's study (1965) was to examine the differences between less creative and more creative people. In pursuit of this aim he studied three groups of architects.

"Architects III" we shall call the conformists; "Architects II," the conscientious; and "Architects I," the self-actualized. He chose architects for his study because this field appeared to require a wide range of competencies. The successful creative architect needs to be something of an artist, scientist, businessman, lawyer, advertiser, journalist, educator, and psychologist.

Five professors of architecture at Berkeley helped him pick the self-actualized group. Each professor, working independently, rated the 40 architects whom they considered the most outstanding in the country. The total list for all the professors included 86 architects. MacKinnon then ranked them from 1 to 86 on the basis of their mean rating. The first 40 were invited to Berkeley to participate in the study. Because some refused, 64 were eventually invited.

The conscientious group of 43 architects were selected in a similar way. None of them were ranked among the top group, but all had had at least two years of work experience with one of the self-actualized architects. This group was picked so that each member matched a member of the self-actualized group who came from the same part of the country and was of the same age.

None of the 41 members of the conformist group had ever worked with any of the self-actualized architects and all had low ratings on creativity. Each member also came from the same part of the country and was of the same age as a member of the self-actualized and a member of the conscientious group.

Measurements   The self-actualized group went to Berkeley and were participants in an intensive three-day personality assessment. In the process, they were interviewed, gave biographical information about themselves, and completed a long battery of psychological tests: the Minnesota Multiphasic Personality Inventory, the Adjective Check List, the California Psychological Inventory, the Taylor Manifest Anxiety Scale, and the Fundamental Interpersonal Relations Orientation-Behavior Questionnaire. Members of the other two groups worked at their homes for more than six hours completing some of the same tests, questionnaires, and inventories that had been taken by the self-actualized group. They did not, however, complete either the timed tests or the intelligence tests that were taken by the self-actualized group at Berkeley.

The data from all these sources were examined with one general question in mind: How did Architects I, II, and III differ and how could their differences be explained? Some of the answers found are included in the following discussion.

SYMPTOMS OF CONSCIENTIOUSNESS

The case of Tony Conrad (*Look*, January 10, 1967) illustrates the slow and painful development from the conforming to the conscientious stage and beyond. The oldest of four children, Tony was born in Baldwin, Maryland, the son of an ex-teacher. As a child, he was close to his mother. He did extremely well in high school and was gifted in both music and mathematics. He was offered scholarships to several dozen colleges. He chose Harvard. In his junior year he took a summer job in Denmark to work with computers.

At the end of the summer, he dismayed his parents by his decision not to return to Harvard. He first visited a center of European avant-garde music and then wandered around Europe for six months. In the fall he returned to Harvard but became interested in economics and modern Russian history. He did poorly and lost his scholarship. He said: "I became obsessed with the idea of an American music that would overthrow present content and form and return to the emotional." After graduation he moved to the East Village in New York: "I paid with poverty and a little discomfort for having literally all the time in the world. I've always needed privacy to contemplate and create." He took temporary jobs mimeographing or opening envelopes to get money to live. He had no bank account, and rode a bicycle to save subway fare.

Of his life in the Village, Tony said:

I'd been inhibited in Baldwin. I was this very sincere kid who thought Tchaikovsky was the grooviest and Bartok too far out. Now that I have gotten into more exotic fields musically, it is very exciting. I felt the same might be true about my inner life. And the people in the underground really stunned me. I respect the idea of communal living: fourteen people in a loft, no possessions, all kinds of amorphous not-too-personal sexuality. I could never appreciate it myself. I've always had one girl and a place. . . . But I have no intention of copping out. I don't feel responsible for upholding old forms of society. But I do feel committed to my own integrity. We are not dropouts really. We are holdouts. We would like to regain our romantic faith in this country. Until we can, we are acting according to personal standards of integrity.

As time passed, he became increasingly worried about how little he had to show for his time. He took a regular job uptown that made use of his technical abilities. In 1966, he cut his hair, married, and received a grant from the Rockefeller Foundation on the basis of his movie *Flicker*, which was shown at the Lincoln Center. The movie consists of light and dark frames with an electric sound track. He is thinking of quitting his job so that he can spend full time on his new movie. He now has two business suits and four neckties.

As Tony moved from the conforming to the conscientious stage, he became more and more self-critical. He struck out on his own in an effort to form goals, ideals, and ethical standards that were his rather than those of society. He gradually assumed new attitudes toward himself and toward the world. New possibilities of development seem to open before him. If he realizes these possibilities, he will become a more competent and creative person. If they are not realized, however, he may remain plagued by self-doubt, feelings of inferiority and guilt, and stay in a chronic and painful state of internal conflict.

Like the conscientious in general, Tony obeys his own internalized rules rather than the external rules of society ("I feel committed to my own integrity"). He is also self-critical rather than smug, original rather than traditional.

Private before Public Laws

The study of architects revealed considerable evidence that the conscientious had internalized their own rules more than the conformists; the self-actualized, more than the conscientious. In the assessment process, all three groups sorted adjectives first to describe themselves in their architectural practice and second to describe the ideal architect. The self-actualized group saw "as most characteristic of themselves and of the ideal architect, some inner artistic standard of excellence and a sensitive appreciation of the fitness of architectural solutions to that standard." The conscientious group placed "more stress upon the efficient execution of architecture, seeing as most saliently characteristic of the ideal the possession of that intellective ability, 'strong powers of spatial visualization,' which clearly is so crucial to the effective practice of architecture." The conforming group "chose as most characteristic of the ideal architect not the meeting of one's own standard but rather the standard of the profession." They showed a stronger sense of responsibility to the group, a weaker sense of responsibility to themselves or to some inner ideal of perfection which was uniquely theirs.

The conformists revealed, in many other ways, their greater dependence upon others. They were members of more social organizations than either the self-actualized or the conscientious groups. They scored highest on scales measuring: Deference, Affiliation, Socialization, Tolerance, Communality, and Social Integration. They scored higher on scales measuring the desire to include others in one's activities, the expressed desire to be included in others' activities, as well as the expressed desire to be controlled. On practically all of these measures, the scores of the conscientious were between those of the conformists and the self-actualized.

Self-Criticism before Self-Approval

The conscientious architects were not merely self-critical, they were so self-critical that they tended to be seriously disturbed (MacKinnon, 1965):

. . . Architects II give evidence of less emotional stability or personal soundness and at the same time manifest more anxiety than either of the other two groups. On the IPAR scale of Personal Soundness (S) they score lower and on the Taylor Manifest Anxiety scale they score higher than both Architects I and Architects III. Although the following differences do not reach statistical significance, they all point in the same direction: Architects II score higher than either Architects I or Architects III on the mean of the eight clinic scales of the MMPI, higher on the Welsh Anxiety factor scale of the MMPI, and higher on two IPAR scales developed by Block: Bimodal Ego Control scale (indicative of vacillation between under- and over-control of impulse) and the scale designed to measure psychoneurotic tendencies (PN). . . . There is, then, unequivocal evidence as well as some suggestive data that Architects II are more conflicted and more psychologically disturbed than either Architects I or III.

The conforming architects avoided such disturbances. They appeared:

. . . to have incorporated into their egos, and into their images of the persons they are and the persons they would like to be, the more conventional standards of society and of their profession. More dependent upon the good opinion of others for their own good opinion of themselves, their goals and ideals are to an important degree those of the group rather than uniquely their own.

The self-actualized, on the other hand, have become the persons they were capable of becoming:

Since they are not preoccupied with the impression they make on others or the demands that others make on them, they are freer than the other two groups to set their own standards and to achieve them in their own fashion. It is not that they are socially irresponsible, but that their behavior is guided by esthetic standards and ethical values which they have set for themselves and which have been effectively integrated into their images of themselves and of their ideals. . . . Confident of themselves and basically self-accepting, they are to an unusual degree able to recognize and give expression to most aspects of inner experience and character, and thus are able more fully to be themselves and to realize their own ideals.

Compensation before Reaction Formation

The lack of self-criticism in the conformist makes him more prone than the conscientious to develop reaction formations—the expression of feelings exactly the opposite of the individual's repressed feelings. Thus, the frightened boy whistles happily as he passes the graveyard at night; an extremely aggressive man, afraid of his own destructive impulses, acts humble; the alcoholic, driven by a desire for liquor, gives temperance lectures; the man who is fascinated by salacious literature becomes the condemning censor. Such behavior suggests repression, but the suggestion may be extremely ambiguous. One may with apparently equal validity ascribe opposite motives to the same person: the mother who protects her child's interests with zeal can be diagnosed as either hating or loving her offspring; the man who is kind and idealistic can be diagnosed as either loving or hating mankind.

One helpful clue in recognizing reaction formation is that the behavior accompanying it is *excessive*. For example, a lawyer has a wife who is an artist. In order to allow her to pursue her career, he has taken over much of the care of the children and the management of the home. Yet he is loud in his admiration of his wife. At dinner parties other husbands (and wives) become irritated by his sole topic of conversation: the artistic achievements of his wife and his pride in them. His legal friends react in the same way and feel something odd about the intensity of his remarks. One remarked: "I think he hates his wife's guts." Another clue to the presence of reaction formation is its fruits: a mother appears to be devoted to her child, yet the child is unhappy and seems to dislike its mother; a fanatical crusader manages to create only resentment and confusion; an extremely polite teacher creates a feeling of distrust and dislike among his students.

The self-criticism of the conscientious often leads them to make heavy use of compensation. When a person feels strong, he relaxes. When he feels weak, he may *compensate*: work harder to become strong and successful. He compensates consciously and unconsciously for biological, psychological, and social weaknesses. When one lung fails, the other lung works harder; when his heart valves weaken, heart muscles compensate by growing thicker; when one eye is lost, the other becomes more adaptable. If his muscles are weak, he exercises to become strong; if he is too emotional, he strives for self-control; if he is not intellectually quick, he studies harder. If his teacher speaks quietly, he listens more intently; if his father was a laborer, he works harder for social success.

Direct compensation is the process of removing a specific weakness by making an unusual effort. The weak boy is compensating directly when he tries to become strong by exercising, by taking vitamins, and by eating well. The student who is weak in mathematics is compensating directly when he tries to become strong by extra study. And the wallflower is compensating directly when she strives to become well-dressed, a skillful dancer, and a master of social conversation.

Overcompensation is the process of molding an outstanding weakness into an outstanding strength. Demosthenes the Athenian, who stammered as a child, became a famous and militant orator. Theodore Roosevelt, asthmatic and often sick as a child, became a Roughrider and a lion hunter. Lord Byron, crippled with infantile paralysis and neglected by his parents, became an athlete, a writer of powerful verse, and a hero to a vast audience.

Substitute compensation is the process of becoming strong in one area because of an outstanding weakness in another. Immanuel Kant, suffering from a sunken chest which restricted the action of his heart and lungs, became a great philosopher. This mechanism is also illustrated by the physically weak student who tries to become an outstanding scholar.

Indirect compensation refers to more devious substitute compensations: a boy steals automobiles to compensate for being humiliated by his parents; a girl becomes sexually promiscuous to compensate for a feeling of being unwanted. The most common form of indirect compensation is that sought by parents through the achievements of their children. Thus, the druggist who wanted to be a doctor enjoys his son's success in medical school. If the child's interests and abilities fit the ambitions of his parents, the result may be good. But many unhappy college students have been pushed into unsuitable programs as a result of the compensatory efforts of their parents.

Creativity
Creativity is originality + social value. The goal of most thinking is set, and it is gained by a method selected from those methods that are already known. The creative process is original: its goals are not clearly defined and cannot be achieved by known methods. For this reason, writing a poem is more original than finding the shortest way to town. Original ideas and products, however, are not necessarily of any social

value. A geometry student may solve the same problem that Euclid did in an original way because he did not know how Euclid did it. The result, however, is of no social value. A poem may be original but lack social value, i.e., no one who reads it feels that it has any merit. Schizophrenics produce many original, and incomprehensible, essays. The paintings of children are typically original but typically lack artistic merit. Social judgments of the value of original ideas and products are sometimes mistaken and sometimes change. Nonetheless, the concept of creativity seems to require social value as an essential element.

In an effort to develop tests that would measure creative potential, Guilford, Wilson, and Christensen (1952) started with a list of abilities that they *thought* would be components of creativity such as sensitivity to problems and flexibility. Then they developed 44 tests, several for each of the hypothetical abilities. They gave all the tests to about 400 air cadets and student officers. Finally, the results were analyzed to determine what abilities were *actually* being measured. Among the factors they discovered were an ability to recognize practical problems, an ability to shift the functions of objects and use them in a new way, and an ability to change one's approach in order to meet new requirements imposed by changing problems. The ability most clearly related to creativity was originality.

The tests of the originality factor had in common the requirement that the subject give uncommon, remote, or clever responses. Thus, the "plot-titles" test required the subject to think of new and clever titles for brief stories. The word-association test required the subject to give uncommon associations to words. The "consequences" test required the subject to think of unusual outcomes of such events as the lengthening of the human life span to 200 years or the sudden repeal of all national and state laws. And the "unusual-uses" test required the subject to think of novel uses for such common objects as a screwdriver.

Tony Conrad, the ex-Harvard student, was certainly original in his musical and movie ideas and his productions had, at least, some social value. The self-actualized architects were not only creative in their work but also showed the openness to new experiences characteristic of creative people. Nine scales given the architects measured some aspect of this openness: the Psychological-Mindedness Scale, the Flexibility Scale, and the Femininity Scale of the California Psychological Inventory; the Feminine Interests Scale of the MMPI; the Barron-Welsh Art Scale; the Welsh Figure Preference Scale; the IPAR Preference for Complexity Scale; the Gough Esthetic Sensitivity Scale; and the Perceptiveness and Intuitiveness Scales of the Myers-Briggs Type Indicator. On all of these scales the self-actualized group scored higher than the conforming group. The conscientious group also scored higher than the conforming group. The conscientious were, in fact, only slightly lower on these measures than the self-actualized.

However, Architects I were selected *because* they were creative, not because they were self-actualized. Generally, the relationship between a person's stage of development and his creativity is uncertain. Many self-actualized persons are creative; some are not. Maslow lists Abraham Lincoln, Eleanor Roosevelt, and Franklin D. Roosevelt among his outstanding self-actualized persons. Their contributions had high social value but they were not particularly original. Dylan Thomas, on the other hand, was very creative but seems to have been more impulse-ridden than conscientious. Maslow resolved this problem by defining creativity not as originality + social value but as a freedom from stereotypes and cliches, as a spontaneous, effortless, innocent, and easy quality.

Maslow (1962) stressed that not only artists, scientists, inventors, and writers could be creative, but anyone who was open to experience and who could avoid the expectations and beliefs that most people confuse with reality. He noted:

. . . one woman, uneducated, poor, a full-time housewife and mother, did none of these conventionally creative things and yet was a marvelous cook, mother, wife, and homemaker. With little money, her home was somehow always beautiful. She was a perfect hostess, her meals were banquets. Her taste in linens, silver, glass, crockery, and furniture was impeccable. She was in all these areas original, novel, ingenious, unexpected, inventive. I just *had* to call her creative. I learned from her and others like her that a first-rate soup is more creative than a second-rate painting, and that, generally, cooking or parenthood or making a home could be creative while poetry need not be; it could be uncreative (p. 128).

This woman, like other creative people, was very original and had high social value—for those who knew her. It seems the creative and the self-actualized have some, but not all, qualities in common. Both, for example, are intelligent. Thus, the highly intelligent may be creative without being self-actualized, or they may be self-actualized without being creative. The attitude of psychologists toward the problem of identifying creative potential is indicated by the following conclusion of a symposium on the subject (Taylor, 1959):

If either traditional intelligence tests or academic grades were adequate measures of creativity, there would be no problem. Or, if the sheer accumulation of information were a sufficient guarantee that the full creative process would occur, the problem would be largely solved. Yet there is abundant evidence that creativity is too rare, a fact which leads to the conclusion that accumulators of old information are not necessarily creators of new things. In face of the evidence, there still is indeed a very large problem of comprehending and identifying creative potential. It is believed by some that, if we err, it should be on the side of over-emphasizing the difference between academic ability and creative potential rather than discounting or ignoring any differences that may actually exist.

Heath (1965) concluded his study of self development among college students on a similar note:

Creativity and maturity may intersect because they share some similar psychological processes (productivity, controlled regression), but the evidence does not support the notion that creativity is a central or necessary defining dimension of maturity. Some of the most mature persons of the college whom I knew well could scarcely be called creative or original—at least not at this point in their developing lives.

DEVELOPMENT TO THE SELF-ACTUALIZED STAGE

Conformists identify with particular people—they feel, think, and act as if they were in the shoes of the people with whom they identify. The conscientious identify with *ideas*—they feel, think, and act as if they were in the shoes of the idea. When their ideas fail, they feel as if they had failed; when their ideals are realized, they feel as if they had succeeded. Their ideas often fail because they are too vague, too unrealistic, or too conflicting. The self-actualized have proceeded beyond coping with conflicts to the reconciliation of conflicts, beyond the frustration of unrealistic goals to the renunciation of what is unattainable, beyond the tolerance of individual differences to the cherishing of these differences, and beyond competence in the playing of social roles to a strong sense of integrated identity. The ideas by which they live seem to have become intensified, illuminated, and harmonized.

As a person becomes more self-actualized, he sees himself as a smaller and smaller part of the universe. Simultaneously, however, his psychological world expands through time and space, and to other people. Unlike the conforming architects, who are focused upon their own status and their particular social groups, the conscientious are concerned with meeting the highest standards of their profession. Unlike the conscientious, the self-actualized are concerned with their own ideals of aesthetic and ethical perfection. The conforming architects seemed most preoccupied with their own immediate group; the conscientious, with architects in general; the self-actualized, with mankind.

Direct Genetic Mechanisms

The development of the self is a slow process of intensifying, clarifying, and harmonizing the differences between oneself and others. How far this development proceeds seems basically determined by the extent to which the ability to symbolize develops. The growth of this ability seems significantly influenced by genetic mechanisms. While words and numbers are not the only symbolic forms, they are the ones that psychologists know the most about and form the major content of most intelligence tests.

Those of low intelligence cannot develop far beyond the conforming stage; those of high intelligence can—but they may not. Terman and Oden (1959) selected more than fifteen hundred California school children who were in the upper 1 percent in intelligence and followed their careers for over twenty years. As adults, they were superior to the average person in almost every respect: two-thirds had obtained college degrees, almost half were in professional occupations, their mortality and divorce rates were below average, their physical and mental health was better, and they were more active in political and social affairs. Some were internationally eminent. Some, however, were unskilled laborers.

Barron (1957) explored the interaction between intelligence and one aspect of self-actualization—originality. He gave Guilford's originality tests to 100 veteran Air Force officers between the ages of twenty-seven and fifty. He combined scores on the tests to obtain a composite originality score. He then selected an "original" group (the 25 officers with the highest scores) and an "unoriginal" group (the 25 officers with the lowest scores). All the officers completed series of aptitude, interest, and personality tests and were rated by staff psychologists on a variety of traits. The original group was:

More impulsive: they obtained higher scores on a scale measuring "impulsivity."

More energetic: the staff rated them higher on "drive."

More integrative in their perceptions: they gave many more "whole" responses on the Rorschach test.

More feminine in their interests: their interest patterns were closer to those of women than were the patterns of the unoriginal group.

More dominating: the staff rated their dominance higher, and they obtained higher scores on a dominance inventory.

The more original officers tended to be more intelligent. However, some original officers were unintelligent and some intelligent officers were unoriginal. The original but unintelligent officers more often described themselves as being aggressive, impatient, sarcastic, demanding, dependent, dominant, forceful, strong, and outspoken. The unoriginal but intelligent officers described themselves as mild, optimistic, pleasant, quiet, and unselfish. Barron (1957) offered the following interpretation using psychoanalytic terms that were defined in Chapter 2:

> Primary process thinking to the exclusion of the secondary process thinking marks the original but unintelligent person, secondary process thinking which carries ego-control to the point where the ego is not so much firm as muscle-bound marks the intelligent but unoriginal person, and easy accessibility of both primary and secondary process marks the person who is both original and intelligent . . .

Indirect Genetic Mechanisms

Degree of eminence is often assumed to be a measure of self-actualization. It is a dubious assumption. If it were true, being born a woman would almost eliminate the possibility of becoming self-actualized. Only 55 of 1,030 eminent English persons were women; only 50 of 2,607 eminent American scientists were women; and only 32 of 1,900 eminent historical figures were women. And these differences incompletely state the sex difference, for lower standards were typically used in judging the eminence of women. Furthermore, the women were much more often visible because of their birth, husbands, philanthropy, tragic fate, beauty, or immortalization in literature. "With the single exception of literature, eminence among women in history seems largely to be associated with circumstantial factors" (Bakan, 1966). Eminence is more a measure of differences between men and women than between those who are and those who are not self-actualized.

Emily Dickinson demonstrates not only that a woman can achieve world eminence as an outstandingly creative person but also the abiding mystery of the process. When she died at the age of fifty-five in 1886, she was "unknown to the world and undreamed of as one of America's great poets" (Anderson, 1960). She grew up in comfort and security as the daughter of a prosperous lawyer in Amherst, Massachusetts. She attended Mount Holyoke Seminary until she was seventeen, and was part of a bookish family by the local standards of the time. Her life, however, was bare of serious literary companionship. Until she was about twenty-five she was active in social life in a New England village at that time: dances, sleigh rides, Valentine verse-writing games, and parties centering around the college Commencement and autumn fair. In her entire life she went to Boston only a few times and once to Philadelphia and Washington, on a trip. She desired to marry but never did and gradually withdrew from village life to her home and garden. In the end, she even avoided calls from intimate friends. In commenting on the striking contrast between her meager cultural life and the richness of her poetry, her biographer (Anderson, 1960) states:

One fumbles in vain at the biographical record in an attempt to discover the sources of her wisdom. There is little if any evidence that she attended concerts, went to theatres and operas, visited museums and art galleries. . . . Yet one poem, sometimes a single line or a glancing reference in a letter, will testify without need of further proof to her precise understanding of some aspect of ballet, the higher criticism, mathematics, music, or Venetian painting. Her formal schooling, with whatever differences, was just about equivalent to that offered by a modern high school. In comparison with what Longfellow enjoyed it seems elementary and provincial, yet somehow she learned God's plenty.

Her thoughts gradually became independent of the everyday events of the village as she became an adventurous explorer of her own inner world. The major themes of her poetry concern the universal questions of religion and philosophy, ecstasy and despair, death and immortality.

General Environmental Mechanisms

Creativity and self-actualization are generally admired in principle but seldom in practice. People at the self-actualized stage see things that others cannot see. While society may tolerate such people, it seldom rewards them. In his story, *The Country of the Blind*, H. G. Wells tells of a man who stumbles into an isolated community where everyone is blind except himself. His vision is not rewarded and he is eventually driven from the country.

The fate of some of the most creative thinkers in the United States supports the conclusion of the story. In his life time, Thoreau was viewed as a second-rate Emerson. Emily Dickinson, now judged to be one of the world's great poets, had only a few poems published during her life. *Moby Dick*, Melville's masterpiece, was judged as inferior to his earlier books and generally ignored for almost a century.

Peirce, judged by Bertrand Russell to be America's most original philosopher, could never get a job in a university. Thorstein Veblen, now considered one of America's most creative economists, never obtained tenure in one.

Criticism and neglect are the common fate of those who engage in "divergent thinking." Highly creative people maintain their creativity at a high cost (Barron, 1959). They are less popular. They receive lower evaluations by teachers and peers than less creative but bright individuals. Those who realize their creative potential do so by persisting in a rebellious attitude, maintaining their independence against considerable social pressure, and developing a tolerance for both physical and social discomforts.

Specific Mechanisms

Can we accelerate the stages of development by training? Piaget, a European authority on psychological development, refers to the desire for instant self-actualization as "the American question." He answers with another question: Should we? He believes that some acceleration may be possible but suggests that a "certain slowness" is desirable. We should not even aim to make the impulse-ridden child into a conformist in a month or the conformist into a self-actualized person in a year. From the point of view of personal happiness such a goal is a questionable one, for, as Loevinger (1966) has emphasized "Every stage has its weaknesses, its problems and its paradoxes, which provides both a potential for maladjustment and a potential for growth."

However, many college students share the plight of the conscientious architects. They are afflicted with self-doubts and internal conflict that make them unhappy. They want to get beyond this stage as soon as they can. Self-analysis is almost forced upon them. Many of the conscientious seek professional help in resolving the problems of being at this stage.

Psychotherapy "Psychotherapy" is an interpersonal relationship in which a person communicates with a qualified therapist to gain help in reducing his anxieties and resolving his conflicts (Figure 12-1). Table 12-1 concerns the reactions of one psychologist who underwent one type of psychotherapy—psychoanalysis. The types of relationships vary, the styles of communication vary, and the qualifications of the therapist vary. All these variations suffer from most of the same general limitations. To make these limitations more concrete, we first examine one effort to evaluate the effectiveness of psychotherapy (Wispe, 1965).

The subjects of the study were 55 psychologists who had had sixty or more hours of psychotherapy. They were selected by their

Figure 12-1 Psychotherapy is a special kind of interpersonal relationship. Beginning with a simple and structured interview, such as the Rorschach Test shown here, the therapist tries to become acquainted with his client. In later sessions, the therapist hopes to develop a warm and trusting relationship with the client, through which psychological growth may be achieved. (Ron Junttonen)

responses to a general questionnaire sent to more than 1,000 psychologists who had received their doctorates from American universities in the period 1945–1951. Of the 966 psychologists who returned the questionnaire, one-third reported that they had received some psychotherapy at one time or another. Two out of three of those selected for the study reported that they had entered psychotherapy for "personal reasons" and had chosen a psychoanalytically oriented therapist. They felt that the experience had increased their "objectivity," "insight," "comfort," and "competence." They also reported that therapy had increased their scholarly productivity.

Did therapy *actually* increase their productivity? The *Psychological Abstracts* includes summaries of practically all published psychological research. The annual publications of the 55 psychologists were checked for the years before and after therapy. A "point" system was used in determining productivity: 1 for a review; 2 for a research article; and 36 for a book. Result: No change. Productivity per

TABLE 12-1   The Psychoanalysis of a Psychologist
Carney Landis, at the time a psychologist at Columbia University, entered into a psychoanalysis to gain a more intimate acquaintance with psychoanalytic phenomena. He hoped that his analysis would aid him in teaching abnormal psychology, in interpreting his own research results, and in solving certain emotional problems of his own. His European analyst, who had been practicing for over twenty-five years, was a close follower of Freud. Landis's report of his analysis was eventually published along with those of other analyzed experimental psychologists on the assumption that their training in psychology would make their comments especially useful in the evaluation of psychoanalysis (American Psychological Association, 1953).

Which of the following statements were true according to Landis's report? Correct answers are given at the end of the chapter.

T F   1. Soon after the analysis started, his anxieties began to decrease.

T F   2. He experienced long periods of irritation and hostility during the analysis.

T F   3. After he was told so by the analyst, he could see that his frequent dreams of locomotives were a death symbol, just as Freud had said.

T F   4. The analyst told him that, even if he were normal at the beginning of analysis, the procedure would tend to make him neurotic.

T F   5. After the analysis, he said: "I wouldn't take a million for the experience or give a nickel for any more of it."

T F   6. Even before his analysis was finished, he had developed an unquestioning belief in the effectiveness of psychoanalytic therapy.

T F   7. The analysis was a happy experience for him.

T F   8. The average analyst is a trained physician who spends more than fifty hours per week sitting in a chair listening to the rambling free associations of neurotic patients.

T F   9. The average analyst is well trained in modern academic psychology.

T F   10. The average analyst knows a great deal about experimentation and experimental controls.

T F   11. Landis remarked that the typical analyst has only the haziest ideas about the logic of science.

T F   12. Some of his acquaintances in nonanalytic psychology told him that he had gone entirely too far into analysis.

T F   13. The analyst encouraged him to discuss current events and the research problems he was working on.

T F   14. Trying to talk to the analyst with nothing appropriate to say sometimes became a nightmare to him.

T F   15. Landis rejected many of the interpretations of his dreams that the analyst made.

year before therapy was 1.4; after therapy, 1.4. Furthermore, there was no relationship between the increases in productivity reported by the psychologists and their *actual* increases: "This interesting lack of relationship cast suspicion upon any unvalidated items which asks respondents to indicate improvements in the quantity of their work." The actual productivity of a matched control group of 55 psychologists for the same period showed an insignificant drop (1.3 to 1.1).

Limitations of money Few people can afford individual psychotherapy. While it is sometimes provided as a free community service, it more often costs over a hundred dollars per hour with fifty dollars per hour being common. The length of successful treatment also varies from a few hours to several years of daily sessions. It is a reasonable estimate that psychotherapy for the 55 psychologists averaged over three thousand dollars for each of them.

The costs almost eliminate psychotherapy as a possible treatment for the mentally ill among the two-thirds of our population in the working and lower classes. A study of mental illness in Connecticut (Hollingshead and Redlich, 1958) showed that three times as much money was spent in the treatment of an upper-class patient as was spent in the treatment of a lower-class patient. One percent of the mentally ill were from the "upper class"; they constituted 3 percent of the general population. On the other hand, 38 percent of the mentally ill were from the "lower class"; they constituted 19 percent of the general population. Members of the upper class not only had proportionally fewer illnesses, but the illnesses they did have were less serious. Thus, only 35 percent of the patients in the upper classes were classified as suffering from schizophrenia, manic-depression, or some other psychotic illness, while 90 percent of the patients in the lower classes were classified as psychotic. Social legislation is spreading the benefits of treatment for the mentally ill, and shorter treatments are being devised. Still, individual psychotherapy is and will remain for the foreseeable future an extremely costly enterprise.

Limitations of training Many are unable to find a professionally trained therapist even when they have the money to pay him. A psychotherapist may be a psychiatrist, a clinical psychologist, or a psychiatric social worker. In the 1950s, only one of any of these were available for every 10,000 people in the United States (Albee and Dickey, 1957). Since then, the gap has become wider—so wide, in fact, that many segments of society have become tired of waiting and have recruited, trained, and already put to work thousands of nonprofessional persons whose major qualification in most instances is a desire to help their fellow man (Matarazzo, 1971):

Figure 12-2 Individual psychotherapy is too expensive for most people (Postgraduate Center for Mental Health, New York)

. . . what began as a trickle of disparate, unorganized, one-man, grass roots programs in a few state hospitals in the decade of the 1950s, and in a few junior colleges in the early 1960s, and in a few inner cities in the latter half of the 1960s, may soon be followed by an avalanche of such programs in still others of these facilities as well as in many of our most prestigious universities. The resulting further reduction in the numbers of patients in our mental hospitals will be but one of the many by-products of these unprecedented developments in the field of mental health manpower.

Limitations of knowledge   For the few who can afford and get a qualified psychotherapist the question becomes: Does it help? The answer of the vast majority of psychotherapists, of course, is that it does and their clients often agree with them. Few facts, however, support their opinions, for research studies of the effectiveness of psychotherapy are rare. These rare studies typically deal with very small numbers of subjects, have generally been forced to employ inadequate experimental designs, and always have unsatisfactory criteria of success. The study of psychologists who had therapy was a rare exception. It used a comparatively large number of subjects (55), a matched control group, and an objective measure of success (research publications). Even here, however, it can be justifiably claimed that gains in research publications are at best an incomplete measure of the success of psychotherapy and at worst a totally irrelevant one.

Research results generally do not support the optimistic opinions of the therapist and their clients. The study of the psychologists, for example, showed *no* relationship between the individual's estimate of the impact of therapy upon his productivity and his actual productivity. Some psychologists claim that there is no evidence that psychotherapy does any good at all (Eysenck, 1952). In general, the early belief that psychotherapy was *the* answer to individual emotional disturbances as well as to the problems of international tensions is waning. Professional therapists are taking increased interest in alternatives to individual therapy: drugs, rehabilitation programs, parental education for more adequate child-rearing practices, community-health projects, and group therapy.

Human relations Psychotherapy is a special kind of interpersonal relationship. There is a growing conviction that its greatest significance may lie in its clarification of the nature of all interpersonal relationships. Carl Rogers (1961), for instance, comments: "I have long had the strong conviction—some might say it was an obsession—that the therapeutic relationship is only a special instance of interpersonal relationships in general, and that the same lawfulness governs all such relationships."

Perhaps the greatest and most enduring contribution of psychotherapy will be its clarification of the kinds of human relationships that encourage the development of the self. In any case, the self is a social and cultural creation. Like the monkeys raised in solitude, the human being raised completely alone could never get beyond the autistic stage. The autistic become impulse-ridden by depending upon others; the impulse-ridden become opportunists by imitating others; the opportunists become conformists by identifying with others; and the conformists become conscientious and self-actualized by identifying with the ideas of others. The individual develops his self through human relationship. However, his development may also be retarded or destroyed by others. What kind of relationships develop the self? This is the question that dominates the next part of this book.

SUMMARY

Self-actualization is not an end but a slow and endless process of intensifying, illuminating, and harmonizing one's view of oneself. Those at the conscientious stage have moved from the identification with people to the identification with ideas. MacKinnon's study of architects showed that those at this stage typically become aware of and disturbed by the conflicts between their identifications with people and ideas, between their ideals and reality, between what they would like to be and do and what they are and are doing. Identification with ideas requires both exposure to and understanding of them. Consequently, it is often the best educated and most intelligent who are most disturbed by these kinds of conflicts. They also more often seek to benefit from professional counseling. However, their opportunity to benefit from such help is limited by their financial resources as well as by the availability of trained counselors and by the limitations of knowledge of even the best trained. In the long run, the major contribution of psychotherapy may be its contribution to our understanding of the kinds of human relationships that are the most help in the development of the self.

SUGGESTIONS FOR FURTHER READING

*Voeks, V. (1964). *On becoming an educated person.* (2nd ed.) Philadelphia: Saunders. This book helps students to do, and to do better, things they feel they should do: "If more incoming freshmen would take the time to read this book, college would be a much more enjoyable and rewarding experience for them. . . . It would save them a lot of time, tears, and traumatic experiences. . . ."

*Blatz, W. E. (1966). *Human security: some reflections.* Toronto: Univ. of Toronto Press. "Thought provoking" is the phrase that students often used to describe their reaction to this book: "Although Blatz did not help me to make any decisions by telling me which side of a specific question is right and which is wrong, reading this book did help me to discover the way in which problems should be faced."

Maslow, A. H. (1954). *Motivation and personality.* New York: Harper. A book that outlines a theory of self-actualization by the psychologist whose name is most intimately linked with it.

Barron, F. (1963). *Creativity and psychological health.* A study of the creativity of 5,000 men and women that ranges from ego strength to violence and vitality.

Answers to Table 12-1: 1. F   2. T   3. F   4. T   5. T   6. F   7. F   8. T   9. F   10. F   11. T   12. T   13. F   14. T   15. T

FOUR

ROLES AS PERSONALITY

All the world's a stage,
And all the men and women merely players:
They have their exits and their entrances;
And one man in his time plays many parts,
His acts being seven stages.

SHAKESPEARE

13

THE DEVELOPMENT OF LOVE

Love is not directed to abstractions, but to persons; not to persons we do not know, nor to numbers of people, but to our own dear ones, our family and neighbours.

CHARLES S. PEIRCE

The trait theory of Part Two focused upon the permanent differences between us here and now; the self theory of Part Three upon the stages that each of us has gone through to reach where we are here and now. The interpersonal theory of love that forms the framework of this part focuses upon how we relate to each other. The stress is not upon how Tom and Mary differ nor upon how each has individually developed but upon how they relate to each other.

A concern with the relationships between people necessarily involves some concern with their traits and with their selves. This comprehensiveness is, in fact, a weakness. Interpersonal theories are so comprehensive that theorists tend to be paralyzed by the vast array of things they need to see, describe, and account for. In overcoming this paralysis, they have more and more concentrated upon "role" as the central concept. So shall we. Furthermore, this part emphasizes just the roles which are most significant in our lives: the roles of man and woman, husband and wife, child and parent, and leader and follower. To begin with, we need to examine what is meant by a role, why we play roles, what determines our success in playing them, and where love fits into the picture.

WHAT IS A ROLE?

A role is *the feelings, attitudes, and behavior that society expects from the holder of a position in some social structure*. From the point of view of radical role theorists, people only *seem* to have stable traits or to be at particular stages of development because they continue to play the same roles. But change their roles and you change their traits and their stage. A role, from their perspective, *has* a personality that awaits whoever enters it.

The power of a man's role in molding him is an everyday observation. People who meet a priest in a clerical collar have common expectations about how he should behave. He learns to speak and to act in accordance with these expectations. People are boxed in by the roles they have learned: young mothers occupied all day with small children tend to talk to adults as if they were children. Grandparents tend to treat their sons and daughters as if they were ten years old. Teachers have difficulty not lecturing to everyone.

We not only quickly learn to act new roles, but also to feel them. John Howard Griffin, a free-lance writer, artifically pigmented his skin and toured the South by bus as a Negro (1960). He quickly began to internalize the expectations of others about himself. Here, for example, is a report of his feelings while driving in the front seat of a white friend's car:

We drove through the darkened streets to his home, talking in a strangely stilted manner. I wondered why, and then realized that I had grown so accustomed to being a Negro, to being shown contempt, that I could not rid myself of the cautions. I was embarrassed to ride in the front seat of the car with a white man, especially on our way to his home. It was breaking the "Southern rule" somehow (p. 72).

Everyone in his time plays many roles. Most of the time, he has a choice in the parts he plays. In the most important roles, however, his choices are extremely limited: everyone must play the role of man or woman, and almost everyone at some time plays the role of spouse, parent, and leader.

We have seen, let us say, two actors play the role of Hamlet. As we think and talk about their separate performances, we might stress the similarities in the way they played the role. On the other hand, we might stress the differences in the way they acted the part. We will give some attention to similarities. Primarily, however, we shall pay attention to the *different* ways in which people play the part of man, woman, husband or wife, leader or follower.

Role Identity

People playing the same role have different *role identities*. A role is the feelings, attitudes, and behavior that society expects from the holder of a social position. A role identity, on the other hand, is the feelings, attitudes, and behavior that the *holder of the position* perceives himself as having or wanting to have. A role identity is generally similar to but never the same as the role. No actual man or woman, husband or wife, leader or follower ever completely matches the standards for holders of these positions. Some deviate quite widely from them. Occasionally, one's role identity may completely contradict the role one is playing as when a man plays a feminine role.

Role players are *not* dishonest con men. Actors in the theater do not live the parts they play when they are off stage. Actors in life's theater, however, must live the parts they play. Playing a role in the social drama means only that the actor is trying to communicate something to his audience. The better he plays his role, the better he communicates what he intends. Thus, the person who is trying to communicate his innermost secrets and his most shameful fears to another is an actor. If he is to communicate effectively, he cannot say or do anything that implies that he is being dishonest or evasive. We can only communicate with others by playing roles. The better we play a role, the better we communicate. The reverse is also true: the better we communicate what we feel, the better we play our roles. Rogers (1961) explains why:

> *In my relationships with persons I have found that it does not help, in the long run, to act as though I were something that I am not.* It does not help to act calm and pleasant when actually I am angry and critical. It does not help to act as though I know the answers when I do not. It does not help to act as though I were a loving person if actually, at the moment, I am hostile. It does not help for me to act as though I were full of assurance, if actually I am frightened and unsure. Even on a very simple level I found that this statement seems to hold. It does not help for me to act as though I were well when I feel ill. . . .
>
> When I am experiencing an attitude of annoyance toward another person but am unaware of it, then my communication contains contradictory messages. My words are giving one message, but I am also in subtle ways communicating the annoyance I feel and this confuses the other person and makes him distrustful though he may be unaware of what is causing the difficulty. When as a parent or a therapist or a teacher or an administrator I fail to listen to what is going on in me, fail because of my own defensiveness to sense my own feelings, then this kind of failure seems to result . . . the most basic learning for anyone who hopes to establish any kind of helping relationship is that it is safe to be transparently real. If in a given relationship I am reasonably congruent, if no feelings relevant to the relationship are hidden either to me or the other person, then I can be almost sure that the relationship will be a helpful one.

WHY WE PLAY ROLES

We play roles to achieve ends that will satisfy ourselves and others. But what ends do we seek? Our specific ends are as variable as our desires. Whatever our ends are, however, their achievement requires that the relationship have some *integration*; i.e., the relationship must last long enough to achieve the ends sought. Indeed, at the extreme, integrative satisfaction, the satisfaction of achieving an enduring relationship, may be the only end sought. Normally, however, we also play roles to achieve some *production*, i.e., to achieve some end that will satisfy needs outside of the relationship—doctors want to make their patients well, generals want to win battles, teachers want to educate their students, ministers want to win converts, and automobile workers want to produce cars and trucks. These integrative and productive ends may be achieved to some degree even when those in the relationship are bored by their roles. To achieve these ends at all, however, the role players must have at least some *morale*, i.e., some degree of intrinsic interest in the parts they are playing.

Integration

The amount of time we need to play a particular role successfully may vary from seconds to years. We can successfully play the role of caller with a telephone operator in seconds; the role of customer in a shoe store, in minutes; the role of tennis player, in hours. The more important the relationship is, however, the more likely it is to demand integration. To be a successful student, parent, or senator requires years of role playing. Such long-term role playing demands not only individual but also organizational integration. The school, the family, and the Senate remain integrated not only long enough to permit one individual to play his role but long enough to permit others to play the same role in his place. Even if the rules which define these organizations change, or particular roles change, or particular role players leave and others join the organizations, their integration must remain high to satisfy the integrative needs of role players in them.

      The desire for integration, the desire to unite with others and to be a part of something larger than ourselves, often is so intense that its satisfaction alone accounts for the endurance of many relationships. The strength of this yearning for union with others is suggested by these student reports:

Tom   I really felt close to a person when I took a "blind walk." I was blindfolded and given instructions not to talk. I set out with a girl I had met only minutes before we proceeded to walk across campus. At first, fear was the dominant feeling but this was erased by my understanding that this person was there and she cared enough to hold your hand and guide you across busy streets and up and down stairs. We walked for an hour and when I finally took off my blind I was ready to ask her to marry me! To me, she was the sweetest thing on earth, when only an hour before she was nothing to me.

Mary   My oldest sister, who is 12 years older than me, and I just don't get along. But when my grandfather died and she came for the funeral, we were really close for awhile. She knew that grandpa meant a great deal to me (much more than he did to her) and that I felt very sad about his death. She gave me spiritual strength and made me feel a lot better. For awhile we really were united.

Thelma   I had known Barbara for a long time but I never felt I understood her. But one night when she left dinner I saw that she was crying so I followed her to her room. She talked about things that get all of us down: Unsympathetic parents, rotten grades, being *forced* to choose one boy friend and let the other go. Each was a petty trouble, but together they overwhelmed her. I pitied her but I didn't *really* feel close to her until she said, "This is all so shitty—I think I'll wash my hair," And she brought me with her so that together we could scrub her hair till it squeaked. I understood her then because she dealt with her personal problems the same way I did. She forced them into herself until they hurt so bad that she had to physically comfort, to mother herself.

William Carlos Williams (1951), poet and physician, has described the integrative satisfaction of being a doctor (p. 357):

It's the humdrum, day-in, day-out, everyday work that is the real satisfaction of the practice of medicine . . . I lost myself in the very properties of their minds: for the moment at least I actually became *them* . . . it is the rest, the peace of mind that comes from adopting the patient's condition as one's own to be struggled with toward a solution during those few minutes or that hour or those trying days when we are searching for causes, trying to relate this to that to build a reasonable basis for action which really gives us our peace . . . often after I have gone into my office harassed by personal perplexities of whatever sort, fatigued physically and mentally, after two hours of intense application to the work, I come out at the finish completely rested (and I mean rested) ready to smile and to laugh as if the day were just starting.

Rogers (1961) has spent thousands of hours working intimately with individuals in personal distress. He has described the integrative rewards of being a psychotherapist:

To understand is enriching in a double way. I find when I am working with clients in distress, that to understand the bizarre world of a psychotic individual, or to understand and sense the attitudes of a person who feels that life is too tragic to bear, or to understand a man who feels that he is a worthless and inferior individual—each of these understandings somehow enriches me. I learn from these experiences in ways that change me, that make me a different and, I think, a more responsive person. Even more important, perhaps, is the fact that my understanding of these individuals permits them to change. It permits them to accept their own fears and bizarre thoughts and tragic feelings and discouragements, as well as their moments of courage and kindness and love and sensitivity. And it is their experience as well as mine that when someone fully understands those feelings, this enables them to accept those feelings in themselves. Then they find both the feelings and themselves changing. Whether it is understanding a woman who feels that very literally she has a hook in her head by which others lead her about, or understanding a man who feels that no one is as lonely, no one is as separated from others as he, I find these understandings to be of value to me. But also, and even more importantly, to be understood has a very positive value to these individuals.

In dramatic terms, our degree of integration depends upon our satisfaction with conditions in the theater in which we play our roles. The more we like the physical conditions in the theater, the other actors, the director, and the way our performance is evaluated, the more likely we are to continue to play our part. The more a wife likes her house, children, husband, and what they and her friends say about her cooking, her housekeeping, and her behavior as a mother and a wife, the higher her integration is likely to be.

In the same way, a student who finds the classroom pleasant, likes the other students in the class, is satisfied with the teacher, and approves of the grading system has high integration (Figure 13-1). As a result, he is unlikely to drop the course, be absent, complain about the course, or fail to take another course.

Integrative satisfaction can be readily measured. Armour (1954), for example, measured differences in integration among 100 students in a psychology class. He gave them attitude scales designed to measure their satisfaction with classroom working conditions, their liking for other students in the class, their liking for the instructor, and their satisfaction with the grading system. Here are some of the items from each of his subscales:

1. I am enthusiastic about the way the psychology classes are conducted.

2. I seldom feel satisfied with the meetings of this class.

3. The students in the course are about the most pleasant I have ever met.

4. I don't think I would care to have these students as classmates again.

5. I find this instructor to be highly stimulating as a teacher.

Figure 13-1 The student who is deeply involved in his role of being a student tends to learn more than one who is not involved. (Ron Junttonen)

6. The teacher of this course is below par as far as I'm concerned.

7. The grading in this course seems quite good, and I am pleased with the mark I'm receiving.

8. I feel the grading in this course is very unfair, and certainly does not show what I know about the work.

Productivity

To survive, we need food, water, shelter, and protection. Man has always related to other men as a means of satisfying these needs. Modern man satisfies them by relating to a clerk to get food or to get a pair of shoes; to a realtor to buy a home; and to a secretary to get a letter written. We not only play roles with others to get things but also to produce changes in ourselves. We play the role of student for a while to produce changes in our knowledge, skills, and attitudes that will be permanent. We play the role of patient with a doctor to produce physical changes; we play the role of client with a psychotherapist to produce personality changes.

The measurement of the production of goods is relatively easy. We can count the number of television sets, cars, or tons of coal produced. The measurement of the production of services is more difficult. However, banks can count the number of checks processed by their employees; restaurants, the number of meals served by their waitresses.

The measurement of productive changes in our knowledge is still more difficult. Teachers give final examinations to determine what changes they have made in their students. One problem with this kind of measurement is that the students may have learned all they know about the subject before they took the course. Armour (1954) solved this problem by giving the final examination to his 100 students on the first day of the course as well as the last day. The gain from the first to the last test was used as a measure of productivity.

The measurement of productive personality changes is most difficult of all. Kurtz and Grummon (1972) solved the difficulty in studying the productivity of psychotherapeutic relationships by using five measures. First, they had 25 clients record their judgments about how helpful counseling had been: (1) extremely harmful; (2) harmed me a lot; (3) harmed me somewhat; (4) indifferent; (5) helped me somewhat; (6) helped me quite a lot; (7) extremely helpful. Second, each of the 25 therapists estimated how productive the relationship had been: (4) successful; (3) partly successful; (2) partly unsuccessful; (1) unsuccessful. This therapist measure was only slightly related to the client measure and not at all related to the following three. Third, three judges with considerable experience in the use of the Minnesota Multiphasic Personality Inventory compared pretherapy and posttherapy scores for each client and rated the changes in the client as follows: (5) satisfactory; (4) partially satisfactory; (3) no change; (2) partly unsatisfactory; (1) unsatisfactory. Finally, pretherapy and posttherapy scores on the Tennessee Self-Concept Scale were compared. This scale provided the fourth and fifth measures of client change, one being a measure of the changes in the client's self-esteem and the other of signs of psychological disturbance. The final composite score gave equal weight to each of these five measures.

Morale

Those in a relationship have high morale when they are involved in the roles they are playing, work hard at them, and say they are very happy in what they are doing. Those with low morale, on the other hand, act as if—and report that—they feel uninvolved, apathetic, indifferent. Some roles produce high morale in almost everyone who plays them while others produce low morale in almost everyone. Commonly, there is an interaction: one person may have great interest in what he is doing while another may have no interest; the latter may be greatly interested in another role that bores the former.

Like integration, morale is relatively easy to measure. Armour (1954) asked his 100 students how interested they were in psychology and how they felt about the student role they were playing. Here are some of the items he used to measure these two aspects of morale:

1.   Psychology is one of the most interesting subjects that I have taken.

2.   The importance of psychology seems to me a bit overrated.

3.   Being a student is just about the most enjoyable thing I have ever done.

4.   I often wish I was not a college student.

The success of all relationships depends on the integration, the production, and the morale of those involved in them. In most relationships, however, one of these is dominant. The integrative goal tends, for example, to dominate family relationships; productivity, work relationships; morale, game relationships. Primarily, we play games because we are intrinsically interested in them. Tennis players, chess players, and golf players participate in these games because they enjoy playing them as an end in itself. In amateur game playing, there is seldom any production goal—no end outside of the game that is achieved by playing it. Only the minimum integration is required— avid players will play with anybody who wants to play and under almost any circumstances.

The Independence of Integration, Productivity, and Morale

Some integration, productivity, and morale is required for any relationship's success. However, the *degree* of success in reaching one of these goals is independent of the others. Integration may be high but productivity and morale low—friends may be delighted to be with each other but bored by what they are doing and accomplish nothing by being together. Productivity may be high, but integration and morale low—a couple may produce many children but dislike their sex roles and want to be divorced. Morale may be high but integration and productivity low—a person may love being a leader but dislike those he is leading and produce nothing by his leadership.

The goals sometimes conflict. In general, however, the relationship between integration and the other two goals is curvilinear: some integration helps, a lot hurts. The relationship between morale and the other goals tends to be linear: the higher the morale, the higher integration and productivity tend to be. Armour (1954) related his four measures of integration to his measure of productivity (gains made in knowledge of psychology). None of these integrative measures had any relationship to productivity—whether a student liked or disliked the class, the instructor, fellow students, or the grading system had no relation to how he learned in the course. Armour also related his measures of morale to productivity. *Both* of these measures were related to productivity—the more interested a student was in psychology in general and the more interested he was in his role as a student, the more he learned in a particular psychology course.

Different people, we are saying, want different kinds of satisfaction in different kinds of relationships at different times. Sometimes they want integration; at other times, productivity or morale. It is rare for people to be completely satisfied in all of these areas. However, it is common for them to be confused about the satisfaction they are getting. When students are getting integrative satisfaction, they are likely to assume that they are also being productive and interested. When managers are achieving production from workers, they are also likely to assume that their workers are integrated and interested. Still others confuse enthusiasm for their role with their feeling of loyalty to the group or their effectiveness in playing the role.

KINDS OF LOVE

What determines our success—how intrinsically interesting, cohesive, and productive is our role playing? The wisdom of the ages tells us that "love" is the answer; i.e., the more a relationship is infused with love, the more successful it will be. Unfortunately, the answer is not clear unless we know what love is.

Hazo (1967), the author of *The Idea of Love*, led a group of more than 25 philosophers in an examination of the concept of love. They considered the use of the idea by ancient philosophers (Plato, Aristotle, and Aquinas) and by modern ones (James, Ortéga, and Lewis), by psychologists (Freud, Jung, Fromm, Menninger), by Darwin, by Adam Smith as well as by many others. One conclusion: "Of all the ideas so far subjected to dialectical analysis by the Institute, the idea of love proved to the most difficult—more difficult than the idea of freedom, and much more difficult than the ideas of progress, justice and happiness."

Hazo reports only four characteristics common to the many views of love. The first of these is that love always implies *interest*, that one cannot be indifferent to what is loved. Love also always implies *preference*, i.e., what is loved is singled out—one loves a particular baby or idea. It also implies *action*, that one does not merely like what is loved but does something about it. Above all, love always implies either potential or actual *good* either in itself or as a means to some good end.

The most fundamental disagreement about love concerns the possibility of altruistic love. All the wise men agreed that love was sometimes selfish. Some, however, felt that love was sometimes completely altruistic; others, that it never was. That is, they agreed that there was impulse-ridden, opportunistic, and conforming love. They disagreed about the frequency of conscientious love and the possibility of self-actualized love.

Autistic Love

The newborn infant loves practically nothing. He gradually develops an interest in eating, a preference for one kind of milk rather than another, acts to reach his mother's breast or a bottle, and benefits from his actions. Later, he develops an interest in and a preference for his mother as a person and acts in ways that will keep her close to him. During this presocial period, however, he has no understanding of his mother and no feeling of accountability for what happens to her.

Autistic adults have some love for some things but little interest in, preference for, or action toward other persons, as the following account of a schizophrenic suggests (Coleman, 1964, p. 277):

> This patient was hospitalized on the complaint of his sister-in-law who stated that he had tried to force her at the point of a gun to have sexual relations with him. On admission to the hospital the patient appeared rather indifferent about the whole matter and explained that it must have been some "temporary impulse" which overcame him.
>
> Although 30 years of age, the patient had been living with his parents and was completely dependent upon them. His educational background was good. He made an A average in high school, but during his first year of college he lost interest in his studies and refused to attend classes despite his parents' pleadings. His parents then did their best to help him achieve some vocational adjustment, but the patient seemed indifferent to their efforts and hopes for him. After leaving college he did take several part-time jobs, including one in a grocery store, which he lost soon after because of his listless attitude and indifference to his duties. Thereafter he would not either look for nor accept work and was quite content to remain dependent upon his parents. Although rather handsome, he had never gone out with girls. When questioned on this subject he stated that "I'm not interested in girls. All they ever do is get you in trouble."

Impulse-ridden Love

In vivid contrast to the autistic, the impulse-ridden has an intense love of others. He has a strong interest in people, marked preferences among

Figure 13-2 The child must learn to love. As he learns through interaction with others of the rewards which relationships can bring, he also learns of the rewards he must supply to others to sustain the relationships with them. (Ron Junttonen)

them, and chronically struggles to be with those he prefers. He feels utterly dependent upon others to supply his needs. He has no feeling, however, of being accountable for what happens to others and little understand or respect for their rights and feelings (Figure 13-2).

The dependent high school student has a similar reliance upon others. He is late when he must get up without being called, late or absent for appointments, and late in getting his homework done. He typically expects others to wait upon him, goes to others for aid or advice, is reluctant to make decisions for himself, is a chronic complainer, and invariably blames others for his difficulties. The dependent adult also shows the clinging quality evident in young children. He is a great borrower. He makes constant requests of others for direction, support, and help. He is extremely gregarious and a chronic joiner of clubs. He makes extraordinary efforts to win the attention and regard of others.

Opportunistic Love

The loves of the opportunist are more discriminating. His interest in and preference for others varies with his estimate of what they are willing to do for him or what he thinks he can get them to do for him. His actions toward others are more precise and differentiated, for he knows something of the rules that others follow and how to use those rules to manipulate them. He can act as if he were considerate and responsible, but he does not feel any respect for others or responsibility for what happens to them. He is dominated by the desire to gain personal and immediate advantage. In the process, lying and deception are used whenever he thinks they will help.

Conforming Love

The opportunist knows the rules but applies them for his immediate advantage. The conformist knows the rules and applies them to himself as well as others, sometimes to his immediate disadvantage. The rules he knows best, however, concern external rather than internal matters, i.e., what he and others say and do rather than what they think and feel like doing. He is preoccupied with the rules that govern physical appearance, formal relationships, status, and prestige. He is a good critic of what is acceptable social behavior, a poor critic of attitudes and of himself. He is concerned with the *surface* of things. If he does not fulfill these superficial requirements, he feels *shame*.

People at the superficial stage may have genuine, reciprocal, and satisfying relationships. They can meet each other's urgent needs for physical and psychological maintenance as well as confirm each other in their views of reality. Their mutual relationships, however, are often limited to those who share their beliefs about how people should look and how they should behave. To those who do not share their values, they may be critical and hostile.

Conscientious Love

The conformist obeys the rules of society; the conscientious, his own rules. When the conformist breaks the rules, he feels *shame*; the conscientious feels *guilt*. The conformist obeys rules because others will know or may know; the conscientious, because *he* will know. The conforming housewife may sweep the dirt under the rug where others cannot see it; the conscientious housewife will not. Like the conformist, the conscientious tends to be judgmental and moralistic. The conscientious, however, places less stress upon the judgment of behavior, more stress upon the judgment of the *motives* of behavior. The conscientious are generally also much more concerned with the motives of their own conduct. The most obvious difference between the conformist and the conscientious is the absence of self-criticism in the former and the excessiveness of self-criticism in the latter.

The conscientious are responsible; i.e., they can *feel* answerable and accountable for what they feel and do and for what others feel and do. Conformists have some sense of responsibility; the more conscientious an individual beocmes, however, the more he is dominated by his sense of responsibility. The conscientious, indeed, often feel responsible in situations where others would not hold them responsible and where the facts could not realistically be interpreted to indicate that they should feel responsible.

The conscientious are often preoccupied with *conflicts* between their responsibilities: their duty to their parents versus their duty to their children, and their obligations to their group versus their obligations to their principles.

Self-actualized Love

As the conscientious become more self-actualized, they develop greater self-understanding, recognize the inevitability of conflict, see more clearly their own weaknesses, and accept their own limited influence on others and on situations. As they do so, they become more aware of the differences between themselves and others, more tolerant of those choosing solutions to conflicts unlike their own solutions, more conscious of the inevitable mutual interdependence of people upon each other, and more filled with an understanding of mankind and of human life.

The feeling of responsibility of the self-actualized fits their actual ability to control people and events. However, their consideration of others, their understanding of human weaknesses and respect for the separateness of others, continues to expand. They move from a tolerance of differences to a love of differences.

Like the conscientious, they are concerned about people. Unlike the conscientious, they recognize the necessity and desirability for others to go their own ways. The conscientious mother, teacher, or leader feels responsible for preventing children, students, or followers from making mistakes. The self-actualized mother, teacher, or leader feels responsible for satisfying the need of others to learn from their own mistakes.

A THEORY ABOUT SUCCESS IN LOVE

We play roles to satisfy our integrative, our productive, and our morale needs. We play a role with a particular person because we love him; i.e., we see the relationship with him as one which will satisfy these needs. The more intense these needs and the more certain we are that our relationship with him will satisfy them, the more we love him, i.e., the more we are interested in him, prefer him, and act to be with him. As the frequent failures of "love at first sight" testify, it is not the intensity of love that determines its success. What does? The theory outlined below and applied in the following chapter asserts that it is the kind of love shown in playing a role that determines the success of the relationship.

The major concepts of the theory are consideration and responsibility. One person's degree of consideration for another is defined as the "degree to which he understands him and respects his rights and feelings." His degree of responsibility is the "degree to which a person feels and acts as if he were holding himself accountable for what happens in a situation or to a person."

The major relationship assumed by the theory is that the degree of consideration that a person shows toward another is *independent* of the degree of responsibility that he will show. This independence is pictured in Figure 13-3. The horizontal line indicates variations from extremely inconsiderate to extremely considerate; the vertical line indicates variations from extremely irresponsible to extremely responsible. The theory assumes that it is just as likely that the considerate person will be irresponsible as it is that he will be responsible and just as likely that the responsible person will be inconsiderate as it is that he will be considerate.

The intersection of these two independent dimensions defines different kinds of love. Thus, love may be inconsiderate and irresponsible. An infant, for example, may be intensely in love with his mother and at the same time be extremely inconsiderate and irresponsible toward her. The equally intense love of a mother for her child may be extremely considerate and responsible. However, it may be extremely inconsiderate but extremely responsible. That is, she may hold herself fully accountable for what happens to her child but at the same time have no understanding of or respect for her child's rights and feelings. Again, she may be extremely considerate but completely irresponsible in her love. She may understand her child without feeling or acting at all responsible. In general, a person in any role may be described in terms of the degree of consideration and responsibility he reveals in playing it.

The degree of success that a person has in a role depends upon the kind of love he shows in playing it. That is, the more considerate *and* the more responsible his role playing, the more integrative, productive, and intrinsically interesting the relationship will be.

Does the Theory Work?

The testing of this theory, like the testing of all theories, requires first measuring the concepts involved and then determining whether the relationships assumed by the theory fit actual relationships. The following chapters explore these problems in relationships between the sexes, between parents and children, and between leaders and their followers. Here is one example of how two psychologists have tried to solve them.

In measuring consideration and responsibility, the role player may estimate his own consideration and responsibility in the relation-

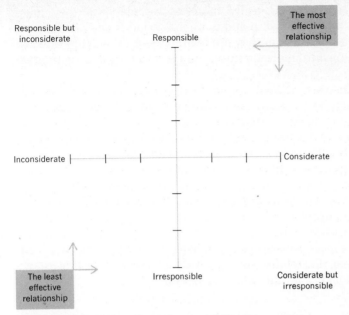

Figure 13-3 Consideration and responsibility theory of love.

ship, the person he is playing the relationship with may estimate his consideration and responsibility, or, finally, observers outside of the relationship may estimate his consideration and responsibility.

Kurtz and Grummon (1972) used all three direct methods in measuring the consideration that 25 counselors showed in playing their roles with their clients. The counselors estimated their consideration by rating themselves after their third interview with their client on statements like the following:

I try to see things through his eyes.

I understand his words but not the way he feels.

After the third interview, the clients also estimated the consideration of their counselor by rating him on statements like the following:

He tries to see things through my eyes.

He understands my words but not the way I feel.

Finally, two independent judges listened to recorded segments of each counselor's sessions with his client and rated the consideration of the counselor.

Are people who are more considerate and responsible in their relationships with others really more successful? Are they more satisfied with the relationship and more interested in the role they are playing? Do those to whom they are relating tend to be more satisfied with the relationship, more interested in their role, and more productive in it?

The answers depends, upon *how* consideration and responsibility are measured. Kurtz and Grummon (1972), we have seen, developed a composite measure of productivity by combining five measures. They also measured the counselor's consideration by means of his self estimate, the estimate of independent observers, and the estimate of the client of his consideration of him. Finally, they correlated each of the consideration measures with therapeutic productivity. The rating by the counselor of his own consideration had no relationship to improvement. The rating by the client of his counselor's consideration did. In fact, it was the *only* measure that did. Conclusion: How loving we think we are in a relationship has little connection with how productive the relationship is likely to be; how loving *others* perceive us to be has an intimate connection.

THE DEVELOPMENT OF SUCCESSFUL RELATIONSHIPS

The more considerate and responsible we are, the happier we are likely to be and the happier we are likely to make others. However, everyone is limited in his ability to be considerate and responsible, many are severely limited, and a few have no capacity to be either. Our ability to be considerate is limited by all the things that limit our understanding of others and their problems. The autistic have no capacity to be considerate because they cannot understand that others have needs separate from their own. The impulse-ridden child can understand some of the problems of his younger brother but few of the problems of his parents. In general, we find it easier to be considerate of those at the same or lower stages of development than we are, harder to be considerate of those at higher stages: the conformist finds it hard to understand the problems that disturb the conscientious.

The limitations on our ability to be responsible are even more strenuous. It is possible to *feel* accountable for what happens to a great many people and in a great many situations, but it is possible to *act* responsible toward only a few. We are limited by our understanding of the person, by our knowledge of what to do about his problem, and, above all, by the time and energy we have and wish to devote to helping him solve his problems.

To achieve more successful relationships, therefore, requires, first of all, developing our ability to select those roles and relationships in which we can be and want to be considerate and responsible. It also requires developing our ability to structure these relationships so that they will be more integrative, productive, and interesting, and developing our skill in communicating our consideration and responsibility to others. These abilities are required for success in every role-playing situation. Psychotherapists have been most aware of this.

The Selection of Role Relationships

The psychotherapist can see only a few of the many people who seek his help. He is, therefore, preoccupied with improving his ability to select those whom he has the best chance of helping. The problem is particularly acute in state hospitals where the patients are many and therapists are few. As the following results indicate, the subjective judgments of the therapist are not necessarily the best method of selection.

Wittman (1941) compared the predictions of success in therapy of 343 schizophrenic patients made by therapists with predictions made by the use of an objective scale. Before therapy began, the therapists rated each of the patients on a scale from most likely to improve to most likely not to improve. After therapy, the patients were classified as: "discharged" (16 percent), "much improved" (19 percent), "improved" (15 percent), "slightly improved" (9 percent), and "unimproved" (41 percent). Their original predictions were correct in 44 percent of the cases.

The second method of predicting the outcome of therapy was by means of a prognosis scale of 30 items. The scale consisted of such items as marital status, duration of psychosis, and anal eroticism versus oral eroticism. The items were picked for inclusion in the scale after a study of the opinions of a variety of writers. The weight given to each item was based on the relative importance accorded it by the authorities consulted. After developing the scale, Wittman rated each of the schizophrenics on it by studying their case records. From the total scores on the prognosis scale Wittman predicted what improvement the patient would make. These predictions were correct in 81 percent of the cases; almost twice as high as the combined judgments of the psychiatric staff!

Are therapists more successful with those who are least like themselves or most like themselves? Sixty therapists saw 60 patients once a week for sixteen weeks (Carson and Heine, 1962). Before therapy, clinicians and patients completed the Minnesota Multiphasic Personality Inventory. Patients were assigned to clinicians on the basis of their similarity or dissimilarity to them. The 60 clinician-patient pairs were divided into five groups, the first group being composed of those with the most similar scores on the inventory and the fifth group being composed of those with the least similar. After therapy, psychologists who had not participated in the therapy sessions rated the success of the therapy for each patient. Both the patients who were least and those who were most like their therapists benefited least from the therapy. Patients who were moderately like their therapists (the three middle groups) benefited the most.

It may be that the therapist has to be enough like his client to be able to understand him. At any rate, the more the therapist improves his understanding of his client, the more the client seems to improve (Cartwright and Lerner, 1963). At the beginning of treatment of 28 patients, their client-centered therapists tried to rate them as they had rated themselves. At the end of therapy, the therapists repeated the process. At this time, 15 of the clients were judged as "improved" and 13 as "unimproved." The therapists of the unimproved patients showed no gain in understanding. The therapists of the improved patients did.

Like the therapist, everyone is limited in the number of people to whom he can relate. The student is forced to choose among the teachers he might have. The husband earns a living and satisfies his own needs as well as the needs of his wife and children. How much of his time should he give to his relationships with his fellow workers? His wife and children? His parents? His friends?

Everyone has difficulty answering such questions and makes some mistakes. Some people, however, seem chronically to make mistakes in their choice of friends, teachers, employers, and spouses. Such people are generally driven by such urgent needs that they see in other people only those qualities that are relevant to their own immediate satisfaction. They "fall in love" with those whom they think can give them what they need. Later, they may be surprised and shocked by the price demanded for getting what they need.

Many people make no conscious effort to select their relationships. They drift. The more conscious a person becomes that he has some choice and some control over whom he relates to, the more effective these relationships are likely to be.

Structure of relationships

"Structure" refers to the form, shape, or pattern given a relationship by the setting of limits and the definition of roles and responsibilities. Relationships may be as unstructured as a pile of bricks or as structured as a skyscraper. The sounder the structure, the more effective the relationship.

The structuring of time is the most obvious way in which a therapist gives form to his relationships. He makes, keeps, and terminates appointments with his clients. The therapist also structures his relationships by the setting of limits. He may, for example, tell the client that he can say anything he wishes but that he cannot be physically aggressive. He structures the relationship in more subtle ways by telling the client the role he will play and then playing that role, and by telling the client the role the client should play and encouraging him to play it.

Therapists vary in the *degree* of structure that they impose upon their relationships. The psychoanalyst, for example, typically provides a high degree of structure by spelling out in detail the times for the relationship, the different roles that he and his client will play, and the different responsibilities that each will have. In group psychotherapy, on the other hand, the structuring may be slight. The length of the group meetings may be left open, few expectations about the regularity of attendance may be communicated, and the roles of the participants may be left undetermined.

The *rigidity* of the structure that the therapist imposes is independent of the degree of structure. Thus, a very unstructured relationship may be rigidly maintained, while a very structured relationship may be easily and quickly changed. For some therapists, the structure of the relationship at the end of therapy is the same as at the beginning. Other therapists plan to change the structure as the relationship progresses. A highly structured relationship may be extremely flexible. Thus, a therapist may have spelled out the details of his and his client's roles but may suddenly switch roles with the client, allowing him to be the therapist and himself the client.

All relationships, whether the participants know it or not, vary in their kind of structure, the degree of structure, and the rigidity of the structure. The more parents and their children, teachers and their students, employers and their employees, and husbands and wives become aware of the structure of their relationships, of their capacity to control the structure, and of their ability to manipulate the structure, the more effective their relationships are likely to be.

Communication of Consideration

The better we understand and respect the feelings, thoughts, and rights of others, the more considerate we are. A basic obstacle to behaving in a considerate way toward others is the unwillingness to accept the separateness of other people. Intellectually, of course, we know that other people are not only physically separate from us but also have their separate backgrounds, separate personalities, separate experiences, and separate paths to follow in fulfilling themselves. Emotionally, it is often impossible to *accept* this separateness (Rogers, 1961):

Can I be strong enough as a person to be separate from the other? Can I be a sturdy respecter of my own feelings, my own needs, as well as his? Can I own and, if need be, express my own feelings as something belonging to me and separate from his feelings? Am I strong enough in my own separateness that I will not be downcast by his depression, frightened by his fear, nor engulfed by his dependency? Is my inner self hardy enough to realize that I am not destroyed by his anger, taken over by his need for dependence, nor enslaved by his love, but that I exist separate from him with feelings and rights of my own? When I can freely feel this strength of being a separate person, then I find that I can let myself go much more deeply in understanding and accepting him because I am not fearful of losing myself.

    . . . Am I secure enough within myself to permit him his separateness? Can I permit him to be what he is—honest or deceitful, infantile or adult, despairing or over-confident? Can I give him the freedom to be? Or do I feel that he should follow my advice, or remain somewhat dependent on me or mold himself after me? In this connection I think of the interesting small study by Farson which found that the less well adjusted and less competent counselor tends to induce conformity to himself, to have clients who model themselves after him. On the other hand, the better adjusted and more competent counselor can interact with a client through many interviews without interfering with the freedom of the client to develop a personality quite separate from that of his therapist. I should prefer to be in this latter class, whether as parent or supervisor or counselor.

The ability of the therapist to accept the separateness of his clients seems to have nothing to do with the kind of formal training he has received. Fiedler (1950*b*) recorded one-hour recordings of therapy sessions of ten different therapists. Four judges listened to the recordings and rated each therapist on his success with the client. Some of the therapists were Adlerians, some Freudians, and some Rogerians. Their point of view, however, had no connection with their success. But success as a therapist was related to experience: the more experienced the therapist, the higher he was rated. Laymen and therapists agree that a successful relationship exists when a client says of his therapist (Fiedler, 1950*a*):

He likes me.

He never seems at all tense or on edge.

He is well able to understand my feelings.

His remarks fit in just right with my mood.

His tone of voice conveys his complete ability to share my feelings.

The more fully a therapist gets such answers from his clients, the more he is communicating consideration.

Communication of Responsibility

To be responsible is to feel and act as if we were holding ourselves accountable for what happens in a situation or to a person. Primarily, we communicate responsibility to others by communicating our liking for them. If we do not like a person, it is nearly impossible to act in a way that convinces him that we do. Even when we do like a person, we are often resistant to communicating our feelings. Rogers (1961) explains why:

Can I let myself experience positive attitudes toward this other person—attitudes of warmth, caring, liking, interest, respect? It is not easy. I find in myself, and feel that I often see in others, a certain amount of fear of these feelings. We are afraid that if we let ourselves freely experience these positive feelings toward another we may be trapped by them. They may lead to demands on us or we may be disappointed in our trust, and these outcomes we fear. So as a reaction we tend to build up distance between ourselves and others—aloofness, a "professional" attitude, an impersonal relationship.

I feel quite strongly that one of the important reasons for the professionalization of every field is that it helps to keep this distance. In the clinical areas we develop elaborate diagnostic formulations, seeing the person as an object. In these ways, I believe, we can keep ourselves from experiencing the caring which would exist if we recognized the relationship as one between two persons. It is a real achievement when we can learn, even in certain relationships at certain times in those relationships, that it is safe to care, that it is safe to relate to the other as a person for whom we have positive feelings.

It is easy to communicate about the external world: "It is raining now." It is hard to communicate about the internal world: "I love you deeply."

Practice in Role Playing

Psychotherapists have long been aware of the value of practice in playing social roles. Moreno (1946) invented the *psychodrama* as a means of providing such practice. The technique permits persons to act out their social roles and emotions under professional guidance. In one case, 20 girls who planned to become salesgirls, waitresses, beauticians, or nurses, met together. Moreno assigned roles to four of them: a visitor to a hospital, a sick child, a nurse on the ward, and a nurse in training. Those who were assigned roles went up on the stage, and the others, for the moment, were part of the audience. The actors then performed their roles as they felt them. The girls learned to respond to the situation, not in terms of previous attitudes and ideas, but in terms of the objective demands of the situation. Psychodrama is flexible: a person may be assigned a role that he avoids in life, he may be assigned a role that requires reliving a painful scene, he may be asked to act out a fantasy, or he may be asked to be part of the audience while one of his problems is acted out by others.

Practice in role playing for those with interpersonal problems not only is beneficial but may be more beneficial than other methods. Lazarus (1966) assigned 75 clients to one of three treatment groups: traditional counseling, direct advice, and role playing. Four 30-minute sessions were devoted to each client's social problem over a period of a month. The measure of success of treatment was the client's report of some behavioral change. For example, a girl who had previously been socially awkward began going on regular dates, a secretary sought and obtained a salary increase, and a husband was able to persuade his wife to move from her parents' to a home of their own. Counseling helped in 32 percent of the cases; advice, in 44 percent; and role playing, *in 92 percent.* Furthermore, more than four-fifths of those that did not benefit from counseling or advice, did benefit when they were later treated by role playing.

We get daily practice playing our social roles. However, much of this practice may be in playing them in an unsuccessful way. What is needed is practice in selecting relationships, practice in structuring them, and practice in communicating consideration and responsibility in them. Individuals may initiate such practice by following the general guidelines given in this and the following chapters. Psychotherapists, as the above example illustrates, are increasingly interested in devising practice that will eliminate undesired ways of playing social roles.

Reevaluation counseling is a recent and radical approach to developing love relationship skills. Its core method is cocounseling. During a session, a pair of participants reverse their counselor and counselee relationships. During the first half of a session, a person is the counselor of his partner; during the second half, his partner becomes the counselor for him. Schiff (1972) has outlined some of the broader implications of this approach:

> Just as Reevaluation Counseling is beginning to serve as the basis of new institutions alternative to existing mental health institutions, it also has other, still larger countercultural implications. The emphasis on the open expression of emotion and

on validation counters, in some fundamental ways, the bureau-cratically-oriented personality style and interpersonal organization prevalent in advanced industrial societies. The legitimation of anger in women contradicts the subordinate position of women not only in the family, but in almost all male-female relationships in the society. Similarly, the legitimation of grief and fear in men suggests a fundamental reorganization of the male role, not only in the family, but in all social institutions.

Like Alcoholics Anonymous, Synanon, Neurotics Anonymous, and other PSHPGs (Peer Self-Help Psychology Groups), reevaluation counseling was not developed and is not run by professional mental health workers. A serious disadvantage of the nonprofessional nature of these activities is that it is hard to obtain evidence of their success.

SUMMARY

This chapter outlines a theory about why we play roles, how we play them, and what determines our success. The theory is used in the following chapters in analyzing role playing between men and women, husbands and wives, parents and children, and citizens and their society. A *role* is a position in a social structure. Society has *standards* (expectations) about how a role should be played. The player has standards about how he should play his role and judgments about how well he is meeting them (*role identity*). We may play roles to achieve *integrative*, *morale*, or *productive* ends, i.e., to achieve a feeling of emotional closeness to others, to engage in activities that are intrinsically interesting, or to satisfy needs outside of the relationship. All three goals are present in every relationship, but in a particular relationship one almost always dominates the others. These goals are independent; i.e., our degree of success in achieving one of them has no necessary relationship to our success in achieving the other two.

The success of a relationship depends, not upon the intensity of love that pervades it, but upon the kind of love. The more consideration and responsibility the players show toward each other in playing their roles, the more successful the relationship is likely to be. *Consideration* is the degree to which a person understands and respects the rights and feelings of another person. *Responsibility* is the degree to which a person feels and acts as if he were holding himself accountable for what happens in a situation or to a person. The degree of consideration and responsibility shown in a relationship depends upon the *selection* of roles and fellow role players, upon the *structure* of their relationship, upon the *communication* between them, and upon the *practice* they have had in playing their roles.

SUGGESTIONS FOR FURTHER READING

Brand, M. (1937). *The outward room*. New York: Simon & Schuster. With the help of another's tenderness and warmth, the heroine gains insight into herself and becomes a happier and more competent person.

Rogers, C. (1961). *On becoming a person*. New York: Houghton Mifflin. In these intimate essays, an outstanding clinical psychologist talks of his convictions about teaching, science, the future, and the art of helping people.

Berne, E. B. (1964). *Games people play*. New York: Grove Press. A best-seller in the field of personality that has also received serious professional attention. Deals with the specific ways in which people avoid love by playing "games."

Adams, H. B. (1964). "Mental illness" or interpersonal behavior? *American Psychologist*, **19**, 191–197. The author of this influential article argues that what is now called "mental illness" is more realistically and helpfully viewed as a disturbance of interpersonal relationships.

14

MAN AND WOMAN

Psychology is not only man-made, as is civilization in general, but masculine in its mentality. Hence, it explains woman also in terms of man . . . Adler's "masculine protest" and Freud's "castration-complex" are attitudes indicative of that masculinized psychology which puts all differences on a sexual basis.

OTTO RANK

Men and women, we all agree, are different. We agree that they differ in such physical characteristics as the size of their breasts, the amount of their hair, and the depth of their voices. They differ in their specific physiological contribution to the reproductive process. Above all, they differ in the standards that society hopes they will meet, in the ways it expects them to play their sexual roles, and in the kinds of identity it assumes they will develop. This chapter examines these differences in standards, in sexuality, and in sex and identities as well as their implications for the development of intersexual love.

SEX-ROLE STANDARDS

A person's standards are his beliefs about the way he should feel, think, and act. His standards affect those of his society. His beliefs that he should be rational, independent, and responsible are learned from his culture as are his beliefs that he should *not* be selfish, dishonest, or violent. Many social standards are about the same for both men and women. "Sex-role standards" concern those traits that are considered good or bad *depending upon whether the person having the traits is a male or a female.* They specify the qualities of the ideal man or woman. They concern physique and dress, sexual and social behavior, and ways of feeling and thinking.

Physical Standards

What kind of female body do males prefer? Nearly a hundred male undergraduates saw nude female silhouettes prepared in such a manner that the size of breasts, buttocks, and legs could be varied systematically. Five different sizes of each body part were employed. Each part was presented with every other part in a way that required the men to indicate which of two sizes he found more attractive. In general, the men showed a preference for well-proportioned women with moderate size breasts, buttocks, and legs (Wiggins, Wiggins, and Conger, 1968).

The men, however, differed widely in their preferences. Furthermore, these differences were related to differences in the personalities and backgrounds of the men. Here are sketches of the men with preferences for the extremes:

> **Large breasts** Men who preferred the figure with the largest breasts were readers of *Playboy* magazine. They tended to date frequently, to have masculine interests, and to read sports magazines. They tended to be heavy smokers.

Small breasts Preference for small breasts was negatively related to the consumption of alcoholic beverages. Men who preferred small breasts tended to hold fundamentalist religious beliefs, to be mildly depressed, and to lack ambition.

Large buttocks Those who preferred large buttocks tended to be business majors, to be neat and orderly, and to be self-critical.

Small buttocks Those who preferred small buttocks were energetic and self-confident. They more often reported that they were breast-fed as infants.

Large legs The personality pattern associated with large-leg preference suggested one of inhibition and restraint in social situations.

Small legs Preference for small legs tended to be accompanied by a strong need for social participation. This preference was associated with smoking but not with drinking, with reading sports magazines but not with reading *Playboy*.

Dress also determines impressions of physical attractiveness. Hamid (1968) showed 21 male and 24 female students eight color photographs of female figures selected from magazines and asked them to rate the women on physical attractiveness. Make-up, glasses, jewelry, neckline, dress color, distance of hemline above the knee, stockings, and shoe color were systematically varied. Those with glasses were rated lower on physical attractiveness; those with makeup, bright colored dresses, and high hemlines were rated higher.

Trait Standards

Our society expects females to be cautious and males to be bold. An overwhelming proportion of fifth graders saw these qualities as typical of females (Oetzel, 1962):

Always does what the teacher says.

Likes to do things for other people.

Is always very polite.

Is easily embarrassed.

Is careful not to hurt other people's feelings.

Likes to act grown up.

An equally large proportion saw these as typical of males:

> Is bossy.
>
> Sticks up for his own rights.
>
> Likes to show off.
>
> Likes noisy fun.
>
> Likes to tease other kids.
>
> Is never afraid of anything.

College students reported similar expectations.

A decade later, people reported the same expectations but with more doubts (Reistrup, 1972). Table 14-1 shows some of the questions asked in a nationwide cross-sectional survey of more than 3,000 men and women. The questions are placed under the trait to which they are most closely related with the percent of women and men answering "true." About 10 percent of the respondents were classified as unsure. The majority of men and women agreed that men were bolder, less emotional, more practical, and less religious in their orientations—though more men than women agreed about these trait differences. These differences are in the same direction as the actual

TABLE 14-1   Trait Standards for Men and Women

	Percent Answering "True"	
Trait	Women	Men
Cautious vs. bold:		
Men have more physical stamina	52	62
Men are more aggressive	51	62
Unemotional vs. emotional:		
Women are more emotional and less logical	58	64
Artistic vs. practical:		
Women have more artistic ability and		
appreciation	58	62
Men are better at economics and business	49	56
Religious vs. scientific:		
Women attach greater value to human life	55	56

(*Source*: Reistrup, 1972)

differences for male and female college students reported on the trait scales in Part Two.

The younger the woman, the less likely she was to agree with any of these statements. Thus, 64 percent of women over fifty agreed that women were more emotional than men but only 46 percent of those under thirty agreed with this statement. Also, the better educated the women, the less they agreed with the statements: 65 percent of women with only an eighth-grade education agreed that women were more emotional than men but only 46 percent of college women agreed with the statement. Obviously, trait standards for men and women are shifting.

Role Standards

Respondents in the survey emphatically agreed that "Women are more sensitive to the problems of the poor and underprivileged than men are." An overwhelming majority of men and women, young and old, uneducated and educated, single and married, and black and white agreed with this statement. More also agreed that women could do a better job than men in public roles concerned with dealing with children and family problems, assisting the poor, dealing with health problems, improving our educational system, or working for peace in the world.

Both boys and girls prefer the male role more than the female role. As early as three, boys show a preference for masculine games and their preference becomes more marked with age. They rarely prefer feminine games. Many girls, on the other hand, prefer masculine games, activities, and objects. They also more often state a desire to be a boy or to be daddy rather than a mommy when they grow up (Brown, 1957).

Whether they like it or not, the vast majority of societies set different role standards for boys and girls and train them to meet them. A study of 110 societies showed consistent and strikingly different standards (Barry, Bacon, and Child, 1957). To begin with, the researchers rated various aspects of the training of infants and then of children in each society after reading enthnographic reports about the society. Whether boy or girl, babies were treated in practically the same way in most cultures.

As Figure 14-1 shows, older boys and girls were trained in quite different ways. In no society were girls given as severe training in self-reliance as boys. In no society were boys given as much training in helping dependent people as girls. For each kind of training, there were a few societies in which there was no reliable evidence of sex differences. In the vast majority of societies, however, boys are given

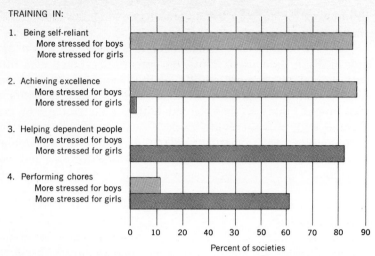

Figure 14-1 Differences in the training of boys and girls in 110 societies. (Data from Barry, Bacon, and Child, 1957)

more training in being self-reliant and achieving excellence than girls; girls are given more training in helping with younger siblings and other dependent persons, as well as in helping with chores in the domestic economy. Thus, our society, like most societies, stresses the development of nurturant and interpersonal skills in girls and independence and achievement in boys.

The differences in sex training in our society are smaller than in most (Barry et al., 1957):

> Our mechanized economy is perhaps less dependent than any previous economy upon the superior average strength of the males. The nuclear family in our society is often so isolated that husband and wife must each be prepared at times to take over or help in the household tasks normally assigned to the other. It is also significant that the conditions favoring low sex differentiation appear to be more characteristic of the upper segments of our society, in socioeconomic and educational status, than of lower segments. This observation may be relevant to the tendency toward smaller sex differences in personality in higher status groups.

Should sex differences in socialization be eliminated? The authors argue that they should not, for a differentiation of sex roles is inevitable in any social group. The reduction may have already gone too far (Barry et al., 1957):

In our training of children, there may now be less differentiation in sex roles than characterizes adult life—so little, indeed, as to provide inadequate preparation for adulthood. This state of affairs is likely to be especially true of formal education, which is more subject to conscious influence by an ideology than is informal socialization at home. With child training being more oriented toward the male than the female role in adulthood, many of the adjustment problems of women in our society today may be partly traced to conflicts growing out of inadequate childhood preparation for their adult role.

One reason why girls may prefer the male role is that it is easier to determine whether one is meeting its standards. The male role may not be easier, but it is easier to determine how well one is playing it, for the criteria are more objective. A boy can determine how strong he is by lifting weights, how good a basketball player he is by how many baskets he can make. A girl has no such performance criteria for determining the strength of her desire to help others or her skill in dealing with others. A girl must have continuous social interaction and feedback to determine how attractive she is, how socially poised, or how helpful.

Another reason girls may prefer the male role is that the standards for the female role are changing with confusing rapidity. Traditional standards are increasingly in conflict with contemporary female standards. Traditional standards stress that under ordinary circumstances women belong in the home, caring for children, and carrying out domestic duties. Contemporary standards hold that the relationship between men and women is ideally egalitarian and that, therefore, women should be willing and able to contribute to the financial support of the family.

MALE AND FEMALE SEXUALITY

The most profound differences between men and women are the complementary parts they play in the sex act. Yet detailed studies of *Human Sexual Response* (Masters and Johnson, 1966) stress the physiological similarities. Both sexes proceed through the same phases during the sex act: (1) the excitement phase; (2) the plateau phase; (3) the orgasmic phase; and (4) the resolution phase. Both sexes demonstrate increases in blood pressure and perspiration, more rapid heart beat, more rapid breathing, and greater muscular tension. The authors conclude (p. 285):

The parallels in reaction to effective sexual stimulation emphasize the physiological similarities in male and female responses rather than the differences. Aside from obvious anatomic variants, men and women are homogeneous in their physiologic responses to sexual stimuli.

Men and women also participate in the same stages in the development of their sexual relationship. Kinsey and associates (1948, p. 540) concluded that as an individual has more contact with a partner, his repertory of sexual experiences increases in a sequential pattern:

> Petting techniques usually expand in a more or less standard sequence, as the partners become better acquainted. Beginning with general body contact, lip kissing, and the deep kiss, it advances to a deliberate manipulation of the female breast, to mouth contacts with the female breast, to manual stimulation of the female genitalia, less often to the manual stimulation of the male genitalia, to the apposition of naked genitalia, to oral stimulation of the male genitalia, and finally to oral stimulation of the female genitalia.

Three separate studies have confirmed this sequence (Podell and Perkins, 1957; Brady and Levitt, 1965; and Bentler, 1968). Bentler derived this sequence from the anonymous replies of 108 college males, mostly unmarried:

1. Kissing with tongue contact

2. Manual manipulation of clad female breast

3. Manual manipulation of nude female breast

4. Oral contact with female breast.

5. Manual manipulation of female genitalia

6. Manual manipulation of your genitalia by a female

7. Heterosexual intercourse: ventral-ventral

8. Oral contact with female genitalia

9. Oral contact with your genitalia by a female

10. Heterosexual intercourse: ventral-dorsal

The experiences are ranked in the order of frequency; i.e., "1" was most frequently reported; "10", least. The scale is also sequential; i.e., those who reported experiencing "10" also reported experiencing all of the more frequent experiences. The other two studies reported practically identical results.

Differences in Sexual Response

The average frequency of the sexual response is much greater in men. Figure 14-2 shows the number of orgasms per week for more than 5,000 American males from adolescence to eighty-five years of age. The typical male has between 2 and 3 orgasms per week. The figures for women are not directly comparable (Kinsey, Pomeroy, and Martin, 1953). It is clear, however, that the frequency for women is considerably less. The range of response among men, however, is much less than among women, although it is still great. Of men, Kinsey et al. (1948, p. 195) report:

There are a few males who have gone for long periods of years without ejaculating: there is one male who, although apparently sound physically, had ejaculated only once in thirty years. There are others who have maintained average frequencies of 10, 20, or more per week for long periods of time: one male (a scholarly and skilled lawyer) has averaged over 30 per week for thirty years.

In general, though, many more women than men have little or no interest in sex. At the other extreme, some women far exceed the maximums obtained by men.

The frequency of sexual responses for men and women also varies differently with age. Figure 14-3 shows the steady decline in sexual activity for married men from adolescence through age sixty. A supplementary study of 126 men over sixty by Kinsey revealed that the gradual decline continues to the eighties. Still, great differences exist at even the oldest ages: 30 percent of the men were sexually inactive at seventy, but the ejaculation rate of one seventy-year-old exceeded that of the average adolescent. In sharp contrast, women's sexual intensity rises more gradually but then stays at the maximum level until after fifty.

Differences in the desire of men and women for sexual intercourse are greatest in youth. At twenty, men have reached their peak while women still have relatively little interest. In the face of this problem, the majority of primitive societies take a permissive attitude toward premarital sexual relationships (Murdock, 1949). Permissiveness in our society, as Table 14-2 indicates, has varied a great deal with social class. Among those single men who have eight grades or less, 53 percent of their sexual outlets are with women companions and

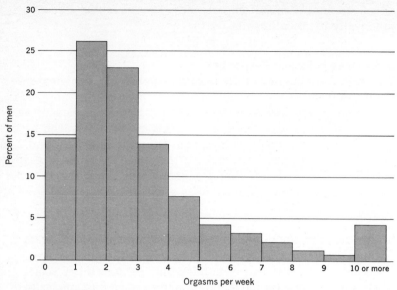

Figure 14-2 Differences in sexual activity of American men. (Data from Kinsey, 1948)

another 13 percent with prostitutes. Among college men, less than 20 percent of their sexual outlets are with companions or prostitutes (Kinsey et al., 1948, p. 378).

Differences in Sexual Motivation

In their sexual relationships, men stress sex; women, love. A study of sexual behavior and dating concluded (Ehrmann, 1959):

> . . . Pleasure among our females is primarily associated with love and among our males with sex. . . . The core of interest in sex education of girls is pregnancy, childbirth, and child rearing, whereas of boys it is sex techniques, sexual intercourse, and probable erotic reactions of the female. . . . love comes to the male with a strongly established erotic orientation, whereas the sex interest of females is aroused within a romantic complex . . .

The greater male stress upon physiology and female stress upon human relationships is vividly shown in the contrasts between male and female homosexuals (Kinsey, Pomeroy, Martin, and Gebbard, 1953, p. 659):

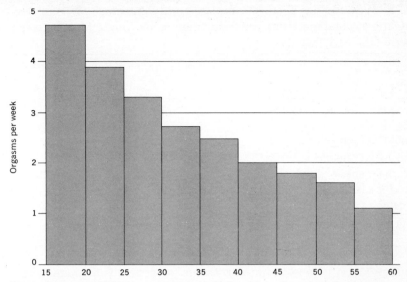

Figure 14-3 Age differences in sexual activity of American men. (Data from Kinsey, 1948)

Homosexual females frequently criticize homosexual males because they are interested in nothing but genitalia; homosexual males, in turn, may criticize homosexual females because "they do nothing" in a homosexual relationship ... homosexual males, in their intensified interest in male genitalia and genital activity, often exhibit the most extreme examples of a typically male type of conditioning.

On motivation for marriage, Kinsey concluded (1953, p. 684):

Our data indicates that the average female marries to establish a home, to establish a long-time affectional relationship with a single spouse, and to have children whose welfare may become the prime business of her life. Most males would admit that all of these are desirable aspects of marriage, but it is probable that few males would marry if they did not anticipate that they would have an opportunity to have coitus regularly with their wives.

Differences in Learning
During the course of human evolution, the control of sexual behavior has moved further and further from physiology and closer and closer to

TABLE 14-2   School Grades Completed and Percentage of Total Sexual Outlets Obtained from Different Sources by Single Men between Twenty-One and Twenty-Five

Source	Number of Grades of School Completed		
	0–8	9–12	13 or More
Intercourse with companions	53	38	18
Masturbation	20	30	53
Intercourse with prostitutes	13	5	1
Homosexual outlets	8	16	4
Nocturnal emissions	5	8	16
Petting to climax	1	3	8
Total	100	100	100

learning. Thus, female chimpanzees are most likely to mate when ovulation is imminent and impregnation most probable. American females have the opposite pattern; i.e., they report the greatest sexual desire when ovulation is not imminent and when impregnation is least probable (Ford and Beach, 1951). In their classic study, these authors present other massive evidence of the dominating role of learning in human sexuality, including the following case (p. 230):

> A young woman, married at 21, engaged in intercourse with her husband once or twice a week for five years until the first child was born. During the first year or two she felt sexual desire but never reached climax. After five years of marriage her desire and responsiveness had grown to be as strong as those of her husband. At this time, however, she discovered that he was unfaithful, and for two years she refused to have intercourse. Following this lapse sexual relations were resumed; but although the wife was easily aroused, she was usually unsatisfied and rarely attained climax. Several years later, after removal of both ovaries, her capacity for complete response returned. At that time the habitual pattern of sexual relations included half an hour of foreplay, and a total of an hour and a half of coitus. She usually had five or six orgasms; less than two left her unsatisfied.

> This single case history illustrates several general points. . . . The first is that full sexual responsiveness including regular orgasm may not appear in the physiologically normal woman until she has had a considerable amount of sexual experience.

The second point is that normal reactivity to erotic stimulation may be lost under circumstances which have no demonstrable effect upon reproductive physiology. The emotional trauma resulting from discovery of her husband's extramarital affairs created a block in this woman's sexual response, with the result that climax became difficult or impossible to attain even though her ovaries were secreting normal amounts of sex hormones. . . . This third and final point illustrated by the example . . . is that complete and satisfactory sexual relations are possible in the human female despite the total absence of ovarian hormones.

The shift of males from homosexual to heterosexual patterns is a practical example of the influence of learning. Feldman and MacCulloch (1965) used instrumental avoidance techniques with homosexuals who requested help in eliminating their homosexual behavior. They showed each homosexual a slide of a male and instructed him to leave the picture on the screen as long as he found it attractive. If he had not switched the slide off within eight seconds he received a strong electric shock. When he began to avoid the shock, he was exposed at random to three kinds of trials: (1) a continuation of the previous trials where the picture disappears when he pressed the switch; (2) the picture and the shock disappears only after he has repeatedly pressed the switch; and (3) the picture and the shock continue even though he continued to press the switch. In addition, on about half of the trials, a female slide appeared as the male slide or the shock disappeared. Upon request, the female slide would remain. The experimenters used a series of male and female slides that the subject had previously ranked from most to least attractive. At the beginning of training, the least attractive male is paired with the most attractive female. At the end of training, the subject is avoiding the most attractive male and approaching the least attractive female. In a follow-up study, 18 of 26 patients had given up homosexual practice entirely and were almost completely without homosexual fantasy. Some of the others reported strong heterosexual fantasies and frequent heterosexual behavior (Feldman, 1966).

MASCULINITY AND FEMININITY

A person's sex role standards are what he believes a good man or a good woman ought to be (Figure 14-4). A person's masculine or feminine identity is how well he or she believes he is meeting the male or female standards. Most roles that we might play have a voluntary element. Sex roles, however, are compulsory. A person has to be, or see himself as being, somewhere on the scale from extremely masculine to extremely

Figure 14-4 The male sex role emphasizes the trait of boldness; the female sex role emphasizes cautiousness. (Michigan Tourist Council; Michigan Department of Mental Health)

feminine. Psychologists have devoted considerable effort to measuring differences in sex role identifications, clarifying their significance, and tracing the path by which infants develop a sex role identity.

Measurement

Mussen and Distler (1960) developed the IT scale to measure the sex role identifications of young children. It consists of 36 picture cards depicting various objects, figures, and activities commonly associated with masculine or feminine roles. The child first looks at a card with a figure drawing that could be either a boy or a girl and is told that this is IT. The examiner then shows the child groups of pictures of toys and paired choices of activities and asks the child in each case to chose what IT would like. The more choices the child makes that are associated with the masculine role, the higher his masculinity score.

Masculinity-femininity scales are the most common method of measuring the sex role identity of adults. The nature of such scales is suggested by the 20 statements shown in Table 14-3. These are the statements from the 200 making up the five trait scales presented in Part 2 which the typical college man answered most differently from

TABLE 14-3 A Masculinity-Femininity Scale

T F	1.	I like ballet performances.
T F	2.	I think I would like to decorate a room with flowers.
T F	3.	I have occasionally had to make an effort not to cry.
T F	4.	I would rather read an article about a famous musician than a financier.
T F	5.	I like to read poetry.
T F	6.	I enjoy going to art galleries very much.
T F	7.	I would like to hear a popular lecture on contemporary painters.
T F	8.	Artistic experiences are of great importance in my life.
T F	9.	I am guided in all of my conduct by firm principles.
T F	10.	I control my sexual impulses by instituting prohibitions and restrictions.
T F	11.	Magazines such as *Arts and Decorations* bore me.
T F	12.	Women should have as much right to propose dates to men as men to women.
T F	13.	The European attitude toward mistresses is more sensible than ours.
T F	14.	I believe I have the disposition of a pleasure seeker.
T F	15.	I am temperamentally more a skeptic than a believer.
T F	16.	In the long run, science provides the best hope for solving the world's problems.
T F	17.	I am really only interested in what is *useful.*
T F	18.	I would rather read *Business Week* than *Atlantic Monthly.*
T F	19.	I like to read scientific articles in popular magazines.
T F	20.	I would rather see a movie than read a book.

the typical college woman. Women much more frequently than men answered "true" to the first 10; men much more frequently than women answered "true" to the second 10. For example, 71 percent of the women answered "true" to the statement "I like ballet performances" whereas only 20 percent of the men answered "true." The statement, "Magazines such as *Arts and Decorations* bore me" was answered "true" by 63 percent of the men but only by 23 percent of the women. Such responses illustrate several assumptions involved in all discussions of the personality differences between men and women.

The study of sex differences in personality concerns the differences between the *typical* man and the *typical* woman. The typical college woman says that she likes ballet performances; the typical college man says he does not. Still, many women (29 percent) say they do not like ballet performances and many men say they do (20 percent). In general, even on the qualities in which men and women differ the most, they overlap a great deal. Many women are more "masculine" than the typical man and many men are more "feminine" than the typical woman.

A difference between men and women does *not* mean, as is often assumed, that heredity is the cause. Indeed, it generally is not. It is hard to imagine a hereditary mechanism that would produce a liking for poetry, movies, or books. Finding a difference does not provide an automatic explanation for the difference. Rather, it stimulates a search for an explanation. In 1959, two-thirds of college men but only one-third of college women agreed that women should have equal rights in proposing dates (Table 14-3, statement 12). In 1973 90 percent of both groups agreed. Why?

We lack confident explanations of sex differences. Consequently, we also lack certainty about the stability of the differences. Would similar differences be found in comparing *non* college men and women? Japanese men and women? The number of men and women answering "true" would certainly vary from group to group and, consequently, the size of the differences would also vary and would sometimes reverse itself.

Is it *better* to like movies or books? Musicians or financiers? *Business Week* or the *Atlantic Monthly?* Value questions like these are the furnace that provides the heat for much of the controversy over sex differences. In the largest context the question becomes: Are men more important than women? College students were asked whether men or women were superior (McKee and Sherriffs, 1957). The answer: 88 percent of the men and 78 percent of the women replied: "Men." On the whole, then, most would agree, it is better for women to be more like men than for men to be more like women—to like movies rather than books, financiers rather than musicians, *Business Week* more than the *Atlantic Monthly.*

One possible outcome of the greater value placed upon men is that women like to be with men more than men like to be with women. An analysis of the vocational interests of women showed one thing which appeared to characterize the various scales for female occupations: "Interest in Male Association" (Tyler, 1956). Betty Friedan's best-seller *The Feminine Mystique* stresses the desirability of women getting away from the bondage of home and child care into the wonderful world of work—and male associations.

Who is better than whom? To answer this question the scientist must first ask: Better for *what?* Are, for example, more masculine men more successful leaders? Porter (1962) related the masculinity scores of executives in small companies with measures of their success. Result: The more masculine their scores, the more effective they were as leaders. He then related the masculinity scores of executives in medium-sized companies with measures of their success. Result: No relationship between masculinity and leadership success. Finally, he related the masculinity scores of executives in large companies (more than 15,000 employees) with their success. Result: The more *feminine* their scores, the more successful they were. Large companies, it seems, need leaders who are more interested in reading books and other intellectual activities (feminine interests) more than they need leaders who are interested in hunting, fishing, and poker playing (masculine interests). The value of feminine or masculine qualities depends upon the problem and the situation. The answer to who is better than whom varies not only with the "what" but also with the "where."

In summary, differences between men and women never apply to all men and women, never are self-explanatory, never are constant from one group of men and women to other groups, and never establish the superiority of masculine or feminine qualities.

Table 14-4 provides the reader with an opportunity to determine his knowledge of what is masculine and feminine, for it is based on the replies of typical men and women to a wide variety of occupations, amusements, and kinds of people. The scores obtained by several hundred college men and women are shown in the norms at the end of the table. The typical student got 22 right on the men test and 27 right on the women test for a combined score of 49 right out of the 80 items.

TABLE 14-4 The Men and Women Test

This is a test of your knowledge of the likes, dislikes, and self-ratings of the typical man (Part I) and the typical woman (Part II). The correct answers are based on the analysis of replies to the *Strong Vocational Interest Blank.** In taking this test the respondent is asked to "disregard considerations of salary, social standing, future advancement, etc. . . . consider only whether or not you would enjoy the interest regardless of any necessary skills, abilities, or training which you may or may not possess."

Part I. Understanding Men
The correct answers are the actual replies of thousands of American men, primarily those in business and professional occupations. They checked whether they would "like" or "dislike" many different occupations, amusements, activities, and kinds of people. They also answered statements about what kind of persons they thought they were.

Likes
Three interests are listed opposite each question below. Only one of the three was liked by *more than half* of the men. Mark on the separate answer sheet the one that you think more than 50 percent of the men said they would "like."

TABLE 14-4   (Continued)

Example

(1) *travel movies* (2) cashier in a bank (3) people who borrow things.

       80% of the men said they liked "travel movies"; 20%, "cashier"; and 2%, "people who borrow things." Therefore, "travel movies" is the correct answer.

1. (1) pet monkeys (2) *geography* (3) military drill
2. (1) civil service employee (2) carpenter (3) *psychology*
3. (1) *literature* (2) botany (3) shop work
4. (1) agriculture (2) typewriting (3) *chemistry*
5. (1) performing sleight-of-hand tricks (2) *educational movies* (3) full-dress affairs.
6. (1) bargaining (swapping) (2) *taking responsibilty* (3) drilling soldiers
7. (1) being pitted against another as in a political or athletic race (2) *meeting and directing people* (3) teaching children
8. (1) spendthrifts (2) cripples (3) *conservative people*
9. (1) J. J. Pershing, soldier (2) *opportunity to make use of all one's knowledge and experience* (3) secretary of a social club
10. (1) head waiter (2) lighthouse tender (3) *emphasis on quality of work*

Dislikes

Only one interest in each group below was actively *disliked* by *more than half* of the men. Mark the one that you think most men said they disliked.

11. (1) factory manager (2) *undertaker* (3) geometry
12. (1) physician (2) *life insurance salesman* (3) economics
13. (1) thrifty people (2) history (3) *music teacher*
14. (1) magazine writer (2) chemist (3) *auctioneer*
15. (1) school teacher (2) *watchmaker* (3) governor of a state
16. (1) *floorwalker* (2) stock broker (3) reporter
17. (1) editor (2) *railway conductor* (3) surgeon
18. (1) author (2) store manager (3) *pharmacist*
19. (1) *auto salesman* (2) interior decorator (3) scientific research worker
20. (1) *printer* (2) wholesaler (3) astronomer
21. (1) making a radio set (2) *pet monkeys* (3) "Atlantic Monthly"
22. (1) repairing a clock (2) *acting as a yell leader* (3) giving first aid
23. (1) interviewing men for a job (2) opening conversation with a stranger (3) *looking at a collection of rare laces*
24. (1) doing research work (2) *climbing along edge of a precipice* (3) looking at shop windows.
25. (1) sick people (2) irreligious people (3) *side show freaks*
26. (1) very old people (2) people who don't believe in evolution (3) *men who use perfume*
27. (1) *people easily led* (2) people who assume leadership (3) deaf mutes

28. (1) *people who get rattled easily* (2) people with protruding jaws (3) people with hooked noses
29. (1) fashionably dressed people (2) *nervous people* (3) emotional people
30. (1) *interest the public in a machine through public address* (2) steadiness and permanence of work (3) chairman, program committee

Self-Ratings
The men also answered statements about what kind of persons they thought they were. Mark the one statement in each group below that you think was answered "yes" by *more than half* of the men.

31. (1) practically never make excuses (2) get "rattled" easily (3) *follow up subordinates effectively*
32. (1) *am approachable* (2) lost my temper at times (3) usually ignore the feelings of others
33. (1) worry very little (2) *win confidence and loyalty* (3) when caught in a mistake usually make excuses
34. (1) tell jokes well (2) *discuss my ideal with others* (3) best-liked friends are superior to me in ability
35. (1) get "rattled" easily (2) worry considerably about mistakes (3) *can correct others without giving offense*
36. (1) *am always on time with my work* (2) loan money to acquaintances (3) have mechanical ingenuity (inventiveness)
37. (1) *stimulate the ambition of my associates* (2) have mechanical ingenuity (inventiveness) (3) best-liked friends are superior to me in ability
38. (1) loan money to acquaintances (2) loan only to certain people (3) *rarely loan money*
39. (1) usually ignore the feelings of others (2) consider them sometimes (3) *carefully consider them*
40. (1) when caught in a mistake usually make excuses (2) *seldom make excuses* (3) practically never make excuses

Part II. Understanding Women
Over 4,000 women, many in professional positions, checked whether they would "like" or "dislike" different occupations, amusements, activities, and kinds of people.

Likes
Three interests are listed opposite each question below. Only one of the three was liked by *more than half* of the women. Mark the one that you think more than 50% of the women said they would "like."
Example
(1) *interior decorator* (2) mechanical engineer (3) cheerleader
Since 65% of the women said they would like being an "interior decorator" this is the correct answer.

41. (1) *wife* (2) office manager (3) music composer
42. (1) probations officer (2) dancing teacher (3) *vocational counselor*

TABLE 14-4   (Continued)

43. (1) confectioner (2) *buyer of merchandise* (3) postmistress
44. (1) solving mechanical puzzles (2)*plays* (3) cashier
45. (1) *Reader's Digest* (2) conventions (3) poker
46. (1) interviewing clients (2) *decorating a room with flowers* (3) open conversation with a stranger
47. (1) organizing a play (2) arguments (3) *looking at shop windows*
48. (1) discussing politics (2) *entertaining others* (3) buying at an auction sale
49. (1) *attending church* (2) doing research work (3) making a speech
50. (1) costume designer (2) emotional people (3) *people who are natural leaders*
51. (1) self-conscious people (2) irreligious people (3) *optimists*
52. (1) methodical people (2) *thrifty people* (3) very old people
53. (1) opportunity to understand just how one's superior expects work to be done (2) *opportunity to make use of all one's knowledge and experience* (3) opportunity for promotion
54. (1) activities of a conservative nature (2) travel with someone who will make the necessary preparations for you (3) *be married*
55. (1) be married with small income (2)*going to a play* (3) order others
56. (1) *psychology* (2) chemistry (3)bible study
57. (1) *geography* (2) bookkeeping (3) calculus

Dislikes

Only one interest in each group below was *disliked* by *more than half* of the women. Mark the one that you think more than 50% of the women said they would "dislike."

58. (1) *factory worker* (2) athletic director (3) physician
59. (1) milliner (2) *life insurance salesman* (3) judge
60. (1) manufacturer (2) *traveling saleswoman* (3) illustrator
61. (1) manager, women's style shop (2) naturalist (3) *dentist*
62. (1) laboratory technician (2) *telephone operator* (3) social worker
63. (1) public health nurse (2) *criminal lawyer* (3) opera singer
64. (1) Y.W.C.A. secretary (2) tea room proprietor (3) *bookkeeper*
65. (1) author of a novel (2) *accountant* (3) graduate general nurse
66. (1) illustrator (2) *typist* (3) interpreter
67. (1) *statistician* (2) secret service woman (3) social worker
68. (1) stage actress (2) *mechanical engineer* (3) editor
69. (1) dean of woman (2) *proofreader* (3) kindergarten teacher
70. (1) *Good Housekeeping* magazine (2) afternoon teas (3) *True Story magazine*
71. (1) *mannish women* (2) surgeon (3) methodical people
72. (1) *absent-minded people* (2) fashionably dressed people (3) people who assume leadership

73. (1) writing personal letters (2) looking at a collection of rare laces (3) *interest the public in building their own homes through public address*

Self-Ratings
The women also answered statements about what kind of persons they thought they were. Mark the one statement in each group below that you think *more than half* of the women answered "yes."

74. (1) *can discriminate between more or less important matters* (2) remember faces and incidents better than the average person (3) can correct others without giving offense
75. (1) usually liven up the group on a dull day (2) loan money to acquaintances (3) *win confidence and loyalty*
76. (1) borrow frequently (2) borrow occasionally (3) *practically never borrow*
77. (1) worry considerably about mistakes (2) *worry very little* (3) do not worry
78. (1) feelings easily hurt (2) *feelings hurt sometimes* (3) feelings rarely hurt
79. (1) have mechanical ingenuity (2) can write a well-organized report (3) *able to meet emergencies quickly and effectively*
80. (1) tell jokes well (2) *smooth out tangles and disagreements between people* (3) feelings easily hurt

	Percentiles										
	LOW										
	0	10	20	30	40	50	60	70	80	90	99
Men test (1–40)	12	16	18	20	21	22	23	25	26	28	38
Women Test (41–80)	12	22	23	25	26	27	28	29	30	32	38
Men + Women (1–80)	28	40	43	45	47	49	51	52	55	58	76

*Correct answers are in italics.

DEVELOPMENT OF SEX-ROLE IDENTITY
Neither masculine nor feminine qualities are "better." However, the individual is much more likely to be happy if he possesses qualities that are standard for his sex. Kayton and Biller (1972) matched 20 normal adult males with 20 schizophrenics, 20 paranoid schizophrenics, and 20 neurotics of the same sex, age and education. All their subjects completed two different masculinity-femininity scales. None of the disturbed groups differed from each other. All, however, received much lower masculinity scores than did the normal group. The authors stressed the "outstanding and pervasive involvement that inadequacies

in sex-role functioning play in a variety of psychological disorders." Most likely, the femininity of the disturbed was a symptom, not the cause, of their difficulties; i.e., the same conditions that made them more feminine also made them more disturbed.

Ways of establishing a sex-role identity are seldom obvious and sometimes not desirable. Zucker (1968) divided almost 400 high school boys and girls into "nondrinkers," "moderate drinkers," and "heavy drinkers" and related these differences in drinking behavior to a variety of measures of sex-role identity. One of these measures was the masculinity-femininity scale of the California Psychological Inventory. Here are a few sample items from this inventory with the feminine answers: "I think I would like the work of a building contractor" (false); "I am inclined to takes things hard" (true); and "I like to be with a crowd who play jokes on one another" (false). The scores of the girls had no relation to whether they drank or not. However, the boys' scores were related: the more masculine the boy said he was, the heavier he drank. Heavy drinking may be one way that adolescent males who have a weak sex-role identity seek to strengthen their masculine identity. Cigarette smoking may be another example, for smoking college men had less muscular physiques than nonsmokers (Plath, 1959).

As boys and girls become men and women they change qualities that are inconsistent with their separate role standards. Kagan and Moss (1962) correlated trait ratings of 35 females and 35 males when they were children with similar ratings of the same men and women after they were 20. Ratings of girls on their passivity and dependence correlated with their passivity and dependence as adults; the ratings of males on the same traits did not. Ratings of boys on the expression of anger and interest in intellectual concerns correlated with their ratings when adults; the ratings of girls on the same traits when they were adults did not.

Changes in the boldness of a boy between two and sixteen illustrate the influence of sex-role standards. At the age of two he behaved in an extremely cautious and passive way (Janis, Mahl, Kagan, and Holt, 1969, p. 486):

> Spent an unhappy week at nursery school. He cried a great deal and looked ready to cry even when he was not actually doing it. He drew away when other children approached him and he seemed afraid of them. Usually he stood around and looked lost.

He was described as having the same qualities when he was four:

This was one of the group's most isolated members. He was non-competitive, unassertive, and sedentary. He shrank from actual physical contact with others, and his relationship with peers was a long distance verbal one. When he was verbally rebuffed he smiled weakly and put his hands behind his back. *S* was the most eclipsed member of the group because of his apprehension, shyness, and inhibition.

By the age of eight, his fear was more disguised. He became less dependent on his family and more committed to hard work in school. He used his intellectual skills as a weapon of power over others. He lectured and bragged to his peers. At age sixteen he realized that he was still afraid of dating girls and decided that there was only one effective way to conquer this fear. He invited to a dance the most popular girl in the school, even though he had never been out with her before.

As this case suggests, differences in masculinity and femininity have genetic as well as environmental determinants. Differences in the sexuality of animals is heavily influenced by genetic endowment. Rasmussen (1952), for example, selected male rats for high versus low sexual responsiveness. By the fifth generation of selection, male rats of the high-drive strain would cross an electrically charged grid to reach a receptive female six times more frequently than would rats of the low-drive strain.

Sexuality in humans is also influenced by genetic differences. However, humans are not rats and sex identity is not sexuality. Some differences between males and females related to masculinity and femininity seem largely genetic. Even in infancy, boys show higher activity levels and girls show more rapid language development. Before they are two, boys show more responsiveness to objects; girls, to persons. By the preschool years, boys are much more physically aggressive than girls. Some of this difference may be environmental, for parents are more tolerant of aggressiveness in boys than girls. Probably more, however, is genetic, for boys are stronger and heavier than girls. Furthermore, similar differences in aggressiveness are found among a number of primate species. In any case, there are wide individual differences. The genes that make a child big, strong, and object-oriented push him toward masculinity; genes that make the child small, weak, and person-oriented push him toward femininity.

Indirect genetic influences are unquestionably larger than direct ones. From birth, the child's sex forms a central aspect of his identity to others. It is reflected in his name, his clothing, his toys, and the traits that others ascribe to him. The degree of masculinity or femininity that a child develops is largely determined by the degree to which he learns to imitate and to identify with his father or his mother. But what determines this?

The Presence of the Father   A child has to be able to observe his mother and father in order to imitate them. Since few families stay together without a mother the amount of contact between children and their mothers is relatively constant. Even the relatively large differences in contact between mothers employed outside the home and those not so employed seem to make little difference in a child's development (Clausen and Williams, 1963). On the other hand, the amount of contact between children and their fathers varies from extensive to almost none (as in the case of fathers in military service). Sons who experience prolonged periods of separation from their fathers are less masculine (Sears, 1951; Lynn, 1959). Separation also affects many other aspects of their development. Thus, Harvard freshmen whose fathers were at home when they were young were more quantitative than verbal; those whose fathers were not at home were more verbal than quantitative (Kuckenberg, 1963). Clinical experience indicates that low masculinity, extending sometimes to transvestism or overt homosexuality, tends to develop in families in which the father is not present or is extremely rejected by the mother.

The development of girls is also markedly influenced by their fathers. Fisher (1973) studied the frequency of orgasm among 300 young, educated, married women in Syracuse. Many factors popularly assumed to be related to sexual responsiveness in women were actually unrelated: parental attitudes toward sex, religious attitudes, source of sex education, premarital and marital experience, husband's technique, traumatic sexual experiences, and general mental health. However, sexual responsiveness *was* related to the early relationships of the women with their fathers. Women who said they rarely reached orgasm were likely to have had fathers who were absent, distant, or irresponsible in raising their daughters. The highly orgasmic women were more likely to have been raised by men who were "real fathers" to their daughters—men who were dependable, caring, demanding and insisting that their daughters meet certain moral standards. It seems that a woman with an undependable father was afraid to "let herself go" with her husband, was unduly fearful of losing the persons she loved and valued, and mistrusted men.

The Power of Reward   A child cannot imitate a parent who is not present; he may not imitate one who is. The son who is in frequent contact with a stuttering father may still learn to speak like his fast-talking mother. On the whole, however, the boy's early realization that he is a boy and the girl's that she is a girl normally lead both to imitate the parent of their own sex. It is only when the parent of their sex is conspicuously absent from the home or notably deficient in playing their parental role that the child identifies with the parent of the opposite sex.

A child is always a blend of the qualities of both parents. But what determines the mixture of the blend? Some psychologists argue that the child imitates most the parent who *gives* the most rewards; others, the parent who *gets* the most rewards; and still others, the parent who *controls* the most rewards. The first of these answers (the secondary-reward hypothesis) assumes that the child identifies most with the parent who satisfies his primary needs for food, water, and physical contact. Once the child perceives the mother or father's behavior as the source of primary reward, he can reward himself by imitating the behavior of that parent. The second answer (the status-envy hypothesis) assumes that the child will identify with the adult in the family who receives the most affection, attention, food, and care. It is assumed that he will envy this adult and play the role of that person in fantasy. The third answer (the social-power hypothesis) assumes that the child will imitate most the parent with the greatest power to reward him.

Bandura, Ross, and Ross (1963) conducted a complex experiment to test the merits of these three answers. The subjects were nursery school children. In the secondary-reward condition, one adult gave attractive toys to a child to play with and ignored the other adult. In the status-envy conditions, one adult asked for and received the toys from the other adult while both adults ignored the child. The children in half the situations were boys, the adult receiver in half the situations was a male, and the adult giver in half the situations was male.

Would the children imitate the adult who gave to him, the adult who was given to, or the adult who was the giver? A surprise game was announced at the end of each condition. The game consisted of guessing which of two boxes contained a picture sticker. In the course of their turns, each model presented the child with a variety of novel responses to imitate. For example, each model selected a "thinking cap" with a different-colored feather. After the adult models had their turns, the child who had been observing took his. The adults left the room but, unknown to the child, raters checked the responses he copied. The social-power hypothesis won: regardless of whether the child himself or the rival adult was rewarded by the controller, the model with the rewarding power was imitated more than either the rewarded or the ignored competing model.

The Amount of Reward   The child identifies with those who have the power to reward him; he also identifies those who *do* reward him.

Payne and Mussen (1956) selected from a large number of high school boys 20 who were closely identified with their fathers and 20 who were little identified with them. They measured the degree of identification by counting the number of items from a 50-item personality inventory that the son and his father answered in the same way. The number of items that the son and his mother had answered in the same way were subtracted from this total. The chief difference between the "high" and "low" identifiers was in their perception of their fathers: Those most like him saw him as a friendly person; those least like him saw him as cold and rejecting.

The development of masculinity and femininity depends not only upon how much a child is rewarded but also upon what he is rewarded *for*. Our culture has a general tendency to equate masculinity with aggression and mastery and femininity with passivity and nurturance. Sears, Rau, and Alpert (1965) explored the identification process in a group of 40 four- and five-year-old children during an eight-week summer nursery school session. The authors concluded: "Masculinity and femininity both appear to be more influenced by parental attitudes toward the control of sex and aggression than by any aspect of the availability or the behavior of models. Masculinity is associated with freedom of expression, and with parental nonpunitiveness, whereas femininity is associated with the opposite" (p. 261). That is, the strongly masculine child is one whose parents tend to reward his aggressive and sexual responses; the strongly feminine child, one whose parents tend to punish his aggressive and sexual responses.

Peers also play an influential role in the development of masculinity and femininity. Boys with brothers obtain higher masculinity scores at all ages through college than do boys with sisters; girls with sisters get higher femininity scores than do girls with brothers (Sutton-Smith and Rosenberg, 1965). Besides serving as models, older siblings often take over the training of the young children and carry it out much more emphatically than the parents. During adolescence, other adults may become important models, especially if they are of higher status than the parents.

In summary, the development of masculinity and femininity is a complex interaction of genetic endowment; of the child's recognition of his sex role and his efforts to elaborate it; of the presence of the father; of the tendency of the mother and father to reward aggressive and sexual responses; and of the amount of influence that siblings, peers, and other adults exert.

THE DEVELOPMENT OF INTERSEXUAL LOVE

Boys and girls segregate themselves. In middle childhood, members of the same sex seek each other out as companions and reject members of the opposite sex. Girls make it clear that they consider boys rough, crude, and generally unacceptable. Boys tell girls they cannot play with them (Figure 14-5). Boys organize themselves around games like baseball and projects like building a fort. Girls place less stress upon games and activities, more stress upon acceptance by the group.

Preadolescents develop a need for intimacy with members of the same sex (Sullivan, 1953). This need pushes the individual from the opportunistic stage ("I play according to the rules of the game, to preserve my prestige and feeling of superiority and merit") to the conforming one—achievement is no longer a personal success but a group performance. The preadolescent's need for intimacy is intensified by experiences of loneliness that drive him out of his protective shell to initiate close relationships with other members of the same sex. This movement toward intimacy is fraught with anxiety and sometimes results in profound psychological disturbances.

In adolescence, the "lust dynamism" erupts as an independent driving force. Girls begin dating by fourteen, and boys, one to two years later. Early heterosexual contacts usually involve mixed-sex parties, without any clear pairing off. Groups of girls and boys attend these parties together to give each other mutual support in this new world. By sixteen or eighteen the vast majority of women have begun to date, and their popularity with men has become a central concern.

The difficult task of the adolescent is to transfer the desire for intimacy from members of the same to members of the opposite sex. The adolescent fails if the intimacy and sexual needs are solely satisfied through members of the same sex. The adolescent achieves only partial success if the intimacy need continues to be satisfied through members of the same sex while the sexual need is satisfied through members of the opposite sex. Full success is achieved when the adolescent can satisfy both his sexual and intimacy needs with members of the opposite sex.

Both boys and girls are dating earlier. Wolfenstein (1953) views this trend with some alarm, for it may interfere with the normal development of intimacy with the same sex. She believes that skipping or abbreviating this development may lead to an incapacity to develop intimate relationships with either sex. Margaret, the eldest of three daughters, illustrates such an incapacity. Her father, an unsuccessful salesman, deserted the family when she was five. Her embittered mother had to work to support them. Margaret did extremely well in her high school work but said later that she "never had a friend." She worked her way through college by being a waitress and taking care of children in the home where she boarded. She was extremely fond of the children and treated them like an affectionate mother. She spent, and continues to spend, hours each day talking on the phone to female acquaintances. However, she leaves the phone off the hook so they

Figure 14-5 In middle childhood, boys satisfy their need for intimacy by seeking each other out as companions; girls are excluded from their games. (Michigan Tourist Council)

cannot interrupt her by calling. After graduation, she had a series of intense but brief relationships with much older men. Later, she married a man several years younger than herself when she became pregnant a few weeks after meeting him. After a year of marriage he left her complaining: "She never pays attention or remembers anything I say or suggest." Margaret seems to have normal sexual desires but no ability to develop intimate relationships with either women or men.

A dating study revealed the power of the lust motive to override the need for intimacy among college students. Nearly 400 freshmen at the University of Minnesota were told they had their dance dates selected for them during "Welcome Week" by a computer (Walster, Aronson, and Abrahams, 1966). In fact, the dates were assigned randomly except that a man was never assigned to a date taller than himself. However, as the freshmen picked up their ticket and their date assignment, each was quickly rated on his or her physical attractiveness by four sophomores. On the basis of the combined rating, each man and woman was classified as: "ugly," "average," or "attractive." Also, a variety of intelligence, achievement, and personality measures were available from the records of the students and from tests taken during freshman week. During the dance intermission, the participants confidentially reported how well they liked their date. Finally, all but 20 of the students were contacted four to six months after the dance to find out how many subsequent dates they had had with their dance date. In the study of dating, measures of all of these variables were available: scores on a social relationships scale, scores on a self-acceptance scale, scores on a scholastic aptitude scale, and percentile ranks in high school. *None* of these measures had a positive relationship to dating. Indeed, the higher a girl's high school percentile rank, the *less* her partner liked her and the less he expressed a desire to date her again; the higher a boy's rank, the less his date liked him or wanted to date him again. In general, the typical man and the typical woman took none of these elements into effective account in their likings or their dating attempts or acceptances: "Sheer physical attractiveness appears to be the overriding determinant of liking."

The higher a woman's rating on physical attractiveness, the more her date liked her. More surprising, the higher a *man's* rating on physical attractiveness, the more his date liked him. For both men and women, the more physically attractive they were, the less attractive they thought their dates were, the less they liked them, and the less they actually dated them. Yet there was *no* relationship between a student's own attractiveness and the attractiveness of those he or she liked and tried to date again. The ugly did not try to date the ugly; they tried to date the most attractive. Those of average attractiveness did not try to date those of average attractiveness; they also tried to date the most attractive. And the most attractive, of course, tried to date the most attractive. Regardless of their own attractiveness, the men asked the most attractive girls for dates. Typically, then, the most physically attractive men got the dates with the most physically attractive women.

Purely sexual relationships may be immediately and intensely satisfying. But, as Jules Feiffer explained in a *Playboy* interview (1971), they rarely endure (p. 96):

If you live with another person, you're going to have to deal with that person, and most of us want to be dealt with rather than deal with. Most of us want to somehow be magically taken care of. There's a thing in all of us that I suppose is part aristocrat and part child; we want to be served, and served without being forced to recognize the existence of the servant, and certainly without dealing with the servant as an entity. What destroys fantasies and gets everybody into trouble early on in relationships is that two people come together each thinking the other is the servant, and they find they've been had. And so it comes to the point where you say, "My God, there's another person in my bed! And she's here under false pretense."

We do not play roles with the opposite sex just to satisfy sexual needs. We also play them to satisfy our enduring needs for intimacy, for playing a role that is intrinsically satisfying, and for producing the means for satisfying needs that exist outside of the sexual relationship. As they develop, men and women become aware of these less obtrusive needs and learn to create more enduring and satisfying relationships. The problems of selecting, structuring, and communicating in these relationships are examined in more detail in the next chapter.

SUMMARY

Males and females differ in their sexual desires, their traits, and their ways of playing their roles. Among animals, these differences are largely genetic in origin; among humans, largely due to the sex-role standards they have learned. Sex-role standards are those physical, psychological, and social qualities that society considers good or bad depending upon whether the person having them is a man or a woman. These standards now seem to be going through a period of rapid change. The sex-role standards that people set for themselves and believe they are meeting determines their masculine or feminine identity. The degree to which a child develops a masculine or a feminine identity is heavily influenced by the presence or absence of the father from the home, by whether the mother or father is seen as having the greater power to give or withhold rewards, and by the degree to which the mother or father actually does reward the child. The development of relationships between the sexes seems to follow an invariable sequence from sexual segregation to intimacy with members of the same sex, to lust relationships with the opposite sex, and, finally, to intimate relationships with the opposite sex. Development may be retarded at any of these stages.

SUGGESTIONS FOR FURTHER READING

Sapirstein, M. R. (1955), *Paradoxes of everyday life: a psychoanalyst's interpretations.* New York: Random House. A readable and original account of many specific problems that modern men and women have in relating effectively to each other. The first essay argues that the current sex manuals do more harm than good.

Wiggins, J. S., Renner, K. E., Clore, G. L., and Rose, R. J. (1971). *The psychology of personality.* New York: Addison-Wesley. Section 5 of this extremely well-written and authoritative textbook views sexuality, in turn, from the biological, experimental, social, and psychometric-trait viewpoints.

Ford, C. S., and Beach, F. A. (1951). *Patterns of sexual behavior.* New York: Hoeber-Harper (paperback available). An animal psychologist and an anthropologist cooperate to describe the physiological and social origins of sexual behavior.

Kinsey, A. C., Pomeroy, W. B., and Martin, C. E. (1948). *Sexual behavior in the human male.* Philadelphia: Saunders. The famous monumental study of sex behavior in the United States.

Masters, W. H., and Johnson, V. E. (1966), *Human sexual response.* Boston: Little, Brown. This scientific best-seller diagnoses sexual problems and makes recommendations based upon the detailed study of the physiology of male and female responses.

15

HUSBAND AND WIFE

Unfortunately, the upholders of the sanctity
of marriage too often . . . prefer to
think of the institution as surrounded with
a divine sanctity which forbids man to touch
or even discuss it, a negative taboo,
instead of leaving the sanctity where it belongs,
namely in the possible beauty of the relationship itself,
and therefore welcoming all
attempts to adapt the institution to human needs and aspirations.

JULIAN HUXLEY

The relationship of husband to wife exists in every society that is or ever was. Marriage combines the functions of reproduction, child care, sexual gratification, and economic cooperation with an over-all efficiency that no alternative arrangement has so far been able to match. Marriage is a necessity for the preservation of society. Consequently, young people are typically encouraged to marry by being told that it will satisfy their *own* needs and by soft-pedalling the fact that society will make strenuous demands upon them when they do so. Like the armed forces, it is easier to enter marriage than to leave it. Most people are happy in their marriages, but many are not. In this chapter we examine marital role standards, the widening differences in the role standards that individuals have, the impact of these differences upon marital happiness, and the problems involved in the development of marital love.

MARITAL ROLE STANDARDS

The reasons why people marry cover the gamut of human desires: to gain sexual satisfaction, to escape feelings of isolation and loneliness, to achieve social status, to play a role that is exciting and fulfilling. Every society has standard ways for its husbands and wives to play their roles to achieve these sexual, integrative, productive, and morale ends. No societies have the same standards and in no society do these standards remain unchanged. As modern societies move from an industrial to a postindustrial stage, however, these standards are changing at a faster rate than ever before.

Sexual Standards

In all societies, marriage is the preferred way of achieving sexual satisfaction. Before marriage, attempts are made to guide sexual impulses into marital channels; after marriage, to limit their expression to the marital relationship. Societies must achieve some success in these endeavors to survive: self-stimulation and homosexuality threaten the procreation of children; promiscuity prevents the proper care of children; incest creates catastrophic forms of sexual competition within the family; and extramarital relationships increase the level of hostility and aggression within the community. Still, societies vary widely in the extent of their sexual restrictions, in the severity of their enforcement, and in the success they have in achieving conformity to them.

Societies are generally more restrictive of extramarital than of premarital relationships, particularly in regard to wives. Although almost half the societies which Murdock (1949) examined in his extensive cross-cultural study permitted some form of extramarital relationship, the forms which it could take were carefully prescribed. Most often, the extramarital liaisons are limited to siblings-in-law, as among the Siriono, where a man may have liaisons with his wife's sisters and with his brother's wives and their sisters and, similarly, a woman has sexual access to her husband's brothers and the husbands of her sisters. Wife lending or wife exchange is also fairly common. Among the Chukchi of Siberia, for example, the men often travel to distant communities. Each married man generally makes special arrangements with some man in each of the communities he has occasion to visit. These arrangements are such that wherever he goes he may engage in a sexual liaison with his host's mate. In return, he permits these men the same privileges when they visit his community.

Societies differ less in the type of sexual restrictions they have than in the methods they use to enforce them. Virtually all societies, for example, limit homosexuality in one way or another, but the penalties for engaging in the practice vary enormously, ranging from mild ridicule to the threat of death. The Mbundu merely make fun of all homosexual practices. Homosexual play among Alorese children is frowned upon, although it may not be punished; adult homosexuality, on the other hand, is strongly discouraged. The Kwoma consider homosexuality unnatural and revolting. The Rwala Bedouins are so strongly opposed to the practice that they sentence male or female offenders to death. Most societies, however, tolerate homosexuality and attempt only to limit it to certain members of the community (Ford and Beach, 1951).

The dominant method of achieving conformity to restrictions in a society may be external or internal. Physical torture, banishment, imprisonment, or death are prime tools in some societies. Although the use of force on an individual seldom reforms him, this is not its essential social function. Its principal purpose is to reaffirm the ideals of the society for the majority, to distinguish for it once again the difference between right and wrong. However, this function does not require the use of severe, cruel, or unusual punishments. The "wrong" of homosexuality, promiscuity, and adultery can be affirmed with mild punishments. This is particularly true in those societies where the more effective methods of conscience and ridicule are highly developed.

American society relies heavily upon internal controls, as large and influential societies generally have. It trains its members from early childhood to control themselves. Although some external punishments are provided, they would not work if most citizens did not control themselves. Thus, by the time that sons and daughters have matured, parents assume, and generally correctly, that the conscience of their children will control their sex behavior so that it stays within the bounds set by social restrictions. However, complete restrictions on premarital sex outlets provide disturbing problems of conscience for young people, particularly women. Ellis and Fuller (1950) analyzed several thousand questions submitted by anonymous student nurses for round-table discussion. The most frequently submitted question was "What do you think of premarital sex relations?" The majority of college women, it seems, do not think much of them.

Few figures exist on the frequency with which sexual restrictions are violated in other societies. Many figures exist for our own. The studies of Kinsey et al. (1948, 1953) show that all the restrictions are sometimes violated and some are violated quite often. In spite of the restrictions on self-stimulation, more than 9 out of 10 American men masturbate to the point of orgasm at least once during their lifetime. In spite of the restrictions on premarital sex relations, 2 out of 3 report having had at least one such experience, most frequently with the girl they eventually marry. In spite of restrictions on extramarital relationships, 1 out of 3 married men had at least one such experience in their lives. And in spite of the severe restrictions on homosexuality, approximately 4 percent of men are dominantly homosexual and about ten times as many have had at least one homosexual experience. For women, the frequencies are of the same order but the percentages are much smaller.

The restrictions are still very effective. The overwhelming majority of sexual outlets occur within the marriage relationship. For most Americans, indulgence in disapproved forms of sexual behavior is an infrequent, unsatisfying, and guilt-arousing experience. The increasing percentage of Americans who marry and the steady decrease in their age enhances the importance of sexual satisfaction as a marital goal.

Since Kinsey's report, there has been much talk of the "sexual revolution" on college campuses. According to Terman's 1938 study, it should now have arrived. He asked more than 600 women if they were virgins at the time they married. Of those born between 1880 and 1889, the answer was "yes" for 87 percent; of those born between 1890 and 1899, 74 percent; and of those born between 1900 and 1909, 51 percent. He concluded that the virgin bride would disappear by 1960.

But Terman seems to have been mistaken in his conclusion, at least about college girls. A 1959 study of girls eighteen to twenty-two at a large coeducational institution showed that the figure was back to that of the 1880s: 87 percent were virgins. An intensive study of 49 girls during their careers in a liberal Eastern college showed that 78 percent were still virgins when they graduated. Eight of the 11 nonvirgins were involved in serious emotional relationships with their partners; three were not. Two of these 3 girls had had relations with 2 men. None of the 11 expressed remorse (Corry, 1966). Other studies at other colleges show a considerably smaller percentage of virgins. None, however, show as small a percentage as that found by Terman among the group born between 1900 and 1909.

Premarital sexual patterns seem to have remained unchanged from the 1920s to the 1960s. During the 1960s, however, the patterns changed radically. Only 28 percent of 205 college women at a large urban university reported having premarital intercourse in 1958. Bell and Chaskes (1970) gave the same inventory to 250 women at the same university in 1968. More than twice as many (61 percent) reported having premarital intercourse. Furthermore, more than twice as many (23 percent versus 10 percent) reported having such experiences in a dating relationship and about half as many (36 percent versus 65 percent) felt they had gone "too far" in having intercourse in this kind of relationship.

Integrative Standards

Nowhere does the desire for physical and emotional intimacy express itself more clearly than in the yearning of men and women to be married to each other (Figure 15-1). The desire is as old as mankind. Greek myth tells us that human beings were once shaped in a circular fashion with four arms and four legs. Their great strength and vigor led them to conspire against the gods. Zeus, in his anger, sliced every one in two. However, they became so apathetic and sad that Zeus eventually allowed the separate parts of the whole person to occasionally and briefly reunite.

To survive, we need physical intimacy. Rats benefit from being handled and so do infants. Children adequately nourished but deprived of intimate physical contact decline physically. The same integrative need is satisfied in more indirect ways among adults (Berne, 1964):

Some people literally stroke an infant; others hug or pat it, while some people pinch it playfully or flit it with a fingertip.

These all have their analogues in conversation, so that it seems one might predict how an individual would handle a baby by listening to him talk. By an extension of meaning, "stroking" may be employed colloquially to denote any act implying a recognition of another's presence. Much of the time in many relationships is devoted to stroking and being stroked.

Marriage also provides satisfaction for the need for psychological and social intimacy. Our survival depends upon understanding the realities in the world and within ourselves. The more confident we are about what is real and what is not real, what is important and what is

Figure 15-1 Mature heterosexual relationships fulfill the need for physical and emotional intimacy. (Michigan Tourist Council)

not important, and what we should and should not do, the more secure and happy we feel. Our confidence in ourselves increases as those closest to us confirm our views about these matters. The goal of confirmation, while rarely expressed by couples, is central to their happiness together.

The disturbances created by failures in confirmation are illustrated by the case of an American-born Japanese husband and his Italian war bride (Seward, 1956):

> Their trouble centered around the husband's feeling of obligation to support and house his parents. With these oriental mores, the Italian wife had neither insight nor sympathy; she moved out of their home rather than share it with her husband's relatives. This behavior intensified the husband's emotional conflict since he had already risked rejection by his Japanese family and friends for marrying outside his ethnic group. Now he was faced with rejection by his occidental wife for not repudiating his family and his deeply entrenched sense of filial duty toward them. Had Mrs. B's relationships with her

own parents been more satisfying, she presumably would have followed the usual Italian pattern of showing deference to her husband's people, even though she might not have comprehended the extent to which Japanese customs carry filial duty. Unfortunately for the marriage, Mrs. B's need to defy her own parents was so great that she "transferred" it to her parents-in-law who not only represented authority, but authority that evoked in her all the greater antagonism because of its strangeness. However, the story had a happy ending. Mr. B. was helped toward insight into some of the conflicting cultural streams that had entered into his own personality and led to his marrying an occidental. . . . He was finally able to accept the solution of having his parents live with some other relatives.

In most societies for most couples the minimum integrative standards have been extremely high. Societies have legally enforced their belief that couples should stay together. They have also been clear in their beliefs that couples should work together, play together, and feel together. The current accelerating divorce rate, however, testifies that these ancient standards are changing.

Productive Standards

The desire for the better satisfaction of economic needs has always been a strong motive for marrying. Most couples in the world still live and die in the same rural area where nearly everything used by the family is produced by the family. Among them there is a crudely equitable division of labor, the women working longer and more continuously; the men working harder and more dangerously.

Men and women desire to improve their social status by marriage. The most basic difference here is that a man gains his status mainly through his job, whereas a woman's status is mainly conferred on her by her husband. Women can gain a tolerable status through work, but a better one can usually be gained more easily through marriage. Men move up most directly by competing for good jobs; women, by marrying men who move up (Scott, 1966).

Given a choice between marrying for love or status, women say "love." But asked what makes a man lovable they tend to say sensitivity, good manners, sophisticated good taste, and interesting conversation—qualities highly related to cultured backgrounds and expensive educational backgrounds. Money is despised in the abstract, admired in the concrete.

The pressure for marrying up produces an imbalance unfavorable to low-status men and high-status women. A low-status man has little wealth or prestige to offer a wife and must compete not only with men of his own status but also with those of higher status as well. A well-born woman can only maintain her status by marrying a man at least equally well born. Such men, however, are likely to place a heavy weight in their choices on physical attractiveness. In this regard, low-status women compete on a fairly equal basis with their high-born sisters. Low-status men are more likely to be bachelors; high-status women, spinsters.

The status pressure also produces inbalances among Catholics. Catholic girls are expected to marry Catholic boys but also want to marry successful men. Protestant men on the average hold higher-ranked positions. As a result, there are more Catholic women who marry Protestants or Jews than Catholic men who do so. The situation is the reverse among Jews, where the men are eminently successful. More Jewish men marry gentiles than do Jewish women.

The impact of these influences is often obscure to young people motivated by the strong feelings engendered by sexual love. Those who take a calculating attitude are likely systematically to misrepresent their age, income, background, and other weaknesses and strengths.They also wear elevator shoes and falsies, tell tall tales and white lies, and misrepresent their intentions.

Men are more concerned with immediate sexual satisfaction than women. Furthermore, their sexual behavior is less intimately related to their social status. Young women, therefore, learn to suspect the verbal expressions of men, which are so often voiced to facilitate seduction. Rather, they estimate the sincerity of a man's intentions by the amount of time and money he invests in the relationship. As a wide age range of men competes for the young and attractive woman, the amounts required tend to be very high. Yet these amounts may work to the disadvantage of the beautiful woman. The pre-professional student who is going places occupationally has little time for dating. He is, therefore, likely to leave the social life to less ambitious campus playboys. The most attractive women, therefore, may marry men of the least achievement. Whatever the result, the aim of much premarital behavior is the same: improvement of social status.

Morale Standards

For most of human history, marital morale has been a dispensable goal. When a husband or wife would be alone or starve without each other, they remain together and work together regardless of their boredom and frustration. However, modern society has made it increasingly possible to obtain sexual satisfaction, companionship, and economic status outside of the marriage relationship. Consequently, morale standards are rising. More and more, couples are demanding that marriage not only provide them with sexual, integrative, and productive satisfactions but also offer them a role that they enjoy playing. This trend is most obvious in the demands of women for new and more flexible standards for their role.

What kind of standards for their role would wives like most? Anne Steinmann and David Fox (1966) had more than 800 American women and more than 400 American men complete a 34-item attitude scale indicating their opinion about the role of women in our society. The items concerned attitudes toward work, marriage, child-rearing, and themselves. As a whole, the scale measured the stress to be placed on activities within the family compared to the stress to be placed on extra-family activities. The women included artists, lawyers, and nurses; blacks and whites; and undergraduates at public and both inexpensive and expensive private schools. As a whole, the women in the group were better educated and more often professionally employed than most.

Undergraduate women at expensive colleges placed most stress on their family role; the artists, most stress on their careers. As a whole, however, the women saw themselves as actually playing a role that placed slightly more stress on their extra-family than on their family role. The women also filled out the scale as they would ideally like their role to be. The ideal role of the undergraduate women at expensive colleges was almost identical with the role they saw themselves as playing. The black professionals saw themselves as playing more of a career role than they would actually like to play, but the discrepancies between their actual and ideal roles were small. In general, the women saw themselves as playing pretty much the roles they would like to play.

What did the men think of this? They were asked to fill out the scale as they would like their ideal woman to fill it out. The ideal woman of the male lawyers was less career oriented than the female lawyers wanted to be; the ideal woman of the male undergraduate was more career oriented than the female undergraduate said she wanted to be. Again, however, there was little difference between the role that women would like to play and the role that men said they wanted them to play.

What did the women think about what men said about their ideal woman? The answer was emphatic: They didn't believe the men. The women were asked to fill out the scale a third time as they thought the typical man would fill it out. Everyone of the female groups thought that men wanted their ideal woman to be much less career oriented and much more family oriented than the women wanted to be. The authors concluded:

The discrepancy between ideas is so great, the gap is so wide and deep that even more than a lack of understanding this discrepancy suggests a real lack of communication between men and women. Evidently both men and women do not understand each one's desires as to what role a woman should assume. . . . The data suggest men are saying to women, "Yes, you are very bright and with this brightness you should do something," but at the point when the women stir themselves and do "something," the men add "but you can't do what you're doing because of the kids." The woman then says to herself, "What does this man want me to do?"

Individual Differences in Standards

The wives of graduate students in the Boston area varied in their marital-role ideology from "traditional" to "contemporary" (Lipman-Blumen, 1972). The traditional ideology is the belief that under ordinary circumstances women belong in the home caring for children and carrying out domestic duties, whereas men are responsible for the financial support of the family. The contemporary ideology holds that the relationships between men and women are ideally egalitarian and that husbands and wives may share domestic, child-rearing, and financial responsibilities. Among the thousand primarily young college wives, about a fourth were traditional; the other three-fourths, contemporary. Among noncollege women, their undoubtedly are many more with a traditional ideology.

Barton and Cattell (1972) made a more detailed factor-analytic study of the dimensions along which men and women varied in their role expectations. Figure 15-2 classifies the resulting dimensions under the headings of sexual, integrative, productive, and morale standards. These dimensions were almost identical with these found in a similar study a decade earlier (Tharp, 1963).

Both the men and women differed markedly in their sexual standards for themselves and for each other. Some considered it very important that "a wife should not have had intercourse with any other man prior to marriage" and that "a husband should not have had intercourse with any other prior to marriage" while others consider premarital chastity of little or no importance. Some considered it extremely important that the husband and wife should be "100 percent faithful in sex" while others considered that sexual fidelity was of little importance. Some considered that "having intercourse when you desire it" as important while others considered it unimportant.

The subjects also differed in their integrative standards. Some considered "sex being bound up with love and affection," "whole family participating together in recreation," "having children," and

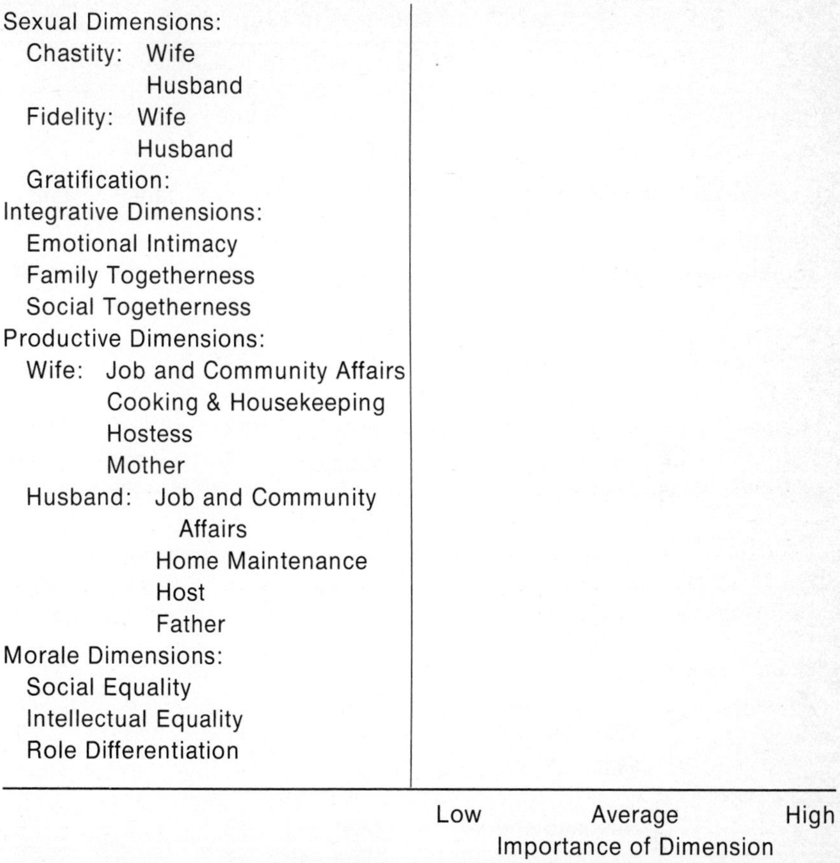

Sexual Dimensions:
  Chastity: Wife
             Husband
  Fidelity: Wife
             Husband
  Gratification:
Integrative Dimensions:
  Emotional Intimacy
  Family Togetherness
  Social Togetherness
Productive Dimensions:
  Wife: Job and Community Affairs
        Cooking & Housekeeping
        Hostess
        Mother
  Husband: Job and Community
          Affairs
          Home Maintenance
          Host
          Father
Morale Dimensions:
  Social Equality
  Intellectual Equality
  Role Differentiation

Low   Average   High
Importance of Dimension

Figure 15-2 Dimensions along which people differ in their marital standards. (Adapted from Barton and Cattell, 1972)

"husband and wife being equally fond of social gatherings" as very important. Others considered emotional, family, and social togetherness of little importance.

Productive standards also varied a great deal. Some considered the wife's ability as a mother, hostess, cook, housekeeper, job holder, and community participant as very important while others did not. There were similar differences of opinion about the importance of a husband's ability "to get ahead on his job," to be a good father, to maintain the home, to be a good host, and to participate effectively in community affairs. Furthermore, there were wide variations in the importance of each of these. Thus, some respondents stressed the importance of the wife being a good cook but did not feel her

TABLE 15-1 The Marital Role Standards of Midwestern Students

Goal area standards			Percent reporting		
			Little or no impor- tance	Moder- ately impor- tant	Very impor- tant
Integrative:					
Emotional:	How well your spouse understands and is con- siderate of you	Men	1	0	99
		Women	0	0	100
Family:	Spouses partici- pate together in recreation	Men	5	16	79
		Women	1	25	74
Social:	Husband and wife should be fond of same friends	Men	16	38	46
		Women	17	36	47
Sexual:					
Fidelity:	Wife should be 100% faithful in sex	Men	17	6	77
		Women	17	4	79
	Husband should be 100% faithful in sex	Men	18	7	75
		Women	17	5	78
Sexual Gratification:	Having inter- course with spouse when you desire it	Men	4	18	78
		Women	4	17	79
Chastity:	Wife should not have intercourse with any other man before marriage	Men	72	13	15
		Women	83	4	13
	Husband should not have inter- course with any other woman before marriage	Men	78	10	12
		Women	84	4	15

Goal area standards			Percent reporting		
			Little or no importance	Moderately important	Very important
Morale:					
Intellectual equality:	Husband should be equal to wife in intelligence	Men	31	24	45
		Women	26	16	58
Social equality:	Husband should be social equal of wife	Men	31	19	50
		Women	38	23	39
Masculine dominance:	Husband should have the final say in most matters	Men	57	25	18
		Women	74	11	15
Productive:					
Parenthood:	Adequacy of wife as mother	Men	9	12	79
		Women	16	7	77
	Adequacy of husband as father	Men	7	12	78
		Women	17	4	79
Work:	Wife should devote major energy to home	Men	47	37	16
		Women	61	23	16
	Importance of husband getting ahead on his job	Men	22	26	52
		Women	27	44	29
Community:	Wife should participate in community affairs	Men	55	29	15
		Women	60	27	12
	Husband should participate in community affairs	Men	56	28	16
		Women	56	31	13

TABLE 15-1   (Continued)

In 1973, the author asked 75 undergraduate women and 68 undergraduate men to rate anonymously the importance they attached to these varying standards. Integration was their overriding motive for marrying. They almost unanimously agreed that having a spouse who was understanding and considerate was "very important." Three-fourths of them felt it was very important that husband and wife should participate together in the same recreations and almost half of them felt it was equally important for them to like the same friends. Two-thirds of them also reported that the fulfillment of integrative standards was more important than the satisfaction of sexual, morale, or productive standards.

The standards of men and women differed very little in the sexual area. About four out of five felt that premarital chastity was unimportant. Almost the same number, however, felt that 100% sexual fidelity in marriage was "very important." About the same number reported that sexual gratification in marriage was of considerable importance.

The standards of men and women differed more in the morale area. Men felt that it was more important for the husband to be the social equal than the intellectual equal of his wife. Women, on the other hand, felt it was more important for the husband to be the intellectual equal than the social equal of his wife. The majority of men thought that it was unimportant whether the husband had the final say in most matters; the *vast* majority of women thought it was unimportant.

A very large majority of both men and women agreed that the adequacy of husband and wife as parents was very important. More women than men felt it was unimportant that the wife devote her major energies to the home. Many more men than women felt that it was important for the husband to get ahead on his job. Most men and women felt it was unimportant whether the husband and wife participated in community affairs. However, a large minority felt it was "moderately important" while more than 1 in 10 felt it was "very important." This probably reflects a retreat from the extreme "privatism" of several decades ago.

Those students who rated one of these standards as "very important" tended to rate the others in the same way, and vice versa. In general, then, the replies of the students reveal agreement or disagreement with traditional marital standards.

---

competence as a hostess was important. Some stressed the importance of the husband being able to maintain the house while others did not feel that this was important at all.

Some men and women were very interested in having the

husband play a different role from the wife and exercising the dominating influence in sexual relations, in interactions with relatives, and in spending the family income. Others wanted to play as similar a role as possible to their spouse, sharing equally in working for an income and in sharing domestic and child-care duties. Men and women also varied in the importance they attached to the husband and wife being social and intellectual equals. The desire for equality was not identical with the desire for role similarity. That is, some husbands and wives who insisted on the importance of social and intellectual equality felt that husbands and wives should play quite different roles.

MARITAL HAPPINESS

The vast majority of American youth expect marriage to provide the major source of their happiness in their future lives. Students at American colleges and foreign colleges were asked: "What three things or activities in your life do you expect to give you the most satisfaction?" (Jacob, 1957). They had six choices: family relations, career, recreational activities, religious activities, community affairs, and participation in national and international affairs. More American students (86 percent) than students from any other country picked family relations. The expectation continues, at least among women. Three-fourths of a large and representative sample of American women said they frequently (56 percent) or occasionally (18 percent) felt that "Having a loving husband who is able to take care of me is much more important to me than making it on my own" (Reistrup, 1972). How well these expectations are realized by a particular husband and wife depends upon how well their sexual, integrative, productive, and morale standards match. They seem to match quite well, for in a national cross-section of several thousand couples in 1971, 58 percent said they were "completely satisfied" with their marriage and only 1 percent said they were "completely dissatisfied."

Sexual Compatibility

Within marriage, it is not the intensity of the sexual needs of husband and wife but the similarity of their needs that is related to marital happiness. As Figure 15-3 indicates, if the passionateness of one partner is decidedly greater than that of the other, then both husband and wife are likely to be unhappy. Consistently, the greater the desire for extramarital relations, the greater the marital unhappiness (Landis, Landis, and Bolles, 1940). The average man manifests a higher sex drive than the average woman (Kinsey, 1953). Thus, the most common sexual problem is that the husband has a greater need for sexual activity than does his wife.

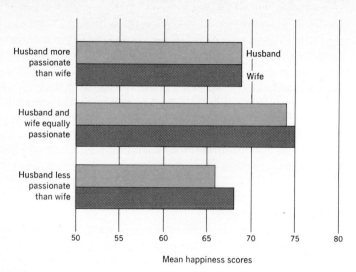

Figure 15-3 Passion of spouses in relation to their marital happiness. (Data from Terman, 1938, p. 286)

Does sexual adjustment determine marital happiness or does marital happiness determine sexual adjustment? It works both ways. On the one hand, the sexual adequacy of the average wife, an important determiner of marital happiness, seems unaffected by experience: early sex shocks, premarital sex activity, pain experienced by wife at first intercourse, frequency of sex intercourse, and contraceptive methods used (Terman, 1938). Also, wide differences in the cultural backgrounds of women have relatively little influence on their sexual behavior (Kinsey, 1953). These findings suggest that the sex drive of the average woman is largely constitutional in nature and relatively uninfluenced by happy or unhappy sex experiences in or out of marriage. On the other hand, what couples *say* about their relative passionateness appears to be determined by their general happiness in being together. Long-married partners who report that they have always had equally intense sex drives contradict findings on the different age curves of sex drives in men and women. Thus, Kinsey reports that the peak of the male's sex drive is before twenty and shows a gradual decline through life, whereas women reach their peak sex drive in the late twenties and remain on a plateau for much of the rest of their lives. Thus, a couple who were equally passionate in their early twenties would not be equally passionate in their forties. It seems that much of what couples say about their sexual adjustment may be a reflection of their general adjustment to each other. People who are happy with each other are likely to find happy ways to deal with differences in their sex drives.

An important aspect of sexual adjustment is the differences in expectations which couples have concerning their sex lives together. The Puritans and the Victorians placed little importance upon sex and expected little happiness from it. As a consequence, they probably were seldom disappointed or seldom considered themselves sexually maladjusted. Today, more couples consider marriage primarily as an avenue to romantic-erotic gratification.

Ort (1950), studying 100 married college couples, gave both partners a list of 88 questions on what they expected of husbands and wives. Here is a sample of the questions about the husband's role:

Should a husband kiss his wife when he leaves for and returns from work?

Should a husband occasionally purchase or make small surprise gifts as tokens of affection for his wife?

Should a husband make it a point to talk to his wife about things he may have done that day so that she may feel more a part of his life?

Ort then counted the conflicting answers which each husband and wife made and compared the total conflicts with ratings of marital happiness. Result: The fewer the conflicting expectations, the greater the marital happiness. The 42 couples receiving the highest happiness ratings averaged only 1 conflict; the 8 couples receiving the lowest ratings averaged 11 conflicts. It seemed more important that couples have the same expectations than that they have any particular expectations. A few couples entered marriage expecting each other to be sexually promiscuous. When these expectations were fulfilled, they still reported themselves as entirely happy in their marriage.

Integration

The dominant marital goal of many is a desire for a close and enduring emotional intimacy with their spouse. For many others, however, these integrative needs seem relatively unimportant. Divorce is the ultimate frustration of these integrative desires. Twenty years ago, well over 25 percent of all marriages in the United States ended in divorce (U.S. Department of Health, Education, and Welfare, 1955), more than in any country in the world (Metropolitan Life Insurance Company, 1952). The rate has continued to climb toward the 50 percent mark.

Unfavorable childhood experiences have an important bearing upon later marital unhappiness. Both Terman (1938) and Locke (1951) found the following four elements significantly related to success in marriage:

1. Lack of conflict with mother

2. Lack of conflict with father

3. Home discipline that was firm but not harsh

4. Parental frankness about matters of sex

Both found that *boys* who had happy parents and *girls* who had a happy childhood were happier. Corsini (1956) successfully used such information to predict the happiness of both men and women (correlation for men: .65, for women, .43).

Why are these childhood experiences related to marital happiness? It seems clear that persons growing up in such an atmosphere will develop favorable attitudes toward the institution of marriage itself. They are more likely to develop favorable attitudes toward their appropriate sex role. They are less likely to develop unconscious hostilities toward the opposite-sex role. They are likely to accept the sexual aspects of marriage with more realism and enthusiasm. The consequence of the absence of such favorable experiences is illustrated by the following family history (Anderson, 1949, pp. 652–653):

> A mother of three daughters had the idea that everyone "had it in for her." She felt that men were "beasts" and were never to be trusted. The eldest daughter married and, after three years of marriage, committed suicide because she was unable to get along with her husband. The second daughter figured in a sensational divorce case that filled the newspapers for weeks. In spite of her allegations, the sympathy of those in the community who knew both parties were with the husband.
>
> The forty-two-year-old husband of the third daughter came to the clinic for advice. He had an important position in an educational organization attached to a church. In addition to his wife, his family consisted of a fourteen-year-old daughter and a twelve-year-old son. His wife had no use for his friends, had quarreled with the neighbors and merchants in her area, interfered constantly in her children's activities and told every one how worthless her husband was. The husband loved his children and was making strenuous efforts to preserve the marriage, but the strain was telling upon him. However, if a divorce were obtained, he would lose his job.
>
> Pearl Harbor arrived. The husband enlisted and was sent overseas. He returned five years later to find his children in college. He secured another position and separated from his wife.

Unfavorable family backgrounds lead a person to take a passive and pessimistic view of marriage and to lack confidence in himself and in his spouse. Such attitudes are likely to make a person unhappy in marriage; they are not likely to make a person seek a divorce. Johnson and Terman (1935) show that it takes boldness to seek and to obtain a divorce. They matched 100 happily married couples with 100 unhappily married couples and with 100 divorced couples. All couples completed an extensive battery of personality tests. Each couple rated their marital happiness and were also rated by their friends. A sample of the items that discriminated between the three groups is incorporated in the Marriage Test (Table 15-2). College sophomores get about 17 right on each part of the test or 34 out of the total of 56. The reader may wish to try making his own predictions before reading further. The correct answers are given at the end of the chapter.

TABLE 15-2 Marriage Test

Directions

The following test measures your ability to identify differences between the typical happily married, unhappily married, and divorced person. Part I deals with men; Part II, with women.

For each of the following statements, *mark the one of the three groups you think is best described by it.*

The correct answers are based on the answers that the groups made on lengthy questionnaires. For example, 100 happily married women, 100 unhappily married women, and 100 divorced women answered the question: "Do you prefer a play to a dance?" Results:

81% of the happily married women answered, "yes."
58% of the unhappily married women answered "yes."
44% of the divorced women answered "yes."

Therefore, the correct answer to the statement "Most apt to prefer a play to a dance" is "happily married women."

Part I. Men
Mark: (1) if you think the correct answer is "happily married men"; (2) "unhappily married men"; or (3) "divorced men."*

1. Most tolerant of sick people.
2. Most prefers to spend a night at home.
3. Most apt to like religious people.
4. Most prefers to make plans with others.
5. Most likely to organize a club or team.
6. Most likely to stress quality in his work.

TABLE 15-2   (Continued)

7. Most apt to like talkative people.
8. Most likes cautious people.
9. Most meticulous and methodical in work.
10. Slowest in making decisions.
11. Most dislikes modern languages.
12. Most apt to be critical of others.
13. Most touchy on most subjects.
14. Most dislikes foreigners.
15. Least often takes the lead to enliven a dull party.
16. Least interested in artistic activities.
17. Least likes symphony concerts.
18. Least often organizes teams or clubs.
19. Most likely to think of himself as radical while actually conservative.
20. Least interested in the occupation of teaching.
21. Most likely to enjoy taking risks.
22. Most apt to make bets.
23. Most prefers fashionably dressed people.
24. Most often experiences feelings of loneliness.
25. Most apt to like the occupation of novelist.
26. Most apt to like the occupation of stockbroker.
27. Most likes the occupation of criminal lawyer.
28. Most likely to enjoy competition.

Part II. Women
Mark: (1) if you think the correct answer is "happily married women"; (2) "unhappily married women"; or (3) "divorced women."

29. Most apt to like old people.
30. Most apt to like religious people.
31. Most apt to like music.
32. Most tolerant of minority groups.
33. Most likes picnics and excursions.
34. Most conservative in social and political opinions.
35. Most dislikes quick-tempered people.
36. Most apt to dislike working isolation.
37. Most apt to like people who never drink.
38. Most often has spells of dizziness.
39. Most apt to arrive late for work.
40. Most often troubled by feelings of inferiority.
41. Most likely to consider themselves as nervous.
42. Least effective in emergencies.
43. Least methodical.
44. Least willing to work things out for themselves.
45. Most interested in avoiding technical responsibilities.

46. Most apt to like psychology.
47. Most prefers working on commission to definite salary.
48. Most willing to be unconventional.
49. Most prefers taking chances to playing safe.
50. Most interested in change and travel.
51. Most prefers work that makes heavy demands.
52. Least likely to blush.
53. Most self-assertive and self-reliant.
54. Most interested in being an inventor.
55. Most ambitious.
56. Most apt to like playing chess.

The typical *happily married man* was the most kindly and tolerant of all groups studied and the least neurotic. He was more amiable, more cautious, less touchy, less grouchy, less irritable, and less critical. He was not very sociable, preferring to spend his evenings at home. The *unhappily married man* appeared to have neither the self-discipline nor the amiability for marriage, nor the aggressive qualities which would enable him to break up the marriage. He rebelled at orders and disliked being told how to do things. The *divorced man* tended to be self-confident, self-sufficient, self-willed, and self-centered. Compared to the married men, he was more radical in his attitudes, more gregarious, and more interested in art and literature.

The typical *happily married woman* regarded marriage as essential to her happiness. She was careful of other people's feelings, insisted less on her own way, and avoided arguments. She was more docile than aggressive, more cautious than daring. The *unhappily married woman* was the most neurotic, indecisive, and unmethodical of all the groups studied. She tended to compensate for her poor family relations with many outside social contacts and activities. The *divorced woman* had qualities more suited to a career than marriage. Compared to the married women, she was more assertive, energetic, enthusiastic, ambitious, aloof, and unsympathetic. She had more clearly defined goals of her own, which tended to be more mercenary and more intellectual.

The happily married husbands and wives had in common a relatively high degree of emotional stability, social adaptability, and conservatism. The unhappily married people were more socially withdrawn, showed more neurotic tendencies, and tended to have intolerant attitudes. The divorced men and women were more dominating, more self-confident, more self-centered, and more radical and artistic in their interests. It is those in this last group who are most frequently misunderstood, for it is implicitly assumed that they will be suffering from the disturbing consequences of being divorced. It is more in accord with the facts to view them as people who have been unhappily married *and* were ready and willing to fight for a divorce. Consistently, Martinson (1955) noted that girls who remained single for at least the first years after high school had the traits of the divorcée: self-confidence, dominance, and a high interest in preserving their personal freedom.

Corsini (1956) discovered even higher relationships between personality items and marital happiness than he found for the biographical items from childhood (for men, a correlation of .65; for women, .68). When he added personality scores to background scores the relationships were still higher (correlations of .68 and .76, respectively).

Productivity

Some integration is necessary for a marriage to survive. Great mutual understanding and emotional intimacy can be a source of great happiness. However, a couple cannot live on togetherness. Someone has to earn a living for the family, cook, do the housekeeping, entertain their friends, take care of the children, and participate to some degree in community affairs; that is, some degree of productivity is necessary for a happy marriage. However, a high degree does not seem to be necessary.

Terman (1938) correlated the family income of his couples with their degree of marital happiness. Result: Almost no relationship was found. A similar study reached a similar conclusion (Burgess and Cottrell, 1939). The prudence with which money matters are handled may be more important than the amount involved. Disagreements over ways of dealing with money are probably most important of all. The husband who feels that he should have complete personal control over family finances is likely to be unhappy and to make his wife unhappy—unless she is an old-fashioned wife.

The critical element is the degree to which husband and wife meet their own and each other's productivity standards.

The impotent husband and the wife unable to have a child are unhappy, for they are willing but unable to do what is expected of them. The prolonged inability of a husband to find work is another potent source of unhappiness for him. Not much less frustrating is his inability to do as well as he and his wife expected in his career. On the other hand, the wife who is a bad cook, a poor housekeeper, and incapable of managing her children may be equally frustrated.

The feminine husband and the masculine wife fail to meet the expectations of society and, generally, their own expectations. The differences between masculine and feminine abilities, traits, interests, and attitudes are clearly marked in our society. Yet there are wide and measurable differences in the extent to which men and women conform to the expected patterns (Gough, 1952). Those who differ greatly in an unexpected direction find it difficult or impossible to play their expected roles.

In a study of role conflicts, 200 wives of all ages in Michigan were first asked to check from a long list of activities ("mending of clothes," "entertaining," "meal planning," "a sexual companion to her husband," "keeping up own appearance," etc.) those which they felt it most important for homemakers in circumstances similar to theirs to perform (Trier, 1959). They checked those that they did perform. A *role conflict* was indicated when a wife felt she should perform an activity but thought she did not. For example, a wife who said it was important to socialize with her neighbors but said she did not, would have a conflict. Result: There were wide differences in the number of conflicts. Of 32 possible conflicts, some wives had as many as 17 and some as few as 2. Wives over sixty had no more conflicts than those under thirty, and wives with family incomes under $4,000 had no more conflicts than those with incomes over $7,000.

The old wives viewed their roles somewhat differently from the young wives. While the young wives more often stressed the importance of being a sexual companion to their husbands and spending time with and enjoying their children, the old wives more often stressed the importance of being a good cook, running an orderly house, and helping their husbands with their jobs. Young or old, rich or poor, those who were stable, optimistic, self-confident, and well organized had few conflicts; those who were pessimistic and disorganized had the most conflicts.

Morale

A couple may have a satisfying sex life, may feel close to each other, be effective in filling their productive responsibilities, but still be unhappy with the roles they are playing. The husband may hate the grind of his dull job; the wife, the repetitiveness of her housekeeping duties and her child-care activities. The wife may resent the fact that she is considered less intelligent and less important socially than her husband. The husband may resent the loss of what he considers his masculine prerogatives. They both may resent the lack of clear differentiation in their roles.

What are the new sources of dissatisfaction among women in modern society? The anthropologist Johnson (1972, *New York Times Magazine*, August 27, pp. 7ff.) cites several. To begin with, the traditional division of labor between the sexes in primitive societies has been radically altered—a woman can drive a pick-up truck with power steering as readily as a man, and a man is as capable of filling and heating a formula bottle as a woman. Women are also living longer and having fewer children. As a consequence, there are many more middle-aged women who have no children in their home and are seeking education and jobs. Finally, many women are dissatisfied because men gain their status by their achievements but women gain theirs through their husbands. In primitive societies, men and women gain their prestige in different ways but by their own efforts and in roughly equal amounts. Thus, a man might gain prestige as a good hunter and a woman gain prestige by bearing many healthy children. In modern society, however, a woman gains prestige primarily through the education, amount of money, and type of job that her husband has.

The Male-oriented Solution   One   proposed   solution   to   increasing female satisfaction is to make women more like men. This solution calls for women to enter the labor force just as men do and for children to be raised in nurseries. Its application requires the gradual elimination of sex-defined jobs so that women will have the same jobs, the same careers, and the same rewards as men. This solution assumes that women can do almost anything that men can do. It also assumes that what men do is more satisfying and more valuable than what women do.

In many situations, women cannot do what men do as well as men do. The Israeli *kibbutzim* were organized in part to put women on an equal footing with men. As it has worked out, men do the heavier work in the fields and orchards while the women do the lighter work in the laundries, kitchens, and children's houses. Most men work on an assembly line, drive a truck, or clerk in a store. Women do not want to do these jobs any more than men want to do them.

The Female-oriented Solution   It may be that the present-day flexible female role may prove to be the model for both men and women in the future. This solution proposes that men should act more like women— should take half-time or undemanding jobs, should become involved with caring for their children and homes, and in general should give free rein to their nurtural impulses. While no one has seriously proposed this solution, it is close to the high-leisure and low-job-involvement ethic that many predict to be the wave of the future.

The solution fits the life-style of blue-collar and lower-echelon white-collar workers. It does not fit the life-style of executives, doctors, and other professional workers. This style requires long, concentrated, and expensive preparation in exchange for high financial and psychological rewards.

The Individual Solution   The United States, with its widely varying regions, religions, and ethnic groups, has always been a pluralistic society. The trend toward pluralism, toward an "alternative life-style" seems to be accelerating. Why not pluralism in male and female roles? Why should not some women be like men, some men like women, and many be somewhere in between? Even if this solution to sex-role standards becomes completely accepted, many may become victims of over-choice. Freedom is not a gift, but a job—and many are not interested in the job and mess it up when they take it on. If there are no standards for playing a sex role, then each individual must decide how he is to play it. It takes a conscientious person to map a course of his own and to stick to it. Even when he does stick to it, he may find he has made the wrong choices and has no one to blame but himself. Fortunately, most of these choices are made in the slow process of developing a satisfactory sex-role identity.

In summary, the trait, self, and role theories each shed a different light upon the complex problem of marital happiness. Happiness is most immediately related to the degree to which husband and wife meet their own and each other's role standards. The standards they have, however, depend upon their traits. Thus, the religious are likely to have traditional while the scientific have contemporary standards. How well a person meets his spouse's standards is heavily dependent upon the stage of his self development. The impulse-ridden cannot meet their spouse's standards, for the only standard they have is the strength of their momentary impulse. The opportunistic will also fail, for they only have standards for their spouse, not for themselves. It takes at least conformists to maintain a happy marriage. However, even the conscientious may be unhappy if they fail to meet their own and each other's standards. A marriage, though, is not static but dynamic. As their marriage endures, couples modify their standards and develop their selves.

THE DEVELOPMENT OF MARITAL HAPPINESS

Individuals are intensely concerned with marrying, and in marriage with the satisfaction of their sexual, integrative, productive, and morale needs. They are rarely consciously preoccupied with the hard task of developing their own personalities in marriage. Indeed, they fight it. They resist facing humiliating facts about themselves that are revealed in the intimacy of marriage. The dependent struggle to remain dependent. Couples cling to their favorable, simple, and unrealistic images of themselves. They try to represent their confusing experiences by clichés learned in childhood instead of seeking more adequate ways of symbolizing them. They desire to maintain the center of their psychological being close to themselves, far from others.

Yet marriage not only provides the most pervasive opportunities for development; it almost forces individuals to develop. The necessity of accommodating oneself to another individual and of finding satisfactory solutions to the inevitable problems may make or break the individual. Above all, the problems of child rearing force parents to face painful facts, to become less dependent, to develop more realistic self-images, to understand themselves and their world more adequately, and to move from egocentric preoccupations to a deeper concern for others. In this sense, the most unrecognized goal is the one most regularly achieved: personality development.

The Selection of a Mate

A husband is happiest whose wife meets his standards; a wife, when her husband meets hers. The selection problem, then, is to find a spouse who *does* match one's standards. The solution is complicated, for it requires knowing what one's standards are and finding out how well a possible mate meets them.

Sexual attractiveness is unlikely to be overlooked; it is likely to be overemphasized. As the results of the dating study (Chapter 14) indicated (Walster et al., 1966) sheer physical attractiveness tends to wash out more important criteria. Even in the sexual area, the matching of standards is more important for marital happiness than physical beauty. The husband who considers premarital chastity important and finds that his wife has not met this standard is unhappy. The wife who thinks it important for husband and wife to be 100 percent faithful in marriage and finds that her husband does not meet this standard is unhappy. A wife who feels that sexual gratification is of little importance makes her husband unhappy if he feels that it is very important.

We like people who are like us; we marry people who are like us; and we are happiest when we marry people who are like us. (Figure 15-4). Three out of four Protestants marry Protestants; nine out of ten Catholics and Jews marry within their faith. Most men marry women who are somewhat younger than themselves. Husbands and wives are similar in height, weight, hair color, and susceptibility to disease. They are similar in intelligence, emotional excitability, and withdrawing and depressive tendencies. They are similar in social behavior, attitudes, and values (Kelly, 1955; Tharp, 1963b).

Hollingshead (1950) studied the race, religion, age, and social class of the more than 2,000 couples married in New Haven, Connecticut, during 1948. Over 500 of these couples were extensively interviewed in their homes. He concludes:

Figure 15-4 A married couple: People marry people like themselves. (Ron Junttonen)

The data presented demonstrate that American culture, as it is reflected in the behavior if newly married couples in New Haven, places very definite restrictions on whom an individual may or may not marry. The racial mores were found to be the most explicit on this point. They divided the community into two pools of marriage mates and an individual fished for a mate only in his own racial pool. Religion divided the white race into three smaller pools. Persons in the Jewish pool in 97.1 percent of the cases married within their own group; the percentage was 93.8 for Catholics and 74.4 for Protestants. . . . One's subculture, and one's race, age, and class position in the society effectively determine the kind of person one will marry, but not the exact individual.

Men marry women like themselves. Further, they *assume* more similarity with their spouses than actually exists. Each member of 36 couples filled out a variety of personality inventories, first for himself and then as he thought his spouse had filled it out (Byrne and Blaylock, 1963). The actual similarities of the responses of each couple were compared with the assumed similarity. Result: The couples assumed more similarity than actually existed, regardless of the length of their marriage. Interpretation: We not only like people who are like us, but also assume that people we like are like us. Thus, couples who like each other tend to assume that they are more alike than they actually are. Contrariwise, those who do not like each other assume *less* similarity than actually exists.

A danger lurks in the assumption of similarity in the mating process. Both men and women like most those of the opposite sex who are physically most attractive. As a consequence, both sexes are particularly likely to assume more similarity between themselves and attractive members of the opposite sex than actually exists. On the other hand, they assume less similarity than actually exists to those who are not physically attractive. The extent to which physical attractiveness rides over all other traits may be a major source of mismatches.

The tendency for individuals to marry those who are similar, or whom they assume are similar, to themselves is so pervasive that it may be asked: Is there *any* quality in which married couples are more different than unmarried ones? Cattell (1965) could find only one: *protension*, a tendency to engage in "self-opinionated, skeptical, jealous, and suspicious behavior, designated in its more abnormal forms as paranoid, but essentially an inner tension accompanied by strong tendencies to projection." Among married couples, if one person is high on this trait the other tends to be low, presumably because no marriage could last where both were protensive.

In some couples traits helpfully balance each other:

An ambitious, well-appearing man of mediocre intelligence and emotional immaturity was attracted to a very brilliant girl of great drive and stability. After marriage he frequently solicited his wife's judgment concerning business matters. In fact, she was the major partner though a silent one. She made most of his major decisions, bolstered him, and assumed the role which his parents previously played. She in turn was very proud of her husband's appearance of the ultimate outcome of his activity. She did not lack insight into her husband's character, but she loved his handsome boyishness (McKinney, 1960, pp. 336–367).

A neurotic engineer married a very stable elementary school principal with whom he shared common religious and political beliefs. He was chronically unhappy, resentful of his children, and irresponsible in his family functions. He alternated trips to therapists with long professional trips away from home, from which he often suddenly returned because of his feelings of loneliness and isolation. In the meantime, his wife maintained her full-time job, ran the family home and social life efficiently and well, and acted as a sympathetic therapist for her husband, whom she admired for his unorthodox and nonconforming way and for his professional achievements?

Note, however, that here we have a trade: beauty for brains, stability for brilliance. Such marriages are more likely to result from trading in the marriage market than from the "attraction of opposites." Winch and his coworkers (1955) have advanced a theory of complementary needs in mate selection, suggested ways of studying them, and provided some evidence that mates do tend to have complementary rather than similar traits. In reviewing all of the evidence, however, Tharp (1963) could find no facts that provided any satisfactory support for this theory.

We do sometimes like people who are different from ourselves. Why do we find no evidence that opposites attract each other in marriage? The answer may be that even the most similar man and woman are quite different enough. They have different goals, different sexual needs, different traits, different personality structures, and different attitudes to interpersonal relationships. It may be only after couples have learned to manage their inevitable differences successfully that the attractions of complementarity arise (Kerckhoff and Davis, 1962).

One reservation on the pervasiveness of similarity: couples may be similar in ways that make them compatible with each other but not with a successful marriage. Benson (1952) studied the common interests checked by engaged couples on an inventory and related these interests to their later reported marital happiness. Those couples who had in common high interest in romantic love, sexual relations, children, and religion tended to be happy in their marriage. On the other hand, the total *number* of common interests had little relationship to their happiness. In fact, those engaged couples who had expressed common interests in drinking, dancing, fame, travel, and commercial entertainment tended to be unhappily married.

In summary, then, people tend to marry people of similar age, physique, religion, education, and background. This thirst for similarity may be viewed as a crude and often unsuccessful way of ensuring the matching of role standards. It may well be that those whose role standards and performances match are happiest even though they are dissimilar in all the other respects. At any rate, those seeking a spouse would achieve a happier outcome if they paid more attention to the matching of standards than they generally do.

Structure

The structure of a marriage relationship is the form given it by the roles that husband and wife agree to play. The basic organizational structure of marriages varies a great deal from society to society. Murdock (1957), for example, has counted the number of societies in which *polygyny* (marriage of one man to more than one woman), *monogamy* (marriage of one man to one woman), or *polyandry* (marriage of one woman to more than one man) is the preferred form of marriage. Table 15-3 shows the results. Thus, the United States, where monogamy is the only acceptable form of marriage, is in the minority. Even in societies where polygyny is preferred, however, it never constitutes the most frequent form of marriage: wives are always scarce and expensive commodities. Furthermore, monogamous societies have been much more successful as measured by the numbers of people in them. Consequently, the vast majority of individuals in the world live in a "one man, one woman" family structure.

Communication

The better husband and wife understand each other and each other's expectations, the happier they tend to be. Married couples, for example, predicted the responses that their spouse would make to 55 statements on a personality inventory (Dymond, 1954). The more accurate their predictions, the happier their marriage: "Married love is not blind, and ignorance is not connubial bliss. The better each partner understands the other's perceptions of himself and his world, the more satisfactory the relationship."

The development of understanding requires intimacy: "The spontaneous game-free candidness of an aware person, the liberation of the eidetically perceptive, uncorrupted child in all its naïveté living in the here and now" (Berne, 1964). Intimacy is so natural and constructive that one might think it would be common among all couples. Yet Berne has shown with convincing clarity the innumerable rituals, pastimes, and above all, "Games People Play" that couples use to avoid intimacy: "If It Weren't for You," "Look How Hard I've Tried," "Harried," and "Courtroom."

TABLE 15-3   Preferred Forms of Marriage in 554 Societies

Form of Marriage	Number of Societies	Percent
General polygyny	415	75
Monogamy	135	24
Polyandry	4	1
Total	554	100

All couples have problems. Some have more, and more serious, problems than others. It is not the presence of problems, however, that separates the happy from the unhappy couples so much as the methods they devise for dealing with them. Couples who expect conflicts, face them, express their feelings about them freely, and learn to modify their expectations to accord with their actual needs and with the realities they face are happier.

All human relationships involve some conflict. Because of the depth and length of marital relationships, serious conflicts in all marriages are inevitable. Acceptance of the inevitability of conflict is an essential step toward dealing with it effectively. The popular ideology of romantic love does not lead to such acceptance, for it assumes complete understanding from the beginning between those in love.

Shocked by an unexpected conflict, a couple may avoid open strife by shirking discussion of it. The avoidance, while eliminating some painful scenes, does not solve the problem which created the conflict. For some conflicts, it may be well to delay discussion; for a few, avoidance may be a poor but still the best way of dealing with the situation. In general, however, avoiding the discussion of a problem tears apart the marital relationship, for as topic after topic becomes taboo, the couple becomes less and less able to understand one another. Eventually the very presence of the mate will become painful because of the strains involved in avoiding so many issues.

For couples who have made too extensive use of avoidance techniques, Moreno (1946) has employed the technique of the psychodrama. The husband and wife are asked to reenact the scene of a painful situation or a quarrel. It is emphasized that they are to put into words all the thoughts which previously had been suppressed. The method facilitates the development of a new point of view by both husband and wife, because they are given more adequate information about the feelings of their mates than they have previously had.

No aspect of marital problems is more important and difficult to deal with constructively than the way the marriage partners handle their hostile feelings toward each other. On the one hand, such feelings always occur in serious conflicts and must be expressed to relieve the hostile partner, to inform his mate, and to provide a basis for solving the conflict which created the hostility. On the other hand, the expression of aggression may create a vicious circle: the husband expresses his anger at his wife; this makes his wife angry, and she retaliates by becoming angry at him; and he becomes still angrier and more aggressive. At the worst, however, partners who fight have a better chance of resolving conflicts than those who avoid facing or expressing their anger.

Ort (1950), who studied the methods which 100 couples used in solving problems, reports that happy couples much less often avoided facing problems than did the unhappy couples. The happy couples also more often used discussion as a method, much less often used aggression or argument. What is the difference between an "aggressive" remark and an "argumentative" one? What is the difference between an "argument" and a "discussion"? The happy couples may have been as aggressive and argumentative as the unhappy couples, but, being more satisfied with the final outcome, tended to think of their behavior as a "discussion."

Happy couples learn to adapt their ways of expressing aggression to fit their own personalities, moods, and problems. Some become angry quickly, enjoy fights, and easily assimilate the aggressions of their partners; others find it very difficult to express their hostility and very painful to receive the hostile remarks of their partner. The same individuals vary, too, in their tolerance of aggression from one time to another, from one place to another, and from one issue to another. In spite of these variations, happy couples expect to feel aggressive sometimes in their marriage, think it desirable to express their aggressions, and feel that marriage should provide special freedom in this regard. Even more important, they expect their partners to feel aggressive, encourage them to express their feelings, and try to develop the ability to assimilate these aggressions with as much equanimity as possible.

A husband becomes angry with his wife if she fails to meet his expectations and angry with himself if he fails to fulfill his expectations of himself, and vice versa. Since much of what a partner expects of himself and his mate he has learned as a child by using his parents as models, he is often only dimly aware of what it is he expects. Self-insight and self-acceptance are key factors in marital happiness. Eastman (1958) correlated the degree of happiness with measures of acceptance among more than 50 married couples. If a husband had high self-acceptance, then he reported himself as happier in marriage and his wife reported herself as happier; similarly, if a wife had high self-acceptance, then both she and her husband were happier. If both had high self-acceptance, then it was still more likely that both would report themselves as happily married.

SUMMARY

Most college students expect marriage to provide the major source of their future happiness, and most couples report that it does. About 1 in 10 couples, however, report that they are seriously unhappy. Male-oriented, female-oriented, and individualistic solutions are being proposed to solve the problems of marital unhappiness. However, it is not the standards themselves that make couples unhappy but rather conflicts between the sexual, integrative, productive, and morale standards of husband and wife. Consequently, the selection of a mate with compatible standards is critical to marital happiness.

Unhappy couples generally report sexual incompatibility, lack of money, or personality conflicts as the source of their unhappiness. The actual source of most unhappiness, however, is related to the attitudes toward marriage and the sex-role identity developed in childhood. Happy couples consistently report that they got along well with their mothers and fathers and that they got along well with each other. The general solution to marital problems lies in the development of more effective communication between couples and the development of flexible family structure which meets the needs, standards, and abilities of both husband and wife.

SUGGESTIONS FOR FURTHER READING

Levy, D. J., and Monroe, R. (1938). *The happy family.* New York: Knopf. How normal, not perfect, couples may achieve a happy marriage. This classic has long been considered by many professionals as the best popular treatment of the subject.

Ibsen, H. *Eleven plays.* New York: Modery Library. In this collection of one of the world's great dramatists, *The doll's house* stresses the consequence of treating a wife as a child; *The wild duck*, of trying to force a couple to face facts about themselves when they are unwilling to do so; and *Hedda Gabler*, judged to be his greatest play, the disastrous influence of an intelligent but discontented wife upon those around her.

LeMasters, E. E. (1957). *Modern courtship and marriage.* New York: Macmillan. Gives summaries of important studies of marriage as well as sage advice—based on research findings—to young people.

Terman, L. M. (1938). *Psychological factors in marital happiness.* New York: McGraw-Hill. A notable study by one of the country's most distinguished research psychologists of the marriages of 792 California couples. The perfection of its methodology has never been duplicated and its major conclusions are consistent with more recent studies.

Answers to **Table   15-2**:

Questions	Answers
1–9	1 (happily married men)
10–20	2 (unhappily married men)
21–28	3 (divorced men)
29–37	1 (happily married women)
38–46	2 (unhappily married women)
47–56	3 (divorced women)

16

FATHER AND MOTHER

If we look at a pine tree growing in the valley
we will notice that it grows differently from one on top of a
mountain. It is the same kind of tree, a pine, but there are
two distinct styles of life. It is much the same way with
human beings. The style of life of a child in a family is fixed
after it is four or five years old and cannot directly be changed.

ALFRED ADLER

Almost all couples want children and many want children more than anything else. In this chapter, we examine the basic needs that parents seek to satisfy by playing their parental roles, the varying ways they try to play their roles to satisfy these needs, the superiority of the authoritative way, and the problems that parents have in finding and following this way.

GOALS OF CHILD REARING

We play roles, we have said, to satisfy our needs for integration, morale, and productivity. Nowhere are these needs more apparent and the desire to satisfy them more intense than in the parental role. The vast majority of young people want to have children. The replies of nearly 200 single college students in Michigan and New York revealed that all but two expected to have children. The men expected to have about three; the women, four. They viewed a childless marriage as "unfortunate, lonely, and unhappy." Only a minority thought that such marriages could be happy (Rabin, 1965). In general, these students saw parenthood as the best, if not the only way of satisfying their integrative and morale needs—their yearnings to be close to others while playing a role that was intrinsically interesting. Morale motives dominated the replies of women. They saw being a mother as "natural," as "fulfilling a basic need," and as "their role and purpose in life." Both men and women agreed that the motives of men were more integrative: to "prove their masculinity," to "carry on their name."

The purpose of some in having children is dominantly integrative. Those who were rejected by their own parents, who are unhappily married, and who have had an only child late in life tend to see their child as a means of satisfying their frustrated yearning to be close to and united with another human being. The morale goal dominates a few. The lives of these are so dull and unhappy that they see parenthood as a relief from their tedium. Most parents, however, are devoted to creating a human being who will become a happy, competent, and mature adult.

The immediate goal of parents is to keep their children alive and healthy. It is not, however, the only goal, for children must eventually learn to take care of themselves. To do so, they must learn who they are, what the world is, and how to deal with it. Parents, therefore, must develop their children's understanding of reality, train them so that they can deal with specific aspects of it, and develop their personalities so that they can deal with it in general in a more competent way. Consequently, as parents are satisfying the maintenance needs of their children they simultaneously teach them what reality is and how to deal with it. It is the ultimate task of parents to contribute to the development of their child—to guide him from the autistic to the impulse-ridden stage and then to the higher stages of personality development.

Autistic to Impulse-ridden

To survive and develop, the infant must learn to perceive his mother in a positive way—to feel dependent upon her, to see her as a source of security and comfort. The development of dependence is so natural a goal for most mothers that they are scarcely aware of the methods they use or the strenuous efforts they make to achieve it. Yet the failure to use effective methods or the lack of motivation to use them has profound and disastrous consequences for the child, as laboratory studies of monkeys convincingly demonstrate.

A mother holds her child to feed it. Is how it is held more important than how it is fed in determining the development of the child's positive attitude toward his mother? For baby monkeys the answer is decisively in the affirmative. Monkeys were raised singly in cages designed to provide a comfortable environment and to take adequate care of bodily needs. Each cage was equipped with two equally accessible artificial mothers (Figure 16-1). The "wire mother" was a cylindrical wire-mesh tube with a block of wood at the head. The "cloth mother" was made from a block of wood covered with sponge rubber and sheathed in terry cloth. Behind each of the mothers was a light bulb that provided radiant heat. Either "mother" could be outfitted with a nursing bottle placed in the center of its "breast." In the critical experiments, the baby was fed on the "wire mother" and not fed on the "cloth mother." Result: The babies still preferred the cloth mother. During the first week, they spent only an hour a day on the wire mother and five hours on the cloth mother. By the third week they were spending no time with the wire mother but eighteen hours per day with cloth mother. Conclusion: "The experimental analysis of the development of the monkey's attachment to an inanimate mother surrogate demonstrates the overwhelming importance of the variable of soft body contact" (Harlow, 1958). A similar conclusion was reached in a study of institutionalized infants (Casler, 1965).

It is not enough for an infant to develop a positive attitude toward something; he must develop a positive attitude toward some person. One group of monkeys were raised with their mothers; other groups were raised under varying types and amounts of isolation (Harlow and Harlow, 1962). As adults, the isolated monkeys were much more submissive and fearful, they played less skillfully and energetically, and were inept in monkey "courtship." So inept were they, in fact, that very few of the isolated female monkeys became pregnant. The crucial period for the monkey was between the ages of three and twelve months. Social isolation before three months pro-

Figure 16-1 Studies of infant monkeys raised with wire and cloth "mothers" demonstrate the overwhelming importance in development of soft-body contact. (H. F. Harlow, Primate Laboratory, University of Wisconsin)

duced little effect. If a monkey was isolated during the crucial period, however, later social experiences had little influence in modifying his behavior. A few minutes of social experience each day during the critical period appeared to be enough to prevent the disastrous emotional and social consequences of isolation.

The vast majority of mothers respond to their infant's need for contact. Still, mothers vary. Levy (1942) classified 72 mothers as low, moderate, or high in their maternal feelings toward their children. The case histories of the mothers low in maternal feeling showed little evidence of maternal tendencies in their earlier lives. For example:

> She had very little interest in dolls and stopped playing with them at about the age of six. When she saw a pretty baby on the street, she was not at all interested. As an adolescent, she never indulged in the fantasy of being a mother and having children. She was ambitious to get married but never thought about having children. As a mother she has felt quite incompetent. She took the children off the breast after two weeks, because she did not like it; she felt like a cow, she said. She still hates the physical care of children, though she is a dutiful mother and rather affectionate. She never was maternal towards men.

Her interests have always been feminine, and she has been quite popular with men.

Mothers who were high in maternal feeling revealed early maternal tendencies:

As a young child, her favorite game was taking care of dolls, dressing them, putting them to bed. She played with dolls until the age of fourteen or fifteen. She used to make visits among her mother's friends to take care of their babies. When she thought of being a mother, she hoped to have six children and have them as soon as possible. When she saw a pretty baby on the street, she had a strong urge to take it in her arms and hug it. She was a "baby-carriage peeker" before and after marriage. In her relations with men she was always maternal—much more, she said, than they liked.

Maternal feelings correlated with length of menstrual flow ($r = .58$). Expressed in another way, the majority of women with four-day periods or less were in the group that was low in maternal feeling; the majority with periods lasting six days or longer were in the group that was high in maternal feeling. While differences in menstruation are probably largely due to genetic differences, they may be influenced—like most physiological functions—by psychological states and experiences.

Every infant requires the "tender and loving care" of a mother. But when and how much? It seems that separation from the mother, particularly during the early weeks of life, may be beneficial.

Today, many infants are routinely separated from their mothers during the first week of life as a result of the central nursery arrangement in modern maternity hospitals. The impact of this separation upon the weight of the child was explored in a Yemenite community in Israel (Gunders and Whiting, 1964). In Yemen, babies were always born at home and spent the first weeks of life in close physical contact with their mothers. Upon arrival in Israel (1949–1950), many Yemenite women were prevailed upon to give birth in maternity wards where conditions of extreme mother-infant separation existed. Many, however, still insisted upon having their children at home. The weights of 150 children born in hospitals were compared periodically with the weights of 150 children born at home. Result: At one month, the average hospital-born child was only a few ounces heavier; at four years, it was almost three pounds heavier.

Height also seems related to separation. Seventy-five societies were ranked according to the typical amount of mother-separation during infancy. Result: The greater the separation in the society, the

Figure 16-2 Maternity hospitals may be having an unexpected beneficial influence on personality development. (Charles Harbutt/ Magnum)

taller its adult males were. Among the females, the greater the separation, the earlier the age at which menstruation began. Among rats, extensive studies indicate that the stress due to separation in infancy accelerates the maturation of the pituitary adrenal system and the production of growth hormones. Separated rats digest their food more efficiently, survive longer under conditions of starvation, learn more quickly, and appear to have greater emotional stability.

Mother love is a necessity for the infant; smother love is not. Occasional separation of mother and infant seems to do no harm. The above evidence indicates that separation at critical periods may do a great deal of good.

Impulse-ridden to Opportunist

The dependent infant has only the strength of his momentary impulses as a guide. These impulses can, and sometimes do, lead to disaster for him or loss for his parents. Accidents are now the leading cause of childhood death. They account for about a third of all deaths in the group ranging from one to fifteen years of age. In the order of their importance, the leading causes of accidental death are: motor vehicles, drowning, burns, bicycles, suffocation, guns, electrocution, hanging, trains, crushing, and poisoning.

Children are destroyers of property. Here are some typical examples (Sears, Maccoby, and Leven, 1957):

A girl broke a bottle of her mother's best perfume.

A boy took his father's watch apart and lost some of the pieces.

A girl went into a neighbor's yard and pulled up his prized tulip bulbs.

A boy started a fire in his mother's bureau drawer and destroyed it and most of his mother's lingerie beyond repair.

A brother and sister, changing the water for their pet turtle, spilled water on the floor which leaked through the ceiling and destroyed the plaster in the room below.

All parents make some effort to control their children's destructive tendencies. Almost none permit their children to jump at will on the furniture, mark on the walls, put their dirty feet on the beds, or play freely with other people's things.

The personality development of any child requires that he be firmly controlled by his parents. It is essential that the impulse-ridden child *not* be permitted to satisfy all of his impulses. If the child can always get what he wants by having temper tantrums, tantrums become a more and more pervasive aspect of his personality. In the end, he may become permanently retarded at the impulse-ridden stage.

Generally, parents do succeed in getting a child to control his impulses by punishing him for expressing them or by rewarding him for controlling them. These methods are simple, obvious, and generally effective. Why? It seems that, like monkeys, children have an irrepressible tendency to imitate those whom they depend upon. At first, they are unselective, imitating anything they can imitate. Gradually, they become more selective, finally imitating only those kinds of behavior that lead to the satisfaction of their needs.

TV Violence When, why, and how imitation works has been clarified by studies of the influence of TV violence on aggressive behavior. In 1960, 427 third graders whose average age was nine, were scored on their three favorite television programs as reported by their mothers from 1 (no violent programs) to 4 (three violent programs). In 1970, the aggressiveness of these same children at the age of nineteen was determined from ratings made by their high school classmates. The ratings consisted of asking each student to nominate any of his classmates on 10 "guess who" items like the following: "Who pushes and shoves other students?"; "Who takes the things of other students without asking?''; "Who starts a fight over nothing?"; "Who says mean things?"

The 184 male subjects were divided on the basis of their viewing habits at age nine into low (bottom 10 percent), medium (middle 80 percent), and high (top 10 percent). The average aggression score of the members of each of these groups at age nineteen was then calculated. The results, shown in Table 16-1, are striking: the more violent TV the child saw at nine the more aggressive he was at nineteen. The aggression scores of those who saw a great deal of violent TV as children were three times as high as the scores of those who saw little or none. Self-ratings of aggression reinforce these results, for the more violence a student saw on TV at nine, the more likely he was to rate himself as more violent at nineteen. Detailed analyses of these and other data led the authors to the conclusion: ". . . a preference for violent television in third grade is the major contributor to thirteenth-grade aggression."

Why did TV violence have such a profound and enduring influence on these boys? In the first place, it deals with one of the most difficult problems for the impulse-ridden to solve. On the one hand, the desire to express hostility and anger is a powerful impulse. On the other hand, the dangers of such expression are so great that every society sets itself the task of teaching its children acceptable forms, intensities, and places for the expression of such behavior. Part of this training demands severe punishment of unacceptable aggression. Children are frequently baffled in their efforts to find expressions of their aggressive impulses that are both acceptable and satisfying. Consequently, they are extremely observant of the behavior of those who seem to have solved the problem. In violent television, they observe prestigious adults expressing extreme aggression in novel ways that are not only unpunished but highly rewarded.

Nine, the age of the subjects in the first phase of the TV study, is close to the peak period for the imitation of relevant behavior. Earlier, as we have suggested, the child imitates both the relevant and irrelevant behavior of those upon whom he feels most dependent. Later, the tendency to imitate declines and other forms of learning increase. In

TABLE 16-1   TV Violence and Behavior

Violent Programs Viewed at Nine	Aggressive Behavior at Nineteen
Low	5.1
Medium	8.1
High	16.5

(*Source:* Eron, Huesmann, Lefkowitz, and Walder, 1972).

the present study, for example, the nineteen-year-olds were asked for their current favorite television programs and were again scored on the violence of the programs they viewed. Their TV violence score at nineteen had no relation to their TV violence score at nine. More important, their TV violence score at nineteen had no relation ($r = -.05$) to their aggression score at nineteen. The authors conclude: "The role of imitation in the formation of the child's personality decreases drastically between ages 9 and 19."

To endure for 10 years, the behavior imitated must have been perceived by the imitators as an appropriate solution for them. Years of exposure to such violent models probably strengthens the conviction of the young viewer that the behavior of these models is socially acceptable, personally satisfying and objectively rewarding. This conviction is dissipated if imitation conflicts with consistent and strong social pressures. It is such pressures that seem to account for the contradictory results for the several hundred girls in the study.

The amount of TV violence the girls saw had no relation to the amount of aggression they expressed. The best explanation for these results is that very early in life girls learn that physical aggression is an undesirable behavior for girls so they acquire other behaviors that are more acceptable. Since they rarely behave in a physically aggressive way, they are rarely either punished or rewarded for being aggressive. Consequently, the physical expression of aggression is a relatively minor problem for them. TV cooperates with society in this respect, for physically aggressive females are seldom shown on television.

Opportunist to Conformist

The opportunistic child knows what his parents expect, he can do what they expect, and he will do what they expect—if he feels he will be caught and punished if he does not. Temporarily, parents may be satisfied with their opportunistic child. In the long run, however, they are not, for he requires their constant and alert supervision. Parents not only become fatigued with being a policeman but they also find it increasingly impossible to exercise the supervision required as the child spends more and more of his time away from home. They want, finally, the child to control *himself.*

To learn to control himself, the child must get beyond acting like his parents to *feeling* like his parents. He must learn not only to imitate his parents but also to feel and think like his parents—to identify with them. That is, he must learn to feel comfortable and think well of himself when he does what his parents would want him to do in the situation and to feel guilty and criticize himself when he does not.

How do parents try to get their children to control themselves?

In their study of 379 New England mothers and their five-year-old children, Sears and his coworkers (1957) found that some stressed *object-oriented* techniques; others, *love-oriented* ones. The former make dominant use of tangible rewards and physical punishment; the latter, of praise, reasoning, isolation, and the withdrawal of love.

Children raised by object-oriented techniques, it seems, can get what they want by just learning to behave in the right way, i.e., by imitating. Children raised by love-oriented techniques cannot get what they want by just by behaving in the right way. They must also learn to feel the right way, i.e., identify.

Table 16-2 shows the variation found among five-year-olds in the degree of guilt feelings they showed when behaving in ways disapproved by their parents. While almost half of them showed little or no evidence of guilt, 3 percent of them felt very guilty. The degree of guilt felt was related to the degree to which love-oriented techniques were used by their parents. Result: The more love-oriented the techniques the guiltier the child.

Beyond Conformity

The conscientious and the self-actualized are more preoccupied with how they feel about themselves than how other people feel about them, more preoccupied with following their own principles than following

TABLE 16-2   Evidence in Five-Year-Olds of the Development of Identification

Evidence	%
No evidence; child hides, denies, does not seem unhappy when naughty	13
Little evidence of conscience	28
Moderate conscience development; may not confess directly, but looks sheepish; seldom denies	38
Considerable conscience	17
Strong conscience; child feels miserable when naughty; always confesses; never denies; strong need for forgiveness	3
Not ascertained	1
Total	100

Note: The influence of object-oriented techniques endures. MacKinnon (Murray, 1938) compared a group of college students who violated a prohibition when they thought no one was watching with a group who did not violate the prohibition. The violators had less conscience: only 29 percent admitted that they often felt guilty, whereas 75 percent of the nonviolators admitted that they often had such feelings. Of the violators, 78 percent said their fathers had used physical punishment; of the nonviolators, 48 percent.
(*Source*: Sears et al., 1957, p. 381).

the principles of others, and more preoccupied with their own individual judgments than with the judgments of others. Few parents are enthusiastic about their children getting to these stages, for it means that their child will be using his own judgment rather than theirs.

Few children really want to get beyond the conforming stage, for conformity has great rewards and conscientiousness is often painful. The conformist feels in harmony with his surroundings and in harmony with himself. He feels that he is doing what he wants to do. He has both the consciousness of individuality and at the same time the feeling of likeness and of unity that makes his relations to the outside world pleasant.

The conscientious person, on the other hand, is confused and troubled. He opposes his will against the will of his parents and against the compulsions of the outside world. He seeks his own attitudes toward himself and toward the world. He has lost his comfortable identification with the people and the world around him; he has not found his own identity. His anxieties are intensified by his increasing sense of separateness. He is plagued by self-criticism, by feelings of guilt, and by a sense of inferiority. The conformist, the conscientious, and the self-actualized are like three men on the bank of a dangerous river. The conformist never plunges in; the conscientious has plunged in but has not reached the other side; and the self-actualized has made it across.

What conditions encourage development beyond the conforming stage? An examination of the life-histories of the self-actualized architects (Chapter 12) indicates in some detail the family and life experiences that encourage the peak development of personality (MacKinnon, 1965):

An extraordinary respect by the parent for the child, and an early granting to him of an unusual freedom in exploring his universe and in making decisions for himself; an expectation that the child would act independently but reasonably and responsibly; a lack of intense closeness between parent and child so that neither overdependence was fostered nor a feeling of rejection experienced, in other words, the sort of interpersonal relationship between parent and child which had a liberating effect upon the child; a plentiful supply in the child's extended social environment of models for identification and the promotion of ego ideals; the presence within the family of clear standards of conduct and ideas as to what was right and wrong; but at the same time an expectation, if not requirement, of active exploration and internalization of a framework of personal conduct; an emphasis upon the development of one's own ethical code; the experience of frequent moving within single communities, or from community to community, or from country to country which provided an enrichment of experience, both cultural and personal, but which at the same time contributed to experiences of aloneness, shyness, isolation, and solitariness during childhood and adolescence; the possession of skills and abilities which, though encouraged and rewarded, were nevertheless allowed to develop at their own pace; and finally the absence of pressures to establish prematurely one's professional identity.

ROLE STANDARDS OF PARENTS

All parents have the same general goals: to satisfy their own integrative and morale needs and to contribute to the personality development of their child. However, they differ widely in the way they go about achieving these ends. What is the simplest and most realistic way of describing differences in the ways that parents play their roles?

In her most recent effort to answer this question, Baumrind (1971) made two home visits to the families of over 100 children enrolled in Berkeley nursery schools. The visits to all families began before the dinner hour and lasted until the child went to bed. In addition, each parent participated in a tape-recorded interview. Later, pairs of psychologists made 75 different ratings of parental behavior based on the typescript of the visit and the transcript of the interviews. By means of factor analysis, these ratings were grouped into a dozen dimensions of parental behavior: firm enforcement, encourages independence and individuality, passive-acceptant, rejecting, self-confidence shown by parents in their behavior, promotion of nonconformity, expect participation in household chores, enrichment of child's environment, discourages emotional dependency, discourages infantile behavior, authoritarian, and directive.

Where parents stood on one of these dimensions was relatively independent of where they stood on the others. Three-fourths of the families, however, could be classified into one of three patterns: Authoritarian, Authoritative, and Permissive. Figure 16-3 shows these patterns in relation to the consideration and responsibility dimensions discussed in Chapter 13. The authoritarian parents were inconsiderate but responsible; i.e., they showed little understanding or respect for the child's feelings but they felt a high degree of accountability for what happened to him. The permissive parents understood and respected their child but made little effort to guide or control his activities. The authoritative parents were both considerate and responsible; i.e.,they respected their child but made firm efforts to enforce his obedience. There were no parents in the study who fell into the inconsiderate and irresponsible pattern, probably because they were all middle-class

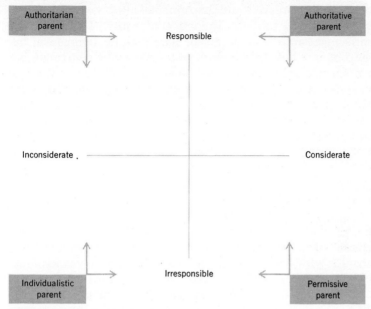

Figure 16-3 Patterns of parental behavior.

whites in a university town who agreed to cooperate in the study.

Here is a composite sketch of parents who fell into each of these patterns, with "she" standing for father and mother (Baumrind, 1971): The *authoritarian* parent attempts:

To shape, control, and evaluate the behavior and attitudes of the child in accordance with a set standard of conduct, usually an absolute standard, theologically motivated and formulated by a higher authority. She values obedience as a virtue and favors punitive, forceful measures to curb the self-will at points where the child's actions or beliefs conflict with what she thinks is right conduct. She believes in inculcating such instrumental values as respect for authority, respect for work and respect for the preservation of order and traditonal structure. She does not encourage verbal give and take, believing that the child should accept her word for what is right.

The *authoritative* parent, by contrast with the authoritarian parent, attempts:

. . . to direct the child's activities but in a rational, issue-oriented manner. She encourages verbal give and take, and shares with the child the reasoning behind her policy. She values both expressive and instrumental attributes, both autonomous self-will and disciplined conformity. Therefore, she exerts firm control at points of parent-child divergence, but does not hem the child in with restrictions. She recognizes her own special rights as an adult, but also the child's individual interests and special ways. The authoritative parent affirms the child's present qualities, but also sets standards for future conduct. She uses reason as well as power to achieve her objectives. She does not base her decisions on group consensus or the individual child's desires; but also, does not regard herself as infallible or divinely inspired.

The *permissive* parent attempts:

> ... to behave in a nonpunitive, acceptant, and affirmative manner toward the child's impulses, desires, and actions. She consults with him about policy decisions and gives explanations for family rules. She makes few demands for household responsibility and orderly behavior. She presents herself to the child as a resource for him to use as he wishes, not as an active agent responsible for shaping or altering his ongoing or future behavior. She allows the child to regulate his own activities as much as possible, avoids the exercise of control, and does not encourage him to obey externally-defined standards. She attempts to use reason but not overt power to accomplish her ends.

None of the parents in the Baumrind study fell into the inconsiderate and irresponsible or what is labelled the "individualistic" pattern in Figure 16-3. This pattern, however, did appear in an earlier study by Schafer and Bayley (1963). They studied the relationships between more than 50 mothers and their sons and daughters over a period of 18 years. The study began with observations made by pediatricians when the children were born and finished with ratings made by psychologists when the children were adolescent. In the intervening years, both mothers and children took tests in many different situations and participated in many intensive interviews.

At the end of the period psychologists who had met neither the children nor their mothers studied the test results and records of the interviews. They rated the relationships between each mother and child on a long series of scales: punitiveness, strictness, irritability, excessive contact, intrusiveness, suppression of aggression, and over-conscientiousness. They then correlated the ratings with each other. These results were then analyzed to determine what independent dimensions were actually being measured by all the scales. Two dimensions appeared as a result of the factor analysis. These two independent dimensions were similar to those found by Baumrind. Parents falling into the authoritarian pattern were rated as "antagonistic," "demanding," and "dictatorial"; in the authoritative pattern, as "accepting," "cooperative," and "democratic"; in the permissive pattern, as "possessive," "overprotective," and "indulgent"; and in the individualistic pattern, as "neglecting," "indifferent," and "detached."

Cross-Cultural Differences

Some parents in our society follow authoritarian role standards; some "authoritative"; some, "permissive"; and a few, the individualistic. Primitive societies also vary in the same way in their role standards. Whiting and Child (1953) studied 47 primitive societies about whose child-rearing practices a good deal was known. Three trained judges asked to study the available written information on these societies. They then classified the customary role standards of parents in five areas: feeding, toilet training, independence training, sex training, and training in the control of aggression. The excerpts are from the original anthropological reports used in making the ratings. In each area, the first example was the most authoritarian pattern found; the second, the most authoritative or permissive. The individualistic pattern did not dominate in any of the societies.

Feeding

MARQUESANS . . . believe that nursing makes a child hard to raise and not properly submissive. Feeding times were irregular and dependent on the convenience of the adult rather than the protests of the child.

KURTATCHI. Weaning is, in the normal course of affairs, a gradual process, other food, beginning with taro, which is given from birth, being gradually increased in quantity and variety.

Toilet training

TANALA. Anal training is begun at the age of two or three months, and the child is expected to be continent at the age of six months. If after this time the child soils its mother, it is severely punished.

SIRIONO. The infant receives no punishment if he urinates or defecates on his parents. . . . The only punishment that an infant is subjected to by defecating on his mother is that of being set aside for a while until she cleans up the mess.

Independence training

AINU. Put into the hanging cradle I have previously described, it was known quite well the poor little creatures could not get out, and for the rest they were free to do whatever they were able. This usually meant a good deal of kicking and screaming until tired of it, followed by exhaustion, repose, and resignation. (See Figure 16-4.)

KWOMA. Kwoma infants up to the time they are weaned are never far from their mothers. . . . At night the infant sleeps cuddled by her side. Whenever she has to move, she carries the child with her cradled in her arm, sitting on her neck, or less frequently, straddling her hip.

Sex training

KURTATCHI. Small children who finger their own genitals or those of their companions are always promptly reproved by an older child or an adult. . . . While they are little, children of both sexes play together, but as soon as the boy reaches the age when he puts up the *upi* . . . he is forbidden to have any close converse with the girls and women.

MARQUESANS. Sexual play was a regular practice among the children from the earliest period. The adult attitude toward it, if not one of active encouragement, was at least that of a mild amusement. Intercourse was frequently witnessed by the children in the dwelling and also at the periods of license which followed the feasts. . . . Sexual techniques were learned through imitation of the adults. Masturbation in childhood was induced by the parents . . .

Aggression

HARNEY VALLEY PAIUTE. If siblings fight among themselves, the older ones are whipped. If a child strikes his parents, they hit him back. Children are told that a big owl or a wildcat will take them off if they do not mind. Over and over again they are told that they should love their parents and their siblings and should not be angry with them nor fight with them. They are severely punished for destroying bird's eggs or hurting any bird or animal.

SIRIONO. Considerable teasing and torturing—such things as pinching the genitals, poking fingers in the eyes and scratching—of young children by older children takes place. A young child most often protects himself from such attacks with a brand of fire or a digging stick, and if he catches off guard the

Figure 16-4 Although the independence training of their children is extremely severe, Ainu parents are generally more indulgent than middle-class American parents. (Courtesy of the American Museum of Natural History)

older child who molested him, he may burn him rather severely or give him a sharp rap on the head.

Permissiveness in one area had little correlation with the degree of permissiveness in other areas. Thus, the Kurtatchi, the most indulgent in nursing, are the least indulgent in sex training; the Marquesans, the least indulgent in nursing, are the most indulgent in sex training. Still, some societies are *generally* permissive. When the indulgence ratings in all five areas were averaged for each society, the Siriono of South America led all the rest.

In comparison with these primitive societies, American parents are extremely nonpermissive. The same three judges made the same kind of indulgence ratings on the basis of recorded interviews with middleclass families living in Chicago in the early 1940s. The Chicago parents were rated as somewhat less permissive than the typical primitive society in the areas of dependency and aggression and much less permissive in the areas of feeding, toilet training, and sex. Overall, the Chicago parents were tied for last place with the Tanala of Madagascar. Material differences between Chicago and primitive societies account for some of the differences in child rearing: mothers in primitive societies without canned baby foods find it safer to indulge their children by the delay of weaning. Even with the benefits of washing machines and diaper service, however, American parents are less permissive about toilet training.

Whether a parent or a society is permissive in the treatment of a particular problem depends a good deal on how serious they think the problem is. That is, they are permissive about unimportant problems; nonpermissive about important ones. However, parents differ with each other about what they consider a serious problem. They also differ with psychologists about the seriousness of problems, as Table 16-3 shows. Thompson (1940) gave 300 parents and 42 child psychologists 24 common behavior problems of children. Each individual in each of the groups ranked the problems from the one that they viewed as most serious (1) to the one that they viewed as least serious (24). Table 16-3 presents the results. The stealing, untruthfulness, and cheating that parents view with most seriousness are viewed as much less serious by the psychologist. The problems that the psychologist sees as most related to the eventual personality development of the child—fearfulness, depression, sensitivity, and shyness—he views as very serious.

THE SUPERIORITY OF THE AUTHORITATIVE PATTERN

What parental role standards are most successful in fostering the personality development of the child? As we have seen, the question cannot be satisfactorily approached in a one-dimensional way. Thus, consideration alone cannot be the answer, for parents who understand and respect their children may act in very irresponsible ways. Neither is responsibility the answer, for responsible parents may be cold and inconsiderate. It is the pattern of consideration and responsibility that influences the child.

Baumrind (1971) observed the influence of authoritarian, authoritative, and permissive parents upon their children. Over a period of three to five months one of a team of seven observers rated children as they engaged in their nursery school activities. Analysis of these ratings showed that the children varied along seven different dimensions: hostile—friendly; resistive—cooperative; domineering—tractable dominant—submissive; purposive—aimless; achievement oriented—not achievement oriented; independent—suggestible.

Finally, the patterns of parental behavior were related to the patterns of behavior of their children in nursery school. The detailed

TABLE 16-3 How Parents and Psychologists Ranked Seriousness of Various Behavior Problems

Problem	Parents	Psychologists
Stealing	1 (most serious)	11
Untruthfulness	2	14
Cheating	3	16
Cruelty	4	5
Disobedience	5	21
Heterosexual activity	6	23
Obscene notes	7	20
Bullying	8	10
Masturbation	9	22
Domineering	10	12
Defiance	11	13
Unsociableness	12	2
Resentfulness	13	9
Impertinence	14	19
Destroying school property	15	18
Suspiciousness	16	4
Truancy	17	17
Overcriticalness	18	15
Fearfulness	19	3
Depression	20	1
Sensitiveness	21	6
Shyness	22	7
Dreaminess	23	8
Puppy love	24 (least serious)	24

(*Source*: Thompson, 1940)

results were complex. The general results, however, were clear and also consistent with those found in an earlier study (Baumrind, 1967). The children of authoritative parents were happiest, most self-reliant, most self-controlled, and most explorative. The children of authoritarian parents were most discontented, most withdrawn, and most distrustful of others. The children of permissive parents were the least self-reliant, the least self-controlled, and the least explorative. In brief, the authoritative pattern facilitated development better than either the authoritarian or the permissive patterns.

The results of Baumrind are limited to the impact of parental patterns upon children before they enter school. Schafer and Bayley (1963) studied the impact of such patterns upon the same children through the age of eighteen. They not only found similar dimensions of parental behavior, but also similar consequences of those patterns.

Each child was rated on a series of scales. The scales for rating children included: shyness, activity level, speed of movements, responsiveness to persons, amount of positive behavior, and happiness. Each of these ratings was correlated with the mother's position on the *hostility—love* and *control—autonomy* dimensions.

The positive influence of the mother's love was clear-cut. The higher her rating on the love scale, the happier, calmer, and more constructive the child; the lower her rating (hostility), the unhappier, more emotional, and more destructive the child. The more the mother loved her infant child, the more constructive the infant. The more the mother loved her adolescent child, the more constructive the adolescent. The positive influence of control was *not* as consistent. The more the mother controlled her infant child, the more constructive the behavior of the infant. The more the mother controlled her adolescent child, the *less* constructive the behavior of the adolescent. The authors conclude: "The child's need for a positive relationship remains constant but his need for autonomy varies from birth to maturity."

Many investigators have isolated a dimension similar to *hostility—love.* They have, however, called it by a variety of names: rejection—acceptance, cold—warm, hostility—affection, and inconsiderate—considerate. The last seems closest to the core of the dimension. A mother's affection or love for her child does normally motivate her to understand and respect him. Sometimes, though, the mother's liking for her child depends upon his behavior satisfying her needs, rather than motivating her to satisfy his needs. In any case, it is not the mother's motivation but her understanding and respect that directly influence the child. "Consideration" accents the understanding and respect rather than the emotions that usually accompany it.

Many investigators have also isolated a dimension similar to *autonomy—control*, but also under a variety of labels: submission—dominance, permissive—restrictive, democratic—authoritarian, and low and high initiation of structure. Their studies also reveal that a person's position on this scale has inconsistent effects upon the one with whom he is relating. Sometimes submissiveness is beneficial, sometimes harmful; and sometimes dominance is beneficial, sometimes harmful. The key to the apparent inconsistency seems to lie in one individual's *intentions* toward another: why is the parent submissive or dominant, permissive or restrictive, democratic or authoritarian, low or high in initiating structure? Whatever his behavior, if it reflects lack of concern for what happens to the child, then the parent's influence will be negative. If, on the other hand, his behavior is motivated by a high sense of responsibility toward the child, then his influence will be positive. That is, the parent who is concerned will sometimes be submissive, democratic, and permissive, and sometimes dominating, restrictive, and controlling, *depending upon the stage of*

development of the child and the situation he is facing. The responsible mother does not permit her toddler to go across a busy street
alone; she does let him, at an older age, drive the car. *Irresponsible—
responsible* stresses the intent of efforts to control or not to control.

The superiority of the "firm but friendly" authoritative pattern
is also emphatically supported by an earlier study of the parents of
delinquents (Glueck and Glueck, 1950). This study (Table 16-4) compared the techniques of control used by the parents of delinquents with
those used by a matched group of parents of nondelinquents.

Thus far, all the studies showing the superiority of the authoritative style depend heavily upon subjective ratings of parental and
consequent child behavior. By contrast, Hurley (1965) used measures
of parental and child behavior that were entirely independent of the
ratings of experts.

His subjects were several hundred parents and their third-grade
children in a rural upstate New York county. In measuring the degree
of authoritarianism of parents, Hurley used three measures of parental
attitudes: (1) answers to a 30-item *Rejection Scale* ("When parents
speak, children should obey"; "It is good for children to sometimes
'talk back' to their parents"; etc.); (2) answers given in an interview to
24 items on a *Punishment Scale* ("If your child got very mad at you,
would you slap him in the face?"; "Would you tell your child you don't
love him for getting very mad at you?"; etc.); and (3) the *judgments* of
the mildness or severity of 13 different kinds of punishment for
children ("giving him an angry look," etc.). He used scores on a
group-administered test of intelligence to measure the impact of
variations in these attitudes on the child.

Result: The more authoritarian the parents, the less intelligent
their children. The result was the same for each of the scales and for
both boys and girls. However, the impact of authoritarianism upon the
intelligence of the girls was greater than its impact upon the intelligence of the boys.

Why are the individualistic, authoritarian, and permissive
styles less successful than the authoritarian? The weaknesses of the

TABLE 16-4   Types of Parental Control and Delinquency

Type of Control	Delinquents, %	Nondelinquents, %
Authoritative ("firm but friendly")	5	60
Authoritarian ("overstrict")	15	5
Permissive ("lax")	42	15
Individualistic ("inconsistent")	38	20
Total	100	100

(*Source*: Glueck and Glueck, 1950)

inconsiderate and irresponsible style of the individualistic parent are so obvious that its extremes are avoided by practically all parents. Baumrind (1971), for example, found *no* parents in Berkeley that fell clearly into this pattern. At worst, such parents hate their children, and are impulsively punitive and completely unconcerned about what happens to them. At best, they are preoccupied with themselves and indifferent to their children.

Abner is a fairly typical product of such parents:

> He was a sixteen-year-old boy of below-average intelligence, referred to the psychiatric clinic by the juvenile court which classified him as "incorrigible." His mother kept a diary of the things she did not like about him. However, her interview with the psychiatrist was less a list of specific dislikes than a long and continuous accusation. His father was less vigorous in his disapproval, confining himself to making specific rather than general accusations. His mother was from a wealthy family and had wanted to be a singer. She felt that Abner, her first child, had sealed her "doom." The clinic recommended that he be placed in a foster home. She objected. However, when Abner tried to burn the house to get away, she yielded.

The Ineffective Punitiveness of the Authoritarian

Authoritarian parents, like authoritative parents, feel responsible for what happens to their children and try to control them. However, they differ a great deal in the amount they try to control, what they try to get their children to do, why they try to get them to do it, and above all, in how they try to get them to do it.

Variations in the Amount of Control   Parents vary enormously in the total amount of control they attempt to exercise over their children. Some parents act as if a child were a reservoir of "good" which needs only the lowering of barriers to find expression. Permissive as well as authoritative parents tend to agree with statements like these:

> A child must learn to do things without the consent of his parents.

> Children should usually be allowed to have their own way.

> A child should have freedom to develop a personality of his own, even though this makes problems for his parents.

It is a good thing for children sometimes to "talk back" to their parents.

Children have a right to play with whomever they please.

Authoritarian parents generally act as if a child were potentially dangerous energy that must be brought under control for the benefit of the child and society. These strict parents tend to agree with statements like these:

Children need some of the natural meanness taken out of them.

Most children need more discipline than they get.

Early weaning and toilet training are important in preparing a child for life.

Children should be expected to take good care of their toys.

Children will neglect their schoolwork if parents do not keep after them.

Variations in What Is Controlled   What parents try to get their children to do and how much pressure they exert to get them to do it varies with the times. Wolfenstein (1953), for instance, has made a comparative study of recommended child-rearing practices in *Infant Care*, a U.S. Children's Bureau bulletin of which nine editions were published between 1914 and 1951. Figure 16-5 summarizes the trends for bowel training and masturbation. In comparing the practices recommended in the 1921 edition for controlling masturbation with those recommended in the 1914 edition, Wolfenstein found the 1921 recommendations more permissive; and in comparing those in the 1929 edition with those of 1921, she found the 1929 recommendations more permissive than the 1921. Thus, as the figure shows, there has been a steady increase in permissiveness toward masturbation. The 1941 edition said masturbation was " . . . an injurious practice . . . easily grows beyond control . . . children are sometimes wrecked for life . . . But it must be eradicated . . . treatment consists in mechanical restraints." The 1951 edition said: "Sometimes a baby handles his genitals when he is sitting on the toilet, or at other times when he is undressed. This is a common thing, and usually will not amount to anything if let alone." Strictness over bowel training reached its peak in the late 1920s and has since declined. Wolfenstein also found that the permissiveness of recommended practices in bladder training, weaning, and thumb-sucking was greater in 1951 than at any of the earlier periods studied.

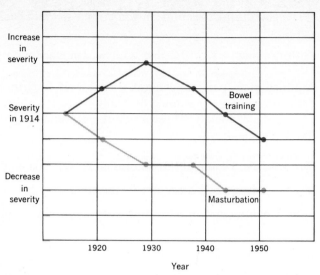

Figure 16-5 Trends in the severity of child-rearing practices. (Ratings by Wolfenstein, 1953)

What *Infant Care* recommended was not necessarily what mothers of the period did. However, it did state what experts felt were the most effective ways of achieving the immediate and long-range goals of child rearing, and these experts undoubtedly both reflected and influenced parental practices. As the widely varying levels of recommended control suggest, experts have been none too stable guides as to what the most desirable level actually is.

Variations in the Success of Controls   The success of parents in controlling their children varies with what they are trying to control. Efforts to control the age at which children walk is unsuccessful. Laboratory studies of identical twins as well as studies of the Hopi, who bind their children to boards for most of the day, show that differences in the age at which children walk depends upon direct genetic mechanisms. In general, parents have nothing to gain and something to lose by making early demands on their children to master such basic skills as sitting, creeping, walking, and the elements of talking. Children do differ in the age at which they gain these skills but the differences are almost entirely due to differences in heredity.

Strictness in the control of aggression is successful. The stricter the parents in controlling the aggressive behavior of their children, the less aggressive the children tend to be (Sears et al., 1957). Physical punishment for aggression, however, produces aggressive children. Peaceful homes are those where the parents make clear that aggression is wrong but head off its expression or deal with it in less punitive ways: isolation, deprivation of privileges, or withdrawal of love.

The "golden mean" is not always successful. A child can be, and often is, successfully weaned during the second six months of his life. On the other hand, if the parents wait until the end of the second year, the average child weans himself. The compromise, weaning the child early in the second year, is difficult and creates emotional disturbances (Sears et al., 1957). Such disturbances may have permanent effects. College students who were weaned early or late were less anxious than those who had been weaned at an intermediate time (Maslow and Szylagyi-Kessler, 1946).

Pediatricians, clinical psychologists, and family counselors have often recommended an extremely permissive system of child care: prolonged breast feeding, gradual weaning, self-demand feeding, and late bowel and bladder training. Still, there is some doubt about whether variations in these practices have any influence on personality development. Data on the way 162 five-year-old children were nursed, weaned, and bowel- and bladder-trained were obtained by interviews with the mothers. Questionaires, projective tests, and ratings made by the mothers and teachers of the children were used as the personality measures. Result: None of the training practices was related to any of the personality measures (Sewell, 1952).

Punitiveness: A Consistent Failure   Authoritarian parents tend to try to control their children too much and, consequently, more often try to control the uncontrollable. However, their primary failures seem to arise from *how* they try to exert control. They operate more often on the principle of "Spare the rod, and spoil the child." Whether punishment is "good" or "bad" for the child is not the problem. The problem is that regular and severe punishment does not work.

Like all parents, authoritarian ones assume that their methods are most likely to result in a well-developed adult. Yet their cold and rigid approach tends to punish their child from the beginning. To develop beyond the autistic stage, warmth and physical contact seem essential. The authoritarian mother is more likely to be a "wire" than a "cloth" mother.

Severe punishment not only does not produce the results desired by the parents; it often produces the *opposite* of what is desired. Sears and his coworkers (1957) who observed 379 New England mothers and their five-year-old children concluded:

The unhappy effects of punishment have run like a dismal thread through our findings. Mothers who punished toilet accidents severely ended up with bed-wetting children.

Mothers who punished dependency to get rid of it had more dependent children than mothers who did not punish. Mothers who punished aggressive behavior severely had more aggressive children than mothers who punished lightly. They also had more dependent children. Harsh physical punishment was associated with high childhood aggressiveness and with the development of feeding problems.

Authoritarian parents use object-oriented techniques: physical punishment and tangible rewards. Such techniques, we have seen, retard the development of identification. Consequently, authoritarian parents are more likely to wind up with children who are retarded at the opportunistic stage.

The Self-Indulgence of the Permissive

Compared to authoritative and authoritarian parents, Baumrind found that the children of permissive parents were notable for their lack of curiosity, self-reliance, and self-control. The explanation seems obvious, for such parents do not try to encourage their children to explore, do not try to train them to be self-reliant, and do not demand that they control themselves. Why don't they?

The desire to be close to and intimate with others is a primary motive for parenthood. When this integrative need is too intense or its satisfaction too long delayed, then parents may become very concerned with the gratification of this need in themselves and unconcerned with the needs of their child. Cases of *maternal overprotection* where the mother treats the child like a baby well beyond the age such treatment is appropriate, are generally of this type. Overprotecting mothers tend to have had an only child late in life, to have been rejected in their own childhood, and to be unhappily married (Levy, 1943). Such parents are afraid to risk alienation from their child by making the demands upon him that neither authoritarian nor authoritative parents hesitate to do.

Ross and Anderson (1965) analyzed the motives of mothers in three unsuccessful cases of adoption. The first mother hoped the "natural pregnancy would follow adoption." The second mother "became bored with collecting antiques and was on the verge of becoming an alcoholic." The third mother had intense fear of many environmental situations and saw the baby as a possible way of helping her avoid such situations. In general, it seems, permissiveness is often a way of satisfying the needs of the parents rather than the needs of the children.

Parenthood has always been a complex and uncertain affair. The worst of parents sometimes succeed in raising happy and competent adults while the best fail. Our effort here has been not only to show that authoritative parents are most likely to succeed but also to show that there are fairly simple reasons why they do.

THE DEVELOPMENT OF AUTHORITATIVE PARENTS

The authoritative parent is the best parent. Such parents understand and accept their children as they are now, but set standards for future conduct. They recognize their children's interests and special ways, but they also recognize their own special rights as adults. They do not base their decisions on their children's momentary desires but they do not regard themselves as infallible or divinely inspired. They want their children to be spontaneous and independent, but they also want them to be capable of disciplined conformity. They exert firm control at critical points, but they do not hem their children with detailed restrictions. They direct their children's activities, but they encourage verbal give and take and share with their children the reasoning behind their directions. They use reason when possible, power when necessary. How do such parents develop?

The Selection of Parenthood

No principle of parenthood is now more widely accepted than that "every child should be wanted." The 1973 Supreme Court decision affirms this principle even to the point of allowing women to terminate a pregnancy if they do not want the child. But wanting a child is not enough. Sloman (1948) tells of 62 planned children who were rejected by their mothers and referred to the Institute for Juvenile Research in Chicago as problem children. Some of the children were rejected because they were not of the hoped-for sex. Some had been planned in order to save a marriage; failing to fulfill this function, the children were rejected. Most of them had mothers who were perfectionistic and compulsive: like everything else they did, these mothers had carefully planned the arrival of their children, and when the child did not fit in with the mother's picture of the ideal child she had hoped to show off to friends and relatives, the child was rejected. Many of these mothers also had had strict religious training, resulting in rigid moral attitudes which could not adapt to the often provocative and negativistic behavior of children. Good parents know why they want children, how to use their strengths, and when to compensate for their weaknesses in helping them.

Structure

Parents vary widely in the degree and rigidity with which they structure relationships with their children. Some parents structure the relationship very little, seldom giving their children any clear idea of what is expected of them. Other parents consistently tell their children exactly what they are to do and how they are to do it. Both permissive and strict parents vary in the rigidity in which they play their roles. From infancy to maturity, the rigid parent is always the "parent," or the "playmate," or, sometimes, the "child." Other parents are much more flexible in the roles that they play in relating to their children, shifting from one to another with considerable ease.

Some children benefit from more, and more rigid, structuring than others (Chess, Thomas, and Birch, 1959). All children, however, vary in their needs for structure. The young child benefits from a highly structured environment in which he knows exactly what is expected of him and what is not—what is permissible and desirable and what is disapproved and punished. Without such structuring, he suffers the chronic frustration of having to test reality in order to find just what he can get away with—trying to find a pattern where none exists. He needs a parent who is always a parent and who is always structuring situations in great detail. As he develops, however, he needs less and less structuring, less and less rigidity.

Here lies the most ancient problem of parenthood: the child requires a changing structure; parents tend to maintain the same degree and rigidity of structure. The permissive and flexible parent may expose his young child to frustration and even to physical dangers, but is likely to have a helpful relationship with him at later ages if the child survives. The strict and rigid parent provides a beneficial early environment for his child; the child, however, may become frustrated and rebellious as an adolescent. The solution to the problem lies in the parent learning to adapt the structure to the age and immediate problems of the child. Since parents are different, the direction from which they approach the solution must be different. The too permissive and too flexible parents must learn to be more strict and rigid; the too strict and rigid, less so.

Communication

A child needs to know and benefits from knowing how his parents feel about him, what they expect from him, and what he can expect from them. If he does not know where he stands, he may be as troubled as one who knows that they are indifferent to him or hate him.

We tell our children much about how we feel about success, little about how he can deal with failure. Child, Potter, and Levine (1946) analyzed the content of children's stories used in the third- and fourth-grade text. As a whole, the stories had an "unrealistic optimism," for they were seldom concerned with failure and often with success. Conclusion: ". . . from the point of view of contribution to the solutions of problems of everyday life, failures ought to receive a large proportion of attention, for it is they that pose problems." Like the textbooks, parents often tell their children about their personal triumphs, rarely about their failures. Yet the stories of parental failures and how the parents dealt with them may be considerably more valuable to their children.

A child needs to learn to express his own feelings freely and appropriately. The parent must lead the way. Emotionally overcontrolled parents have overcontrolled children. Even the violent expression by parents of feelings that are painful to the child has one great advantage—it teaches the child that he, too, can express his violent feelings. If it is all right for his parents, it is all right for him.

Children often cannot or will not talk about their problems. *Play therapy* attempts to overcome this difficulty. It employs puppet shows, finger painting, drawing, modeling with clay, toys, and dolls. An atmosphere of permissiveness is essential for the child to bring his feelings to the surface in his playing (Axline, 1947). Consequently, the child is encouraged to do what he feels like doing so long as he does not attack the therapist or destroy the toys. Thus, a child who had frequent car sickness but who refused to talk about it placed a mamma doll and a boy doll in a toy streetcar. He said that the boy felt sick because he feared a truck would hit the car and hurt the mamma. In another situation, he said a small boy doll would not go to sleep alone in a dark room because he was afraid that the father doll, who did not live with the mother doll, would come and steal him. In such situations the child not only learns to express his feelings but also learns that these feelings are accepted by an adult.

Parental Role Training

There is a growing recognition that parenthood is too important to be left to either nature or professionals. Birth control clinics, prenatal counseling, and child-care training programs are accelerating. Courses for undergraduates that involve supervised experience in caring for children are increasingly common. In one such course, students are made responsible for the toddlers attending a day-care center (Fitzgerald, Ledesma, Swarthout, and Parker, 1972). The course guides for interacting with the children try to make concrete the authoritative style in dealing with them:

Guides to Interaction

1.   The children come FIRST!

2.   Be positive!

3. Interact when you can add something to the child's discovery or growth—be a catalyst not an answer!!

4. Help children to formulate *their* rules in *their* world. Use questions to aid their reasoning. Ex. What are teeth for? . . . We use them to eat with.

5. OBSERVE AND LISTEN—children's actions "talk." Tune in through involvement with children (save adult conversation for later).

6. We don't have good and bad children, RATHER we have acceptable and nonacceptable behavior. When disciplining, discuss the issue not the child per se.

7. Praise has great powers in influencing behavior (remember how it feels).

8. Always send a child *TO* an activity NOT *FROM* an activity.

9. Help children be responsible for their toys, clothes, and actions.

10. Communicate in concrete specific terms. Ex. "Put the book on the shelf," not "Let's clean up."

11. Bend or kneel down to the child and speak to him face to face. If necessary turn his face gently towards you, or say "Look at me" in a gentle voice.

12. Use statements when the child doesn't have a choice; don't communicate in question form. Ex. "It's time for our naps," not "Do you want to take a nap?"

The difference between using power in an authoritative rather than an authoritarian way is suggested by the following guides for the successful disciplining of children:

1. Do you provide experiences that help the child develop responsibility for his own behavior, experiences that help him to evaluate himself realistically, experiences that are aimed at helping him to *direct his own life* using good judgment?

2. Do you treat each child with as much *respect* as you expect him to show you?

3. Do you help each child to consider the *justice of his own acts* as well as acts directed toward him?

4.   Do you treat children according to their own *individual needs* or do you treat them "all the same"?

5.   Do you help children see *alternate ways* to satisfy their needs and make these ways seem possible and worthy?

6.   Do you discipline a child by *redirecting his behavior* and activity rather than punishing or scolding him?

7.   Do you let children know what is expected of them in *advance* of a new experience?

8.   Can you control a situation without letting a child be a threat to your emotions and *without producing resentment* on his part?

9.   Do you help set up limits to behavior that seem reasonable to the child?

10.   Are you *consistent* in your expectations and demands of children?

Almost as many male students enroll for this course as females and are at least as successful as the women. Among both males and females, however, there are wide differences in enthusiasm and aptitude for the job.

Professional counseling for parents with disturbed children is an old story. The new story is the training of parents of disturbed children to be therapists for their *own* children (Stollak, 1966). In this training, small groups of mothers meet weekly with a professional therapist. In the initial meetings, the mother is asked to be as understanding of her child as she can, to put herself as much as she can in the child's place, to express what she thinks the child is feeling to him, and to try to convey her acceptance of these feelings to the child. She is told to let him play as he wishes, to refrain from offering suggestions, and to refrain from either blaming or praising the child for what he says or does. In other sessions, the therapist demonstrates the technique with children and the mothers bring in their own children and practice playing the role before the therapist and the group. Throughout the training sessions the mothers are encouraged to ask questions, to express their doubts, and state their personal reactions freely. In spite of the fact that these mothers were suffering from serious problems themselves, they showed dramatic changes in the ways that they interacted with their children. In turn, the children showed similar changes in the way they responded to their mothers.

The program for mothers led to a program to train undergraduates as play therapists (Stollak, 1973). Graduate students trained as play therapists supervise the training of the undergraduates in small groups. The aims of the program are to improve the abilities of the student to follow the lead of the child, to pay attention to his activities, and to communicate his acceptance of these activities to the child.

SUMMARY

The vast majority of couples see the role of parent as highly desirable and satisfying. Personally, they judge their success in the role by their feelings of closeness to their children and their interest in the activities required by the role. Socially, however, their success is judged by the personality development of their child. Individualistic parents do the least to enhance this development. Permissive and authoritarian parents are likely to be successful in promoting development through the autistic, impulse-ridden, and opportunistic stages but unlikely to be successful in promoting development beyond the conforming stage. Authoritative parents are likely to be most successful in encouraging their child's development, for they are most realistic in adapting the structure of their relationship with their children to fit their needs and in communicating most fully and effectively with them.

SUGGESTIONS FOR FURTHER READING

Leader, P. (1931). *And no birds sing*. New York: Vanguard. The story of a sensitive girl who grows deaf in her efforts to escape the constant threats and condemnation of her parents.

*Neill, A. S. (1960). *Summerhill*. New York: Hart. All but 1 of 30 students who reported on this book enjoyed it very much. Although they were generally "turned off by his extreme Freudian views" and doubted very much that the program "would work anywhere except in a controlled environment such as his school," they felt that the kind of freedom that the author talks about "would most certainly bring about a happy child and that what our society needs is more happy people."

Sears, R. R., Maccoby, E. E., and Levin, H. (1957). *Patterns of child rearing*. New York: Harper & Row. The study of 379 New England mothers of five-year-old children referred to in this chapter. An excellent synthesis of original research, lively writing, and wise advice.

17

LEADER AND FOLLOWER

One fine day it occurred
to the Members of the Body that they
were doing all the work and the Belly
was having all the food. So they held a
meeting, and after a long discussion, decided to strike
work till the Belly
consented to take its proper share of the work.
So for a day or two, the Hands refused to
take food, the Mouth refused
to receive it, and the Teeth had no work to do. . . .

AESOP'S FABLES (ca 900 B.C.)

We seek out members of the opposite sex, marry them, and have children with them to satisfy our yearnings to be close to others, to play roles that we enjoy, and to satisfy our material needs. In none of the roles we play have the elements that determine the success of relationships been more carefully studied than in the work relationships between leaders and their followers. It is, then, the goals that we try to achieve in these relationships, the standards that we set for our leaders, and their varying success that is the concern of the present chapter.

THE GOALS OF GROUPS

Individuals have integrative, morale, and productive goals. An organization is a group of people brought together to help achieve such goals. Consequently, every group has similar goals. In our sexual, marital, and parental relationships, integrative needs tend to dominate. In work relationships, however, productivity dominates. The production of a group is its output of goods or services. *Productivity is output per unit of labor input.* The measurement of productivity is relatively easy in companies that produce raw materials like oil or coal or such material products as cars or planes. Production under these circumstances is the quantity and quality of output; productivity, the output divided by the number of man-hours required to produce it. Measurement is more difficult in a bank or a restaurant, where services rather than goods are produced. The bank, however can count the number of checks processed by its clerks per hour and the restaurant can count the number and size of checks handled by different waitresses per evening. In any case, service organizations have profit and loss statements that provide valuable information about productivity. In churches, government bureaus, universities of other non-profit organizations, development of adequate measures of productivity becomes very difficult.

Productivity cannot be the only goal of a company, for a business not only must be productive now, but must continue to be so. In order to maintain its productivity, it must at least maintain and at best increase its integration. *The integration of a company is its ability to maintain its structure and function.* If a company is losing its workers and losing its ability to function effectively, its integration is declining. If it is keeping its workers and its effectiveness, it is maintaining its integration. If it is improving its ability to keep its workers and improving its organizational effectiveness, its integration is increasing.

Executives may feel they are forced to be concerned with immediate productivity at the expense of integration. Often, for example, a man is placed in charge of a department or plant knowing that the more he increases productivity, the better are his chances for advancement. Sometimes he can show a phony improvement by juggling the inventory or by failing to maintain the plant. That is, he can increase productivity in the short run by liquidating the physical resources of his organization. The reward system of the company may also encourage him to liquidate the human resources. He pressures his subordinates to push production up so that at the end of the year the figures show him to be a "fine manager." He is promoted to another job and repeats the performance. Meanwhile, back at the first plant, his high-pressure methods show up in decreased loyalty to the company, lack of motivation to do a job, labor turnover, slowdowns, scrap loss, and inability to meet emergencies effectively. His replacement, who finds the organization falling apart, may be handicapped for years by the deep-seated distrust and hostility generated by the "fine manager."

Integration or the lack of it is easier to see in small than in large groups. It is easier, for example, to observe in a football team than in a corporation. The degree of integration and its value are also easier to observe in a crisis than in normal times. At a critical point in a difficult game, the coach can sometimes almost see his team falling apart.

Companies are larger than teams and operate in a routine rather than a crisis atmosphere. It is not surprising, therefore, that company executives are often too little aware of the importance of company integration or of the actions that raise or lower it. Whether an executive is aware of it or not, however, the level of integration in his organization is determining his and his organization's success. Integration is, in other words, an essential company goal.

Morale is the worker's intrinsic interest in what he is doing as measured by his work effort, initiative, and satisfaction. An individual or a group has high morale when there is a high level of involvement in the task to be done, great effort expended, and considerable happiness with the work itself. Low morale exists when the individual or group acts and feels apathetic, uninvolved, and indifferent about the work and its outcomes. Morale lies in the *interaction* between a worker and his work. That is, one employee may be interested and another uninterested in the same work, and some work may be more interesting to all workers than other work.

ROLE STANDARDS FOR GROUP LEADERS

How do people differ in the standards they set for their ideal leader? To find out, Doré (1960) developed the Attitudes toward Leadership scale shown in Table 17-1. The first part is a measure of how considerate people want their leader to be. Consideration is the degree to which a leader understands and respects the rights and feelings of his followers. In the abstract, nearly everyone would rather have a considerate than an inconsiderate leader. In a concrete situation, however, one is generally forced to decide whether one wants a leader who

---

TABLE 17-1   Attitudes toward Leadership

Directions   In each question are two statements of things that a leader can do. Choose the one you feel it is more *important* for him to do. If you feel that both alternatives are poor, choose the one you think is less poor.

It is more important for a leader:

Consideration
1. (1) To make decisions independently of the group.
   (2) To really be a part of his work group.*
2. (1) To let workers take time out from the monotony when they wish.*
   (2) To allow workers to make decisions only when given explicit authority by the leader.
3. (1) To take an interest in the worker as a person.*
   (2) To maintain definite standards of performance.
4. (1) To have his workers do their work they way they think is best.*
   (2) To rule with a firm hand.
5. (1) To decide in detail how the work shall be done by the workers.
   (2) To let workers make decisions whenever they feel competent.*
6. (1) To make it clear that he is the leader of the group.
   (2) To have workers settle by themselves most of their job problems.*
7. (1) To have the workers settle by themselves most problems.*
   (2) To have scheduled rest periods.
8. (1) To have his workers do their work they way they think is best.*
   (2) To assign specific responsibilities and duties daily.
9. (1) To do the important jobs himself.
   (2) To have workers take their rest periods when they wish.*
10. (1) To feel he belongs in his group.*
    (2) To reward the good worker.
11. (1) To have his workers do the work the way they think is best.*
    (2) To have the worker depend upon him to make decisions.
12. (1) To get the work done on time.
    (2) To be friendly toward his workers.*
13. (1) To act as he thinks best, regardless of the views of his workers.
    (2) To be proud of his work group.*
14. (1) To give the workers the power to act independently of him.*
    (2) To assign workers to particular tasks.
15. (1) To do the important jobs himself.
    (2) To let the workers decide how to do each task.*
16. (1) To leave it up to each worker to get his share of the work done.*
    (2) To set up most projects himself.

Responsibility
17. (1) To call the group together to discuss the work.†
    (2) To work right alongside the workers.
18. (1) To pitch right in with the workers.
    (2) To plan the work carefully.†

19. (1) To explain carefully each worker's duties to him.†
    (2) To spend some of his time helping get the work done.
20. (1) To work hard himself.
    (2) To schedule the work of the men carefully.†
21. (1) To be an authority in the type of work the group does.
    (2) To tell poor workers when their work isn't measuring up to what it should be.
22. (1) To do the same work as his men whenever time allows.
    (2) To plan how his men will do the job.†
23. (1) To call the group together to discuss the work.†
    (2) To attempt to make his work not too different from the work of his men.
24. (1) To be respected as a man of high technical skill in his field.
    (2) To spend over half his time in supervisory activities such as planning and scheduling.
25. (1) To let his workers know how they are doing on their jobs.†
    (2) To spend some of his time helping get the work done.
26. (1) To pass along to his workers information from higher management.†
    (2) To help get the work done.
27. (1) To be known as a man of great technical skill in the field.
    (2) To schedule the work to be done.†
28. (1) To meet with the workers to consider proposed changes.†
    (2) To pitch right in with the workers to help make changes.
29. (1) To explain the duties of each worker's job to him until he really understands them.†
    (2) To pitch right in with the workers.
30. (1) To perform the same work as the workers whenever possible.
    (2) To plan his day's activities in considerable detail.
31. (1) To be known as a skillful trainer.†
    (2) To set an example by working hard himself.
32. (1) To work right alongside his workers.
    (2) To try out new ideas on the work group.†

*Indicates high-consideration response.
†Indicates high-responsibility response.

stresses being considerate of the members of the group or a leader who stresses getting the job done. The first 16 items of the scale force the respondent to choose whether he prefers a leader who stresses consideration for the members of the group or one who stresses the work to be done. Under these circumstances, as Figure 17-1 shows, college men vary a great deal in their standards. Among these men, some gave the worker-oriented response to only three of the statements while others gave the worker-oriented response in 16 out of the 16 statements. The typical student gave the worker-oriented response in 9 out of the 16. This score of 9, which is the 50th percentile, is shown in the middle of the figure.

Items 16 through 32 are a measure of how responsible people want their leader to be. The responsibility of a leader is the degree to

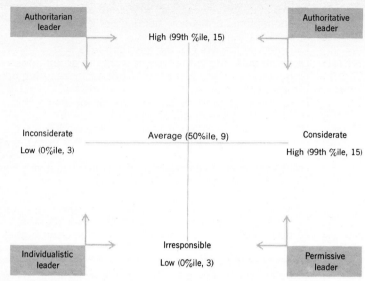

Figure 17-1   The measurement of the role standards of college men for their leaders. (Smith, 1973)

which he feels and acts as if he were holding himself accountable for what happens to the members and to the group as a whole. Perhaps we all like people who *feel* responsible for what happens to us. We do not always like those who *act* responsibly toward us, for that requires them to play a different role than we do. The responsible leader cannot play the same role as we for he has to spend most of his time setting the goals for the group, planning and organizing the activities of the group, and instructing or explaining things to it. Thus, the items in this part of the scale ask the respondents whether they prefer a leader who plays an undifferentiated role or one who plays a differentiated role. As the figures along the vertical line in Figure 17-1 show, college men have quite different standards in regard to how differentiated a role their ideal leader would play. Some prefer a leader who does just what his followers do while others prefer a leader who plays an entirely different role. The typical student takes a moderate view. He chose the differentiated role option in 9 out of the 16 statements. This 50th percentile position is shown at the intersection of the consideration and responsibility dimensions in the figure. The typical college woman has slightly greater preference for leaders who are more considerate and less responsible than those preferred by college men.

Like students, workers observe the consideration and respon- sibility of their leaders. Fleishman and Salter (1963) had subordinates in a variety of work settings rate their supervisors on these two dimensions. Typical of the items in the final consideration scale were the following:

He sees that a person is rewarded for a job well done.

He makes those in the group feel at ease when talking with him.

He backs up his men in their actions.

Negative items in the scale were the following:

He refuses to give in when people disagree with him.

He changes the duties of people without first talking it over with them.

He doesn't give credit when it is due.

Fleishman and Salter describe the general quality of these items as including ". . . behavior indicating mutual trust, respect, and a certain warmth and rapport between the supervisor and his group. This does not mean that this dimension reflects a superficial 'pat-on-the-back,' 'first-name-calling' kind of human relations behavior. The meaning of this dimension goes more deeply into respect for the individual and includes such behavior as allowing subordinates more participation in decision making."

Typical items in the final responsibility scale were the following:

He offers new approaches to problems.

He asks for sacrifices for the good of the entire department.

He assigns people to particular tasks.

He criticizes poor work.

He encourages slow-working people to greater effort.

These statements are described as including ". . . behavior in which the supervisor organizes and defines group activities and his relation to the group. Thus he defines the role he expects each member to assume, plans ahead, establishes ways of getting things done, and pushes for production."

As used in practice, the two scales are completed by the subordinates of a supervisor. While each of the scales has high internal consistencies, scores on them have no relationship. These scales were developed in work situations. However, the dimensions appear not only in all leadership situations but also in all human relationships:

teaching, counseling, parent-child relations, etc. With slight changes in wording, the scales can be fitted to these situations. In all these situations, however, the measurement is made by the subordinate, not by the leader; by the client, not the counselor.

Consideration and responsibility are independent: one cannot predict how important the consideration of a leader is to a follower from knowing how important leader responsibility is to the follower. Each follower, in other words, has his own preferred "mix" of consideration and responsibility. The preferences of followers for their leaders and for leaders for themselves fall into four distinguishable patterns. The names given to these patterns are shown in Figure 17-1 and briefly described below.

The Authoritative Leader

(High consideration; high responsibility). Such a leader is *both* considerate and responsible. He stresses the worker rather than the work and he also plays a role quite different from that played by his followers. He is perceived by his followers as trusting and respecting them and also as organizing and defining the group's activities (Figure 17-2).

The Permissive Leader

(High consideration; low responsibility). Such a leader acts as if the needs of his followers were more important than getting the work done. He also tries to play a role as much like that of his followers as possible. He does not accept the responsibility of planning and organizing the activities of the group.

The Individualistic Leader

(Low consideration; low responsibility). The leader who follows this pattern shows little interest in the personal problems of his followers or in their advice. He may criticize the contributions of others, but feels no responsibility to "pull things together" for the group.

The Authoritarian Leader

(Low consideration; high responsiblity). The leader who follows this pattern pays little attention to the needs and suggestions of followers and concentrates on getting the job done. He spends most of his time planning and organizing the work and solving the problems that interfere with its completion.

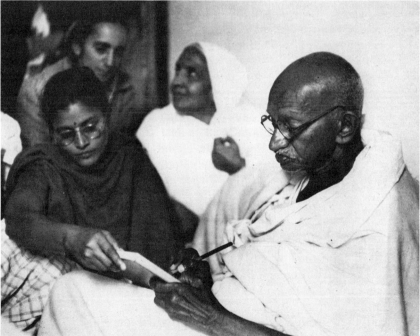

Figure 17-2 De Gaulle and Ghandi: these world leaders of the past had vastly different leadership styles. De Gaulle was authoritative—responsible and moderately considerate. Ghandi was permissive—seldom responsible but very considerate. (Henri Cartier-Bresson/Magnum)

THE SUCCESS OF LEADERSHIP

Some leaders are authoritative; some, permissive; some, individualistic; and some, authoritarian. What determines the success of a leader's style? Is one style more successful than the others?

The Standards of Followers

The success of a leader's style depends upon the expectations of his followers. The more followers want an authoritative leader, the more successful an authoritative leader is likely to be. The more they want an authoritarian leader, the more successful an authoritarian leader is likely to be. Army rifle squads, for example, were asked how they thought an ideal squad leader should act. They were also asked how they thought their own leader acted. The differences between the ideal and the real for each man were calculated and became his *discrepancy score.* The scores for men in a squad were averaged to find the squad's discrepancy score for a particular leader. When the discrepancy scores of different leaders were related to the effectiveness of their squads, it was found that the lower the discrepancy, the higher the effectiveness. That is, the more the leader acted the way the average member of his squad thought a good leader should act, the more effective the unit was. This held true even though different squads and different men in the same squad varied greatly in their ideals. The investigators concluded that the successful leader is able to meet the varying expectations of the men under him. He varies his leadership behavior to fit the expectations of each of his followers (Havron and McGrath, 1961).

The theoretical necessity of an interaction view is suggested by the results of a laboratory study of 4-man groups. Before the groups were formed, all participants took a test that measured their "authoritarian" tendencies, that is the extent to which they desired a clear-cut authority structure in social situations. The participants were then divided into 4-man groups. One of the four was appointed by the experimenter as the leader. Four different kinds of groups were set up: (1) High authoritarian leaders with high authoritarian followers; (2) high authoritarian leaders with low authoritarian followers; (3) low authoritarian leaders with high authoritarian followers; and (4) low authoritarian leaders with low authoritarian followers. The leaders influenced their followers: compared to the low authoritarian leaders, the high authoritarian leaders had groups with a more formal structure and more unequal division of work. However, followers also influenced their leaders. Regardless of whether they had low or high authoritarian tendencies, leaders with authoritarian followers behaved more autocratically with them than they did with nonauthoritarian followers (Haythorn, 1958).

Leadership Style versus Group Goal

The permissive style seems most successful in achieving integrative ends, least successful in achieving productive ends. Rodin and Rodin (1972) studied the success of a dozen instructors of sections of a large introductory calculus course. An instructor's integrative score was measured by having his students grade him: "What grade would you assign to his total teaching performance?" His productive score was measured by the number of 40 calculus problems solved correctly by his average student. Allowances were made for their knowledge of calculus at the beginning of the course. Integrative and productive scores were correlated. Result: The higher the integrative score, the *lower* the productive score ($r = -.75$). The students of the instructor who gave him the highest grade did most poorly on the final examination. It seems that most of the students had low morale, i.e., had only moderate interest in learning about calculus. Consequently, they preferred instructors who stressed integration rather than productivity, i.e., a pleasant and friendly instructor who did not push them to learn more than they cared to know about calculus.

The individualistic style would seem best adapted to achieving morale ends. It is, however, not so much a leadership style as a nonleadership style. A "leader" following this style tends to ignore the members of the group, makes little or no effort to organize its activities, and just concentrates on doing his "thing." Consequently, the other members of the group are free to do what interests them most—until the group fails.

The authoritarian style is most successful in achieving productive ends, least successful in achieving integrative ends. The management of a large corporation was anxious to increase the productivity of the 500 clerical workers in four divisions who were engaged in the same billing operation. The amount of billing to be done by these divisions was a constant. The only way of increasing efficiency, therefore, was by increasing the amount of work done by each clerk. A study by the methods department showed that billing divisions were overstaffed by about 30 percent except during the occasional peak-load periods. The question was: How can the number of workers be decreased without decreasing the volume of work done? Two of the divisions set up an authoritarian system for solving the problem. The general manager of the corporation ordered the managers of the billing units to cut their staff by 25 percent. However, no one was to be dismissed in the process: workers were to be transferred or not replaced. The supervisors in these divisions were given an intensive training program that informed them about the company organization and policies. Above all, the training stressed the importance of supervisors obediently carrying out the instructions given them by their superiors. A check on the level at which decisions were made before and after training showed that the training had a significant influence on the day-to-day behavior of the supervisors. After training, more decisions were made at a higher level. The program achieved its goal of improving efficiency. A comparison of salary costs for the year before and for the year after the program was installed showed a decline of 25 percent.

The other two billing divisions set up an authoritative system for solving the problem. The aim of their program was to give employees more freedom of action in planning and doing their work. The supervisors were instructed to involve their subordinates in more activities, allow them to make decisions, and to supervise the details of their work less. The salary comparison showed that this program also improved efficiency, but not quite as much. Salary costs declined 20 percent. Psychologists also measured employee attitudes before and after the group system was installed. After the program, the employees felt more responsible, more favorably inclined toward high producing employees, closer to their supervisors, and more confident that their supervisors were pulling for them.

The shift in attitudes in the divisions under the authoritarian system was exactly opposite. After this system was installed, the employees felt less responsible for getting the work done, less favorable toward high producers, less close to the managers, and less confident that their supervisors were pulling for them. Thus, while this division was advancing toward the goal of *productivity*, it was retreating from the goal of *integration*, the cohesiveness and soundness of the organized structure, and from the goal of *morale*, the intrinsic interest of the workers in what they were doing.

Likert (1958) concluded that "if the company had had an accounting procedure which showed the investment in the human organization, it would have shown . . . the value of the human organization was less at the end of the experimental year than at the beginning. In other words, some of the increased productivity was achieved actually by liquidating part of the investment which the company had in the human organization . . . the increase in productivity should have been charged with this cost."

The productive success of the authoritarian leader is limited by the complexity of the tasks his group has to perform—the more complex the tasks, the less successful he is likely to be. Five men were each given five solid-colored marbles (Leavitt, 1958). Their problem was to find the one color that they all had in common. They were only allowed to communicate with others by writing notes: "I have red, green, yellow, blue, and brown," etc. Some groups were organized in the authoritarian pattern: one of the five was the leader and the other four could only write notes to and receive notes from him. Other groups were organized so that they could communicate with the other members as well as the leader. Although the members of the authoritarian system were bored (except the leader), they solved problems more quickly and more accurately. Some groups, however, were given odd shades of marbles that were hard to describe (one member might call a marble greenish-blue while another would call the same marble aqua). With these complex problems, the members of the authoritarian groups were not only more dissatisfied with what they were doing but were also slower and less accurate.

The more time the followers of an authoritarian leader have to do their jobs the way they want, the more integrated their group tends to be, i.e., the more they tend to be satisfied with him. Vroom and Mann (1960) used the F-scale to measure the authoritarianism of 52 supervisors in a single plant of a large delivery company. The F-scale (for fascist) is composed of 40 statements like "There are two kinds of people: the strong and the weak." As a whole, the scale measures the readiness of the respondent to condemn and punish anyone who violates conventional standards, to stress the importance of dominance and power, to assert his personal toughness, and to believe that the world is wild and dangerous.

Of the 52 supervisors, 28 were in charge of groups of drivers; the other 24 were in charge of groups of positioners. There were 30 to 50 drivers under each supervisor. Each driver checked in with his supervisor in the morning between 8:30 and 9, got his truck loaded, delivered his packages, and then reported back in the afternoon when he had finished. The positioners remained at the plant all day and worked in small groups, taking packages from conveyor belts, getting them ready to load into trucks, and actually loading them.

The satisfaction of the drivers and the positioners with their work group, with their overall work situation, with their supervisor, with their pay system, and with higher management was measured by means of attitude scales. The average score of each of 28 groups of drivers and 24 groups of positioners was then determined. Finally, these satisfaction scores were related to the authoritarianism scores of the respective supervisors. Table 17–2 shows the correlations.

The most surprising result was the difference between the drivers and positioners. Among the drivers, the more authoritarian their supervisor, the better they liked him and other aspects of their jobs as well. Among the positioners, the case was the opposite. Why? The two groups were not in the same situation: the drivers saw their supervisors for only a short time each day; the positioners saw their

TABLE 17–2. Authoritarian Leadership and Worker Satisfaction

Satisfaction with:	Correlation with F-scale	
	Drivers	Positioners
Work group	.47	.01
Overall work situation	.42	−.37
Supervisor	.42	−.41
Payment	.29	−.19
Higher management	.22	−.23

(Source: Vroom and Mann, 1960)

supervisors and their fellow positioners for most of the day. The variations in job *situations* seem to account for the radical differences in the effectiveness of authoritarian leaders.

The Superiority of Authoritative Leadership

Permissive leadership achieves integration; individualistic leadership, morale; and authoritarian leadership, productivity. However, a group almost never has only an integration, or only a morale, or only a production goal. Generally, it has goals in all three areas. Consequently, as the study of the clerks in the billing division showed, the degree of success of a leadership style is most realistically measured by its integrative, morale, *and* productive achievements.

The most successful style of leadership, then, is one which *simultaneously* increases integration, morale, and production, i.e., makes the members more interested in what they are doing and more loyal to the group while it is increasing the productivity of the group. The authoritative style meets these requirements, for it is one which many members expect and practically all can accept, it is one which fits a wide variety of situations, and it is one which does not achieve one goal at the expense of others.

Dawson (1970) showed how successful the authoritative style could be in the classroom. He taught the same course during one quarter to four different groups under four different styles of leadership: *high* consideration, *high* responsibility; *high* consideration, *low* responsibility; *low* consideration, *high* responsibility, and *low* consideration, *low* responsibility. At the end of the course his students rated him on the following kinds of statements:

Low Consideration

He treats his students without considering their feelings.

He refuses to explain his actions.

He acts without consulting his students first.

High Consideration

He puts suggestions that are made by students into operation.

He is willing to make changes.

He makes students feel at ease when talking with him.

Low Responsibility

He lets students do their work in the way they think best.

He does not criticize poor work.

He does not emphasize quantity of work.

High Responsibility

He insists that his students follow a standard way of doing things.

He decides in detail what shall be done and how it shall be done.

He emphasizes meeting deadlines.

His student ratings on the statements consistently fitted his intended style. He used three measures to determine the success of his role playing under the four conditions. He used reports of student satisfaction as a measure of integration; the results of objective examinations as a measure of productivity; and amount of participation in voluntary projects outside of class as a measure of morale. The high consideration and high responsibility class was highest on all three of these measures.

Dawson started with varying styles of leadership and then determined their relative success. Kahn and Katz (1953) reversed the process. They started with leaders of varying degrees of success and then determined their styles of leadership. They systematically studied hundreds of supervisors in a variety of business organizations: supervisors of female clerical workers in an insurance company, supervisors of laborers on railroad section gangs, and supervisors of production workers in a tractor plant. They used a variety of objective criteria for measuring the productivity of each unit supervised by each supervisor: the average woman-hour cost of writing policies in the insurance units, the average rating by superintendents of the section gangs, and productivity on the tractor assembly line. These criteria showed marked differences in the effectiveness of the supervisors in the three companies. Finally, in each company, a group of high-producing and a group of low-producing supervisors were identified.

An intense effort was made to account for these differences in effectiveness. The supervisors, the people under them, and the people over them filled out questionnaries regarding their attitudes and beliefs. Intensive interviews with these groups were recorded and then analyzed. Finally, the attitudes and behavior of high-producing units were compared with the attitudes and behavior of low-producing units. In all these studies as in the original study of the insurance company, the findings showed that high-producing supervisors were more considerate than low-producing supervisors. To begin with, they were more *interested* in their men. In the tractor factory, for example, workers were asked, "How much interest does your foreman take in you off the job?" Of the men in groups whose productivity was 100 percent of standard, 24 percent answered "a great deal" or "quite a lot." Of the men in groups whose productivity was 70 percent or lower, only 14 percent gave this answer. Workers in high-producing units in the insurance company and on the railroad also more often said their supervisors took a personal interest in them and their off-the-job problems. The high-producing supervisors themselves more often said that their subordinates wanted them to take a personal interest. The low-producing supervisor had such poor relationships with his subordinates that they did not want him to know about their personal problems.

High-producing supervisors were more interested in worker problems than work problems; low-producing supervisors were more interested in work problems than worker problems. That is, the high-producing supervisors were *employee-oriented* while the low-producing supervisors were *work-oriented*. In the insurance company, a typical low-producing and work-oriented supervisor said:

> I apportion the *work* to the people in my section and generally supervise the *work*. If a clerk is out, I have to make arrangements to have her *work* handled. The *work* must go on, even though there are absences. This involves getting the *work* redistributed to those who are there. That is all you are supposed to do. But I am from the old school and believe the head should *work* too.

In the same company, a high-producing and employee-oriented supervisor said:

> My job is dealing with human beings, rather than with the work. . . . The chances are that people will do a better job if you're really taking an interest in them. Knowing the names is important and helps a lot, but it's not enough. You really have

to know each individual well, know what his problems are. Most of the time I discuss matters with employees at their desks, rather than in the office. Sometimes I sit on a wastebasket or lean on the files. It's all very informal (Kahn and Katz, 1953).

The high-producing supervisors were also more responsible than the low-producing supervisors. That is, they spent more of their time planning, organizing, training, and helping the workers. For example, insurance company, tractor factory, and railroad section-gang supervisors were asked, "How much of your time do you spend in supervising the men, planning the work, making out reports, and dealing with people outside your section?" The answer of high-producing and low-producing supervisors, divided into those who said they spent more than half their time in supervising activities and those who spent less than half, are shown in Table 17–3. In all three companies, the high-producing supervisors spent more time in supervising. Thus successful leaders play a *differentiated* rather than an undifferentiated role. That is, they do not play the role of a worker and do the same things he does. Rather, they take on tasks their subordinates cannot do as well: organizing the work, planning on-the-job training, trying to obtain promotions for subordinates, informing subordinates about policies, etc. Every leader, of course, spends *some* of his time in undifferentiated activity, and leaders in some situations spend more time in undifferentiated activity than leaders in other situations. In the same situation, however, good leaders spend more time than poor leaders in differentiated activites.

Workers see and appreciate the results of supervisory planning. The men in the railroad section gangs, for example, were asked, "How good is the foreman at figuring work out ahead of time?" Ten percent of the men under low-producing supervisors answered "not very good" for their supervisor; only 2 percent of men under high-producing

TABLE 17–3.   Which Supervisors Spent More than Half Their Time in Supervising Activities?

Company	Percent of supervisors		
	High-producing	Low-producing	Difference
Insurance company	75	33	42
Tractor company	69	47	22
Railroad company	55	25	30

(*Source:* Kahn and Katz, 1953)

supervisors gave this answer. Workers of planning supervisors also more often felt that they were a part of their group and that their group was better than most in getting a job done.

It is not enough for a leader to try to be considerate. He must actually *be* considerate. That is, the most successful leader is one who best understands his followers. Rifle squad leaders answered the following questions about each of the 10 infantry trainees under them:

1. What is his first name?

2. Has he been on KP during the past week?

3. Has he been on sick call during the past week?

4. Has he had a pass during the past week?

5. What is his rifle qualification score?

6. How many years of schooling has he completed?

7. What was his job before entering the army?

8. What is his principal hobby or interest?

9. What is his ambition for a future civilian career?

A leader's knowledge of his men was measured by the total number of these questions he answered correctly for his squad. His effectiveness as a military leader was measured by (1) ratings by his subordinates; (2) rating by his sergeant; (3) rating by his platoon leader; and (4) his score on a standardized leader reaction test. Conclusion: The greater a squad leader's knowledge of his men, the greater his effectiveness as a leader (Showel, 1960).

It is also not enough for a leader to try to be responsible. He must actually *be* effectively responsible. That is, the most successful leader is one who best understands the job that has to be done and how to organize the work and the workers so that it gets done.

The principles of effective structuring seem to be the same in a wide range of jobs. The Air Force, for example, developed a test of knowledge of such principles consisting of 150 multiple-choice questions like the following (Carp, Vittola, and McLanathan, 1963):

1. Which one of the following is the best reason for the proper use of controls in an organization?
   (a) to maintain discipline in the organization
   (b) to eliminate poor workers and retain good ones
   (c) to assure quality and quantity of production
   (d) to regulate the work flow in a unit

2. Which one of the following is the first factor to consider in
    the preparation of a training problem?
    (a) equipment available
    (b) instructors available
    (c) scheduling the training
    (d) objective of the mission

The leader who tries to be considerate and responsible may not succeed. However, he is not only more likely to be given "A" for effort by his followers but also more likely to succeed in the long run than the leader who does not try. Daw and Gage (1967) had 151 principals in California rate how high they would like their teachers to rate them on each of the following aspects of consideration and responsibility:

Consideration

1. Encourages teachers with a friendly remark or smile.

2. Gives enough credit to teachers for their contribution.

3. Does not force opinions on teachers.

4. Demonstrates interest in pupil progress.

5. Interrupts the classroom infrequently.

6. Displays much interest in teachers' ideas.

Responsibility

7. Enforces rules consistently.

8. Criticizes without disparaging the efforts of teachers.

9. Informs teachers of decisions or actions which affect their work.

10. Gives concrete suggestions for improving classroom instruction.

11. Enlists sufficient participation by teachers in making decisions.

12. Acts promptly in fulfilling teacher requests.

Each principal was then shown the ratings actually given him by his teachers. Two months later, his teachers rated him again. The typical principal (who wanted to be seen as more considerate and responsible by his teachers than they originally saw him) had improved his rating on all the items.

In summary: The success of a leadership style varies with the expectations of those led, with the problems the group faces, with the ability of the leader to play the role the way he wants to, and with whether integration, morale, or productivity is the primary measure of success. However, the authoritative style is most often preferred by group members, is most flexible, and is suited for achieving goals in different areas.

THE DEVELOPMENT OF SUCCESSFUL GROUPS

Everyone is a member of many social groups and has a stake in their success. Everyone, though, has had the experience of being in both effective and ineffective groups. McGregor (1960) contrasted the characteristics of effective and ineffective groups in the following manner:

Effective group	Ineffective group
1. The *atmosphere* tends to be informal, comfortable, and relaxed.	1. The atmosphere reflects boredom, indifference, and tension.
2. Everyone *participates* in the discussion and the discussion remains pertinent to the task of the group.	2. A few people dominate the discussion and often make contributions that are way off the point.
3. The task of the group is well *understood and accepted* by the members.	3. Different members have different, private, and personal objectives that are in conflict with each other and the group's task.
4. The members *listen* to each other! Every idea is given a hearing.	4. Ideas are ignored and overridden and members make speeches intended to impress someone rather than to solve the problem at hand.
5. There is *disagreement* but no "tyranny of the minority." Individuals who disagree do not try to dominate the group or express hostility.	5. Disagreements are either suppressed by a leader who fears conflict, or cause open warfare, or are "resolved" by a vote in which a small majority wins the day.

6. Most decisions are reached by a *consensus* in which it is clear that everybody is in agreement or at least willing to go along.

6. Decisions are often made prematurely before the real issues are examined or resolved.

7. *Criticism* is frequent, frank, and oriented toward removing obstacles.

7. Criticism is present, but is embarrassing and tension-producing. It involves personal hostility and the members are unable to cope with this.

8. Members are *free in expressing their feelings.* Little pussy-footing, few "hidden agendas."

8. Personal feelings are hidden rather than being out in the open.

9. When action is taken, *clear assignments* are made and accepted.

9. Action decisions are often unclear so that no one really knows who is going to do what.

10. There is little evidence of a struggle for *power.* The issue is not who controls but how to get the job done.

10. The formal chairman may be weak or strong but he always sits "at the head of the table."

The leader is the one who has the most obvious influence on the effectiveness of a group. However, followers have the most profound influence, for they determine whom they will follow, how the group will be structured, and whether the communication system works. Consequently, the better everyone understands what leadership is and what conditions determine its success, the more effective groups are likely to become.

What Leadership Is
Leadership is the effort of A to influence B by communication to move toward a goal. Social scientists have been long in coming to general agreement on the usefulness of such an interaction definition. They have been reluctant to give up the individual orientation to leadership. They have slowly learned, however, that it is hard to find traits that consistently distinguish leaders from followers. They have found that many successful leaders have been remarkable for their emotional

control; they have also found, however, that many successful leaders have been remarkable for their *lack* of emotional control. They have found that successful leaders differ from society to society: the leaders among the Manus in Oceania are notable for their aggressiveness; the leaders among the Iroquois are notable for their generous cooperation. They have found that successful leaders differ from organization to organization in our own society: in some organizations the successful leaders have masculine interests; in others, feminine ones (Porter, 1962). They have found that successful leaders may differ from one part of the same organization to another: in one part of a large distributing company, the most successful leaders were the most authoritarian; in another part, the *least* authoritarian (Vroom and Mann, 1960).

The qualities of successful leadership do not lie in either A or B; they lie in the interaction between them. The status of an individual is related to the probability that he will exercise leadership. Leadership, however, is clearly distinguishable from status. Those in the status of parent, for example, normally exercise more leadership than their child; the child, however, sometimes influences his parents more than they influence him.

Leadership is *shared.* While A is trying to influence B, B is also generally trying to influence A. It is impossible for A to influence B without B influencing him in some way. "Followers" may be leaders, lead their "leader," select their leader, and reject their leader. Consider a supervisor directing a subordinate to go on vacation from July 1 to July 20. We note that the supervisor is influencing his subordinate. We may not note, however, that the subordinate is a technician who is hard to replace, and that he has previously told his supervisor that he will quit unless he gets his vacation when he wants it. Who is leading whom?

We influence each other in countless unconscious ways: the man who yawns may cause others to yawn; the speaker who is tense may cause his listeners to become tense; and, in general, many of the things we do may influence what others do without our having any interest or intention of influencing them. We may also influence others by force, e.g., a mother may restrain her child by locking him in his room or a policeman may push a prisoner into a paddy wagon. It is more useful to limit the concept of leadership to influence by communication and by intent, excluding from it unconscious or forceful influence.

Leadership in the home, in the classroom, in the army, as in business, is a process of interaction. The leader influences his followers; his followers influence him. Consequently, the effectiveness of a leader depends most directly upon how he interacts with his followers. The success of this interaction depends, in turn, upon how the group and its leader are selected, how the group is structured, and how the members communicate with each other.

The Selection of the Group

A group can be fitted together on the basis of age, sex, nationality, and local factors which are known to be sources of conflict. Employees of similar seniority generally fit together more readily than those with wide differences in seniority. The placement of men and women in the same work group must be handled with care. The employment of blacks and whites on some jobs must be planned with understanding if it is to be successful.

Sociometry can be a valuable aid in fitting teams together. In its simplest form, it consists of asking (privately) each member of a potential work group to list in order the names of the people he would like to work with. The simplest use of the answers consists in fitting pairs of workers together. This method was used to group 74 carpenters and bricklayers who were working on a large construction project in the Chicago area (Van Zelst, 1952). They were all experienced men on a fixed-wage scale. They were constructing homes in identical rows of eight each, half on one side of the road, half on the other. Before the introduction of the sociometric procedures, careful records of labor turnover and material costs were compiled.

The sociometric procedure was started by assembling the men and giving them the following instructions:

You are now working with a partner who was not chosen by you, nor were you chosen by him. You are now given an opportunity to choose the persons with whom you would most like to work. You can choose any of the individuals in your own group. Write down your first choice, then your second and third choices in order.

On the basis of these choices, the men were first arranged in pairs and then in groups of four. Since the work was of the type that seldom required more than four men to work as a team, the procedure did not go beyond this point. The greater satisfaction of the workers under the new arrangement was suggested by the comments of a typical worker:

Seems as though everything flows a lot smoother. It makes you feel more comfortable working—and I don't waste any time bickering about who's going to do what and how. We just seem to go ahead and do it. The work's a lot more interesting too when you've got your buddy working with you. You certainly like it a lot better anyway.

Highly significant reductions in costs and turnover were found: "The end result in this study has been a happier, more productive worker, who has given management a 5% saving in total production cost."

Groups need leaders. Should one be picked by someone outside the group or by the group itself? The members of a group sometimes pick a poor leader. On the whole, however, they seem to make faster and better choices than anyone else, even in unlikely situations. Ratings by Marine trainees were "a more valid predictor of success in Officer Candidate School and of combat performance" than ratings by superiors. Among Signal Corps trainees, "nominations by class appear to be better measures of the leadership factor than any other variable." Ratings by Air Force trainees were "the most promising OCS criterion found" (Hollander, 1954). Buddy ratings not only predicted success better, but also earlier. For example, buddy ratings predicting which Naval Aviation cadets would complete flight training were as valid as officer ratings that were made a year later. In another study involving military personnel, buddy ratings obtained at an early stage of training proved to be valid predictors of promotion at several successive stages in the soldier's military career. They not only indicated who would be a good non-commissioned officer but also predicted who would be a good officer later on (Amir, Kovarsky, and Sharan, 1970).

Mayfield (1970) asked insurance agents to nominate three other agents in their group for supervisory positions. More than two years later 154 of these agents had been promoted to the position of assistant manager. The superiors who promoted them had no knowledge of the nominations they had previously received from fellow agents. The researcher then compared the assistant managers' rating by superiors after six months on the job with their original rating by fellow agents. Only a third of those who had been given low ratings by their buddies were considered successful. Two-thirds of those who had been given high ratings were considered successful.

It is necessary that leaders want to lead. It is, however, not sufficient. Of 17 studies where boldness scores were related to leadership, 11 showed a positive relationship, 2 showed no relationship. In 4, the most dominating individuals were rejected as leaders (Stogdill, 1948). The importance we attach to boldness in our leaders also varies with the situation. In extracurricular activities, for example, the bolder college girls were, the more likely they were to be leaders. In sororities, however, the bolder they were, the *less* likely they were to be in leadership positions (Guilford, 1959).

The members of a group quickly learn to separate those who are eager to lead men from those who are able to. Sometimes, however, they get stuck with the willing but unable. More often, they have the problem of persuading the able but unwilling member to take the leader's job.

Once selected, followers and leaders need to *stay* selected. The members of a group require time to get to know each other and to develop the close ties upon which support is built. For, like family ties, work ties develop slowly. How much time is suggested by a study of aircraft workers in southern California during World War II (Mayo and Lombard, 1944). Three types of groups were discovered:The *organized* group grew out of the efforts of a skillful supervisor to create a cohesive and cooperative team; the *natural* group was one limited to not more than seven workers on closely related jobs; and the *family* group was one of larger size that was based on a core of relatively long-service workers whose behavior set an example for new workers. The formation of an effective family group took about 6 months. This period of time seemed necessary in order for the example of the older group to be communicated to the newer workers. The departments with the best-developed groups had both good attendance and good output records.

When the stability of groups was about the same, differences in the type of leadership made big differences in the cohesiveness and productivity of the groups. For example, the high cohesiveness and productivity in one department seemed largely due to the efforts of one "leadman." He was a college graduate who did not rank as a supervisor. This man tried to help the individual worker in such ways as listening to him, introducing him to his companions, getting him congenial work associates, and helping him to handle his personal problems. He helped the workers with their technical problems and acted as contact man in the group's relationships with inspectors, time-study men, and the department foreman. Among other things, he arranged trips for the worker to other parts of the plant so that he could see, in place on finished assemblies, the parts he produced.

The Structure of the Group

Groups are popularly supposed to do what someone organizes them to do. It is nearer the truth to say they organize to do what they decide to do. In 1924, the Hawthorne plant of the Western Electric Company in Chicago began an apparently simple experiment to answer the question: What is the best work lighting? The results, however, were hard to understand. For example, workers in an experimental group had their illumination increased from 24 foot-candles to 72 foot-candles. Their production increased significantly, but so did the production of a control group whose illumination remained at 24 foot-candles.

The final illumination experiment led to the conclusion that a new approach was necessary. In this experiment, a group of workers was asked to comment on different intensities of illumination. An electrician came in daily to change the bulbs to increase the illumination. The workers commented favorably on the changes. Experimenters then instructed the electrician to act as if he were changing the bulbs, but actually to put back the same bulbs. The girls commented as favorably on the *apparent* change.

The puzzling results, the persisting desire of the experimenters to solve the puzzle, and the support of the Western Electric Company's management led to a series of experiments lasting more than 10 years. In the relay assembly-room experiments, the work behavior of six girls was intensively studied for several years. Several more years were spent in conducting, recording, and analyzing more than 20,000 interviews with employees and supervisors. For 6 months a single observer recorded the activities of 14 workers in the bank-wiring room as they wired, soldered, and inspected electrical connections. And over a period of years, a personnel counseling program for the plant was planned, developed, and installed.

In 1939, Roethlisberger and Dickson published *Management and the Worker,* the major report of results. It had been preceded by Mayo's *Human Problems of an Industrial Civilization* in 1933 and by Whitehead's *The Industrial Worker* in 1938. All were long and detailed reports. In general, however, the studies showed that groups organize to do what the members informally decide to do rather than what they are formally organized to do. Thus, the way a group is organized to set its goals is an extremely important aspect of its structure.

Letting a group decide on its own production goals is the most certain way of getting the group to accept them. In addition, performance standards the group sets for itself may be higher than those management sets. A psychologist, for example, met with three different groups of workers on the same job, each of whose normal production was 70 units per man-hour. In two of the groups, he discussed the desirability of setting higher goals, but the groups did not decide on specific goals for the following week. Their productivity did not change over the next 3 weeks. In the third group, the desirability of setting higher goals was not only discussed, but a decision to reach 90 units per man-hour the following week was made by the group.Productivity the following week was 86 units; the next week, 92 units; and the third week, 87 units (Bavelas, 1946).

Letting a group decide its own production goals is worker-management cooperation at its highest level. It seldom reaches this level. Managers are least willing to allow workers to make decisions in areas directly concerned with production: the setting of output standards, the planning of production, the utilization of machinery, or the innovation of technological changes. They are more willing to allow them to make decisions that directly concern the worker: on lateness, absenteeism, employee health, discipline, etc. They are most willing to allow them to make decisions in areas where workers and management have an obvious common goal, i.e., accident prevention (Dale, 1949).

Whether managers are willing or not, however, groups *do* make informal but effective decisions about production goals. The following are examples:

In one company, a long assembly line with 1,100 employees assembled exactly 1,500 units on the day shift. The company scheduled higher production and sought to achieve it, but volume stayed at 1,500 units. The hourly production often varied, and by midafternoon, the number of units might be appreciably more or less than that required for a 1,500 day, but by the end of the shift there were always 1,500 units, no more and no less.

In a company with much of its work on either individual or group piece rates, virtually no employee produces above 150 percent of standard. An appreciable number of workers are at the level of 145 to 149 percent of standard, but the decision has been made—and not by management—that it is undesirable to reach or exceed 150 percent of standard (Likert, 1961, p. 211).

The setting of goals is important. It is equally important, however, that workers be motivated to achieve them.

Giving a group information about its performance is one of the most effective ways of increasing its goal achievement. The earlier it can get this information, the better. For example, a company manufactured a heavy boardlike material for the siding of houses. The quality of the material was tested as it came off a long machine. Thus, if something was wrong with the mixture at the beginning of the machine, over 6,000 square feet of the material had to be scrapped. Now the company tests the material in the very early stages, so that workers can make corrections in the mixture if necessary. As a result of this shortened feedback cycle, only a few hundred square feet at most ever have to be scrapped. Without this early information, the group could not have improved its scrap record.

COMMUNICATION

The better the members of a group communicate, the more successful the group is likely to be. Communication is the giving or exchanging of information, ideas, and feelings through talking, writing, or signs. The goal of communication is to deliver the goods: freight or ideas. Both can use a variety of vessels: motorboats or steamships, conversations or telephone calls. The vessels travel in different directions: upstream or downstream, from followers to leader or from leader to followers. Finally, the goods may be accepted or rejected: the receiver may refuse to accept the delivered goods; the group member may accept or reject the suggestions of his leader.

Workers often fail to communicate their feelings to their leader. Table17-4 summarizes data in a study in which workers were asked, "Different people want different things out of their jobs. What are the things you yourself feel are *most important* in a job?" The table shows the percent of 2,499 men who named the listed items as being among their first three preferences. The foremen of the men were also asked to answer as they themselves felt. In addition, they were asked to answer as they thought their men would respond. It is the latter answers by 196 foremen that appear in the table (Kahn, 1958).

The results are clear: Foremen overestimate the importance of economic factors and underestimate the importance of interpersonal relations and morale factors to the worker. The foremen would have been more correct if they had assumed that the workers' ratings would be the same as their own. For example, 39 percent of the foremen and 36 percent of the workers rated "getting along well with people I work with" as among the three most important aspects of the job. Exactly the

TABLE 17-4 Differences between What Foremen Think Their Men Will Say They Want and What Their Men Do Say They Want

Things That Were Important on the Job	As foremen thought men would	As men actually did	Difference
Getting along well with people I work with	17%	36%	−19
Getting along well with my supervisor	14%	28%	−14
Good chance to do interesting work	22%	12%	+10
Good chance to turn out quality work	16%	11%	+ 5
Pensions and other benefits	17%	13%	+ 4
Steady work and steady wages	79%	61%	+18
High wages	61%	28%	+33

(*Source*: Kahn, 1958)

same proportion of foremen and workers (28 percent) rated "getting along well with my supervisor" as important, and so on.

Workers also fail to communicate their feelings to college students. The author asked students to answer the 20 statements in Table 17-5. In all 20 statements, the "true" answer reflects more favorably on the group than a "false" answer. The average college student answers "true" for the 10 statements about the typical college student. He is correct, for the typical college student does answer "true" to all the statements. The average college student answers "false" for the 10 statements about the typical worker. He is entirely mistaken, for the typical worker answers "true" to all the statements about workers.

The problem is not a matter of fact but a matter of feeling. It is not, for example, whether a student or a worker actually takes pride in his work; it is a question of whether he feels and says that he takes pride in it.

In part, good communication in a group depends upon *how* the members try to communicate with each other. The words they use must be easy enough so they can understand each other. The words must also not be subject to *mis*understanding. Thus, a supervisor asked a female employee "to pull with the team." She was insulted because she felt she was being compared to an animal.

In general, however, *what* is communicated is much more important than how it is communicated. The leader who communicates a lack of understanding, respect, or concern for his followers will be ineffective no matter what words he uses. The leader who communicates understanding, respect, and a feeling of accountability for what happens to his followers will be successful no matter what words he uses or how he acts, as the following case illustrates:

The mechanical superintendent in a small manufacturing company was the prototype of the "bull of the woods" manager. He swore at his men, drove them, disciplined them, behaved superficially like a Napoleon. He was the despair of the staff group who were carrying on a program of supervisory training in human relations, Yet, oddly, his subordinates appeared to have high regard for him. They said, "Oh, his bark is worse than his bite." Morale and productivity in his department were both high.

Probing revealed some significant facts. He was known as a "square shooter" who dealt with his men with scrupulous fairness. Despite his superficial toughness he was sincerely and warmly interested in his subordinates. When they were in trouble—whether it was a simple matter of a few dollars to tide

TABLE 17-5   A Demonstration of Poor Communication

The Typical Student

A group of undergraduates was asked to give their impression of the typical undergraduate student here by answering the following statements. Some of the group answered "true" and some answered "false" to each of them. Answer each of these statements, not as you would, but as *you think the majority of the group answered them.**

T F   1. The average student really enjoys learning.
T F   2. He takes pride in his work.
T F   3. He rarely worries about being suspended.
T F   4. He thinks he should learn as much as he can while in college.
T F   5. He believes his education is supported because society will benefit from it.
T F   6. He believes that everyone would benefit if each student did the best he could.
T F   7. He is more interested in relevant than in "snap" courses.
T F   8. He would rather be graded on his performance than on some automatic grading system.
T F   9. He thinks the future of society will be influenced by how much students get out of college.
T F   10. He is seriously interested in learning rather than in just "getting by."

The Typical Worker

Several thousand workers in 150 small and large companies, some of which were unionized and some of which were not, answered the statements below. Some of the group answered "true" and some answered "false" to each of them. Answer each of these statements, not as you would, but as *you think the majority of the workers described the typical worker.*

T F   11. The average worker really enjoys his work.
T F   12. The average worker takes pride in what he does on his job.
T F   13. The average worker thinks that wages are increased primarily because he is able to produce more and needs more to live.
T F   14. The average worker only occasionally worries about being laid off.
T F   15. The average worker feels that the company's investment in new labor-saving equipment generally makes it possible for him to earn more money.
T F   16. The average worker thinks he should be advanced by ability rather than by seniority.
T F   17. The average worker in a plant should turn out as much work as he can.
T F   18. The average worker feels that his company's growth and prosperity depend upon whether he does his work well or not.

T F 19. The average worker feels that his work is important to the company's customers.

T F 20. The average worker believes that everyone on the job would benefit if each worker did the best he could.

a man over until payday, or a family crisis—he helped out in a matter-of-fact way that left no uncomfortable feeling of being patronized.

Most important of all, he was known to be ready to go to bat for his men on any occasion when he felt that they had not been accorded a fair break by higher management. The men spoke with awe of two occasions during a ten-year period when he had stormed into the office of the big boss to demand that a decision be altered because it was unfair to "his boys." When he was refused in one of these instances, he resigned on the spot, put on his hat, and left. His superior actually followed him out to the gate and capitulated (McGregor, 1960, p. 134).

Whether the members of a group and their leader are well matched, whether they have enough power to make their own decisions, and whether they communicate feelings of consideration and responsibility for each other generally depends upon the qualities of the larger organization of which the group is only a part. In turn, the qualities of the larger organization reflect those of the society. In the last chapter, therefore, we turn to the present and future qualities of our society.

SUMMARY

Leadership is the effort of one person in a group to influence its members by communicating with them to move toward goals. The success of the group depends upon the kinds of goals it has, the style of its leader, the leadership standards of the group, and the way in which leaders and followers are selected, the way in which the group is structured, and the way in which the members communicate with each other.

Leaders may have an individualistic style (low consideration and high responsibility), a permissive style (high consideration and low responsibility), an authoritarian style (low consideration and high responsibility), or an authoritative style (high consideration and high responsibility). The individualistic style is likely to be most successful in reaching morale goals; the permissive, in reaching integration goals; and the authoritarian, in reaching short-term production goals. The authoritative style is most likely to be successful in reaching all of these goals, especially if the style is fully accepted by the group. The most successful groups are those in which the members are fitted together, participate in the selection of their leaders, are given detailed information about their performance, are allowed to make decisions on their own, and communicate feelings of consideration and responsibility toward each other.

SUGGESTIONS FOR FURTHER READING

McGregor, D. (1960). *The human side of enterprise.* New York: McGraw-Hill. A brief and informal discussion of the topic by an organizational psychologist who became a college president.

Walker, C. R., and Guest, R. H. (1952). *The man on the assembly line.* Cambridge, Mass.: Harvard Univ. Press. A lucid account of an empirical study of the problems of repetitive work with realistic proposals for their solution.

Roethlisberger, F. J. and Dickson, W. J. (1939). *Management and the worker.* Cambridge, Mass.: Harvard Univ. Press. The final account of the decade of studies at the Western Electric Company that altered the form and spirit of American business organizations.

18

CITIZEN AND SOCIETY

The "hot" issues in America's insurrection against itself, numerous
as they are, form a cohesive and coherent whole within which no
one issue can be separated from the others. These issues are as
follows: a radically new approach to moral values; the black revolt;
the feminist attack on masculine domination; the rejection by young
people of exclusively economic and technical goals; the general
adoption of noncoercive methods in education; the acceptance of
the guilt for poverty; the growing demand for equality; the rejection
of an authoritarian culture in favor of a critical and diversified
culture that is basically new, rather than adopted from the
old cultural stockpile; the rejection both of the spread of
American power abroad and of foreign policy; and a determination
that the natural environment is more important than
commercial profit.

JEAN-FRANCOIS REVEL,
WITHOUT MARX OR JESUS

As man or woman, husband or wife, father or mother, leader or follower, we select the roles we play and decide how we will play them. Society, though, offers the roles from which we select, and sets the standards for playing them. We live in a time of momentous changes in these standards. They are not only changing rapidly, but the speed of change is accelerating. Changes in the physical universe are slow: major changes in the sun, for example, are measurable in billions of years. Changes in the biological world are faster: Ancestral horses changed the size of their bones about 10 percent in a million years. Primitive man evolved still faster: It took him only a half million years to perfect stone implements. The settled life, permanent buildings, and written language of civilized man reduced the time scale to decades. Today, major changes take place in years.

This final chapter seeks to clarify the changing goals we have in playing our social roles, the changing social structures in which we are playing them, and the changing kinds of leaders we are selecting to run these structures. These changes, as we shall see, are forcing more and more responsibilities upon the individual citizen.

THE CHANGING GOALS OF SOCIETY

Society seeks eternally to satisfy the yearnings of people to feel united with others, to engage in activities that are exciting and interesting, and to produce helpful changes that will endure beyond the immediate relationship. However, the priorities within each of these goal areas are temporary: what is seen as the most important product to make, what is seen as the best way of getting people together to make it, and what is seen as the best way of interesting people in making it is always changing. Even more important, the priorities among these areas are constantly changing: sometimes production goals dominate; sometimes, integrative goals; and sometimes, morale goals. Today, these priorities are changing more rapidly than ever before.

The Productive Revolution

All of us see, hear, smell, and use the radical changes that have been wrought by the production revolution. What was a walk toward change has become a trot. Man has always tried to make his work easier to do. He has slowly developed better tools for making use of his energy: the caveman's sharpened stone evolved into a knife. Man has developed ways of controlling the release of his muscular energy to fit his ability to regenerate it: the lever, the inclined plane, and the pulley let him use his energy at a lower rate. He has developed substitutes for his muscles: i.e., animals, water power, and, finally, the power machinery that represented a sharp break with the past and set the stage for the industrial revolution. Over the past few decades, man has developed substitutes for his senses: mechanical seeing, hearing, touching, and even smelling devices that control his mechanical muscles. Now, most revolutionary of all, he is developing substitutes for his brain: computers that receive the mechanical sensations and control the mechanical muscles.

What was a trot is becoming a run. Most social theorists believe that we are in the midst of a major social transformation that is taking us into the postindustrial society of the future. As many see it, it will be a highly productive, automated, and rationalized society that will be characterized by more individual choices, rapid social change, and the demand for high levels of education among those who occupy positions of leadership. It will be a society of large-scale organizations, global communications, and technical approaches to the solution of human problems.

These theorists explain the current rebellion among some of the young as a resistance to the postponed gratification of their needs that the new society demands of them. They must stay in school for many years to gain the highly specialized technical skills that will be required tomorrow. The new society will need systems analysts, computer programmers, high-level scientists, and trained administrators. Some of the young are also rebelling because they feel that they are obsolete, that they have no salable skills, personality, or value orientations that will be useful in this world. Consequently, they rebel in a generally destructive way against rationalism, organization, discipline, and all of the requisites of the postindustrial society. The theorists agree that while the revolt of the young may be destructive in the short run, the rapid movement toward the superindustrial state is unstoppable.

The computer, however, is beginning to side with the young rebels. An international team of physicists, biophysicists, engineers, and computer experts simulated the world situation (Meadows et al., 1972). From this simulation the computer predicted the collapse of world society within a century by the following stages:

1. As population grows, industrial production rises along with rising demands for oil, metals, and other resources.

2. As wells and mines are exhausted, prices go up and money for investment goes down.

3. As investment goes down, industry collapses along with agriculture and services.

4. Finally, population declines rapidly through starvation and disease.

Figure 18-1 Computers can extend the capacity and speed of man's mind, but technical approaches to man's problems are bringing even more prob- lems. (Michigan State University Information Services)

Technological progress will not solve the problem, for pollu- tion will become overwhelming (Figure 18-1). Technological progress + pollution control will not solve the problem, for production will drop to starvation levels. Even technological advance + pollution control + increased agricultural productivity + birth control would eventually grind the world to a halt with rising pollution, falling food output, and falling population. The study found that even the stabiliza- tion of population and of industrial growth would not avoid the eventual disaster (Figure 18-2). It would take zero population growth + zero industrial growth + a "Copernican revolution of the mind" that would shift mankind's attention from economic to religious, artistic, and scientific development to save us from disaster in the next century.

Davis (1970) concludes that the United States is not immune to this disaster. In fact it is peculiarly susceptible to it. Using the amount of natural resources consumed by the average citizen of India in a year, he finds that the average American is consuming these resources at the rate of 25 "Indian equivalents." In terms of Indian equivalents the population of the United States is already over four billion and our

Figure 18-2 In Hong Kong, as well as in many other areas, overpopulation has already drastically reduced the quality of life. (Amy Wegner)

present birth rate is increasing the consumption of resources 10 times faster than that of India. Like living organisms, civilizations vary in their metabolic rates as widely as the hummingbird and the giant turtle. Hummingbird America may be the first to die.

Our production goals, however, are changing as rapidly as goods are being produced. All societies produce not only goods but services: protection as well as food, medical care as well as houses, and education as well as cars. Through history, the production of food has occupied most of the energies of mankind. In the United States today, only 1 in 20 workers is on the farm. Furthermore, over half of the nonfarm workers now wear the white collar of service rather than the blue collar of goods. For the first time, workers in retail trade, administration, communications, research, education, and medical care outnumber the producers of goods. The goal is shifting from the production of "better things for better living" to the production of better people for better living.

Skinner (1971) speaks on behalf of the production of better people:

To contain a population explosion we look for better methods of birth control. Threatened by a nuclear holocaust, we build bigger deterrent forces and anti-ballistic-missile systems. We try to stave off world famine with new foods and better ways of growing them. Improved sanitation and medicine will, we hope, control disease, better housing and transportation will solve the problems of the ghettos, and new ways of reducing or disposing of waste will stop the pollution of the environment. We can point to remarkable achievements in all these fields, and it is not surprising that we should try to extend them. But things grew steadily worse, and it is disheartening to find that technology itself is increasingly at fault. Sanitation and medicine have made the problems of population more acute, war has acquired a new horror with the invention of nuclear weapons, and the affluent pursuit of happiness is largely responsible for pollution.

What we need is a technology of behavior. We could solve our problems quickly enough if we could adjust the growth of the world's population as precisely as we adjust the course of a spaceship, or improve agriculture and industry with some of the confidence with which we accelerate high-energy particles, or move toward a peaceful world with something like the steady progress with which physics has approached absolute zero (even though both remain presumably out of reach) (p. 3-5).

The Disintegrative Revolution

We relate to others to obtain food, to gain shelter, to protect ourselves from physical harm. Fromm (1956) has stressed that above and beyond all of these needs man yearns to feel united with others:

> This awareness of himself as a separate entity, the awareness of his own short life span, of the fact that without his will he is born and against his will he dies, that he will die before those whom he loves, or they before him, the awareness of his aloneness and separateness, of his helplessness before the forces of nature and of society, all this makes his separate, disunited existence an unbearable prison. He would become insane could he not liberate himself from this prison and reach out, unite himself in some form or other with men, with the world outside.

The revolutionary rise in productivity has been accompanied by a revolutionary decline in integration. The cohesiveness of our day-to-day living, of our social order, rests on trust: buying gasoline, paying taxes, or going to the dentist. As trust weakens, integration collapses. Rotter (1971) defined trust as "an expectancy held by an individual or a group that the word, promise, verbal or written statement of another individual or group can be relied on." The items in his measure ask the respondent to indicate how much he trusted teachers, other students, judges, newspaper writers, politicians, etc. People, of course, trust some people much more than others— physicians more than used-car salesmen. However, every year from 1964 through 1970 students in the same elementary psychology class showed a significant decline in trust from the year before. The greatest delines included those in the areas of politics, peace keeping, and communication.

Toffler (1970) pictures the disintegration in a more dramatic way:

The United States is a nation in which tens of thousands of young people flee reality by opting for drug-induced lassitude; a nation in which millions of their parents retreat into a video-induced stupor or alcoholic haze; a nation in which legions of elderly folk vegetate and die in loneliness; in which the flight from family and occupational responsibility has become an exodus; in which masses tame their raging anxieties with Miltown, or Librium, or Equanil or a score of other tranquilizers and psychic pacifiers.

The longer we know people, the more likely we are to trust them. Thus, Rotter (1971) found no decline in students' trust of their parents and those whom they knew well. However, the duration of interpersonal relationships is rapidly declining. The people the feudal villager saw on one day were the same people he had known and would know all of his life. Practically none of the people the active New Yorker sees in a day has he ever seen before or will ever see again. The rapid rise in geographic, occupational, educational, and social mobility has resulted in a rapid decrease in the duration not only of acquaintanceships, but of work relationships, friendships, and marriages.

The longer and more frequently we interact with a person, the more likely we are to like and feel close to him. The feeling that man is in sympathetic relationship with all of nature, that all men are brothers, and that there is a "Fundamental and indelible *solidarity of life* that bridges over the multiplicity and variety of its single forms" seems to be the core around which all religions have formed (Cassirer, 1944). Those of strong religious beliefs seem to be more trusting (Rotter, 1971). At any rate, the modern return to religion may be a reaction to the rising tide of alienation.

In every social organization there is a continuous tension between tradition and innovation. Churches, more than any other kind of institution, have always been heavily weighted in favor of tradition. They still are, but the balance may be rapidly shifting toward a Tom Paine (1945, p. 285) point of view:

> I believe in one God, and no more; and I hope for happiness beyond this life.
>
> I believe in the equality of man; and I believe that religious duties consist in doing justice, loving mercy, and endeavoring to make our fellow creatures happy.
>
> I do not believe in the creed professed by the Jewish church, by the Roman church, by the Greek church, by the Turkish church, by the Protestant church, nor by any church that I know of.
>
> My mind is my own church.

The titles of new books suggest this trend: *The New Religion, What the Religious Revolutionaries Are Saying, The Jesus Trip, The Politics of God, Quotations from Chairman Jesus, Yoga, Youth and Reincarnation,* etc. It is suggested by the wide interest and involvement with drugs as a way to mystical experiences: *The Sacred Mushroom and the Cross.* Dunnette (1969) concludes from his extensive review of T-Group research that the accelerating participation in such groups is dominated by a very personal religious quest. The new ways to religion, in any case, seem to reflect man's old desire for integration and the increasing frustration of this desire in modern society.

The Morale Revolution

Maslow (1948) suggests that human needs are arranged in a hierarchy from low to high. The lower needs are more urgent and take precedent over the higher ones. However, as the concern for the satisfaction of these lower needs wanes, concern for the satisfaction of higher needs emerges:

> It is quite true that man lives by bread alone—when there is no bread. But what happens to man's desires when there is plenty of bread, and when his belly is chronically filled? At once other (and higher) needs emerge and these, rather than physiological hungers, dominate the organism. And when these in turn are satisfied new (and still higher) needs emerge and so on.

The need for self-actualization, the need to become what one is capable of becoming, is the highest of all needs. It is the need to play a role that is intrinsically satisfying because it is self-developing:

> When I was a young engineer I designed a bridge which stands over one of the rivers around Pittsburgh. I got a tremendous

feeling of satisfaction from seeing the bridge actually arise out of the plans I had drawn. I still feel wonderful every time I pass the bridge and point to it and say, "I built that."

A salesman tells about visiting a building in which materials on which he had "worked" were a part of the construction. It made him feel very good to see this because "I sweated out a lot of stuff working the thing out. It really gave me a new inspiration; I really had a feeling that I had a function, that I was an important part of the job."

An accounting supervisor reports that he felt wonderful during the period he was working on installing new IBM equipment. He felt especially good when it turned out after a period of time that the equipment was working, statements were going to come through on time, and a real difference had been made in the functioning of his section (Herzberg, Mausner, and Snyderman, 1959).

As the production revolution has increased the satisfaction of lower needs, higher needs have come to the fore. Husbands and wives now sometimes leave each other, not because they are starving or because they hate each other, but because they bore each other. Assembly-line workers strike, not because the pay is too low or the working conditions uncomfortable, but because the work they are doing is so intrinsically uninteresting. The goal of self-fulfillment and development has increasingly become prominent in the playing of social roles.

To some old institutions like the family and the school, the development of the self has a familiar ring. To most institutions, however, the idea seems strange. The army is set up to win wars, not to provide interesting activities; the factory is run to produce cars, not personalities; and the farm is run to raise food, not to develop the selves of the hired hands. Yet wars cannot be won, cars produced, or food grown by those who will not do what they are supposed to do. More and more of our citizens are acting as if they agreed with Thoreau: "Most of the luxuries, and many of the so-called comforts of life, are not only not indispensible, but positive hindrances to the elevation of mankind." For some, the idea that roles should be designed so that they are interesting to those who must play them is revolutionary. But in the family, in the school, and at work the idea is more and more forced into practice.

The ideal society, then, like the ideal family or team, is one which simultaneously increases productivity, integration, and morale. It is one in which the citizens feel closely bound in deep sympathy with each other, are interested in and developed by the roles they play, and produce the goods and services that in the long run best serve them and their society. Unfortunately, these goals are not only in-dependent but often in conflict—increasing production may decrease integration and morale, increasing integration may decrease produc-tion and morale, and increasing morale may decrease production and integration.

How can society be organized to better achieve all of these goals? It cannot be done, though it has often been tried, by stressing one of these goals and ignoring the others. The behaviorist B. F. Skinner (1948) has described in his novel, *Walden Two*, how he thinks it might be done. His proposal has been violently condemned by many as the preface in Table 18-1 indicates. Desirable or undesirable, the chances that a community anything like the one he describes will ever be created is extremely dim, as he himself more recently has admitted in *Beyond Freedom and Dignity* (1971). What is needed is not the invention of a Utopia but the discovery of the best way to move toward one.

TABLE 18-1   At Walden Two

In 1948, the Harvard psychologist B. F. Skinner published a novel, *Walden Two*. It pictures an imaginary community of several thousand members located about 30 miles from the largest city in a Midwestern state. A fictional psychologist, who describes himself in the novel as "conceited, aggressive, tactless, and selfish," developed the community by applying psychological principles in solving the personal, economic, and political problems involved in social organization. One of his basic principles was that people are happiest and learn best when they are rewarded for doing the correct thing. The community is self-supporting, taxpaying, and monogamous. Its mem-bers vote, serve in the Armed Forces, and are happy. But the fictional philosopher who visits the community calls the psychologist a "fascist."

Life magazine called the book "a menace . . . a travesty on the good life." Joseph Wood Krutch said: "Of all the dictatorships espoused by utopists, this is the most profound, and incipient dictators might well find in this utopia a guidebook of political practice." The clinical psychologist Carl Rogers claims that the book exhibits a "denial, misunderstanding, or gross under-estima-tion of the place of ends, goals or values in their relationship to science." Which of the following statements are true of *Walden Two* and which are false?*

T F   1. Everyone in the community was allowed to choose his own work and might change his choice from time to time.

T F   2. Men and women in the community performed quite different kinds of work.

T F   3. Most men and women married before they were twenty.

T F   4. Seniority was an important determinant of status in the community.

T F   5. Artistic activities consumed a good part of the energies of the community.

T F   6. Members were encouraged to adopt an experimental attitude toward every habit and custom of the community.

T F   7. The lecture was the most commonly employed teaching method.

T F   8. The six members of the Board of Planners were required to do some laboring work every day.

T F   9. School children were not taught specific subjects but only how to learn.

T F   10. The community provided for little personal privacy.

T F   11. Workers who did poorly on their jobs were sometimes expelled from the community.

T F   12. The Board of Planners and the Managers could use the threat of force to ensure compliance with their regulations.

T F   13. Parents were free to give their children any religious training they wished.

T F   14. Propaganda and songs glorifying the community were used to maintain a favorable attitude toward the community.

T F   15. The study of history was considered an essential part of the education of every member of the community.

*Answers are given at the end of the chapter.

THE GROUP SYSTEM OF ORGANIZATION

Social organizations are human inventions designed to reach human goals. Consequently, the revolutionary changes in goals are being accompanied by revolutionary changes in social organizations. More new organizations have been created in the past 20 years than in the entire history of the human race: new universities, new schools, clinics, research institutes, businesses, governmental agencies, and communes.

The half-life of new organizations is short—more likely to be weeks than years. About three-fourths of new organizations fail within the first five years (Sarason, 1972). Some fail because they overlook the tensions and frictions, the contrasts and conflicts between the goals of production, integration, and morale. They may also fail because of their antique organizational patterns.

An "organization" is an arrangement of interdependent parts, each having special functions and relationships to the whole. The critical parts of a social organization are its members. The critical problem of a social organization is finding effective ways of relating its members to each other and to the whole. As mankind has found more effective ways, it has progressed from the tribe, to the city state, to the nation, and, now, to a growing world organization. Our present institutions reflect, in varying degrees, past solutions: the man-to-man system and the bureaucratic system. Slowly, however, these solutions are giving way to the more effective group system of organization. Man-to-man systems stress the individual member and his responsibilities. Decisions are made by individuals, individuals are rewarded for performing their functions well, and the obedience of one individual to another is emphasized. Families may be organized on a man-to-man system. The father makes the decisions: "I am older and more experienced and therefore it is my responsibility to make the decisions." He deals with the members of his family one at a time and relies on his knowledge of them as individuals rather than on his knowledge of them as a social group. He rewards and punishes each individual for his performance and is relatively unconcerned about how his treatment of one individual will affect the other members of the family.

The man-to-man system works best when the problems are simple. The more complex they become, the more ineffective the system becomes. The production manager of a company organized on the man-to-man system went to the president to recommend a model change. The president called in the sales manager, asked for his opinion, made the decision to produce the new model, and gave orders to implement the change. Unknown to the president, however, the production manager had withheld information about a better model that would be harder to produce. The sales manager knew about this but went along with the decision. He thought he could get the president to set a price on the model that would make it easy for him to sell it, although it would be hard for the company to make a profit. When the heads of other departments heard about the decision, they began to plan how they could protect themselves. The man-to-man system resulted in the setting of low goals and the distorting of communication. Bureaucratic systems stress rules rather than individuals. Decisions are made by the rule book, rewards are given for following the rules regardless of the consequences, and loyalty to the rules and to the "bureau" which makes them up has the highest priority. The child in the bureaucratically run family is most aware of the rules he is expected to follow, learns that if he can show that he followed these rules he is safe, and often develops a fanatical loyalty to the "rule book." In general, members feel safer in a bureaucratic than in a man-to-man system. Their effectiveness on both simple or complex problems tends to be less than in the man-to-man system. The members devote too much time and attention to following the rules and too little to achieving ends.

The group system is a happy compromise. The leader in a group system sees his primary task as the development of a productive and well-integrated group with high morale. He sees his real power as arising from group customs and codes. He feels that written rules are a source of authority only when they are understood and accepted by the group.

An episode in the life of an institution organized on the group system shows how it works. The president of a subsidiary of a large corporation was younger (forty-two) than most of his staff and much younger than two of his vice-presidents (who were sixty-one and sixty-two). The subsidiary had done quite well under its previous president, but the young president was eager to have it do still better. In his first two years as president, his company showed substantial improvement. He found, however, that the two older vice-presidents were not effectively handling their responsibilities. Better results were needed from them if the company was to achieve the record performance which the president and the other vice-presidents sought.

The president met the situation by using his regular staff meetings to analyze the company's present position, evaluate its potential, and decide on goals and the action required to reach them. The president had no need to put pressure on his coasting vice-presidents; the other vice-presidents did it for him. One vice-president in particular, slightly younger but with more years of experience than the two who were dragging their feet, gently but effectively pushed them to commit themselves to higher performance goals. In the regular staff meetings, progress toward objectives was watched and new short-term goals were set as needed. Using this group process, steady progress was made. The two oldest vice-presidents became as much involved and worked as enthusiastically as the rest of the staff.

We know the principles of missiles and television. We know much less about the principles of effective human organization and how to apply them. The principles that have been learned from organizations producing missiles and television sets can be applied to the problems of family, school, church, and governmental organizations. The problems are complex. The directions in which we should look for solutions, however, seem clear: give the members of a group all the responsibilities they want and can meet; give the groups all the responsibilities they want and can meet; find the best ways of organizing to encourage these ends. But how can the development of such organizations be encouraged?

The Decentralization of Decision Making

In theory all the responsibility and authority for making decisions in a social institution rests with its head. In practice, however, final decisions on what specific responsibilities are to be assumed and how they are to be met can be made and are made at every level of the organization. The lower the typical level at which such decisions are made, the more decentralized the institution. The more decentralized the institution, the greater the responsibilities of the groups that compose it.

The physical separation of the parts of a large organization encourages decentralization (Figure 18-3). When the units of an organization are hundreds of miles apart, the local units must necessarily make final decisions on many matters. Such physical separation, however, may create more of an illusion of decentralization than a reality. With nearly instant electronic communication and jet planes, those high in the organization can still conveniently make and enforce decisions on the most minor matters. With or without physical separation, many institutions are deliberately decentralizing their organizations to achieve the benefits of giving larger responsibilities to their groups.

Almost accidentally, but fortunately, automation increases the importance of the jobs assigned to groups. Three-fourths of the workers transferred to an automated engine plant said they preferred their new job to the old one, and the more automated the new job, the more they liked it (Faunce, 1958). Ninety-four percent of the workers transferred from an old power plant to a more automated one were more satisfied with their new jobs (Mann and Hoffman, 1960). They said they liked the increased freedom to move around, they liked the increased opportunity to learn while on the job, and above all, they liked their greater responsibilities.

Accelerating change is forcing decentralization. As machines take over routine tasks and changes increase the amount of novelty in the organization, the organization is more and more preoccupied with the solution of nonroutine problems. This requires a degree of imagination and creativity that bureaucracy, with its man-in-a-slot organizations, its permanent structures, and its hierarchies, does not have. Consequently, the more an organization is caught up in the stream of technological and social change, the more decision-making power it must give to its groups to survive.

The Flattening of Organizations

As organizations grow in size, their structure tends to pyramid: one group has one leader; two groups each have a leader and a leader to lead the leaders; the leaders of a hundred groups in the same organization often have twenty leaders to lead the group leaders, four leaders to lead the leaders of the group leaders, and one big leader to lead the leaders of the group leaders. An extremely flat organization, by contrast, would have just one leader of the hundred group leaders. In general, the flatter an organization, the fewer the levels of supervision it has between the top and the bottom. The apparent weakness of the flat

Figure 18-3 A wounded Vietnamese child and the Concord Battle of the American Revolution. The guerilla warfare tactics of the Viet Cong and the similar strategy of the American revolutionaries were highly successful in achieving the goals of war. These armies were most effective because of their decentralized decision-making processes, flattened organizational structure, and the subsequent generalization of responsibility. The small and autonomous groups of fighters were more potent than the larger and better-equipped opposing armies because of the difference in structure. (Wide World Photos; New York Public Library)

organization is that it is impossible for a single leader to know, except in the most general way, what his hundred subordinates are doing. As a consequence, he cannot assign detailed responsibilities to them. The actual strength of the flat organization is that it *is* impossible for the leader to exercise detailed control. This impossibility means that the groups have more responsibilities. And with more responsibilities, they can make more and bigger mistakes. Yet, the more responsibilities that are assigned to a group, the more responsibilities they are likely to accept, struggle to fulfill, and actually succeed in fulfilling. The radical flattening of an organization can, and has, worked. Sears, Roebuck and Company is an example of an organization that deliberately and successfully flattened its organizational structure (Worthy, 1950).

The Generalization of Responsibilities

Generalizing the responsibilities of a group is the most intangible and yet the most comprehensive way of increasing its decision-making power. Consider, for simplicity, an imaginary organization that packs and ships apples, baubles, and cables. Assume, also that the organization is so large that it requires three groups to pack the apples, three to pack the baubles, and three to pack the cables. How can it best organize itself to meet its goals? It might—and if it followed traditional organizational principles, it would—specialize organizational responsibilities. That is, it would have an apple division with three groups of apple packers, a bauble division with three groups of bauble packers, and a cable division with three groups of cable packers. Such a scheme has the advantages of specialization. It does, however, require a higher level of organization to coordinate the activities of the apple, bauble, and cable divisions.

The higher level of organization can be eliminated. Each division might have a group packing apples, a group packing baubles, and a group packing cables. Compared to the traditional scheme, each division would then be independent and have more general responsibilities. The scheme does not fit present trends; it does fit the needs of human beings for enlarged responsibilities.

In sum, we have said, the most cohesive, productive, and interesting modern organizations are likely to be those built upon small and autonomous groups. The development of a society made up of such organizations is encouraged by the flattening of organizations, the generalization of responsibilities, and the decentralization of decision making. To most people, such a society is, at best, an unrealizable ideal. To Toffler (1970), such a society is not only necessary but inevitable:

> One of the most persistent myths about the future envisions man as a helpless cog in some vast organizational machine. In this nightmarish projection, each man is frozen into a narrow, unchanging niche in a rabbit-warren bureaucracy. The walls of this niche squeeze the individuality out of him, smash his personality, and compel him, in effect, to conform or die. . . . In the United States everyone "knows" that it is just such

faceless bureaucrats who invent all-digit telephone numbers, who send out cards marked "do not fold, spindle or mutilate," who ruthlessly dehumanize students, and whom you cannot fight at City Hall. . . .

The kinds of organization these critics project unthinkingly into the future are precisely those lease likely to dominate tomorrow. For we are witnessing not the triumph, but the breakdown of bureaucracy. We are, in fact, witnessing the arrival of a new organizational system that will increasingly challenge, and ultimately supplant bureaucracy (p. 124–125).

THE NEED FOR BETTER LEADERS AND BETTER FOLLOWERS

The country is now on a binge of social reorganization powered by snowballing success in the production of things, by the need to improve the cohesiveness in the society, and by the drive for self development through the changing of role standards. Billions are being plowed into new and old organizations designed to help the poor, the retarded, and the culturally deprived. Individuals and groups come together with money, expertise, enthusiasm, and altruism to solve these problems. The results, on the whole, are disappointing. The disappointment may arise from the effort to create man-to-man or bureaucratic organizations instead of group ones. It may also arise from the failures of leadership and followership.

In the family and in groups, we have seen in the last two chapters, authoritative leaders are most successful. A permissive pattern of leadership can be successful in achieving integration; the individualistic pattern, in raising morale; and the authoritarian pattern, in achieving short-run and simple production goals. However, the over-all success of a group depends upon its ability to achieve integration, morale, *and* productivity. Whether raising children, raising wheat, or raising buildings, it is the authoritative leader who is most likely to achieve this over-all success for it is only the authoritative leader who combines understanding of followers with the knowledge and the ability to get the work of his organization done.

The need for authoritative leadership is increasingly essential in the higher levels of social organizations of which groups are parts. As groups assume more power, they become increasingly separated from each other. As they do, the linking-pin function becomes more critical. The critical linking-pin function in a group system or organization is illustrated in Figure 18-4: The triangles represent the hierarchy of groups in the organization, the small circles the men with a linking-pin function, and the arrows the directions in which these men work.

The top leader who is fulfilling his linking-pin function holds

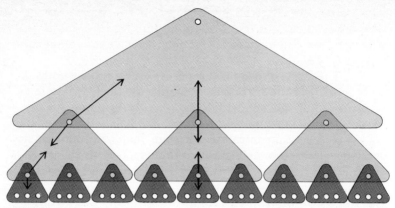

Figure 18-4 The linking pin in the group system of orgnization. The triangles show the groups in the organization; the arrows, the linking pin function. (From Lickert, 1961, p. 113)

frequent meetings with his immediate subordinate. He also holds occasional meetings with the leaders below his subordinate to see if there is any breakdown in the linking process. He may, for example, observe in such meetings that the men are reluctant to talk, that they never question any policy, and that they give evidence of being fearful. These signs suggest to him that his subordinate is failing in the linking function and needs help in building work groups which trust their leaders.

As the group system takes over, leaders must become increasingly skillful in performing their linking-pin function. They must also become increasingly experimental. As the revolutions continue, organizations must change. But the changes they make may not result in improvement. The entrapped leader is one who is committed to the changes he has made rather than to the goals he is trying to achieve by making them. The experimental leader is one who justifies a change on the basis of the importance of the goal, not the certainty of his proposal for reaching it. Consequently, he is ready to go on to other possible solutions if the one first tried fails.

How are the new kind of leaders to be selected? Increasingly, by their followers. On the whole, as we saw in the last chapter, the members of a group make better choices than anyone else. Even if they did not, the leader selected by his followers has the great advantage of having followers who want him to succeed and will help him to do so. In any case, the unobtrusive but increasing prevalence of group systems or organizations is placing more responsibility for the selection of leaders upon the members of the group. It is important for the success of their selection that followers expect and demand that their leaders play a different role from theirs. It is even more important for them to recognize that what they do is more important in determining the success of their organization than what their leaders do.

The Influence of Followers

Followers have a profound influence on their leaders, so much so that one social scientist has suggested:

There is some justification for regarding the follower as the most crucial factor in any leadership event and for arguing that research directed at the follower will eventually yield a handsome payoff. Not only is it the follower who accepts or rejects leadership, but it is the follower who *perceives* both the leader and the situation and who reacts in terms of what he perceives. And what he perceives may be, to an important degree, a function of his own motivations, frames of reference, and "readiness" (Sanford, 1950, p.4).

"Followers" may be leaders, lead their leaders, select their leaders, or reject their leaders because they do not meet expectations. Bowers and Seashore (1967) believe it is a necessary function of the work group to provide leadership to its own members and also to supplement the leadership that the formal hierarchy of the organization provides.

In a democratic society, followers have power over their leaders. The leaders have felt so keenly the power of their followers that they have devised intricate ways of keeping secret what they are doing. Followers, however, are battering at these devices. A psychologist turned politician (Gardner, 1972) organized in 1970 a nonpartisan group in *Common Cause* to find ways of opening the meetings of leaders to citizens and of getting them to reveal who voted for what and why. In a year, the national membership had grown to several hundred thousand and in three years to over a million.

Followers will not follow if they find their problems too simple. If they feel that they face few problems, if they feel they can solve these few with ease, and if they are highly satisfied with things as they are, they cannot be led. This is most often the situation with skilled and experienced groups, for problems that seem hard to the unskilled and inexperienced may seem easy to them (Bass, 1960). As groups continue to meet, leadership acts decrease; as combat crews progress in their training, the trainees participate more and the instructors criticize less; and as intelligence increases, the influence of propaganda decreases.

The closer a group is to its maximum productivity, integration, and morale, the less leadership is possible or necessary; the further a group is from the maximums, the more leadership is possible and desirable. In general, the maximum effective leadership can occur when the problems faced by a group are not so difficult that the members withdraw from them or so easy that little change in behavior is necessary to solve them. Thus, among 45 air crews of 10 members each who discussed work problems, the number of efforts to exercise interpersonal influence correlated with ratings of problems difficulty. That is, as the problems progressed from easy to hard, the number of interactions in the group increased (Ziller, 1955). Again, as problems were made systematically more difficult for 51 ROTC groups of 5 members each, the number of successful leadership attempts increased (Bass and Flint, 1958). When the problems faced by business and government conference participants are made more difficult by the failure of chairmen to lead, more acts of leadership are attempted by the other participants (Crockett, 1955).

Leadership, we have said, is the effort of A to influence B by communication to move toward a goal. The success of leadership is less and less dependent upon whether A is the "leader" or "follower" and more and more dependent upon the amount and, above all, upon the quality of the communication.

THE REVOLUTION IN COMMUNICATION

Revolutions fill the history books. What is different about the modern one? Keniston (1971) concludes that it is the spectacular growth in the "knowledge sector" of our society:

> This sector includes not only universities, scientific laboratories, research institutes, and the world of creative artists but a much broader set of enterprises including corporate research and development, the communications industry, data analysis and processing, the major higher professions, advertising, merchandising, administrative science and personnel management, entertainment, systems analysis and so on. So defined, the knowledge sector is clearly that sector of contemporary industrialized societies which has grown most rapidly in size and power. Often exploited, yet more often manipulating, immensely powerful yet vastly vulnerable; an interest group, but one that possesses unprecedented power, the knowledge sector must be recognized as new.

The accelerating influence of the knowledge sector is reflected in the accelerating growth in formal education. In 1940, less than 40 percent of the work force had a high school diploma; in 1950, 50 percent; in 1960, more than 60 percent; and very likely the percentage will rise to 75 to 80 percent by 1980. At the same time, according to one estimate, the number of bachelor's and first professional degrees awarded in 1980 is expected to be nearly twice the number of such degrees awarded in 1965 (Tickton, 1968), an increase that far exceeds the expected rate of growth of the population. Young revolutionaries are predominantly children of the knowledge sector—the sons and daughters of ministers, artists, scientists, media executives, personnel managers, and advertising men (Keniston, 1971).

The revolution in knowledge is the mainspring driving the wheels of change ever faster in the family and school, in business and art, in church and state. The changes are reflected in new machines and buildings, new music and movies, new attitudes toward abortion and cremation, new forms of organization and leadership.

The conflicts growing out of these rapid changes are intensifying. The new is in conflict with the old and one kind of change conflicts with other kinds. Above all, however, is the problem of adjusting to the *amount* of change. The solution to this problem, suggests Toffler (1970), is anticipatory democracy: the development and use of a new kind of knowledge, a knowledge of what people want their future to be like:

The time has come for a dramatic reassessment of the directions of change, a reassessment made not by the politicians or the sociologists or the clergy or the elitist revolutionaries, not by technicians or college presidents, but by the people themselves. We need, quite literally, to "go to the people" with a question that is almost never asked of them: "What kind of a world do you want ten, twenty, or thirty years from now?" We need to initiate, in short, a continuing plebiscite on the future.

SUMMARY

Rapid increases in productivity, decreases in integration, and increases in morale expectations are hallmarks of the modern revolution in American society. The decline of man-to-man and bureaucratic institutional structures and the rise of group systems of organization are causing, reflecting, and augmenting these accelerating changes. The development of group systems is encouraged by the decentralization of decision making, by the flattening of organizational structures, and by the generalization of the responsibilities of individuals. All of these changes are placing greater power in the hands of individual citizens and are demanding the growth of anticipatory democracy to reduce the disintegrative effects of too chaotic and too much change.

SUGGESTIONS FOR FURTHER READING

*Grier, W. H., and Cobbs, P. M. (1969). *Black rage*. New York: Basic Books (paperback, Bantam). A psychological study of the effects of racism on black America written by two black psychiatrists: " . . . an important book . . . tremendously enlightening."

*Skinner, B. F. (1948). *Walden two*. New York: Macmillan. A utopian novel written by the best known American behaviorist that reveals his ideas about the good society. Far more students were against than for his ideas, but the book makes them think and feel: " . . . an infuriating, frightening novel . . . Walden Two has a different race of man than the outside world. They don't fight, war, whore, get mad, yell, and may not even think."

Toffler, A. (1970). *Future shock*. New York: Bantam. The runaway best seller that projects present trends into the future, dramatizes the human problems being created by these changes, and offers solutions for them.

Smith, H. C., and Wakeley, J. (1972). *Psychology of industrial behavior*. New York: McGraw-Hill (3rd ed.). An elaboration of the problems of social organization outlined in this section and possible solutions to them in work settings.

REFERENCES

Abegglen, J. C. (1958). Personality factors in social mobility: a study of occupationally mobile businessmen. *Genet. Psychol.Monogr.*, **58**, 101–159.

Adams, H. B. (1964). "Mental illness" or interpersonal behavior? *Amer. Psychologist*, **19**, 191–197.

Ainsworth, M. D. S. (1967) *Infancy in Uganda*. Baltimore: Johns Hopkins Press.

Albee, G. W., and Dickey, M. (1957). Manpower trends in three mental health professions. *Amer. Psychologist*, **12**, 57–70.

Allen, G. (1968). Hate therapy: sensitivity training for "planned change." *Amer. Opinion*, **11**, 73–86.

Allport, G. W. (1937). *Personality*. New York: Holt.

Allport, G. W. (1945). Catharsis and the reduction of prejudice. *J. soc. Issues*, **1**, 3–10.

Allport, G. W. (1954). *The nature of prejudice*. Reading, Mass.: Addison-Wesley.

Allport, G. W., Vernon, P. E., and Lindzey, G. (1951). *Study of values: manual of directions.* Boston: Houghton Mifflin.

American Psychiatric Association (1952). *Diagnostic and statistical manual: mental disorders.* Washington, D.C.: Amer. Psychiat. Assoc.

American Psychological Association (1953). *Psychoanalysis as seen by analyzed psychologists: a symposium.* Washington, D.C.: Amer. Psychiat. Assoc.

Amir, Y., Kovarsky, Y., and Sharan, S. (1970). Peer nominations as a predictor of multistage promotions in a ramified organization. *J. appl. Psychol., 54,* 462–469.

Anastasi, Anne (1958). Heredity, environment, and the question "How?" *Psychol. Review, 65,* 197–208.

Anderson, C. R. (1960). *Emily Dickinson's poetry: stairway of surprise.* New York: Holt.

Anderson, J. E. (1949). *The psychology of development and personal adjustment.* New York: Holt.

Anderson, N. H. (1968). Likeableness rating of 555 personality-trait words. *J. pers. and soc. psychol., 9*(3), 272–279.

Andrews, M. G. (1965). Peer imitation by three- and four-year-old children as a function of the conditions of task familiarity. Unpublished doctoral dissertation, Michigan State Univ.

Anonymous (1955). Case report: an autobiography of a schizophrenic experience. *J. abnorm. soc. Psychol., 51,* 677–689.

Armour, J. B. (1954). Student attitudes in relation to classroom achievement. Unpublished Master's thesis, Michigan State Univ.

Artiss, K. L., Bullard, D. M., and Rioch, D. M. (1962). *Milieu therapy in schizophrenia.* New York: Grune & Stratton.

Asch, S. E. (1946). Forming impressions of personality. *J. abnorm. soc. Psychol. 41,* 258–290.

Asch, S. E. (1952). *Social psychology.* Englewood Cliffs, N. J.: Prentice-Hall.

Aserinsky, R., and Kleitman, N. (1953). Regularly occurring periods of eye motility and concomitant phenomena during sleep. *Science, 118,* 273–274.

Ausubel, D. P., and Schiff, H. M. (1955). A level of aspiration approach to the measurement of goal tenacity. *J. gen. Psychol., 52,* 97–110.

Axline, Virginia M. (1947). *Play therapy.* Boston: Houghton Mifflin.

Bacon, Margaret K., Child, I. L., and Barry, H., III (1963). Cross-cultural study of crime. *J. abnorm. soc. Psychol., 66,* 291–300.

Bacon, S. D., and Straus, R. (1953). *Drinking in college.* New Haven, Conn.: Yale.

Bakan, D. (1966). *The duality of human existence: an essay on psychology and religion.* Chicago: Rand McNally.

Bandura, A., and Huston, A. C. (1961). Identification as a process of incidental learning. *J. abnorm. soc. Psychol., 63,* 311–318.

Bandura, A., Ross, D., and Ross, S. A. (1963). A comparative test of the status envy, social power, and secondary reinforcement theories of identificatory learning. *J. abnorm. soc. Psychol., 67,* 601–607.

Barker, R. G. and Wright, H. F. (1951). *One boy's day.* New York: Harper.

Barron, F. (1957). Originality in relation to personality and intellect. *J. Pers., 25,* 730–742.

Barron, F. (1969), *Creative person and creative process.* New York: Holt.

Barry, H., Bacon, Margaret K., and Child, I. L. (1957). A cross-culture survey of some sex differences in socialization. *J. abnorm. soc. Psychol., 55,* 327–332.

Barton, K. and Cattell, R. B. (1972). Marriage dimensions and personality. *J. Pers. and soc. Psychol., 21,* 369–375.

Bass, B. M. (1960). *Leadership, psychology, and organizational psychology.* New York: Harper & Row.

Bass, B. M. and Flint, A. W. (1958). Some effects of power, practice, and problem difficulty on success as a leader. *Tech. Rep. 18* (Contract N70NR35609) Baton Rouge, La.: Louisiana State Univ. Press.

Baumrind, D. (1967). Child care practices anteceding three patterns of preschool behavior. *Genet. Psychol. Monogr., **75**, 43–88.

Baumrind, D. (1971). Current patterns of parental authority. *Developmental Psychol. Monogr.*, **4**, no. 1, part 2.

Bavelas, A. (1946). Group decision in setting goals. In N. R. F. Maier, *Psychology in industry*. Boston: Houghton Mifflin, 264–266.

Bayley, Nancy (1955). On the growth of intelligence. *Amer. Psychologist*, **10**, 805–818.

Bayley, Nancy, and Oden, Mellita H. (1955). The maintenance of intellectual ability in gifted adults. *J. Gerontol.*, **10**, 91–107.

Beers, C. W. (1948). *A mind that found itself*. New York: Doubleday.

Bell, R. R. and Chaskes, I. B. (1970). Premarital sexual experience among coeds 1958 and 1969. *J. Marriage and the Family*, **32**, 81–84.

Benedict, Ruth (1946). *The chrysanthemum and the sword*. Boston: Houghton Mifflin, p. 223.

Bennett, L., Jr. (1964). *What manner of man?* Chicago; Johnson.

Benson, P. (1952). The interests of happily married couples. *Marriage and Family Living*, **14**, 276–280.

Bentler, P. M. (1968). Heterosexual behavior assessment: I. Males. *Behavior Research and Therapy*, **6**, 21–25.

Berdach, E. and Bakan, P. (1967). Body position and the free recall of early memories. *Psychotherapy*, **4**, 101–102.

Berne, E. B. (1964). *Games People Play*. New York: Grove Press.

Berry, J. L., and Martin, B. (1957). GSR reactivity as a function of anxiety, instructions, and sex. *J. abnorm. soc. Psychol.*, **54**, 9–12.

Berry, T. W. (1967). Independence and conformity in subsistence level societies. *J. Pers. and soc. Psychol.*, **7**, 415–418.

Bond, E. D., and Braceland, F. J. (1937). Prognosis in mental disease. *Amer. J. Psychiat.*, **94**, 263–274.

Bossard, J. H. S., and Boll, Eleanor S. (1955). Marital unhappiness in the life cycle. *Marriage and Family Living*, **17**, 10–14.

Bowers, D. G. and Seashore, S. F. (1967). Peer leadership within work groups. *Personnel Admin.*, **30**, 45–50.

Brady, J. P., and Levitt, E. E. (1965). The scalability of sexual experiences. *Psychol. Record*, **15**, 275–279.

Braley, L. S., and Freed, N. H. (1971). Modes of temporal orientation and psychopathology. *J. consult. and clin. Psychol.* **36**, 33–39.

Bridges, K. M. B. (1932). Emotional development in early infancy. *Child Developm.*, **3**, 324–341.

Bronfenbrenner, V. (1961). Some familial antecedents of responsibility and leadership in adolescents. In L. Petrullo and B. M. Bass (eds.), *Leadership and interpersonal behavior*. New York: Holt.

Brown, D. G. (1957). Masculinity-femininity development in children. *J. consult. Psychol.*, **21**, 197–202.

Bruner, J. (1956). Freud and the image of man. *Amer. Psychologist*, **11**, 463–466.

Buhler, Charlotte (1933). The social behavior of children. In C. Murchison (ed.), *Handbook of child psychology*. Worcester, Mass.: Clark Univ. Press.

Burckhardt, J. (1960). *The civilization of the renaissance in Italy*. New York: New American Library.

Burgess, S. S., and Cottrell, L. S., (1939). *Prediction success or failure in marriage*. Englewood Cliffs, N. J.: Prentice-Hall.

Burks, Barbara S., and Roe, Anne (1949). Studies of identical twins reared apart. *Psychol. Monogr.*, **63** (5).

Burnstein, E., Stotland, E., and Zander A. (1962). Similarity to a model and self evaluation. *J. abnorm. soc. Psychol.* **62**, 257–264.

Burrow, T. (1927). *The social basis of consciousness*. New York: Harcourt, Brace.

Byrne, D., and Blaylock, Barbara (1963). Similarity and assumed similarity of attitudes between husbands and wives. *J. abnorm. soc. Psychol.*, **67**, 636–640.

Byrne, D., Clore, G. L. Jr., and Worchel, P. (1966). Effect of economic similarity-dissimilarity on interpersonal attraction. *J. Pers. and soc. Psychol.*, 4, 220–224.

Caldwell, W. C. (1968). *L.S.D. psychotherapy.* New York: Grove Press.

Cameron, N. A., and Magaret, Ann (1951). *Behavior pathology.* Boston: Houghton Mifflin.

Cannon, W. (1932). *The wisdom of the body.* New York: Norton.

Carp, F. M., Vittola, B.M., and McLanathan, F. L. (1963). Human relations knowledge and social distance set in supervisors. *J. appl. Psychol.*, **41**, 78–80.

Carson, R. C., and Heine, R. W. (1962). Similarity and success in therapeutic dyads. *J. consult. Psychol.*, **26**, 38–43.

Cartwright, Rosalind D., and Lerner, Barbara (1963). Empathy, need to change and improvement with psychotherapy. *J. consult. Psychol.*, **27**, 138–144.

Casler, L. (1965). The effects of extratactile stimulation on a group of institutionalized infants. *Genet. Psychol. Monogr.* **71**, 137–175.

Cassirer, E. (1944). *Essay on man.* New Haven, Conn.: Yale.

Castle, Cora S. (1913). A statistical study of eminent women. *Archives of Psychology.* New York: Science Press, No. 27.

Cattell, R. B. (1956). Validation and intensification of the 16 personality factor questionnaire. *J. clin. Psychol.*, **12**, 205–214.

Cattell, R. B. (1965). *The scientific analysis of personality.* Baltimore: Penguin.

Chance, June E., and Meaders, W. (1960). Needs and interpersonal perception. *J. Pers.*, **28**, 200–210.

Chess, S., Thomas, A., and Birch, H. (1959). Characteristics of the individual child's behavioral response to the environment. *Amer. J. Orthopsychiat.*, **29**, 791–802.

Child, I. L. (1965). Personality correlates of aesthetic judgment in college students. *J. Pers.*, **33**, 476–511.

Child, I. L., Potter, E. H., and Levine, E. M. (1946). Children's textbooks and personality development: an exploration in the social psychology of education. *Psychol. Monogr.*, **60** (279).

Childs, B. (1965). Genetic origins of some sex differences among human beings. *Pediatrics*, **35**, 798–812.

Chinard, G. (1957). *Thomas Jefferson.* Ann Arbor: Univ. of Michigan Press.

Chodorkoff, B. (1954). Self-perception, perceptual defense and adjustment. *J. abnorm. soc. Psychol.*, **49**, 508–512.

Clausen, J. A., and Williams, J. R. (1963). Sociological correlates of child behavior. In H. W. Stevenson (ed.). *Child psychology.* Sixty-second Yearbook of the National Society for the Study of Education, Univ. of Chicago Press, 62–107.

Clore, G. L., and McMillan, K. L. (1970). Role playing, attitude change, and attraction toward a disabled other. In: Wiggins, J. S., Renner, K. E., Clore, G. L. and Rose, R. J. (1971). *The psychology of personality.* Reading, Mass.: Addison-Wesley, 106–07.

Cofer, C. N., and Dunn, J. T. (1952). Personality ratings as influenced by verbal stimuli. *J. Pers.*, **21**, 223–227.

Cohen, D., Whitmyre, J. W., and Funk, W. H. (1960). Effect of group cohesiveness and training upon creative thinking. *J. appl. Psychol.*, **44**, 319–322.

Coleman, J. C. (1964). *Abnormal psychology and modern life.* (3rd ed.) Chicago: Scott, Foresman.

Conrad, J. (1912). *A personal record.* New York: Harper.

Corry, J. (1966). Current sexual behavior and attitudes. In Ruth and Edward Brecher (eds.), *An analysis of human sexual response.* New York: New American Library.

Corsini, R. J. (1956). Understanding and similarity in marriage. *J. abnorm. soc. Psychol.*, **52**, 327–332.

Cortes, J. B., and Gatti, Florence M. (1965). Physique and self-description of temperament. *J. consult. Psychol.*, **29**, 432–439.

Cottle, T. (1967). The circle test: an investigation of perceptions of temporal relatedness and dominance. *J. proj. tech. and Pers. Assessment*, **31**, 58–71.

Court-Brown, W. M. (1968). Males with an XYY sex chromosome complement. *J. Med. Genet.*, **5**, 341–359.

Cox, C. M. (1926). *Genetic studies of genius: II. The early mental traits of three hundred geniuses*. Stanford, Calif.: Stanford Univ. Press.

Coyle, E. (1955). Psychology and slychology. *Amer. Psychologist*, **10**, 87.

Crockett, W. H. (1955). Emergent leadership in small, decision-making groups. *J. abnorm. soc. Psychol.*, **51**, 378–382.

Crutchfield, R. S. (1955). Conformity and character. *Amer. Psychologist*, **10**, 191–198.

Dale, E. (1949). Greater productivity through labor-management cooperation. *Amer. Managem. Assoc. Research Reports*, **14**.

Danish, S. J. and Kagan, N. (1971). Measurement of affective sensitivity toward a valid measure of interpersonal perception. *J. counseling psychol.*, **18**, 51–54.

Darley, J. G. (1937). Tested maladjustment related to clinically diagnosed maladjustment. *J. appl. Psychol.*, **21**, 632–642.

Darley, J. G. (1957). Tested maladjustment related to clinically diagnosed maladjustment. *J. appl. Psychol.*, **21**, 632–642.

Davidson, M., McInnes, R., and Parnell, R. (1957). The distribution of personality traits in seven-year-old children: a combined psychological, psychiatric and somatotype study. *Brit. J. educ. Psychol.*, **27**, 48–51.

Davis, W. H. (1970). Overpopulated America. *New Republic*, January 10.

Daw, R. W., and Gage, N. L. Effect of feedback from teachers to principals. *J. educ. Psychol.* 1967, **58**, 181–188.

Dawson, J. E. (1970). Consideration and ICS: Instructor leadership influencing student performance. Unpublished master's thesis, Michigan State Univ.

Dewey, J. (1939). *Art as experience.*. New York: Putnam.

Dollard, J. (1942). *Victory over fear*. New York: Reynal & Hitchcock.

Doré, R. (1960). The development and validation of forced-choice scales measuring attitudes toward leadership methods. Unpub. master's thesis, Michigan State Univ.

Dubois, Cora (1955). The dominant value profile of American culture. *Amer. Anthrop.*, **57**, 1232–1239.

Dunnette, M. D. (1969). People feeling: joy, more joy, and the "Slough of Despond." *J. appl. behavioral Sci.*, **1**, 26.

Dymond, Rosalind (1949). A scale for measurement of empathic ability *J. consult. Psychol.*, **13**, 127–133.

Dymond, Rosalind (1954). Interpersonal perception and marital happiness. *Canad. J. Psychol.*, **8**, 164–171.

Eastman, D. (1958). Self-acceptance and marital happiness. *J. consult. Psychol.* **22**, 95–99.

Eaton, J. W., and Weil, R. J. (1955). *Culture and mental disorders*. New York: Free Press of Glencoe.

Edwards, A. L. (1954). *Edwards personal preference schedule*. New York: Psychological Corp. (manual).

Edwards, D. A. (1968). Mice: fighting by neonatally androgenized females. *Science*, **161**, 1027–1028.

Egner, R. E., and Dennon, L. E. (eds.) (1962). *The basic writings of Bertrand Russell*. New York: Simon and Schuster.

Ehrlich, H. J., and Lipsey, C. (1968). Affective style as variable in person perception. *J. Pers.*, 522–540.

Ehrmann, W. W. (1959). *Premarital dating behavior.* New York: Holt.

Eiduson, Bernice T. (1958). Artist and non-artist: a comparative study. *J. Pers.*, **26**, 13–28.

Ellis, A., and Fuller, E. W. (1950). The sex, love, and marriage questions of senior nursing students. *J. soc. Psychol.*, **31**, 209–216.

Ellson, D. G. (1941). Hallucinations produced by sensory conditioning. *J. exp. and soc. Psychol.* **28**, 1–20.

Erickson, M. H. (1939). Experimental demonstrations of the psychopathology of every-day life. *Psychoanal. Quart.*, **8**, 338–353.

Eron, L. D., Huesmann, L. R., Lefkowitz, M. M., and Walder, L. (1972). Does television violence cause aggression? *Amer. Psycholgist*, **27**, 253–263.

Ewalt, J. R., Strecker, E. A., and Ebaugh, F. G. (1957). *Practical clinical psychiatry.* New York: McGraw-Hill.

Eysenck, H. J. (1952). The effect of psychotherapy: an evaluation. *J. consult. Psychol.*, **16**, 319–324.

Fairweather, G. W., Sanders, D. H., Maynard, H., Cressler, D. L., and Bleck, D. S. (1969). *Community life for the mentally ill.* Chicago: Aldine.

Farber, L. H. (1966). Ours is the addicted society. *New York Times Magazine*, December 11, p. 43ff.

Faris, R. E.L., and Dunham, H. W. (1939). *Mental disorders in urban areas.* Chicago: Univ. of Chicago Press.

Farrell, J. T. (1954). *Reflections at fifty and other essays. New York: Vanguard Press.*

Faunce, W. A. (1958). *Automation and the automobile worker. Soc. Problems*, **6**, 68–78.

Feldman, M. P. (1966). Aversion therapy for sexual deviations: a critical review. *Psychological Bull.* **65**, 65–79.

Feldman, M. P. and MacCulloch, M. J. (1965). The application of anticipatory avoidance learning to the treatment of homosexuality: I. Theory, technique, and preliminary results. *Behavior Research and Therapy*, **2**, 165–183.

Feldman, P. E. (1957). Clinical evaluation of chlorpromazine therapy for mental illness. *J. clin. and exp. Psychopathology*, **18**, 1–16.

Feshbach, S. (1955). The drive-reducing function of fantasy behavior. *J. abnorm. soc. Psychol.*, **50**, 3–11.

Feshbach, N. D. and Roe, K. (1968). Empathy in six- and seven-year-olds. *Child Developm.*, **39**, 133–45.

Feiffer, J. (1971). Playboy interview. *Playboy*, September, 81.

Fever, G., and Broadhurst, P. L. (1962). Thyroid function in rats selectively bred for emotional elimination: III. Behavioral and physiological changes after treatment with drugs acting on the thyroid. *J. Endocrinology*, **24**, (4), 385–396.

Fiedler, F. E. (1950a). The concept of an ideal therapeutic relationship. *J. consult. Psychol.*, **14**, 239–245.

Fiedler, F. E. (1950b). A comparison of therapeutic relationships in psychoanalytic, nondirective and Adlerian therapy. *J. consult. Psychol.*, **14**, 463–445.

Fisher, C., and Dement, W. C. (1963). Studies on the psychopathology of sleep and dreams. *Amer. J. Psychiatry*, **119**, 1160–1168.

Fisher, S. C. (1948). Relationships in attitudes, opinions, and values among family members. Univer. Calif. Publ. Culture Soc., **2**, 29–100.

Fisher, S. (1973). *The female orgasm.* New York: Basic Books.

Fitzgerald, H.E., Ledesma, S., Swarthout, W., and Parker, A. (1972). Orientation manual for trainees in infant-toddler day care. *Institute for Family and Child Study*, Michigan State Univ.: Lansing.

Fitzgibbon, C. (1965). *The life of Dylan Thomas.* Boston: Little, Brown.

Fitzgibbons, D. J., and Shearn, C. R. (1972). Concepts among mental health professionals: a factor analytic study. *J. consult. and clin. Psychol.*, **38**, 288–295.

Fleishman, E. A. (1953). The description of supervisory behavior. *J. Psychol.*, **37**, 1–6.

Fleishman, E. A., and Salter, J. A., (1963). Relation between the leader's behavior and his empathy toward subordinates. *J. indust. Psychol.*, **1**, 79–84.

Ford, C. S., and Beach, F. E. (1951). *Patterns of sexual behavior*. New York: Hoeber-Harper.

Freud, S. (1961). *Civilization and its discontents*. New York: Norton.

Friedan, Betty (1964). *The feminine mystique*. New York: Norton.

Fromm, E. (1956). *The art of loving*. New York: Harper. (Bantam ed., 1963).

Gagné, R. M., and Fleishman, E. A. (1959). *Psychology and human performance*. New York: Holt.

Galton, F. (1909). *Memories of my life*. New York: Dutton.

Galvin, J. A. V., and MacDonald, J. M. (1959). Psychiatric study of a mass murder. *Amer. J. Psychiat.*, **115**, no. 12, 1057–1061.

Gardner, J. W. (1972). *In common cause*. New York: Norton.

Geller, J. J. (1950). Current status of group psychotherapy practice in the state hospitals for mental disease. *Group Psychother.*, **3**, 231–240.

Gerard, D. L., and Houston, G. (1953). Family setting and the social ecology of schizophrenia. *Psychiat. Quart.*, **27**, 90–101.

Giedt, F. H. (1955). Comparison of visual content and auditory cues in interviewing. *J. consult. Psychol.*, **19**, 407–416.

Giedt, F. H. (1958). Cues associated with accurate and inaccurate interview impressions. *Psychiatry*, **21**, 405–409.

Gillespie, J. M. (1954). In G. W. Allport, *The nature of prejudice*. Reading, Mass.: Addison-Wesley.

Ginsbury, G. B., and Alee, W. C. (1942). Some effects of conditioning on social dominance and subordination in inbred strains of mice. *Physiol. Zool.*, **15**, 586–606.

Given, W. B., Jr. (1949). *Bottom-up management*. New York: Harper & Row.

Glavis, L. R., Jr., (1946). Bombing mission number fifteen. *J. abnorm. soc. Psychol.*, **41**, 189–198.

Gleason, W. J. (1957). Predicting army leadership ability by modified leaderless group discussing. *J. appl. Psychol.*, **41**, 231–235.

Glueck, S., and Glueck, E. (1950). *Unravelling juvenile delinquency*. Cambridge, Mass.: Harvard.

Goethals, G. W., and Klos, D. S. (1970). *Experiencing youth*. Boston: Little, Brown.

Goffman, E. (1952). On cooling the mark out: some aspects of adaptation to failure, *Psychiatry*, **15**, 451–463

Goldfarb, W. (1949). Rorschach test differences between family-reared, institution-reared, and schizophrenic children. *Amer. J. Orthopsychiat.*, **19**, 624–633.

Gollin, E. (1954). Forming impressions of personality. *J. Pers.*, **23**, 65–76.

Gottesman, I. (1963) I. Heritability of personality: a demonstration. *Psychol. Monogr.*, **77**, No. 9 (Whole No. 572), pp. 1–21.

Gough, H. G. (1952). On making a good impression. *J. educ. Res.*, **46**, 33–42.

Gough, H. G. (1954). A preliminary guide for the use and interpretation of the California psychological inventory. Berkeley, Calif.: Univ. Calif. Inst. Pers. Assessment Res. (manual).

Griffin, J. H. (1960). *Black like me*. Boston: Houghton Mifflin.

Grinder, R. E., and McMichael, R. E. (1963). Cultural influence on conscience development: resistance to temptation and guilt among Samoans and American Caucasians. *J. abnorm. soc. Psychol.*, **66**, 503–507.

Grinker, R. R., and Spiegel, J. P. (1945). *Men under stress*. New York: McGraw-Hill.

Grossman, B. A. (1963). The measurement and determinants of interpersonal sensitivity. Unpublished master's thesis, Michigan State Univ.

Grossman, B. A. (1967). Evaluation of a training program to improve the ability to differentiate between people. Unpublished Ph.D. thesis, Michigan State Univ.

Guilford, J. P. (1940). *An inventory of factors STDCR.* Beverly Hills, Calif.: Sheridan Supply.

Guilford, J. P. (1959). *Personality.* New York: McGraw-Hill.

Guilford, J. P., and Martin, H. (1944). Age differences and sex differences in some introvertive and emotional traits. *J. gen. Psychol.,* **31,** 219–299.

Guilford, J. P., Wilson, R. C., and Christensen, P. R. (1952). A factor-analytic study of creative thinking: II. Administration of test and analysis of results. *Rep. psychol. Lab.,* no. 8.

Gunders, S. M., and Whiting, J. W. M. (1964). The effects of periodic separation from the mother during infancy upon growth and development. Paper presented at Int. Congr. of Anthropological Ethnological Sciences, August, 1964.

Hall, C. S. (1938). The inheritance of emotionality. *Sigma Xi Quart.,* **26,** 17–27.

Hall, C., and Van de Castle, R. (1965). An empirical investigation of the castration complex in dreams. *J. Pers.,* **33,** 2–29.

Hall, J. F., Warren, J. M., and Harlow, H. F. (1955). The effects of reserpine (Serpasil) on the delayed response in monkeys. *J. Psychol.,* **40,** 159–161.

Hamid, P. N. (1968). Style of dress as a perceptual cue in impression formation. *Perceptual motor skills,* **26,** 904–906.

Hamilton, Edith (1964). *The Greek way.* New York: Norton.

Handler, L., and Rehyer, J. (1966). Relationship between GSR and anxiety indexes in projective drawings. *J. consult. Psychol.,* **30,** 6–67.

Hansel, M. (1966). *ESP: a Scientific evaluation.* New York: Scribner.

Harding, L. W. (1944). A value type generalization test. *J. soc. Psychol.,* **40,** 324–328.

Harding, W. R. (1965). *The days of Henry Thoreau.* New York: Knopf.

Harlow, H. F. (1958). The nature of love. *Amer. Psychologist,* **13,** 673–685.

Harlow, H. F., and Harlow, M. R. (1962). Social deprivation in monkeys. *Sci. Amer.,* **207** (5), 136–146.

Harlow, H. F., Harlow, M. K., Dodsworth, R. O., and Arling, G. L. (1966). The maternal behavior of rhesus monkeys deprived of mothering and peer associations in infancy. *Proceeding of the American Philosophical Society,* **110,** 58–66.

Hartshorne, H., and May, M. A. (1928). *Studies in deceit.* New York: Macmillan.

Hastorf, A. H., and Cantril, H. (1954). They saw a game: a case study. *J. abnorm. soc. Psychol.,* **49,** 129–134.

Hattwick, L. A. (1937). Sex differences in behavior of nursery school children. *Child Develpm.,* **8,** 343–355.

Havron, M. D., and McGrath, J. E. (1961). The contribution of the leader to the effectiveness of small military groups. In L. Petrullo and M. B. Bass (eds.), *Leadership and interpersonal behavior.* New York: Holt.

Haythorn, W. (1958). The effects of varying combinations of authoritarian and equalitarian leaders and followers. In E. E. Maccoby, T. M. Newcomb, and E. L. Hartley (eds.), *Readings in social psychology.* (3rd ed.) New York: Holt.

Hazo, R. G. (1967). *The idea of love.* New York: Praeger.

Healy, W., Bronner, A. F., and Bowers, A. M. (1931). *The Structure and Meaning of Psychoanalysis.* New York: Knopf.

Heath, D. H. (1965). *Explorations of maturity.* New York: Appleton-Century-Crofts.

Helson, R. (1965). Childhood interest clusters related to creativity in women. *J. consult. Psychol.,* **29,** 352–361.

Henry, W. E., Sims, H. H., and Spray, S. L. (1971). *The fifth profession.* New York: Jossey-Bass Behavior Science Series.

Hertz, M. R. (1942). Personality patterns in adolescence as portrayed by Rorschach ink-blot method: I. Movement factors. *J. gen. Psychol.,* **27,** 119–188.

Herzberg, F., Mausner, B., and Capwell, D. F. (1957). *Job attitudes: review of research and opinion.* Pittsburgh: Psychological Services of Pittsburgh.

Herzberg, F., Mausner, B., and Snyderman, B. (1959). *The motivation to work.* New York: Wiley.

Hirsch, Ada C. (1953). Possibilities of self-analysis. Summary of lecture 73 delivered before the Auxiliary Council to the Ass. for the Advancement of Psychoanal.

Hoffer, A., and Osmond, H. (1959). The adrenochrome model and schizophrenia. *J. nerv. and ment. Dis.*, **128**, 18–35.

Hogan, R. and Manking, D. (1970). Personality correlates of undergraduate marijuana use. *J. consult. and clin. Psychol.* **35**, 58–73.

Hollander, E. P. (1954). Buddy ratings: military research and industrial implications. *Personnel Psychol.* **7**, 385–393.

Hollingshead, A. B. (1942). *Children above 180 IQ.* New York: Harcourt, Brace & World.

Hollingshead, A. B. (1950). Cultural factors in the selection of marriage mates. *Amer. sociol. Rev.*, **15**, 619–627.

Hollingshead, A. B., and Redlich, F. C. (1958). *Social class and mental illness.* New York: Wiley.

Hollister, L. E., Traub, L., and Beckman, W. G. (1956). Psychiatric use of reserpine and chlorpromazine: results of double-blind studies. In N. S. Kline (ed.), *Psychopharmacology.* Washington, D.C.: Amer. Ass. for the Advancement of Sci., pp. 65–74.

Holmes, Frances B. (1936). An experimental investigation of a method of overcoming children's fears. *Child. Develpm.*, **7**, 6–30.

Honzik, Marjorie P. (1963). A sex-difference in the age of onset of the parent child resemblance in intelligence. *J. educ. Psychol.*, **54**, 231–237.

Hoppock, R. (1935). *Job satisfaction.* New York: Harper.

Horton, D. (1943). The functions of alcohol in primitive societies; a cross-cultural study. *Quart. J. Stud. Alcohol.*, **4**, 199–320.

Hudson, J. (1947). The new orthodoxy and human progress. In H. Wieman, *Religious liberals reply.* Boston: Beacon Press.

Hurley, J. R. (1965). Parental acceptance-rejection and children's intelligence. *Merrill-Palmer Quarterly*, **11**, 19–31.

Huxley, A. (1932). *Brave new world.* New York: Harper.

Jack, L. M. (1934). An experimental study of ascendant behavior in preschool children. *Univ. Iowa Stud. Child Welf.*, **9** (3), 4–18.

Jacob, P. E. (1957). *Changing values in college: an exploratory study of the impact of college teaching.* New York: Harper.

Jacobs, P. A., Brunton, M., Melville, M. M., Brittain, R. P., McClemont, W. F. (1965). Aggressive behavior, mental subnormality and the XYY male. *Nature*, **209**, 1351–1352.

Jacobs, P. A., Brunton, M., Melville, M. H., Brittain, R. P., and Whatmore, P. B. (1968). Chromosome studies on men in a maximum security hospital. *Annals of Human Genetics*, **31**, 339–351.

James, W. (1890). *Principles of psychology.* New York: Holt.

James, W. (1929). *Varieties of religious experience.* New York: Modern Library.

James, W. (1955). *Pragmatism.* New York: Meridian Books.

James, W. (1956). *The will to believe and other essays in popular philosophy.* New York: Dover Publishers.

James, W. T. (1951). Social organization among dogs of different temperaments, terriers and beagles, reared together. *J. comp. physiol. Psychol.*, **47**, 71–77.

Janis, I. L., Mahl, G. F., Kagan, J., and Holt, R. R. (1969). *Personality: dynamics, development, and assessment.* New York: Harcourt, Brace & World.

Joad, C. E. M. (1928). *Matter, life and value.* London: Oxford Univ. Press.

Johnson, S. K. (1972). A woman anthropologist offers a solution to the woman problem. *New York Times Magazine*, August 27, p. 7ff.

Johnson, W. B., and Terman, L. M. (1935). Personality characteristics of happily married, unhappily married and divorced persons. *Charact. & Pers.*, **3**, 290–311.

Jones, E. (1957). *Life and work of Sigmund Freud*. 3 vols. New York: Basic Books.

Jowett, B. (h.d.). *The works of Plato*. New York: Tudor.

Jung, C. G. (1965). *Memories, dreams, reflections*. New York: Vintage Books.

Kagan, J. (1966). Reflection-impulsivity: the generality and dynamics of conceptual tempo. *J. abnorm. soc. Psychol.*, **71**, 17–24.

Kagan, J. and Moss, H. A. (1962). *Birth to maturity: a study in psychological development*. New York: Wiley.

Kahn, R. L. (1958). Human relations on the shop floor. In E. M. Hugh-Jones (ed.), *Human relations and modern management*. Amsterdam: North Holland Publishing Company.

Kahn, R. L., and Katz, D. (1953). Leadership practices in relation to productivity and morale. In D. Cartwright and A. Zander (eds.), *Group dynamics*. New York: Harper & Row.

Kallman, F. J. (1953). *Heredity in health and mental disorder*. New York: Norton.

Kapp, F. T., Rosenbaum, M., and Romano, J. (1947). Psychological factors in men with peptic ulcers. *Amer. J. Psychiat.*, **103**, 700–704.

Karp, S. A., Poster, Dorothy, C., and Goodman, A. (1963). Differentiation in alcoholic women. *J. Pers.*, **31**, 386–393.

Kayton, R. and Biller, H. B. (1972). Sex-role development and psychopathology in adult males. *J. consult. and clin. Psychol.* **38**, 208–210.

Keller, H. (1908). *The story of my life*. New York: Doubleday (with supplementary account).

Kelley, H. H. (1955). Warm-cold variable in first impressions. *J. Pers.*, **18**, 431–439.

Kelly, E. L. (1955). Consistency of the adult personality. *Amer. Psychologist*, **10**, 659–681.

Keniston, K. (1971) *Youth and dissent*. New York: Harcourt, Brace, and Jovanovich.

Kerckhoff, A. F., and Davis, K. E. (1962). Value consensus and need complementarity in mate selection. *Amer. Sociol. Rev.*, **27** (3), 295–303.

Kety, S. (1959). Biochemical theories of schizophrenia. *Science*, **129**, 1528–1532.

Kinsey, A. C., Pomeroy, W. B., and Martin, C. E. (1948). *Sexual behavior in the human male*. Philadelphia: Saunders.

Kinsey, A. C., Pomeroy, W. B., Martin, C. E., and Gebbard, P. H. (1953). *Sexual behavior in the human female*. Philadelphia: Saunders.

Kipnis, D., and Resnick, J. H. (1971). Experimental prevention of underachievement among intelligent impulsive college students. *J. consult. and clin. Psychol.*, **36**, 53–60.

Klugman, S. F. (1948). Emotional stability and level of aspiration. *J. gen. Psychol.*, **38**, 101–118.

Knapp, R. H., and Goodrich, H. B. (1952). *Origins of American scientists*. Chicago: Univ. of Chicago Press.

Kohlberg, L. (1969) Stage and sequence: the cognitive-developmental approach to socialization. In D. A. Goslin (ed.), *Socialization theory and research*. Chicago: Rand McNally, 347–380.

Kuckenberg, C. (1963). The effects of early father absence. Unpublished master's thesis, Harvard University.

Kukuk, W. (1960). Traits of college drinkers. Unpublished master's thesis, Michigan State Univ.

Kurtz, R. R., and Grummon, D. L. (1972). Different approaches to the measurement of therapist empathy and their relationship to therapy outcomes. *J. consult. and clin. Psychol.*, **39**, 106–115.

Landis, C., and Hamwi, V. (1954). Some prognostic criteria for recovery from psychosis following psychosurgery. *Psychiat. Quart. Suppl.*, **28**, 78–83.

Landis, C., Landis, A. T., and Bolles, M. M. (1940). *Sex in development*. New York: Hoeber-Harper.

Lang, P. J., and Lazovik, A. D. (1963). Experimental desensitization of a phobia. *J. abnorm. soc. Psychol.*, **66**, 519–525.

Langer, S. (1962). The cultural importance of art. In: *Philosophical Sketches*. Baltimore: Johns Hopkins Press.

Lansing, A. (1959). *Endurance*. New York: McGraw-Hill.

Lazarus, A. A. (1966). Behavior rehearsal vs. nondirective counseling vs. advice in effecting behavior change. *Behavior Research and Therapy*, **4**, 209–212.

Lear, J. (1972). Where is society going? *Saturday Review*, April 15, 34–39.

Leavitt, H. J. (1958). *Managerial psychology*. Chicago: Univ. of Chicago Press.

Levy, D. M. (1942). Psychosomatic studies of some aspects of maternal behavior. *Psychosom. Med.*, **4**, 223–227.

Levy, D. M. (1943). *Maternal overprotection*. New York: Columbia Univ. Press.

Lewin, K. (1951). Field theory in social science: selected theoretical papers. New York: Harper.

Lewis, N. D. C., and Pietrowski, Z. A. (1954). Clinical diagnosis of manic-depressive psychosis. In P. H. Hoch and J. Zubin (eds.), *Depression*. New York: Ronald. Pp. 389–412.

Likert, R. (1958). Measuring organizational performance. *Harvard Business Rev.*, **36**, 41–50.

Likert, R. (1961). *New patterns of management*. New York: McGraw-Hill.

Likert, R., and Katz, D. (1948). Supervisory practices and organizational structures as they affect employee productivity and morale. *Amer. Mgmt. Ass. Personnel Ser.*, no. 120.

Lieberman, M. A., Yalom, I. D., and Miles, M. B. (1973). *Encounter groups: first facts*. New York: Basic Books.

Linden, J. (1965). The self-centered orientation in interpersonal relationships. Unpublished master's thesis, Michigan State Univ.

Lipman-Blumen, J. (1972). How ideology shapes women's lives. *Sci. Amer.* **226**, 34–42.

Lipscomb, A. A., and Bergh, A. E. (eds.) (1903). *The writings of Thomas Jefferson*. Vol. 14. Thomas Jefferson Memorial Ass. Pp. 48–50.

Locke, H. J. (1951). *Predicting adjustment in marriage*. New York: Holt.

Loevinger, Jane (1966). The meaning and measurement of ego development. *Amer. Psychologist*, **21**, 195–206.

Look Magazine. January 10, 1967.

Loranger, A. W., Prout, C. T., and White, Mary Alice (1961). The placebo effect in psychiatric drug research. *J. Amer. Med. Ass.* **176**, 920–925.

Lykken, D. T. (1959). The GSR in the detection of guilt. *J. appl. Psychol.*, **43**, 385–388.

Lynn, D. B. (1959). A note on sex differences in the development of masculine and feminine identification. *Psychol. Rev. 66*, 126–135.

MacArthur, R. S. (1955). An experimental investigation of persistence in secondary school boys. *Canad. J. Psychol.*, **9**, 42–54.

MacKinnon, D. W. (1965). Personality and the realization of creative potential. *Amer. Psychologist*, **20**, 261–281.

McClelland, D. C. (1961). *The achieving society*. Toronto: Van Nostrand.

McClelland, D. C., Atkinson, J. W., Clark, R. A., and Lowell, E. L. (1953). *The achievement motive*. New York: Appleton-Century-Crofts.

McCollom, I. N. (1971). Psychological thrillers: psychology books students read when given freedom of choice. *Amer. Psychologist*, **26**, 921–927.

McFall, R. M. and Marston, A. R. (1970). An experimental investigation of behavior rehearsal in assertive training. *J. abnorm. Psychol.* **76**, 295–303.

McGehee, W., and Owen, E. B. (1940). Authorized and unauthorized rest pauses in clerical work. *J. appl. Psychol.*, **24**, 605–614.

McGinnies, E., and Bowles, W. (1949). Personal values as determinants of perceptual fixation. *J. Pers.*, **18**, 224–235.

McGregor, D. M. (1960). *The human side of enterprise.* New York: McGraw-Hill.

McKeachie, W. J. (1952). Lipstick as a determiner of first impressions of personality: an experiment for the general psychology course. *J. soc. Psychol.*, **36**, 241–244.

McKee, J. P., and Sherriffs, A. C. (1957). The differential evaluation of males and females. *J. Pers.*, **25**, 356–371.

McKinney, F. (1939). Personality adjustment of college students as related to factors in personal history. *J. appl. Psychol.*, **23**, 660–668.

McKinney, F. (1960). *Psychology of personal adjustment.* New York: Wiley.

Maddy, Nancy R. (1943). Comparison of children's personality traits, attitudes and intelligence with parental occupation. *Genet. Psychol. Monogr.*, **27**, 3–65.

Mahut, Helen (1958). Breed differences in the dog's emotional behavior. *Canad. J. Psychol.*, **12**, 35–44.

Mann, F. C., and Hoffman, L. R. (1960). *Automation and the worker.* New York: Holt.

Mann, L. and Janis, I. L. (1968). A follow-up study of the long-term effects of emotional role playing. *J. pers. and soc. Psychol.* **8**, 339–342.

Mansfield, Katherine (1928). *Journal of Katherine Mansfield.* New York: Knopf.

Marquis, D. G., Kelly, E. L., Miller, J. G., and Rapoport, A. (1957). Meprobamate and other agents used in mental disturbances: experimental studies of behavioral effects on normal subjects. *Ann. N. Y. Acad. Sci.*, **67**, 701–711.

Martinson, F. M. (1955). Ego deficiency as a factor in marriage. *Amer. sociol. Rev.*, **20**, 161–164.

Marx, M. H. (1951). The general nature of theory construction. In M. H. Marx (ed.), *Psychological theory.* New York: Macmillan.

Masling, J. M. (1957). The effects of warm and cold interaction on the interpretation of a projective protocol. *J. proj. Tech.*, **21**, 377–383.

Maslow, A. H. (1942). Self-esteem (dominance-feeling) and sexuality in women. *J. soc. Psychol.*, **16**, 259–294.

Maslow, A. H. (1948). Some theoretical consequences of basic need gratification. *J. Pers.*, **16**, 402–416.

Maslow, A. H. (1954). *Motivation and personality* New York: Harper. P. 203.

Maslow, A. H. (1962). *Toward a psychology of being.* Princeton: Van Nostrand.

Maslow, A. H., and Mittel, B. (1951). *Principles of abnormal psychology.* (rev. ed.) New York: Harper.

Maslow, A. H., and Szylagyi-Kessler, I. (1946). Security and breast-feeding. *J. abnorm. soc. Psychol.*, **41**, 83–85.

Masters, W. H., and Johnson, Virginia E. (1966). *Human sexual response.* Boston: Little, Brown.

Matarazzo, J. D. (1971). Some national developments in the utilization of nontraditional mental health manpower. *Amer. Psychologist*, **26**, 363–372.

Maugham, W. S. (1938). *The summing up.* New York: Doubleday, London: Heinemann.

Mayfield, E. C. (1970). Management selection: buddy nomination. *Personnel Psychol.* **23**, 377–391.

Mayo, E. (1933). *The human problems of an industrial civilization.* New York: Macmillan.

Mayo, E. and Lombard, G. F. F. (1944). Teamwork and labor turnover in the aircraft industry of southern California. Boston: Harvard Univ. Research Bureau.

Mead, Margaret (1928). *Coming of age in Samoa.* New York: Morrow.

Mead, Margaret (1935). Sex and temperament in three primitive societies. New York: Morrow.

Mead, Margaret (1954). Some theoretical considerations on the problem of mother-child separation. *Amer. J. Orthopsychiat.*, **24**, 471–483.

Meade, R. D. (1966). Achievement motivation, achievement, and psychological time. *J. Pers. and soc. Psychol.*, **4**, 577–580.

Meadows, D. H., Meadows, D. L., Randers, J., and Behrens, W. W. III. (1972). *The limits of growth.* New York: Potomac Associates.

Meadows, A., Parnes, S. J., and Reese, H. (1959). Influence of brain-storming instructions and problem sequence on a creative problem solving test. *J. appl. Psychol.*, **43**, 413–416.

Megargee, E. I. (1966). Undercontrolled and overcontrolled personality types in extreme antisocial aggression. *Psychological Monogr.* **80**, No. 3 (Whole No. 611).

Melville, H. (1961). *Moby Dick: or the white whale.* New York: New American Library.

Metropolitan Life Insurance Company. (1952). Postwar divorce rates here and abroad. *Statist. Bull.*, **33** (6), 6–8.

Meyer, R. G., and Karon, B. P. (1967). The schizophrenogenic mother concept and the TAT. *Psychiatry*, **30**, 173–179.

Miller, H. (1962) *Tropic of capricorn.* New York: Grove Press.

Mintz, E. (1971). Therapy techniques and encounter techniques: comparison and rationale. *Amer. J. Psychotherapy*, **25**, 104–109.

Mishima, Sumie (1941). *My narrow isle: the story of a modern woman in Japan.* Toronto: McClelland.

Money, J. (1962). *Reading disability: progress and research needs in dyslexia.* Baltimore: Johns Hopkins.

Moreno, J. L. (1946). *Psychodrama.* New York: Beacon House.

Morris, C. W. (1956). *Varieties of human value.* Chicago: Univ. of Chicago Press.

Moss, H. A., and Kagan, J. (1964). Report on personality consistency and change from Fels longitudinal study. *Vita Humana*, **7**, 127–138.

Moss, T., Chang, A. E., and Marc, L. (1970). Long-distance ESP: a controlled study. *J. abnorm. Psychol.*, **76**, 288–294.

Mossher, E. C. (1954). *The life of David Hume.* Austin, Tex.: Univ. of Texas Press.

Mowrer, O. H., and Kluckhohn, C. (1944). Dynamic theory of personality, In J. McV. Hunt (ed.), *Personality and behavior disorders.* New York: Ronald.

MSU Reporter (1959). Five troubled students. September, pp. 12–13.

Mueller, W. J. (1966). Need structure and the projection of traits onto parents. *J. pers. and soc. Psychol.*, **3**, 63–72.

Murdock, G. (1949). *Social structure.* New York: Macmillan.

Murdock, G. (1957). World ethnographic sample. *Amer. Anthrop.*, **59**, 669–687.

Murphy, G. (1947). *Personality.* New York: Harper.

Murray, H. A. (1938). *Explorations in personality.* New York: Oxford Univ. Press.

Murray, H. A. (1959). Vicissitudes of creativity. In H. H. Anderson, *Creativity and its cultivation.* New York: Harper & Row.

Murray, J. L., and Jackson, D. N. (1964). Impulsivity and color-form abstraction. *J. consult. Psychol.*, **28**, 518–522.

Mussen, P. H., and Distler, L. (1960). Child-rearing antecedents of masculine identification in kindergarten boys. *Child Developm.*, **31**, 89–100.

Nelson, E., and Nelson, N. (1940). Student attitudes and vocational choices. *J. abnorm. soc. Psychol.*, **35**, 279–282.

Newbigging, P. L. (1954). The relationship between reversible perspective and imbedded figures. *Canad. J. Psychol.*, **8**, 204–208.

Newcomb, T. M. (1956). The prediction of interpersonal attraction. *Amer. Psychologist*, **11**, 575–586.

Newcomb, T. M. (1963). Stabilities underlying changes in interpersonal attraction. *J. abnorm. soc. Psychol.*, **66**, 376–386.

Newman, H. H., Freeman, F. N., and Holzinger, K. J. (1937). *Twins: a study of heredity and environment*. Chicago: Univ. of Chicago Press.

Oetzel, R. M. (1962). Sex typing and sex role adoption in relation to differential abilities. Unpublished master's thesis, Stanford Univ.

Ort, R. S. (1950). A study of role-conflicts as related to happiness in marriage. *J. abnorm. soc. Psychol.*, **45**, 691–699.

Oskamp, S. W. (1965). Overconfidence in case-study judgments. *J. consult. Psychol.*, **29**, 261–265.

Owens, W. A. (1953). Age and mental abilities; a longitudinal study. *Genet. Psychol. Monogr.*, **48**, 3–54.

Paine, T. (1945). *The selected work of Tom Paine*. New York: Duell, Sloan, and Pearce.

Payne, D. E., and Mussen, P. H. (1956). Parent-child relations and father identification among adolescent boys. *J. abnorm. soc. Psychol.*, **52**, 358–362.

Peirce, C. S. (1955). *Philosophical writings of Peirce*. New York: Dover Publications.

Peltz, D. C. (1952). Influence: a key to effective leadership in the first-line supervisor. *Personnel*, **29**, 209–217.

Perry, R. B. (1954). *The thought and character of William James*. Boston: Atlantic–Little, Brown.

Plant, W. T., and Minium, E. W. (1967). Differential personality development in young adults of markedly different aptitude levels. *J. educ. Psychol.*, **58**, 141–152.

Plath, D. W. (1959). Physique and personality differences between male college cigarette smokers and non-smokers. Unpublished master's thesis, Michigan State Univ.

Podell, L., and Perkins, J. C. (1957). A Guttman scale for sexual experience: a methodological note. *J. abnorm. Soc. Psychol.*, **54.**, 420–422.

Porter, A. (1962). Effect of organization size on validity of masculinity-femininity score. *J. appl. Psychol.*, **46**, 228–229.

Premack, A. J., and Premack, D. (1972). Teaching language to an ape. *Sci. Amer.*, **227**, 92–99.

Price, W. H., and Whatmore, P. B. (1967). Behavior disorders and pattern of crime among XYY males identified at a maximum security hospital. *British Medical Journal*, **1**, 533–536.

Proust, M. (1922) *Swann's way*. London: Chatto & Windus.

Provence, S., and Lipton, R. (1962). *Infants in institutions*. New York: International Universities Press.

Rabin, A. I. (1958). Infants and children under conditions of "intermittent" mothering in the Kibbutz. *Amer. J. Orthopsychiat.*, **28**, 577–586.

Rabin, A. I. (1965). Motivation for parenthood. *J. proj. Tech. and Pers. Assessment*, **29**, 405–411.

Rabin, A. I., and Goldman, Hanna (1966). The relationship of severity of guilt to intensity of identification in the Kibbutz and non-kibbutz children. *J. soc. Psychol.*, **69**, 159–163.

Radke, Marjan, Trager, H. G., and Davis, H. (1949). Social perceptions and attitudes of children. *Genet. Psychol. Monogr.*, **40**, 327–447.

Raifman, I. (1957). Level of aspiration in a group of peptic ulcer patients. *J. consult. Psychol.*, **21**, 229–231.

Rank, O. (1941). *Beyond psychology*. New York: Dover.

Rasmussen, E. W. (1952). The relation between strength of sexual drive and fertility as evident from experimental investigation. *Proceedings 2nd International Congress of Animal Reproduction*. (Copenhagen), **1**, 188–191.

Raushenbush, S. (1939) *The march of fascism*. New Haven, Conn: Yale Univ. Press.

Raven, B., and French, J. R. D. (1958). Group support, legitimate power, and social influence. *J. Pers.*, **26**, 400–409.

Rees, T. P. (1957). Back to moral treatment and community care. *J. ment. Sci.*, **103**, 303–313.

Reistrup, J. V. (1972). Women still cool to lib. *Washington Post*, March 24, p. 1.

Rheingold, H. L. (1956). The modification of social responsiveness in institutional babies. *Monographs of the Society for Research in Child Development.* **21**, (No. 63).

Robinson, Mary, and Freeman, W. (1954). *Psychosurgery and the self.* New York: Grune & Stratton.

Rodin, M., and Rodin, B. (1972). Student evaluation of teachers. *Science*, **177**, 1164–1166.

Roe, Anne (1953). A psychological study of eminent psychologists and anthropologists, and a comparison with biological and physical scientists. *Psychol. Monogr.*, **67** (352).

Roethlisberger, F. J., and Dickson, W. J. (1939). *Management and the worker*. Cambridge, Mass.: Harvard.

Rogers, C. R. (1939). *The clinical treatment of the problem child*. Boston: Houghton Mifflin.

Rogers, C. R. (1942). *Counseling and psychotherapy*. Boston: Houghton Mifflin.

Rogers, C. R. (1947). Some observations on the organization of personality. *Amer. Psychologist*, **2**, 358–368.

Rogers, C. R. (1951). *Client centered therapy*. Boston: Houghton Mifflin.

Rogers, C. R. (1957). The necessary and sufficient conditions of therapeutic personality change. *J. consult. Psychol.*, **21**, 95–103.

Rogers, C. R. (1961). *Becoming a person*. Boston: Houghton Mifflin.

Rogers, C. R., Kell, B. L., and McNeil, H. (1948). The role of self-understanding in the prediction of behavior. *J. consult. Psychol.*, 174–186.

Ross, D. (1966) Relationship between dependency, intentional learning, and incidental learning in preschool children. *J. pers. and soc. Psychol.*, **4**, 374–381.

Ross, Adelaide, and Anderson, A. S. (1965). An examination of motivation of adoptive parents. *Amer. J. Orthopsychiat.*, **35**, 365–377.

Rotter, J. B. (1971). Generalized expectancies for interpersonal trust. *Amer. Psychologist*, **26**, 443–452.

Royce, J. R. (1955). A factorial study of emotionality in the dog. *Psychol. Monogr.*, **69** (407).

Ruben, L. S. (1957). The psychopharmacology of lysergic acid diethylamide (LSD 25). *Psychol. Bull.*, **54**, 479–489.

Rundquist, E. A. (1933). The inheritance of spontaneous activity in rats. *J. comp. physiol. Psychol.*, **16**, 415–438.

Sackett, G. P. (1968) Innate mechanisms, differential rearing experiences, and the development of social attachments by rhesus monkeys. Paper presented at the annual meeting of the Amer. Psychol. Assoc., San Francisco.

Sackett, G. P., Porter, M., and Holmes, H. (1965). Choice behavior in rhesus monkeys: effects of stimulation during the first month of life. *Science*, **154**, 1468–1472.

Sanford, F. H. (1942). Speech and personality. *Psychol. Bull.*, **39**, 811–845.

Sanford, F. H. (1950). *Authoritarianism and leadership*. Philadelphia: Inst. Res. in Human Relations.

Santayana, G. (1955). *The sense of beauty*. New York: Modern Library.

Sarason, S. B. (1972). *The creation of settings and the future societies*. San Francisco, Calif.: Josey Bass, Inc.

Sarnoff, I., and Zimbardo, P. G. (1961). Anxiety, fear and social affiliation. *J. abnorm. soc. Psychol.*, **62**, 356–363.

Sarvis, Mary, and Garcia, Blanches (1961). Etiological variables in autism. *Psychiatry*, **24**, 307–317.

Scarr, S. (1966). The origins of individual indifferences in Adjective Check List scores. *J. consult. Psychol.*, **30**, 354–357.

Scarr, S. (1968). Environmental bias in twin studies. *Eugenics Quarterly*, **15**, 34–40.

Schacter, S. (1971). Some extraordinary facts about obese humans and rats. *Amer. Psychologist*, **26**, 129–144.

Schafer, E. S., and Bayley, Nancy (1963). Maternal behavior, child behavior, and their intercorrelations from infancy through adolescence. *Monogr. Soc. Res. in Child Developm.*, **28**, no. 3.

Schaller, G. B. (1963). *The mountain gorilla: ecology and behavior*. Chicago: Univ. of Chicago Press.

Scheler, M. (1923). *Wesen und formen*. Quoted from Cassirer, E. (1957). *The phenomenology of knowledge*. New Haven: Yale Univ. Press, p. 89.

Schiff, T. J. (1972). Reevaluation counseling: social implications. *J. Humanistic Psychol.* **12**, 1–13.

Schutz, W. C. (1958). *FIRO: a three-dimensional theory of interpersonal behavior*. New York: Rinehart.

Scott, J. F. (1966). Marriage is not a personal matter. *New York Times Magazine*, October 30, pp. 27 ff.

Sears, P. S. (1951). Doll play aggression in normal young children: Influence of sex, age, sibling status, father's absence. *Psychological Monogr.*, **65**, 1–42.

Sears, R. R., Maccoby, Eleanor E., and Leven, H. (1957). *Patterns of child rearing*. New York: Harper & Row.

Sears, R. R., Rau, L., and Alpert, R. (1965). *Identification and child rearing*. Palo Alto, Calif.: Stanford Univ. Press.

Sears, Roebuck and Co. (1962). The Sears experience in investigation, description, and prediction of executive behavior. Unpubl. Rep. of Psychological Res. and Serv. Sect.

Secord, P. F. (1958). Facial features and inference processes in interpersonal perception, In R. Tagiuri and L. Petrullo (eds.), *Person perception and interpersonal behavior*. Stanford: Stanford Univ. Press.

Seward, Georgene H. (1956). *Psychotherapy and culture conflict*. New York: Ronald.

Sewell, W. H. (1952). Infant training and the personality of the child. *Amer. J.Sociol.*, **548**, 150–159.

Shaffer, L. F., and Shoben, E. J. (1956). *The psychology of adjustment*. Boston: Houghton Mifflin.

Sheldon, W. H. (1954). *Atlas of men: a guide of somatotyping the adult male of all ages*. New York: Harper.

Sheldon, W. H., Stevens, S. S., and Tucker, W. B. (1940). *The varieties of human physique*. New York: Harper.

Sheldon, W. H., and Stevens, S. S. (1945). *The varieties of temperament*. New York: Harper.

Shirley, Mary (1931). *The first two years: a study of twenty-five babies*. Minneapolis: Univ. of Minn. Press.

Showel, M. (1960). Interpersonal knowledge and rated leader potential. *J. abnorm. soc. Psychol.*, **61**, 87–92.

Singer, J. L. (1960). The experience type: some behavioral correlates and theoretical implications. In M.R. Rickers-Ovsiankina (ed.), *Rorschach psychology*. New York: Wiley.

Singer, J. L. (1961). Imagination and waiting ability in young children. *J. Pers.*, **29**, 396–413.

Singer, J. L. (1966). *Daydreaming: an introduction to the experimental study of inner experience*. New York: Random House.

Singer, J. L., and McCraven, V. (1962). Some characteristics of adult daydreaming. *J. Psychol.*, **51**, 151–164.

Singer, J. L., and Schonbar, H. (1961). Correlates of daydreaming: a dimension of self-awareness. *J. consult. Psychol.*, **25**, 1–6.

Skinner, B. F. (1948). *Walden two.* New York: Macmillan.

Skinner, B. F. (1971). *Beyond freedom and dignity.* New York: Knopf.

Slater, E. (1953). Psychotic and neurotic illnesses in twins. Med. Res. Council. Rep. Ser., no. 278.

Sloman, Sophie S. (1948). Emotional problems in "planned for" children. *Amer. J. Orthopsychiat.*, **18**, 523–528.

Smart, R. G., and Fejer, D. (1972). Drug use among adolescents and their parents: Closing the generation gap in mode modification. *J. abnorm. Psychol.* **79**, 153–160.

Smith, H. C. (1964). *Psychology of industrial behavior,* (2nd ed.) New York: McGraw-Hill.

Smith, H. C. (1973). *Sensitivity training.* New York: McGraw-Hill.

Smith, H. C., and Dunbar, D. S. (1951). The personality and achievement of the classroom participant. *J. educ. Psychol.*, **42**, 65–84.

Spiro, M. E. (1956). *Kibbutz: venture in utopia.* Cambridge, Mass.: Harvard.

Stagner, R. (1958). The gullibility of personnel managers. *Personnel Psychol.*, **11**, 347–352.

Stanley, J. C. (1951). Insight into one's own values. *J. ed. Psychol.*, **42**, 399–480.

Steckle, L. C. (1957). *Problems of human adjustment.* New York: Harper.

Steinman, A., and Fox, D. J. (1966). Male-female perceptions of the female role in the United States. *J. Psychol.*, **64**, 265–276.

Stephenson, W. (1950). A statistical approach to typology: the study of trait-universes. *J. clin. Psychol.*, **6**, 26–38.

Stern, Edith M. (1951). Why couples quit after 20 years. *Nation's Business*, August, **47–49**, 76.

Stockard, C. R., Johnson, A. L., Vicari, E. M., James, W. T., and Anderson, O. D. (1941). Genetic and endocrine basis for differences in form and behavior. *Amer. anatom. Mem.*, no. 19.

Stodgill, R. M. (1948). Personal factors associated with leadership: a survey of the literature. *J. Psychol.*, **25**, 35–71.

Stollak, G. E. (1966). Filial therapy and the use of non-professionals as therapeutic agents. Presented at a workshop on new therapy techniques, Univ. of Wisconsin at Milwaukee.

Stollak, G. (1973). Undergraduates as play therapists: The effects of training and personal characteristics. *Professional Psychol.*

Stollak, G. E. (1973). Undergraduates and children: an integrated undergraduate program in the assessment, treatment, and prevention of child psychopathology. *Professional Psychol.* In Press.

Stotland, E., and Dunn, R. E. (1963). Empathy, self-esteem, and birth order. *J. abnorm. soc. Psychol.* **66**, 532–540.

Streb, J. M., and Smith, K. (1955). Frontal lobotomy and the elimination of conditioned anxiety in the rat. *J. comp. Physiol.*, **48**, 126–129.

Strickberger, M. W. (1968). *Genetics.* New York: Macmillan.

Sullivan, H. S. (1953). *The interpersonal theory of psychiatry.* New York: W. W. Norton.

Sutton-Smith, B., and Rosenberg, B. G. (1965). Age changes on the effects of ordinal position on role identification. *J. Genet. Psychol.*, **107**, 61–73.

Taylor, C. W. (1959). The identification of creative talent. *Amer. Psychologist*, **14**, 100–102.

Taylor, C., and Combs, A. W. (1952). Self-acceptance and adjustment. *J. consult. Psychol.*, **16**, 89–91.

Terman, L. M. (1938). *Psychological factors in marital happiness.* New York: McGraw-Hill.

Terman, L. M., and Oden, Mellita (1959). *Genetic studies of genius: V. The gifted group at mid-life: thirty-five years' follow-up of the superior child.* Stanford, Calif.: Stanford Univ. Press.

Tharp, R. G. (1963*a*). Dimensions of marriage roles. *Marriage and Family Living,* **25,** 389–404.

Tharp, R. G. (1963*b*). Psychological patterning in marriage. *Psychol. Bull.,* **60,** 97–117.

Thomas, C. (1957). *Leftover life to kill.* Boston: Little, Brown.

Thompson, C. E. (1940). The attitudes of various groups toward behavior problems of children. *J. abnorm. soc. Psychol.,* **35,** 120–125.

Thompson, W. R., and Melzack, R. (1956). Early environment. *Sci. Amer.,* **194,** 38–42.

Thoreau, H. D. (1950). *Walden.* New York: Modern Library.

Thornton, G. R. (1943). The effect upon judgments of personality traits of varying a single factor in a photograph. *J. soc. Psychol.,* **18,** 127–148.

Thornton, G. R., and Guilford, J. P. (1936). Reliability and meaning of Erlebnistypus scores in Rorschach test. *J. abnorm. soc. Psychol.,* **31,** 324–330.

Thorpe, A. C. (1955). How married college students manage. In M. B. Sussman (ed.), *Source book in marriage and the family.* Boston: Houghton Mifflin.

Thurstone, L. L. (1938). Primary mental abilities. *Psychometric Monogr.,* no. 1.

Thurstone, L. L. (1944). *A factorial study of perception.* Chicago: Univ. of Chicago Press.

Tickton, S. G. (1968). The magnitude of American higher education in 1980. In A. C. Burich (ed.), *Campus 1980.* New York: Dell.

Todd, J. E. (1941). Social norms and the behavior of college students. *Teach. Coll. Contr. Educ.,* no. 833.

Toffler, A. (1970). *Future shock.* New York: Bantam Books.

Tolstoi, L. N. (1960). *What is art?* New York: Liberal Arts Press.

Trier, H. E. (1959). Sociological variables, personality traits, and buying attitudes related to role perceptions and conflicts among 242 Michigan wives. Unpublished doctoral dissertation, Michigan State Univ.

Trollope, A. (1923). *An autobiography by* . . . New York: Oxford Univ. Press.

Trumbo, D. (1955). The development and analysis of a test of the ability to predict behavior. Unpublished master's thesis, Michigan State Univ.

Twain, Mark, ed. C. Neider (1961), *Autobiography.* New York: Washington Square Press, p. 71.

Tyler, Leona (1956). *The psychology of human differences.* New York: Appleton-Century-Crofts.

Uleman, J. S. (1966). Influence, a new power-related motive: development and validation of a TAT measure. Presented at the meeting of Midwestern Psychol. Ass., Chicago, May 5.

U. S. Department of Health, Education, and Welfare. (1955). *Marriages and divorces 1953.* Washington, D.C.: Public Health Service.

Vaillant, G. C. (1963). Twins discordant for early infantile autism. *Arch. gen. Psychiat.,* **9** (2), 163–167.

Van Zelst, R. H. (1952). Sociometrically selected work teams increase production. *Personnel Psychol.,* **14,** 9–38.

Vaught, G. M. (1965). The relationship of role identification and ego strength to sex differences in rod-and-frame test. *J. Person.,* **33,** 271–283.

Vroom, V. H., and Mann, F. C. (1960). Leadership, authoritarianism and employee attitudes, *Personnel Psychol.,* **13,** 115–141.

Walker, C. R., Guest, R. H., and Turner, A. N. (1956). *The foreman on the assembly line.* Cambridge, Mass: Harvard.

Walster, Elaine, Aronson, Vera, and Abrahams, Darcy (1966). Importance of physical attractiveness in dating behavior. *J. pers. soc. Psychol.*, **4**, 508–516.

Watson, G. (1930). Happiness among adult students of education. *J. educ. Psychol.*, **21**, 79–109.

Watson, W. S., and Hartmann, G. W. (1939). Rigidity of basic attitudinal frame. *J. abnorm. soc. Psychol.*, **34**, 314–336.

Wegner, D. (1971). Self-other differentiation: Field dependence and assumed similarity. Unpublished master's thesis, Michigan State Univ.

Weitz, J. (1958). Selecting supervisors with peer ratings. *Personnel Psychol.*, **11**, 25–35.

White, K., and Allen, R. (1971). Art counseling in an educational setting: self-concept changes among pre-adolescent boys. *J. school Psychol.*, **9**, 218–225.

White, R. W. (1959). Motivation reconsidered: the concept of competence. *Psychol. Rev.*, **66**, 297–333.

Whitehead, A. N. (1929). *Aims of education and other essays.* New York: Macmillan.

Whitehead, A. N. (1933). *Adventures of ideas.* New York: Macmillan.

Whiting, J. W. M. (1959). Sorcery, sin, and the superego: a cross-cultural study of some mechanisms of social control. In M. R. Jones (ed.), *Nebraska symposium on motivation*, 174–194.

Whiting, J. W. M. (1960). Resource mediation and learning by identification. In I. Iscoe and M. Stevenson (eds.), *Personality development in children.* Austin, Tex.: Univ. of Texas Press.

Whiting, J. W. M., and Child, I. L. (1953). *Child training and personality: a cross-cultural study.* New Haven, Conn.: Yale.

Whyte, W. H., Jr. (1956). *The organization man.* New York: Simon and Schuster.

Wiggins, J. S., Benner, K. E., Clore, G. L., and Rose, R. J. (1971). *The psychology of personality.* Reading, Mass.: Addison-Wesley.

Wiggins, J. S., Wiggins, N., and Conger, J. C. (1968). Correlates of heterosexual somatic preference. *J. pers. and soc. Psychol.*, **10**, 82–90.

Williams, W. C. (1951). *Autobiography.* New York: Random House.

Winch, R. F., Ktsanes, T., and Ktsanes, V. (1955). Empirical elaboration of the theory of complementary needs in mate-selection. *J. abnorm. soc. Psychol.*, **51**, 508–513.

Wispe, L. G. (1965). Impact of psychotherapy on the productivity of psychologists. *J. abnorm. Psychol.*, **70**, 188–193.

Witkin, H. A., Lewis, H. B., Hertzman, H., Machover, K., Meissner, P. B., and Wapner, S. (1954). *Personality through perception.* New York: Harper.

Witryol, S. L., and Kaess, W. A. (1957). Sex differences in social memory tasks. *J. abnorm. soc. Psychol.*, **54**, 343–346.

Wittman, M. P. (1941). A scale for measuring prognosis in schizophrenic patients, *Elgin Papers*, **4**, 20–33.

Wolfenstein, Martha (1953). Trends in infant care. *Amer. J. Orthopsychiat.*, **23**, 120–130.

Wolman, B. B. (ed.) (1965). *Handbook of clinical psychology.* New York: McGraw-Hill.

Woolley, Helen, T. (1925). A dominant personality in the making. *Pedagog. Seminar*, **32**, 569–598.

Worthy, J. C. (1950). Organizational structure and employee morale. *Amer. Socio. Rev.*, **15**, 169–179.

Yerkes, R. M. (1927). The mind of a gorilla. *Genet. Psychol. Monogr.*, **2**, 1–191, 377–551.

Ziller, R. C. (1955). Leader acceptance of responsibility for group action under conditions of uncertainty and risk (abstract). *Amer. Psychologist*, **10**, 475–476.

Zucker, R. A. (1968). Sex-role identity patterns and drinking behavior of adolescents. *Quart. J. Studies on Alcohol.* **29**, 868–884.

GLOSSARY

The definitions below include most of the important terms and some of the minor ones used in this book, particularly those that are used in a special or more restricted sense than is usually employed by either psychologists or people in general. Since most of these terms are more fully defined and exemplified in the text, the reader may also wish to check under the subject index. For other meanings of these terms and for terms not used in this book, see English, H. B. and A. C. A *comprehensive dictionary of psychological and psychoanalytical terms.* New York: Longmans, Green, 1958.

ADAPTATION   The relationship that exists between an individual and his environment, especially his physical environment, in the attempt to satisfy his needs.

ADJUSTMENT   The relationship that exists between an individual and his environment, especially his social environment, in the attempt to satisfy his needs.

AGGRESSION   Feelings of anger or hostility which are reflected in conscious or unconscious efforts to hurt or destroy what is seen as the source of frustration.

ANALYTIC PSYCHOLOGY   The theory of psychoanalysis and psychotherapy developed by Jung.

ANXIETY   A vague fear aroused by internal conflicts. Antonym: Fear.

ARTISTIC   One extreme of the artistic versus practical trait. Compared to the practical, the artistic are more introverted in their orientation, more aesthetic in their attitudes, and more artistic in their interests.

AUTHORITARIAN LEADER   One who is low in consideration but high in responsibility toward his followers.

AUTHORITATIVE LEADER   One who is both high in consideration and high in responsibility toward his followers.

AUTISM   The tendency to have thoughts and feelings that do not correspond to perceptual reality and that are strongly determined by a person's wishes and needs.

AUTISTIC STAGE   The earliest stage of personality development, at which the individual lacks awareness of himself as a self and cannot discriminate between what is him and not him.

AUTONOMY   The tendency for a person's decisions to be determined by his self-structure rather than by his reaction to forces in the external environment.

BOLD   One extreme of the cautious versus bold trait. Compared to the cautious, the bold are more dominating, confident, optimistic, energetic, and gregarious.

BUREAUCRACY   The form of social organization that puts primary emphasis upon following rules.

CASTRATION COMPLEX   In general, the often unconscious fear of bodily injury or loss of power at the hands of authority. More specifically, a child's fear or delusion of genital injury at the hands of the parent of the same sex.

CATATONIC TYPE The form of schizophrenia characterized by states of muscular rigidity that may remain fixed for hours.

CAUTIOUS   One extreme of the cautious versus bold trait. Compared to the bold, the cautious are submissive, pessimistic, inactive, aloof, and lacking in self-confidence.

COMPENSATION The defense mechanism by which an individual compensates for a frustrated drive, inadequacy, or imperfection by substituting or stressing another drive, trait, or function.

COMPETENCE   The state of being functionally adequate or of having sufficient knowledge, judgment, skill, or strength. Synonyms: Maturity, Self-Actualization, Ego Strength.

CONFORMING STAGE The stage of personality development at which the individual is ruled by social rules, feels shame rather than guilt when he breaks them, and has superficial interpersonal relationships. The stage is preceded by the impulse-ridden stage and followed by the conscientious stage.

CONFORMITY   The tendency to be influenced by group pressure and acquiesce to group norms.

CONSCIENTIOUS STAGE   The personality stage following the conforming stage at which the individual's inner standards take precedence over group-sanctioned rules. He feels guilt when these standards are violated and becomes responsible in his interpersonal relationships.

CONSIDERATION   The tendency to know and respect the rights and feelings of others.

CORRELATION COEFFICIENT   A number between +1.00 and −1.00 that represents the relationship between two sets of measurements arranged in pairs and where .00 represents no relationship and 1.00 represents a perfect relationship.

CROSS-IDENTIFICATION The process by which a child models himself after the parent of the opposite sex.

DEPENDENCE   The often unconscious feeling of one person needing another that is identifiable by the person's relaxation in the presence of, and anxiety in the absence of, the other.

DESENSITIZATION   A weakening of a response as a result of repeated exposure. More specifically, the method used in psychotherapy to enable a person to be comfortable in situations in which he was previously fearful or anxious.

DIFFERENTIATED ROLE   In general, the tendency of an individual to play a social role different from the roles played by those around him. Specifically, the tendency of a leader to perform tasks different from those of his followers.

DIFFERENTIATION   The physical, biological, psychological, or social process by which the many develop from the one, the complex from the simple, and the heterogenous from the homogeneous.

DISPLACEMENT   A transfer of libidinal energy from its original object to a person or idea that is more acceptable to the ego.

EGO   The psychoanalytic term referring to the largely conscious part of the personality that is derived from the id through contacts with reality. It mediates the demands of the id, of the superego, and of external everyday reality.

EGO STRENGTH   The capacity of the individual to integrate the conflicting demands of the id, superego, and external reality. Synonyms: Self-Confidence, Self-Esteem, Boldness.

EMOTIONAL   One extreme of the unemotional versus emotional trait. Compared to the unemotional, the emotional have wider-ranging, more frequent, and more intense emotional states that they more freely express.

EMPATHY   In general, the imaginative projection of a subjective state into an object so that the whole appears to be infused with it. Specifically, empathy with another person is the tendency to assume that another's feelings and thoughts are similar to one's own.

EXTRASENSORY PERCEPTION (ESP)   Perception that purportedly takes place outside sensory channels, as in mental telepathy.

FACTOR ANALYSIS   A general statistical method, involving coefficients of correlation, that isolates the few independent factors in a large number of test scores, ratings, or other measurements.

FANTASY   Daydreaming and imagining a world of one's own, a tendency that may be used as a defense mechanism.

FEAR   The emotional state aroused by external threats. Antonym: Anxiety.

FIELD INDEPENDENCE   The ability to use internal and abstract stimuli as well as external ones in the perception and manipulation of the external world. Antonym: Field Dependence; Synonyms: Flexibility of Closure, Autonomy, Independence.

FUTURE-MINDED   One extreme of the present-minded versus future-minded trait. Compared to the present-minded, the future-minded live more in the future, set harder goals for themselves, and are more organized in their daily lives.

GALVANIC SKIN RESPONSE (GSR)   A change in the electrical resistance of the skin occurring in emotional and certain other conditions.

GROUP THERAPY   A technique of psychotherapy in which a therapist guides a group of individuals as they discuss their personal problems together.

GUILT   A painful emotion caused by the awareness that one has violated one's own principles regardless of whether others know or care about the violation. Antonym: Shame.

HEBEPHRENIA   A variety of schizophrenia characterized by childishness and regressive behavior.

HOMEOSTASIS   The tendency of the body to maintain a balance among internal physiological conditions, such as temperature and sugar. Synonyms: Adaptation, Adjustment.

ID   In psychoanalytic theory, the aspect of personality concerned with immediate gratification of needs with little regard for the consequences or the realities of life.

IDENTIFICATION   The process by which an individual molds his feelings and attitudes to match the feelings and attitudes of another person.

IMITATION   The process by which an individual molds his external behavior to match the external behavior of another person.

IMPULSE-RIDDEN STAGE   The stage of development at which the individual does not know the social rules, is dominated by his immediate impulses, and views others as sources of supply.

INDIVIDUALISTIC LEADER   One who is low in consideration and low in responsibility toward his followers.

INTEGRATION   An individual's degree of interest in and satisfaction with the theater in which he plays his roles and with the other role players.

INTERNAL CONSISTENCY   The degree to which different parts of a measure agree with each other.

INTERVENING VARIABLE   In personality, theoretical concepts that "intervene" between those used to describe the stimuli impinging upon an individual and those used to describe the response he makes.

LEVEL OF ASPIRATION   The level at which a person sets certain goals.

LINKING PIN   The process by which the activities of one group in an organization are coordinated with the activities of other groups in the same organization.

LOVE   The generally beneficial process of singling out, becoming interested in, and acting in behalf of a specific thing, idea, or, particularly, person. The variations from infantile to mature love can be discriminated by the degree of consideration and responsibility that the lover shows toward what he loves.

MANIC-DEPRESSION   Psychotic reactions marked by extremes of depressed or elated moods.

MASCULINE PROTEST   A tendency to compensate for feelings of inferiority by exaggerating one's overt aggressiveness.

MECHANISM   A genetic or environmental process that determines differences in traits, selves, or role playing.

MILIEU THERAPY   An approach to psychotherapy that views the disturbed as people disrupted in their social roles and, therefore, stresses the development of therapeutic social environments.

MORALE   An individual's degree of interest in and satisfaction with the activities involved in a role he is playing.

NEGATIVISM   Defense mechanism characterized by extreme and irrational resistance to accepting the suggestions of others.

NEUROSIS   A behavior disorder—less severe than a psychotic reaction—in which a person is unusually anxious, miserable, ineffective in his work and interpersonal relationships, and an excessive user of defense mechanisms. Synonyms: Psychoneurosis, Psychoneurotic Reaction.

NONDIRECTIVE COUNSELING   Psychotherapy dominated by the view that the client must solve his own problems; the client is given maximum encouragement and opportunity to express himself and guide the course of his therapy.

NORMS   Scores of specified classes of persons on a specified test.

OPPORTUNISTIC STAGE   The stage of development preceded by the impulse-ridden and followed by the conforming stage in which the morality of the individual is purely expedient, his interpersonal relations are manipulative, his conscious preoccupation is with gaining advantage by deception, and feelings of shame or guilt are absent.

OVERCOMPENSATION   Excessive reaction to a feeling of inferiority or guilt leading to an exaggerated attempt to overcome the feeling.

PARANOIA   Psychotic disorder marked by extreme suspiciousness in an individual, often taking the form of elaborate but erroneous beliefs that others are plotting against him.

PERCENTILE   The value of the statistical variable that marks the boundary between any two consecutive intervals in which each interval contains 1 percent of the total population.

PERCEPTUAL DEFENSE   The tendency of a person not to see or hear that which is threatening or disturbing him.

PLAY THERAPY   A technique for the study of personality and for the treatment of personality problems that permits a child to express his feelings and conflicts by the use of dolls or other playthings.

PLEASURE PRINCIPLE   The tendency to satisfy the impulses of the id.

POLYANDRY   The rare form of marriage permitting one woman to be married to more than one man.

POLYGYNY   Marriage of one man to more than one woman.

PRESENT-MINDED   One extreme of the trait of present-minded versus future-minded. Compared to the future-minded, the present-minded are more concerned about the present moment, more impulsive, and more disorganized.

PRODUCTIVITY   An individual's degree of interest in and satisfaction with the objective results he achieves by playing a particular role.

PROJECTION   In general, the attribution to other people and to objects of one's own ideas, feelings, and attitudes. Specifically, the externalization of blame and guilt for one's actions or thoughts as an unconscious mechanism to defend the ego against anxiety.

PSYCHODRAMA   A technique of psychotherapy in which patients act out roles, situations, and fantasies relevant to their personal problems, often before a small audience of patients.

PSYCHOPATH   A disorder of behavior in which an individual perceives reality but does not feel any sense of responsibility or moral obligation toward other individuals or society.

PSYCHOSES A broad category of behavior disorders that are more severe than neuroses and generally require hospitalization. *See:* Manic-depression, Schizophrenia, Paranoia.

PSYCHOSURGERY Cerebral surgery, particularly lobotomy, employed in treating psychic symptoms.

PSYCHOTHERAPY Treatment of behavior disorders by psychological means, especially those involving verbal communication as in psychoanalysis, nondirective counseling, hypnosis, or psychodrama.

RATIONALIZATION The defense mechanism which involves giving good reasons to explain one's behavior when the real reasons are different and unknown or unconscious.

REACTION FORMATION The defense mechanism in which an attitude, trait, or behavioral tendency substitutes for or conceals a diametrically opposite tendency.

REALITY PRINCIPLE The tendency for an individual to defer the gratification of id impulses to achieve longer-range goals or to deal with pressures from the physical or social environment.

REALITY TESTING A process of the ego in which acts are explored so that the individual will be aware of their consequences.

REGRESSION Reversion in behavior, thinking, or attitudes to an earlier stage of development.

RELIGIOUS One extreme of the religious versus scientific trait. Compared to the scientific, the religious believe more in abstract principles, and in traditional religious and social forms and are more resistant to change.

REPEAT (TEST-RETEST) RELIABILITY The agreement of scores on the same test taken by the same people at two different times.

REPRESSION The defense mechanism whereby wishes or impulses are kept from or made inaccessible to consciousness except in disguised form as in dreams.

RESPONSIBILITY The tendency for a person to feel and act as if he were holding himself accountable for what happens in a situation or to a person.

ROLE The feelings, attitudes, and behavior that society expects from the holder of a position in some social structure.

ROLE IDENTITY The feelings, attitudes, and behavior that the holder of a position in a social structure perceives himself as having or wanting to have.

RORSCHACH TEST   A psychological test consisting of ten standard inkblot designs that the subject describes in terms of what they look like to him, revealing through the selectivity of his responses the manner in which intellectual and emotional factors are integrated in his perception of environmental stimuli.

SCIENTIFIC   One extreme of the religious versus scientific trait. Compared to the religious, the scientific put more faith in facts, are readier for change, and are more skeptical and individualistic.

SCHIZOPHRENIA   A psychotic disorder of complex etiology that occurs in simple, catatonic, hebephrenic, and paranoid forms. Characterized by disturbances in the usual logical relationships between ideas, by emotional manifestations that are inappropriate to actual situations, and by withdrawal from interpersonal relationships.

SELF   A person as he feels, perceives, and thinks of himself.

SELF-ACTUALIZED STAGE   The highest stage of personality development, at which the individual reconciles earlier conflicts, renounces goals that are unattainable, loves the differences between people, and develops a strong identification with mankind.

SELF-IMAGE   One's conception of oneself and of one's role.

SELF-INSIGHT   The completeness and accuracy of a person's understanding of himself.

SELF-OTHER DIFFERENTIATION   The process by which the individual learns to discriminate his physical, psychological, and social self from the external world.

SEX-ROLE STANDARDS   Those traits that a society considers good or bad depending upon whether the person having the traits is a male or a female.

SHAME   A painful emotion caused by the awareness that others know or may know of one's shortcomings or violations of social norms. Antonym: Guilt.

SHOCK THERAPY   The treatment of behavior disorders by some agent—such as insulin, metrazol, or electric shock—causing convulsion or coma.

STABILITY   The component of personality structure indicating the degree to which an individual is consistent from one time and place to another in his view of himself, his approach to problems, and in his attitudes and behavior.

STABILITY OF SELF-IMAGE   The degree to which the individual is capable of resisting or recovering from the disorganizing effects induced by either external sources or information about himself, so that he appears to others to be dependable and consistent from one time to another.

STATUS ENVY   Envy of the social role of another, especially a child's envy of the position of his father or mother.

SUPEREGO   In psychoanalytic theory, the section of the psyche that develops out of the ego through the advice and punishment of authority figures, especially parents, and that reflects parental conscience and the rule of society. *See also:* Id and Ego.

SUPPRESSION   The intentional exclusion from consciousness of a thought or feeling. *Contrast with:* Repression.

SYMBOL   A word, act, sound, or material object having cultural significance and the capacity to represent an experience or objectify a response.

SYMBOLIC REPRESENTATION   The component of competence reflecting the individual's ability to represent his internal and external experiences effectively through the use of verbal, quantitative, visual, and other kinds of symbols.

TACHISTOSCOPE   An apparatus for the brief exposure of visual stimuli.

THEMATIC APPERCEPTION TEST (TAT)   A projective technique in which personality assessments are based on the subject's verbal responses to a series of ambiguous black and white pictures.

THEORY   A set of concepts with assumed relationships between them.

TRAIT   Aspects of behavior or experience in which individuals differ from each other.

UNEMOTIONAL   One extreme of the unemotional versus emotional trait. Compared to the emotional, the unemotional have fewer and less intense emotional states and are less inclined to express those they have.

VALIDATION   The process of determining the degree of validity of a measuring device.

VALIDITY   The concern with what a test or other instrument measures and how well it does so.

NAME INDEX

SUBJECT INDEX